Focus on Computer Graphics

Tutorials and Perspectives in Computer Graphics

Edited by W.T. Hewitt, R. Gnatz, and W. Hansmann

Springer
Berlin
Heidelberg
New York
Barcelona
Budapest
Hong Kong
London
Milan
Paris
Tokyo

G. Sakas P. Shirley S. Müller (Eds.)

Photorealistic Rendering Techniques

With 155 Figures, 16 Colour Plates,
and 14 Tables

 Springer

Focus on Computer Graphics

Edited by W. T. Hewitt, R. Gnatz, and W. Hansmann
for EUROGRAPHICS –
The European Association for Computer Graphics
P. O. Box 16, CH-1288 Aire-la-Ville, Switzerland

Volume Editors

Georgios Sakas
Stefan Müller

Fraunhofer Institute for Computer Graphics
Wilhelminenstraße 7
D-64283 Darmstadt, Germany

Peter Shirley

Indiana University
Department of Computer Science
Lindley Hall
Bloomington, IL 47405, USA

CR Subject Classification (1991): I.3.7, I.3.3, I.6.7

ISBN-13: 978-3-642-87827-5

Library of Congress Cataloging-in-Publication Data
Photorealistic rendering techniques /G. Sakas, P. Shirley, S. Müller, eds.   p. cm.
(Focus on computer graphics)
Includes bibliographical references.
ISBN-13: 978-3-642-87827-5   e-ISBN-13: 978-3-642-87825-1
DOI: 10.1007/978-3-642-87825-1
1. Computer graphics–Congresses, I. Sakas, Georgios. II. Shirley, P. (Peter), 1963 -
III. Müller, S. (Stefan), 1965 -   . IV. Series.
T385.P493 1995 006.6–dc20 95-23397 CIP

Cover: Künkel + Lopka, Ilvesheim, Germany
Typesetting: Camera-ready copy from the authors/editors
SPIN 10085230   45/3143-5 4 3 2 1 0 – Printed on acid-free paper

Preface

This book contains the final versions of the proceedings of the fifth EUROGRA-PHICS Workshop on Rendering held in Darmstadt, Germany, between 13-15 June 1994. With around 80 participants and 30 papers, the event continued the successful tradition of the previous ones establishing the event as the most important meeting for persons working on this area world-wide. After more than 20 years of research, rendering remains an partially unsolved, interesting, and challenging topic.

This year 71 (!) papers have been submitted from Europe, North America, and Asia. The average quality in terms of technical merit was impressive, showing that substantial work is achieved on this topic from several groups around the world. In general we all gained the impression that in the mean time the technical quality of the contributions is comparable to that of a specialised high-end, full-scale conference. All papers have been reviewed from at least three members of the program committee. In addition, several colleagues helped us in managing the reviewing process in time either by supporting additional reviews, or by assisting the members of the committee.

We have been very happy to welcome eminent invited speakers. Holly Rushmeier is internationally well known for her excellent work in all areas of rendering and gave us a review of modelling and rendering participating media with emphasis on scientific visualization. In addition, Peter Shirley presented a survey about future rends in rendering techniques.

The book covers a wide spectrum of topics within the field of Photorealistic Rendering Techniques and includes not only the "classic" topics such as Radiosity, Ray Tracing, Meshing/Sampling, Monte Carlo and Viewing Solutions, but also some new areas of increasing interest. The excellent quality of the Participating Media contributions shows that sufficient work exists here, which should be exploited from future applications. Dynamic Solutions & Walkthroughs intend to show ways that results can become fast and accurate enough in order to become unable and incorporated in existing systems. And finally, Wavelets show a new approach promising to solve several existing problems in an innovative way.

Georgios Sakas, Peter Shirley, Stefan Müller

Contents

Part III: Ray Tracing and Monte Carlo

Part IV: Radiosity

Part V: Wavelets

Part VI: Dynamic Solutions and Walkthrouhgs

Part I

Viewing Solutions

Results of the 1994 Survey on Image Synthesis

Peter Shirley[1], *Georgios Sakas*[2]

[1] Indiana University, Bloomington IN 47405, USA
[2] Fraunhofer-IGD, Wilhelminenstr. 7, 64283 Darmstadt, Germany

1 Introduction

At the 1992 Rendering Workshop in Bristol, Michael Cohen presented the results of what he called a very unscientific survey of image synthesis researchers. This survey stimulated a great deal of discussion, so we ran a second survey (again distributed by email), and collected twenty-two responses from researchers with an average of ten years experience in image synthesis. The results of this survey, along with the results of Cohen's survey are given here.

Since this was an informal survey, we can certainly draw no hard conclusions from the results. However, we do feel the results are useful for getting a feel for what are perceived to be important research areas. For new researchers in rendering it the results may be helpful in identifying areas that are viewed as being largely solved.

2 Survey Responses

When asked to define image synthesis, we got a number of responses similar to those described by Cohen: "make an image indistinguishable from a photo". Several respondents commented that we probably should have asked about "realistic image synthesis", and gave a broader definition for image synthesis. Some extracted phrases from this second class of responses are:

- Displaying (or somehow outputting) the image (or idea) we have in our mind.
- Photorealism is a subclass of image synthesis.
- The creation of a visual representation intended to communicate an idea.
- The generation of images from information.

The next question was: *What are the key issues that are still unanswered or not answered well in realistic image synthesis? Rate each issue as unsolved (0) to solved (5).* We used the same eight subquestions as Cohen (a-h) and added subquestions (i-k).

	1992 $\bar{x}$	1992 σ	1994 $\bar{x}$	1994 σ
(a) dealing with environmental complexity	1.47	1.14	1.55	0.89
(b) dealing with human perceptual issues	1.47	0.92	1.59	0.94
(c) rendering caustics	1.67	0.72	2.43	1.05
(d) dealing with color	2.58	1.03	3.14	0.69
(e) parallelization	2.60	1.02	2.95	0.57
(f) local reflection models	3.09	1.09	3.27	0.69
(g) the hidden surface problem	3.84	0.65	4.05	0.82
(h) mapping results to display devices	2.88	1.18	2.86	1.14
(i) participating media			2.00	0.74
(j) time/space complexity of rend. algorithms			2.27	0.75
(k) implementation issues for image synthesis			2.81	0.90

The next question asked the extent to which the respondent agreed with the statement: *the MAIN problem remaining in image synthesis is simply that we cannot model, with sufficient detail, the environments we want to create images of.* Cohen's mean response was 2.9 out of 5.0 with a standard deviation of 1.5. The 1994 respondents had an average of 2.61 with a standard deviation of 1.33. One respondent summarized: "This is half of the main remaining problem. The other half is that, if we could model the environment with sufficient detail, we couldn't render it".

The next two questions asked how far the respondents thought the image synthesis field come in solving the image synthesis problem, *and* how far the graphics community as a whole think the field has come in solving the image synthesis problem. Cohen's results were means of 2.6 and 4.0 (the graphics community thinks the problem is more solved than researchers in the area do), and the 1994 means were 2.8 and 3.74.

The respondents were given the opportunity to identify the most important problem to work on in image synthesis. Responses were:

- Dealing with high complexity, dealing with perceptual issues.
- Creating a standard scene description language for physically-based rendering. Renderers should be a commodity, and we need some kind of standard to make this happen. RIB is not it, nor is Inventor, or any of the many other non-physical description languages out there. Geometry is well-understood and people generally agree on how to describe surfaces and volumes, but materials and light behavior have so far been treated with rampant disrespect.
- Efficient storage and reconstruction of accurate, complex world-space global illumination solutions.
- Area-Area Visibility.
- Solving for global illumination with arbitrary reflection models and anisotropic light sources.
- This is a matter of personal taste. I personally think scientific and data visualization is an important area, with unsolved problems in visualizing

3D vector fields, and multiple related scalar fields in a way that the human visual system can use them to gain understanding.

- We need to understand how to communicate ideas that are richer than simulated photographs. Image synthesis today is like dynamics: set it up and let it go, and pray for the right result. Nobody uses pure dynamics for animation, because it doesn't let you say what you want to say; we use constraints and other methods to get the dynamics we want (though pure dynamics is good for secondary motion and pure physical simulation). We need to put the same hooks into rendering, so we can control it to convey our message. It's important to understand what those hooks are. Artists know some of that answer, but they don't express it mathematically and algorithmically. We've been wonderfully successful at translating the physics literature into algorithms; now comes the next step of doing the same for artistic knowledge.
- Interactive environments.
- The design of rendering systems (not algorithms).
- Improve convergence speed.
- Modelling of complex dynamic environments, including geometry and surface properties and movement, using a "levels of detail" approach based on suitably defined error metrics so that the transition between low-quality interactivity to extremely precise high-quality renderings is well-defined.
- Usability. I really care about publications which talk about better general algorithms for rendering or surface simulation or other aspect of image synthesis (increased speed in processing, speed in user interface, quality, etc).
- What computations are necessary to give a "correct" impression of a scenery? I think we spend a lot of work/time in calculating things "very correct" which can not be seen: 1280x1024 pixels, 24 bit RGB NOT calibrated, ... printing of this images most parts of a scenary are never seen, interreflection of light under a desk.
- Parallel processing - sufficient computing power would overcome most of the existing shortcomings of graphic techniques. Only parallel processing will be able to provide these computational needs.
- The entire pipeline with respect to high complexity environments. (not just modeling, as suggested in 3.)
- Complex reflection functions in global illumination and time complexity.
- Handling complexity. A critical and related problem is integrating perceptual criteria into algorithms, since one of the key ways of reducing computation will be to concentrate effort on those aspects of the solution that improve perceived accuracy the most.
- Complexity and efficiency, this is the type of problem that I like I don't know that much about physics and perception.
- Modeling.
- Interactive environments and modelling natural phenomena. In the future, Virtual reality systems will need to include accurately modelled natural phenomena.
- Modeling and rendering complex environments: that is, modeling (maybe capturing in the case of existing models) a number of objects of varied shapes,

and being able to predict their appearance to a photographic level of realism.
- Realistic rendering of complex outdoor scenes (trillions of primitives).

2.1 Miscelleneous Respondent Comments

- A key problem now is that we actually can make quite realistic images. The problem is that we cannot do it efficiently or robustly. This is the main reason for the misconception as indicated by question (5) above.
- Conclusions about neither science nor art should be drawn from polls. Does computer graphics aspire to either of these?
- I think that the major unsolved problem is to have interactive environments. This is not necessarily the same thing as having detailed environments. A very beautifully rendered but static/passive image is ultimately not using the real potential of the computer. See how quickly yesterday's CG images are discarded.
- What I would like to see in the following years, is an algorithm able to go from a real-time awful draft picture to a perfectly polished one (ie with complete global illumination, textures, and so one) using a continuous progressive refinement scheme, with minimal recomputations.
- Realism will not only be achievable by advanced illumination models. I think we still are a long way from understanding (and thus being able to accurately model) human perception of environments.
- Applications based on image synthesis must be generalized.
- I have found an elegant solution to this problem, which this margin is too small to contain.

Acknowledgents

Thanks to the respondents of the survey: Alan Chalmers, Kenneth Chiu, Michael Cohen, George Drettakis, Veronique Gaildrat, Andrew Glassner, Eric Haines, Toby Howard, Roger Hubbold, Erik Jansen, Bob Lewis, Martin Lob, Nelson Max, Christophe Schlick, Francois Sillion, Kelvin Sung, A. Augusto de Sousa, Ben Trumbore, Samuel Uselton, John Wallace, Greg Ward.

Quantization Techniques for Visualization of High Dynamic Range Pictures

Christophe Schlick

Laboratoire Bordelais de Recherche en Informatique
351 cours de la libération, 33405 Talence, France

Abstract

This paper proposes several techniques that enable to display high dynamic range pictures (created by a global illumination rendering program, for instance) on a low dynamic range device. The methods described here are based on some basic knowledge about human vision and are intended to provide "realistic looking" images on the visualization device, even with critical lighting conditions in the rendered scene. The main features of the new techniques are *speed* (only a handful of floating point operations per pixel are needed) and *simplicity* (only one single parameter, which can be empirically evaluated has to be provided by the user). The goal of this paper is not to propose a psychovisual or neurological model for subjective perception, but only to described some experimental results and propose some possible research directions.

1 Motivations

The last task of the rendering step in computer graphics is to display the computed picture on some visualization device. More precisely, it implies to quantize every floating point "intensity" value (expressed either as radiance or luminance) computed during the rendering process, in order to map to one of the N single integer values accepted by a typical visualization device (cathodic monitor, laser printer). This step is far from being trivial, the main difficulty is to find a good *quantization function* which bypasses the limitations of the device (limited color gamut, limited dynamic range) in order to display a picture that evokes the same visual sensation as the equivalent real scene [8]. Several comprehensive solutions, using work done in color science [13], have been proposed for color gamut limitations [9, 6, 10]. But, except two very recent papers [3, 12], dynamic range limitations have usually been ignored or solved only for specific cases.

This paper proposes some fast and simple quantization techniques to display high dynamic range pictures on low dynamic range devices. For simplicity, the algorithms are first explained on greyscale pictures (Section 3 and 4) before being extended to color pictures (Section 5). Notice that these techniques do not pretent to be a comprehensive solution based on a more or less complex psycho-visual model for subjective perception, but only some better alternatives to the "gamma-corrected clamping technique" that is widely used in the global illumination community. Every quantization technique detailed here will be tested on the two pictures shown on Fig. 1. For the first one, the ratio between the highest and the lowest intensity value (*ie* dynamic range) is 2 500, whereas for the second one the dynamic range is 30 000. Such dynamic ranges are common both in real life and in computer imagery generated by global illumination. Therefore finding a technique to display correctly these pictures on current visualization devices should be of great interest for the global illumination community.

Fig. 1. High dynamic range test pictures
(a) Abstract picture showing stripes and circles of different intensities
(b) Room with a table and a wooden floor lit by an incandescent bulb[1]

2 Quantization of Greyscale Pictures

As recalled in the introduction, every intensity value *Val* of the computed picture has to be quantized in order to map one of the N single values in $[0, N-1]$ accepted by a typical visualization device. This process uses a so-called *tone reproduction function* (TRF, for short) F and can be formulated as :

$$Q\ (Val) = \lfloor N\ F(Val)\rfloor \quad \text{where} \quad F : [0, HiVal] \longrightarrow [0,1] \tag{1}$$

With Equation 1, $F(Val) = 1$ maps to the out-of-range value N. This particular case can be easily detected, and *Val* be remapped to $N-1$. Despite this annoying additional test, we find Equation 1 preferable to the more usual $Q(Val) = \lfloor (N-1)\ F(Val) + 0.5\rfloor$ because it provides N equal quantization steps.

Finding a good TRF is a complex task which involves many different fields such as anatomy of the human eye, technology of the visualization device, color science, principles of subjective perception [8]. As said, until very recent papers [12, 3], most work on TRF functions in computer graphics has been done on color reproduction, usually ignoring brightness reproduction. The most widely used TRF in computer graphics is *gamma-corrected linear mapping* :

$$F_q\left(Val\right) = \left(\frac{Val}{HiVal}\right)^{1/q} \quad \text{where} \quad q \in [1,3] \tag{2}$$

In fact, two successive operators are applied in that function : first, a linear scaling (*ie* division by HiVal) which brings the intensity values into the range [0,1] and second, a gamma-correction which compensates for the non-linear response of the visualization device (usual values for q range from 1 to 3). The result of gamma-corrected linear mapping on our pictures (see Fig. 4, Left Line) shows the inadequacy of this quantization for high dynamic range pictures: almost the whole scene (except the luminaires) is mapped to black or very dark gray.

A second popular TRF in computer graphics is *gamma-corrected clamping* :

$$F_{p,q}\left(Val\right) = \begin{cases} \left(Val/p\right)^{1/q} & \text{if } Val < p \\ 1 & \text{otherwise} \end{cases} \quad \text{where} \quad p \in [LoVal, HiVal] \quad q \in [1,3]$$

$$\tag{3}$$

The main limitation of clamping is that a satisfying value for p can almost never be found. Either it is too high (see Fig. 4, Middle Line) and then dark features (woodgrain of the floor, for instance) of the scene are all mapped to black, or it is too low (see Fig. 4, Right Line) and then bright details (the bulb and its neighborhood) are all mapped to white. A "magic formula" that circulates in the global illumination community is to give to p the value of the brightest object which is not a luminaire (Middle Line of Fig. 4 has been obtained so). But notice that such a formula implies that the quantization is done directly by the rendering process, because it is the only place where the luminaire/non-luminaire information is available.

Another TRF that has been often recommended but rarely implemented [2] is *logarithmic mapping* :

$$F_{p,q}\left(Val\right) = \left(\frac{\log\left(1 + p\ Val\right)}{\log\left(1 + p\ HiVal\right)}\right)^{1/q} \quad \text{where} \quad p \in [0, \infty) \quad q \in [1,3] \tag{4}$$

Logarithmic mapping has been proposed in the literature with or without gamma-correction. This fact can be explained when plotting the curves of logarithm mapping (see Fig. 2a) and gamma-correction (see Fig. 2b) : the shapes are almost identical. It means that gamma-corrected logarithmic scaling can be simulated with simple logarithmic scaling by giving a larger value to p. Applied on our test pictures, nice results are obtained (see Fig. 5, Left Line) showing both the woodgrain on the floor and the details near the bulb.

Theoretical justifications of logarithm mapping are usually based on an old result in human vision, dating from the beginning of the century, known as Weber's law [7]. This law follows from experimentation on brightness perception that consists of exposing an observer to a uniform field of intensity *Val* in which a disk is gradually increased with a quantity ΔVal. The value ΔVal from which

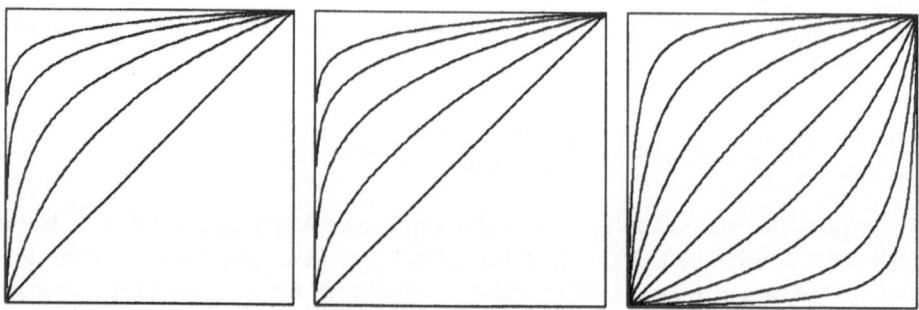

Fig. 2. Mapping functions for different values of p
(a) Logarithmic mapping   (b) Exponentiation mapping   (c) Rational mapping

the observer perceives the disk is called brightness discrimination threshold, and Weber noticed that $\Delta Val/Val$ is constant for a wide range of intensity values.

More complete and more recent experimentation [11, 5] have shown that Weber's experimental results (valid for the discrimination threshold) cannot be integrated to derive a logarithmic law (valid throughout the range of brightnesses). In fact, the actual law looks more like an exponentiation law ($\Delta Val/Val^k$ is constant) where $k \in [0, 1]$ depends on the intensity of the surrounding environment and the dynamic range of the picture. Thus, a possible TRF including both brightness perception and gamma-correction could be *exponentiation mapping* :

$$F_{p,q}\,(Val) = \left(\frac{Val}{HiVal}\right)^{p/q} \quad \text{where} \quad p \in [0,1] \quad q \in [1,3] \tag{5}$$

Consequently, what we have here is a gamma-corrected linear scaling with a new gamma factor $q' = q/p$ where nice results may be obtained by a judicious value for p (see Fig. 5, Middle Line). In other words, it means that the natural reflex (which everyone has succumbed to one day) of pushing the gamma factor over the value recommended by the manufacturer of the visualization device when displaying dark pictures, has got at least some theoretical justifications.

3 Uniform Rational Quantization

Though they can provide very good results, logarithmic and exponentiation mapping suffer from a serious weak point : there is no good rule to generate automatically a value for parameters p and q. Of course, q is theoretically given by the manufacturer but, as noted in [4], the gamma law is a first order approximation, usually only valid for a specific surrounding luminance and a specific setting of the device contrast and brightness. Moreover, as recalled in many technical manuals of printers or monitors, the gamma value is fluctuating under environment changes (heat, hygrometry, atmospheric pressure). Therefore finding some satisfying values implies a wasteful try-and-look process for almost every picture (more than 20 trials have been needed to get Left and Middle Line of Fig. 5).

In order to correct this weak point, we propose a new quantization scheme using a so-called *rational mapping* function :

$$F_p\,(Val) = \frac{p\,Val}{p\,Val - Val + Hi\,Val} \quad \text{where} \quad p \in [1, \infty) \tag{6}$$

This TRF is intended to account for the non-linear response of both the visualization device and subjective perception. When looking at the shape of the function for different values of p (see Fig. 2c), one can see that very similar curves are obtained compared to logarithmic or exponentiation (the same figure also shows that symmetric curves according to the first diagonal can be obtained by replacing p by $1/p$; this property will be used in Section 4). Therefore when applying rational mapping on our test pictures, results are almost identical to the previous techniques (see Fig. 2, Right Line), but the new function needs only 1 division, 1 multiplication, 1 subtraction and 1 addition, which is very economic compared to logarithm or exponentiation.

Automatic Generation of Parameter But the most interesting feature of the new TRF is that we propose a scheme to generate automatically the value of p. As this parameter controls how the non-linear response of the visualization device and subjective perception is accounted for, it should ideally depend on all the factors that are involved in a specific combination of observer, device and viewing conditions.

A possible solution is to use a scheme similar to the one proposed by Tumblin & Rushmeier [12] where 7 different parameters enable to control the shape of the TRF : gamma factor, maximum device contrast, maximum device luminance and the degree of adaptation in both the real world observer and display observer. While this technique is very comprehensive and does provide impressive results, we find it a bit too complex to become of general use for computer graphics. Indeed, the role of some parameters is hard to understand for a non-specialist user; and even for a specialist, giving a meaningful value to some of these parameters implies to use specific measuring instruments such as a photometer. Therefore, the user is more or less forced to work with the default values provided in [12], giving a sort of unflexible TRF hard to adapt to specific viewing conditions.

The automatic parameter generation process that we propose is based on the assumption that what really changes on a visualization device when several viewing parameters are modifed (average brightness of the surrounding environment, contrast and brightness setting for the device, observation distance...) is the value M of the darkest gray level that can be clearly distinguished from black. This value M could be used in the following manner : almost every rendering program includes an "epsilon" value (beneath which computed intensities are considered as negligible) that usually generates the smallest non-zero intensity value $Lo\,Val$ of the picture. Therefore, it seems natural that a quantization process should map the smallest non-zero intensity of the picture to the darkest non-black gray of the device : $Q(Lo\,Val) = M$

With our rational mapping function, it gives :

$$p = \frac{M\ HiVal - M\ LoVal}{N\ LoVal - M\ LoVal} \simeq \frac{M\ HiVal}{N\ LoVal} \tag{7}$$

The value of M can be easily provided by the user without any measuring instrument. For instance, we use the following process on our workstation : a black window is displayed on the screen, in which several squares of various intensities are drawn at random positions (see Fig. 3) — randomness insures that no spatial regularity would bias the perception. The user simply clicks on the darkest square he is able to see; the intensity of the selected square gives the value of parameter M. In a similar way, by printing or photographing the resulting pattern, the same process may be used to find the value of M for a given printer or camera setting.

This automatic generation of p using Equation 7 has been tested on numerous images and/or viewing conditions, and it always enabled to display a picture where all the desired details were visible. Therefore, the main result illustrated on Fig. 5 is not the similarity between the results provided by the three quantization techniques, but rather the fact that rational mapping enables to obtain these results, without any guesswork or hand fitting.

The reader may ask why the process $Q(LoVal) = M$ could not be used with logarithmic or exponentiation mapping in order to generate automatically the value of p. In fact, we have tried it, but in general, it does not provide very good results. We think that the reason lies on the symmetry of the rational mapping curves along the second diagonal (see Fig. 2c), symmetry that does not exist with logarithmic or exponentiation mapping. This symmetry implies that low and high values are treated in a reciprocal way (when the dynamic range of low values is multiplied by a given factor, the dynamic range of high values is divided by the same factor) and therefore a somewhat smoother mapping is provided.

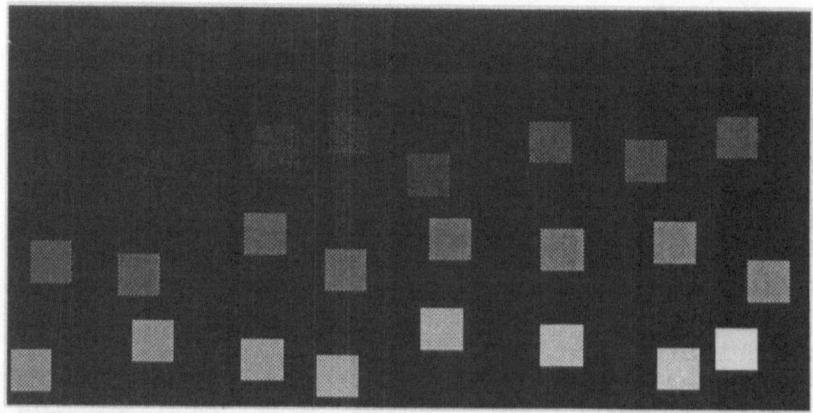

Fig. 3. Selection of the darkest non-black gray level.

4 Non Uniform Rational Quantization

The quantization process presented in Section 3 can be called *uniform* in the sense that each pixel intensity is quantized with the same tone mapping function. Therefore two pixels intensities Val_1 and Val_2, with $Val_1 \leq Val_2$, will be mapped to quantized values Q_1 and Q_2, such as $Q_1 \leq Q_2$. In real life, this is not always true because the subjective brightness of an object is highly dependent on the average surrounding brightness — everyone knows the classical optical illusion in which two identical gray squares put on different backgrounds appear with different subjective brightnesses. Chiu et al. [3] were the first in computer graphics to consider this property and stated that a quantization technique should be spatially *non-uniform*.

This non-uniform subjective perception is usually explained in vision science by the fact that an observer does not view a scene as a whole [1]. In fact, his eyes are continuously moving from one point to another, and for each point on which the eye focuses, there exists a surrounding zone that creates some local visual adaptation and thus modifies brightness perception. If we want to display a picture that evokes the subjective perception of the scene, this eye behaviour has to be included during the visualization process.

We propose the following empirical scheme to account for non-uniform subjective perception. For each pixel, an intensity value $Zo Val$ is computed corresponding to the average intensity of a given zone surrounding the pixel. This value $Zo Val$ is then used to modify parameter p of Equation 6, in order to create a specific parameter p' (and thus a specific TRF) for each pixel. According to the rules governing subjective perception [7, 5] when $Zo Val$ is low (resp. high), the pixel should appears brighter (resp. darker) to the observer, which means that p' should be smaller (resp. larger) than p.

Because of the (quasi-)logarithmic response of subjective brightness perception, a fundamental quantity of our picture is the geometrical mean :

$$MiVal = \sqrt{Lo Val \, Hi Val} \tag{8}$$

which divides the dynamic range into two equal sub-ranges :

$$\frac{Hi Val}{Mi Val} = \frac{Mi Val}{Lo Val} = \sqrt{\frac{Hi Val}{Lo Val}} \tag{9}$$

Therefore the ratio $Zo Val/Mi Val$ characterizes the brightness of a zone : if it is smaller (resp. larger) than 1, the zone will be considered as dark (resp. bright). In our scheme, this ratio is used to modify parameter p in the following manner :

$$p' = p \left(1 - k + k \frac{Zo Val}{Mi Val}\right) \quad \text{with} \quad k \in [0, 1] \tag{10}$$

where k represents the weight of non-uniformity that is included in the TRF (*ie* when $k = 0$, the mapping is uniform). Giving a meaningful value to k is difficult because, to our knowledge, the relative importance of global vs. local

Fig. 4. LEFT: Linear quantization, MIDDLE: Clamping with a large value, RIGHT: Clamping with a small value.

brightness perception has never been studied (we have used $k = 0.5$ in our experimentations).

So, to get a complete non-uniform quantization technique, the only point that remains to solve is to find a scheme to compute $Zo\,Val$ for each pixel. In fact, we have tested three different schemes (low pass filtering, micro-zone, segmentation) which are detailed in the next paragraphs.

Low-Pass Filtering Because we want to compute the average intensity value $Zo\,Val$ of a zone surrounding a pixel, a natural idea is to apply a low-pass filter on the picture. Thus, $Zo\,Val$ will be computed as a weighted sum of neighboring intensities; the weights as well as the extent of the neighbourhood are given by the convolution matrix of the filter. Such a process has been used by Chiu et al. [3] in their non-uniform mapping scheme. We have tried a similar idea, and though we have used a different convolution matrix and a different mapping function, we came to the same conclusion : non-uniform quantization driven by a low-pass filtered picture creates some unacceptable artifacts.

A low-pass filtered version of our test pictures can be seen on Fig. 5, Left Line. Using the intensity values $Zo\,Val$ provided by that filtered image to control the non-uniform mapping with Equation 10 yields bad results (see Fig. 6, Middle Line) where unnatural dark bandings are visible. Nevertheless, it should be noted that, if low-pass filtering is inadequate for our quantization scheme, we have found it very useful to simulate another specific phenomenon involved in human vision : dazzling effects (see Fig. 6, Right Line) can be obtained by

Fig. 5. LEFT: Logarithmic quantization, MIDDLE: Exponentiation quantization, RIGHT: Rational quantization.

simply reversing the transformation of parameter p in the non-uniform mapping (*ie* replacing $ZoVal/MiVal$ by $MiVal/ZoVal$ in Equation 10).

Micro-Zones When reducing the size of the convolution matrix, dark artifacts progressively vanish. Finally best results are obtained when the size of the matrix is one, which means that the surrounding zone of a pixel is reduced to a micro-zone composed of the pixel itself, and thus $ZoVal = Val$. This result is somewhat surprising because reducing to surrounding zone to one pixel provides in fact a uniform mapping.

Comparing the result of such a mapping (see Fig. 7, Left Line) with the previous rational mapping on our test pictures (see Fig. 7, Right Line) shows much nice results for the former (the woodgrain appears much better and the light bulb is better antialiased). We think that this result comes from the fact that the new uniform mapping creates larger dynamic ranges (which may eventually overlap) for specific parts of the picture. Notice that by precomputing $1-k$ and $k/MiVal$, this new rational mapping function involves only an additional cost of 2 multiplications and 1 addition per pixel, compared to the rational mapping function presented in Section 3.

Segmentation The last scheme that we have tried is to segment the picture into zones of similar intensity values. For each zone, the average intensity $ZoVal$ is computed and each pixel of the zone will get the same $ZoVal$. Image segmentation

Fig. 6. LEFT: Low-pass filtered image, MIDDLE: Low-pass quantization, RIGHT: Inverse low-pass quantization.

Fig. 7. LEFT: Micro-zone quantization, MIDDLE: Segmented image, RIGHT: Segmentation quantization.

is a complex problem and an algorithm dealing with every configuration has not yet been found. But we have here a simplified case (greyscale picture where only a few number of zones are wanted) and therefore classical techniques such as gradient or histogram thresholding should work for most pictures.

A segmented version of our test pictures id shown on Fig. 7, Middle Line. Using the value *ZoVal* provided by that segmented image to control the non-uniform mapping with Equation 10 yields nice results (see Fig. 7, Right Line). But compared to the micro-zone technique, differences can hardly be seen (a bit less saturation around the light bulb) and therefore, we think that the improvement is not worth the overhead involved by the segmentation step.

5 Extension to Color Pictures

In this section, we propose to extend our quantization scheme to color pictures. Only images created with a trichromatic model during the rendering step are considered here, but the technique can be straightforwardly adapted to spectral models [6, 9]. The only imperative is to be able to compute the Y coordinate of the CIE XYZ color system.

Let's suppose that we have created a color picture using three floating point values per pixel (Val_r, Val_g, Val_b), one for each primary color R,G,B. A naive extension of the quantization scheme could be to compute 3 dynamic ranges, 3 parameters (p_r, p_g, p_b) and 3 rational mapping functions $F_{p_r}(Val_r)$, $F_{p_g}(Val_g)$ and $F_{p_b}(Val_b)$. Because dynamic ranges may be very different for each primary color, the resulting mapping functions may have very different shapes and then many color shifts are likely to be created by such a process.

One has to remember that our tone mapping function is intended to compensate for non-linear response of both the visualization device and subjective brightness perception. When looking at technical characteristics of trichromatic devices, one can see that the response is nearly identical for the three primary colors. When looking at the conclusions of experimentation on subjective perception, one can see that the brightness discrimination law yields, more or less, throughout the visible spectrum, depending only on the relative sensitivity of the eye to the tested color. These two results tend to prove that, in a first order approximation, the tone mapping operator should probably be achromatic.

Starting from that presumption, we propose the following extension of our TRF for color pictures. For each pixel (Val_r, Val_g, Val_b), the corresponding achromatic intensity *Val* is computed. *Val* is in fact the Y coordinate of the CIE XYZ color system (*ie* luminous efficiency of human eye across the visible spectrum). Therefore, if the XYZ coordinates of the primary colors used by the visualization device are provided by the manufacturer, they could be used. If these coordinates are not available, *Val* could be computed according to some television color standard. For instance, with NTSC[2] is gives [6] :

$$Val = 0.299 \ Val_r + 0.587 \ Val_g + 0.114 \ Val_b \tag{11}$$

This operation creates a greyscale picture for which the tone mapping function $F_p(Val)$ is defined by Equations 6, 7 and 10. This TRF insures that $Val' = F_p(Val)$ will be the new (normalized) intensity of the pixel. Therefore, what we want is to find (Val'_r, Val'_g, Val'_b) such as

$$Val' = 0.299 \ Val'_r + 0.587 \ Val'_g + 0.114 \ Val'_b \tag{12}$$

There is an infinite number of solutions that fulfill Equation 12. Work done on a similar problem for color gamut [6, 10] has shown that minimal color shifts occur when the ratios between primary colors are preserved during the tranformation :

$$\frac{Val'_r}{Val_r} = \frac{Val'_g}{Val_g} = \frac{Val'_b}{Val_b} \tag{13}$$

Let's suppose that $max \ (Val_r, Val_g, Val_b) = Val_r$. It means that

$$\exists \ (u, v) \in [0, 1]^2 \ / \ \ Val_g = u \ Val_r \ \ \text{and} \ \ Val_b = v \ Val_r \tag{14}$$

We have

$$Val = Val_r \ (0.299 + 0.587 \ u + 0.114 \ v) \tag{15}$$

and according to Equation 13, we want

$$Val' = Val'_r \ (0.299 + 0.587 \ u + 0.114 \ v) \tag{16}$$

thus

$$Val'_r = \frac{Val'}{0.299 + 0.587 \ u + 0.114 \ v} \qquad Val'_g = u \ Val'_r \qquad Val'_b = v \ Val'_r \tag{17}$$

which defines the TRF for color pictures.

6 Conclusion

This paper has reported some experimentations about quantization techniques for visualization of computer generated pictures, leading to the following conclusions :

- Arbitrary high dynamic ranges (greyscale or color) pictures can be displayed on arbitrary low range devices by the use of an original rational tone mapping function F_p.

---

[2] Equation 11 is valid for an additive color device (e.g. CRT) with R,G,B as primary colors. For a subtractive color device (e.g. printer) with C,M,Y as primary colors, Val is given by : $1 - 0.402 \, Val_c + 0.174 \, Val_m - 0.772 \, Val_y$.

- A possible technique has been proposed (called *micro-zone rational mapping*) which uses a specific function F_p for which parameter p is changed according to the intensity of each pixel.
- One main feature of the quantization is *speed* : for a color picture, only 4 divisions, 12 multiplications and 5 additions per pixel are required.
- Another main feature is *simplicity* : the algorithm is controlled by only 3 parameters, the highest intensity *HiVal* of the picture, the lowest non-zero intensity *LoVal* (which can either be provided by the user or computed by a first pass on the picture) and the value M of the darkest non-black gray visible on the device under the current viewing conditions.

7 Pictures

Each picture (see picture plates, below) is composed of three columns where one column represents one quantization technique. For each technique, four images are shown : an abstract picture composed of lines and circles, an room with a table and a wooden floor lit by an incandescent bulb, as well as two close-ups of specific parts of this latter image (the light bulb and the rightmost table foot).

Aknowledgments

Special thanks to Pete Shirley for providing the room test picture, to Holly Rushmeier for making available her technical report before publication and to Jean-Philippe Domenger for numerous contructive discussions. The present work is supported by the *Université Bordeaux I*, the *Centre National de la Recherche Scientifique* and the *Conseil Régional d'Aquitaine*.

References

1. J.Armington, *Visual Psychophysics and Physiology*, Academic Press, 1978
2. J.Blinn, *Dirty Pixels*, IEEE Computer Graphics & Applications, v9, n3, p100-105, 1989
3. K.Chiu, M.Herf, P.Shirley, S.Swamy, C.Wang, K.Zimmerman, *Spatially Non Uniform Scaling Functions for High Contrast Images*, Proceedings of Graphics Interface 93, p182-191, 1993
4. W.Cowan, *An Inexpensive Scheme for Calibration of a Colour Monitor in Terms of CIE Standard Coordinates*, ACM Computer Graphics, v17, n3, p315-321, 1983
5. E.Gordon, *A Power Law for Contrast Discrimination*, Vision Research, v21, p457-467, 1981
6. R.Hall, *Illumination and Color in Computer Generated Imagery*, Springer Verlag, 1989
7. D.Jameson, L.Hurvich, *Handbook of Sensory Physiology*, Springer Verlag, 1972
8. G.Meyer, H.Rushmeier, M.Cohen, D.Greenberg, K.Torrance, *An Experimental Evaluation of Computer Graphics Imagery*, ACM Transactions on Graphics, v5, n1, p30-50, 1986

9. G.Meyer, *Wavelength Selection for Synthetic Image Generation*, Computer Graphics & Image Processing, v41, p57-79, 1988

10. B.Smits, G.Meyer, *Simulating Interference Phenomena in Realistic Image Synthesis*, Proceedings of First Eurographics Workshop on Rendering (Rennes, France), p185-194, 1990

11. S.S.Stevens, J.C.Stevens, *Brightness Function : Effects of Adaptation*, Journal of Optical Society of America, v53, n3, p375-385, 1963

12. J.Tumblin, H.Rushmeier, *Tone Reproduction for Realistic Computer Generated Images*, IEEE Computer Graphics & Applications, v13, n6, p42-48, 1993

13. G.Wyszecki, W.Stiles, *Color Science*, Wiley & sons, 1967

Rendering, Complexity, and Perception

Kenneth Chiu, Peter Shirley

Indiana University, Bloomington IN 47405, USA

1 Introduction

Computer graphics researchers have spent great effort in the last ten years on strengthening the physical foundations of computers graphics. We now need to step back and examine the nature of scenes our end-users wish to render, and what qualities these rendered images must possess. Humans view these images, not machines, and this crucial distinction must guide the research process, lest we become an increasingly irrelevant enclave, divorced from the users we profess to serve.

In *Is Image Synthesis a Solved Problem?*[Coh92], Cohen examined the degree to which current realistic rendering methods solve problems encountered in real applications. He concluded that these methods do not adequately deal with complexities in scene geometries, reflection properties, and illumination; and with issues involving human perception. In his informal survey of rendering researchers, the two areas of image synthesis that were considered the "least solved" were: dealing with environmental complexity, and dealing with perceptual issues. In this paper, we propose a rendering system that is designed around these two problems. We do not claim to have a solution, rather we have a partial solution made from current technology, and a direction for future development.

In Section 2 we examine the qualities required by typical computer graphics applications. In Section 3 we discuss how these qualities impact our modeling techniques. In Section 4 the importance of perception is expanded. In Section 5, the requirements for future renderers are discussed. In Section 6, we present our framework for a renderer satisfying these requirements.

2 Applications of Future Renderers

The primary purpose of most computer graphics imagery is to communicate with the viewer. This communication may simply be knowledge or information about the data being rendered, such as what a traffic safety engineer might need, or it can take on a deeper, more emotional form, such as that used by the entertainment industry.

The effectiveness of this communication depends critically on realism. Different applications require different kinds of realism, but we believe that all fall under two broad categories: *perceptual realism* and *visceral realism*. Such categorization is useful because design decisions affect these kinds of realism differently.

- **Perceptual realism.** An image is perceptually realistic if a viewer of the image synthesizes a mental image similar to that synthesized by a viewer of the real scene. For example, parts of the scene too dark to be visible to an actual viewer should also be too dark in the image. Likewise, areas of the scene where the actual viewer is blinded by glare should be washed out in the image. These and other effects would need to be simulated accurately for applications such as safety engineering, architectural simulation, or set design. To correctly model them requires a full, quantitative model for human perception, something not yet available, although incomplete models have been shown to be useful[MG88, NKON90, TR93, SW91, GFMS94, CHS+93].

- **Visceral realism.** A viscerally realistic image suspends our disbelief in the same way that a good movie convinces us that it is really happening. Viewers need to have a deep, intuitive sense that the objects in the image actually exist, even if they are fantastic or improbable. Such images would be necessary for training simulations, entertainment, artistic applications, etc. We believe that the key quality for visceral realism is complexity. This complexity can take many forms. It includes complexity of the material as well as geometric complexity. Images need to be rich and detailed. Objects need to be worn, dirty, cracked, weathered, etc. Some elements of perceptual realism such as glare are also important.

For most applications, both forms of realism are important. For example, in a military training simulator, correctly reproducing the visibility or invisibility of objects is very important. But inducing the stress that the trainee would encounter in a real situation is also very important, and for this the trainee must feel, intuitively, that what he is experiencing is real. The former is a component of perceptual realism, and the latter is visceral realism.

3 Modeling Issues

Texture-mapping, bump-mapping, solid textures are several well-known methods for adding complexity to an image[BM93]. While computationally practical and very effective for some kinds of complexity, they suffer from some fundamental limitations.

First, they do not actually extend the geometry. So any kinds of detail where the viewpoint is close enough to actually see the geometry cannot be rendered with these techniques. Second, they cannot handle self-shadowing. Carpets and fur are two examples that are difficult to render accurately without self-shadowing. Lastly, they have a difficult time handling dynamic objects. Replacing a field of wheat waving in the wind with a texture map would require that the map be accurately recomputed for every frame.

Texels[Kaj89] are somewhat less limiting. They include self-shadowing, and thus can produce convincing images of things like fur. Extension to geometric complexity that is significantly non-isotropic would greatly increase memory usage, however, since the scalar density in each cell must be replaced with a higher tensor quantity. Like texture maps, texels also cannot be used in areas where the details of the geometry are distinguishable. Texels also have problems with dynamic objects because the an immense quantity of information must be processed.

For convincing complexity then, actual geometry is often necessary. Unfortunately, this produces an enormous number of primitives. Just correctly modeling the carpet in a large room can involve millions of primitives. To reduce the number of primitives, multiple levels of detail are commonly used[FS93]. In this technique, an object has more than one representation. The representations have different degrees of detail. Depending on various factors such as the screen size of the object, the appropriate level of detail is selected. Thus, an object that covers only one pixel will be represented with many fewer primitives than that same object when it covers half the image.

This strategy can work well with static images, but when applied to dynamic objects in an animation, several problems arise. First, avoiding "jumps" when changing from one level of detail to another is difficult. Second, even given that we have some method to change smoothly, generating enough intermediate representations to avoid disturbing transitions from one level of detail to a much different level of detail can be a considerable amount of work. Lastly and most importantly, producing intermediate representations for dynamic objects with arbitrary reflection characteristics can be extremely difficult.

For an intermediate representation to produce good results, it must have the same average reflective properties as the actual, full resolution object. For example, suppose an image contains a forest that is far enough away so that a tree is smaller than a pixel. In this case, a tree can be perhaps be represented by a sphere. Now suppose we zoom in so that the trees are now approximately four pixels in size. At this point, a slightly more detailed representation of the tree should be used. In order to avoid a disturbing color shift, this slightly more detailed representation must have the same average reflective properties as the sphere representation, and both of these must have the same average reflective properties as the full representation of the tree.

Although perhaps feasible for static scenes, the above requirement becomes prohibitively difficult for arbitrary, dynamic objects[BM93]. For example, creating a coarse representation of a patch of wheat that could be used to produce an animation of a plain of wheat waving in the wind would be difficult without actually modeling the structure of an individual plant. But if the structures of the an individual plant are actually modeled, then the level of detail is not very low, and we have lost most of the advantage of using different levels of detail.

The above problems can all be eliminated if everything is always represented in its full level of detail. This immediately brings other problems, however. First, storing such a large number of primitives would be very expensive. A detailed model of a tree might require a million primitives. Scenes containing billions if not trillions of primitives are easily imaginable. Consider a large plain covered with prairie grass. Assume that every square meter contains one hundred plants. If 10,000,000 square meters are visible, then 1 billion plants must be rendered. If each plant is modeled with 1000 primitives, then the scene contains 1 trillion primitives total.

The question then arises: why stop at the leaves? Why is it not necessary to model the microfacets of surfaces? The answer is that the depth to which it is necessary to model the actual geometry depends upon the application. Three questions are important. First, is the geometry distinguishable? If we are making an animation from the viewpoint of a virus, then modeling the microfacets is important because they can actually be seen. Second, does a good analytical model exist for the BRDF of the surface? For a complex surface such as skin, modeling the cellular structure might be necessary to capture the proper appearance[HK93]. But if a suitable analytical function exists, such as for brushed steel, then the microfacets need not be modeled. Lastly, in the time frame of application, is the surface changing appreciably? If we are generating a one-minute animation of a room with a wooden floor, modeling the microstructure of the wood is probably not necessary. If we wish to generate a realistic depiction of wood weathering over a five-year period, however, modeling the microstructure might be important.

Since we are primarily interested in rendering in the human spatial and temporal scale, for our purposes we do not need to model most microstructure as long as a satisfactory analytic approximation can be found for the BRDF. Even in those cases where such a function cannot be found, tabulated results from Monte-Carlo simulations can be substituted for the microstructure[HK93].

The extremely large number number of primitives required for convincing complexity imply that procedural models must be used. By procedural model, we mean that not only are the primitives generated by an algorithm, but that in addition the primitives are generated only on demand, and not explicitly stored. Some examples of high complexity procedural models are [Pru93, PH89, FS90].

Procedural models have other important advantages besides storage cost. Through procedural models, users can produce highly detailed and complex scenes with relatively sparse input. Without this capability, users would be burdened with having to provide an overwhelming amount of data about the exact geometric and physical properties of each and every object. Procedural models can also communicate with each other. Thus, the vegetation model underneath a tree model can understand that it is in shade rather than sunlight, and modify its growth accordingly[AGW86].

4 Perceptual Issues

The human visual process involves the synthesis of many different signals into an internal mental image. The original input to this process is the light coming from the various surfaces in the scene. Our goal is to generate an image that, when viewed on a display device, results in the same internal mental image.

Note that the two human visual systems are not necessarily identical. For example, suppose we have an 80-year old man encountering a pedestrian while driving a vehicle. His visual system processes the light entering his eye into an internal mental image. Now, we have a traffic engineer sitting at his workstation. He wishes to know whether or not that 80-year old man can see the pedestrian. We need to generate an image that, when processed through *his* visual system, results in the synthesis of an identical internal mental image (Figure 1).

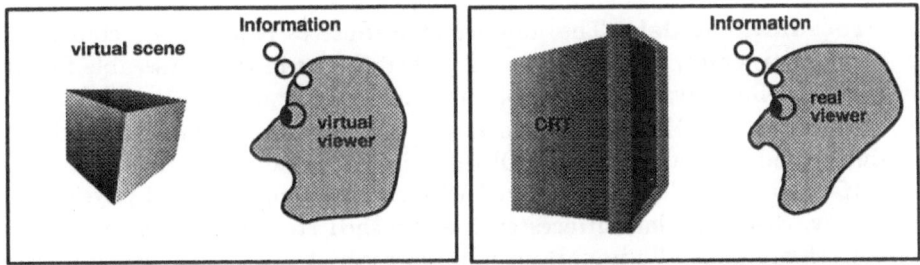

Fig. 1. Virtual person views a virtual screen and real viewer views a monitor.

Producing an exact match would probably require a perfect display device.[1] Lacking this for the forseeable future, we can only hope to produce an image that results in a similar internal mental image. Ideally, we could develop a error metric that weights differences between the two internal mental images in a way appropriate for the application. Part of the rendering process would then involve finding a perceptual transform on the computed radiance values that minimizes this error.

Lacking the necessary perceptual model of the human visual system, researchers have aimed at producing somewhat weaker forms of perceptual realism. Rather than trying to duplicate the visual experience of the virtual viewer, we can aim at determining only which parts of the scene are visible and which parts are invisible, and displaying an image that reproduces this visibility condition for the computer user. Meyer has similar results for color-blind virtual viewers[MG88]. A viewer of the resulting image is unable to distinguish different colors where a color-blind person is also unable to distinguish different colors. Tumblin and Rushmeier have investigated the more difficult problem of imitating the effects of dark adaptation under low-light conditions[TR93]. Nakamae et al. simulated glare effects to cause an impression of high-intensity luminaires

---

[1] If we had a perfect display device, and both human visual systems were identical, this would be trivial. We could simply use a physically accurate renderer to compute the light that would enter the eye of the actual viewer of the real scene. The perfect display device would then send the exact same light into the eye's of the device user. Since both viewer's eyes receive the same light, they will perceive the same image. Real display devices, however, have a limited dynamic range, a limited color gamut, and do not provide a full field-of-view.

on a low-intensity display[NKON90]. Ultimately, all of these effects must be used in an integrated framework.

5 Requirements of Future Renderers

From the above discussion, we can make some statements of what capabilities a renderer must have to meet the realism requirements of current and future applications.

- **Procedural models.** The number of primitives required for convincing complexity simply cannot be stored, either now or in the foreseeable future. The modeling advantages of procedural models are also essential.
- **Arbitrary BRDFs.** Real surfaces are not some combination of perfectly diffuse and perfectly specular. Objects simply do not look real unless their surfaces are modeled and rendered with a convincing degree of physical accuracy. Near-specular surfaces such as brushed steel, semi-gloss paint, and varnish are especially important in many scenes.
- **Global illumination.** Indirect lighting is a very important component to realism. For example, the ceiling in a room lit with recessed ceiling lights would be black without including indirect lighting in the illumination computations. Other effects, such as caustics and color-bleeding, are somewhat less crucial, but can be an important contributor to realism.
- **Many luminaires.** Indoor scenes are commonly lit with only a few lights. Outdoor scenes, however, may have thousands or even millions of lights.
- **Perceptual transform.** To meet requirements of perceptual realism, a perceptual transform must be performed at some stage of the rendering process.
- **Parallelizeable.** Current computer hardware already utilizes parallel architectures to improve performance. Future hardware is also likely to include parallel architectures, perhaps to a very high degree.
- **Physical accuracy.** In applications where the image is being used to preview a proposed design, such as set design, or architectural simulations, the calculated radiometric values must be accurate if the image is to be useful as a preview. For other applications, where perhaps visceral realism is more important, a larger degree of error is tolerable, but the accuracy must still be high enough to provide a convincing approximation to actual materials[War92, WAT92].

A balanced perspective must be used when evaluating the last requirement. While calculations should have a solid grounding in physics, we must not produce a renderer that reduces the complexity of the scene to make possible the generation of accurate radiometric values. For visceral realism especially, complexity is often more important that physical accuracy, as can be seen by the commercial success of movies such as *Jurassic Park*.

Different algorithms divide their computational resources between physical accuracy and complexity in different ways. A radiosity algorithm, for example, can produce extremely accurate physical results, but only for a fairly limited number of perfectly diffuse primitives. A classical ray-tracing program can produce images of much lower physical accuracy, but for a correspondingly much greater number of primitives. We propose that more effort should devoted to developing a renderer that sacrifices some of the accuracy of radiosity methods for complexity. Figure 2 diagrams the trade-offs between physical accuracy and complexity.

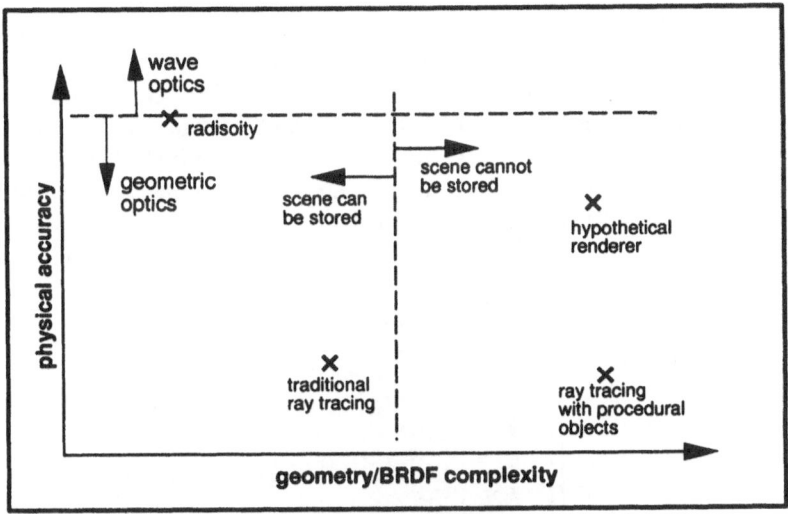

Fig. 2. Qualitative graph of the target rendering algorithm.

6 A Framework

In this section we outline what we believe a renderer that meets the above requirements will look like. Our framework is only a proposal, and other frameworks may certainly meet our requirements.

Any method that requires all primitives to fit into memory at the same time will fail on scenes with sufficiently rich procedural objects. This includes most, if not all, radiosity methods. Hierarchical schemes may manage to reduce the working set size of a renderer, but the introduction of general BRDFs into most radiosity methods greatly increases the memory storage required. We propose that a raytracing-based scheme will be more flexible, easier to program, and ultimately faster. This is an extension of arguments made by Kajiya at SIGGRAPH '88[Kaj88].

To expend resources where they will provide the most benefit, some kind of multi-stage adaptive sampling is probably required, An initial set of samples through a pixel gathers information about what is seen through that pixel and decides whether more rays need to be sent. Kirk and Arvo point out that the difficulties of adaptive sampling are more subtle than one might anticipate[KA91a], but Glassner, in his survey of adaptive sampling methods determines that adaptive sampling can perform well in practice[Gla94]. Previous adaptive sampling methods are also surveyed in [vWvNJ91].

To adaptively sample we need to know the accuracy desired at a given pixel. If we know how a pixel radiance value will be mapped to a display intensity then we know the approximate accuracy needed for that pixel and can then adaptively sample that pixel. However, we have a "chicken-and-egg" problem because we don't know the mapping to display intensities for any of the pixels until all pixel radiances have been calculated. But if we had a approximate idea of what the mapping to display intensities was, this would provide information to allow us to conservatively apply adaptive sampling. This suggests the surprising strategy of taking the initial samples at every pixel, and using this noisy image to estimate the mapping to display intensity for every pixel. Then pixels that have insufficient accuracy can be sampled in an adaptive phase. The architecture for such a strategy is illustrated in Figure 3.

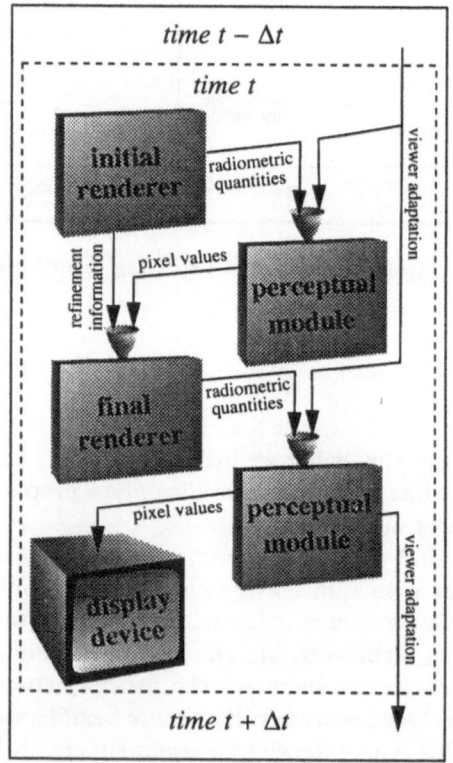

Fig. 3. Modules active during the generation of one frame.

The initial set of samples in the adaptive sampling gives enough information to approximate the perceptual transform. This tells us what the error metric is in a pixel space and can give us an estimate of sampling goals. The final renderer decides the effort needed to render each pixel based on the adapted image and the symbolic information passed by the initial renderer. The rendered image then filters through the perceptual module to produce the displayed image. Our images are computed with full spectral resolution, and are stored as XYZ chromaticities and a fourth channel containing the rod response as detailed in the Appendix.

This strategy assumes that the degree of acceptable error at a pixel depends not on the strict radiance of that pixel, but rather on the perceived brightness as produced by the visual system. Though we believe this assumption to be true, the acceptable error at each pixel may be independent of nearby pixels. In this case, no feedback loop would necessary, and the architecture would be a much simpler linear pipeline.

A variety of renderers have been developed for general BRDFs. Two-pass methods are very numerous, and these are surveyed in [JC93]. Many of the methods have generated quite successful scenes (e.g., [KJ92]), but they still use shadow rays and will fail in highly complex scenes where virtual luminaires are important.

Interestingly, the only rendering algorithm that can compute the global illumination in an arbitrarily complex environment is Kajiya's path-tracing algorithm[Kaj86] and even his algorithm breaks down for scenes with many luminaires. Ward's *Radiance* program performs fairly well in the presence of dozens or hundreds of luminaires, but degenerates to Kajiya's algorithm for global illumination if the variation in surface normals in the scene is high, as is common in outdoor scenes.

We are aware of only two methods that do not use shadow rays: Glassner's[Gla93], and Kirk and Arvo's [KA91b]. But both of these force sampling of luminaires on the hemisphere. Virtual luminaires,[2] however, especially non-planar virtual luminaires, makes determining where the luminaires are in the first place computationally expensive. We believe that in a highly complex environment, treating anything as a special case is only marginally beneficial. So we reach the surprising conclusion that *Kajiya's path-tracing method is not too brute-force, but rather not brute-force enough.* We need a method such as Kajiya's path-tracing with no shadow rays, which is really just the random-walk methods of the 1940s. Figure 4[3] is an example image created with such a technique.

Our current research focuses on smarter brute-force methods that maintain the principle of no shadow rays. The "smartness" of the method will undoubtably focus on the use of low-resolution environments[RPV93, Kok93]. We believe all future rendering methods will use such low-resolution environments for at least the indirect lighting calculation.

---

[2] A virtual luminaire is a luminaire that does not generate its own light, but rather specularly reflects or refracts the light from other luminaires.

[3] This figure is available in ppm format on ftp.cs.indiana.edu in as /pub/chiu.ppm. A version gamma-corrected (with a gamma of 2.3) is available as chiu_gamma.ppm.

Fig. 4. Brute force rendering with 4800 rays per pixel.

7 Conclusion

We believe that future applications will increasingly require perceptual accuracy in addition to physical accuracy. Without it, we cannot assure an architect that the walkthrough we have generated is anything at all like what a real person walking through the real building will experience. This is certainly not a new idea, but is one that needs to influence the focus of our rendering research. This is the fundamental difference between rendering research and heat-transfer research.

Future applications will also require a primitive database with too many primitives to store explicitly. We believe that this will be the only viable way to realize the goal of generating an animation that is as effective at suspending the viewer's disbelief as a normal motion picture. Such a large number of primitives probably means that physical accuracy must be selectively sacrificed.

To some degree, this implies that brute-force methods will become increasingly more useful. A field of grain waving gently in the wind would be difficult to model with multiple scales of resolution, especially as we change parameters such as moisture on the grain, species, time-of-day, cloud cover, season, soil type, terrain, etc. General techniques that consider all primitives at full resolution will become increasingly attractive as hardware performance increases, and as physical and biological models become increasingly common.

Realism of some kind has always been the goal of computer graphics, and physical accuracy has been implicitly assumed to be synonymous with realism. Perhaps this would be true in a world with fantastic computing power and display technologies, but in our world we must remember that our viewers are humans, not measuring instruments. As such, we believe that much current research efforts fail to reflect that for many applications, perception is as important as physics, and that for many other applications, accuracy should be subordinate to complexity. Understanding and attention to physical accuracy are undoubtedly crucial, but maintaining a balance between perceptual transforms, scene complexity, and physical accuracy must become our primary concern. In our quest for realism, we should not let ourselves become slaves of physical accuracy to the detriment of other important qualities.

Appendix: Implementation Issues

Because we want our rendering software to be applied to real problems, we must make an effort to support as many standards of measure and file format as possible.

For input, we must support luminaire distribution data that is supplied by manufacturers. The most common format in use now is the IES file format for far-field photometry[oNA91]. This format is also reviewed in Glassner's book[Gla94]. To approximate near-field photometry, we assume the power leaves the surface of the luminaire with equal radiance at each point.

Traditionally, integer-valued output files such as *ppm* have been used for computer graphics. For output format, we store floating point values. The new ray tracer instead outputs files with floating point values (4 bytes—3 bytes for 3 mantissas and one byte for a shared exponent). The file I/O routines are based on Greg Ward's *Radiance* format, and have proven to be very convenient to use, especially given the tools Ward makes freely available. Instead of display dependent RGB files, we output tristimulous XYZ response in SI units $(lm/(m^2 sr))$. This unit is sometimes called the *nit*[Ins86]. You will also see luminances reported in *Lamberts*, which are $\pi/1000$ nits each. There is also a concept of scotopic (night/rod) luminance, which has the same units as photopic luminances. Because we are interested in viewing night scenes, we produce a second floating point file containing the scotopic luminance at each pixel. This brings up the question of whether a four mantissa format is needed.

A question we should have is when do we use the photopic XYZ values for display, and when do we use photopic? At luminances above 3 cd/m^2 we are in the photopic region, where colors can be distinguished and fine detail can be seen. From 0.01 to 3 cd/m^2 we are in the mesopic region, where some color and detail is visible. Below 0.01 cd/m^2 we are in the scotopic region where cones are inactive so there is no color vision[Rea93].

Another question we should ask is whether the one byte mantissa and exponent give us enough dynamic range. The brightest commonly seen object is the Sun, which has an average luminance of is about 1600×10^6 cd/m^2 viewed from sea level[Rea93]. This is well within the capabilities of the format.

The biggest hole in standardization now is scene file format. However, we do not yet understand how material properties or procedural models and textures are likely to be specified at an abstract level, so it is probably too early to work on a standard unless it is extensible.

8 Acknowledgements

Thanks to Changyaw Wang and Kurt Zimmerman who helped develop code used in this work. Thanks to Jack Tumblin and Holly Rushmeier for making their tone mapping work available to us early. Thanks to many members of the Cornell Program of Computer Graphics who gave valuable feedback on a presentation related to this work. Thanks to Greg Ward for software and guidance. Thanks to Andrew Glassner for helping us to ask the right questions about our own work. Thanks also several excellent anonymous SIGGRAPH reviewers who commented on an earlier version of this paper.

This work was supported Indiana University and by NSF grant *True Virtual Reality Systems* NSF-CCR-92-09457.

References

[AGW86]   Phil Amburn, Eric Grant, and Turner Whitted. Managing geometric complexity with enhanced procedural models. *Computer Graphics*, 20(4):189–195, August 1986. ACM Siggraph '86 Conference Proceedings.

[BM93]   Barry G. Becker and Nelson L. Max. Smooth transitions between bump rendering algorithms. *Computer Graphics*, pages 183–190, August 1993. ACM Siggraph '93 Conference Proceedings.

[CHS+93] K. Chiu, M. Herf, P. Shirley, S. Swamy, C. Wang, and K. Zimmerman. Spatially nonuniform scaling functions for high contrast images. In *Graphics Interface '93*, pages 245–244, May 1993.

[Coh92]   Michael F. Cohen. Is image synthesis a solved problem? In *Proceedings of the Third Eurographics Workshop on Rendering*, pages 161–167, 1992.

[FS90]   Mark Friedell and Jean-Louis Schulmann. Constrained grammar-directed generation of landscapes. In *Graphics Interface '90*, pages 244–251, May 1990.

[FS93]   Thomas A. Funkhouser and Carlo H. Sequin. Adaptive display algorithm for interactive frame rates during visualization of complex virtual environments. *Computer Graphics*, pages 247–254, August 1993. ACM Siggraph '93 Conference Proceedings.

[GFMS94] Andrew Glassner, Kenneth P. Fishkin, David H. Marimont, and Maureen C. Stone. Device-directed rendering. *ACM Transactions on Graphics*, 0(0):0–0, November 1994. To appear.

[Gla93]   Andrew S. Glassner. Dynamic stratification. In *Proceedings of the Fourth Eurographics Workshop on Rendering*, pages 5–14, 1993.

[Gla94]   Andrew S. Glassner. *Principles of Image Synthesis*. Morgan-Kaufman, 1994.

[HK93]   Pat Hanrahan and Wolfgang Krueger. Reflection from layered surfaces due to subsurface scattering. *Computer Graphics*, pages 165–174, August 1993. ACM Siggraph '93 Conference Proceedings.

[Ins86]   American National Standard Institute. Nomenclature and definitions for illumination engineering. ANSI Report, 1986. ANSI/IES RP-16-1986.

[JC93]   Frederik W. Jansen and Alan Chalmers. Realism in real time? In *Proceedings of the Fourth Eurographics Workshop on Rendering*, pages 27–46, 1993.

[KA91a]   David Kirk and James Arvo. Unbiased sampling techniques for image sysnthesis. *Computer Graphics*, 25(4):153–156, July 1991. ACM Siggraph '91 Conference Proceedings.

[KA91b]   David Kirk and James Arvo. Unbiased variance reduction for global illumination. In *Proceedings of the Second Eurographics Workshop on Rendering*, 1991.

[Kaj86]   James T. Kajiya. The rendering equation. *Computer Graphics*, 20(4):143–150, August 1986. ACM Siggraph '86 Conference Proceedings.

[Kaj88]   James T. Kajiya. An overview and comparison of rendering methods. *A Consumer's and Developer's Guide to Image Synthesis*, pages 259–263, 1988. ACM Siggraph '88 Course 12 Notes.

[Kaj89]   James T. Kajiya. Rendering fur with three dimensional textures. *Computer Graphics*, 23(3):271–280, July 1989. ACM Siggraph '89 Conference Proceedings.

[KJ92]   Arjan J. F. Kok and Frederik W. Jasen. Adaptive sampling of area light sources in ray tracing including diffuse interreflection. *Computer Graphics forum*, 11(3):289–298, 1992. Eurographics '92.

[Kok93]   Arjan F. Kok. Grouping of patches in progressive radiosity. In *Proceedings of the Fourth Eurographics Workshop on Rendering*, pages 221–231, 1993.

[MG88]   Gary W. Meyer and Donald P. Greenberg. Color-defective vision and computer graphics displays. *IEEE Computer Graphics and Applications*, 8(9):28–40, September 1988.

[NKON90]   Eihachiro Nakamae, Kazufumi Kaneda, Takashi Okamoto, and Tomoyuki Nishita. A lighting model aiming at drive simulators. *Computer Graphics*, 24(3):395–404, August 1990. ACM Siggraph '90 Conference Proceedings.

[oNA91]   Illumination Engineering Society of North America. Ies standard file format for electronic transfer of photometric data and related information. IES Lighting Measurement Series, 1991. IES LM-63-1991.

[PH89]   Ken Perlin and Eric M. Hoffert. Hypertexture. *Computer Graphics*, 23(3):253–262, July 1989. ACM Siggraph '89 Conference Proceedings.

[Pru93]   Przemyslaw Prusinkiewicz. Modeling and visualization of biological structures. In *Graphics Interface '93*, pages 128–137, May 1993.

[Rea93]   Mark S. Rea, editor. *The Illumination Engineering Society Lighting Handbook*. Illumination Engineering Society, New York, NY, 8th edition, 1993.

[RPV93]   Holly Rushmeier, Charles Patterson, and Aravindan Veerasamy. Geometric simplification for indirect illumination calculations. In *Graphics Interface '93*, pages 227–236, May 1993.

[SW91]   Maureen C. Stone and William E. Wallace. Gamut mapping computer generated imagery. In *Graphics Interface '91*, pages 32–39, June 1991.

[TR93]   Jack Tumblin and Holly Rushmeier. Tone reproduction for realistic computer generated images. *IEEE Comp. Graphics and Applic.*, 13(7), 1993.

[vWvNJ91]   Theo van Walsum, Peter R. van Nieuwenhuizen, and Frederik Jansen. Refinement criteria for adaptive stochastic ray tracing of textures. In *Eurographics '91*, pages 155–166, September 1991.

[War92]   Gregory J. Ward. Measuring and modeling anisotropic reflection. *Computer Graphics*, 26(4):265–272, July 1992. ACM Siggraph '92 Conference Proceedings.

[WAT92]   Stephen H. Westin, James R. Arvo, and Kenneth E. Torrance. Measuring and modeling anisotropic reflection. *Computer Graphics*, 26(2):255–264, July 1992. ACM Siggraph '92 Conference Proceedings.

Part II

Participating Media

Rendering Participating Media:
Problems and Solutions from Application Areas

Holly Rushmeier

National Institute of Standards and Technology, Gaithersburg, MD 20899, USA

Abstract

Physically accurate rendering of radiatively participating media is an extremely demanding computational task. In this paper, current and potential applications requiring such renderings are reviewed. Some ideas for a practical rendering system, based on insights from application areas, are presented.

1 Introduction

Images of radiatively participating media are aesthetically appealing – curls of smoke, sunsets, fires and clouds. Generating physically accurate, rather than artistic, images of participating media is an extremely challenging computational problem. What applications require physically accurate image of participating media? How accurate does a rendering of a volumetric medium need to be? What are the main practical problems in generating an image? What is the best way to organize the solution? In this paper, the current and potential applications for rendering participating media are reviewed to try to address these questions.

1.1 Defining The Problem

A reasonable place to begin is to define the problem of physically accurate rendering of participating media. The geometry of rendering a scene containing a participating medium is shown in Fig. 1.

As in rendering any realistic scene, the image is computed by finding the radiance (energy per unit time, solid angle and projected area) $L(s)$ which would pass through an image pixel to the eye. To form a final image, a weighted average of this value must be found across the pixel (for antialiasing) and the spectral radiance distribution must be mapped to the gamut of the display. In this paper, we will concentrate on the problem of determining $L(s)$, bearing in mind though that display transformations will ultimately need to be made.

Unlike the surface problem, in which it is adequate to find the radiance of the closest visible surface, in the presence of a participating medium an integral

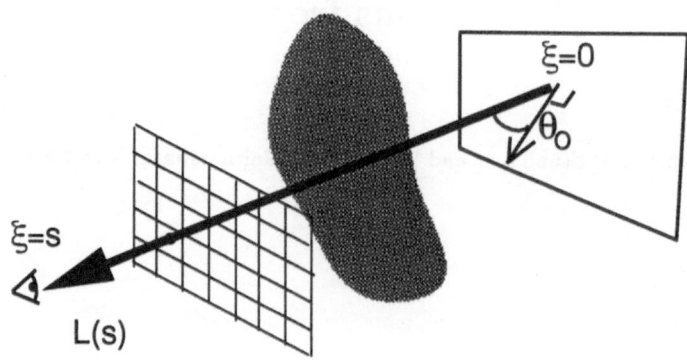

Fig. 1. The geometry of rendering a scene with a participating medium. An image is formed by computing the radiance L(s) that reaches the eye through a pixel by integrating along the line of sight.

along the line of sight must be evaluated. Assuming that light transport in the environment is adequately modelled by geometric optics, the integral to be evaluated for each wavelength sample is:

$$L(s) = L(0)\tau(s) + \int_0^s J(\xi)\tau(s - \xi)k_t(\xi)d\xi \qquad (1)$$

In Eq. 1, $L(0)$ is the radiance of the closest opaque surface, which is at the origin of the line integral. $\tau(s)$ is the transmittance (fraction transmitted) along the path of length s. $J(\xi)$ is the source radiance in the medium. The source radiance increases the radiance along the path, and is the result of either emission or inscattering at point ξ along the path. k_t is the extinction coefficient, the fraction by which radiance is reduced by absorption and scattering per unit length in the medium. k_t is large for a dense medium, and small for a sparse medium.

The transmittance τ accounts for the attenuation by absorption and scattering along a path through a participating medium. In terms of the extinction coefficient, τ is given by the following path integral:

$$\tau(s) = exp(-\int_o^s k_t(\xi)d\xi) \qquad (2)$$

The surface radiance $L(0)$ is given by:

$$L(0) = L_e(\theta_o, \phi_o) + \int_i f_r(\theta_o, \phi_o, \theta_i, \phi_i)L_i(\theta_i, \phi_i)cos(\theta_i)d\omega_i \qquad (3)$$

In Eq. 3, the angles θ and ϕ are spherical coordinates based on the surface point. The subscript o indicates the direction leaving the surface in the direction of the line integral coordinate s. The subscript i indicates an incoming direction from the hemisphere of solid angle ω_i above the surface. The function $f_r(\theta_o, \phi_o, \theta_i, \phi_i)$ is the bidirectional reflectance distribution function (BRDF) of the surface. The incident radiance $L_i(\theta_i, \phi_i)$ is itself determined by a line integral of the form of Eq. 1 in which the line is in the direction θ_i, ϕ_i.

The product $k_t(\xi)d\xi$ is a dimensionless measure of how much the medium affects the radiance at point ξ. Requirements for thermal equilibrium [46] give the result that $k_t(\xi)d\xi$ is a measure of the amount the medium can increase radiance along the path, as well as the amount the medium can decrease radiance. The product $J(\xi)k_t(\xi)d\xi$ in the integral on the right of Eq. 1 is the differential increase to radiance along the differential path length $d\xi$. The factor $\tau(s-\xi)$ appropriately attenuates this contribution for the rest of the path from ξ to the end of the path s.

The source radiance $J(\xi)$ is given by the sum of the emitted radiance and in-scattered radiance:

$$J(\xi) = J_e(\xi) + \frac{\Omega(\xi)}{4\pi} \int_i P(\theta_i, \phi_i, \theta_o, \phi_o) L_i(\theta_i, \phi_i) d\omega_i \qquad (4)$$

In Eq. 4, J_e is emitted radiance. Ω is the scattering albedo of the medium. While k_t measures the overall effect of the medium on radiance, Ω measures what fraction of this effect is scattering rather than absorption. P is the scattering phase function. By definition P is equal to one for all directions for isotropic scatter. For anisotropic scatter, $P(\theta_i, \phi_i, \theta_o, \phi_o)$ is the ratio of the incident radiation from direction (θ_i, ϕ_i) scattered into the direction (θ_o, ϕ_o) to the the amount scattered into the same direction by an isotropic scatterer.

In addition to the input data required for a surface-only problem, the definition of a problem containing a participating medium requires the definition of J_e, P, Ω, and k_t as a function of position in the medium. Unlike the surface problem in which geometry and reflectance properties are treated entirely separately, the definition of the geometry of a participating medium and its properties are closely coupled. If k_t is given directly as a function of location, the geometry of the medium is implied. The distribution of the medium may also be specified by giving partial pressure, volume fraction, or the density of the medium as a function of location. The values of k_t then are computed by converting these quantities to densities, and using the mass coefficients of extinction (i.e. (fraction extinction/length)/(mass density)). The values of P and Ω can be specified directly, or they can be computed from the size of the particles in the medium and their complex index of refraction [5].

1.2 What Makes Rendering Participating Media Hard?

Obviously, the participating medium problem is hard because a third dimension is added. Rather than just computing radiance on surfaces, source radiance needs to be computed throughout space. Rather than forming an image by finding a visible point, a line integral has to be performed.

The problem is also hard because of the geometric complexity of some media. In turbulent media such as flames and cumulus clouds variations in k_t vary over time and length scales of many different orders of magnitude. Obtaining geometric models for these media is problematic. Complete solutions for these geometries from first principles of fluid mechanics are not feasible. For many types of media empirical observations and a statistical methods must be used to model input geometry (e.g. see [48]).

The problem is not hard however, in the sense that given the numerical description of the medium we do have methods for solving solving Eq. 1 in all generality. The reverse Monte Carlo method outlined by Kajiya for surfaces [24] can readily be extended to participating media [39]. While feasible, reverse Monte Carlo methods are far from being "real time". The key to improving the efficiency of rendering participating media is to recognize that Eq. 1 does not need to be solved in full generality to high accuracy for every portion of every scene.

1.3 Approximations vs. Hacks

A lot of graphics rendering methods originated as "tricks" or "hacks". Mathematical techniques, generally inspired by some physics, were developed to generate images that looked good. There are certainly many artistic applications in graphics in which such techniques are extremely powerful and useful.

To some extent, physics-based rendering has taken the approach that anything less than a full first-principles simulation is a "hack". The result has been to generate solutions of higher and higher accuracy (and complexity), regardless of whether such accuracy is necessary. This approach has also resulted in powerful and useful techniques. However it views the lighting simulation apart from the full process of image synthesis, which can be viewed as in Fig. 2.

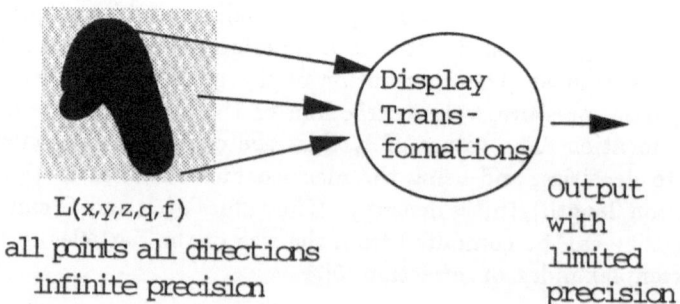

L(x,y,z,q,f)
all points all directions
infinite precision

Output with limited precision

Fig. 2. The full simulation problem for generating an image, of which light transport simulation is only a part. Because output with only limited precision is required, only limited precision is required in $L(x, y, z, \theta, \phi)$.

What we seek in image synthesis is not a perfect simulation of the light transport process. This is pointless when we understand that we will never have perfect input for such an simulation. But also, perfect simulation of the radiance in every point an direction is unnecessary. We only want to *approximate* the light transport to the extent that it affects the image to the level of accuracy of required of that image for a particular application.

In other problem areas, such as heat transfer, approximations have been made to simulate radiative transfer in participating media to the level of accuracy required by the problems in those areas. The result has been a variety of finite volume methods such as the zonal, discrete ordinate and P-N methods [23]. In the zonal method, isotropic scatter is assumed, and the value of J is computed for each discrete volume. In the discrete ordinate and P-N methods the directional distribution of L is estimated at each volume. In the P-N methods the directional variation is expressed as a series of spherical harmonics, while in the discrete ordinate method the sphere around each point is discretized into a small number of solid angles.

Because different levels of accuracy, expressed in different forms, are required in other problem areas, these methods can not just be applied "as is" to image synthesis. A better understanding of the accuracy requirements of image synthesis is needed to assess and modify these various methods.

In this paper we will examine what types of approximations make sense for the rendering of participating media problem by considering various applications.

2 Applications from the Graphics Literature

As a start, it should be acknowledged that applications for rendering participating media have not been ignored in computer graphics research. Several papers that have appeared in the graphics literature about the rendering of participating media have addressed specific applications. Not surprisingly, these application oriented papers have presented far more tractable rendering methods than more theoretically oriented papers (e.g. [25], [42]).

An early model for a physically based lighting solution by Blinn [4] was directly motivated by the need to realistically image the atmosphere above planetary surfaces. Blinn's approach was based on models from the classic radiative transport text by Chandrasekhar [12]. The method described in [4] uses plane parallel atmospheres. While this approach is certainly not generally applicable, it is a good approximation for the problem of rendering planets, in which the extent of the medium – over the whole surface - is essentially infinite relative to the height of of the atmosphere above the planet. A more detailed model using Blinn's ideas for rendering the earth viewed from space for space flight simulators has recently been presented by Nishita et al. [36]. By carefully modelling the spectral distributions of sunlight, atmospheric single scatter and cloud single scatter, Nishita et al. obtained results which compare favorably with photographs taken from the space shuttle.

Gardner [19] presented a cloud simulation method for use in fight simulators. Gardner developed a method that is appearance based, rather than physics based, for efficiency. An important contribution of [19] is the representation of clouds as three dimensional procedural textures, a mathematical representation that can also be used in physics based systems. It is also noted in [19] that clouds are classified by appearance – cirrus, stratus, and cumulus. Given the limitations on attempting to compute solutions for turbulent flows, modelling the shape of clouds using shapes observed in nature is not necessarily less physically accurate than attempting to model cloud formation from first principles of thermodynamics and fluid mechanics.

Yeager et al. [51] presented a more elaborate model of a planetary atmosphere to generate images for the film "2010". As in Gardner's work, the emphasis was on visual simulation. However the method of modelling the medium was essentially physics based. The starting point for the simulation was actual photographs of Jupiter's surface. The atmosphere was animated using simple fluid mechanics models. Since no views were ever to be generated very close to the planet, a simple two dimensional simulation was performed. Overall this work suggests an important idea – that even if a medium truly is 3-D, for a particular application there may be no loss in accuracy in using a 2-D map of radiances to represent the medium. The sky is a participating medium, but for accurately rendering the light coming through a window we don't have to model all of the Rayleigh scattering in the atmosphere, we can use measurement based models of a 2-D map of sky radiance (e.g. as the CIE standard clear sky model [15]or [26] is used in the *Radiance* package [49].)

Nishita et al. [35] consider the rendering of participating media for studio lighting and driving simulators. The model considers only attenuation and single scatter from light sources. For most of the examples they give – night scenes and dark stages with spotlights, neglecting other surface/volume interchange is an accurate approximation. Clearly, single scatter is a good approximation for low albedo media. It is also a good approximation for optically thin media – in which the transmittance through the entire medium is nearly one. Several of the examples they show are optically thin – a light haze outdoors or a small plume of smoke. For scattering phase function Nishita et al. use simple functions fit to experimental data for particle scattering, rather than Mie theory. Using experimental data for irregularly shaped particles, rather than calculating the Mie scattering for equivalent spherical particles, is just as (or even more) physically accurate.

Beyond these examples, there are many more applications that could potentially benefit from physically accurate renderings of participating media. A sampling of these applications from fire research, remote sensing, defense and transportation will now be considered.

3 Applications from Fire Research

Understanding combustion and the products of combustion is fundamental to the development of systems for the effective prevention and control of fires. Smoke and flames are participating media. Because they are complicated both spatially and temporally, it is difficult to understand smoke and flames from

point measurements or calculations. Increasingly imaging is an important tool
for acquiring data about fires and for understanding fires.

3.1 Smoke

The dispersion of smoke is important both in interior and exterior applications.
In both cases, the visibility of the smoke produced in a fire is one of the issues
being studied.

Exterior Fires An important outdoor study of smoke dispersion is the in-situ
burning of spilled oil [18]. Cleaning up oil spills by burning has the advantages
of preventing oil from reaching shore, and limiting the effect of oil on plant and
animal life. However, it is important to determine what impact the products of
combustion will have on the environment.

To determine smoke dispersion, fluid flow models such as the Large Eddy
Simulation (LES) [1] have been developed. In a typical simulation, particulate
density in $\mu g/m^3$ is computed for a 192x768x2400 grid covering a 6x1.5x10 km
volume occupied by the plume. Such a simulation requires on the order of a
couple hours on a typical work station.

There are two motivations for generating accurate visual images of the results of the simulation. The first is for comparison with experimental results.
Large scale tests are performed of these types of fires. Instrumentation for detailed measurements of particle densities in these tests are not feasible. A major
source of information from the physical tests are photographs of the plume. By
generating physically accurate images of the simulation a meaningful comparison could be made with these photographs. Currently, the simulation results are
visualized with representations such as density isosurfaces, as shown in Fig. 3.

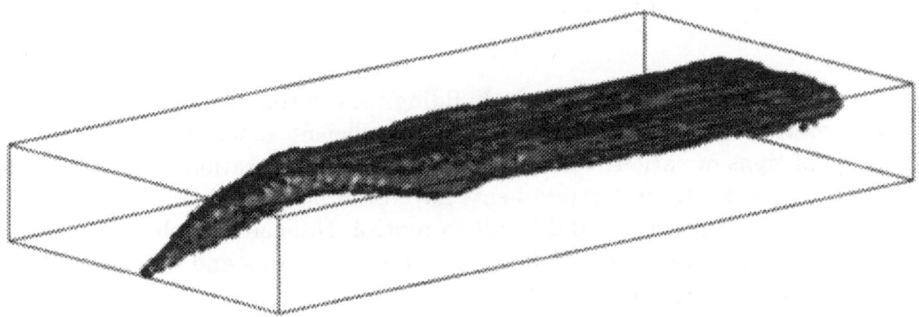

Fig. 3. The result of a LES calculation displayed as a density isosurface (image
generated by Kevin McGrattan, BFRL, NIST).

A second reason for physically accurate images is that one of the significant environmental impacts of burning is its effect on visibility. Answering questions such as how far away the plume will be visible is one of the purposes of the simulation. Currently rough estimates are made using relatively simple assumptions about plume optics. A realistic rendering would require not only modelling the radiation within the plume, but also merging the model with an accurate radiance map of the background terrain, and accounting for atmospheric effects between the plume and the viewer.

Oil fires are just one instance of particulate plumes for which visibility is a concern. A symposium on "Plumes and Visibility: Measurement and Model Components" was head in Grand Canyon National Park in November 1980 [50]. A variety of plumes were discussed including plumes from power plants [2]. One of the goals of the symposium was to encourage modular components for computing visibility. The growing concern for air quality in the 1970's resulted in many computer programs which attempted to simulate the overall visibility problem. The goal was to break down these simulations into individual modules, each of which could be verified by experiment.

Besides quantity of data, a major obstacle to generating accurate images of smoke plumes is that the optical properties of the collections of complex aggregate soot particles are unknown. One function of the visual simulations would be to examine the visual impact of using different models for the absorption and scattering by the particles.

The measurement of the optical properties of smoke is itself an active area of research. One class of instruments for making these measurements are nephelometers. In nephelometers, photodetectors are used to measure the light scattered from a beam passing through a uniform particle suspension. In the design of such an instrument questions remain regarding the effect of finite size of the overall apparatus, the size of the detector and the angular response of the detector. Currently analytical models are used to assess such effects [33]. Algorithms developed in computer graphics for efficiently calculating transfer in participating media could be a useful in evaluating various instrument designs.

Interior Fires A safety concern in building fires is the visibility of exit signs. Efforts continue to develop effective, energy efficient signs. To determine the visibility of signs of various color, luminance and configuration under clear and smoky conditions, physical experiments have been performed [16]. Clearly, such experiments are expensive and difficult to control. Difficulties include generating and characterizing smoke, controlling the ambient lighting and testing the large number of potentially important factors.

Because of the difficulties involved with physical experiments, some computational simulations have been performed. Roysam et al. [37] developed a Monte Carlo method for the exit sign problem for a general participating medium. In Roysam's method, light is followed from the exit sign to the receiver, as shown in Fig. 4. Assuming parallel projection, the sign is discretized into pixels. Photon bundles are followed through the medium using a relatively standard Monte

Carlo technique. Phase functions are used both from experimental measurements and from numerical calculations of Mie scattering. The photon paths end when they either escape the medium or hit the receiver.

Fig. 4. Geometry of Monte Carlo simulation of exit sign visibility.

Even with this simple parallel geometry, the number of calculations to form an image is enormous. Since Monte Carlo simulations are completely parallelizable, the simulation was implemented on a 32,768 processor Connection Machine. Time for image generation was on the order of tens of minutes.

Despite some obvious restrictions in this approach, this study illustrates the potential of simulation for this application. It also demonstrates the flexibility and parallelism of the Monte Carlo approach.

A much more demanding future interior application of smoke rendering is in virtual reality systems for fire fighter training. An ongoing project at NIST is the development of CFAST – a comprehensive model of fire growth and smoke transport [17]. CFAST combines a variety of models of fluid mechanics, heat transfer, and chemistry to predict quantities such as "Available Safe Egress Time" for each room in a structure, and the burning behavior of individual items in a room. Currently CFAST input and results are displayed using simple 2-D graphic representations of floor plans. Long term future plans are to take CAD building descriptions as input, and produce 3-D output of the smoke transport results. One application of such 3-D output would be in fire fighter training, to reduce the training time required in actual hazardous burning structures.

3.2 Flames

Flames of concern in fire prevention and control are difficult to study because they are non-steady, turbulent and have complicated emission spectra. The structure of flames is studied to answer questions such as, how much does radiative feedback from a flame contribute to continued fuel vaporization? Will irradiation from the flame ignite other materials near but not touching the flame?

Currently temperatures, pressures and soot concentrations in flames are measured with immersive probes [14]. Only time averaged measurements can be obtained. Rushmeier et al. [40] did a short study of these measurements by producing physically accurate images. The cylindrical structure of the flame constructed from measurements is shown in Fig. 5. Rays were followed through the structure, and the data for length and measured values for each segment was collected. The line integration was performed using the RADCAL program [20]. RADCAL accurately calculates the radiation taking into account the detailed spectral properties of CO_2, H_2O, CH_4, CO, N_2, and O_2. Figure 6 shows images that were produced to illustrate the magnitude of radiation from combustion gases versus the magnitude of radiation from the soot cloud above the fuel. Images were also used to study the fall-off of irradiance with distance and orientation, and the impact of using time averaged, rather than instantaneous data. The same ray tracing used for imaging was used for calculating irradiance for actual pool fire experiments. At a minimum, the images were a useful tool for validating the ray tracing used to produce the irradiance results.

RADCAL considers only absorption and emission along the path – not scattering, since the effect of scattering is negligible for the problem of thermal radiation in combustion products. RADCAL assumes local thermodynamic equilibrium (LTE), which is an accurate assumption for the radiative transfer of interest in thermal problems. It should be noted that non-LTE radiation, luminescence which occurs by excitation other than thermal agitation, is responsible for a significant amount of visible radiation (particularly that which is blue in color) in some flames. Yellow, orange and red visible radiation in most fires, such as the heptane pool fire considered in the study described above, are dominated by LTE radiation from soot particles.

Besides illustrating the importance of gas emission, Fig. 6 also serves to highlight the inadequacy of current measurements for obtaining the temporal/spatial structure of flames. Time averaged measurements are inherently limited in the spatial structure that they can capture. Variations that occur on small length scales occur in short time scales.

Because of the limitations of immersive probes, increasingly computer tomography is being considered for studying combustion [32]. Tomographic techniques can potentially provide much more detailed temporal/spatial descriptions of flame structure. Physically accurate images of the large quantities of data available from such techniques will potentially play in important role in understanding flames. Furthermore, the detailed structures obtained may be useful as input to visual simulations for training.

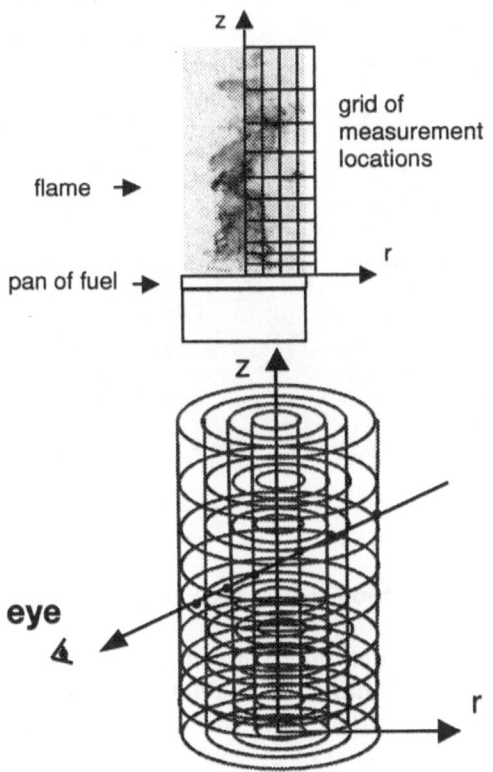

Fig. 5. Measurements are made in one plane only. A volume of data is defined as a stack of concentric rings.

4 Applications in Remote Sensing

In remote sensing images of land surfaces are acquired by airborne or satellite sensors for the purpose of classifying and identifying features. The problem is difficult enough if the image is formed by unperturbed radiance from the earth's surface. The problem is made more difficult though by atmospheric effects that attenuate and blur the view from the sensor to the surface.

4.1 Blurring

Blurring by the atmosphere is usually modelled as a point spread function (PSF). If the PSF in the atmosphere is known, its inverse can be used to deblur images. Many PSF's are assumed to be symmetric, and are limited in the viewing angles to which they can be applied. Borel and Gerstl [6] have developed a variation of the zonal method [42] to compute PSF's for arbitrary viewing angles. Images

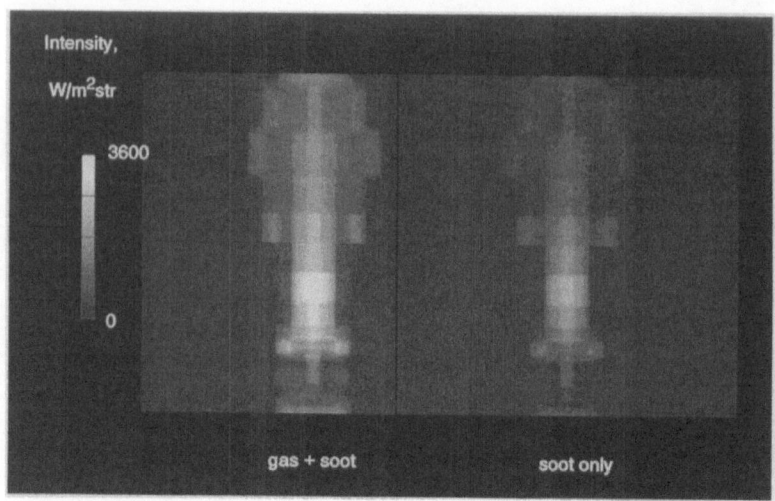

Fig. 6. Infrared images of radiation from soot and gas, versus soot alone.

generated using the zonal method are used to verify the modelling of the blurring effect.

In Borel and Gerstl's model, diagrammed in Fig. 7, direct sunlight only is considered (since indirect illumination is relatively small). The earth reflects light diffusely, and the flat surfaces can not view one another, so the surface radiances (which will be the values of $L(0)$ in all of the line of sight integrations) are determined by the angle of the sun and atmospheric attenuation only.

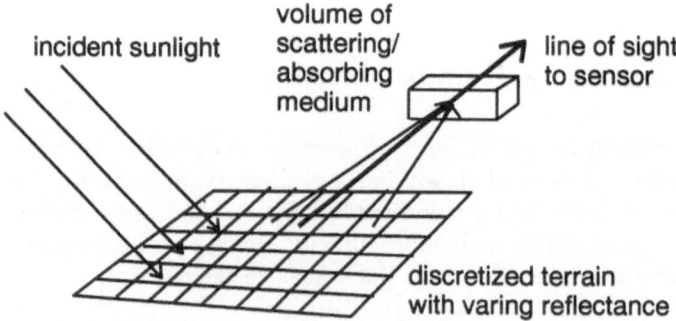

Fig. 7. Geometry of modified zonal method for computing PSF to account for atmospheric blurring.

Exchange factors $S_i V_j$ are computed from each surface S_i on the earth to each volume V_j in the atmosphere. The source radiance J for each volume then in the path from the earth to the sensor is calculated by summing the effect of inscattering of light from the earth's surface. That is, one scattering event from the surface to the sensor is accounted for, and the directionality of the scattering phase function is accounted for in this scattering.

Using this model Borel and Gerstl were able to successfully reproduce blurring effects observed in satellite images. They were able to develop a PSF for vertically varying non-isotropic atmospheres for arbitrary view angles. They also report [7] that work is continuing to develop an extended zonal method to account for additional surface/surface, volume/volume, and surface/volume interactions of importance in the remote sensing problem. They are continuing to develop the zonal, rather than Monte Carlo method, because their application requires many different views of the same environment.

4.2 LOWTRAN

Because attenuation and scattering through the atmosphere is so important in remote sensing applications, there is an extensive body of literature on this topic. For computation, many of the models for the transport of radiation have been included in the program LOWTRAN [27]. LOWTRAN is one of the most-used large scale scientific programs, and is cited widely in the remote sensing literature. Typical, kilometers long, lines of sight for which LOWTRAN is used to compute transmittance and radiance through the atmosphere are shown in Fig. 8.

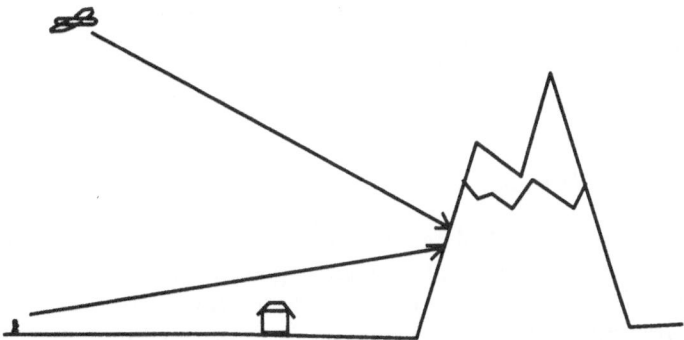

Fig. 8. The LOWTRAN code is typically used to compute the effect of the atmosphere on individual, kilometers long, lines of sight.

LOWTRAN was developed over decades at the Air Force Geophysics Laboratory (AFGL) to include a wide range of phenomena. A variety of model atmospheres can be selected, e.g. tropical, subartic summer, etc. Many different types of aerosols can be included such as fog, volcanic dust and typical desert aerosols. Clouds of different types can be specified. Different models for rain can be used. The various models used for the properties of various atmospheric components are detailed in a long series of technical reports from AFGL.

The name "LOWTRAN" comes from the relatively low spectral sampling for many atmospheric applications. The sampling is at 5 cm^{-1}, which is a low rate at the far infrared (wavenumber 20 cm^{-1} at λ of 500 μm). In the visible range (wave numbers on the order of 20,000 cm^{-1}), it is a relatively high sampling rate for graphics researchers accustomed to sampling 3 wavelengths.

LOWTRAN covers many phenomena and wavelengths (into the ultraviolet and out into the infrared) which are not of interest in visible image synthesis. And, as a FORTRAN program which has evolved over many years, the code itself is unwieldy to work with. However, for building a renderer for atmospheric effects, the LOWTRAN documentation is a good starting point for understanding the important effects to model, and the LOWTRAN code could be used to check the accuracy of line intergration of a visible image renderer.

5 Defense Applications

Simulating the visual effect of both naturally occurring participating media and deliberately introduced smoke screens is an important issue in defense related research. Most of this work is reported either in government laboratory technical reports (e.g. [29]) or in defense oriented conferences (e.g. [11], [28]).

Simulations of the atmosphere and smoke plumes are generally embedded in large integrated systems which also include modules for modelling background terrains, target vehicles, and sensors. Such systems can be used alternatively for testing new designs for sensors, targets or obscurants. Because these are extensive systems used for rerunning many scenarios, the calculations must very fast. However, because the results are being used for design, the results must also be accurate. All of the models used have to be verified by physical measurements.

5.1 Battlefield Plumes

An example of the types of phenomenon modeled in these systems is battlefield smoke plumes [9], [22]. These plumes are a good example of how the geometry of a medium can be built from physical observations without a complete first principles simulation. The basic geometry is shown in Fig. 9. The basic plume centerline is modeled with the plume height equal to downwind distance raised to a power – with the coefficient and power based on experimental observations of various plumes. The basic centerline is then perturbed according to a model of wind conditions. The basic particulate concentration of the plume is a Gaussian distribution from the centerline. The width of the distribution increases along the centerline, and depends on an estimated rate of entrainment of ambient fluid into the plume. The base distribution is then perturbed by sinosoidal fluctuations in concentration. These fluctuations simulate turbulent eddies of various length scales. The amplitude of these fluctuations is inversely related to their spatial frequency to emulate the observed "energy cascade" in turbulent flows (an effect more recently introduced as a graphics animation tool in [43], [47]).

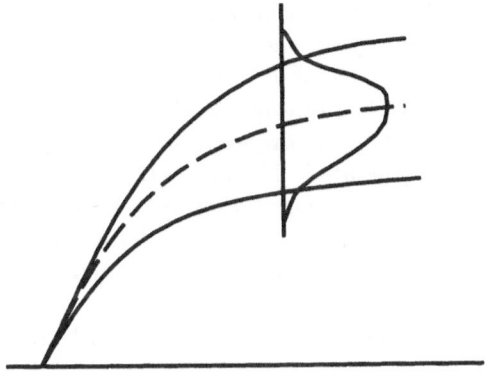

Fig. 9. Baseline battlefield plume definition. The centerline is defined with the height equal to downwind direction raised to a power. The concentration in the plume is a Gaussian of distance from the centerline.

In [22], given this geometry, reasonable images can be produced computing τ from the given concentration distribution and assuming a uniform value for J. However, in the same paper, the need is cited for practical methods to more accurately render clouds under a variety of conditions.

5.2 Atmospherics

As in remote sensing, atmospheric effects are also important in defense simulation systems. LOWTRAN is frequently used in these simulations [10]. Because of the computation expense of LOWTRAN, an average values of k_t and J. are computed for just two lines of sight – one for the target, and one for the background. In computing the image $L(0)$ for the closest surface is evaluated pixel by pixel. The value of $L(0)$ at each pixel is then attenuated using the appropriate average k_t value and depth information at each pixel. Finally, the effect of source radiance is added in using the data for the appropriate line of sight. This approach produces acceptable results because atmospheric effects vary relatively little over distances of just a few meters.

6 Applications in Transportation

Determining visibility and simulating operating conditions are important in the design of transportation systems and in training of vehicle operators. In the graphics literature Nakamae et al. [34] describe a driving simulation program that takes into account many effects, including single scatter in fog as mentioned in the paper cited in Section 2 [35].

Outside of the graphics literature, at least a couple of papers have appeared examining visibility for transportation systems taking into account multiple scattering. Rozé et al. [38] describe a Monte Carlo system to assess visibility of objects in fog on a roadway. In their simulations, the goal is to examine the relative contrast between target objects (such as the fog light on a car ahead on the highway) and the light from overhead lights and a car's own headlights which are scattered back into the driver's view. A simple contrast ratio then, rather than an image, is generated. The geometry of these simulations is shown in Fig. 10. The fog luminance is calculated by a forward Monte Carlo simulation from the overhead lights and the car head lights. The path of each photon bundle ends when it is either absorbed or hits the detector. In this instance the detector is the driver's eye. Assuming that the fog luminance will vary slowly with distance, the eye is modelled as a 0.8m radius disk to facilitate convergence of the solution.

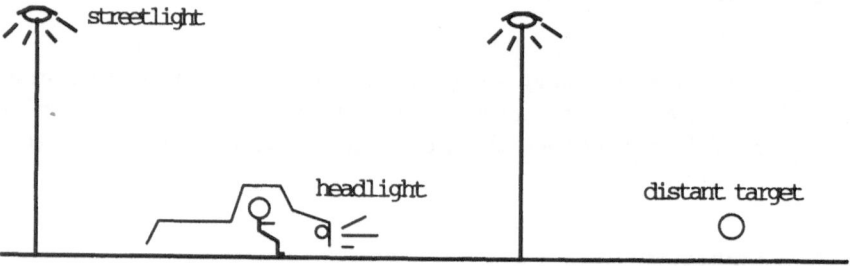

Fig. 10. Geometry for simulating roadway visibility in fog. (Adapted from Rozé et al.)

Because visibility of a specific object is critical in this study, Rozé et al. include a discussion of adaptation luminance and differential luminance threshhold that give some insights into how accurate the light transport simulations have to be.

Bresciani et al. [8] describe the development of a progressive refinement zonal method for computing luminance in participating media for studying visibility on airport runways and for roadway lighting. While this work is still in progress, some experimental verification of results have been made. Light measurements were made in a black-walled room filled with an artificial fog illuminated with a single light source. Good correspondence with simulated values was found, even using a crude mesh, and simple differential-to-differential form factors.

7 Implications

Clearly then, there are real world problems that require physically accurate rendering of environments containing participating media. For the most part, a great deal of work needs to be done in these problem areas to increase the accuracy and speed of image generation.

Applications provide us with insights that can be useful for a designing a multi-purpose rendering system for participating media. As urged in the "Plumes and Visibility" symposium [50], such a system should be composed of individual modules, each of which can be validated independantly. Basic components which are needed are a materials data base, a description of the geometry of the medium, a ray casting module, and a method for estimating radiance at points within the medium.

7.1 Materials Data Base

Because of important applications such as remote sensing and combustion studies, there is a tremendous amount of property data available for participating media. The major problem is assembling it all. In other disciplines, the way property data has been collected for general use is in computer programs for computing individual line of sight radiances such as RADCAL and LOWTRAN. Embedding property data in a light of sight module is too restrictive. In some problems k_t, Ω, J_e and P may be defined directly. In other problems these quantities will need to be computed from a materials data base.

Examining the documentation for programs like RADCAL and LOWTRAN is a good starting point in building a properties data base for visible image synthesis. Besides the actual property values these programs can provide insight into the many ways these property values are represented. A general system should allow other types of property values to be stored, and provide functions for converting these properties to the forms needed for rendering. For example, it should be possible to store k_t for a material as a function of either partial pressures, mass densities or volume fractions. It should also be possible to store complex index of refraction, particle shapes and sizes for computing scattering properties from electromagnetic theory. A system should also allow storing P as a function of incident and exitant angles which fits data obtained from physical experiments.

A significant gap in currently available data is how to obtain J_e if it is not given directly. For thermal emission J_e can be computed from temperature and absorption coefficient. However, some models are needed for computing non-LTE emission for gases under various conditions.

7.2 Geometry

There are several methods of modelling the geometry of participating media. Some detailed fluid models are now available – such as the Large Eddy Simulations used for the oil plume problem. In these models, the participating media will

generally be represented by concentration values on a grid. Because of the varying length scales that are important in participating media, a general rendering
system should have the capability of storing the data on an irregular grid.

As demonstrated by the battlefield plumes, physically accurate models of
media can be built in terms of measurable quantities such as overall shape
and statistical variations, rather than strictly from first principles simulation.
In this type of representation the concentrations are represented as continuous
functions. The system could allow functions entirely user specified. Parametric
representations of clouds and plumes could also be offered – e.g. allowing the user
to specify a few parameters that determine a plume center-line and magnitude
of fluctuations.

As in the LOWTRAN software, a number of "standard" atmospheres could
be defined. The user could choose from a predefined, expandable list of 1-D
atmospheres.

More detailed geometries may soon be come available from physical measurements as methods from computer tomography are used to study phenomena
such as pool fire flames. Considering the recent visualization work in computing
volume views as Fourier slices, perhaps a new form of storing volume geometries
will be developed.

In any of the above cases the rendering system would need to ensure that
the data used to specify geometry is adequate to compute k_t, P, Ω and J_e from
the materials data base.

7.3 Ray Casting

In all applications, the basic calculation to be performed is the evaluation of the
line integral in Eq. 1. A general system needs to be able to efficiently cast a ray
through any of the possible geometric descriptions, and evaluate k_t, P, Ω and
J_e at any point along the ray.

A naive, but general, reverse Monte Carlo renderer could be written with
relatively little code beyond the ray casting and accessing the properties of the
medium. However, in every application some simplification can be made. A practical rendering system should be capable of using a number of different strategies
for computing radiance.

7.4 Computing Radiance

Not only should a system be capable of using different computational strategies,
it should also be capable of determining which is most appropriate for a given
input. A series of rules should be developed to determine the strategy requiring
the minimum computational effort required for a particular application.

The most time consuming quantity to compute for participating media is the
source radiance due to scattering. In imaging flames, scatter could be ignored.
In computing the PSF for remote sensing, single scatter was adequate. In computing visibility through fog for drivers, multiple scattering was important. As

a prelude to the calculations, it should be determined whether multiple, single or no scattering calculations are required.

One option is to let the user determine the type of scattering calculations performed. However, a reasonable determination can be made by the rendering system based on the input data. In absolute terms, there is almost always some scattering. Because there is a limit to the accuracy needed though, the effect of scattering should be assessed *relative* to other lighting effects. For example, if the product of average values of Ω, k_t and path length through the medium is orders of magnitude smaller than the average surface reflectance, scattering can be neglected. More work is needed to determine appropriate parameters involving average values of the properties of the medium to the average surface properties to make a more detailed determination of the extent to which scattering affects the image.

In determining direct visibility and the effects of direct illumination, τ nearly always needs to be computed. For very thin media though, in which the average value of τ is nearly one, it may be a good approximation to neglect attenuation as well as scattering for computing multiple interreflections.

When scattering is important in the medium, there is a choice between computing the complete radiance L or just the source radiance J as a function of location and direction everywhere in the medium. The advantage of estimating L everywhere in the medium is that in rendering, only the closest point in the medium needs to be found. The value of L accounts for the line integral and opaque surfaces further away. One disadvantage is that L needs to be computed with a high level of spatial detail for media with spatially detailed distributions of k_t. Another disadvantage is that L needs to be computed with a high level of directional detail if opaque objects are visible through the medium. Most visibility applications do not attempt to compute L everywhere. One application where this approach can be useful is rendering clouds viewed at a distance. Because they are viewed at a distance, high spatial resolution is not required. Because they are nearly opaque, high directional resolution is not required either. In animated sequences cloud geometry changes slowly relative to other motion, so the same values of L can be reused for many frames without recomputing any line integrals.

For volumes which are less dense, or viewed at closer range, estimating J throughout the medium is often preferable because of the lower resolution required. In the battlefield plume example, a single estimate of J was found to be adequate. The modified zonal method for computing PSF in remote sensing and zonal method for the airport/roadway visibility used relatively crude discretizations for computing J. The zonal methods though are limited to either single scatter for anisotropic media, or to isotropic media for multiple scatter. Since multiple scatter in anisotropic media is important in applications such as the exit sign visibility problem, more work is needed to efficiently compute J for general scattering functions. Possible approaches include a forward Monte Carlo simulation [3], a modified discrete ordinate method [30],[31] or a modified P-N method.

Steep spatial gradients in J occur when there are shadow boundaries. Shadow boundaries are important when rendering beams of light from head lights or spotlights as in [35]. If scattering is important for these cases the portion of J due to indirect illumination only could be computed on a coarse grids. A two pass method analogous to the method described by Shirley for surfaces [44] could be used to interpolate the portion of J due to indirect illumination, and compute the direct portion separately. For one strong light source it is efficient to propagate the direct illumination through a fine grid in the mesh [25]. For multiple light sources – such as the streetlights in the driving visibility problem – a modification of Shirley and Wang's Monte Carlo method for direct lighting would be more appropriate [45].

Even for indirect illumination a high level of discretization might be required. For cases which have a high spatial variation in J, a reverse Monte Carlo method could be used with values of J on a coarse mesh used to estimate higher order scattering, analogous to the methods for surfaces described in [13] and [41]. This type of method could exploit the the slower temporal changes associated with spatially averaged data noted in the discussion of flames by computing the values of J only for relatively large time steps in animated sequences.

Any method that computes J rather L directly needs an efficient sampling method along the ray for evaluating the line integral in Eq. 1. Haas and Sakas [21] have performed some studies on the tradeoffs in speed and image quality for various sampling strategies.

8 Conclusion

Currently there is no all purpose rendering system, either public domain or commercial, that includes physically accurate renderings of general participating media. That is partly true because unlike architectural and lighting design applications for surface-only systems, specific applications for such a system haven't been clearly identified. It is also partly true because of the complexity of the calculation.

It is hoped that this paper will lead to the design of a general, modular, flexible, rendering system for participating media. A flexible system would allow for a variety of representations of properties and geometries, and for a variety of solution strategies. It would also include rules for determining what approximations are appropriate for particular data input and viewing conditions. Such a system would make physically accurate rendering accessible to a wide range of applications. It would also facilitate future research, by allowing researchers to concentrate on improving specific components of the rendering process, rather than rebuilding an entire rendering system.

References

1. H.R. Baum, K.B. McGrattan, and R.G. Rehm. Simulation of smoke plumes from large pool fires. In *The Proceedings of the Twenty-fifth International Symposium on Combustion*. The Combustion Institute, 1994.

2. R.W. Bergstrom, C. Seigneur, B.L. Babson, H.-Y. Holmer, and M.A. Wojcik. Comparison of the observed and predicted visual effects caused by power plant plumes. *Atmospheric Environment*, 15(10/11):2135–2150, 1981.

3. P. Blasi, B. Le Saëc, and C. Schlick. A rendering algorithm for discrete volume density objects. In *Proceedings of Eurographics 1993*, 1993.

4. J.F. Blinn. Light reflection functions for simulation of clouds and dusty surfaces. In *Proceedings of Siggraph 1982*, pages 21–29. ACM SIGGRAPH, 1982.

5. C. F. Bohren and D. R. Huffman. *Absorption and Scattering of Light by Small Particles*. Wiley, 1983.

6. C.C. Borel and S.A.W. Gerstl. Atmospheric corrections of land imagery using the extended radiosity method. In *Proceedings of the International Geoscience and Remote Sensing Symposium '92*. IEEE and URSI, 1992.

7. C.C. Borel and S.A.W. Gerstl. Remote sensing applications of the extended radiosity method. In *Proceedings of the International Geoscience and Remote Sensing Symposium '92*. IEEE and URSI, 1992.

8. F. Bresciani and G. Rossi. A computational method to simulate light propagation in fog: Theory experimental verification and applicability to road lighting systems analysis. In *LUX EUROPA 1993 Proceedings, Vol. II*, 1993.

9. D. Bruce. A realistic model for battlefield fire plume simulation. In *Characterization, Propagation and Simulation of Sources and Backgrounds*, pages 231–236. SPIE, 1991.

10. J.M. Cathcart and A.D. Sheffer. Generation and application of high resolution infrared computer imagery. *Optical Engineering*, 30(11):1745–1755, November 1991.

11. B.A. Chance. Synthetic imagery to simulate camouflage effectiveness. In *Proceedings of the IEEE 1989 National Aerospace and Electronics Conference: NAECON 1989*, pages 2098–2102. IEEE, 1989.

12. S. Chandrasekhar. *Radiative Transfer*. Dover, 1960.

13. S.-E. Chen, H. Rushmeier, G. Miller, and D. Turner. A progressive multi-pass method for global illumination. In *Proceedings of Siggraph 1991*, pages 165–174. ACM SIGGRAPH, 1991.

14. M.Y. Choi, A. Hamins, H. Rushmeier, and T. Kashiwagi. Simultaneous optical measurement of soot volume fraction, temperature and CO_2 in heptane pool fire. In *The Proceedings of the Twenty-fifth International Symposium on Combustion*. The Combustion Institute, 1994.

15. CIE. Standardization of luminance distribution on clear skies. CIE Publication No. 22, 1973.

16. B. Collins. Visibility of exit signs in clear and smoky conditions. *Journal of the Illumination Engineering Society*, pages 69–83, Winter 1992.

17. R.D. Peacock et al. CFAST: the consolidated model of fire growth and smoke transport. NIST Technical Note 1299, 1993.

18. D.D. Evans, W.D. Walton, H.R. Baum, K.A. Notarianni, J.R. Lawson, H.C. Tang, K.R. Keydel, R.G. Rehm, D. Madrzykowski an R.H. Zile, H. Koseki, and E.J. Tennyson. In-situ burning of oil spills: Mesoscale experiments. In *The Proceedings of the Fifteenth Arctic and Marine Oil Spill Program*, pages 593–657. contributed by the National Institute of Standards and Technology, 1992.

19. G.Y. Gardner. Visual simulation of clouds. In *Proceedings of Siggraph 1985*, pages 297–303. ACM SIGGRAPH, 1985.

20. W.L. Grosshandler. RADCAL: A narrow-band model for radiation calculations in a combustion environment. NIST Technical Note 1402, 1993.

21. S. Haas and G. Sakas. Methods for efficient sampling of arbitrary distributed volume densities. In *Proceedings of the Eurographics Workshop on Photosimulation, Realism and Physics in Computer Graphics*, pages 215–227. INRIA-IRISA, 1990.

22. D.W. Hoock. Modeling time-dependent obscuration for simulated imaging of dust and smoke clouds. In *Characterization, Propagation and Simulation of Sources and Backgrounds*, pages 164–175. SPIE, 1991.

23. J. Howell. Thermal radiation in participating media: The past, the present and some possible futures. *The Journal of Heat Transfer*, 110:1220–1229, November 1988.

24. J.T. Kajiya. The rendering equation. In *Proceedings of Siggraph 1986*, pages 143–150. ACM SIGGRAPH, 1986.

25. J.T. Kajiya and B.P. Von Herzen. Ray tracing volume densities. In *Proceedings of Siggraph 1984*, pages 165–174. ACM SIGGRAPH, 1984.

26. John Kaufman, editor. *IES Lighting Handbook, 1984 Reference Volume*. IESNA, NYC, 1984.

27. F.X. Kneizys, E.P. Shettle, G.P. Anderson, L.W. Abreu, J.H. Chetwynd, J.E.A. Selby, S.A. Cloug, and W.O. Gallery. *LOWTRAN 7 COMPUTER CODE : USER'S MANUAL AFGL-TR-88-0177*. Air Force Geophysics Laboratory, Hanscom AFB, MA, 1988.

28. W. Kreiss, W. Lanich, and E. Niple. Electro-optical aerial targeting workstation. In *Proceedings of the IEEE 1989 National Aerospace and Electronics Conference: NAECON 1989*, pages 902–908. IEEE, 1989.

29. US Army Atmospheric Sciences Laboratory. Electro-optical system atmosphere effects library 1987. technical report, 1987.

30. E. Languénou, K. Bouatouch, and M. Chelle. Global illumination in presence of participating media with general properties. In *Proceedings of the 5th Eurographics Workshop on Rendering*, 1994.

31. N. Max. Efficient light propagation for multiple anisotropic volume scattering. In *Proceedings of 5th Eurographics Workshop on Rendering*, 1994.

32. M.P. Mengüç and P. Dutta. Scattering tomography and its application to diffusion flames. *Journal of Heat Transfer*, pages 144–151, February 1994.

33. G.W. Mulholland and N.P. Bryner. Radiometric model of the transmission cell-reciprocal nephelometer. *Atmospheric Environment*, 28(5):873–887, 1994.

34. E. Nakamae, K. Kaneda, T. Okamoto, and T. Nishita. A lighting model aiming at drive simulators. In *Proceedings of Siggraph 1990*, pages 395–404. ACM SIGGRAPH, 1990.

35. T. Nishita, Y. Miyawaki, and E. Nakamae. A shading model for atmospheric scattering considering luminous intensity distribution of light sources. In *Proceedings of Siggraph 1987*, pages 303–308. ACM SIGGRAPH, 1987.

36. T. Nishita, T. Sirai, K. Tadamura, and E. Nakamae. Display of the earth taking into account atmospheric scattering. In *Proceedings of Siggraph 1993*, pages 175–182. ACM SIGGRAPH, 1993.

37. B. Roysam, A.R. Cohen, P.H. Getto, and P.R. Boyce. A numerical approach to the computation of light propagation through turbid media: Application to the evaluation of lighted exit signs. *IEEE Transactions on Industry Applications*, pages 661–669, May/June 1993.

38. C. Rozé, B. Maheu, and G. Gréhan. Evaluations of the sighting distance in a foggy atmosphere by monte carlo simulation. *Atmospheric Environment*, 28(5):769–775, 1994.

39. H. Rushmeier. *Realistic Image Synthesis for Scenes with Radiatively Participating Media*. PhD thesis, The Sibley School of Mechanical and Aerospace Engineering, Cornell University, 1988.

40. H. Rushmeier, A. Hamins, and M.Y. Choi. Case study: Volume rendering of pool fires. In *The Proceedings of Visualization '94*. IEEE, 1994.

41. H. Rushmeier, C. Patterson, and A. Veerasamy. Geometric simplification for indirect illumination calculations. In *Proceedings of Graphics Interface 1993*, pages 227–236. Canadian Human – Computer Communications Society (CHCCS), May 1993.

42. H. Rushmeier and K.E. Torrance. The zonal method for calculating light intensities in the presence of a participating medium. In *Proceedings of Siggraph 1987*, pages 293–302. ACM SIGGRAPH, 1987.

43. G. Sakas. Modeling and animating turbulent gaseous phenomena using spectral synthesis. *The Visual Computer*, 9:200–212, 1993.

44. P. Shirley. A ray tracing method for illumination calculation in diffuse-specular scenes. In *Proceedings of Graphics Interface 1990*, pages 205–212. Canadian Human – Computer Communications Society (CHCCS), May 1990.

45. P. Shirley and C. Wang. Monte carlo techniques for the direct lighting calculation. submitted for publication.

46. R. Siegel and J. Howell. *Thermal Radiation Heat Transfer*. Hemisphere Publishing Corporation, 1981.

47. J. Stam and E. Fiume. Turbulent wind fields for gaseous phenomena. In *Proceedings of Siggraph 1993*, pages 369–376. ACM SIGGRAPH, 1993.

48. H. Tennekes and J.L. Lumley. *A First Course in Turbulence*. The MIT Press, Cambridge, MA, 1972.

49. G.J. Ward. The RADIANCE lighting simulation and rendering system. In *Proceedings of Siggraph 1994*. ACM SIGGRAPH, 1994.

50. W.H. White, D.J. Moore, and J.P. Lodge, editors. *Proceedings of the Symposium on Plumes and Visibility: Measurement and Model Components*, 1980. in a special issue of Atmospheric Environment, vol. 15,1981.

51. L. Yeager, C. Upson, and R. Myers. Combining physical and visual simulation – creation of the planet jupiter for the film "2010". In *Proceedings of Siggraph 1986*, pages 85–93. ACM SIGGRAPH, 1986.

A Model for Fluorescence and Phosphorescence

Andrew S. Glassner

Xerox PARC, 3333 Coyote Hill Road, Palo Alto, CA 94304 USA

1 Introduction

If you are indoors and reading this document on paper, then the page may be lit by a *fluorescent* light bulb. The gases inside the bulb absorb high-energy electrons, and then *fluoresce*, or re-radiate that absorbed energy at a different frequency. The particular gases in common fluorescent bulbs are chosen to be efficient at re-radiating this energy in the visible wavelengths. If you are reading this document on-line, then you're probably reading it on a cathode-ray tube (CRT). The face of the CRT is lined with *phosphors*, which absorb the high-energy electrons directed at them, and gradually release that energy over time in the visible band. The two phenomena of *fluorescence* and *phosphorescence* are not as common as simple reflection and transmission, but do have an important part to play in the complete description of macroscopic physical behavior that should be modeled by image synthesis programs. This paper presents a mathematical model for global energy balancing which includes these phenomena.

We phrase the discussion in the context of the Rendering Equation as presented by Kajiya [Kajiya86], which can be derived by using ideas from transport theory [Arvo93]. In general, one may consider rendering to be a light transport problem which is solved for a dynamic equilibrium solution. This matches our intuitive experience of the world: when we turn on the lights in a room, then unless something moves the illumination quickly settles down into a stable distribution. In other words, the number of light particles of each frequency that are flowing through a volume of space remains constant.

In this paper we quickly summarize the transport equation that describes this dynamic equilibrium in a scene of surfaces within a participating medium. We show how it can be easily extended to include fluorescence and phosphorescence, and then discuss implementation issues.

2 The Full Radiance Equation

We can consider photons to be particles that occupy a *phase space*, built from the Cartesian product of a 3D volume space $\mathcal{R}^3$ and a 2D direction space $\mathcal{S}^2$.

Each point $(\mathbf{r}, \omega)$ in this phase space represents a particle at some point $\mathbf{r} \in \mathcal{R}^3$ and traveling in some direction $\omega \in \mathcal{S}^2$. The direction vector ω may be taken as constant length because the speed of light is a constant. When working with non-relativistic phenomena this vector may be simply considered to have length 1.

We will focus on the energy that leaves a point on a surface (called the shading point), since that is often a quantity of interest for rendering; the "surface" may be considered a point in space for rendering gaseous and volumetric objects. Basically the light that leaves the surface is a combination of the light generated at the surface itself, plus the light that arrives elsewhere and is then propagated by the surface.

The classical equation representing this energy is the integral form of the transport equation. This can be written in many different ways. We will use the *incident* formulation, where we solve for the light that strikes the shading point. Using the notation of [Glassner94], we write the incident flux $\Phi(\mathbf{r}, \omega)$ at phase-space point $(\mathbf{r}, \omega)$ by finding the first surface point visible from $\mathbf{r}$ in the direction $-\omega$. This point, $\mathbf{s}$, is found by the *ray-tracing function* $\mathbf{s} = \nu(\mathbf{r}, \omega)$, and is located at a distance h from the shading point $\mathbf{r}$. Thus, as illustrated in Figure 1a, the light arriving at $\mathbf{r}$ is a combination of the light leaving $\mathbf{s}$ towards $\mathbf{r}$, minus that percentage that is absorbed and out-scatted along the way.

Fig. 1. (a) Light from a surface. (b) Light from a volume.

We will say that the surface point $\mathbf{s}$ emits light $\epsilon(\mathbf{s}, \omega)$, and that this light is attenuated by absorption and out-scattering by a factor $\mu(\mathbf{s}, \mathbf{r})$. The light that leaves $\mathbf{s}$ is also due to the surface-scattering properties of $\mathbf{s}$, typically embodied in the BRDF f_r. We can simply write $k(\mathbf{s}, \omega' \rightarrow \omega)$ to capture the propagation of light striking $\mathbf{s}$ along direction ω' and propagated into direction ω. Such light can arrive from all directions around $\mathbf{s}$, and is then reflected or transmitted appropriately. Rather than deal with the two domains separately, we integrate the scattering function k over the entire sphere of incident directions. We write this sphere $\Theta_i^i(\mathbf{s})$; note that this set of directions is more specific than $\mathcal{S}^2$, since each direction $\omega' \in \Theta_i^i(\mathbf{s})$ is directed inwards towards the the shading point. In particular, $\omega \notin \Theta_i^i(\mathbf{s})$, since ω points away from $\mathbf{s}$. So the flux $\Phi(\mathbf{s}, \omega)$ propagated by $\mathbf{s}$ can be found by determining the incident flux $\Phi(\mathbf{s}, \omega')$ falling on $\mathbf{s}$ from each incident direction ω', modulating that by the surface function k, and integrating this over all incident directions.

Similarly, we can consider each point $\mathbf{a} = \mathbf{r} - \alpha\omega$ for $\alpha \in (0, h)$; this is the set of all points along the path between **s** and **r**, as in Figure 1b. At each point **a**, there can be some volumetric emission towards **r**, and some inscattering of light that strikes **a** in some incident direction ω' and is redirected towards **a** along ω. Just as with the shading point **r**, we integrate the volume-scattering kernel $k(\mathbf{a}, \omega' \rightarrow \omega)$ against the incident flux $\Phi(\mathbf{a}, \omega')$. We add the volume emission and inscattering terms together, and then multiply by $\mu(\mathbf{r}, \mathbf{a})$ to account for the absorption and outscattering of that flux as it travels from **a** to **r**.

The total contribution to **r** along ω is then the sum of the light emitted and propagated by the surface point **s** towards **r** (and lost along the way), plus the light emitted and propagated by the volume point **a** (and lost along the way). Gathering this all together mathematically, we write

$$\Phi(\mathbf{r}, \omega) = \mu(\mathbf{r}, \mathbf{s}) \left[\epsilon(\mathbf{s}, \omega) + \int_{\Theta_i^!(\mathbf{s})} k(\mathbf{s}, \omega' \rightarrow \omega) \Phi(\mathbf{s}, \omega') d\omega' \right] +$$

$$\int_0^h \mu(\mathbf{r}, \mathbf{a}) \left[\epsilon(\mathbf{a}, \omega) + \int_{\Theta_i^!(\mathbf{a})} k(\mathbf{a}, \omega' \rightarrow \omega) \Phi(\mathbf{a}, \omega') d\omega' \right] d\alpha \qquad (1)$$

where $\mathbf{a} = \mathbf{r} - \alpha\omega$. By omitting the first term entirely and generalizing the scattering function to handle both surfaces and volumes, we could phrase this equation as a single integral. However, it's often computationally convenient to separate the surface and volume contributions as we've done here. We can formulate this equation in terms of the *radiance L* by noticing that the radiance is proportional to the flux times the energy carried by each particle: $L = E\Phi$. To use bidirectional propagation functions, we need to replace $\Phi(\mathbf{p}, \omega)$ with $L(\mathbf{p}, \omega) \cos\theta$, where θ is the angle between ω and the normal to the surface at **p**. When **p** is a point in space, the "normal" is the direction in which we're integrating.

We also use the *bidirection scattering distribution function* (or BSDF) f, which is a combination of the *bidirectional reflection distribution function* (or BRDF) f_r, and the *bidirectional transmission distribution function* (or BTDF), f_t. To satisfy BDFs that depend on polarization, we will also include an *ellipsometric vector* **e** in the description of the radiance $L(\mathbf{r}, \omega)$. Anisotropic functions are handled implicitly by the dependence of f on both **r** and ω.

This has been a very intuitive and schematic summary of Equation 1; a much more detailed development of all the component terms and how they fit together may be found in [Glassner94].

3 Phosphorescence

Phosphorescence is a phenomenon whereby a material traps incident energy for longer than about 10^{-8} seconds before re-emitting it as visible light. Generally this re-emission has no directional character but is radiated uniformly in all directions; that is, it appears like perfect diffuse emission.

To model phosphorescence we will break down the emission term in Equation 1 into a *blackbody* (or *thermal* or *incandescent*) term ϵ_b and a *phosphorescent* term ϵ_p:

$$\epsilon(\mathbf{p}, t, \lambda) = \epsilon_b(\mathbf{p}, \omega, t, \lambda) + \epsilon_p(\mathbf{p}, \omega, t, \lambda) \tag{2}$$

The incandescent term comes from the standard blackbody radiation formula [Born64], which gives the light from a blackbody in terms of its temperature T and the surrounding index of refraction $\eta(\nu)$. We will write the temperature as a function of position $\mathbf{p}$ and time t. Normally incandescent radiation has no preferred direction; it is isotropic. But it is very convenient in computer graphics to associate directional characteristics with light sources; these can be due to low-level geometric and physical properties that we don't want to explicitly include in our models. The easiest way to include these terms is to include a modulating function $m_b(\mathbf{p}, \omega)$ into the expression for the blackbody emission, giving us

$$\epsilon_b(\nu, \mathbf{p}, \omega, t) = m_b(\mathbf{p}, \omega) \frac{2\pi h \nu^3}{c^2} \frac{1}{\exp[h\nu/kT(\mathbf{p}, t)] - 1} \tag{3}$$

(recall $\nu = c/\lambda$). For convenience, rather than work with the energy given by ϵ_b we will work with its related radiance L^e.

The phosphorescent terms comes from simply modeling the behavior of phosphorescent materials. At any given moment, the energy absorbed at a point $\mathbf{p}$ at wavelength λ is determined by the energy arriving from every direction $\omega \in \Theta_i^i$ at λ, times a *phosphorescence efficiency* function $P_p(\lambda)$. This energy decays over time as it is radiated according to a decay function $d(t)$. So the radiance at a given moment is the result of all the energy absorbed in the past times how long it's been since that energy was absorbed. We model the absorption term by integrating the irradiance over all directions (giving us the total energy absorbed at that wavelength), and then scaling the result by the efficiency of the material at that wavelength. The total phosphorescent emission at a given time is given by an integral over all time, which weights the absorption at a given time by the decay function since then. Like the incandescent term, we can add a modulation function m_p into the definition to account for fine surface geometry. In symbols,

$$\epsilon_p(\mathbf{p}, \omega, t, \lambda) = m_p(\mathbf{p}, \omega) \int_{-\infty}^{t} d(t - \tau) P_p(\mathbf{p}, \lambda) \int_{\Theta_i^i} L(\mathbf{p}, \omega', \lambda, \tau) \cos\theta' \, d\omega' \, d\tau \tag{4}$$

where θ' is the angle made by ω' with respect to the normal at $\mathbf{p}$.

Equation 4 is missing a *saturation* component. After a certain point, the material cannot store any more energy at a given wavelength, and the excess is converted to heat or is not absorbed at all. So P_p should depend on how much room is left for storing energy at a given wavelength. Introducing this nonlinearity would make the expression more complex; our approximation is reasonable at low illuminations.

A good candidate for d at a time t due to an incident radiance L_0 is given by a model proposed by Leverenz [Leverenz68], which combines several different physical mechanisms into one expression:

$$L(t, L_0) = \frac{1}{b\left(\dfrac{1}{\sqrt{L_0 b}} + t\right)^2} \tag{5}$$

A material with no phosphorescence may be modeled with a discrete delta function $d(\tau) = \delta[t - \tau]$; that is,

$$d(\tau) = \begin{cases} 1 & t = \tau \\ 0 & \text{otherwise} \end{cases} \tag{6}$$

4 Fluorescence

Fluorescence is a phenomenon whereby a material absorbs light at one frequency and then re-radiates it at another frequency within about 10^{-8} seconds. Like phosphorescence, this re-emission has no directional character.

To model fluorescence we change the scattering function to account for this transfer of energy from one wavelength to the next. Rather than simply integrating over all incident directions and weighting the energy at each one, we also integrate over all visible wavelengths (represented by the domain $\mathcal{R}_V$) and scale by a *fluorescence efficiency* $P_f(\lambda' \rightarrow \lambda)$ which models the transfer of energy from λ' to λ. In other words, we look in each direction and scatter not just the energy at λ, but the energy at all other λ' which will be absorbed and re-radiated at λ. Symbolically, the scattering term becomes

$$\int_{\Theta_i^!} (\mathbf{p}) f(\mathbf{p}, \omega' \rightarrow \omega) \int_{\mathcal{R}_V} P_f(\mathbf{p}, \lambda' \rightarrow \lambda) L(\mathbf{p}, \omega', \lambda') \, d\lambda' \, d\omega' \tag{7}$$

If a material has no fluorescence, then P_f may be modeled with a discrete delta function $P_f(\lambda' \rightarrow \lambda) = \delta[\lambda - \lambda']$.

4.1 The Radiance Equation

We can now put together the pieces above. We assume that there is no fluorescence-phosphorescent interaction; that is, energy absorbed at a wavelength λ for fluorescent re-radiation at λ' does not contribute to later phosphorescent re-radiation at λ'. There's no mathematical reason not to model such an effect, but I have not seen it reported in the literature on luminescence [Harvey57].

To build the complete radiance equation we can replace the emission and scattering terms in Equation 1 with Equation 4 and Equation 7 respectively. This gives us the following complete (but formidable) result for the radiance at wavelength λ arriving at a point $\mathbf{r}$ from a direction $\boldsymbol{\omega}$ at time t:

$$
\begin{aligned}
L\left(\mathbf{r}, \boldsymbol{\omega}, \lambda, \mathbf{e}, t\right) = \mu(\mathbf{r}, \mathbf{s}) & \left[L^e(\mathbf{s}, \boldsymbol{\omega}, t, \lambda) \right. \\
& + m_p(\mathbf{r}, \boldsymbol{\omega}) \int_{-\infty}^{t} d(t - \tau) P_p(\mathbf{s}, \lambda) \int_{\Theta_i^-(\mathbf{s})} L(s, \boldsymbol{\omega}', \lambda, \mathbf{e}, \tau) \cos \theta' \, d\boldsymbol{\omega}' \, d\tau \\
& \left. + \int_{\Theta_i^-}(s) f(\mathbf{s}, \lambda, \boldsymbol{\omega}' \to \boldsymbol{\omega}) \int_{\mathcal{R}_\nu} P_f(\mathbf{s}, \lambda' \to \lambda) L(s, \boldsymbol{\omega}', \lambda', \mathbf{e}, t) \, d\lambda' \, \cos \theta' \, d\boldsymbol{\omega}' \right] \\
+ \int_0^{h(\mathbf{r}, \boldsymbol{\omega})} \mu(\mathbf{r}, \mathbf{a}) & \left[L^e(\mathbf{a}, \boldsymbol{\omega}, t, \lambda) \right. \\
& + m_p(\mathbf{a}, \boldsymbol{\omega}) \int_{-\infty}^{t} d(t - \tau) P_p(\mathbf{a}, \lambda) \int_{\Theta_i^-(\mathbf{a})} L(s, \boldsymbol{\omega}', \lambda, \mathbf{e}, \tau) \cos \theta' \, d\boldsymbol{\omega}' \, d\tau \\
& \left. + \int_{\Theta_i^-}(\mathbf{a}) f(\mathbf{a}, \lambda, \boldsymbol{\omega}' \to \boldsymbol{\omega}) \int_{\mathcal{R}_\nu} P_f(\mathbf{a}, \lambda' \to \lambda) L(\mathbf{a}, \boldsymbol{\omega}', \lambda', \mathbf{e}, t) d\lambda' \cos \theta' d\boldsymbol{\omega}' \right] d\alpha
\end{aligned}
$$

$$(8)$$

where

$$
\mathbf{a} = \mathbf{r} - \alpha\boldsymbol{\omega}
$$
$$
f(\mathbf{s}, \lambda, \boldsymbol{\omega}' \to \boldsymbol{\omega}) = \text{is the surface BDF at } \mathbf{s}
$$
$$
f(\mathbf{a}, \lambda, \boldsymbol{\omega}' \to \boldsymbol{\omega}) = \text{is the volume BDF at } \mathbf{a}
$$

Equation 8 is *The Full Radiance Equation*, which we refer to simply as the FRE [1].

The FRE can be tamed a bit by putting it into operator notation. This doesn't make it any easier to solve, but it is a bit easier to take in all the steps at once. The definitions of the operators come directly from their use in Equation 8. The operator form of the FRE may be written

$$
L = (\mathcal{M} + \mathcal{V})[L^e + \mathcal{P}AL + \mathcal{K}\mathcal{F}L] \tag{9}
$$

where

$\mathcal{M}$ represents the attenuation of radiance from point $\mathbf{s}$

$\mathcal{V}$ represents the attenuation of radiance from point $\mathbf{a}$

between $\mathbf{r}$ and $\mathbf{s}$

---

[1] The name *full radiance equation* is similar to, but deliberately distinct from, the name *rendering equation* used by Kajiya [Kajiya86]. Although Equation 8 could reasonably be called a "rendering equation", the formula given that name by Kajiya corresponds to my Equation 12, which is derived after a set of additional assumptions. I think that re-assigning an existing name to a new equation is likely to cause confusion, so I have chosen a new name.

$\mathcal{P}$ is the phosphorescence operator

$\mathcal{F}$ is the fluorescence operator

$\mathcal{A}$ is the absorption operator

$\mathcal{K}$ is the BDF operator

There is no hope of solving the full radiance equation analytically for the function L, even if we had all of the other functions in a reasonable form. Much of practical image synthesis has been devoted to finding efficient and accurate approximations to solutions of this equation, either by approximating the solution, the equation, or both. That is, since an exact solution to the exact equation is intractable, we instead seek out exact solutions to an approximate equation, approximate solutions to the exact equation, or (most commonly) approximate solutions to an approximate equation.

5 TIGRE

The FRE in Equation 8 is enough to challenge even the strongest of heart. Since we know that an exact solution to the exact equation is unlikely to be found for a non-trivial environment, we need to start cutting corners somewhere. The most common approximation is to eliminate the terms for polarization, phosphorescence, and fluorescence.

Eliminating polarization means that we are assuming that all light in the image is unpolarized. If we avoid coherent light sources like lasers we can start without polarized light, but we know from Fresnel's laws that at Brewster's angle light will reflect off of a surface linearly polarized. If polarization is important for a particular image then one can run linearly independent simulations and then combine them.

By eliminating fluorescence we are asserting that all wavelengths are *decoupled*. This is, the solution to the radiance at wavelength λ is independent of the solution at some other λ'. This means that we can compute a color image by solving a simplified radiance equation several times at several different wavelengths, and then combining the results. It also makes it much easier to compute color images using basis functions rather than spectral samples, since we don't introduce arbitrary transformations on the bases. We can't leave out the wavelength altogether, since the index of refraction depends upon it, so it remains in the expression for the scattering function. The result is called a *monochromatic* or *gray* equation.

By eliminating phosphorescence we are asserting that every instant of time is the same as every other instant for the system. The underlying 3D model may change at each moment, but when we solve the rendering equation we assume that the model has been frozen in position in an enclosed environment without any illumination, and that when the simulation begins the lights are only then turned on. In signal-processing terms, this means that the modified radiance equation is *time-invariant*.

The resulting simplified equation is then:

$$L(\mathbf{r}, \omega) = \mu(\mathbf{r}, \mathbf{s}) \left[L^e(\mathbf{s}, \omega) + \int_{\Theta_i^:(\mathbf{s})} f(\mathbf{s}, \omega' \to \omega, \lambda) L(\mathbf{s}, \omega') \cos \theta' \, d\omega' \right] +$$

$$\int_0^{h(\mathbf{r}, \omega)} \mu(\mathbf{r}, \mathbf{a}) \left[L^e(\mathbf{a}, \omega) + \int_{\Theta_i^:(\mathbf{s})} f(\mathbf{a}, \omega' \to \omega, \lambda) L(\mathbf{a}, \omega') \cos \theta' \, d\omega' \right] d\alpha$$

(10)

Equation 10 is the *Time-Invariant, Gray Radiance Equation*, or TIGRE, illustrated in Figure 2a. Notice that TIGRE contains volumetric terms, so it accommodates *participating media* such as smoke and fog, as well as volumetric objects defined not by surfaces but by fields in space. In operator notation, TIGRE may be written

$$L = (\mathcal{M} + \mathcal{V})[L^e + \mathcal{K}L]$$

(11)

Fig. 2. (a) Geometry of TIGRE. (b) Geometry of OVTIGRE.

6 VTIGRE

The formulation of TIGRE in Equation 10 is much simpler than the full radiance equation, but it is often simplified even further by assuming that all synthesis occurs in a vacuum. Under vacuum conditions, the entire right-hand term on the right side of Equation 10 goes to zero: there is no volumetric emission, so $L^e(\mathbf{a}, \omega) = 0$, and no scattering or absorption, so $f(\mathbf{a}, \omega' \to \omega, \lambda) = 0$, and $\mu(\mathbf{r}, \mathbf{s}) = \exp\left[\int_0^{\|\mathbf{r}-\mathbf{s}\|} 0 d\tau \right] = e^0 = 1$ [Glassner94].

The result is then

$$L(\mathbf{r}, \omega) = L^e(\mathbf{s}, \omega) + \int_{\Theta_i^:(\mathbf{s})} f(\mathbf{s}, \omega' \to \omega, \lambda) L(\mathbf{s}, \omega') \cos \theta' \, d\omega'$$

(12)

Equation 12 is the *Vacuum, Time-Invariant, Gray Radiance Equation*, or VTIGRE. This equation expresses the same physics as the *rendering equation* due to Kajiya [Kajiya86]. We chose not to use that name here because this is a special case of the FRE (see footnote on page 65).

In operator notation, VTIGRE may be written

$$L = L^e + \mathcal{K}L \tag{13}$$

When we are in a vacuum then we can refer to the radiance at $\mathbf{r}$ coming from $\mathbf{s}$ by simply indicating the direction vector ω along which light from $\mathbf{s}$ would arrive. Then we can write VTIGRE in a slightly modified form that describes the light radiated from $\mathbf{r}$ in an outgoing direction ω in terms of the incident radiance from all directions and the emission at $\mathbf{r}$ itself.

This modified form is then

$$L(\mathbf{r}, \omega^o) = L^e(\mathbf{r}, \omega^o) + \int_{\Theta_i^i(\mathbf{r})} f(\mathbf{r}, \omega \rightarrow \omega^o, \lambda) L(\mathbf{r}, \omega) \cos \theta_r \, d\omega \tag{14}$$

where $\omega^o \in \Theta_o^o(\mathbf{r})$, and θ_r is the angle between the normal at $\mathbf{r}$ and ω. Note that we are now integrating the sphere of incoming directions around $\mathbf{r}$, not $\mathbf{s}$. This form is sometimes a more useful starting place for rendering algorithms. We call this the OVTIGRE form, since it represents the *outgoing* form of the VTIGRE assumptions. It is illustrated in Figure 2b.

7 Implementation

The most straightforward implementation of fluorescence and phosphorescence is to build a rendering system which attempts to directly find numerical solutions to the full rendering equation of Equation 8 using Monte Carlo and other sampling methods. I expect that as computers continue to become faster and cheaper, there will come a day when this brute-force approach will be the most attractive way to compute images. In the meantime, other techniques must be used.

Most of today's rendering systems actively exploit the suppression of these two phenomena to achieve improved performance. When there is no fluorescence, each wavelength of light is independent of all other wavelengths, so rendering at different wavelengths (or bands of wavelengths) may proceed in parallel. When there is no fluorescence, each frame of an animation is independent of all other frames, and thus may also be rendered in parallel. When these phenomena are included, the simplification that allows this parallelism is replaced by a model that requires time- and frequency-serial computation.

Phosphorescence may be added to most rendering systems without requiring any architectural changes. Each material contains a surface parameter b that controls its decay curve, and each object maintains a cache of its current un-radiated energy at different wavelengths or wavelength bands (as many as are required by the system). Any object with an appreciable amount of energy to be radiated should be considered a "light source" in a ray-tracing system; in a radiosity system this energy is simply added to the material's emission.

Fluorescence may be harder to incorporate because it violates the assumption made by most renderers that simulations at different wavelengths are independent. To model the effect, each material contains a surface parameter M, which is a matrix that represents the transfer of energy from one wavelength (or band of wavelengths) to another. In general, this means that one must solve for all wavelengths simultaneously, just as one solves for all objects simultaneously. However, for most physical materials this matrix is triangular: that is, energy absorbed at any wavelength is consistently re-radiated with less energy. In this case one can still render in wavelength-independent passes, proceeding from the highest to the lowest energies. After each pass the energy absorbed at that wavelength is propagated through the matrix and added to the energy to be radiated at lower wavelengths. As with phosphorescence, this means for ray-tracers that objects with an appreciable amount of energy to be emitted at a given wavelength must be considered as light sources; radiosity handles this condition naturally.

I have added both of these phenomena to Craig Kolb's *Rayshade* public-domain ray-tracing package with just a few relatively small modifications. The only architectural change was converting the renderer from an RGB color model to a denser sampling of the visible range, and making sure that these wavelengths were scanned in order of decreasing energy. Since *Rayshade* is a ray tracer, I had to scan the list of all objects before each pass to identify those with appreciable energy to emit and turn them into (temporary) area light sources. Adding the new material coefficients and changing the shading model was straightforward.

Color plate 1 (*see color section*) shows phosphorescence displayed by a watch with hands that glow in the dark (the small white balls that mark the hours are not phosphorescent). The phosphorescent decay of the hands was computed using the time in seconds elapsed since the removal of illumination, and a decay value of $b = 1 \times 10^{-5}$. The first image shows the watch at 1:00:00, when the illumination is removed. Successive images show the watch face 1 second after illumination was shut off, and continued figures after total lapses of 90, 640, 2,608, and 5,691 seconds. In the final figure the radiance is down to 0.003 percent of its initial amplitude, and is so faint that the watch would be invisible but for a small amount of background illumination.

Color plate 2 (*see color section*) demonstrates fluorescence, first with a room illuminated by an overhead bulb of roughly white light, and then illuminated by a so-called "black-light" bulb, which is really just a bulb whose emission contains mostly blue and ultraviolet radiation. This radiation is absorbed, modulated, and re-radiated by the fluorescent ink in the posters, which explains why they have a significant amount of middle- and long-wavelength radiation despite the fact that they are receiving no illumination at those wavelengths. I modeled the transfer matrices of the inks empirically.

8 Conclusion

The full radiance equation (FRE) offers a single expression that explicitly combines surface and volumetric reflection and transmission, including polarization, frequency, phosphorescence, and fluorescence in a participating medium. It suffers from the same restrictions shared by all methods based on geometrical optics: diffraction and interference are not accounted for at all, and can only be added in with special additional models. However, it does offer a convenient summary of the particle-based physics of light transport. This equation may be solved with small changes to the ray-tracing and radiosity methods that have been developed to solve VTIGRE, the more specific equation for transparent, stationary, gray surfaces and non-participating media. It is interesting to note that the parallelism often exploited by ray-tracing systems is not inherent in the algorithm, but is a result of simplifying the physics so that frequency crosstalk (fluorescence) and sustained release (phosphorescence) are ignored.

9 Acknowledgements

This paper contains some material from my forthcoming book; thanks to Mike Morgan for supporting the publication of this material here.

References

[Arvo93]   James Arvo: Transfer Equations in Global Illumination. August 1993, in Paul Heckbert, ed., Siggraph 1993 Global Illumination course notes

[Born64]   Max Born and Emil Wolf: Principles of Optics, Second Revised Edition. Pergamon Press, Cambridge, 1964

[Glassner94] Andrew S. Glassner: Principles of Digital Image Synthesis. Morgan-Kaufmann Publishers, San Francisco, 1994

[Harvey57]   E. Newton Harvey: A History of Luminescence. The American Philosophical Society, Philadelphia, 1957

[Kajiya86]   James T. Kajiya: The Rendering Equation. Computer Graphics (Proc. Siggraph '86), 20(4), August 1986, pp. 143–150

[Leverenz68] Humboldt W. Leverenz: An Introduction to Luminescence of Solids. Dover Publications, New York, 1968

Global Illumination in Presence of Participating Media with General Properties

Eric Languénou, Kadi Bouatouch, Michael Chelle

IRISA, Campus de Beaulieu, 35042 Rennes Cedex, France

Abstract

In the recent years a number of techniques have been devised by computer graphics researchers for rendering participating media like haze, fog, clouds, dust... Due to the complexity of the underlying physics, strong assumptions (isotropy, single scattering, no spontaneous emission...) are often made to make these techniques tractable. In this paper, we propose a method which lifts these assumptions. It relies on the discrete ordinate method and allows light transfer simulation in an environment made up of diffuse objects and participating media.

1 Introduction

Significant progresses have been made in the field of rendering techniques through the use of global illumination model which describes the light transport mechanism between the surfaces of an environment. To simulate reality, these models rely on physics, optics, reflection and transmission models, photometry and colorimetry. Multiple reflections and transmissions as well as glossy surfaces can now be handled by the rendering techniques using these illumination models. In comparison to these latter, the existing models for simulating light transfer in participating media are still underdeveloped. Due to the complexity of the physical phenomenon related to these media, the existing methods make strong simplifying assumptions on the physical properties of the used media such as isotropy, anisotropy but with a low albedo (single scattering), no emission,etc.

On the other hand, in thermal engineering, several methods have been devised for simulating thermal radiative transfer within a medium having any physical properties. It turns out that the method known as *discrete ordinate method* is the most efficient one for such simulation. Thermal engineers consider a medium as delimited by a boundary, and calculate the energy exchange between this boundary and the medium. Whereas in this paper, the proposed method considers several media included in an environment also containing diffuse objects, and performs a global lighting simulation by accounting for the energy exchange between the participating media and the diffuse object surfaces. The used technique for simulating light transfer within a medium is a modified version of the discrete ordinate method, and does not make any assumption on the media. In this way, the described method is capable of handling anisotropy, multiple scattering and spontaneous emission. In addition, several effects can be rendered: shadows due to and cast onto media and objects, illumination contribution between objects, media, and between objects and media.

The paper is organized as follows. After a theoretical background on the physics of participating media, previous works on the rendering of these media are outlined and discussed. Then details on our method are given, followed by results, a conclusion and appendices.

2 Theoretical Background

In a participating medium, radiation traveling along a path is attenuated by absorption and scattering and is enhanced by emission and scattering in from other directions. The radiance value of this radiation at any point of the medium is given by the solution of the *equation of radiative transfer* (ERT) which is (figure 1) [12]:

$$\frac{dL_\lambda(S)}{dS} = - \underbrace{a_\lambda L_\lambda(S)}_{\text{absorption}} + \underbrace{a_\lambda L_{\lambda b}(T)}_{\text{emission}} - \underbrace{\sigma_\lambda L_\lambda(S)}_{\text{scattering}}$$

$$+ \underbrace{\frac{\sigma_\lambda}{4\pi} \int_{\omega_i=4\pi} L_\lambda(S, \theta, \phi)\Phi_\lambda(\theta, \phi)d\omega_i}_{\text{in-scattering}}$$

This ERT describes, for each wavelength λ, the radiance $L_\lambda(S)$ (emitted flux per unit surface and per unit projected solid angle) at any position S along a path C_S through a participating medium. It gives the change of radiance $\frac{dL_\lambda(S)}{dS}$ as the radiation passes through distance dS. This change is due to emission, absorption, scattering and in-scattering. The terms a_λ and σ_λ are the absorption and scattering coefficients respectively, while $\Phi_\lambda(\theta, \phi)$ is the phase function associated with the medium. If this function is constant then the medium is isotropic, otherwise it is anisotropic. $a_\lambda L_{\lambda b}(T)$ is due to the spontaneous emission in the medium along dS, when this medium is compared to a blackbody at a temperature T. $L_\lambda(S, \theta, \phi)$ is the incident radiance at position S coming from direction (θ, ϕ). $d\omega_i$ is the differential solid angle corresponding to this incident radiance.

The terms responsible for the gain in energy at position S will together be called *Source term G* and expressed as:

$$G_\lambda(S) = a_\lambda L_{\lambda b}(T) + \frac{\sigma_\lambda}{4\pi} \int_{\omega_i=4\pi} L_\lambda(S, \theta, \phi)\Phi_\lambda(\theta, \phi)d\omega_i.$$

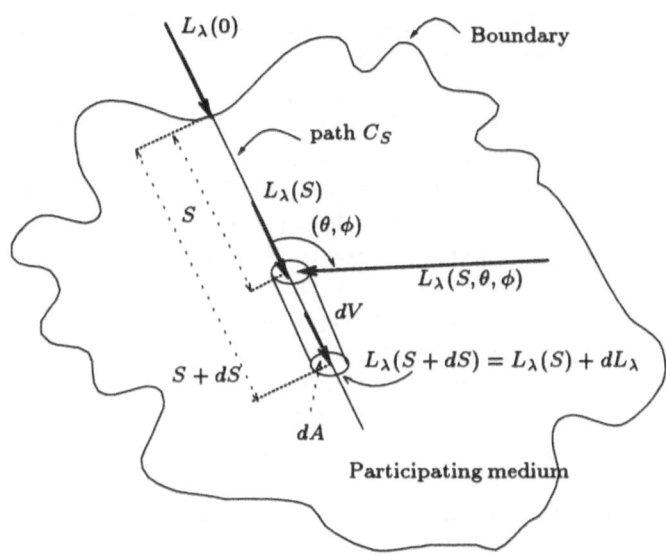

Fig. 1. Radiative transfer within a medium.

The extinction coefficient is defined as $K_\lambda = a_\lambda + \sigma_\lambda$ and the albedo as $\Omega_\lambda = \frac{\sigma_\lambda}{K_\lambda}$. The optical depth for a path S is given by $\kappa_\lambda(S) = \int_0^S K_\lambda(S')dS'$.

Note that the ERT gives only the local radiance at a position S in the medium. To determine the energy balance within the medium, this equation has to be solved over the entire medium. Several approaches have been attempted to solve it. They are outlined in the next section.

3 Previous Works

This section outlines different methods aiming at solving the ERT. These methods can be referred to as analytical, zonal, statistical, P-N or discrete ordinate.

The analytical methods [3, 8, 11] try to analytically solve the ERT by making strong simplifying assumptions (isotropy, single scattering, uniform density, point light source...). A projective rendering technique or ray tracing is used in the rendering step.

In case of isotropic media, the zonal method has been proposed by Hottel [5] in thermal engineering and applied by Rushmeier [10] to computer graphics. This method is an extension of the radiosity method to volumes. The medium is subdivided into volume elements and the ERT is transformed into a system of linear equations whose unknowns are patch and volume radiosities. The coefficients of the system matrix are surface-surface, surface-volume and volume-volume form-factors. This method has been extended by Rushmeier to anisotropic media having a low albedo (single scattering).

The objective of the statistical methods is to simulate the light transfer within a medium with the help of the Monte-Carlo method [10, 9, 2]. Even though these methods handle anisotropic media, they are time expensive and do not give a means of appraising the computation accuracy.

The P-N method transforms the ERT, which is an integro-differential equation, into a differential equation by expanding the radiance L_λ in an orthogonal series of spherical harmonics truncated after N terms. The medium is subdivided into small volumes and the ERT is expressed in each volume element. This results in a system of differential equations to be solved. This method has been used in thermal engineering [4, 13] and in computer graphics [6, 1] only for $N = 1, 2, 3$. To accurately handle anisotropic media, N has to be significantly increased, which limits this method practically.

In the discrete ordinate method [14, 12], the 4π solid angle about a location is divided into a finite number of small solid angles, each corresponding to one discrete ordinate direction. Therefore, integrals over solid angles are represented by sums over the ordinate directions. The ERT is then represented by a differential equation for the average radiance over a finite number of directions. Furthermore, in order to transform the differential equation (ERT) into an algebraic one, a discretization of the 3D space is performed. This is done by subdividing the participating medium into small volumes so that the scattering and absorption coefficients as well as the radiance for any given direction are assumed to be constant in a volume. When no assumption is made on the used participating medium, the discrete ordinate method seems to be the most interesting because of its tractability. For this reason, the method we have developed for simulating the light transfer in a medium is based on the discrete ordinate method. It is described in the next section.

4 Our Method

The objective of our method is to simulate light transfer within a medium without making assumptions on its physical properties (multiple scatterings, any albedo, spectral approach...). Our simulation approach relies on the discrete ordinate method and requires both angular (ordinate directions) and spatial discretizations.

4.1 Angular and Spatial Discretization

The ERT can be written for a finite number n_d of ordinate directions as:

$$\mu_m \frac{\partial L_m}{\partial x} + \xi_m \frac{\partial L_m}{\partial y} + \eta_m \frac{\partial L_m}{\partial z} = -K L_m + a L_b + \frac{\sigma}{4\pi} \sum_{m'=1}^{n_d} w_{m'} \Phi_{m'm} L_{m'}, \quad (1)$$

where L_m is the radiance in direction V_m, K the extinction coefficient, V_m and $V_{m'}$ the incoming and outgoing angular directions indexed by m and m', $(m, m' \in [1, n_d])$, (μ_m, ξ_m, η_m) the direction cosines for direction V_m, and $w_{m'}$ is the small solid angle associated with the angular direction $V_{m'}$. The subscript λ has been omitted for a reason of clarity. The obtained ERT is differential and can be spatially discretized by using the control volume method which consists in subdividing the rectangular enclosure of the medium into a set of rectangular volumes also called voxels (grid of voxels).

Let the six faces of a voxel be denoted $X_-, X_+, Y_-, Y_+, Z_-, Z_+$. The subscripts $-$ and $+$ correspond to the incoming and outgoing faces with respect to the incident light direction. To set up a numerical solution, a voxel form for the ERT is derived by multiplying equation (1) by $dxdydz$ and integrating over a voxel P to obtain:

$$\mu_m(L_{mX+} - L_{mX-})A_X + \xi_m(L_{mY+} - L_{mY-})A_Y$$

$$+ \eta_m(L_{mZ+} - L_{mZ-})A_Z = aV_PL_{bP} - KV_PL_{mP} + V_P\frac{\sigma}{4\pi}\sum_{m'=1}^{n_d} w_{m'}L_{m'P}\Phi_{m'm},$$

$$(2)$$

where A_X, A_Y, A_Z are the areas of faces X, Y, Z of voxel P respectively, V_P the volume of P, L_{mP} and $L_{m'P}$ the average radiances for P and for direction V_m and direction $V_{m'}$ respectively.

Note that boundary equations (corresponding to boundary conditions) have to be added to this system of equations. It is easy to see that the numerical solution to this system for each of the n_d directions is iterative, each iteration corresponding to one scattering. The first iteration gives the radiances at the boundary, and for the iterations that follow the radiances of each voxel is computed progressively from voxel to voxel. This resolution results finally in radiances at each voxel obtained after a certain number of scatterings. This resolution strategy is adopted in thermal engineering. It is easy to see that this strategy is not well suited to computer graphics. Suppose that ray tracing is used during the rendering step. When a ray is traced from the viewpoint it may intersect the medium. Only the closest intersection point I lying on the medium boundary has to be considered. The radiance L_{mI} at point I (in all directions V_m) has been already computed by the discrete ordinate method. As the direction I-to-viewpoint is not likely to be a discrete direction, the radiance L_{mI} toward the viewpoint has to be interpolated. This interpolated radiance cannot be computed accurately because of the limited number of discrete directions and of the fact that the radiance on a face of a voxel lying on a boundary is assumed to be constant over this face and for one direction. As a consequence, the objects lying behind the medium look fuzzy. In addition, this resolution method may provide negative radiance values, which has no sense. Thermal engineers usually set these values to 0.

For all these reasons, we have modified the classical discrete ordinate method to adapt it to computer graphics. Indeed, we are interested in computing the *Source terms* rather than the radiances, except for the boundary faces. Note that a boundary face at the same time lies on a medium boundary and belongs to a boundary voxel. In the following, we will see that the boundary conditions are accounted for in a way different from that used in thermal engineering.

Furthermore, certain weighting coefficients are computed more precisely by our method (see appendices B and C).

4.2 Principle

The *Source term* in its discrete form is given for each voxel P by:

$$G_{m'P} = aL_{bP} + \frac{\sigma}{4\pi} \sum_{m=1}^{n_d} w_m L_{mP} \Phi_{mm'}. \tag{3}$$

Recall that it represents the gain in energy by emission and scattering in. In each voxel, this *Source term* for a given direction together with the physical properties of the medium are assumed to be constant. In this way, $G_{m'P}$ represents the average *Source term*, L_{mP} the average incident radiance and L_{bP} the average radiance due to emission. The first goal of our method is to compute, for each voxel and for all directions $V_{m'}$, the average *Source term* after multiple scatterings in the medium. The second is the calculation of the radiances at the boundary faces. These boundary radiances are used to compute their contribution to the objects lying in the environment. For each given direction V_m, light is propagated along V_m and scattered in all directions $V_{m'}$ (see figure 2), which enhances the *Source terms* as:

$$G_{m'P} + = \frac{\sigma}{4\pi} w_m L_{mP} \Phi_{mm'}.$$

The energy of this light is also transferred from voxel to voxel through the common faces for which the average radiances are computed.

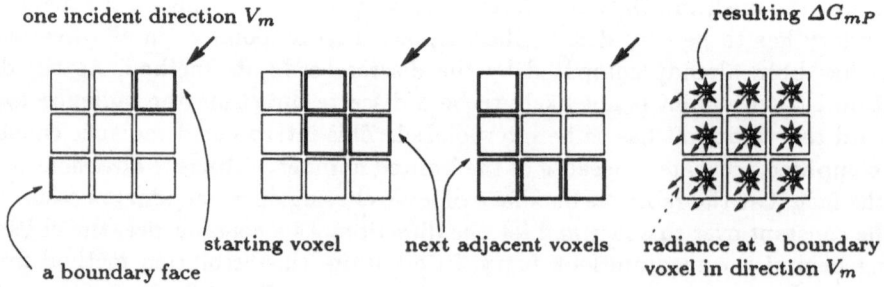

one incident direction V_m resulting ΔG_{mP}

starting voxel   next adjacent voxels   radiance at a boundary

a boundary face   voxel in direction V_m

Fig. 2. Grid traversal.

Traversing the Voxel Grid Assume that the radiance for a given direction over a voxel face is constant. This assumption holds since the voxels are small enough. Let us denote L_{mJ-} and L_{mI+} the radiances for the incoming and outgoing faces of a voxel for direction V_m respectively. The subscripts J and I are equal to X, Y or Z. For example, L_{mX-} is the radiance at the incoming face perpendicular to the X axis. For a given voxel P, if the *Source term* and the radiances L_{mJ-} of the incoming faces are known, the radiances L_{mI+} at the outgoing faces are computed with the help of the ERT (see appendix B). Indeed, as within a voxel P the *Source term*, for a given direction V_m, is $G_m(x) = G_{mP} = constant$ and $K(x) = K = constant$, then the solution of the ERT for a path of length s is:

$$L_m(s) = L_m(0)e^{-Ks} + \frac{G_{mP}}{K}(1 - e^{-Ks}) \tag{4}$$

As seen later on, this formula will be used to evaluate the light energy propagated from voxel to voxel. Now, let us see how this propagation is performed, say how the voxel grid is traversed. For an incident direction V_m, the traversal starts at one of the voxels that has 3 incoming faces lying on the boundary (figure 2). To carry out the grid traversal, a referential R is defined and oriented $(\mu_m > 0, \xi_m > 0, \eta_m > 0)$ so that the increments for each axis may be computed appropriately. This referential is constructed by the procedure *init_referential()*.

The three incoming boundary faces of the starting voxel have a radiance equal to 0 for all directions, but their *Source term* is calculated by accounting for the contribution of the environment's objects. This contribution is computed by the initialization procedure we call *init_source_term ()* and described in appendix A. This procedure also calculates the *Source terms* for all the grid voxels. At this time, these *Source terms* $\Delta(G_{mP})^1$ correspond to the first order scattering plus the spontaneous emission (the superscript 1 means first scattering).

Next, for the second scattering, the calculated *Source term* of the starting boundary voxel is used to compute the radiance at its outgoing faces L_{mI+} with the help of the procedure *propagate_radiance()*. These radiances also are those of the incoming faces of the adjacent voxels in direction V_m. This process is repeated for these adjacent voxels. Note that the incoming radiances for these voxels are no more equal to 0. This process proceeds till all the voxels have been considered. This is performed similarly for all the n_d directions. As a result of this iterative process, the *Source terms* calculated by the procedure *init_source_term ()* are propagated throughout the medium, and the boundary faces are assigned radiances. During this process, new average radiances $\Delta(L_{mP})^1$ and new average *Source terms* $\Delta(G_{mP})^2$ of all the voxels are calculated. To handle the subsequent orders of scattering, the overall process is repeated with these new average radiances and new average *Source terms* according to the following scheme (the superscript n being the scattering order):

$$\forall m \quad \Delta(L_{mI-})^n \text{ and } \Delta(G_{mP})^n \Rightarrow \Delta(L_{mI+})^n \text{ and } \Delta(L_{mP})^n$$
$$\Delta(L_{mP})^n \Rightarrow \Delta(G_{m'P})_m^{n+1} \forall m'$$

where:

- Δ means the contribution of one scattering.
- $\Delta(G_{m'P})_m^{n+1}$ the contribution of scattering of order $n + 1$ in direction $V_{m'}$ for an incident radiance in direction V_m of order n.

- $\Delta(G_{mP})^n$ is the sum of all the contributions of the n order scattering in direction V_m for all incident directions $V_{m''}$ ($\Delta(G_{mP})^n = \sum_{m''=0}^{n_d} \Delta(G_{mP})_{m''}^n$, $\forall m \in [0, n_d]$).

The overall process stops when the convergence criterion is met.

Resolution Algorithm `medium_resolution()`
`begin`
$n = 1$; /* first scattering already handled by *init_source_term()* */
repeat /* scattering loop */
   $\Delta(G_{mP})^{n+1} = 0, \forall m$ and $\forall P$
   for m from 1 to n_d /*incident directions loop */
      `init_referential`(V_m) ;
      for each voxel P in the traversal direction
         for faces $I- \in \{X-, Y-, Z-\}$
            if boundary$(I-, P)$ *then* $\Delta(L_{mI-})^n = 0$
            else $\Delta(L_{mI-})^n = \Delta(L_{mI+})^n(P')$
            /* P' being the preceding voxel with
            respect to the incident direction V_m */
         EndFor
         $(\Delta(L_{mX+})^n, \Delta(L_{mY+})^n, \Delta(L_{mZ+})^n) =$ `propagate_radiance`
               $(P, \Delta(L_{mX-})^n, \Delta(L_{mY-})^n, \Delta(L_{mZ-})^n, \Delta(G_{mP})^n)$;
         $\Delta(L_{mP})^n =$ `compute_average_radiance`
               $(P, \Delta(L_{mX-})^n, \Delta(L_{mY-})^n, \Delta(L_{mZ-})^n, \Delta(G_{mP})^n)$;
         for m' from 1 to n_d /* loop of scattering directions */
            $\Delta(G_{m'P})^{n+1} += \frac{\sigma}{4\pi} w_m \Phi_{mm'} \Delta(L_{mP})^n$;
            $G_{m'P} += \frac{\sigma}{4\pi} w_m \Phi_{mm'} \Delta(L_{mP})^n$;
         EndFor
         if outgoing_boundary_face(P, V_m)
         then load_boundary$(P, \Delta(L_{mX+})^n, \Delta(L_{mY+})^n, \Delta(L_{mZ+})^n)$;
      EndFor
   EndFor
   $n++$; /* next scattering */
until convergence /* end of scattering loop */
`end`

Note that G_{mP} and $\Delta(G_{mP})^1$ are initialized by the procedure *init_source_term()* before each call to *medium_resolution()*, and the total *Source term* $G_{m'P}$ of each voxel P is calculated by summing all the $\Delta(G_{m'P})_m^n$, $n = [1, N]$, N being the number of scatterings. *init_source_term()* is used by *progressive_radiosity()* at each shooting iteration.

- **boundary()** returns a boolean taking the value *true* if the incoming face of the current voxel lies on the medium boundary.

- **outgoing_boundary_face()** returns *true* if the outgoing face of the current voxel lies on the medium boundary.

- **propagate_radiance()** computes the radiances of the outgoing faces of the current voxel as a function of the radiances of the incoming faces and the *Source term* (see appendix B).

- **compute_average_radiance**() returns the average radiance of a voxel as a function of the radiances of the incoming faces and the *Source term* (see appendix C).

- **load_boundary**() updates the radiance at the boundary faces by summing the contributions due to the propagations corresponding to the different orders of scattering.

4.3 Global Illumination Algorithm

The goal of the global illumination algorithm is to simulate light transfer in an environment including diffuse objects as well as several participating media having any physical properties (any albedo, anisotropy, spontaneous emission...). This algorithm is iterative and consists of three processings.

Progressive Radiosity This first processing consists in applying the classical progressive radiosity approach to the objects' surfaces to calculate the energy exchange between these surfaces via multiple interreflections and emission. This iterative process stops when the convergence criterion is met: the sum of the unshot patches energies is below a certain threshold. The method of form factor calculation makes use of a hemisphere as a projection surface and ray tracing.

A hemisphere is placed at the center of a patch p and is discretized by sampling the two polar angles θ and ϕ. The hemisphere is then discretized into surface elements ΔS, each one corresponds to a small form-factor called delta form-factor. To calculate the form-factors and solve the visibility problem, a ray is cast from the hemisphere center and through each surface element ΔS, i.e. in directions (θ_i, ϕ_j).

As the environment contains media, when a ray goes through a medium, we compute the associated attenuation depending on the optical depth. In this way, the cast rays may not correspond to the same delta form-factor.

Note that, during the shooting process, for each emitter patch the energy contribution of this patch to each voxel P is calculated by gathering, and the corresponding average *Source term* G_{mP} is derived. This is done by making use of the procedure *init_source_term()*. This procedure is given in appendix A.

Resolution for each Medium Our modified discrete ordinate system is carried out for each medium with the help of the procedure *medium_resolution()*. This results, for each medium, in a set of total average *Source terms* G_{mP}'s associated with the voxels, these terms giving the energy gain after multiple scatterings. Another result is the total radiances at all the boundary faces. Recall that these radiances are used to transfer the media's energies to the objects within the environment.

Emission of the Boundary Faces The radiances at the boundary faces of
the media are emitted toward the environment's objects by using the procedure
boundary_emission(). This emission is performed as follows. Like for the form-
factor calculation, a hemisphere is placed around a boundary face of area A
and is discretized into small surfaces. A ray is cast from the hemisphere center
through each of these small surfaces. The direction of a ray is not likely to
be a discrete angular direction V_m. To cope with this problem, the radiance
L_{ray} of the emitting boundary face in the ray direction is calculated by simple
interpolation. Let us denote ω the small solid angle associated with a ray. The
flux emitted by the emitting boundary face within ω is given by :

$$Flux = L_{ray} \times A \times \cos\theta \times \omega,$$

where θ is the angle formed by the normal at the boundary face and the ray
direction. This formula holds since the radiance in one direction at a face boundary is assumed to be the same for each point of this face (average radiance as
seen in appendix B), and since this radiance for all directions within the small
solid angle ω is assumed to be constant.

Note that if another medium M lies between the emitter boundary face
and the receiving object, *Flux* is multiplied by an attenuation factor and the
contribution to the *Source terms* of the voxels belonging to M is calculated.

4.4 Global Algorithm

Global illumination in presence of participating media is performed by the following algorithm.

```
global_algorithm()
 begin
   repeat /* global convergence loop
      progressive_radiosity() ; /* first processing*/
      for each participating medium M
         medium_resolution(M) ; /* second processing*/
      EndFor
      for each participating medium M
         boundary_emission(M) ;/*third processing*/
      EndFor
   until global_convergence /*end of global convergence loop*/
 end
```

At each iteration of the global convergence loop the environment's objects
firstly shoot their energy. Then, if the sum of the unshot patch energies is below
a given threshold, the global convergence is met.

4.5 Rendering

The rendering step consists in tracing a ray from the viewpoint through each
pixel and computing the associated radiance by accounting for the attenuations
along participating media and for the calculated *Source terms*.

The radiance along each ray is obtained by applying equation (4) for each voxel traversed by the ray as shown in the following algorithm.

```
radiance(P, ray,In )
 P : voxel ; ray : ray ; In : boolean ;
 /* Sp is the distance covered by the ray in the voxel P */
  begin
   if not In then
     object = ray_inter(ray) ;
     radiance = object.radiosity / π
   else
     next_voxel(ray,P',In) ;
     radiance = radiance(P', ray,In )
  EndIf
 end
```

$$\text{radiance} = \text{radiance}(P', ray,In)\ \times e^{-K_P S_P} + \frac{(1-e^{-K_P S_P})}{K_P} \times G_{mP}$$

Before calling the procedure *radiance()*, In is initialized to true and P to the entry voxel if the ray intersects one of the media. *next_voxel(ray,P',In)* is a procedure which returns the next voxel P' (P' may belong to another medium) along the ray and a boolean "In" which indicates if the ray still is in a medium. The procedure *ray_inter()* returns the closest object intersected by a ray.

5 Results

To show the different physical phenomena and effects handled and rendered by our method, we have chosen a simple test scene which is a room containing a medium either dense or sparse. This scene is illuminated by a single directional light source which lights the medium either directly (in directions perpendicular to the source plane) or indirectly. Four wavelength samples have been used [7] to express radiances, fluxes, *Source terms*, the absorption coefficients (0.01, 0.01, 0.01, 0.01) and the scattering coefficients (0.8, 0.8, 0.5, 0.5). The Mie phase function has been chosen to model the medium anisotropy. The medium enclosure has been subdivided into 30x30x30 voxels. The number of discrete directions is 64. Figure 5 (for all following figures see color plate 3) is the image of the scene without medium. In figure 6 only the direct contribution of the light source is accounted for, which corresponds to the first scattering. We can see that the medium is partially illuminated. Indeed, only the portion, included in the volume subtended by the light source, is lit. Image of figure 7 is the result of the direct light source contribution and of ten scatterings. Compared to figure 6, the medium borders are now illuminated by multiple scattering. As for figures 8 and 9, in addition to the light source all the environment's objects have emitted their energy to the medium. We can see that the medium borders take the color of the floor (green and blue respectively). Figure 10 is a complete image obtained after multiple scattering and emission of both objects and boundary faces. We can ascertain that the boundary faces really illuminate the scene's objects. For figure 11, the light source is oriented so that it indirectly illuminates the medium through a wall. The effect of spontaneous emission is shown in figure 12, where the medium is dense. Finally, figure 13 shows colored cast shadows due to a dense medium with scattering coefficients $(0.9, 0.5, 0.05, 0.05)$.

6 Conclusion

The method presented in this paper relies on the discrete ordinate technique for simulating light transfer within a medium. This technique is the most efficient and accurate one and is often used by thermal engineers. We have adapted it to computer graphics and improved it by computing more accurately the weighting coefficients necessary for the evaluation of the *Source terms* as well as the radiances at the outgoing voxel faces. Unlike in thermal engineering where the medium exchanges energy with its boundary through boundary conditions, our method allows diffuse objects to interact with several participating media with general properties.

The effects generated are: shadows due to and cast onto media and objects, illumination contribution inter-objects, intra-media, and between objects and media. Future works will consist in accounting for specular and transparent objects.

Appendix

A Initializing the Source Terms

The role of the procedure *init_source_term()* is to compute by gathering the average *Source term* $\Delta G_{m'P}$ due to the objects of the environment, for each voxel P and each direction $V_{m'}$:

$$\Delta G_{m'P} = \frac{1}{V_P} \int_{p \in P} G_{m'p} dV,$$

where V_P is the volume occupied by voxel P.

To evaluate this term as accurately as possible, each voxel P is uniformly subdivided into n subvoxels P_i (figure 3). We have then:

$$\Delta G_{m'P} = \frac{1}{n} \sum_{i=1}^{i=n} \Delta G_{m'P_i}.$$

For a patch E, its contribution to P_i is given by:

$$\Delta G_{m'P_i} = \frac{\sigma}{4\pi} \int_{\Omega_E^i} \Phi_{m'm} L_{m,i}^E d\omega, \tag{5}$$

and

$$L_{m,i}^E = L_m^E \times e^{-\int_{s=0}^{s=s} K dS}.$$

where L_m^E is the radiance of patch E in direction V_m as seen by the center of P_i, and s the distance traveled in the medium within Ω_E^i. To move $\Phi_{m'm}$ out of the integral in equation (5), patch E is subdivided into subpatches E_j so that $\Phi_{m'm}$ and the optical depth weakly vary when the incident direction V_{m_j} lies within the solid angle $\Omega_{E_j}^i$ subtended by E_j and whose apex is the center of P_i. We obtain then:

$$G_{m'P_i} = \frac{\sigma}{4\pi}\Phi_{m'm_j}L_{m,i}^{E_j}\Omega_{E_j}^i e^{-\int_{s=0}^{s=s}KdS}.$$

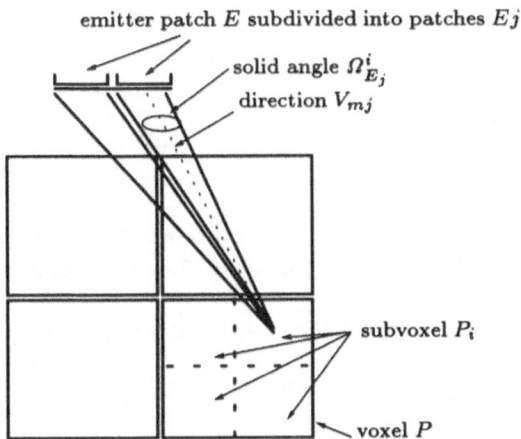

emitter patch E subdivided into patches Ej

solid angle $\Omega_{E_j}^i$

direction V_{mj}

subvoxel P_i

voxel P

Fig. 3. Source terms initialization.

B Computing the Radiances at the Outgoing Faces

Let see how the procedure *propagate_radiance()* calculates the radiance L_{mI+} at the outgoing faces of a voxel, given the radiances at the incoming faces L_{mJ-} and the source term ΔG_{mP} (see figure 4).

We consider the average radiance L_{mI+} :

$$L_{mI+} = \frac{1}{A_{I+}}\int_{I+} L_{mi}\, di,$$

where $I+ \in (X+, Y+, Z+)$, $i \in I+$ and A_{I+} the total area of $I+$. As there are at most three incoming faces $J-$ and three outgoing faces $I+$ then:

$$L_{mI+} = \frac{1}{A_{I+}}\sum_{J-\in(X-,Y-,Z-)}\int_{A_{I,J}} L_{mi}di, \qquad (6)$$

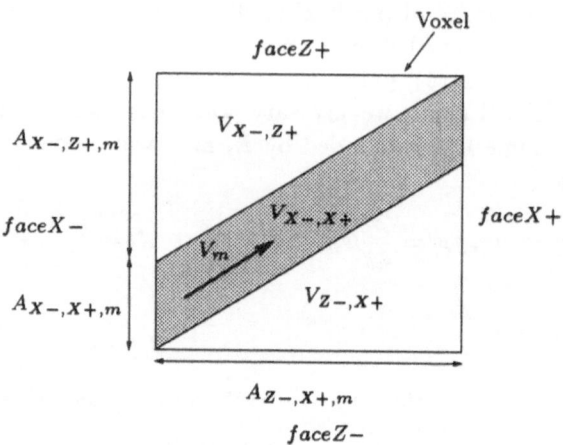

Fig. 4. Weighting coefficients for a voxel.

where $A_{I,J}$ is the projection of face $J-$ onto face $I+$ in direction V_m. Each point $i \in I+$ is the projection of one point $j \in J-$ according to direction V_m. The distance from i to j is denoted s_i.

Recall that the integrated ERT over a path of length s is:

$$L_{ms} = L_{m0}e^{-Ks} + \frac{\Delta G_{mP}}{K}(1 - e^{-Ks})$$

Using this integrated ERT and equation (6), and assuming $L_{mj} = L_{mJ-} = constant$, $\forall j \in J-$ for one given direction V_m, we get:

$$L_{mI+} = \frac{\Delta G_{mP}}{K} + \sum_{J-} \frac{A_{I,J}}{A_{I+}}(L_{mJ-} - \frac{\Delta G_{mP}}{K})\frac{1}{A_{I,J}} \int_{A_{I,J}} e^{-Ks_i}di,$$

where, $\frac{A_{I,J}}{A_{I+}} \times \frac{1}{A_{I,J}} \int_{A_{I,J}} e^{-Ks_i}di$ is weighting coefficient associated with the contribution of $J-$ to $I+$. These coefficients take into account the variability of the optical depth in the whole voxel. In thermal engineering, the average radiance at one outgoing face is taken as the radiance at its center calculated by integrating the ERT over a single path starting at one point of one incoming face and arriving to this center.

Experiments have shown $\frac{1}{A_{I,J}} \int_{A_{I,J}} e^{Ks_i}di \approx e^{-Ks_{av(I,J)}}$ for small $K's$, where $s_{av(I,J)} = \frac{1}{A_{I,J}} \int_{A_{I,J}} s_i di$, which is easy to precompute for each pair $(J-, I+)$ and each incident direction V_m.

C   Computing the Average Radiance of a Voxel

Given the *Source term* ΔG_{mP} and the radiances L_{mJ-} at the incoming faces of a voxel P, the procedure *compute_average_radiance()* computes the average radiance for P as:

$$L_{mP} = \frac{1}{V_P} \int_{p \in P} L_{mp} dV,$$

where

$$L_{mp} = L_{mJ-} e^{-K_s} + \frac{\Delta G_{mP}}{K}(1 - e^{-K_s}),$$

and s represents the distance covered in direction V_m by a point $j \in J-$ to reach a point $p \in P$. As a voxel P has at most three incoming and three outgoing faces, then the average radiance L_{mP} of P is:

$$L_{mP} = \frac{1}{V_P} \sum_{J-} \sum_{I+} \int_{J-} \int_{I+} (L_{mJ-} e^{-K_s} + \frac{\Delta G_{mP}}{K}(1 - e^{-K_s})) dV,$$

or

$$L_{mP} = \frac{\Delta G_{mP}}{K} + \sum_{J-} \sum_{I+} ((L_{mJ-} - \frac{\Delta G_{mP}}{K}) \frac{V_{J,I}}{V_P} \times \frac{1}{V_{J,I}} \int_{V_{J,I}} e^{-K_s} dV),$$

where $V_{J,I}$ is the volume swept by the points $j \in J-$ when they move to face $I+$ along direction V_m (figure 4).

$\frac{V_{J,I}}{V_P} \times \frac{1}{V_{J,I}} \int_{V_{J,I}} e^{-K_s} dV$ are weighting coefficients giving the contribution of one incoming face $J-$ to L_{mP}. They account for the variability of the optical depth. In thermal engineering, L_{mP} is calculated as the radiance as the center of P by using linear interpolation, which is not correct.

Experiments have shown that $\frac{1}{V_{J,I}} \int_{V_{J,I}} e^{-K_s} dV \approx e^{-K_{s_{av}(I,J)}}$ for small $K's$, where $s_{av(I,J)} = \frac{1}{A_{I,J}} \int_{A_{I,J}} \frac{s_i}{2} di$, which is easy to precompute for each pair $(J-, I+)$ and for each direction V_m.

References

1. N. Bhate and A. Tokuta. Photorealistic volume rendering of media with directional scattering. In *EUROGRAPHICS'92 Conference Proceeding*, pages 228–245. EUROGRAPHICS, may 1992.
2. P. Blasi, B. Le Saec, and C. Schlick. A rendering algorithm for discrete volume density objects. In *Proceedings of Eurographics'93*, Barcelona, Spain, Septembre 1993.
3. J. F. Blinn. Light reflection functions for simulation of clouds and dusty surfaces. In *SIGGRAPH'82 Conference Proceeding*, pages 21–29, august 1982.
4. A. Draoui. *Etudes numériques des transferts de chaleur couplés rayonnement-conduction et rayonnement-convection dans un milieu semi-transparent bidimensionnel*. PhD thesis, INSA Lyon, FRANCE, 1989.
5. H.C. Hottel and A.F. Sarofim. *Radiative Transfert*. McGraw–Hill, 1967.
6. J.T. Kajiya and V. Herzen. Ray tracing volume densities. In *Proceedings of SIGGRAPH'84 in computer graphics*, pages 165–174. SIGGRAPH, July 1984.
7. Gary W. Meyer. Wavelength selection for synthetic image generation. *Computer Vision, Graphics, and Image Processing*, 41:57–79, 1988.

8. T. Nishita, Y. Miyawaki, and E. Nakamae. A shading model for atmospheric scattering considering luminous intensity distribution of light sources. In *SIG-GRAPH'87 Conference Proceeding*, pages 303–310. ACM, July 1987.

9. S. N. Pattanaik. *Computational Methods for Global Illumination and Visualisation of Complex 3D Environments*. PhD thesis, NCST, Bombay, India, 1993.

10. H. Rushmeier. *Realistic image synthesis for scenes with radiatively participating media*. PhD thesis, Cornell University, USA, 1988.

11. G. Sakas. Fast rendering of arbitrary volume density. In *EUROGRAPHICS'90 Conference Proceeding*, pages 519–530. EUROGRAPHICS, 1990.

12. R. Siegel and J.R. Howel. *Thermal radiation heat transfert - Third Edition*. Hemisphere, 1992.

13. M.P. Mengüc. *Modeling of radiative heat transfert in multidimensional enclosures using spherical harmonics approximation*. PhD thesis, Purdue University, E.U., August 1985.

14. N. El Wakil. *Etude des transferts de chaleur par conduction, convection et rayonnement couplés dans des milieux semi-transparents fluides ou poreux. Elaboration de modèles en géométrie bidimensionnelle*. PhD thesis, INSA Lyon, FRANCE, 1991.

Efficient Light Propagation for Multiple Anisotropic Volume Scattering

Nelson Max

University of California, Davis, and Lawrence Livermore National Laboratory

Abstract

Realistic rendering of participating media like clouds requires multiple anisotropic light scattering. This paper presents a propagation approximation for light scattered into M direction bins, which reduces the "ray effect" problem in the traditional "discrete ordinates" method. For a regular grid volume of n^3 elements, it takes $O(Mn^3 \log n + M^2 n^3)$ time and $O(Mn^3 + M^2)$ space.

1 Introduction

To render realistic images of clouds, one must take into account absorption and multiple scattering of incoming illumination. In addition, to produce the bright edges surrounding a cloud when the sun is behind it, one must account for the anisotropic, mainly forward, scattering of light from the water droplets.

In 1984, Jim Kajiya and Brian Von Herzen [Kaj84] proposed two methods for rendering clouds. The first was the two-pass "slab" method, which accounted only for single scattering. The first pass deposited flux from the light source into the cloud voxels one horizontal layer at a time, taking into account the attenuation by the opacity in each layer. The second pass gathered the scattered flux along each viewing ray, taking into account the attenuation between the scattering event and the viewpoint. Voss [Voss83] used a similar method to produce fractal clouds in terrain scenes. Nishita, Miyakawa, and Nakamae [Nish87] have considered anisotropic single scattering in fog, and Inakage [Inak89] has included cases where the density and phase function of the scattering material varies from point to point. Kaneda *et al.* [Kan90] also simulate anisotropic scattering in clouds and fog, including one case of double scattering: first Raleigh and Mie scattering to determine a fixed sky illumination, and then one more scattering of this illumination within a fog.

Kajiya's second method was an application of the multiple scattering ideas of Chandrasekhar [Chan50], which use spherical harmonics to expand, at each point, the light intensity as a function of direction. The scattering phase function is also expanded in Legendre polynomials, resulting in a set of coupled partial differential equations for the spherical harmonic coefficients of intensity as functions of the spatial coordinates. Kajiya attempted to solve these equations for the case of isotropic scattering, but it is unclear whether he succeeded, since all the pictures in [Kaj84] were produced by the simpler "slab" method.

The transport equations Kajiya used, described in the next section, have a long history in radiation heat transfer in mechanical engineering, and in particle transport in nuclear engineering. Siegel and Howell [Sie92] give a good summary of solution techniques. Holly Rushmeier [Rush87, Rush88] applied two of these solution techniques to computer rendering of *participating* (*i.e.* absorbing, emitting, and scattering) *media*. One was the Monte Carlo method, where a random collection of photons or flux packets are traced through the volume, undergoing random scattering and absorption. This method can accurately model all the physics of scattering, but may take an impractical number of random trials to converge to a useful solution. Blasi *et al.* [Blas93] have used the Monte Carlo method to render volume densities of anisotropically scattering material.

The other was the *zonal* method for isotropic scattering only, which divides the volume into a number of *finite elements* which are assumed to have constant radiosity. This requires the calculation of a *form factor* between every pair of elements. In a cube of $N = n^3$ elements, there will be $N^2 = n^6$ such pairs of elements. In the *Galerkin* finite element scheme, each form factor involves a double integral over points in both elements, as well as along the path between the two points, giving a total of 7 integration variables. Rushmeier approximates this by an inverse square factor and a 1-D integral of opacity along the path connecting the element centers. If each of the $O(n)$ intervening elements has different scattering properties, this 1-D integral takes time $O(n)$. Using an iterative method for solving the resulting matrix equation which converges in $O(1)$ iterations, the total computational cost is $O(n^7)$. This cost can be reduced somewhat by grouping adjacent elements into larger interaction pairs, in the style of Hanrahan, Salzman, and Aupperle [Hanr91], as was done by Bhata [Bhat93]. Rushmeier [Rush88] also considers anisotropic scattering, but only in the single scattering case.

Zhiquiang Tan [Tan89] applied the ideas of finite element analysis to the solution for the spherical harmonic coefficients in the case of multiple anisotropic scattering. If there are M terms in the expansion, this results in a matrix of size $M^2 N^2$. Tan uses the *point allocation* (or *point collocation*) method, which allows the representation of non-constant basis functions. He points out that this requires integrals over only one 3-D position, reducing the number of integration variables by 3. This simplification has been misinterpreted by Siegel and Howell [Sie92], who incorrectly claimed that the method is $O(N)$. Bhata [Bhat92] has applied this method to computer rendering, but could deal with only a small number of voxels, due to the $O(n^7 + M^2 n^6)$ cost.

Another approach is to allocate the radiosity leaving each volume element into a collection of M direction bins of constant intensity. Assuming the interaction between two elements involves only one direction bin for flux transit (reasonable only for distant pairs of elements), this reduces the number of nonzero matrix elements to MN^2, and the cost to compute them to $O(n^7 + Mn^6)$.

Sparse matrix solution methods are then available, as in Immel *et al.*[Imm86].

In the *discrete ordinates* method in radiation transfer, [Sie92, Chan50], the M direction bins are represented by M discrete directions, chosen to give optimal Gaussian quadrature in the integrals over a solid angle. Lathrop [Lath68] points out that this process produces ray effects, because it is equivalent to shooting the energy from an element in narrow beams along the discrete directions, missing the regions between them. He presents modifications to avoid these ray effects, but the resulting equations are mathematically equivalent to the ones mentioned above for the spherical harmonic coefficients. This implies that M properly distributed direction bins specify the directional intensity distribution to the same detail as M spherical harmonic coefficients.

The current paper presents an approximation to the discrete ordinates method, which reduces the ray effect by shooting radiosity into the whole solid angle bin, instead of in a discrete representative direction. As a shooting method, it is similar to the progressive radiosity method of Cohen *et al.* [Coh88], and can be shown to converge for albedo less than one. (See [Gort93] and section 6 below.) Patmore [Patm93] has used a discrete ordinates shooting algorithm (subject to ray effects) for a multiple-scattering rendering of clouds, and his paper inspired the current one. Langer *et al.* [Lang93] have implemented the discrete ordinates method on a massively parallel SIMD machine, and included surface reflections. (See section 10 below.)

My chief enhancement is to spread the shot radiosity throughout the direction bin in an efficient way which handles a whole plane of source elements simultaneously, while reducing the ray effect. Another enhancement treats multiple scattering within a single receiving element before the next shooting step. I use $O(MN)$ space to store the total radiosity in each direction bin at each element, and also the unshot radiosity. The direction-bin-indexed matrix representing the anisotropic scattering function takes an additional $O(M^2)$ space. The computation for each pass through the M shooting directions takes time $O(Mn^3 \log n + M^2 n^3) = O(MN \log N + M^2 N)$. This large speedup compared to the other methods discussed can only be achieved with a regular cubical grid. Since it makes essential use of the homogeneity of the grid, my method will not work on more general finite element meshes.

2 Transport Equations

In thermal radiation heat transport, a participating medium which absorbs radiation heats up, and re-emits "black body" radiation isotropically. This effect is usually not important in rendering, and I will neglect it below for simplicity, and deal only with absorption and scattering. More complete discussions are available from [Sie92] and [Rush88].

Let $I(x,\omega)$ be the intensity at position x flowing in direction ω, and let $k_t(x)$ be the extinction coefficient of the participating medium. This is the total opacity (absorption plus scattering) per unit length, so $k_t(x)I(x,\omega)ds$ is the intensity removed along an infinitesimal ray segment ds at x. Let the *albedo*,

a, be the fraction of this removed intensity scattered in other directions, and let the *phase function*, $f(\omega, \omega')$, be the directional distribution function for this scattered intensity, so that $\int_B f(\omega, \omega')d\omega'$ is the fraction of the scattered intensity from direction ω that ends up in solid angle B. Then

$$ak_t(x)ds \int_{4\pi} f(\omega', \omega)I(x, \omega')d\omega'$$

is the intensity scattered into the direction ω along the ray segment ds from other directions ω' in the 4π unit sphere. (This is the *source function* [Sie92] in the absence of volume emission.) The integro-differential equation for $I(x, \omega)$ is thus

$$\frac{dI(x, \omega)}{ds} = -k_t(x)I(x, \omega) + ak_t(x) \int_{4\pi} f(\omega', \omega)I(x, \omega')d\omega'$$

Using an integrating factor (see [Sie92], [Rush88], or [Will92]), this can be integrated along a path $x'(s) = x - s\omega$, from $x = x'(0)$ to $x_0 = x'(s_0)$ at the edge of the medium, to give the integral form

$$I(x, \omega) = I(x_0, \omega) \exp\left(-\int_0^{s_0} k_t(x'(s))ds\right) \tag{1}$$

$$+a \int_0^{s_0} \left[k_t(x'(s)) \exp\left(-\int_0^s k_t(x'(t))dt\right) \int_{4\pi} f(\omega', \omega)I(x'(s), \omega')d\omega'\right] ds$$

Now assume that the region under study is divided into a collection of cubical volume elements V_k, which I also call cells, voxels, or, in 2-D, pixels. Assume that the unit sphere is divided into a number of direction bins B_l, and that $I(x, \omega)$ is constant for x in V_k and ω in B_l. In the implementation, these constant values are represented by a matrix through[k][l], which stores the intensity multiplied by the solid angle of bin B_l, size[l]. I assume that the extinction coefficient k_t is constant in each element V_k, and stored in an array kt[k]. The input values for kt[k] are produced by a cloud modeler, described briefly in section 8. I assume that the albedo a is constant everywhere, to avoid creating an extra array. Let x lie in cell V_i, and ω lie in angle bin B_j. Then with these assumptions, we can integrate equation (1) over B_j to get

$$\text{through[i][j]} = \int_{B_j} I(x, \omega)d\omega \tag{2}$$

$$= \int_{B_j} d\omega \left\{ \frac{\text{through}[n(s_0)][l(\omega)]}{\text{size}[l(\omega)]} \exp\left(-\int_0^{s_0} kt[n(s)]ds\right) + \right.$$

$$a \int_0^{s_0} \left[kt[n(s)] \exp\left(-\int_0^s kt[n(t)]dt\right) \right.$$

$$\left.\left. \int_{4\pi} f(\omega', \omega) \frac{\text{through}[n(s)][l(\omega')]}{\text{size}[l(\omega')]} d\omega' \right] ds \right\}$$

where $n(s)$ is the index of the volume element containing $x'(s)$, and $l(\omega)$ is the index of the angle bin containing ω. Suppose, for simplicity, that all rays from x

to cell V_k lie in angle bin j. (The algorithm described in the following sections takes special account of interactions involving two or more bins.) Geometric arguments (see [Rush88]) show that

$$Geom_{ijk} = \int_{B_j} d\omega \int_{n(s)=k} ds \cong \frac{\text{Volume}(V_k)}{r_{ik}^2} \qquad (3)$$

where r_{ik} is the distance between the centers of cells i and k. Thus the multiplier giving the contribution of through[k][l] to the last term in equation (2) is the "form factor"

$$F_{klij} \cong a \frac{\text{Volume}(V_k)}{r_{ik}^2} \text{kt[k]} \exp\left(-\int_0^r (\text{kt}[n(t)])dt\right) \int_{B_l} d\omega' \frac{f(\omega', \omega)}{\text{size[l]}} \qquad (4)$$

I precalculated by Simpson's rule integration the $M \times M$ matrix version of the phase function:

$$\text{bintobin[l][j]} = \int_{B_j} d\omega \int_{B_l} d\omega' \frac{f(\omega', \omega)}{\text{size[l]}}$$

giving the fraction of the flux from bin l directions scattering into bin j. Replacing the factor $\int_{B_l} d\omega' \frac{f(\omega', \omega)}{\text{size[l]}}$ in equation (4) by its average value $\frac{\text{bintobin[l][j]}}{\text{size[j]}}$, we get

$$F_{klij} \cong a \frac{\text{Volume}(V_k)}{r_{ik}^2 \text{size[j]}} \text{kt[k]} \exp\left(-\int_0^r \text{kt}[n(t)]dt\right) \text{bintobin[l][j]} \qquad (5)$$

In the implementation, I take the unit of length to be the side of a cubic cell V_k, so that the factor Volume(V_k) drops out. Note that this effects the extinction coefficients kt[n], whose units are inverse length.

Using these form factors, one can write the usual system of linear equations for the unknown fluxes through[k][l]. I have developed an approximate solution method which accumulates opacity on the fly, as the flux is propagated in a shooting procedure. As in progressive radiosity for surface illumination [Coh88], I use an auxiliary array unshot[k][l] of size $MN = Mn^3$, to store the flux waiting to be propagated, and need not store the $M^2N^2 = M^2n^6$ form factors. The most difficult part in evaluating equation (5) is in computing $\exp(-\int_0^r(\text{kt}[n(t)]))dt$ by integrating along a straight line joining the pixel centers. My method approximates each such term as a weighted sum of similar terms, obtained by integrating over piecewise linear paths that lie near the straight line (see figure 1). This permits sharing of calculations to compute the effect of the M^2N^2 form factors in time $O(MN\log N + M^2N)$, as described in the next section.

For my test images, I used the Henyey-Greenstein phase function [Heny40]

$$f(\omega', \omega) = f(\omega, \omega') = \frac{1}{4\pi} \frac{1 - g^2}{(1 + g^2 - 2gx)^{3/2}}$$

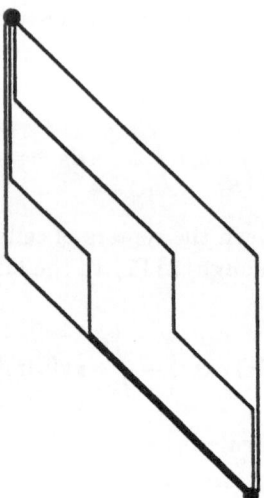

Fig. 1. Paths connecting two pixels.

where x is the dot product of the two unit direction vectors ω and ω', and g is an adjustable parameter between -1 and 1, which is positive for forward scattering, negative for backwards scattering, and 0 for isotropic scattering. For an appropriate choice of g, this is a good approximation to the exact Mie scattering [Mie09] from spherical water droplets. Except for the first bounce from the light source, and the last bounce to the viewpoint, which use one exact direction each, all intermediate bounces are via the array bintobin, so any phase function can be used efficiently.

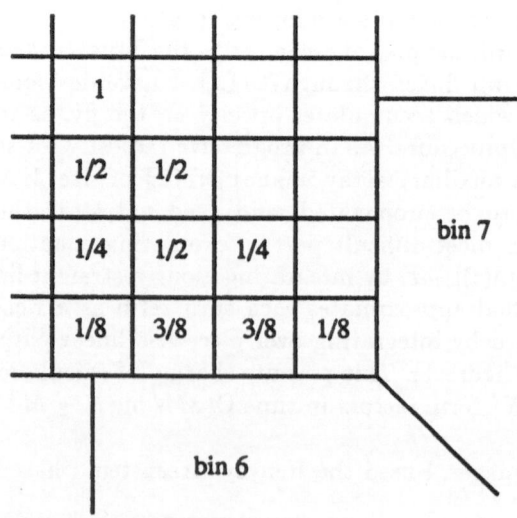

Fig. 2. Binomial weight distribution.

3 Simultaneous Shooting

Consider a unit cube of un-normalized direction vectors, with each face divided into $2m \times 2m$ equal bins, giving a total of $M = 24m^2$ direction bins. The previous section assumed that the flux through[k][l] is uniformly distributed in the direction bin B_l, so that the intensity is constant for any direction inside the bin. From now on, I assume that the flux within a single bin is proportional to surface area on the unit direction cube. This assumption is necessary for the efficient method, described next, for propagating the flux incrementally from a cell to its close neighbors. It introduces some error in the light distribution, but the error decreases with decreasing bin size.

For simplicity, I will first discuss the method for the 2-D, $m = 1$ case. There are $M = 8m = 8$ direction bins (four square sides, each with $2m = 2$ bins). Two of these bins are shown in figure 2. I will first describe a simple scheme for propagating the flux which gives a binomial distribution, and then show how to modify it to give a uniform distribution. Consider the bin between 270° and 315° (bin 6 counting from 0), and suppose the shooting pixel at the upper left has a unit flux leaving within this bin. Approximately half of this flux enters the pixel below, and half enters the one diagonally below and to the right, so these two pixels are marked in figure 2 with the weights 1/2. If each of these pixels distributes its flux in the same (1/2, 1/2) scheme to the row below, the flux in that row would be 1/4, 1/2, 1/4, as shown. The third row below the shooting pixel has the pattern 1/8, 3/8, 3/8, 1/8.

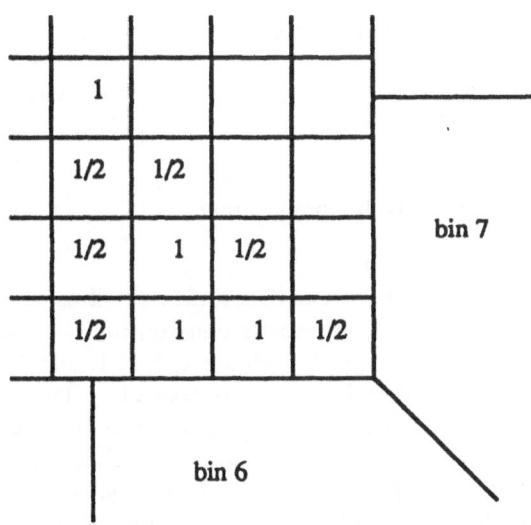

Fig. 3. Bin 6 from figure 2, with desired weight distribution.

In general, at pixel (i, n), the ith pixel in the nth row below the shooting pixel at $(0, 0)$, the weight is $\frac{1}{2^n} \binom{n}{i}$, giving a binomial distribution. The binomial coefficient $\binom{n}{i} = \frac{n!}{i!(n-i)!}$ counts the number of n-step paths from $(0, 0)$ to (i, n), obtained by taking any i of the steps in a diagonal direction, and the rest directly downwards, as in figure 1.

```
/* Initialize with unshot radiosity from row i0. */
for (j = 0; j < columns; ++j) {
    work[j] = unshot[i0][j];
    corner[0][j] = unshot[i0][j];
    corner[1][j] = unshot[i0][j];}
for (i = i0 + 1; i < rows; ++i) {
/* Propagate radiosity to row i. */
    s = i - i0;
    for (j = 0; j < columns; ++j) {
        tempwork[j] = .5 * work[j];
        if (j > 0) tempwork[j] += .5*work[j-1];
        receive[i][j] = tempwork[i][j]/s;
/* Adjust tempwork using corner arrays. */
        tempwork[j] += .5 * corner[0][j];
        if (j > 0) tempwork[j] += .5 * corner[1][j-1];}
/* Update work & corners, to account for transparency. */
    for (j = 0; j < columns; ++j) {
        transparency = exp( - raylength * kt[i][j] );
        work[i][j] = tempwork[i][j] * transparency;
        corner[0][j] *= transparency;
        if (j > 0)
            corner[1][j] = corner[1][j-1] * transparency;
        else corner[1][j] = 0.; } }
```

Fig. 4. Code fragment for 2-D flux propagation

This binomial $(1/2, 1/2)$ scheme distributes the flux across the bin, but not in the uniform way desired. The desired distribution is shown in figure 3, with the pixels in row 3 marked with the weights $1/2$, 1, 1, and $1/2$. The outer pixels are counted half in this bin and half in adjacent bins. The sum of these weights is 3, so they must be normalized by dividing by 3 to give the portion of the bin's flux reaching each pixel. To propagate this weight pattern to the next row below, first add $1/2$ to each of the outer two pixels, to get a pattern of all 1's. Then add each of these 1's, half to the pixel below, and half to the pixel below and to the right. The result is the desired pattern $1/2$, 1, 1, 1, $1/2$ in the fourth row.

This pattern of weights, when normalized, shows the proportion of the shot flux reaching a receiving pixel in the absence of intervening opacity. To account for opacity, each value is multiplied by the transparency at the current pixel, before propagating by the (1/2, 1/2) scheme, so that the opacity is accumulated along the propagation path. The added adjustment to the left-most pixel is similarly attenuated by the opacities in the column above it, and the adjustment to the right-most pixel, by the opacities along a 45° diagonal. The iterative process actually starts with the outgoing flux to be shot in a direction bin, instead of the unit flux discussed above. In row s, it builds a pattern of $s + 1$ appropriately weighted and attenuated values, which are divided by s and added into the **receive** array at that row. The arithmetic involved in this iteration is independent of the horizontal displacement between the shooting and the receiving pixel, so it can be done simultaneously for each pixel in a horizontal row, as indicated by the code fragment in figure 4.

The actual implementation contains subscripts indicating the bin direction and starting row, not shown in the fragment. These let multiple directions and starting rows be propagated together, permitting multiple bounces per pass, as discussed below.

The array **work[]** stores the flux on a row propagating in the direction bin 6 in figure 3. It is initialized with the unshot flux from row $i0$, **unshot[i0][]**. The array **corner[0][]**, named after its 3-D use, stores the flux propagating directly downward, used to adjust the left- most numbered pixel in figure 3, and the array **corner[1][]** stores the flux propagating diagonally, to adjust the right-most pixel. The constant raylength is the average length of a ray/ pixel intersection segment, and depends on the direction bin index.

For a square collection of pixels, with **rows** = **columns** = n, this code fragment computes the $O(n^3)$ interactions of the shooting row with the pixels below it in time $O(n^2)$, instead of the $O(n^4)$ time which would be required to accumulate the opacity for each interaction along a straight path of length $O(n)$. However this n^2 savings factor comes at a cost in accuracy. The attenuation is not accumulated only along the straight path between a shooting and receiving pixel, but instead along the many possible propagation paths of downward and diagonal steps connecting them. Several of these paths are shown in figure 1, filling out a parallelogram.

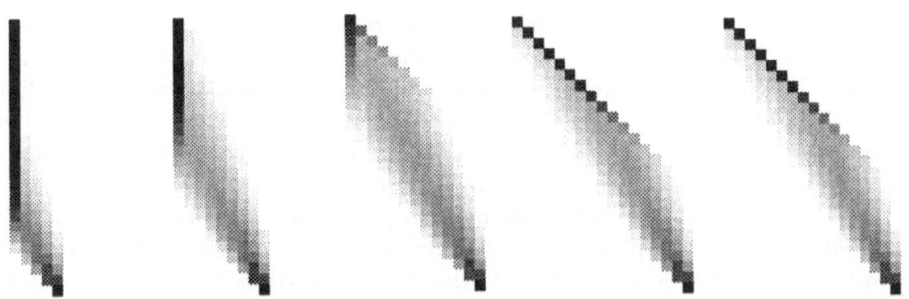

Fig. 5. The number of paths passing through each cell.

The opacities at all the pixels in this parallelogram will influence the occlusion of the flux shot from pixel $(0, 0)$ and received at pixel (i, n). The opacity at pixel (j, k) contributes according to the number of propagation paths passing through it. Paths belonging to the simple $(1/2, 1/2)$ scheme are weighted by $1/2^n$, while those which first go l steps along one of the two **corner** arrays, being divided by 2 only on the last step, are weighted by $1/2^{n-l+1}$. Thus, neglecting the nonlinearity of the exponential function, the opacity contribution from pixel (j, k), when $0 < j < k$, is

$$\frac{1}{2^n} \binom{n-k}{i-j} \left[\binom{k}{j} + \sum_{l=1}^{k-j} 2^{l-1} \binom{k-l}{j} + \sum_{l=1}^{j} 2^{l-1} \binom{k-l}{j-l} \right]$$

The binomial coefficient outside the square brackets represents the number of paths from (j, k) to (i, n). The three binomial coefficients in the square brackets represent the number of paths from $(0, 0)$ to (j, k) using, respectively, the $(1/2, 1/2)$ scheme alone, l steps of vertical **corner** propagation, or l steps of diagonal **corner** propagation. If $k = 0$ or $k = j$, other terms must be added to include the extra weighted **corner** paths.

Figure 5 shows this opacity contribution as a function of the location (j, k), with k increasing downwards, for $n = 25$, and for $i = 5, 9,$ and $13, 17,$ and 21 in left to right order. Black denotes the greatest contributions, and the palest grey is used for any non-zero contribution. The center $i = 13$ case shows mainly the effect of the binomial $(1/2, 1/2)$ scheme alone. The weight is concentrated near the straight path, but spread somewhat, blurring the shadows. For the other i shown, the summation giving the contributions from one of the **corner** arrays biases the contribution towards that **corner** direction, giving extra weight to shadowing objects in that direction. I believe these continuously varying shadow errors are less serious than the discontinuous illumination errors due to the ray effect.

4 The 3-D Case

In the 3-D case, the flux in a direction bin shot from a central voxel spreads out across the faces of a cubical shell. Figure 6 shows the weights for one of the 24 direction bins in the $m = 1$ case, marked on a surface layer of a $7 \times 7 \times 7$ cubical shell. Voxels shared between two adjacent bins are marked with weight $1/2$, and those shared between four adjacent bins are marked with weight $1/4$. Only voxels at the eight cube corners are shared between three adjacent bins, and are marked with weight $1/3$. These corners require a separate correction.

First consider the case where all four corners have weight $1/4$. The analogy to the 2-D case should be clear. The pattern of weights of value $1, 1/2,$ and $1/4$ can easily be constructed from the smaller pattern of all 1's in the next shell inwards. Simply divide each value in the smaller pattern by 4, and add it to the appropriate four direct or diagonal neighbors. The procedure to reconstruct the all 1's pattern is a little more complicated, since four whole edges of weight

				1/4	1/2	1/2	1/4
				1/2	1	1	1/2
				1/2	1	1	1/2
				1/4	1/2	1/2	1/3

Fig. 6. Weights for a layer in a 3D bin.

1/2 must be added on. The needed **edge** arrays can be maintained by the 2-D procedure described in the preceding section. These 2-D iterations require four **corner** arrays, along the four corners of the direction bins. The four **corner** arrays are also used to adjust the corner values of the pattern of weights to exactly 1, since the addition of the **edge** arrays leaves them off by 1/4. The weighted attenuated **work** values s layers beyond the shooting plane are divided by s^2 and added into the **receive** array at that layer. Finally, $1/(12s^2)$ times the **corner** array, if any, corresponding to a cube main diagonal direction is added to **receive** to make the final weight 1/3. The temporary **work**, **edge**, and **corner** arrays are initialized with the n^2 unshot direction bin flux values in a shooting plane, and propagate their flux to $O(n^3)$ receiving elements, using $O(n^3)$ time to produce $O(n^5)$ interactions. Thus the total cost for propagating a single direction bin for the n shooting planes is $O(n^4)$. This last factor of n can be reduced to $O(\log n)$ by maintaining these temporary arrays from all the shooting layers, as the receiving layer progresses through the volume, and recursively consolidating them when the resulting error is small, as described next.

The only computational difference between the treatment of the various shooting layers is the inverse square factor $1/s^2$, corresponding to $1/r_{ik}^2$ in equation (5). Suppose we take the flux in the **work**, **edge**, and **corner** arrays for a shooting layer at separation s from the current receiving layer, and at each entry, put half the flux into the corresponding entry in the array for the shooting layer at separation $s-a$, and half into the corresponding entry for separation $s+a$. These two layers each have their own inverse square factor, so the effective inverse square factor will become

$$\frac{1}{2(s-a)^2} + \frac{1}{2(s+a)^2} = \frac{s^2+a^2}{(s^2-a^2)^2} = \frac{1}{s^2}\left(\frac{1+a^2/s^2}{(1-a^2/s^2)^2}\right) = \frac{1}{s^2} + \frac{3a^2}{s^4} + O\left(\frac{1}{s^6}\right)$$

$$(6)$$

We start with $a = 1$, and redistribute layers with odd separations into layers with even separations. Given an error tolerance e, we can find a separation s_0 beyond which this consolidation results in a "form factor" error of less than e. This flux consolidation can be continued recursively. At the ith level of recursion, we redistribute the flux in layers representing separation $s = t_0 + 2^{i+1} + 2^i k$, for $k = 1, 3, 5, \ldots$, onto layers for separations $s - a$ and $s + a$, with $a = 2^i$. Using equation (6), one can show that for sufficiently large t_0, independent of the volume array side n, the total error introduced is less than e. The number of layers remaining after this consolidation is $O(\log n)$.

It is actually possible to reduce the $O(\log n)$ factor to $O(1)$ by consolidating the voxels within a layer, as well as between adjacent layers, in the manner of [Hanr91] and [Bhat93]. The additional errors would not be large, because the occlusion effects at large distances become fuzzy, as shown in figure 5. I have not coded this enhancement, because the practical differences between $O(\log n)$ and $O(1)$ are small.

5 The $m > 1$ Case

For $m > 1$, the propagation is more complicated. The work, edge, and corner arrays are maintained only for separations s divisible by m. For cells i and k with separations less than m, more accurate galerkin-type geometric form factors $Geom_{ijk}$ are precomputed using Monte Carlo integration, in place of the approximation in equation (3). These are used to propagate the flux from the work, edge, and corner arrays at separations lm, for $l = 0, 1, 2, \ldots$, to get the receive flux at cells at separations $lm + 1$ up to $(l+1)m - 1$, and to account for the effect of the opacities in these cells on these arrays. The work, edge, and corner are then updated as discussed above, to propagate the flux to cells at separation $(l+1)m$. I have implemented the $m = 2$ case, with 96 direction bins in 3-D, and used it to produce all the results in this paper.

6 Scattering of Received Flux

Once the flux in a direction bin is received in a cell, it must be added to the tally in through, for use in a final extra bounce towards the viewpoint during rendering. It must also be scattered into the unshot flux in each of the M direction bins at the receiving cell, using one row of the $M \times M$ scattering matrix bintobin. This costs time M, so the total cost per direction bin is $O(n^3 \log n + Mn^3)$. The factor $\log n$ is missing from the second term, since the flux from all shooting layers is maintained during one pass through the volume, and consolidated into receive. A pass through all M direction bins costs time $O(Mn^3 \log n + M^2 n^3)$.

Note that in equation (5), the product of all the factors after the albedo a is less than 1, so after k bounces, the flux is decreased by a factor of at least a^k. For a fixed albedo a less than 1, the error can thus be made smaller than a set tolerance after a number of passes that depends only on a, and not on n, that is, in $O(1)$ passes. For scattering from water droplets in clouds, a is very close to 1, which would theoretically make the O(1) iteration count very large. In practice, the flux leaks out at the edges of the cloud, so there is reasonable convergence even when $a = 1$.

The finite element implementations of Rushmeier set the form factor between a volume element and itself to zero [personal communication], because her inverse square approximation to the form factor had a singularity in this case. However, to approximate dense clouds with large enough elements for practical computation, it is necessary to account for scattering within a single element. To do so, I assume exactly forward scattering, a fairly good approximation for water droplets, in order to calculate the probability of higher order scattering. The multiple scattering events are then governed by a Poisson distribution [Fell68]. Let l be the average length of the intersection of a ray in the incoming direction bin with a volume element cube of extinction coefficient k_t, and let $\lambda = k_t l$. Then the probability that the ray emerges unscattered is $e^{-\lambda}$ and the probability of emerging after b bounces is $\lambda^b e^{-\lambda}/b!$. At each cell the flux in `receive` from direction bin B_i is distributed as unshot and through flux into all bins B_j for that cell by the factors

$$\sum_{b=1}^{B} \frac{a^b \lambda^b}{b!} e^{-\lambda} \texttt{bintobin}^b \texttt{[i][j]},$$

where a is the albedo, and the powers of the `bintobin` matrix are precomputed. The number B of terms required depends on a and the range of k_t but is O(1) as a function of n. For the images in the results section, I used $B = 12$ terms.

This approximation was checked by comparison with the Monte Carlo simulation described by Hanrahan and Krueger [Hanr93], and agreed well even when the scattering was not forward. (The box on page 170 of [Hanr93] giving the Monte Carlo simulation has three errors, confirmed by the authors. The absolute value signs around $2g$ in the expression for $\cos j$ should be removed, the last row in the vector $\bar{t}$ should be $-\cos\phi\sin\theta$, and there is no need to adjust the weight using the distance to the boundary if d causes the particle to leave the layer.)

The multiple scattering within one cell speeds up the convergence of the iteration. Another way to speed up the convergence is to process multiple scattering events at different cells during one sweep through the volume. The $4m^2$ shooting bins in one of the six faces of the direction cube are processed together as the receiving planes sweeps along the corresponding axis direction. The energy scattered from one direction bin to another in the same cube face can then be processed for further transmission and scattering during the same sweep. When the scattering is predominately forward, the scattered flux is likely to end up in a direction in the same cube face.

In order to maintain the $O(\log n)$ temporary arrays of size n^2 for each of the $O(M)$ directions on a cube face, $O(Mn^2 \log n)$ storage is required. This is asymptotically less than the $O(Mn^3)$ needed for the `through` and `unshot` arrays.

7 Final Gathering Pass

The final rendering uses an evaluation of the integral form (1) of the transport equation along a ray through each pixel, as a summation over the ray/element intersection segments, representing an extra scattering of the flux in **through**. In this final gathering step, I displaced the volume cells so that their vertices were at the centers of the original elements, and used interpolated values of **through** to give smoother shading. To use the exact direction ω of the viewing ray, instead of just its direction bin, I computed the integrals

$$\int_{B_l} f(\omega', \omega) d\omega'$$

for each bin B_l once per viewing ray, or else once per volume element, depending on which are less numerous. This gives a smooth variation of the scattering with the viewing angle.

Similarly, the **unshot** flux is initialized from the attenuated light source flux array **en**, using integrals involving the exact direction to the light source. To compute **en**, many illumination rays are traced through the volume, enough to cross each volume element multiple times. The ray/element intersections are processed in the order of light propagation, to attenuate the intensity by the element opacity, and to add the flux into **en**.

Note that the light source flux in **en** is not transferred to **through**. The final gathering pass computes the single scattering contribution using this accurately attenuated direct illumination, without the shadow blurring caused by the spread out opacity weighting shown in figure 5. For this single scattering contribution, the phase function is evaluated using the exact directions of both the viewing and the direct illumination rays.

8 Cloud Model

The geometry of the cloud is determined by the density array **kt**. Kajiya and Von Herzen [Kaj84] computed this density with a meteorological simulation. Instead, for the purposes of test rendering, I used a variant of the visual cloud model of Gardner [Gard84]. Gardner rendered the surfaces of ellipsoids with a 3-D transparency texture based on a pseudo-fractal trigonometric series. I wanted an analogous 3-D density function. I took quadratic polynomials of the form

$$d - \frac{(x - x_0)^2}{a^2} - \frac{(y - y_0)^2}{b^2} - \frac{(z - z_0)^2}{c^2}$$

whose contours are ellipsoids, and used the maximum of several such ellipsoidal functions with different parameters to define the union of ellipsoidal clouds. I then added on a version of Ken Perlin's $1/f$ noise function [Perl85], to roughen and randomize the edges. Like Gardner, when the volume function was negative, I let **kt** = 0, giving complete transparency. More sophisticated cloud turbulence models are given in [Sak93] and the references therein.

9 Results

Figure 7 (please refer to the color plate 4 in the color section for the rest of the figures) shows a cloud with the sun behind it, rendered with multiple anisotropic scattering. Note that the cloud edges are brightest near the direction of the sun. Figure 8 shows the same cloud from a different direction, with the green "grass" background color added for orientation. For comparison, figure 9 shows the view in figure 8 with only single anisotropic scattering, and figure 10, the difference of figure 8 minus figure 9, indicates the contribution of the higher order scattering.

The cloud was defined on a $24 \times 24 \times 18$ voxel volume. The initial illumination pass, with approximately 1000 illumination rays per voxel, took 120 seconds on an SGI 4D/35. The albedo was .99, and the Henyey-Greenstein phase function had $g = .55$, for forward scattering. I used 96 direction bins. Each of the 15 scattering passes took 15 minutes. The final rendering at 500×384 resolution took 5 minutes per frame. Once the multiple scattering flux in **through** has been computed, frames can be rendered from any viewpoint, so the 300×225 resolution frames on a videotape in which the simulated camera looped around the cloud took an average of two minutes each.

Figure 11 shows a side view of the cloud at sunset, using two light sources, an orange one from near the horizon representing the sun, and another bluish one representing the sky illumination. This image took twice as long for the two passes. For the sky illumination, I used the CIE standard clear sky directional luminance function [CIE73] to initialize the **unshot** array on an extra shell of cells on the top and sides of the volume. Figure 12 shows a top view of another cloud, using an orange point source for the setting sun, and a blue point source for the sky.

10 Future Work

This method should be applicable to thermal engineering computations if black body emission is included in the flux propagation, an easy modification.

Rushmeier [Rush88] and Kajiya [Kaj84] have pointed out that after a number of scattering events, even a narrow forward phase function becomes more isotropic. This means that the later scattering passes through the volume could use a smaller number of direction bins, for greater speed, and still maintain accuracy.

Rushmeier [Rush87, Rush88] handles surface and volume radiosity in a unified framework. I currently do not handle surface radiosity, but it should be possible to include surface elements in this method. In a common engineering application, the only surfaces are on the enclosure of the participating medium. In this straightforward case, a directional pass through the volume begins with the unshot flux leaving a shooting surface, as described above for the sky illumination, and the flux exiting the sides or left over at the end is deposited on the appropriate receiving surface.

Langer *et al.* [Lang93] have applied the discrete ordinates method to general surface geometries, using "surface nodes" with a bidirectional reflection distribution function at voxels containing surfaces. Langunou *et al.* [Lang94] combine discrete ordinate methods on volumes with traditional radiosity on surfaces external to the participating medium, as in the previous paragraph. These two groups can thus include anisotropic surface reflections, as well as isotropic volume scattering and absorption. Their flux propagation, like mine, is along a discrete cube of directions, and could be enhanced by my method to reduce the ray effects.

11 Acknowledgments

This work was performed under the auspices of the U. S. Department of Energy by Lawrence Livermore National Laboratory under contract W-7405-ENG-48. I would like to thank Holly Rushmeier, John Howell, Roger Crawfis, and Charles Grant for helpful conversations, Chris Patmore, Steven Zucker, and Neeta Bhate for preprints of [Patm93], [Lang93] and [Bhat93], respectively, anonymous Siggraph and Eurographics reviewers for suggesting improvements and pointing out references [Blas93], [Sak93], and [Kan90], and Peter Shirley and Kurt Zimmerman for reformatting this paper from Framemaker into LaTeX.

References

[Bhat92] N. Bhate and A. Tokuta, "Photorealistic Volume Rendering of Media with Directional Scattering", Third Eurographics Conference on Rendering (May 1992) Consolidation Express, Bristol England, pp. 227-245

[Bhat93] Neeta Bhate, "Application of Rapid Hierarchical Radiosity to Participation Media," in "ATARV-93: Advanced Techniques in Animation, Rendering, and Visualization" (B. Özgüç and V. Akman, eds.), Bilkent University (July 1993) pp. 43 - 53

[Blas93] P. Blasi et al. "A Rendering Algorithm for Discrete Volume Density Objects," Eurographics '93, Computer Graphics Forum Vol. 12 No. 3 (1993) pp. C-202 - 210

[CIE73] CIE Technical Committee 4.2: Standardization of Luminance Distribution on Clear Skies, CIE Publication 22, Commission International de l'Eclairage, Paris (1973) p. 7

[Chan50] Subrahmanyan Chandrasekhar, "Radiative Transfer," The Clarendon Press, Oxford, (1950) (or Dover Press, New York, 1960)

[Coh88] Michael Cohen, Shenchang Eric Chen, John Wallace, and Donald Greenberg, "A Progressive Refinement Approach to Fast Radiosity Image Generation," Computer Graphics Vol. 22 No. 4 (August 1988) pp. 75 - 84

[Fell68] William Feller, "An Introduction to Probability Theory and its Applications, Volume I, Third Edition," John Wiley & Sons, Inc., New York (1968)

[Gard84] Geoffrey Gardner, "Simulation of Natural Scenes using Textured Quadric Surfaces," Computer Graphics Vol. 18 No. 3 (July 1984) pp. 11 - 20

[Gort93] Steven Gortler, Michael Cohen, and Philipp Slusallek, "Radiosity and Relaxation Methods: Progressive Radiosity is Southwell Relaxation," Technical Report, Computer Science Dept., Princeton University (shortened version to appear in IEEE CG&A, 1994)

[Hanr91] Pat Hanrahan, David Salzman, and Larry Aupperle, "A Rapid Hierarchical Radiosity Algorithm," Computer Graphics Vol. 25 No. 4 (July 1991) pp. 197 - 206

[Hanr93] Pat Hanrahan and Wolfgang Krueger, "Reflection from Layered Surfaces due to Subsurface Scattering," Computer Graphics Proceedings, Annual Conference Series (1993) pp. 165 - 174

[Heny40] G. L. Henyey and J. L. Greenstein, "Diffuse Radiation in the Galaxy," Astrophysical Journal Vol. 88 (1940) pp. 70 - 73

[Imm86] David Immel, Michael Cohen, and Donald Greenberg, "A Radiosity Method for Non-Diffuse Environments"' Computer Graphics Vol. 20 No. 4 (1986) pp. 133 - 142

[Inak89] M. Inakage, "An Illumination Model for Atmospheric Environments" in "New Advances in Computer Graphics: Proceedings of C. G. International '89," (R. A. Earnshsaw and B. Wyvill, eds.) Springer Verlag, Tokyo (1989) pp. 533 - 548

[Kaj84] James Kajiya and Brian Von Herzen, "Ray Tracing Volume Densities", Computer Graphics Vol. 18 No. 3 (July 1984) pp. 165 - 174

[Kan90] Kazufumi Kaneda, Takashi Okamoto, Eihachiro Nakamae and Tomoyuki Nishita, "Highly Realistic Visual Simulation of Outdoor Scenes under Various Atmospheric Conditions," CG International '90, (T. S. Chua and T. L. Kunii, eds.) Springer-Verlag, Tokyo (1990) pp. 117 - 131

[Kauf87] Arie Kaufman, "Efficient Algorithms for 3D Scan-Conversion of Parametric Curves, Surfaces, and Volumes," Computer Graphics Vol. 21 No. 4 (July 1987) pp. 171 - 179

[Lang93] Michael Langer, Pierre Breton, and Steven Zucker, "Parallel Radiosity without Form Factors," report TR-CIM-93-22, McGill Research Center for Intelligent Machines, McGill University, Montreal, Quebec, Canada (December 1993)

[Lang94] Eric Langunou, Kadi Bauatouch, and Michel Chelle, "Global Illumination in Presence of Participating Media with General Properties," in this volume.

[Lath68] K. D. Lathrop, "Ray Effects in Discrete Ordinates Equations," Nuclear Science and Engineering Vol. 32 (1968) pp. 357 - 368

[Mie09] Gustav Mie, "Optics of Turbid Media," Ann. Physik Vol. 25 No. 3 (1908) pp. 377 - 445

[Nish87] Tomoyuki Nishita, Yasuhiro Miyakawa, and Eihachiro Nakamae, "A Shading Model for Atmospheric Scattering Considering Luminous Intensity Distribution of Light Sources," Computer Graphics Vol. 21 No. 4 (July 1987) pp. 303 - 310

[Patm93] Chris Patmore, "Simulated Multiple Scattering for Cloud Rendering" in "Graphics, Design, and Visualization: Proceedings of the International Conference on Computer Graphics -ICCG93" (S. P. Mudur and S. N. Pattaniak, eds.) Elsevier Science Publishers (1993) pp. 29-40

[Perl85] Ken Perlin, "An Image Synthesizer," Computer Graphics Vol. 19 No. 3 (July 1985) pp. 287 - 296

[Rush87] Holly Rushmeier and Kenneth Torrance, "The Zonal Method for Calculating Light Intensities in the Presence of Participating Media," Computer Graphics Vol. 21 No. 4 (July 1987) pp. 293 - 302

[Rush88] Holly Rushmeier, "Realistic Image Synthesis for Scenes with Radiatively Participating Media," Ph.D. Thesis, Cornell University (May 1988)

[Sak93]   Georgios Sakas, "Modeling and Animating Turbulent Gaseous Phenomena
          using Spectral Synthesis," The Visual Computer Vol. 9 No. 4 (January 1993)
          pp. 200 - 212

[Sie92]   Robert Siegel and John Howell, "Thermal Radiation Heat Transfer, Third
          Edition," Hemisphere Publishing Corp., Washington (1992)

[Tan89]   Zhiqiang Tan, "Radiative Heat Transfer in Multidimensional Emitting, Ab-
          sorbing, and Scattering Media – Mathematical Formulation and Numerical
          Method," Journal of Heat Transfer Vol. 111 (February 1989) pp. 141 - 147

[Voss83] Richard Voss, "Fourier Synthesis of Gaussian Fractals: $1/f$ Noises, Lands-
          capes, and Flakes," Tutorial on State of the Art Image Synthesis, ACM
          Siggraph Course Notes (1983)

[Will92] Peter Williams and Nelson Max, "A Volume Density Optical Model," Pro-
          ceedings, 1992 Workshop on Volume Visualization, ACM Press, New York
          (1992) pp. 61 - 68

Clustering and Volume Scattering for Hierarchical Radiosity Calculations

François Sillion

iMAGIS / IMAG, B.P. 53, F-38041 Grenoble Cedex 9, France

Abstract

This paper introduces a new approach to hierarchical radiosity computation, making it practical for the simulation of energy exchanges in very complex environments. Results indicate that the new formulation allows the effective simulation of environments of significant complexity, containing several thousands of surfaces or volumes.

In this new technique a hierarchy is constructed in a *bottom-up* fashion, in effect grouping together nearby surfaces for the purpose of evaluating their energy exchanges with distant objects. This clustering approach eliminates the need for an $O(n^2)$ initial linking stage, by establishing connections between abstract entities that behave like volumes.

A general hierarchical transfer algorithm for volumes is first derived and its adaptation to clustered environments is then discussed. In particular the mechanisms required to efficiently simulate the radiant interactions between surfaces and clusters are reviewed.

1 Introduction

The recent introduction of hierarchical formulations of the radiosity method has been a major step in allowing rapid simulation of energy exchanges between surfaces. Hierarchical algorithms attempt to limit the amount of subdivision of surfaces by selecting the proper level of detail needed to represent each energy transfer within a given error tolerance. The exchange of energy between a pair of surfaces is represented using a hierarchy of *links* that connect some of their components. Links are created in an adaptive refinement procedure that recursively attempts to link two sub-surfaces. The error incurred when representing the energy transfer using a single link is estimated (a variety of error measures are available to choose from) and the link is actually established if that error falls below some threshold. Otherwise one of the two sub-surfaces is subdivided and the procedure is called recursively for each of the new components.

The benefit of hierarchical radiosity methods is that the number of links created in the adaptive procedure is linear with respect to the final number of surface elements [4]. This is a major advantage compared to the quadratic matrix of form factors needed to completely represent the possible energy transfers with "conventional" radiosity. However, all hierarchical radiosity methods to date proceed in a *top-down* fashion, by selectively subdividing a set of input surfaces. Each pair of input surfaces must still be linked in a preliminary "initial linking" stage, resulting in a quadratic cost with respect to the number of input surfaces. Furthermore, no exchange of energy is computed until the entire "initial linking" phase has terminated.

When complex scenes are to be simulated, this quadratic cost rapidly becomes overwhelming, and a bottom-up hierarchical method becomes necessary. One possibility to avoid the quadratic cost is to compute energy exchanges (i.e. establish links) between groups of objects in a single operation. This concept is commonly referred to as "clustering", since it creates abstract objects that act as representatives of a group (or cluster) of neighboring objects in lighting calculations.

Clustering works by introducing a hierarchy *above* the input-surface level, creating a set of abstract entities that exchange energy. Since these entities contain several surfaces of arbitrary orientation, they can be represented as volumetric objects. Previous efforts to simplify the radiosity algorithm have either attempted to treat subsets of the scene independently in a divide-and-conquer approach [17, 1], or manually constructed groups of patches used as representatives for their contents [12, 8]. In this paper we propose a new hierarchical algorithm that borrows ideas from volume scattering methods to express the hierarchical exchanges between clusters, and completely automates the creation of clusters.

The paper is organized as follows. First we show how energy exchanges in a radiatively participating medium can be computed using a hierarchical algorithm. We then present a clustering method that models groups of surfaces as volumes of equivalent optical density. This model works well for collections of small objects. Finally we discuss the creation of a hierarchy for a scene containing surfaces of arbitrary size. The specific issues encountered in estimating the volumetric properties of clusters are reviewed and solutions are suggested.

2 Hierarchical Simulation of Volume Scattering in Isotropic Media

In this section we present a hierarchical formulation for the simulation of energy exchanges in an isotropic scattering medium. This can be seen as a combination of the zonal method [13] and the hierarchical radiosity algorithm[1] [5]. Specific issues raised by the combination of both methods are highlighted.

2.1 Energy Transfer in Volume Densities

The properties of an isotropic participating medium are expressed using an *extinction coefficient* κ, which measures the rate of attenuation per unit length due to absorption and scattering, and the *albedo R* representing the fraction of that attenuation due to scattering.

Transmittance Consider a pencil of light traveling from the origin to a point at distance s in a participating medium. the fraction of light that passes through the medium without being absorbed nor scattered is called the *transmittance* and is given by:

$$\tau(s) = e^{-\int_0^s \kappa(u)du} .$$ (1)

2.2 Diffuse Energy Transfers Between Surfaces and Volumes

The zonal method models the exchange of energy between diffuse surfaces and isotropically scattering media by the following equation [13, 11]:

$$B_\alpha = E_\alpha + \rho_\alpha \sum_\beta F_{\alpha\beta} B_\beta$$ (2)

Here the summation is carried out both over a set of surface patches, and a set of volume elements, each of which is assumed to possess a uniform radiosity value. ρ denotes either the diffuse reflectance (for a surface) or the albedo (for a volume). The expression of the form factor $F_{\alpha\beta}$ depends on the physical nature of elements α and β. In the following formulæ, indices i and j are used for surfaces, and k and m for volumes.

$$\text{Surface–Surface: } F_{ij} = \frac{1}{A_i} \int_{A_i} \int_{A_j} \frac{\tau \cos\theta_i \cos\theta_j}{\pi r^2} dA_j dA_i$$ (3)

$$\text{Surface–Volume: } F_{jk} = \frac{1}{A_j} \int_{A_j} \int_{V_k} \frac{\tau \kappa_k \cos\theta_j}{\pi r^2} dV_k dA_j$$ (4)

$$\text{Volume–Surface: } F_{ki} = \frac{1}{V_k} \int_{V_k} \int_{A_i} \frac{\tau \cos\theta_i}{4\pi r^2} dA_i dV_k$$ (5)

$$\text{Volume–Volume: } F_{mk} = \frac{1}{V_m} \int_{V_m} \int_{V_k} \frac{\tau \kappa_k}{4\pi r^2} dV_k dV_m$$ (6)

---

[1] Since the first version of this paper was written, it was brought to our attention that a similar approach is described in [2] for a homogeneous medium. The algorithm described here is more general in that it accommodates arbitrary density distributions.

τ is the transmittance between differential elements, A_i is the area of patch i and V_k is the volume of volume k. This presentation differs from the original zonal method in that it favors the simplicity of the transfer equation over that of the form factor and the reciprocity relations. The resulting equation is identical to the surface radiosity equation [14] and allows a very smooth integration of surfaces and volumes in a universal algorithm. Note that the total power emitted by an element is given by

$$P_i = \quad A_i B_i \quad \text{for a surface element} \tag{7}$$
$$P_k = 4\kappa_k V_k B_k \text{ for a volume element} \tag{8}$$

Thus the quantity $4\kappa V$ can be seen as the "equivalent area" of a volume element[2].

Once a solution of (2) is found, an image can be computed by evaluating a line integral for each view direction to obtain the radiance reaching the eye. Assuming a surface is visible through a medium at a distance s from the eye, the image radiance is given by

$$L(s) = L(0)\tau(s) + \int_0^s B(u)\tau(s-u)\kappa(u)du \,. \tag{9}$$

2.3 A Hierarchical Algorithm for Isotropic Volumes

In this section we show that the hierarchical radiosity algorithm is easily adapted to the case of volumes. Thus we consider a scene with no surfaces, described by the distribution of the extinction coefficient. We assume that the volume enclosing the scene can be represented using a hierarchical data structure. In our implementation we have used a k-d tree but the algorithm is largely independent of the specific representation used. Octrees, BSP trees, or hierarchies of bounding volumes could be used as well, and our presentation is done with a generic data structure. The original hierarchical radiosity algorithm is also assumed to be well known to the reader [5].

Refinement of the Links The core of the hierarchical radiosity algorithm is a recursive refinement procedure: considering two volumes, it decides whether the transfer of energy is correctly represented at the current level, otherwise it subdivides one of the volumes. The procedure for volumes is almost identical to its surface-based counterpart. It first computes a bound on the error incurred by a link at the current level. This can be done either by bounding the error on the form factor alone[4], or by bounding the radiosity transfer (BF refinement)[3] [5].

Based on the error estimates for the energy transfers in both directions, a decision is made to either subdivide one of the volumes (which one depends on the relative magnitude of both estimates) or establish a link between the

---

[2] In particular it has units of $m^{-1}m^3 = m^2$.

[3] Importance weighting is also possible [16]. Our current implementation uses BF refinement.

volumes. Establishing a link requires the computation of a form factor. Note that the transmittance factor in (6) is the "equivalent" of the visibility term in surface form factors. It can be ignored in the computation of an upper bound of the form factor, but must be evaluated for the final form factor estimate. Transmittance is computed by traversing the hierarchical structure (possibly for a number of sample rays) while accumulating opacity along the way, and then evaluating the negative exponential.

Initial Linking and Self-Linking In surface-based radiosity, surfaces are generally not allowed to interact with themselves. Thus no form factor is computed from one surface to itself, and no link is established from a patch to itself. For volumes the situation is different, and in general there must be a link from a volume to itself (called a *self-link*), representing all the interactions taking place *inside* the volume. In fact the entire initial linking phase is replaced by the creation of a single link, from the root of the hierarchy to itself. This link is then refined by the recursive procedure described above.

The subdivision of a self-link is slightly different from that of a link between two different volumes: In this case links must be created between all possible pairs of hierarchical children, thus including a self-link for each child, as illustrated in Fig. 1.

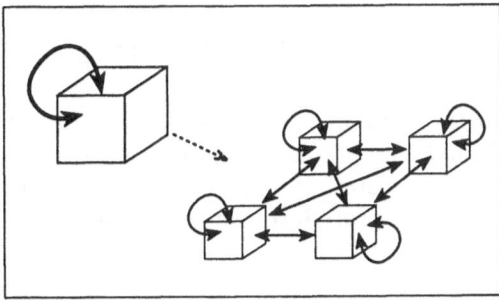

Fig. 1. Subdivision of a self-link.

Energy Transfer Once links have been established, energy transfers are computed in a gathering step, and a bidirectional traversal of the hierarchical structure ensures that a correct representation of radiosity is obtained at all levels (Push-Pull procedure).

Another difference with surface-based radiosity is the fact that volumes are not homogeneous in nature: they contain a variety of densities and albedos. This is in contrast to the typical assumption in radiosity that a patch has a uniform reflectance. Therefore care must be taken to always use the proper albedo value to weight incoming energy.

In practice, this issue is easily solved by gathering *irradiance* values at each node of the hierarchy, that is, incoming energy per unit area. Irradiance is then pushed down to the leaves of the hierarchy, where it is multiplied by the appropriate albedo value. The resulting radiosity values are then pulled up the hierarchy and averaged at each level. The weighting coefficients are proportional to $4\kappa V$, which acts as the effective area of a volume element. Note that this modified Push-Pull procedure also solves the problem of non-uniform reflectance across surfaces, and therefore allows the accurate treatment of textured surfaces in hierarchical radiosity.

Results The images in Fig. 3 and 4 demonstrate the application of the hierarchical radiosity algorithm to volumes. The cloud data is the 64^3 dataset provided for this workshop. In these images, the walls and obstacles were modeled as a thin layer of an optically thick material. Note that shadowing by the cloud and shadowing of the cloud (both by obstacles and by itself) is simulated.

For the images in Fig. 3 and 4, solutions took between 2 and 8 minutes to compute on an SGI Indigo. 30,000 to 800,000 links were established (out of a total of about 2.5 billion potential links). The images were then produced by a volume renderer –based on ray tracing– operating on the 3D solution according to (9).

3 A Simple Clustering Algorithm Using Isotropic Volumes

Let us now turn to the issue of clustering surfaces to reduce the complexity of hierarchical radiosity. The preceding discussion introduced some of the key elements for a successful clustering strategy. These are the notion of self-link, and the modified Push-Pull procedure using irradiance.

3.1 Creating a Volume Model

We first consider the case of a large number of "small" objects. This model could be used to represent a number of natural situations such as foliage, as noted by Patmore [10]. The value of this model is that, as objects become smaller, the behaviour of the medium resembles more and more that of a density distribution. In this section we therefore model the radiative properties of surface clusters using equivalent isotropic scattering volumes.

In order to use the above algorithm, a transition from surface clusters to equivalent volumes must be modeled. Rushmeier et al. compute reflectance properties of manually constructed clusters using Monte Carlo simulation [12]. Since we are using a large number of automatically constructed clusters, we need a faster correspondence between surfaces and volume densities, which can be based on the notion of "equivalent area". As noted above, an isotropic scattering volume element has an equivalent area of $A = 4\kappa V$. Reciprocally, if a number of objects of total surface area A are placed in a volume V, an equivalent extinction coefficient is computed as[4]

$$\kappa = \frac{A}{4V} \, . \tag{10}$$

3.2 Isotropic Clustering

Replacing a collection of small surfaces by an equivalent volume density allows two major performance improvements for hierarchical radiosity calculations. First, the cost of visibility computation is dramatically lowered by the use of semi-transparent volumes. In addition, links and energy exchanges are computed between clusters in a top-down manner, thus no initial linking of the surfaces is needed.

The isotropic clustering algorithm proceeds by computing the distribution of the extinction coefficient in the volume of the scene, according to (10). The hierarchical algorithm of Sect. 2.3 is then applied to the scene.

Visibility Calculation All transmittance factors are computed using the extinction coefficients, in effect performing a statistical average over the distribution of objects. Compared to a surface visibility calculation, the computation of volume transmittance is cheaper by more than one order of magnitude.

Obtaining Surface Radiosity After the hierarchical radiosity algorithm has finished, volume radiosity is transferred to the surfaces in each leaf cell of the hierarchical structure. Because of the isotropic assumption for the volume, radiosity is simply copied from the volume to the contained surfaces.

3.3 Results

The scene shown in Fig. 5 contains 1000 small cubes of random orientation. The image on the left was obtained in 17 minutes using an accelerated version of the surface hierarchical radiosity algorithm [7] (the original algorithm would require more than 6 hours of initial linking!). The image on the right was obtained by the isotropic clustering method. The volume radiosity solution took 4 minutes.

Note that because the radiance of a volume element is assumed isotropic, it is much lower than the radiance that a single surface would have when subjected to the same irradiance (by a factor of four, since the same energy is equally distributed in 4π sr, instead of being distributed in a hemisphere according to $\cos\theta$, with an integral of π). In addition, all faces of a cube are shaded according to the same volume, thus the three-dimensional nature of the objects is not apparent. Both these issues are addressed in the next section.

However the impact on the environment is similar when a large number of cubes is considered. In particular, consider the fact that the entire volume of

---

[4] Note that in the case of a distribution of infinitely small spheres or cubes, this formula is exact in that it gives the probability of interception of a ray per unit length [6].

the cluster participates in secondary transfers, which compensates for the lower radiosity. This suggests that the solution of the volume algorithm is valuable to compute global interreflection effects, even though a "local" shading phase is necessary to improve the accuracy on the visible surfaces [9].

4 A General Clustering Strategy

The representation of complex groups of surfaces is often impossible using isotropic volumes. Perhaps the main reason for this is that when surfaces are not infinitely small, the visibility (transmittance) function becomes more of a binary quantity. Thus the approximation of clusters by isotropic media is only valid in the limit of extremely small surfaces. A general clustering algorithm must therefore incorporate a mechanism that computes visibility using either surfaces or volumes, whichever is the most appropriate.

Another important issue with finite-sized surfaces is that the radiance distribution leaving a cluster is generally not isotropic. One possibility to alleviate this difficulty, which is not discussed here, would be to represent directional information at the cluster level.

We now describe how to compute energy exchanges between surfaces of arbitrary size using clusters.

4.1 Constructing the Hierarchy of Clusters

We model a general hierarchical scene as a mixture of surfaces and volumes, by allowing a volume element in a hierarchical subdivision of space to contain children surfaces in addition to its normal hierarchical children (Fig. 2).

One possibility, similar to the idea of "virtual walls" to accelerate radiosity calculations [17, 3], is to attach surfaces only to leaves of the hierarchical volume description.

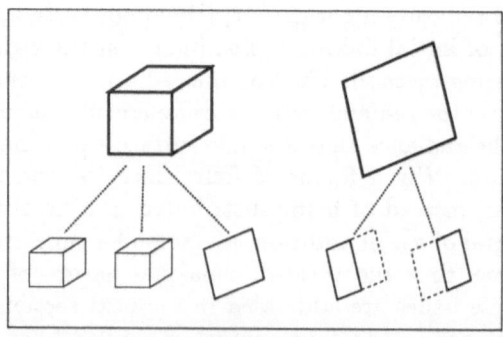

Fig. 2. Hierarchical structure: volumes can have both surface and volume children (left), while surfaces only have surface children (right).

In our implementation, we take a different route and attach surfaces at the lowest level of the volume hierarchy that contains them entirely. This avoids potential problems when a surface straddles a subdivision boundary, and has additional advantages in terms of visibility testing: By traversing the structure in breadth-first order, potential occluders are tested roughly in order of decreasing size.

4.2 Interfaces Between Surfaces and Clusters

Link Refinement An abstract data type, the "hierarchical element", is used in the hierarchical algorithm to represent either volumes or surfaces. Form factors between elements are computed using (3–6), with the appropriate equation automatically chosen through the C++ overloading mechanism. When a cluster is subdivided for refinement, it produces a list of children elements that can consist of volume children (if the cluster is not a leaf of the hierarchy) and/or surface children (if surfaces are contained in the cluster).

Representing Energy Exchanges at the Cluster Level Figure 5 shows that the simple replication of the cluster radiosity among its children surfaces produces unacceptable results. This is a negative effect of the isotropic assumption.

A relatively simple way around this drawback is to change the behaviour of clusters to allow "smart" energy exchanges between contained surfaces and the cluster. This is accomplished by modifying the refinement routine, the energy gathering routine and the bidirectional sweep routine used to distribute energy in the hierarchy. The goal is to model the following phenomena in the interaction between two clusters:

- How the radiosity of each surface (and sub-cluster) of the cluster contributes to the energy leaving the cluster.
- How the irradiance on the receiving cluster is distributed among the surfaces and sub-clusters.

As a first approximation, we can ignore all visibility relationships in a cluster and simply take into account the relative orientation of each individual element, with respect to the general direction of transfer. Thus the dot product of each surface's normal vector and the direction of transfer is used to modulate the irradiance or radiosity. Since the transmittance factor is still only evaluated between the clusters, the additional cost remains reasonable[5]

Better criteria can probably be devised, but should remain very simple to implement, to avoid losing all the benefits of clustering. Current work includes the definition of adaptive criteria taking into account a degraded notion of visibility inside the cluster.

---

[5] Independent work by Smits et al. establishes interesting complexity bounds on a variety of clustering mechanisms [15]. In this case for clusters with m and n objects, a naive cost of $O(mn)$ is replaced by $O(m + n)$.

Visibility and Transmittance In our current implementation, transmittance is computed using either volumes or surfaces. Thus the choice is between a fast and approximate method (with volumes and their "equivalent extinction"), and an expensive but more accurate one. A natural extension of this work consists of developing better visibility algorithms that switch automatically from one description to the other. In particular, importance methods [16] should be used to select the appropriate representation for each surface.

4.3 Results

Figure 6 (see colour section) shows the result obtained with the improved clustering algorithm. The right-hand image displays the hierarchy of clusters, color-coded according to their computed extinction coefficient. This solution took 6 minutes, and should be compared to the one in Fig. 5.

Figures 7 and 8 show the application of the clustering algorithm to a scene with 6250 polygons. The solution (one iteration) took 56 seconds. For all these images visibility was performed using volumes only, resulting in approximate shadows. Note however that the quality of the shadows is much better for Fig. 6. This is to be expected since the distribution of surfaces mimics a density distribution.

5 Conclusions and Future Work

A hierarchical formulation of the zonal method for the simulation of energy exchanges in isotropic participating media was presented. This volume algorithm can be applied in all fields that require accurate simulation of volume illumination. It also provides an avenue for the development of efficient clustering algorithm, by establishing a correspondence between volumes and groups of surfaces.

Results were presented for two automatic clustering methods, showing that clustering can significantly accelerate radiosity calculations by effectively removing the need for a complete initial linking phase.

Work in progress at iMAGIS includes the study of better criteria to distribute energy from a cluster to its elements (and reciprocally), and the development of efficient algorithms for the calculation of visibility and transmittance factors. In particular we hope to use the automatic correspondence between surfaces and volumes to compute error bounds on transmittance estimates. In general the use of mixed representations combining surfaces and volumes is a promising area of research. Each representation can then be used in specific areas of computation.

6 Acknowledgements

This research was greatly accelerated by the courtesy of several colleagues who kindly shared some of their code with the author. Much of the comprehension of hierarchical algorithms was gained by studying a program provided by Pat

Hanrahan. The hierarchical subdivision code using a *k-d* tree is based on software developed by Kevin Novins, Jim Arvo and David Salesin. Kevin Novins provided the ray tracer used to create the images in Fig. 3 and 4.

Fig. 3. The same density model is used for the three clouds, with different extinction coefficients (direct lighting only). Note the variation in the shadow of the cloud, and the change in the illumination of the cloud itself.

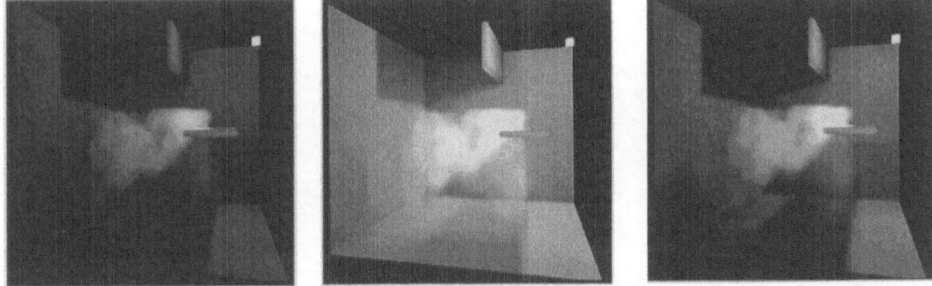

Fig. 4. Global illumination in volumes: images obtained after 1, 2 and 5 BF refinement stages. Note the gradual propagation of light through the cloud. The horizontal obstacle has a transmittance of 25%, and the vertical obstacle is virtually opaque ($\tau \approx 1\%$).

Fig. 5. Comparison of surface radiosity and isotropic clustering (volume radiosity) on a scene with 1000 cubes. Left: surface radiosity (17 min.). Right: image created by generating flat-shaded surfaces according to the volume solution (4 min.).

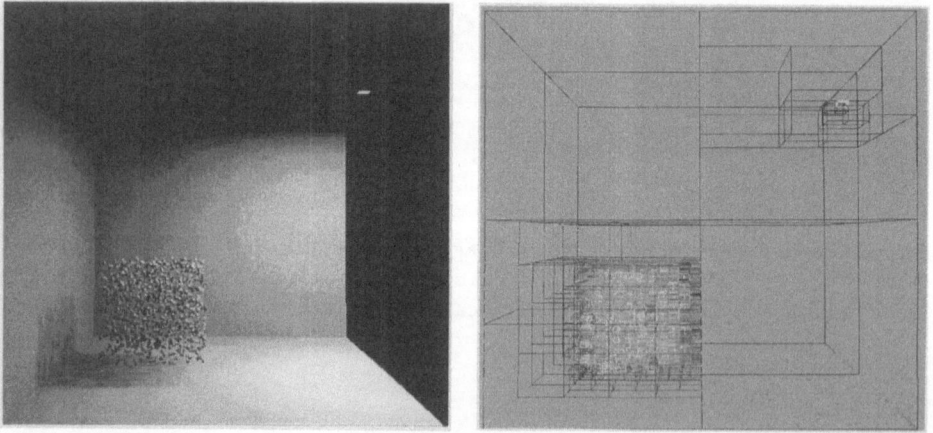

Fig. 6. General clustering solution (left, 6 min.) and corresponding clusters (right).

Fig. 7. Clustering solution (56 sec.).

Fig. 8. Corresponding hierarchical clusters.

References

1. Bruno Arnaldi, Xavier Pueyo, and Josep Vilaplana. On the division of environments by virtual walls for radiosity computation. In P. Brunet and F.W. Jansen, editors, *Photorealistic Rendering in Computer Graphics*, pages 198–205. Springer Verlag, 1993. Proceedings of the Second Eurographics Workshop on Rendering (Barcelona, Spain, May 1991).
2. Neeta Bhate. Application of rapid hierarchical radiosity to participating media. In *Proceedings of AATRV-93: Advanced Techniques in Animation, Rendering, and Visualization*, pages 43–53. Bilkent University, July 1993.
3. Alain Fournier, Eugene Fiume, Marc Ouellette, and Chuan K. Chee. Fiat lux. Technical Report 90-1, University of Toronto, Dynamics Graphics Project, January 1990.

4. Pat Hanrahan and David Saltzman. A rapid hierarchical radiosity algorithm for unoccluded environments. In C. Bouville and K. Bouatouch, editors, *Photorealism in Computer Graphics*. Springer Verlag, EurographicSeminars series, 1992.

5. Pat Hanrahan, David Saltzman, and Larry Aupperle. A rapid hierarchical radiosity algorithm. *Computer Graphics*, 25(4):197–206, August 1991. Proceedings SIGGRAPH '91 in Las Vegas (USA).

6. Nicolas Holzschuch. Personal communication, 1994.

7. Nicolas Holzschuch, François Sillion, and George Drettakis. An efficient progressive refinment strategy for hiearchical radiosity. In *Fifth Eurographics Workshop on Rendering*, Darmstadt, Germany, June 1994. In these proceedings.

8. Arjan J. F. Kok. Grouping of patches in progressive radiosity. In *Proceedings of Fourth Eurographics Workshop on Rendering*, pages 221–231. Eurographics, June 1993. Technical Report EG 93 RW.

9. Dani Lischinski, Filippo Tampieri, and Donald P. Greenberg. Combining hierarchical radiosity and discontinuity meshing. In *Computer Graphics Proceedings, Annual Conference Series:* SIGGRAPH '93 (Anaheim, CA, USA), pages 199–208. ACM SIGGRAPH, New York, August 1993.

10. Chris Patmore. Illumination of dense foliage models. In *Proceedings of Fourth Eurographics Workshop on Rendering*, pages 63–71. Eurographics, June 1993. Technical Report EG 93 RW.

11. Holly Rushmeier. Solution methods for radiatively participating media, August 1992. SIGGRAPH Course notes (# 18, "Global Illumination").

12. Holly Rushmeier, Charles Patterson, and Aravindan Veerasamy. Geometric simplification for indirect illumination calculations. In *Proceedings Graphics Interface '93*. Morgan Kaufmann, 1993.

13. Holly E. Rushmeier and Kenneth E. Torrance. The zonal method for calculating light intensities in the presence of a participating medium. *Computer Graphics*, 21(4):293–302, July 1987. Proceedings SIGGRAPH '87 in Anaheim (USA).

14. François Sillion and Claude Puech. *Radiosity and Global Illumination*. Morgan Kaufmann, San Francisco, 1994.

15. Brian Smits, James Arvo, and Donald P. Greenberg. A clustering algorithm for radiosity in complex environments. In *Computer Graphics Proceedings, Annual Conference Series:* SIGGRAPH '94 (Orlando, FL). ACM SIGGRAPH, New York, 1994.

16. Brian E. Smits, James R. Arvo, and David H. Salesin. An importance-driven radiosity algorithm. *Computer Graphics*, 26(4):273–282, July 1992. Proceedings of SIGGRAPH '92 in Chicago (USA).

17. H. Xu, Q. Peng, and Y Liang. Accelerated radiosity method for complex environments. *Eurographics '89*, pages 51–61, September 1989.

Part III

Ray Tracing and Monte Carlo

Adaptive Splatting for Specular to Diffuse Light Transport

Steven Collins

Trinity College Dublin, Ireland

Abstract

We present an extension to existing techniques to provide for more accurate re-solution of specular to diffuse transfer within a global illumination framework. In particular this new model is adaptive with a view to capturing high frequency phenomena such as caustic curves in sharp detail and yet allowing for low frequency detail without compromising noise levels and aliasing artefacts. A 2-pass ray-tracing algorithm is used, with an adaptive light-pass followed by a standard eye-pass. During the light-pass, rays are traced from the light sources (essentially sampling the wavefront radiating from the sources), each carrying a fraction of the total power per wavelength of the source. The interactions of these rays with diffuse surfaces are recorded in illumination-maps, as first proposed by Arvo [Ar86]. The key to reconstructing the intensity gradients due to this light-pass lies in the construction of the illumination maps. We record the power carried by the ray as a splat of energy flux, deposited on the surface using a Gaussian distribution kernel. The kernel of the splat is adaptively scaled according to an estimation of the wavefront divergence or convergence, thus resolving sharp intensity gradients in regions of high wavefront convergence and smooth gradients in areas of divergence. The 2nd pass eye-trace modulates the surfaces radiance according to the power stored in the illumination map in order to include the specular to diffuse light modelled during the first pass.

1 Introduction

Ultimately, to produce realistic renderings of a scene, we wish to determine the radiance at every point in the scene visible to the viewer. The radiance at any point in the scene may be expressed using a recursive integral:

$$L\left(x, \theta, \phi, \lambda\right) = L_e\left(x, \theta, \phi, \lambda\right) + \int_{\Omega} \rho_{bd}\left(\theta, \phi, \theta', \phi', \lambda\right) L\left(x, \theta', \phi', \lambda\right) \cos\theta d\omega \quad (1)$$

$L(x, \theta, \phi, \lambda)$ is the radiance (energy per unit time per unit projected area per unit solid angle per wavelength) leaving point x in direction (θ, ϕ) and is defined in terms of the radiance emitted by the surface in that direction $L_e(x, \theta, \phi, \lambda)$, and the radiance impinging on point x from all other directions (θ', ϕ') scaled by the *bi-directional reflectance distribution function* (BRDF) which is a function of the incoming and outgoing angles and the wavelength. Existing algorithms, ray tracing and radiosity, solve for many of the modes of light transport but not all. The most notable omission is that of specular to diffuse light transport, or light that reaches a surface through one or more specular interactions (either reflection or refraction).

Classic ray-tracing simulates only the **LDS*E|LS*E** paths (using Heckbert's notation [He90]) whereas the radiosity technique simulates **LD*E** (although extensions to the radiosity techniques to include specular transfer ([ICG86], [WCG87]) have extended this path classification). The technique presented here is based upon a 2-pass method first proposed by Arvo [Ar86] and later augmented by Heckbert [He90] to model the **LS⁺DE** transport as a first pass, tracing rays from the light sources as they interact with specular surfaces and depositing power on these surfaces if they exhibit diffuse characteristics and terminating at a purely diffuse surface (or when the power falls below a pre-defined threshold). A subsequent eye-pass backward-traces paths of the form **DS*E** and extracts the power deposited on the diffuse surfaces during the first pass. A major problem with this method is the large numbers of light-pass rays required to produce an adequate image. We propose a solution which uses information about the local divergence/convergence of the wavefront to reduce the number of these rays.

2 Tracing LS*D Paths

The task of tracing these paths is a 3-fold operation:

1. Trace rays from the light sources, assigning a fraction of the total light source power, Φ_s, to each ray.
2. Record the rays collisions with diffuse surfaces by depositing this power, Φ_r, on the surface.
3. Reconstruct the power distribution during the eye-pass by modulating the radiance from the surface according to the power stored on the surface.

We will now discuss the details of each of these phases and their implementation in the current system.

2.1 Light Ray Tracing

We trace rays originating at the light sources in the scene and record the interactions of these rays and the surfaces in the scene, depositing power on diffuse surfaces along the rays paths. In order to record this power, illumination maps in the spirit of Arvo [Ar86] are used.

Illumination Map Resolution Determination We must first determine the resolution of the illumination map associated with each diffuse surface. Heckbert proposes tracing rays to the surfaces and recording the distance between these rays with the surface, using this information in the later light-pass in order to determine the threshold for quadtree subdivision during illumination map adaptation. Chen et al. [CRMT91] propose a similar scheme, where the distance between intersections during this initial *size pass* is used to specify the resolution for uniform caustic maps. However, this gives a view dependent solution and in general is not appropriate for a general pre-process, the results of which we wish to use subsequently in a walk through visualisation system.

Illumination maps are assigned to diffuse surfaces that are in the path of light pass rays. Thus surfaces which are not indirectly irradiated via specular transfers are not encumbered with expensive maps. An estimate of convergence/divergence of the wavefront emanating from the light source is used to determine the resolution of the map. This estimate is also used to determine the distribution of power deposited on the surfaces illumination map and is outlined in section 2.2. The surface keeps track of the average behaviour of the wavefront as it interacts with the surface and increases the resolution of the map if the power distribution exhibits high frequencies. The illumination maps, if required, are simply doubled in resolution to simplify the power redistribution. A map with an original resolution of (r_x, r_y) will have its resolution increased to $(2r_x, 2r_y)$ with the each original cell being redistributed over 4 new cells, thus the new power per cell is simply:

$$\frac{\Phi_{cell\_old}}{4} \tag{2}$$

Light Ray Distribution In order to determine the solid angles (about the light sources within the scene) subtended by specular surfaces, we use a technique similar to the item buffer of [WHG84] and the hemicube of [CG85]. We wish to trace light-rays only in directions that will potentially give rise to some from of specular to diffuse transfer, so we first determine the directions in which specular surfaces are visible from the light source. All the objects in the scene are projected onto a unit cube centred at the light source with Z- buffers attached to its faces (Fig. 1). During the light pass, we sample only those "pixels" on the cube's faces that can "see" a specular surface. The number of rays sent to each cube pixel is determined by the solid angle subtended by the pixel and a user specified sample density (specified in rays per steradian). The delta solid angle per pixel is derived in a similar manner to the hemicube delta form-factor (see Fig. 2):

$$x = \frac{h_x + 0.5}{R_x}$$
$$y = \frac{h_y + 0.5}{R_y}$$

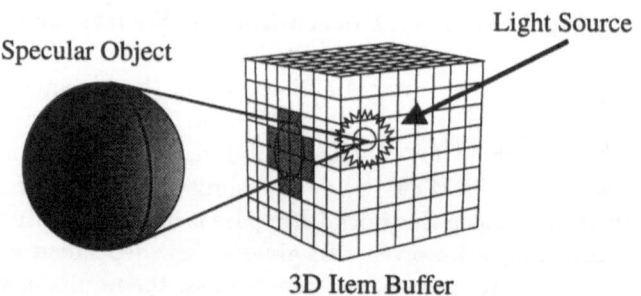

Fig. 1. Item buffer construction.

$$\cos\theta = \frac{1}{\sqrt{x^2 + y^2 + 1}}$$

$$A = \frac{4}{R_x R_y},$$

$$r = \sqrt{x^2 + y^2 + 1}$$

$$\Delta\omega = \frac{\cos\theta}{Ar^2}$$

$$= \frac{R_x R_y}{4 * \left[\sqrt{x^2 + y^2 + 1}\right]^3} \tag{3}$$

Because of the cube's symmetry, we only need to compute $\Delta\omega$ for one quarter of one face. (R_x, R_y) is the resolution of the cube faces, (h_x, h_y) is the co-ordinate of the cube pixel in cube-space, θ, the angle between the face normal and the direction of $\Delta\omega$, r, the distance to the centre of the cube and A the area of the cube-pixel.

Each ray carries with it a fraction of the total power of the source. This fraction is proportional to the solid angle subtended by the ray at the source. The power shot towards each cube-pixel for a point light source is:

$$\Phi_p = \frac{\Phi_s \Delta\omega}{\omega_s} = \frac{\Phi_s \Delta\omega}{4\pi} \tag{4}$$

This power is evenly distributed among the rays shot through the pixel. Note that this distribution of rays will produce a bias towards the centre of the cube faces. This bias may be reduced by stratifying the sampling of the cube faces, whereby the area of the cube pixels are proportional to the solid angle they subtend, rather than the uniform area used here. To reduce aliasing artefacts, the rays are jittered within their sub-pixels in order to approximate a Poisson distribution on the cube face.

2.2 Wavefront Behaviour Tracking

We model the behaviour of the wavefront emanating from the light source by examining the distribution of ray hits across surfaces. On a given surface we are

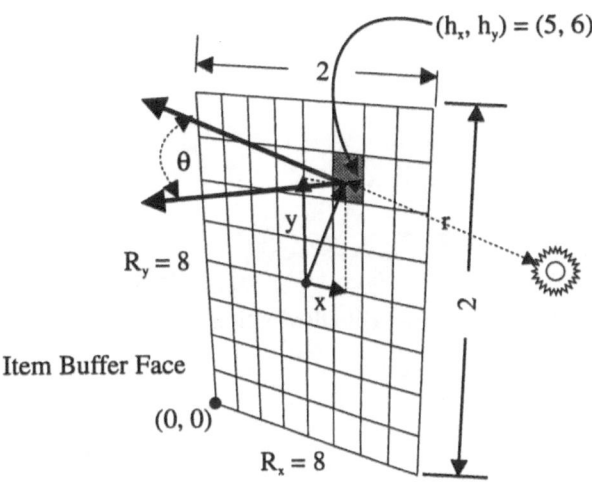

Fig. 2. Delta solid angle per ray determination.

interested in the convergence/divergence of the wavefront locally. Rather than attempt to reconstruct the shape of the wavefront by applying a post-filter to the intersection points we maintain connectivity information between rays. By tracking arrays of rays from the light source, we associate with each ray some fraction of the solid angle of the source. When these rays intersect surfaces we examine the distances between neighbouring rays to determine the shape of the wavefront. We use this information to determine how to distribute the power on the receiving surface.

Figure 3 demonstrates the problem of reconstructing the wavefront interaction with a surface. The distribution of the hit points is such that if the power distribution is determined by examining a set of nearst neighbour collisions, the intensity will be biased close to the sample points, and due to the coincidence of these sample points, we get a skewed estimate of the power distribution. Using connectivity information between rays, we can determine the area over which each ray must deposit its power and thus eliminate the bias introduced through the locality based filter schemes.

Deposit Area Determination We maintain neighbourhood information between rays through the use of a dynamic caching system for each surface where the most recent set of rays and their collisions with the surfaces are recorded, thus for any new ray colliding with a surface, we can estimate local wavefront density by examining the last few ray hits. If enough information does not exist to determine the spread, deposition of power is postponed until new rays provide the required information.

Figure 4 depicts a subset of the rays from a light source incident on a surface, having passed through the scene, possibly interacting with specular surfaces. Only when ray number 4 hits the surface do we have enough information to

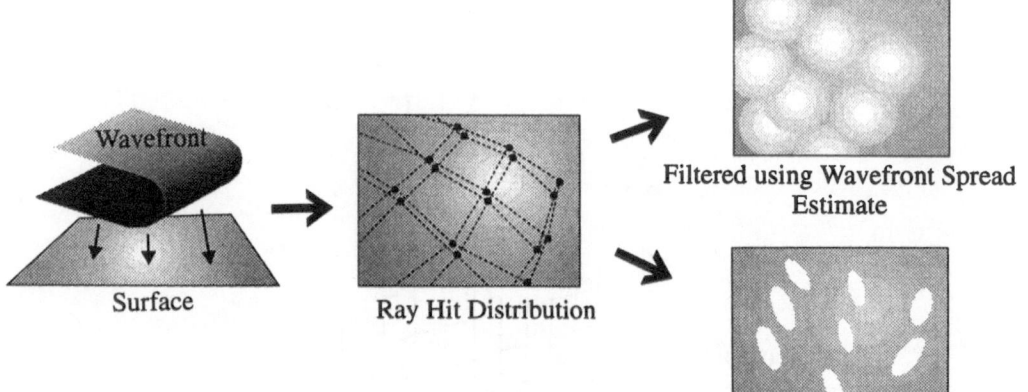

Filtered using Wavefront Spread
Estimate

Filtered using Nearest Neighbour Set
Estimate

Fig. 3. Effects of different filtering approaches.

estimate the spread of the wavefront. Rays 1 to 3 are cached until 4 arrives, and the estimated spread is used for all 4 deposits (as there will not be enough information to independently determine an estimate for rays 1 to 3). The spread estimate is simply the area of the polygon defined by the 4 ray hit points. This area is effectively the area over which we wish to deposit the power being carried by the ray.

Note that this area is proportional to the square of the distance the ray has travelled and also the cosine of the angle between the ray direction and the normal to the surface. Thus when we are depositing the ray's power onto the surface we need not scale it by the usual cosine and distance squared factor.

Power Deposition using Gaussian Kernels Having determined the area over which we wish to deposit the power, we must now decide how to distribute this power across that area. Rather than distribute the power uniformly which tends to result in aliasing at the edges of the regions (see [Wa90]) we deposit the power as a *splat*. This technique has been used to implement a progressive refinement algorithm for volume rendering [LP91] where Gaussian splats are used to represent a volume's octtree and the footprint of the splats scaled to match the projected area of the voxels making up the octtree. We deposit power, therefore, with the following kernel:

$$w(x, y) = e^{-\frac{z^2}{2\sigma}} \tag{5}$$

The footprint of the Gaussian kernel is scaled to match the areas defined by the ray collisions. Intuitively we felt that we might further improve the estimate by adaptively scaling the Gaussian spread factor, σ, according to our estimate of convergence/divergence. This surprisingly gave less accurate results as detailed in

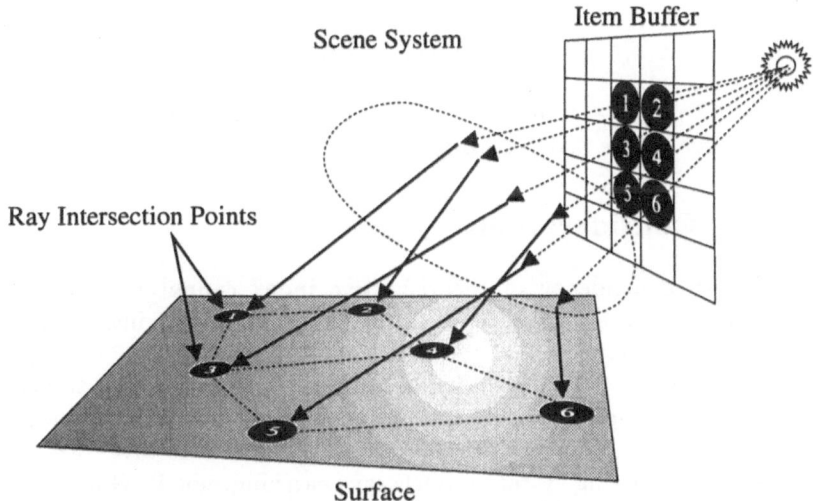

Fig. 4. Wavefront spread determination using ray intersection information.

section 4. Although the Gaussian is generally accepted as a good choice of kernel for filtering what is essentially a warped image [GH86], we have also investigated box, disc and cone kernel topologies. Based on the relative performance of the various kernels (see section 4), the Gaussian was deemed the best choice.

In order to deposit the kernel of power on the surface, the kernel must be warped into the parameter space of the surface. The kernel is then sampled by the illumination map to extract the power from the kernel and store it in the map pixels. Having sampled the kernel, thus necessitating re-normalisation of the kernel, the application of the splat is a 2 pass procedure:

1. Sample the kernel into a temporary buffer.
2. Normalise the buffer and apply it to the illumination map.

The current implementation assumes a rectilinear illumination map, thus the problem of warping is simplified to one of scaling. In order to speed up deposit times, an array of kernels is created before tracing begins. The problems presented by illumination maps on curved surfaces such as spheres have not been addressed. An improved kernel based on rotated elliptical Gaussians ([Go93]), designed to match the orientation and aspect ratio of the regions defined by ray-surface intersections is currently under investigation.

2.3 Eye Pass

During the eye pass, the illumination map is queried in a similar fashion to a texture map (though, unlike texture maps, it is not subject to shadowing). The power in each pixel of the illumination map is converted to intensity (with the assumption that the surface exhibits a constant BRDF):

$$L(x, y, \lambda) = \frac{\Phi_{(x,y)}}{\pi A_{(x,y)}} \qquad (6)$$

$\Phi_{(x,y)}$ is the power accumulated in pixel (x, y) of the illumination map and $A_{(x,y)}$ is the area of the pixel in world-space.

3 Spectral Considerations

The wavelength dependency of the refractive index cannot be ignored when attempting to render accurate representations of wavefront interactions with transparent media.

As a consequence of the *dispersion* of light as it passes through transmittive material we must sample the spectrum of light in order to correctly model light transmission. The sampling resolution is critical in order to resolve correct colour separation. The rendering system models rays carrying, not R, G and B values, but rather a spectral power curve, represented by n sample points.

3.1 Spectral Sampling

The choice of n is not clear. Musgrave, in his modelling of the rainbow, [Mu89], uses 13 samples, spread uniformly across the visible spectrum. Meyer [Me88], having examined a number of different sampling schemes, derived a new colour space, AC_1C_2, and using Gaussian quadrature techniques to integrate low order sampling polynomials applied to the spectral curve, samples into this new colour space. Having tried a number of sampling schemes, Meyer suggests a scheme where 4 samples are used.

For the sake of computational efficiency, we have opted for 7 sample points. The distribution of these sample points is driven by our desire to accurately capture dispersive effects that are commonly visible in real scenes. Our sample points are located around the wavelengths corresponding to the 7 colours of the rainbow. This clearly does not represent a definitive sampling scheme, however it produces satisfactory results. Figure 10 (see color plate 5) shows the effects of different spectral sampling resolutions. The test scene, Fig. 10(5) shows a prism and sphere of silicate flint glass. The prism is illuminated by a thin beam of white light which is dispersed to produce the spectrum on the back wall. Figure 10(a) details the results of 2 sampling schemes. The top 6 spectra result from initial rays hitting the prism being refracted, generating a number of new rays distributed (jittered) through the visible spectrum. The bottom 6 spectra detail a "fairer" scheme where each initial ray spawns only 1 refracted ray, the wavelength of which is determined stochastically.

All computations are performed with respect to these 7 sample points. For final image display however, we must convert to RGB space. This is achieved ([Ha89], [Pe93]) by multiplying the reconstructed spectrum by the CIEXYZ tristimulus matching curves, using Riemann summation to evaluate the integral, and finally converting the XYZ triplet to RGB space using chromaticity data for the monitor phosphors.

3.2 Light Source Data

Clearly to model the interaction of light with surfaces at a spectral level we need information regarding the spectral power curve of the light source and the frequency dependent refractive index curve for the surfaces. The light source data is usually obtainable from manufacturers and is available in the form of spectral energy distribution curves ($\Phi(\lambda)$) and the total luminous light power and must first be converted to spectral power (from luminous power) using the relationship ([LT92]):

$$\Phi_L = 683 \int_{380}^{780} \Phi(\lambda)V(\lambda)d\lambda \tag{7}$$

Φ_L is the luminous power, $\Phi(\lambda)$ the spectral power, $V(\lambda)$ the *spectral luminous relative efficiency curve* describing the sensitivity of the eye and 683 is a conversion factor from Watts to Lumens (the Lumen having been defined in 1979 at a meeting in Paris of the General Conference on Weights and Measures as the amount of light of monochromatic radiation whose frequency is $540 * 10^{12}$ Hz. and whose power is 1/683 Watt.).

3.3 Material Data

The *mean dispersion* ($\eta_f - \eta_C$) of a material defines the change of index of refraction of that material with respect to frequency and the following ratio is used to define the dispersive behaviour of a material (usually glass):

$$v = \frac{\eta_d - 1}{\eta_F - \eta_C} \tag{8}$$

η_F and η_C are the refractive indices of the material at the F and C Fraunhofer lines (the emission lines of hydrogen at 486.1nm(blue) and 656.3nm(red) respectively) and η_d the refractive index at the yellow d line of helium (587.6nm) rather than the sodium D doublet (589.3nm) used in older literature. This ratio is *Abbe's number*, also called the *v-value* or *V-number* of the material. A high V-number indicates a material of low mean dispersion. Manufacturers classify glass by a six digit code (the *glass number*), the first three digits of which is the refractive index $\eta_d - 1$ and the last three digits Abbe's number scaled by 10. For example a glass with number 523588 has a refractive index of $\eta_d = 1.523$ and mean dispersion of 58.8 [Me89]. Glasses with low mean dispersion (V-number above 55) are called crowns and glasses of high dispersion (V- number below 50) are called flints.

Using this information we can reconstruct a curve relating frequency and refractive index, and sample this curve at our spectral sample points to determine the index to use for our light-rays. Another approach is to adopt one of the many attempts to formulate a quantitative relationship between refractive index and frequency such as that of Herzberger [He59]:

$$\eta = A + B\lambda^2 + \frac{C}{\lambda^2 - \lambda_0^2} + \frac{D}{(\lambda^2 - \lambda_0^2)^2} \tag{9}$$

A, B, C and D are empirically determined constants, and λ_0 is set at 168nm. Values for A, B, C, and D are, unfortunately, difficult to come by and therefore the glass number is a more convenient representation. The glass used in the example scenes included in this paper has been modelled on Silicate Flint Glass with glass number 635577.

4 Results

Table 4 demonstrates the effect of light ray density on rendering times[1]. The corresponding images are shown in Fig. 5.

Fig. 5. Effects of increasing light-pass ray density.

Table 1. Effect of light pass ray density on image quality and rendering times

	Image A	Image B	Image C
Ray Density (rays\Sr)	7957.7	79577.5	795775.7
No. of Light Rays	3467	34680	346813
Light-Pass Time	11.57 secs.	53.27 secs.	379.22 secs.
Eye-Pass Time	148.33 secs.	144.72 secs.	135.96 secs.

In order to demonstrate the effects of illumination map resolution on the image quality, we have fixed the illumination map to three separate resolutions in Fig. 6. The images were rendered with illumination maps of (30,30), (100,100) and (300,300) respectively. The resolution differences have little effect on the rendering times.

---

[1] All the images were rendered and timings taken on a 486 66Mhz PC running BSD Unix. (©Berkeley Software Design Inc.)

Fig. 6. Effects of increasing illumination map resolution.

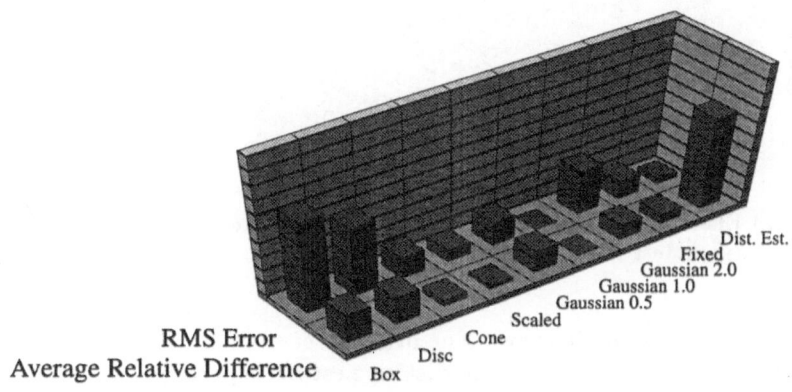

Fig. 7. Relative performace of various filter topologies and size.

Figure 7 details the relative performance in terms of RMS error and average relative difference (ARD) of some different choices of filter shape (box, disc, cone, Gaussians with $\sigma = 0.5, 1.0, 2.0$, adaptive) and size (scaled according to distance travelled by the ray, and a fixed size kernel). RMS error and ARD error are defined as:

$$\text{RMSerror} = \sqrt{\sum (I_s - I_r)^2} \qquad (10)$$

$$\text{ARDerror} = \frac{1}{n} \sum \frac{|I_s - I_r|}{I_r} \qquad (11)$$

I_r is the intensity of the reference map (centre of Fig. 8(a)), I_s the intensity of the source map, and n the number of pixels in the map.

Figure 8(a) depicts visually the performance of the filters with Fig. 8(b) indicating the test scene used to generate the data. As can be seen the Gaussian kernel with $\sigma = 1.0$ performs most satisfactorily. Note how the fixed kernel size results in an image that is indistinct, failing to capture the high frequency

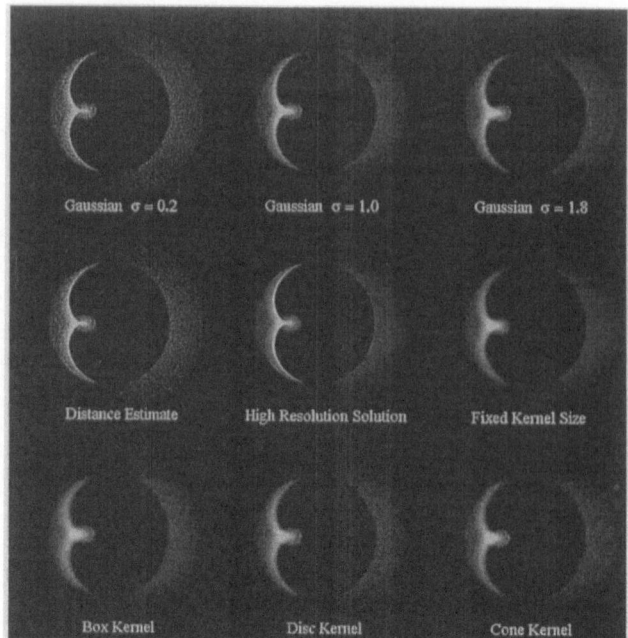
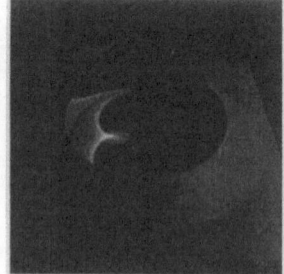

Fig. 8. (a) Effect of using different kernel shapes and size criterion with (b) showing the scene used to test the kernels.

aspects of the epicycloidic curve. The other filter shapes also fail to capture the clarity of the Gaussian kernel. The distance estimate performs surprisingly well in terms of RMS error, but results in a noisy image captured by the ARD error metric indicating that the error was present despite a low error variance.

Figure 9(a) shows the decrease in error as the number of rays increase. Figure 9(b) depicts the relationship between image quality and Gaussian spread factor σ. The error is at a minimum when $\sigma = 0.9 \ldots 1.0$.

To demonstrate the application of the system on complex objects, a classic example of caustic formation, the swimming pool floor, was rendered following the example of [Wa90]. Figure 11(a) (see color plate 5) is a view from above, and Figure 11(b) a view from below the surface of the water. As remarked by Watt, the triangular patch resolution of the waters surface is amplified by the caustic image, requiring very high patch subdivision resolutions. To avoid this we modelled the surface as a single polygon having a bump map composed of overlapping cosine terms [Ma81].

5 Conclusions

We have presented an algorithm extending existing specular to diffuse transport models with a view to capturing both high and low frequency artefacts through the use of adaptive Gaussian kernels or splats. We also extend the method to

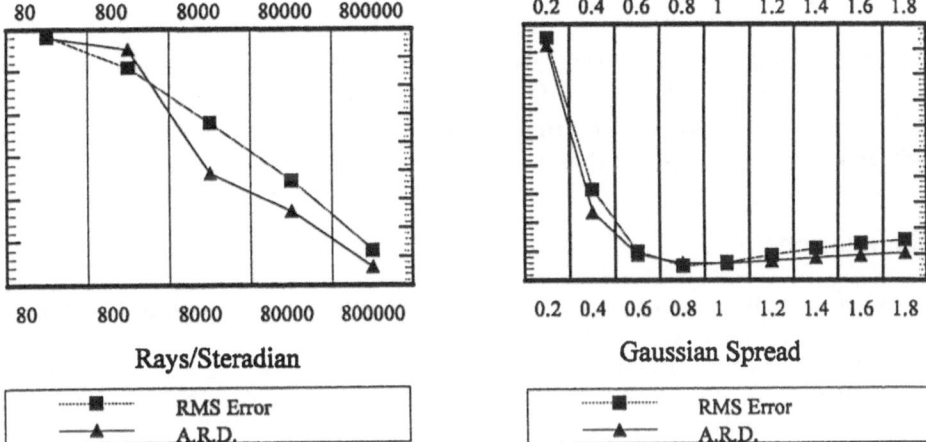

Fig. 9. Left image quality with varying numbers of light-pass rays and right different Gaussian kernel spread factors.

allow for accurate modelling of frequency dependent refraction of light with a view to capturing the beauty of dispersion. The algorithm has been designed to produce illumination maps to be used as texture maps in a real-time walk-through simulation system but can be used as part of a general purpose global illumination algorithm as an extension to existing ray-tracing/radiosity systems.

Through the use of the item buffer we can cut down on the number of first generation light rays and by adaptively scaling the illumination maps according to the average splat size we concentrate expensive map memory where it is most needed.

Many problems remain. In order to successfully handle surfaces with non linear parameter space we must warp the Gaussian kernels to the parameter space of the surface before applying the kernel. Our current implementation assumes rectilinear texture maps.

More intelligently constructed item buffers should be used in order not to introduce bias into the distribution of energy from the light source.

The illumination maps are typically very expensive in terms of memory usage, despite the adaptive strategy adopted here. We feel that a hybrid approach might be used analogous to that adopted for ray tracing space subdivision, where the best speeds have been achieved by a shallow octree of uniform grids. This would entail the illumination maps being added to surfaces as surface details (similar to the approach of [Wa90]), with potentially many illumination maps spread across the one surface.

The current spectral sampling scheme is quite primitive and could be improved through more attention to perceptual issues [Me88]. By importance sampling the spectrum of visible light with sample distribution proportional to the spectral luminous relative efficiency curve of the eye, more work will be done where the eye will perceive the difference.

6 Acknowledgements

I wish to thank my supervisor, Dr. Dan McCarthy for his continuous advice and support, Prof. John Byrne for continuing to support and fund this work, Pete Shirley for helpful information regarding global illumination and finally my colleagues in the Image Synthesis Group, Trinity College Dublin.

References

[Ar86] Arvo J., Backward Ray Tracing, *SIGGRAPH '86 Developments in Ray Tracing seminar notes*, Vol. 12, Aug. 1986.

[CRMT91] Chen S.E., Rushmeier H.E., Miller G., Turner D., "A Progressive Multi-Pass Method for Global Illumination", *Computer Graphics*, Vol. 25, No. 4, pp. 165-174, July 1991.

[CG85] Cohen M.F., Greenberg D.P., "The Hemi-Cube; A Radiosity Solution for Complex Environments", *Computer Graphics*, Vol. 19, No. 3, pp. 31-40, July 1985.

[Go93] Gotsman C., "Constant Time Filtering by Singular Value Decomposition", *Proceedings of the 4th Eurographics Workshop on Rendering*, pp. 145-155, June 1993.

[GH86] Green N., Heckbert P.S., "Creating Raster Omnimax Images from Multiple Perspective Views using the Elliptical Weighted Average Filter", *IEEE Computer Graphics and Applications*, Vol. 6, No. 11, pp. 21- 29, 1986.

[Ha89] Hall R., *Illumination and Color in Computer Generated Imagery*, Monographs In Visual Communication, Springer Verlag, pp. 45-62, 1989.

[He90] Heckbert P., "Adaptive Radiosity Textures for Bidirectional Ray Tracing", *Computer Graphics*, Vol. 25, No. 4, pp. 145-154, August 1990.

[He59] Herzberger M., "Colour Correction in Optical Systems and a New Dispersion Formula", *Opt. Acta (London)*, Vol. 6, pp. 197-215, 1959.

[ICG86] Immel D.S., Cohen M.F., Greenberg D. P., "A Radiosity Method for Non-Diffuse Environments", *Computer Graphics*, Vol. 20, No. 4, pp. 133-142, August 1986.

[LT92] Languenou E., Tellier P., "Including Physical Light Sources and Daylight in a Global Illumination Model", *Third Eurographics Workshop on Rendering*, pp. 217-226, May 1992.

[LP91] Laur D., Hanrahan P., "Hierarchical Splatting: A Progressive Refinement Algorithm for Volume Rendering", *Computer Graphics*, Vol. 25, No. 4, pp. 285-288, July 1991.

[Ma81] Max N.L., "Vectorised Procedural Models for Natural Terrain: Waves and Islands in the Sunset", *Computer Graphics*, Vol 15, No. 3, pp 317-324, August 1981.

[Me88] Meyer G.W., "Wavelength Selection for Synthetic Image Generation", *Computer Vision, Graphics & Image Processing*, Vol. 41, pp 57-79, 1988.

[Me89] Meyer-Arendt J.R., *Introduction to Classical and Modern Optics*, Third Edition, Prentice-Hall International, pp. 13-26, 1989.

[Mu89] Musgrave F.K., "Prisms and Rainbows: a Dispersion Model for Computer Graphics", *Graphics Interface '89*, pp. 227-234, 1989.

[Pe93] Peercy M.S., "Linear Color Representations for Full Spectral Rendering", *Computer Graphics Proceedings, Annual Conference Series 1993*, pp. 191-198, August 1993.

[WCG87] Wallace J.R., Cohen M.F., Greenberg D.P., "A 2-Pass Solution to the Rendering Equation: A Synthesis of Ray Tracing and Radiosity Methods", *Computer Graphics*, Vol. 21, No. 4, pp. 311-320, July 1987.

[Wa90] Watt M., "Light Water Interaction using Backward Beam Tracing", *Computer Graphics*, Vol. 24, No. 4, pp. 377-385, August 1990.

[WHG84] Weghorst H., Hooper G., Greenberg D.P., "Improved Comutational Methods for Ray Tracing", *ACM Transactions on Graphics*, Vol. 3, No. 1, pp. 52-69, January 1984.

Rayvolution: An Evolutionary Ray Tracing Algorithm

Brigitta Lange, Markus Beyer

Fraunhofer Institute for Computer Graphics, D–64283 Darmstadt, Germany

1 Introduction

In computer graphics the accurate simulation of radiant light transfer is an essential to realistic rendering. In general, for every elementary surface area within a scene the total irradiance incident from the entire half–space has to be accounted for. In a mathematical formulation this leads to a complex system of integral equations, referred to as *Rendering Equation* [Kaj86]. Since usually it is not possible to find a closed form analytical solution, the Rendering Equation is solved approximately by defining a probabilistic model of the radiation exchange process and applying *Monte Carlo methods*.

Monte Carlo integration is performed by *stochastic ray tracing*[Lan91], where the integration domain, i.e. the half–space of irradiance, is sampled by a finite set of random rays. The integral then is estimated by the weighted average of irradiance values calculated for each sample ray direction. The major problem of Monte Carlo integration is to determine the optimal location and density of samples in order to guarantee some bound on the variance of the estimate, which is equivalent to finding a probability density function that is a good primary estimator for the function being integrated. In general, this is impossible, since the irradiance distribution over the hemisphere above a point on a surface has many local peaks of different magnitude and both, location and magnitude of these local flux density maxima are unknown in advance.

Even well known variance reduction techniques, which will be discussed in the following, have to rely on a priori assumptions about the irradiance distribution and fail to adapt their sample distribution optimally to a particular lighting situation, because they neglect information gained from former samples. Therefore, the simulation process has to be optimized in such a way, that the irradiance information gained during sampling is exploited effectively, allowing the system to adapt itself to the actual irradiance distribution.

The technique presented here contributes towards a solution to this problem by means of *Evolutionary Algorithms* (EA). Rayvolution gives the stochastic process a direction by adaptively exploiting irradiance information. In analogy to nature a *population* of *ray individuals* evolves towards an optimal sample ray distribution by application of *genetic operators* and *selection* mechanisms. As a result we achieve an *implicit stratification* of the hemisphere into different regions which are sampled according to the irradiance information they provide. The simulation process now becomes self–organizing which allows the system to adjust itself to a particular lighting situation without having to make any assumptions about the irradiance distribution in advance. Thus a better convergence of the estimate towards the accurate value of the Rendering Equation is achieved which in turn results in an improvement of image quality.

In Section 2 we discuss classical variance reduction techniques for Monte Carlo simulation of radiant light transfer. In Section 3 we introduce Evolutionary Algorithms and present Rayvolution as a new approach to optimize the sample distribution by means of evolution. In Section 4 we examine the results and develop an alternative evolution model for the approximation of the Rendering Equation.

2 Monte Carlo Simulation

For a given point on a reflecting surface the total hemisphere of incoming radiation has to be accounted for in order to calculate the emitted radiance. Thus the radiance L_{out} of an elemental projected surface area $d\omega$ emitted in direction (θ_r, ϕ_r) is obtained by integrating the incident radiation over all directions (θ, ϕ) of the total hemisphere Ω, which leads to the following alternative form of the Rendering Equation:

$$L_{out}(\theta_r, \phi_r) = L_e(\theta_r, \phi_r) + \int_\Omega \rho(\theta_r, \phi_r, \theta, \phi)\, L_{in}(\theta, \phi) \cos\theta_{in}\, d\omega_{in} \qquad (1)$$

where $L_e(\theta_r, \phi_r)$ is the emitted radiance in direction (θ_r, ϕ_r) and $\rho(\theta_r, \phi_r, \theta, \phi)$ is the bidirectional reflectance of the surface.

Since it is impossible to follow all incident directions necessary for an accurate simulation, we use Monte Carlo methods and *path tracing* [Kaj86] and sample the hemisphere of incident radiation by a finite set of randomly selected rays. Although it is possible to approximate the Rendering Equation using uniform stochastic sampling and sample–mean Monte Carlo integration [Rub81], the convergence under most conditions is so slow, that such a solution is impractical.

The key to optimal convergence lies in variance reduction. This is achieved by altering the probability density in such a way, that the information gained from each sample is maximized. There have been made several attempts to increase the efficiency of the Monte Carlo solution through variance reduction techniques like *importance sampling* and *stratification* ([Dre91], [Kir91], [Shi91], [War92]). Importance sampling distributes the random variables according to the surfaces reflection properties but usually does not consider the irradiance distribution. Stratification is preformed explicitly by estimating the integrals of direct and indirect irradiance independently. This may become inefficient if there are too many light sources in the scene, because in this case it is very difficult to generate a set of appropriate sample rays. Although these variance reduction techniques reduce the number of samples, they have to rely on a priori assumptions about irradiance distribution. In order to reduce the variance of the estimated irradiance to tolerable levels for arbitrary surfaces, it still requires tracing thousands of rays, even if a combination of importance sampling and stratification is used. This is due to the fact, that the irradiance usually is a multimodal function, thus it is hard to determine a good primary estimator without any previous knowledge.

Another fundamental problem of classical variance reduction techniques is, that the information gained during the simulation process is not sufficiently exploited. The samples are distributed only once according to a predefined probability density function. Furthermore the irradiance information gained from each sample ray decreases with respect to the total number of sample rays. Therefore an adaptive sampling technique is needed which is superior to Monte Carlo sampling, in that it efficiently exploits irradiance information gained during the sampling process itself, thus giving the stochastic process a direction and improving the simulation process towards optimal convergence.

In the past Evolutionary Algorithms have proven to be powerful methods for global optimization problems in different fields of research, not using any predefined internal model of the objective function. They are robust even in the case of multimodal objective functions and provide mechanisms for self–adaptation. Due to these properties they are well suited to optimize the simulation of global illumination.

3 Evolutionary Algorithms

In nature, evolution, which is the process of adaptation of living organisms to their environment, can be regarded as a very powerful optimization method. Thus developing nature analogous problem solving strategies seems to be promising.

Evolutionary Algorithms are directed search techniques with a great versatility, that mimic the effects of evolution and natural selection. The most important ones being *Evolution Strategies* ([Rech73], [Schw75], [Schw77]) and *Genetic Algorithms* ([Gol89], [Hol75]). Each of these approaches is based upon a collective learning process within a population of individuals representing points in the search space of potential solutions to a problem given by the objective function. The individuals of an arbitrarily initialized start population adapt to their environment, by evolving towards better and better regions of the search space (in terms of the objective function) by means of probabilistic *selection* and *genetic operators* (*mutation* and *recombination*) in such a way, that the average quality of the individuals increases. Each individual is assigned a quality value which usually depends on the objective function. Selection is an operator of the evolutionary process that favors individuals of higher fitness to reproduce more often than those of lower fitness, thus guaranteeing survival of the fittest, and giving the process a direction. The recombination operator allows the exchange of genetic information, whereas the mutation operator accounts for genetic innovation.

This informal description leads to the rough outline of a general Evolutionary Algorithm depicted in Fig. 1. Here t denotes the generation number and $P(t) = (a_1, \ldots, a_\mu)$ is the population at generation t consisting of μ individuals $a_1, \ldots, a_\mu$.

```
t := 0;
initialize (P(t));
evaluate (P(t));
while not terminate (P(t)) do
        t := t + 1;
        P(t) = select (P(t - 1));
        recombine (P(t));
        mutate      (P(t));
        evaluate    (P(t));
od
```

Fig. 1. General Evolutionary Algorithm.

Evolutionary Algorithms have shown to be useful methods for the exploration of large search spaces using simulated systems of variation and selection. They achieve much of their breadth by ignoring information except that concerning payoff and they can tolerate extremely noisy function evaluation. Furthermore they find near optimal results quickly after searching only small portions of the search space. Due to these properties they seem to be well suited for the optimization of the sample ray distribution in order to approximate the Rendering Equation.

First we will examine how Evolutionary Algorithms apply to the calculation of irradiance and then the implementation concept of Rayvolution is presented.

3.1 Evolving Ray Distributions

If we want to apply Evolutionary Algorithms to the problem of calculating the total radiation incident to a given point, we first have to formulate the radiation calculation as an optimization problem. As mentioned earlier, the approximation accuracy in the context of Monte Carlo integration strongly depends on the sample ray distribution. This means we are looking for an optimal distribution in order to reduce the variance of the estimate.

Next, we have to find a suitable evolutionary model for the optimization problem above and define an Evolutionary Algorithm to solve it. The algorithm has to be designed in such a way, that it produces successively better approximations to the irradiance equation by exploring the total hemisphere of incident radiation; searching for those regions or sample ray directions that contribute significantly to the irradiance. Thus increasing the average information gained from each sample and converging towards an optimal sample ray distribution.

In contrast to the classical design of an EA, we have not chosen every individual to be a full representation of the solution. This would imply a population of ray distributions, which seems rather impractical, not only from the computational efficiency point of view, but also from the difficulties in defining an appropriate quality measure for individual ray distributions, as well as difficulties in designing suitable genetic operators.

In a figurative sense our approach can be described as follows: the hemisphere of incident radiation to an object point represents the biosphere for a population of ray individuals. These ray individuals now have to adapt to their environment by finding optimal living conditions for themselves. Thus they have to search for attractive places to settle down. With increasing attractiveness of their actual residence on the hemisphere their willingness to move decreases. The attractiveness or quality of life at a certain place depends on the irradiance at that place ("sunny places preferred") as well as on the population density of its surroundings [Bey94].

The goal of this settlement process is to find a suitable settlement structure, where the living conditions for all ray individuals are approximately equal. In contrast to classical Evolutionary Algorithms, where at last only one individual representing the optimal solution is searched for.

The process of finding an optimal settlement structure corresponds to the ability of the EA to exploit the information gained by individuals during the settlement process. In order to have no loss of irradiance information accumulative cartographic irradiance maps are produced during the settlement process. The process terminates if the irradiance map of the hemisphere has a certain state of accuracy.

In order to find all attractive regions of the hemisphere quickly and at the same time achieve an overall representative settlement structure, the Evolutionary Algorithm has to be implemented in such a way that there is always a balance between exploration of the hemisphere and exploitation of the information gained by it.

3.2 Implementation Concept

In the evolutionary model outlined above, a ray individual is defined by its ray direction (θ, ϕ) related to the local sphere coordinate system with cone angle θ and circumferential angle ϕ. This representation is appropriate, since it allows a problem specific design of the genetic operators. Furthermore individuals that are close to each other in the representation space are also close in the problem space [Mich92].

According to Fig. 1 the evolutionary ray tracing algorithm first assigns an initial population P_0 of μ ray individuals representing a set of random ray directions equally or stochastically distributed over the total hemisphere of a given surface point within the scene:

$$P_0 = \{(\theta_1, \phi_1), (\theta_2, \phi_2), \ldots, (\theta_\mu, \phi_\mu)\}, \tag{2}$$

where

$$\theta_i \in \left[0 \ldots \frac{\pi}{2}\right], \ \phi_i \in [0 \ldots 2\pi] \ (\forall i \in \{1, \ldots, \mu\}).$$

The evaluation of the initial population P_0 is performed in four steps, one for the calculation of the irradiance incident from each individual ray direction and three to calculate a fitness value for each ray individual.

The irradiance $L_{in} : \mathbb{R}^3 \times I \to C$ (where $C = \mathbb{R}^3$ is the color space of RGB triplets) associated with each ray individual corresponds to the objective function of the general EA.

The fitness $f_{fit} : C \times I \to [0 \ldots 1]$ of a single ray individual is determined by the difference between the individual's irradiance and an assumed background radiance for that direction. Since the overall contribution of the background radiance to the total irradiance can be calculated in advance, the main effort of the evolutionary search procedure can be spend on those regions of the hemisphere, where the irradiance differs significantly from the background radiance, i.e. regions, where the gain in information for the evaluation of the reflected radiance is high. In combination with the selection procedure, f_{fit} is responsible for the exploitation of information gained during the Rayvolution process, thus conducting a local search for regions considered to be important for the total reflected radiance.

The fitness value f_{fit} only depends on the irradiance value measured by ray tracing. Therefore it does not describe the living conditions of each ray individual completely according to the settlement model defined above. In order to satisfy this model, also the population density distribution over the hemisphere has to be taken into account. The sharing function $f_{share} : [0 \ldots 1]^\mu \to [0 \ldots 1]^\mu$ considers the distance between all individuals within the population and reduces the fitness value calculated for each ray individual by f_{fit} according to the population density of its neighborhood. Therefore it also reduces the fitness difference within the population, and in combination with the selection procedure it leads towards a global search process exploring the total hemisphere.

In order to achieve an appropriate balance between exploration and exploitation, i. e. between global and local search, the fitness values given by f_{fit} are scaled by the scaling function $f_{scale} : [0 \ldots 1]^\mu \to [0 \ldots 1]^\mu$ before f_{share} is applied. f_{scale} is constructed in such a way that the minimum fitness value $f_{fit_{min}}$ within the population remains unchanged whereas all other fitness values are scaled linearly so that the maximum scaled fitness value $f_{scale_{max}}$ does not exceed $f_{fit_{min}}$ times a constant factor m_{scale}.

The functionality described so far allows to initialize and rate the population of rays which then will evolve until a termination condition is reached. If for a number of successive generations there is no significant change in the radiance value estimated, then there is no more gain in information and the process terminates.

A new population is derived from the old one by first generating an intermediate generation of $\mu + \lambda_o$ individuals, where λ_o is the number of offsprings. Then from this intermediate generation the μ best individuals are selected in terms of their scaled and shared fitness values.

The offsprings are produced by randomly selecting a subpopulation of λ_o parents and applying a genetic mutation operator $m : I^{\lambda_o} \rightarrow I^{\lambda_o}$.

The mutation operator is the most important operator of the process. It is designed in such a way that it models a directed search for attractive regions of the hemisphere, thus allowing the individuals to move around with the goal to find a place with higher quality of life. It produces new individuals through altering the ray directions of the parents in dependence of their scaled and shared fitness values.

Based on the observation that the indirect irradiance tends to change slowly over a surface [War92], the start population P_0 for a given object point can be initialized with the evolved ray distribution of a neighboring object point. Thus information is exploited not only during the sampling process but also within the image space.

4 Results

With the evolutionary algorithm described above it is possible to evolve sample ray distributions which adapt themselves to the lighting situation at a given object point, thus achieving an implicit and flexible stratification of the hemisphere of that point suitable for reducing the variance of the estimated total irradiance value.

Figure 2 (see color plate 6) compares a typical final sample ray distribution produced by the Rayvolution algorithm to a Monte Carlo sample ray distribution, where only importance sampling is performed according to the surface reflection properties (For the geometry of the corresponding scene refer to Fig. 4, color plate 6).

Comparing both ray distributions it is evident that the Monte Carlo algorithm spends a lot of its effort in regions of the hemisphere, where the irradiance information is low. In contrast, the Evolutionary Algorithm directs the sampling process towards those regions with large payoff in irradiance information. Particularly the concentration of rays in the range of the white light source becomes evident.

Rayvolution's optimized sample ray distribution has a positive influence on the image quality which becomes noticeable in a significant reduction of overall noise in case of diffuse surfaces.

One problem of the Rayvolution algorithm, however, lies in the calculation of the estimated total irradiance based on the final sample ray distribution. In contrast to the Monte Carlo sample distribution there exists no analytical description of the probability density function. Therefore the integral has to be evaluated by mapping the evolved ray individuals to a hemispherical grid or by performing a *Delaunay*-triangulation of the hemisphere, which leads to an undesirable increase of computational cost. In order to avoid the explicit mapping of rays to solid angles, we have developed an alternative evolutionary algorithm, where solid angles are implicitly accounted for. The concept here is to maximize the confidence in our estimate by an evolutionary stratification of the hemisphere. Thus the hemisphere represents a population of irradiated solid angles, i.e. spherical triangles with sample rays at their vertices, see also Fig. 3(color plate 6). The quality of life for each individual triangle depends on its size, the associated mean irradiance and its variance with respect to neighboring triangles, thus being a measure for confidence. The goal now is to reduce the variance by achieving a stratification of the hemisphere into solid angles of equal confidence. The genetic operators model a population growth by cell–splitting, i.e. subdividing the individuals into triangles, until all individuals have an almost equal quality of life, see Fig. 3 (color plate 6). The advantages of this method are fast convergence and computational efficiency, since the evolution process and the evaluation of the integral can be effectively combined by using the same data structures. It produces successively better approximations to the integral equation by exploring the hemisphere, searching for those solid angles that contribute significantly to the total irradiance. Thus increasing the average information value of the samples and converging towards the best approximation, which in turn results in an improvement of image quality (see Fig. 4, color plate 6).

The evolutionary algorithms described above have been implemented within an open configurative test and visualization environment in order to enable the comparison to different Monte Carlo sampling techniques and to other possible evolutionary and non–evolutionary simulation methods.

5 Conclusions

The main objective approximating the Rendering Equation is to minimize the variance of the estimate. This implies an optimization of the sample ray distribution used. Since the irradiance distribution over the hemisphere is unknown in advance, Monte Carlo sampling techniques, which use predefined probability density functions, have to rely on a priori assumptions and are mostly inefficient. Adaptive sampling techniques are superior, because they use information gained during the sampling process itself to generate a subset of new samples in each adaptation step. We have shown that in order to exploit this information nature analogous techniques like the evolutionary sampling algorithms described above can be successfully applied. In contrast to classical Monte Carlo methods Rayvolution achieves a self–adaptation of the sample ray distribution to a particular lighting situation. In order to avoid computational effort for the final evaluation of the integral, an alternative evolutionary approach has been investigated. In this approach not sample directions but solid angles are subject to evolution. The confidence in the estimate is maximized by evolutionary subdividing the integration domain according to local and regional irradiance information, which in turn results in a fast convergence towards the optimum.

6 Acknowledgements

The authors would like to thank Dr. Christoph Hornung for his comments and useful discussions on the topic.

References

[Bey94]   Beyer, Markus: *Approximation der Rendering Equation durch Evolutionäre Algorithmen*. Technische Hochschule Darmstadt, Diplomarbeit, 1994.

[Dre91]   Drettakis, G.; Fiume, E.: *Structure–Directed Sampling, Reconstruction and Data Representation for Global Illumination*. Proceedings of the Second Eurographics Workshop on Rendering, 1991.

[Gol89]   Goldberg, David E.: *Genetic Algorithms in Search, Optimization and Machine Learning*. Reading, Massachusetts: Addison–Wesley, 1989.

[Hol75]   Holland, John H.: *Adaptation in natural and artificial Systems*. Ann Arbor, Michigan: The University of Michigan Press, 1975.

[Kaj86]   Kajiya, James T.: *The Rendering Equation*. In: Computer Graphics (SIGGRAPH '86 Proceedings) 20(4), August 1986, S. 143–150.

[Kir91]   Kirk, David; Arvo, James: *Unbiased Variance Reduction for Global Illumination*. Proceedings of the Second Eurographics Workshop on Rendering, 1991.

[Lan91]   Lange, Brigitta: *The Simulation of Radiant Light Transfer with Stochastic Ray–Tracing*. Proceedings of the Second Eurographics Workshop on Rendering, 1991.

[Mich92] Michalewicz, Zbigniew: *Genetic Algorithms + Data Structures = Evolution Programs*. Berlin; Heidelberg: Springer, 1992.

[Rech73] Rechenberg, Ingo: *Evolutionsstrategie*. Stuttgart: Frommann–Holzboog, 1973.

[Rub81]   Rubinstein, Reuven Y.: *Simulation and the Monte Carlo Method*. New York: Wiley & Sons, 1981.

[Schw75] Schwefel, Hans–P.: *Evolutionsstrategie und numerische Optimierung*. Technische Universität Berlin, Fachbereich Verfahrenstechnik, Dissertation, 1975.

[Schw77] Schwefel, Hans–P.: *Numerische Optimierung von Computer–Modellen mittels der Evolutionsstrategie*. Basel, Birkhäuser, 1977.

[Shi91]   Shirley, Peter S.: *Physically Based Lighting Calculations for Computer Graphics*. Urbana, University of Illinois, PhD Thesis, 1991.

[War92]   Ward, Gregory J.: *The RADIANCE Lighting Simulation System*. Global Illumination, ACM SIGGRAPH'92; Course Notes of the 19th Annual Conference & Exhibition on Computer Graphics and Interactive Techniques, July 1992.

Bidirectional Estimators for Light Transport

Eric Veach, Leonidas Guibas

Computer Science Department, Stanford University

Abstract

Most of the research on the global illumination problem in computer graphics has been concentrated on finite-element (radiosity) techniques. Monte Carlo methods are an intriguing alternative which are attractive for their ability to handle very general scene descriptions without the need for meshing. In this paper we study techniques for reducing the sampling noise inherent in pure Monte Carlo approaches to global illumination. Every light energy transport path from a light source to the eye can be generated in a number of different ways, according to how we partition the path into an initial portion traced from a light source, and a final portion traced from the eye. Each partitioning gives us a different unbiased estimator, but some partitionings give estimators with much lower variance than others. We give examples of this phenomenon and describe its significance. We also present work in progress on the problem of combining these multiple estimators to achieve near-optimal variance, with the goal of producing images with less noise for a given number of samples.

1 Introduction

Many techniques have been proposed for solving the problem of global illumination in computer graphics. By far the simplest of these algorithms are the *pure Monte Carlo* (MC) methods. These methods have several other advantages: they guarantee that the *expected* value of the solution at each image pixel is correct (compared with the true mathematical solution); they require almost no storage beyond the scene model itself; and they can be applied to arbitrary surface geometries and reflectance functions in a clean, uniform way. The interface to the scene model is particularly nice—all operations access the scene as an object-oriented *black box*, allowing truly procedural geometric and reflection models. Pure MC methods do not suffer from many of the artifacts and limitations that must be addressed by radiosity techniques[8, 9, 10] ("blocky" appearance, Mach bands, missing shadows, limited reflectance models), making them an excellent choice for the validation of other methods.

However, Monte Carlo methods have one well-known drawback: *noise*. The focus of this research is to determine to what extent this noise is an inherent limitation. That is, how far can MC methods be taken in terms of variance reduction, without adding bias to the solution? Many techniques for variance reduction have been described in the Monte Carlo literature[1, 2] (e.g. importance sampling, stratified sampling) and have long been used by the computer graphics community[3, 6, 7, 5]. Yet even with these techniques, there are many reasonable scenes for which current MC algorithms are not practical. Our goal is the development of new variance reduction methods that exploit the special properties of global illumination.

In this paper, we restrict ourselves to *pure* Monte Carlo methods for global illumination. These are methods which

- give an unbiased estimate at every pixel,
- have no correlation between the errors at different pixels,
- work for general surface geometries and reflectance functions, and
- do not require any data structures in object space (such as a subdivision of surfaces into patches).

For example, MC methods which express the solution as a linear combination of basis functions are not pure, since this introduces correlations between the errors at different pixels. Pure methods are attractive because the only image artifact is noise; thus if an image we compute does *not* appear to be noisy, we have strong reason to believe that it is correct. Pure methods include distribution ray tracing[3] and path tracing[6]. Many variants on these techniques are possible[4, 6, 5].

All *pure* MC techniques described in the literature have one feature in common: rays are traced only from the eye, not from the light sources. Techniques such as *light ray tracing*[15, 13], *bidirectional ray tracing*[16, 12], and *Monte Carlo radiosity*[14, 11] all use the light rays to deposit energy on surface patches. Since this requires a mesh in object space, these methods are not "pure" for the purpose of this paper. Also, these techniques do not extend well to environments with many small patches[17] or to non-diffuse surfaces[18, 19, 20].

Lafortune and Willems[21] have independently developed a "bidirectional path tracing" technique which uses some of the ideas presented in this paper. However their framework does not recognize explicitly the multiple estimators for each path length, or the problem of optimally combining them.

Let's consider a specific cause of noise in MC images: highly non-uniform incoming illumination. The problem is that the outgoing illumination L_o is essentially the product of the incoming illumination L_i with a reflection term; generally we can obtain accurate local information about the reflection term but not about L_i. For this reason, existing methods sample where the reflection term is large (importance sampling). However if L_i is highly non-uniform (for example 99% of the light comes from only 1% of the hemisphere of solid angles), this strategy is a poor predictor of the important sampling directions, leading to high variance.

In this paper we investigate pure MC methods which *balance* between sampling where the reflection function is large and where the incoming illumination is large. These methods build transport paths in two parts, one starting from a light source and the other from the eye. We show that there are k ways to evaluate the light flowing on transport paths of length k, according to where we break the path between the eye and light portions. We are also experimenting with techniques for *partitioning* the transport paths between the k methods to reduce the variance of our estimates.

Our results generalize the *direct lighting calculation*[6, 5], a common optimization for MC methods. Rather than following paths all the way back to the light sources, this optimization handles the last path segment specially. Our partitioning technique gives a rule for when the direct lighting calculation should be applied; there are some situations where it is not beneficial. More generally, our techniques address the problem of noise due to highly non-uniform *indirect* lighting. We demonstrate that noise from bright indirect light in typical MC images is due to following transport paths only from the eye.

This paper is organized as follows. Section 2 gives an outline of our rendering algorithm, along with several examples which demonstrate how it works. Section 3 describes a reformulation of the rendering equation as an integral over rays. We have found this useful in describing and analyzing the algorithm. Section 4 discusses the problem of partitioning transport paths among the rendering methods to reduce variance, and describes several ideas we are currently experimenting with to solve this problem. Finally, the Appendix describes a recursive formulation of the bidirectional sampling, and gives some additional mathematical details.

2 Outline of the Algorithm

The desired value at a pixel P can be expressed as an integral

$$\int_\Omega f(x)d\mu(x)$$

over the space Ω of all transport paths x, where the weight $f(x)$ is proportional to the contribution made to P by the light flowing along x (see Sect. 3,4). The largest contributions typically come from short paths, so we can either ignore paths whose length exceeds some threshold, or use *Russian roulette*[4] to terminate long paths without adding bias. This lets us partition the estimate at P into a finite sum; we estimate separately the contribution due to each path length k.

To estimate the contribution for a particular k, we use MC integration (Sect. 4). This involves randomly generating a path x of length k which potentially contributes to P, and scoring the contribution $f(x)/p(x)$ where $p(x)$ is the differential probability with which we generated x. To reduce the variance, we repeat the whole process M times and take the average (see Fig. 1).

```
1   ESTIMATE-PIXEL(P)
2       S ← 0
3       for n ← 1 to M
4           for k ← 1 to Max-length
5               x ← CHOOSE-PATH(P, k)
6               S ← S + f(x)/p(x)
7       return S/M
```

Fig. 1. Simplified pseudocode for estimating the value at a pixel P. CHOOSE-PATH(P, k) generates a path x of length k which potentially contributes to P. $f(x)$ is the differential contribution to P of light flowing along x, and $p(x)$ is the probability density with which CHOOSE-PATH generates x. In practice, the estimates for each k are not independent; we can incrementally add a segment to partial paths from the previous step(s), and save the effort of generating an entire path each time.

How should we go about generating paths of length k? In typical MC algorithms, paths are generated by following random bounces backward starting from the eye. The key feature of our algorithms is that they construct transport paths starting from *both* the light sources and the eye. The transport paths have the form

$$y_0 \rightarrow y_1 \rightarrow \cdots \rightarrow y_n$$
$$\rightsquigarrow x_m \rightarrow x_{m-1} \rightarrow \cdots \rightarrow x_0$$

consisting of a *light portion* $y_0, \ldots, y_n$ starting at a point y_0 on a light source, followed by an *eye portion* $x_m, \ldots, x_0$ ending at a point x_0 on the lens aperture. All x_i, y_i lie on surfaces of the scene S (see Fig. 2).

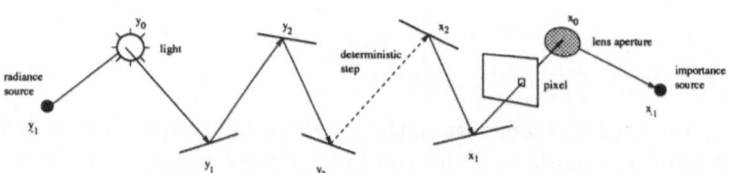

Fig. 2. A complete transport path. For symmetry with the first two light steps, we draw the lens aperture and film plane in the opposite order from a real camera.

The eye portion of a transport path is built by following a chain of m random bounces starting from the eye; this is "backward" relative to the direction light travels. Similarly the light portion is built by following n random bounces forward from the light source. The connecting segment $y_n \rightsquigarrow x_m$ is *not* chosen randomly; it is completely determined by the choice of y_n and x_m. Of course it is possible that segment $\mathbf{y}_n \to \mathbf{x}_m$ is occluded, in which case no light flows along this path.

By controlling the number of steps taken in each direction, there are k different methods for path generation; each segment is a possible breakpoint between the eye and light portions. That is, by taking m steps from the eye and n steps starting from a light source, we can generate a path of length $m+n+1=k$. The choice of m and n can have a large effect on the probability distribution of randomly generated paths; for example if we take all steps from the eye, the path distribution does not depend on the light source locations. This fact is crucial in obtaining good MC estimates, since the more closely the path distribution $p(x)$ matches the contributions $f(x)$ made by these paths, the lower the final variance will be (see Sect. 4).

In effect, each of the k partitioning choices leads to a different rendering algorithm for the light flowing on paths of length k. We define a notation for these algorithms: an (m, n)-*method* is one that generates transport paths by taking exactly m eye steps and n light steps (where $m+n+1=k$). Examples are given below.

2.1 Area Lights and Lens Apertures

Note that Fig. 2 refers to two additional points $\mathbf{x}_{-1}$ and $\mathbf{y}_{-1}$. These points do not belong to the scene S; they are *artificial* points that allow our algorithms to extend naturally to area light sources and finite-area lens apertures.

To model area light sources, we consider $\mathbf{y}_{-1}$ to be a point *radiance source* which distributes light energy to the emitting surfaces of the scene. We can think of $\mathbf{y}_{-1}$ as having a directional distribution on the rays $\mathbf{y}_{-1} \to \mathbf{y}$ for each point $\mathbf{y}$ of the scene. Since the point $\mathbf{y}_{-1}$ is entirely artificial, we can *define* the behavior of the light transport kernel K on these rays. In particular we define K so that after one "bounce"[1] the energy emitted along rays $\mathbf{y}_{-1} \to \mathbf{y}$ is scattered into exactly the desired emitted distribution L_e. This is like applying light transport in reverse; given an arbitrary distribution L_e, we define an artificial kernel that produces L_e after one bounce from a single point light source.

Similarly, we can model the effects of an arbitrary lens system as a scattering function from the external lens surfaces to an artificial *importance source* $\mathbf{x}_{-1}$. The directional distribution at $\mathbf{x}_{-1}$ assigns importance to the light arriving at each point on the lens surface.

In effect, this modification gives us two extra places to break the transport paths, since choosing a point on the area light source/lens aperture is considered a "step". It lets us handle problems involving arbitrary emitted light distributions and filter functions with the same methods that we use for a single point light source and a single pinhole lens. It is purely a formalism, in the sense that an implementation must still handle these cases specially. We can include multiple cameras and motion-blur effects with the same technique.

---

[1] We define a *bounce* as a single application of the light transport operator determined by K (section 3).

A *complete* transport path is now a sequence

$$\mathbf{y}_{-1} \to \mathbf{y}_0 \to \cdots \to \mathbf{y}_{n-1}$$
$$\leadsto \mathbf{x}_{m-1} \to \cdots \to \mathbf{x}_0 \to \mathbf{x}_{-1}$$

consisting of $k = m+n+1$ segments, where we maintain the convention that an (m, n)-method takes m eye steps and n light steps. The first light step $\mathbf{y}_{-1} \to \mathbf{y}_0$ chooses a random point on a light-emitting surface; the second chooses a direction in which light is emitted. Similarly the first two eye steps (from $\mathbf{x}_{-1}$) choose a point on the lens aperture, and a sampling direction that contributes to the current pixel P.

2.2 Algorithms for One Bounce

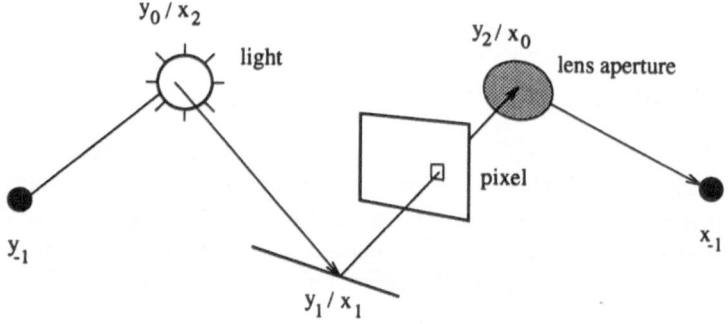

Fig. 3. This transport path leaves the light source, bounces off a surface, and passes through the lens aperture onto the film plane. We can generate paths of this kind in four ways, by taking differing numbers of eye and light steps.

Let's qualitatively examine the rendering algorithms we obtain for paths with $k = 4$. Such paths account only for light which bounces exactly once on the way from a light source to the eye (the bounces at $\mathbf{x}_0$ and $\mathbf{y}_0$ are artificial). Since there are four possible segments where we could break between eye and light portions, there are four possible rendering algorithms.

A. The (0,3)-method (see Fig. 3). The light steps are: choose a point $\mathbf{y}_0$ on a light source, choose a direction to get an emitted ray $\mathbf{y}_0 \to \mathbf{y}_1$, and follow it through one random bounce to get $\mathbf{y}_1 \to \mathbf{y}_2$. A non-zero contribution occurs only if this ray happens to pass through the lens aperture and strike the film plane near the pixel P. This is exactly what happens with a real camera.

B. The (1,2)-method. The two light steps choose an emitted ray $\mathbf{y}_0 \to \mathbf{y}_1$. The eye step chooses a point $\mathbf{x}_0$ on the lens aperture. To contribute, y_1 must be visible to x_0 in the small range of directions corresponding to pixel P (and of course $y_1 \leadsto \mathbf{x}_0$ must be unobstructed).

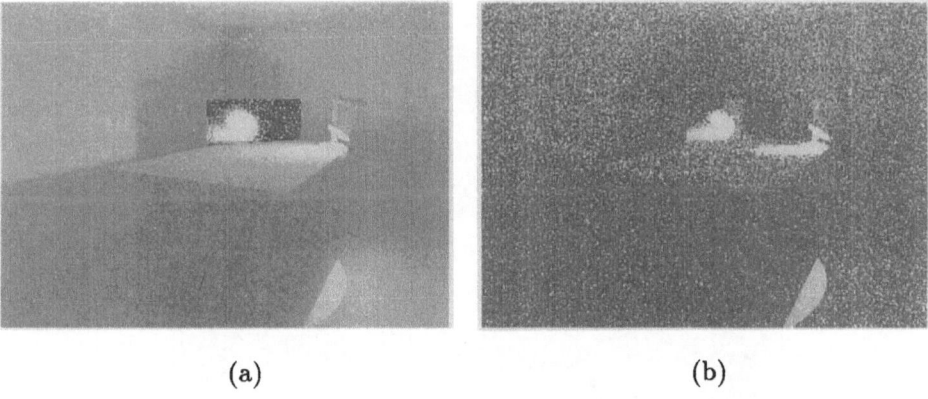

(a)   (b)

Fig. 4. (a) An image computed by building transport paths starting from the lights (in this case, a single point source inside the lamp shade). **(b)** The same scene using standard MC path tracing from the eye. See figures 13 and 14 for more detailed images.

C. The (2,1)-method. The light step chooses a point y_0 on a light source. The eye steps choose an aperture point and direction. To contribute, x_1 and y_0 must be mutually visible. This technique is the one normally associated with MC ray tracing, which follows paths backward from the eye, but computes the direct lighting separately.

D. The (3,0)-method. The eye steps choose a sample ray and follow it through one bounce. To contribute, the path must land on a light source. This technique is naive MC ray tracing with no direct lighting component.

Note that to get a sample contribution with any of these methods, not only must the connecting segment be unobstructed, but also the BRDF's at both ends must reflect some light along it.

Methods A and B seem impractical. However if we allow point light sources and perfect mirrors, it is easy to construct examples where these are the *only* methods (of the four) capable of producing a reasonable result. To see this, note that two or more eye steps result in a sample ray that is guaranteed to miss any point light sources. This deficiency is often seen in Monte Carlo or ray-traced images, where the effects of a point light source are visible but the light itself is not. (Depending on the filter function used over the image plane, a point source should be blurred over several pixels.)

A more practical example comes from the direct lighting calculation, i.e. the difference between methods C and D. It is well-known that if we view an area light source through a perfect mirror, the direct lighting calculation fails. Only a single point on the light source contributes to a transport path ending on the mirror; the probability of randomly choosing this point is zero. It is much better to follow the transport path backward through an additional bounce. More generally, if the surface is *almost* a mirror, the direct lighting "optimization" will give much noisier estimates than the naive method (although both have the

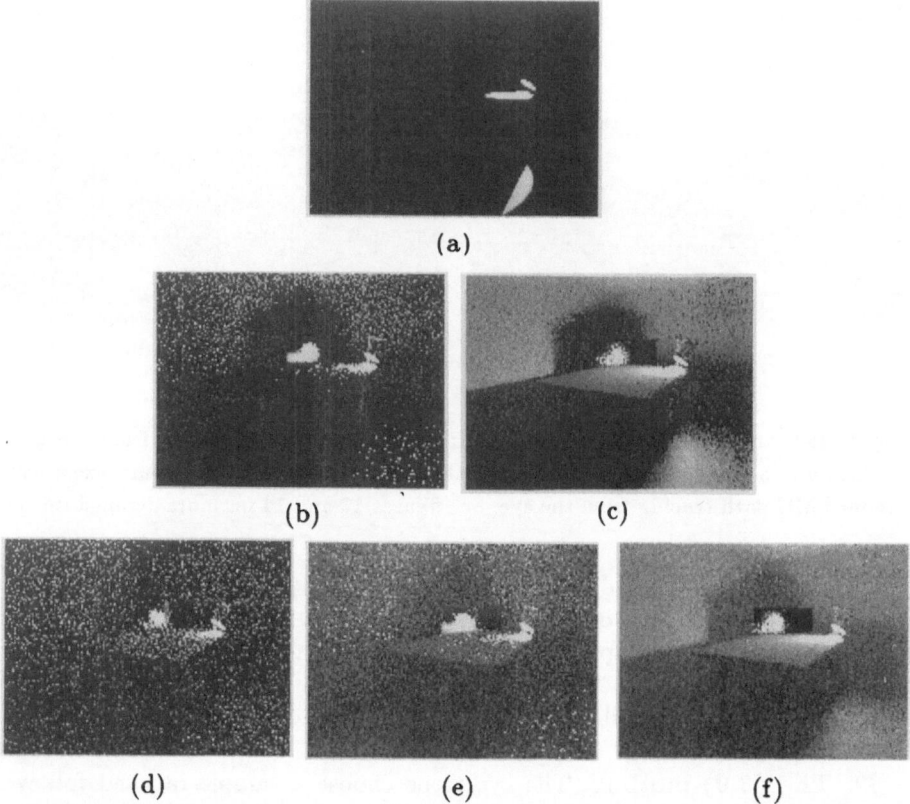

Fig. 5. (a) The direct lighting component (light which bounces exactly once on its way from the light source to the eye). It is rendered with the $(2, 1)$-method: two eye steps (to choose a viewing ray) and one light step (choosing the point on the light source). **(b,c)** The two-bounce component. The left image shows the $(3, 1)$-method, the right image shows the $(2, 2)$-method (i.e. the right image takes an additional light step). **(d,e,f)** Three bounces. From left to right, we have the $(4, 1)$, $(3, 2)$, and $(2, 3)$-methods.

correct expected value).

We emphasize that we are not claiming that these techniques (when $k = 4$) are practical in most scenes; they are simply examples of the methods which come naturally from our formulation of bidirectional sampling. For larger k, we *do* claim that the new methods can be superior in practice; the following section presents some evidence of this.

2.3 Two or More Bounces

As an example we have chosen a scene that is very challenging for pure Monte Carlo methods, to emphasize the differences between various techniques. The best images produced by our preliminary implementation are still quite noisy.

All images were computed with 50 samples per pixel.

The scene in Fig. 4(a) consists of a table, a desk lamp, and a shiny slab of metal in a closed room. All surfaces are diffuse, except for the metal slab which is Phong-specular. All light in the scene comes from a single point light source located in the lamp shade (the "bulb filament"). Because of this, almost all lighting is indirect. Most light is reflected one or more times within the lamp shade, and then it strikes the table top before illuminating the rest of the scene. This image was made with the new techniques described in this paper; it is the union of all $(2, k)$-methods (all steps taken from the lights, except for the choice of initial viewing ray).

A standard MC image made with the same number of samples is substantially more noisy and darker (Fig. 4(b)). The reason is clear when we examine the surfaces that are lit directly (Fig. 5(a)). Even with the direct lighting optimization, a transport path must randomly strike one of these directly lit regions to make any contribution, and most of the light energy after one bounce is concentrated on the interior of the lamp shade and a small area of the table. In terms of the (m, n) notation defined above, this image is the union all $(k, 1)$-methods.

Note that Fig. 4(a) and (b) should have the same average brightness, since both give the correct expected value at each pixel. The reason for the discrepancy is that most white pixels in Fig. 4(b) are actually much brighter than could be displayed, and have been truncated at a maximum value.

Fig. 5 shows various possibilities for rendering the light due to one, two, and three physical bounces (the first 3 components of the steady-state solution). The $(k, 1)$-methods correspond to standard Monte Carlo with the direct lighting optimization. Our implementation does not yet support the $(0, k)$- and $(1, k)$-methods, although this should be easy to do. The images have been computed at low resolution (160 by 120) so that individual pixels can be seen. It was necessary to brighten these images relative to Fig. 4, since each image accounts for only a fraction of the light in the scene.

3 Light Transport in Ray Form

To analyze our algorithms, we have found it useful to reformulate the rendering equation[6] as an integral over *rays*. This leads to a very simple expression for the kernel; the geometric terms are hidden in the *measure function* we use for the inner product. We find that the *ray measure* simplifies the description of bidirectional sampling, and is very useful when dealing with general filter functions and light distributions.

3.1 Local Form

Pat Hanrahan has written an excellent development of the following material which can be found in [22]. Please consult this reference for an explanation of terms not defined here.

Light transport is described by an integral equation of the form:

$$L_o(\mathbf{x}, \boldsymbol{\omega}_o) = L_e(\mathbf{x}, \boldsymbol{\omega}_o) + \tag{1}$$
$$\int_{\Omega_{4\pi}} K_L(\mathbf{x}, \boldsymbol{\omega}_o, \boldsymbol{\omega}_i) L_i(\mathbf{x}, \boldsymbol{\omega}_i)\, d\omega_i \ .$$

We call this the *local* form of light transport equation, because all quantities are expressed in terms of $\mathbf{x}$. It expresses the relation between incoming and outgoing light at a particular point $\mathbf{x}$ on a surface of the scene S.

The function K_L is called the *kernel* of the integral equation, and describes how light is scattered. For reflectance functions from surfaces, K_L has the form

$$K_L(\mathbf{x}, \boldsymbol{\omega}_o, \boldsymbol{\omega}_i) = f_r(\mathbf{x}, \boldsymbol{\omega}_o, \boldsymbol{\omega}_i) \cos(\theta_i)$$

where f_r is the bidirectional reflectance distribution function (BRDF) and θ_i measures the angle between ω_i and the surface normal at $\mathbf{x}$. Physically accurate surface reflection models lead to a symmetric BRDF, i.e. $f_r(\mathbf{x}, \boldsymbol{\omega}_o, \boldsymbol{\omega}_i) = f_r(\mathbf{x}, \boldsymbol{\omega}_i, \boldsymbol{\omega}_o)$ due to a physical principle known as *Helmholtz reciprocity* [22].

3.2 Three-Point Form

We can express L_i in terms of L_o via a change of variables to get the *three-point* form of the rendering equation (note that $\mathbf{x}$ is now $\mathbf{x}'$, and L_o is now L):

$$L(\mathbf{x}' \to \mathbf{x}'') = L_e(\mathbf{x}' \to \mathbf{x}'') + \tag{2}$$
$$\int_S K_3(\mathbf{x} \to \mathbf{x}' \to \mathbf{x}'') L(\mathbf{x} \to \mathbf{x}')\, d\mathbf{x} \ .$$

The integration is now over the scene S, and the kernel is given by

$$K_3(\mathbf{x} \to \mathbf{x}' \to \mathbf{x}'') = f_r(\mathbf{x} \leftrightarrow \mathbf{x}' \leftrightarrow \mathbf{x}'')\, V(\mathbf{x} \leftrightarrow \mathbf{x}')$$
$$\cdot \frac{\cos(\theta) \cos(\theta')}{\|\mathbf{x} - \mathbf{x}'\|^2} \ .$$

3.3 Ray Form

Note that the domain of L is a 4-dimensional space, the space of all *rays*. However, the integration in (2) is taken only over a 2-dimensional subset (those rays $\mathbf{x} \to \mathbf{x}'$ where $\mathbf{x}'$ is fixed). It seems natural to integrate instead over the domain of all rays, which leads to the *ray* form of the rendering equation:

$$L(\mathbf{x}) = L_e(\mathbf{x}) + \int_R K_R(\mathbf{x}, \mathbf{y}) L(\mathbf{y})\, d\mu(\mathbf{y}) \tag{3}$$

where $\mathbf{x} = \mathbf{x} \to \mathbf{x}'$ and $\mathbf{y} = \mathbf{y} \to \mathbf{y}'$ are rays, and R contains all rays with $\mathbf{y}, \mathbf{y}' \in S$. Not all rays contribute equally; this is controlled by the measure function

$$d\mu(\mathbf{y} \to \mathbf{y}') = V(\mathbf{y} \leftrightarrow \mathbf{y}') \cdot \frac{\cos(\theta) \cos(\theta')}{\|\mathbf{y} - \mathbf{y}'\|^2}\, d\mathbf{y}\, d\mathbf{y}'$$

where $V(\mathbf{y} \leftrightarrow \mathbf{y}')$ is 1 if $\mathbf{y}$ and $\mathbf{y}'$ are mutually visible and 0 otherwise. The quantity $d\mu(\mathbf{y} \to \mathbf{y}')$ is known as the *throughput* of a differential beam[22]. Finally, the kernel K_R describes the fraction of light travelling along $\mathbf{y}$ which is scattered along $\mathbf{x}$. For scattering to take place, we need a delta function which says that one ray terminates where the next begins:

$$K_R(\mathbf{x} \to \mathbf{x}', \mathbf{y} \to \mathbf{y}') = f_r(\mathbf{y} \leftrightarrow \mathbf{x} \leftrightarrow \mathbf{x}')\delta(\mathbf{y}' - \mathbf{x}) \ .$$

It is useful to think of the integration as an inner product:

$$\langle f, g \rangle \equiv \int_R f(\mathbf{x})g(\mathbf{x}) \, d\mu(\mathbf{x}) \tag{4}$$

and to think of K_R as defining a *light transport operator*

$$(T L)(\mathbf{x}) = \langle K_R(\mathbf{x}, \cdot), L \rangle \ . \tag{5}$$

T has an intuitive meaning: it describes the way light bounces (for the given scene S). If L is any light distribution, then $T L$ is the distribution after exactly once bounce. Using this notation, (3) has a very simple form: $L = L_e + T L$.

This is the essence of the ray form: a simple form for the kernel K_R, and a symmetric, intuitively meaningful inner product over the space of all rays. The framework is more general than the three-point form, since operators described in this way are closed under composition. (For example, the three-point form cannot represent the transport operator T^2.) This lets us think about general linear operators, where the output on a given ray depends linearly on the entire input distribution.

3.4 Filter Functions on Rays

In computer graphics, the goal is to compute intensity values at a discrete set of *pixels*. The value at pixel P is computed by integrating the solution L with a *weighting* or *filter* function W_P. Normally the filter for a given pixel is equivalent to point-sampling a convolution over the image plane.

The inner product over rays provides a simple way to manipulate more general filter functions. Rather than specifying a filter over the image plane, we supply a weighting coefficient $W_P(\mathbf{x} \to \mathbf{x}')$ for each ray. The integration to obtain a pixel value is written as $\langle W_P, L \rangle$, using the inner product over all rays. Note that W_P also models the effects of the imaging system. For example, we can model a simple finite-aperture "lens" by taking a standard pinhole camera and making the hole a little larger. The rays that contribute to W_P all pass through the aperture A and meet the film plane near P (see Fig. 6). For a pinhole aperture, W_P has a component which is a two-dimensional δ-function, reducing the inner product to a 2D integration over the film plane.

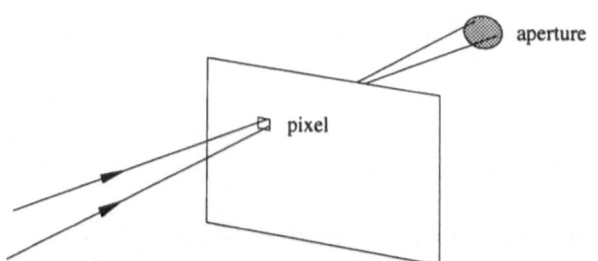

Fig. 6. Rays that contribute to the filter function for a given pixel P. For symmetry with area light sources, we have drawn the lens aperture behind the film plane (they obviously occur in the other order in a real camera!).

3.5 Importance Transport

Adjoint methods for the solution of integral equations have long been used in other fields, such as neutron transport[23, 24, 2]. A continuous adjoint formulation for radiance transport was first proposed in the computer graphics literature by [25], based on earlier work in [26] and [27]. We review this material here for two reasons: first, we believe that the inner product on rays helps to clarify the relationship between the rendering equation and its adjoint. Second, the idea of building paths from the light sources can be viewed as a direct solution method for the adjoint rendering equation. This idea has been applied in neutron transport problems[24], where in fact "direct" and "adjoint" methods have the opposite meaning they are given in computer graphics. Appendix A develops this relationship further. To our knowledge the bidirectional Monte Carlo techniques proposed by this paper have not been explored elsewhere.

Two linear operators $\mathcal{O}$ and $\mathcal{O}^*$ are *adjoint* if $\langle f, \mathcal{O}g \rangle = \langle \mathcal{O}^* f, g \rangle$ for all f and g, where $\langle f, g \rangle$ in an inner product (we use the inner product defined by (4)). The adjoint is not a complex notion; the corresponding idea for matrices of real numbers is the transpose operator.

If T is light transport operator defined by $(TL)(\mathbf{x}) = \langle K_{\mathrm{R}}(\mathbf{x}, \cdot), L \rangle$, then it is easy to verify that its adjoint is defined by

$$(T^*W)(\mathbf{x}) = \langle K_{\mathrm{R}}(\cdot, \mathbf{x}), W \rangle \tag{6}$$

where the only difference between T and T^* is the order of the arguments to K_{R}. What is the meaning of T^*? Just as T describes one bounce of a light distribution L, T^* describes a way to bounce the *filter function* W such that $\langle W, TL \rangle = \langle T^*W, L \rangle$. We speak of W as an *importance* distribution when it is propagated by T^* in this way.

We give a simple proof here of a result from [25], that except for a change in ray orientation, radiance and importance are propagated in the same way. We have

$$K_{\mathrm{R}}(\mathbf{x} \to \mathbf{x}', \mathbf{y} \to \mathbf{y}') = f_{\mathrm{r}}(\mathbf{y} \leftrightarrow \mathbf{x} \leftrightarrow \mathbf{x}')\delta(\mathbf{y}' - \mathbf{x})$$
$$= f_{\mathrm{r}}(\mathbf{x}' \leftrightarrow \mathbf{y}' \leftrightarrow \mathbf{y})\delta(\mathbf{x} - \mathbf{y}')$$

$$= K_{\mathrm{R}}(\mathbf{y'} \to \mathbf{y}, \mathbf{x'} \to \mathbf{x})$$

from which we see that (5) and (6) are the same except for the orientation of the rays. This shows that the importance on a given ray is propagated just as light flowing in the opposite direction. This is not to be confused with the notion of a self-adjoint linear operator $T = T^*$, since this requires a *symmetric* kernel K_{R}.

4 Partitioning for Variance Reduction

As in Sect. 2, we focus on the problem of estimating the contribution to a pixel P from light that travels on paths of length k. As outlined there, we have k methods for generating the transport paths, which lead to k algorithms for estimating the contribution to P. In the terminology of statistics, we have k different *estimators* for the same quantity. It is natural to ask under what conditions each of these k estimators has the lowest variance, or more generally how to combine them to get the best features of each one. In this section we describe several ideas we are experimenting with.

4.1 What Makes a Good Estimator?

First, let's examine how the estimators are constructed and why they should have different variances. We will need a basic principle of MC integration, namely that if X is a random variable with probability distribution $p(x)$ (with respect to a measure μ), then

$$\int_{\Omega} f(x)\, d\mu(x) = \int_{\Omega} \frac{f(x)}{p(x)} p(x)\, d\mu(x)$$
$$= E\left[\frac{f(X)}{p(X)}\right]$$

provided that $f(x)/p(x) < \infty$ for all x. Essentially this says that to estimate an integral $\int f$, we sample a point x chosen from an arbitrary probability distribution $p(x)$, and take $f(x)/p(x)$ as our estimate.

We need to relate this to the estimators for paths of length k. In our case, x is a transport path of length k, and Ω is the space of all such paths. The integral $\int f(x)\, d\mu(x)$ is just a reformulation of the inner product $\langle W_P, T^k L_e\rangle$ (see Sect. 3.4) as an integral over these paths:

$$\langle W_P, T^k L_e\rangle = \int_{\Omega} f(x)d\mu(x) \tag{7}$$

where $f(x)$ is proportional to the light flowing along x, (we call this the *transport coefficient* of the path), and $d\mu_k(x)$ measures the throughput of the path (we omit the details in this discussion). Finally, $p(x)$ is the probability density with which we generate x, which is different for each of the k estimators. Each estimator works by generating a path x, computing $f(x)$ and $p(x)$ for this path, and scoring a contribution $f(x)/p(x)$ (we average several samples from estimator to reduce the variance).

Let's examine why the methods generate transport paths with different probabilities. Each path is built by taking a number of steps, where at each step we randomly choose a local direction ω in which to extend the path. Let $\mathbf{y}$ be the current path endpoint, and let $p(\omega)$ be the probability distribution we use to extend the path. The probability density of extending the path to a point $\mathbf{y}'$ is

$$p(\omega)\,d\omega = \frac{p(\omega)\cos(\theta')}{\|\mathbf{y}-\mathbf{y}'\|^2}\,d\mathbf{y}' \; . \tag{8}$$

So we see the probability of generating a given path segment depends on the geometry (i.e. the length of the segment and the surface normals at its endpoints), as well as the choice of $p(\omega)$. Note that the probabilities of generating $\mathbf{y} \to \mathbf{y}'$ and $\mathbf{y}' \to \mathbf{y}$ could be very different, and this is exactly the distinction between using a light step or an eye step to generate this segment. Most important, for each of the k methods there is a path segment that does *not* need to be generated randomly (the connecting segment $\mathbf{y}_n \rightsquigarrow \mathbf{x}_m$).

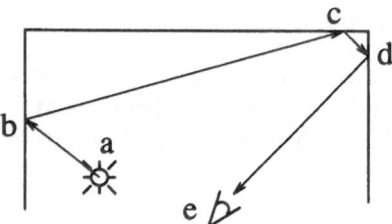

Fig. 7. The choice of breakpoint between light and eye steps has a large effect on the probability of generating this path.

For example, consider the path of length 4 in Fig. 7. What is the probability of generating this path if we take two light steps and one eye step, vs. one light step and two eye steps? In the first case we must generate **bc** but not **cd**, and in the second we must generate **dc** but not **cb**. Since **dc** is much shorter than **bc** in this example, by (8) the second method is more likely to generate the path **abcde** (other things being equal). It is this effect that causes the noise visible in figure 13 where two walls meet; there are important transport paths which are generated with very low probability.

Finally, we need to understand the relationship between a probability distribution on paths and the variance of the corresponding estimator. Let F be one of the *original estimators* $f(X)/p(X)$ described above. One way to write the variance of F is

$$\mathrm{Var}[F] = E[F^2] - E[F]^2$$

and since $E[F]$ is the fixed quantity we are trying to estimate, we want to minimize the second-order moment $E[F^2]$. If $E[F^2]$ is large, our image will be noisy. Examining $F = f(X)/p(X)$, it is clearly undesirable to have $p(x)$ small where $f(x)$ is large, since this makes a large contribution to $E[F^2]$. This effect is responsible for the large amounts of noise observed in figure 14.

4.2 A Discrete Analogy

Here is a simple analogy which demonstrates one idea that we are experimenting with. Suppose that only four transport paths contribute to the pixel we are evaluating (rather than an infinite number), and we have three methods A,B,C of path generation (i.e. these are paths of length three). We show the probability distribution of each method as a bar graph (Fig. 8). The paths are shown as bars with different shadings; each path appears in all three graphs (since each method can generate all the paths). However the bars have different shapes: the *width* of a bar is the probability $p(x)$ of generating path x; the *height* is the sample value $f(x)/p(x)$ (recall $f(x)$ is the transport coefficient for the path). Note that the bar corresponding to a path x has the same area $f(x)$ in all three graphs. This is necessary for the methods to be unbiased.

We want to combine these estimators in a way that remains unbiased (each path x occupies the proper area $f(x)$), but also has a lower variance. First we need to decide what sort of estimator combinations we will allow. A natural way to combine the estimators is a *partitioning*, where three new estimators A', B', C' each estimate the integral over a subset of the paths, and the final estimate has the form $S = A' + B' + C'$. The estimator A' uses the same method for path generation as A; however A' has the flexibility to discard samples when this is desirable, as long as the discarded paths are accounted for by one of B' or C'. We would like to find a way to minimize the variance of S over all such partitionings.

4.3 A Partitioning Heuristic

We noted above that minimizing $\text{Var}[S]$ is equivalent to minimizing $E[S^2]$ since $E[S]$ is fixed. This is the second-order moment of a sum $A' + B' + C'$. It turns out to be much easier to minimize the sum of the second-order moments, $E[(A')^2] + E[(B')^2] + E[(C')^2]$. This is not the same as minimizing the variance, but it is similar. To understand what this does, examine Fig. 8. Geometrically, the expected value $E[A']$ is the sum over each path of its rectangle area. Similarly the second-order moment $E[(A')^2]$ is the sum of each rectangle's area *times its height*. Intuitively, minimizing the second-order moment is good because it penalizes tall, thin rectangles; these "spikes" can make a large contribution to the variance.

How do we partition the paths to minimize this sum? Since each path x must be assigned to one of A', B', C', and the area of x is the same in all cases, we want to place x where it has the *greatest width*, i.e. the highest probability of being generated. We call this the *maximum heuristic*, which assigns each path x to the estimator that generates it with highest probability.

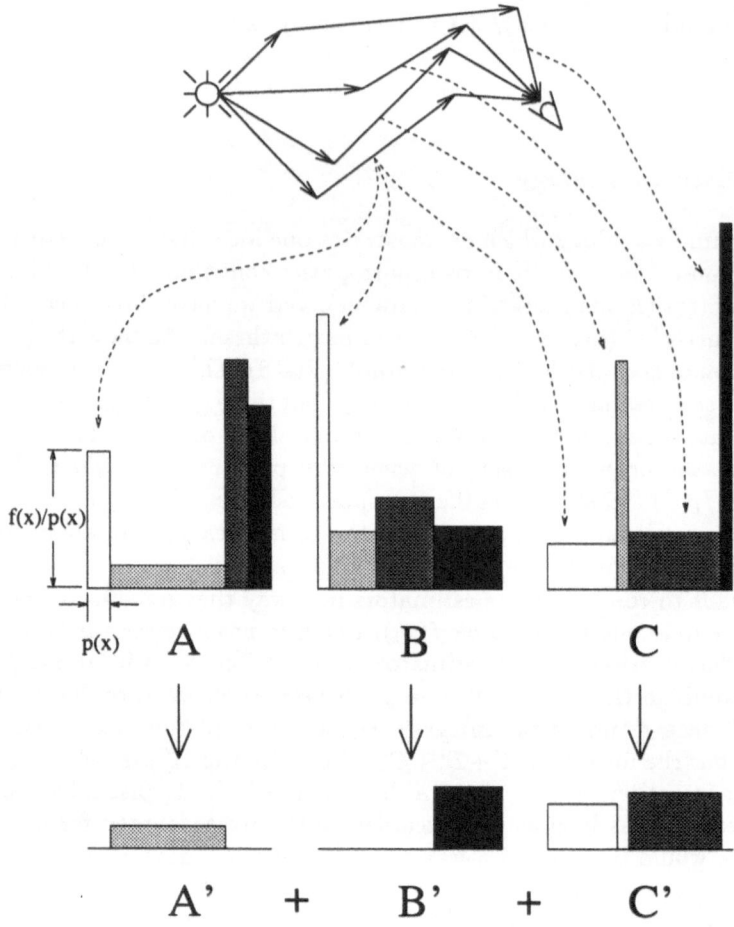

Fig. 8. The upper bar graphs show a discrete probability distributions on four paths for three estimators A, B, C. The lower bar graphs show a partitioning of the paths among new estimators A', B', C' which minimizes the sum of their second-order moments.

Pixel estimation using the maximum heuristic is outlined in Fig. 9. The basic idea (for $k = 3$) is to take one sample from each of A', B', C' and sum the results. Sampling from an estimator A' is easy: we simply take a sample x from A, then we compute the probabilities $p_A(x), p_B(x), p_C(x)$. If $p_A(x)$ is not the largest of these, we reject x and return zero. Note that once a path x has been chosen, it is easy to compute the probability with which any of the other methods generates it.

We are experimenting with several other heuristics that combine the original estimators in more general ways. For example, we can try to minimize the variance over all *weighted partitionings* of the paths. In our discrete example, this corresponds to splitting the rectangle area $f(x)$ among the new estimators, for each path x. We have some preliminary theoretical results about these heu-

```
1   MAXIMUM-HEURISTIC(P)
2       S ← 0
3       for k ← 1 to Max-length
4         for i ← 1 to k
5           x ← CHOOSE-PATH(P, k, i)
6           if p_i(x) ≥ p_j(x)  ∀j ≠ i
7               then   S ← S + f(x)/p_i(x)
8               else   (Discard x and score 0)
9       return S
```

Fig. 9. The *maximum heuristic* for combining estimators. CHOOSE-PATH(P, k, i) chooses a path contributing to pixel P of length k, using segment i as the breakpoint between the eye and light portions. Note that for efficiency, path generation for length k will reuse the eye and light portions from smaller path lengths.

ristics, but have not yet verified their effectiveness in practice. The goal is to automatically combine the best features of all the original estimators.

5 Acknowledgements

Thanks to Marc Levoy and Brian Curless for reviewing early drafts of this paper. Thanks also to Jorge Stolfi and Stephen Harrison for many stimulating discussions. This work was supported by the National Science Foundation (CCR-9215219), the Digital Systems Research Center, and the Digital External Research Program.

A Recursive Formulation

In this appendix we develop further the relation between bidirectional sampling and light/importance transport. The key is to show how taking a light or eye step reduces the estimation of $\langle W_P, L \rangle$ to a problem of the same form.

Recall that T denotes the light transport operator (5). As long as $\|T\| < 1$ (satisfied by all physically valid models), the formal solution to $L = L_e + TL$ is given by the *Neumann series*[2],

$$L = L_e + T L_e + T^2 L_e + \cdots \ .$$

The term $T^i L_e$ in the expansion represents the contribution of light which bounces exactly i times. Note that $\|T^i L_e\|$ necessarily decreases as i grows. For convenience we define the *solution operator*

$$S \equiv (I - T)^{-1} = I + T + T^2 + \cdots \tag{9}$$

(where I is the identity operator), so that the solution to the light transport equation is now just $L = S L_e$, and our goal is to estimate $\langle W_P, S L_e \rangle$.

A.1 Notation for Eye and Light Steps

We assume that W_P represents a pinhole lens with the point aperture located at x_0, and that the emitted light L_e is due to a single point light source at y_0. It will be convenient to define W_P and L_e as "slices" of the kernel K_R, i.e. as functions $K_R(x, y)$ where one of x or y is held fixed. In particular, we define $K_R(x_0 \to x_{-1}, x \to x') = W_P(x \to x')$ and $K_R(y \to y', y_{-1} \to y_0) = L_e(y \to y')$. We can think of the emitted light distribution L_e as the result of scattering energy flowing along a single (artificial) ray $y_{-1} \to y_0$, and similarly for W_P. We can still handle arbitrary light sources and filter functions by using the artificial point sources x_{-1}, y_{-1} as described earlier. However to describe these emitted distributions as slices of the kernel, we must take this one step further: the initial light is concentrated on a single ray $y_{-2} \to y_{-1}$ which is scattered into the distribution at y_{-1} by the first bounce.

For each eye step our algorithm will define an associated weighting function W_i, where $W_0 = W_P$. Similarly each light step introduces a new emitted radiance function L_j where $L_0 = L_e$. The algorithm works by estimating a sequence of inner products $\langle W_i, SL_j \rangle$, starting with the original problem $\langle W_P, SL_e \rangle$. The sequence of functions W_i and L_i will always have the following form ($i \geq 0$):

$$W_i(x) = K_R(x_i, x) \tag{10}$$
$$L_i(y) = K_R(y, y_i)$$

where $y_i \equiv y_{i-1} \to y_i$ and $x_i \equiv x_i \to x_{i-1}$ (Fig. 2). Thus each W_i is a "slice" of the kernel K_R that weights incoming rays $x \to x_i$ according to how much light they reflect along the outgoing ray $x_i \to x_{i-1}$, and similarly for L_i. Property (10) is an important invariant maintained by the following algorithm.

A.2 The Eye Step

To estimate $\langle W_i, SL_j \rangle$, we first apply the identity $S = I + TS$ (see (9)):

$$\langle W_i, SL_j \rangle = \langle W_i, L_j \rangle + \langle W_i, TSL_j \rangle .$$

We now need to estimate each of the two terms. By the assumption of (10), $\langle W_i, L_j \rangle$ can be evaluated exactly. In fact W_i and L_j can interact along only a single ray (Fig. 10):

$$
\begin{aligned}
&\langle W_i, L_j \rangle \\
&= \int_R K_R(x_i, x) K_R(x, y_j) \, d\mu(x) \\
&= f_r(y_j \leftrightarrow x_i \leftrightarrow x_{i-1}) f_r(y_{j-1} \leftrightarrow y_j \leftrightarrow x_i) \\
&\quad \cdot V(y_j \leftrightarrow x_i) \frac{\cos(\theta) \cos(\theta')}{\|y_j - x_i\|^2}
\end{aligned}
\tag{11}
$$

where θ and θ' are the angles between the ray $y_j \to x_i$ and the surface normals at y_j and x_i respectively. All terms in (11) can easily be evaluated.

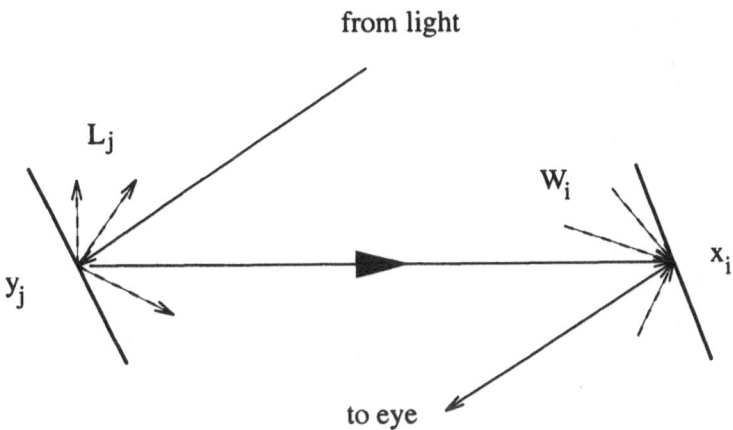

Fig. 10. The inner product $\langle W_i, L_j \rangle$.

To evaluate the second term $\langle W_i, \mathcal{T} \mathcal{S} L_j \rangle$, we use Monte Carlo sampling. Since W_i is zero except on rays of the form $\mathbf{x} \rightarrow \mathbf{x}_i$, we choose a probability distribution p_i which gives positive weight to rays of this form. (In practice, p_i is a distribution on the set of directions out of $\mathbf{x}_i$, i.e. the possible directions to extend our transport path). As long as $W_i(\mathbf{x})/p(\mathbf{x}) < \infty$ for all $\mathbf{x}$, we have

$$\langle W_i, \mathcal{T} \mathcal{S} L_j \rangle = E \left[\frac{W_i(\mathbf{x}_{i+1})(\mathcal{T} \mathcal{S} L_j)(\mathbf{x}_{i+1})}{p_i(\mathbf{x}_{i+1})} \right] \tag{12}$$

where $\mathbf{x}_{i+1}$ is randomly distributed according to p_i. The new ray is $\mathbf{x}_{i+1} \rightarrow \mathbf{x}_i$ where $\mathbf{x}_{i+1}$ is first surface point intersected in the randomly chosen direction (which we are following backwards relative to the direction that light travels).

All that remains is to evaluate the parenthesized expression in (12), which requires that we estimate $(\mathcal{T} \mathcal{S} L_j)(\mathbf{x}_{i+1})$. This is simply the problem we started with, in disguise:

$$\begin{aligned} (\mathcal{T} \mathcal{S} L_j)(\mathbf{x}_{i+1}) &= \langle K_{\mathrm{R}}(\mathbf{x}_{i+1}, \cdot), \mathcal{S} L_j \rangle \\ &\equiv \langle W_{i+1}, \mathcal{S} L_j \rangle \ . \end{aligned}$$

We have a new weighting function W_{i+1}, whose form is the same "slice" of K_{R} (10) that we assumed for W_i. The eye step is illustrated in Fig. 11.

We can apply this operation as many times as we like, building a transport path extending backward from the eye. We are actually building a family of transport paths, since each prefix of the path contributes to the sample value. At each step, the term $\langle W_i, L_j \rangle$ *connects* the current prefix and suffix to build a complete transport path from the light to the eye.

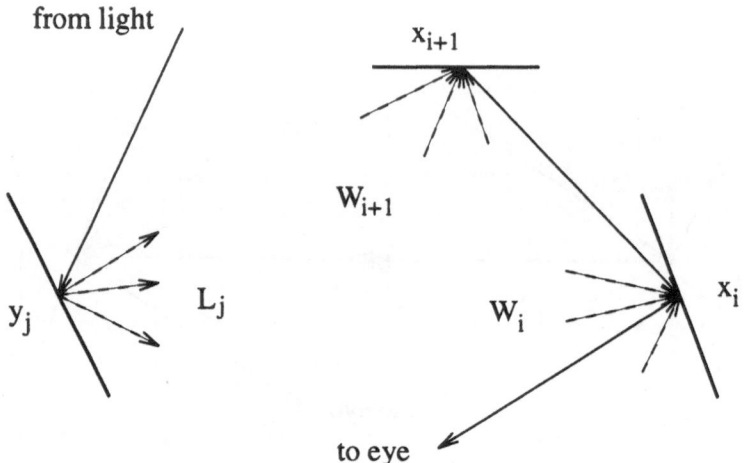

Fig. 11. The eye step replaces W_i by a new emitted importance function W_{i+1}.

A.3 The Light Step

To take a light step, we use the adjoint transport operator (see Sect. 3.5). Rather than estimating $\langle W_P, \mathcal{S}L_e \rangle$, we estimate $\langle \mathcal{S}^* W_P, L_e \rangle$, where $\mathcal{S}^* = [(\mathcal{I} - \mathcal{T})^{-1}]^* = (\mathcal{I} - \mathcal{T}^*)^{-1}$. To understand $\mathcal{S}^*$, consider the importance transport equation $W = W_P + \mathcal{T}^* W$. Its solution is the steady-state importance distribution $W \equiv \mathcal{S}^* W_P$. The value $W(\mathbf{x})$ is proportional to the contribution that radiance emitted along $\mathbf{x}$ eventually makes to the final solution $\langle W_P, \mathcal{S}L_e \rangle$. Thus we have two choices: we can either solve for the steady-state radiance L and compute $\langle W_P, L \rangle$, or solve for the steady-state importance W and compute $\langle W, L_e \rangle$. In fact we have more choices, since we can choose whether to propagate light or importance at each step of building a transport path. It is this observation that leads to k estimators for paths of length k.

We are now ready to describe a *light step*. Again we want to estimate $\langle W_i, \mathcal{S}L_j \rangle$, but this time we apply the identity $\mathcal{S}^* = \mathcal{I} + \mathcal{T}^* \mathcal{S}^*$:

$$\langle \mathcal{S}^* W_i, L_j \rangle = \langle W_i, L_j \rangle + \langle \mathcal{T}^* \mathcal{S}^* W_i, L_j \rangle \ .$$

The term $\langle W_i, L_j \rangle$ is evaluated exactly as before. For the other term, we have

$$\langle \mathcal{T}^* \mathcal{S}^* W_i, L_j \rangle = E\left[\frac{(\mathcal{T}^* \mathcal{S}^* W_i)(\mathbf{y}_{j+1}) L_j(\mathbf{y}_{j+1})}{q_j(\mathbf{y}_{j+1})} \right] \tag{13}$$

where $\mathbf{y}_{j+1}$ is a ray chosen randomly according to q_j (a sampling distribution for the rays contributing to L_j). Finally we need to estimate

$$(\mathcal{T}^* \mathcal{S}^* W_i)(\mathbf{y}_{j+1}) = \langle \mathcal{S}^* W_i, K_{\mathrm{R}}(\cdot, \mathbf{y}_{j+1}) \rangle$$
$$\equiv \langle \mathcal{S}^* W_i, L_{j+1} \rangle$$

which has the same form we started with, except for the new emitted radiance distribution L_{j+1}. The light step is illustrated in Fig. 12.

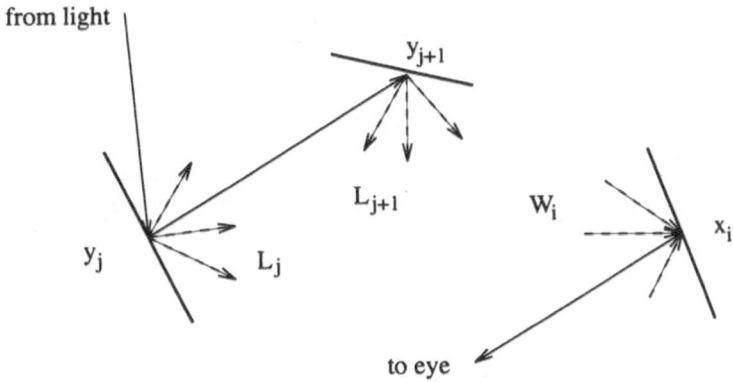

Fig. 12. The light step replaces L_j by a new emitted radiance function L_{j+1}.

Since both eye and light steps leave us with an estimation problem of the same form, we can apply some of each. A complete transport path consists of a prefix $y_0 \rightarrow \cdots \rightarrow y_n$ built by taking light steps, a suffix $x_m \rightarrow \cdots \rightarrow x_0$ built by taking eye steps, and a segment $y_n \rightarrow x_m$ that deterministically connects them.

Fig. 13. This image was computed using a pure Monte Carlo method which generates transport paths starting from the source. Single light source in the lamp shade. 900 x 675 pixels, 50 samples per pixel.

Fig. 14. The same scene computed using standard Monte Carlo path tracing, which builds transport paths starting from the eye. The scene is very noisy even with 50 samples per pixel, because most light comes *indirectly* from small, bright surfaces. Many of the white pixels are much brighter than that could be displayed (which is why the image is darker).

References

1. J. Hammersley, D. Handscomb, *Monte Carlo Methods*, Chapman and Hall, 1964.
2. M. Kalos, P. Whitlock, *Monte Carlo Methods, Volume I: Basics*. J. Wiley, New York, 1986.
3. R. Cook, T. Porter, L. Carpenter, Distributed ray tracing. *Computer Graphics (SIGGRAPH '84)*, **18**, 137–146 (1984).
4. J. Arvo, D. Kirk, Particle transport and image synthesis, *Computer Graphics (SIGGRAPH '90)*, **24**, 63–66 (1990).
5. P. Shirley, C. Wang, Luminaire sampling in distribution ray tracing. Technical Report 343, CS Dept., Indiana University, Jan 1992. Also appears in: *SIGGRAPH '93* Global Illumination Course Notes.
6. J. Kajiya, The rendering equation. *Computer Graphics (SIGGRAPH '86)*, **20**, 143–150 (1986).
7. D. Kirk, J. Arvo, Unbiased sampling techniques for image synthesis, *Computer Graphics (SIGGRAPH '91)*, **25**, 153–156 (1991).
8. F. Sillion, J. Arvo, S. Westin, D. Greenberg, A global illumination solution for general reflectance distributions. *Computer Graphics (SIGGRAPH '91)*, **25**, 187–196 (1991).
9. D. Baum, S. Mann, K. Smith, J. Winget, Making radiosity usable: automatic pre-processing and meshing techniques for the generation of accurate radiosity solutions. *Computer Graphics (SIGGRAPH '91)*, **25**, 51–60 (1991).

10. D. Lischinski, F. Tampieri, D. Greenberg, Combining hierarchical radiosity and discontinuity meshing. *Computer Graphics (SIGGRAPH '93)*, **27**, 199–208 (1993).

11. S. Pattanaik, S. Mudur, Efficient potential equation solutions for global illumination computation. *Computers and Graphics*, **17** (4), 387–396 (1993).

12. S. Chen, H. Rushmeier, G. Miller, D. Turner, A progressive multi-pass method for global illumination. *Computer Graphics (SIGGRAPH '91)*, **25**, 165–174 (1991).

13. M. Watt, Light-water interaction using backward beam tracing. *Computer Graphics (SIGGRAPH '90)*, **24**, 377–385 (1990).

14. P. Shirley, A ray tracing method for illumination calculation in diffuse-specular scenes. *Graphics Interface '90*, 205–212 (1990).

15. J. Arvo, Backward ray tracing. *SIGGRAPH '86* "Developments in Ray Tracing" course notes (1986).

16. P. Heckbert, Adaptive radiosity textures for bidirectional ray tracing. *Computer Graphics (SIGGRAPH '90)*, **24**, 145–154 (1990).

17. P. Shirley, Time complexity of Monte-Carlo radiosity. *Eurographics '91 Proceedings*, 459–465 (1991).

18. P. Shirley, K. Sung, W. Brown, A ray tracing framework for global illumination. *Graphics Interface '91*, 117–128 (1991).

19. B. Le Saec, C. Schlick, A progressive ray-tracing based radiosity with general reflectance functions. *Eurographics Workshop on Photosimulation, Realism, and Physics in Computer Graphics*, 1990.

20. G. Ward, F. Rubinstein, R. Clear, A ray tracing solution for diffuse interreflection. *Computer Graphics (SIGGRAPH '88)*, **22**, 85–92 (1988).

21. E. Lafortune, Y. Willems, Bidirectional path tracing. *CompuGraphics Proceedings* (Alvor, Portugal), 145–153 (Dec. 1993).

22. M. Cohen, J. Wallace, *Radiosity and Realistic Image Synthesis*. Academic Press, 1993.

23. Lewins, Jeffery, *Importance, The Adjoint Function: The Physical Basis of Variational and Perturbation Theory in Transport and Diffusion Problems*. Pergamon Press, New York, 1965.

24. J. Spanier, E. Gelbard, *Monte Carlo Principles and Neutron Transport Problems*, Addison-Wesley, 1969.

25. P. Christensen, D. Salesin, T. DeRose, A continuous adjoint formulation for radiance transport. *Fourth Eurographics Workshop on Rendering*, 1993.

26. S. Pattanaik, S. Mudur, The Potential Equation and Importance in Illumination Computations. *Computer Graphics Forum*, **12** (2), 131–136 (1993).

27. B. Smits, J. Arvo, D. Salesin, An importance-driven radiosity algorithm. *Computer Graphics (SIGGRAPH '92)*, **26**, 273–282 (1992).

The Ambient Term as a Variance Reducing Technique for Monte Carlo Ray Tracing

Eric P. Lafortune, Yves D. Willems

Department of Computer Science, Katholieke Universiteit Leuven, Celestijnenlaan 200A, 3001 Heverlee, Belgium

Abstract

Ray tracing algorithms often approximate indirect diffuse lighting by means of an ambient lighting term. In this paper we show how a similar term can be used as a variance reducing technique for stochastic ray tracing. In a theoretical derivation we prove that the technique is mathematically correct. Test results demonstrate its usefulness and effectiveness in practice.

1 Introduction

The original ray tracing technique as introduced by Whitted [1] was the first to be able to render some more complex lighting effects such as reflections and refractions. The resulting images often look spectacular albeit a bit artificial due to the limitations of the lighting simulation. Only perfectly specular reflections and direct diffuse lighting contributions are computed explicitly. Indirect diffuse contributions are approximated by a user-defined ambient lighting term.

Realistic rendering has come a long way since then. Cook et al. [2] presented distributed ray tracing which also renders glossy reflections by stochastically sampling the reflected directions. Kajiya later gave a theoretical foundation to the technique by introducing the rendering equation [3]. From this point of view stochastic ray tracing – or its special case path tracing – is simply a Monte Carlo method to solve an integral equation. Several other researchers have elaborated on this idea [4, 5]. Its advantages are its elegancy and generality. Monte Carlo ray tracing can render a host of lighting effects including depth of field and motion blur, all in a physically and mathematically correct way. Unfortunately the basic technique is slow to converge. Various optimised sampling techniques try to alleviate this problem [6, 7, 8, 9], but rendering typical global illumination effects such as indirect diffuse reflections still requires a lot of computational effort.

This paper presents a new optimisation which further reduces the variance and therefore improves on the required computation time. It elaborates on the idea of an ambient lighting term as it is used in the original ray tracing technique.

Rather than being used as a 'fudge factor' though, it will be shown that it lowers the variance without influencing the expected value of the result. Notably it improves the rendering of diffuse lighting effects.

First we will present the technique from a theoretical point of view. We will discuss the general principle as it is described in literature about Monte Carlo methods and subsequently apply it to the rendering equation. We will discuss what we can and what we cannot expect in terms of improvements. In the last section the theory will be verified by means of some practical test results.

2 Mathematical Principle

The basic idea of the technique is well-known in general Monte Carlo literature as *control variates* [10, 11] or *extraction of a regular part* [12]. Consider for instance the computation of a definite integral of a one-dimensional function $f(x)$ (Fig. 1):

$$I = \int_a^b f(x)dx$$

An estimate for the integral can be found by taking randomly distributed samples x_i over the domain (possibly stratified), evaluating their function values and taking a weighted sum:

$$\langle I \rangle = \frac{(b-a)}{N} \sum_{i=1}^N f(x_i)$$

Now suppose one knows a function $g(x)$ which more or less closely approximates $f(x)$ and which can be integrated analytically over the given domain:

$$J = \int_a^b g(x)dx$$

The original integral can then be rewritten as:

$$I = \int_a^b [f(x) - g(x)]dx + \int_a^b g(x)dx = \int_a^b [f(x) - g(x)]dx + J$$

Sampling the integral in the first term now yields another estimate:

$$\langle I \rangle = \frac{(b-a)}{N} \sum_{i=1}^N [f(x_i) - g(x_i)] + J$$

One can see intuitively that if $g(x)$ approaches $f(x)$ (by some metric) the variance of this estimate will go to 0. Finding an approximating function which can be integrated therefore may be worthwhile for Monte Carlo integration. Note that a constant control variate $g(x) = C$ does not change the value of the estimate at all and therefore cannot offer any improvement. This will have some consequences later for our application to the rendering equation.

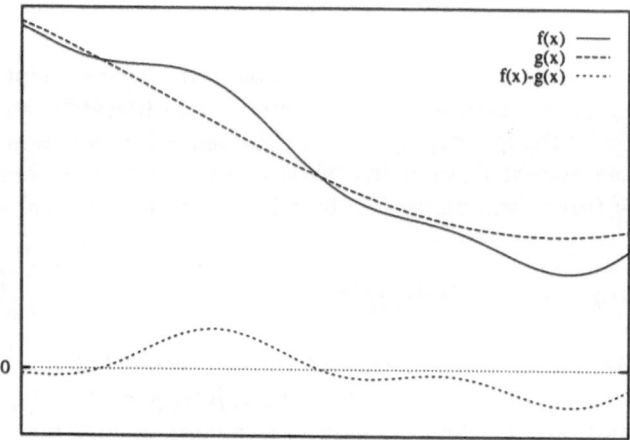

Fig. 1. Computing a definite integral of a function $f(x)$ using a Monte Carlo method. A function $g(x)$ which approximates $f(x)$ and which can be integrated analytically can serve as a control variate. It is more efficient to sample the difference between the functions rather than $f(x)$ itself to compute an estimate.

3 Application to the Rendering Equation

From a mathematical point of view Monte Carlo ray tracing samples the outgoing radiance values from surfaces that are seen through a given pixel. The radiance leaving a point x along direction Θ_x is determined by the rendering equation:

$$L(x, \Theta_x) = L_e(x, \Theta_x) + L_r(x, \Theta_x)$$
$$= L_e(x, \Theta_x) + \int_{\Omega_x^{-1}} f_r(x, \Theta_y, \Theta_x) L(y, \Theta_y) |\Theta_y \cdot N_x| \, d\omega_y$$

where:

- $L(x, \Theta_x)$ = the emitted radiance at point x along direction Θ_x [W/m²sr],
- $L_e(x, \Theta_x)$ = the self-emitted radiance at point x along direction Θ_x [W/m²sr],
- $L_r(x, \Theta_x)$ = the radiance reflected at point x along direction Θ_x [W/m²sr],
- Ω_x^{-1} = the set of incoming directions around point x,
- $f_r(x, \Theta_y, \Theta_x)$ = the bi-directional reflection distribution function (*brdf*) at point x for light coming in from direction Θ_y and going out along direction Θ_x [1/sr],
- $|\Theta_y \cdot N_x|$ = the absolute value of the cosine of the angle between the direction Θ_y and the normal to the surface at point x,
- y = the point that 'sees' point x along direction Θ_y,
- $d\omega_y$ = a differential angle around Θ_y [sr].

In order to reduce the variance light sources are usually treated separately from other surfaces. For this purpose the terms in the rendering equation are rewritten. The reflected radiance $L_r(x, \Theta_x)$ is split up in a direct term $L_d(x, \Theta_x)$ and an indirect term $L_i(x, \Theta_x)$:

$$L_r(x, \Theta_x) = L_d(x, \Theta_x) + L_i(x, \Theta_x)$$

where:

- The direct term can be found by integrating over the light sources instead of over all incoming angles. It is usually estimated by sampling the surface area of the light sources.

$$L_d(x, \Theta_x) = \int_{\Omega_x^{-1}} f_r(x, \Theta_y, \Theta_x) L_e(y, \Theta_y) |\Theta_y \cdot N_x| d\omega_y$$

$$= \int_{A_l} f_r(x, \Theta_y, \Theta_x) L_e(y, \Theta_y) \frac{|\Theta_y \cdot N_y| |\Theta_y \cdot N_x|}{r^2} v(x, y) d\mu_y$$

- The indirect term, which is of greater concern to us now, is:

$$L_i(x, \Theta_x) = \int_{\Omega_x^{-1}} f_r(x, \Theta_y, \Theta_x) L_r(y, \Theta_y) |\Theta_y \cdot N_x| d\omega_y$$

Monte Carlo ray tracing proceeds by recursively sampling the latter integral. It is in this sampling process that the variance reducing technique can be applied. As an approximation for the integrand – which is two-dimensional now – we select the *brdf* times a constant ambient radiance L_a. As in the one-dimensional example the indirect term can then be written as:

$$L_i(x, \Theta_x) = \int_{\Omega_x^{-1}} f_r(x, \Theta_y, \Theta_x)[L_r(y, \Theta_y) - L_a] |\Theta_y \cdot N_x| d\omega_y$$

$$+ \int_{\Omega_x^{-1}} f_r(x, \Theta_y, \Theta_x) L_a |\Theta_y \cdot N_x| d\omega_y$$

$$= \int_{\Omega_x^{-1}} f_r(x, \Theta_y, \Theta_x)[L_r(y, \Theta_y) - L_a] |\Theta_y \cdot N_x| d\omega_y + \rho(x, \Theta_x) \times L_a$$

where $\rho(x, \Theta_x)$ is the total reflectivity for light reaching point x along direction Θ_x. This factor only depends on the local reflective properties of the surface. It can be computed analytically for many models of *brdfs*. The general theory for control variates predicts that sampling the integrand in the new expression for $L_i(x, \Theta_x)$ will yield a smaller variance than with the original expression, on the condition that the approximation of the integrand is close enough.

4 Analysis for Specific Sampling Approaches

There are several alternatives for sampling the original and the new integral expressions. These influence the effectiveness of the variance reduction technique. The parameters that determine the sampling approach are the factors in which the integrand, $f_r(x, \Theta_y, \Theta_x)L_r(y, \Theta_y)|\Theta_y \cdot N_x|$, is split up:

- the probability P that the recursion is continued,
- the probability density function $pdf(\Theta_y)$ that is used to sample the reflected direction over the hemisphere (for the given (x, Θ_x)),
- the weight that forms the resulting estimate $\langle L_i(x, \Theta_x)\rangle$ for the sample if the recursion is continued.

Some of the most notable techniques use the following parameters:

- $P = 1$, $pdf(\Theta_y) = |\Theta_y \cdot N_x|/\pi$, $\langle L_i(x, \Theta_x)\rangle = \pi f_r(x, \Theta_y, \Theta_x)\langle L_r(y, \Theta_y)\rangle$ yields a straightforward technique without importance sampling. The recursion has to be cut off at a certain point, which theoretically introduces a bias. The ambient term may be expected to reduce the variance of the sampling process.
- $P = 1$, $pdf(\Theta_y) = f_r(x, \Theta_y, \Theta_x)|\Theta_y \cdot N_x|/\rho(x, \Theta_x)$, $\langle L_i(x, \Theta_x)\rangle = \rho(x, \Theta_x)\langle L_r(y, \Theta_y)\rangle$ yields an importance sampling technique. Again the recursion has to be cut off artificially. Importance sampling can be seen as a transformation of the integral. After transformation the $brdf$ times the ambient term is reduced to a constant. As noted in the general discussion the ambient term therefore does not offer any improvement here. The technique on its own is not optimal though, since a lot of computational effort may be put in samples with small weights.
- $P = \rho(x, \Theta_x)$, $pdf(\Theta_y) = f_r(x, \Theta_y, \Theta_x)|\Theta_y \cdot N_x|/\rho(x, \Theta_x)$, $\langle L_i(x, \Theta_x)\rangle = \langle L_r(y, \Theta_y)\rangle$ yields an importance sampling technique with Russian roulette to end the recursion. This approach does not introduce a bias and samples are used more sparingly. Because of the Russian roulette the ambient term will affect the variance here.

If the ambient term is introduced the constant $\rho(x, \Theta_x)L_a$ is added to the estimate $\langle L_i(x, \Theta_x)\rangle$ and all occurrences of the estimate $\langle L_r(y, \Theta_y)\rangle$ are replaced by the delta term $\langle L_r(y, \Theta_y)\rangle - L_a$. This principle can be applied at each recursion level. The ambient radiance L_a may vary with the position in the scene.

For a path tracing algorithm which only takes a single sample at each recursion level the eventual estimate for the radiance $L(x, \Theta_x)$ with the last technique looks like:

$$\langle L(x, \Theta_x)\rangle = L_e(x, \Theta_x) + \langle L_d(x_0, \Theta_{x_0})\rangle + \rho(x_0, \Theta_{x_0})L_a(x_0)$$

$$+ \sum_{k=1}^{n}[\langle L_d(x_k, \Theta_{x_k})\rangle + \rho(x_k, \Theta_{x_k})L_a(x_k) - L_a(x_{k-1})]$$

where n is the depth of the recursion. Note that a value of 0 for L_a yields the original path tracing technique.

5 Results

We have verified our theoretical findings by means of an implementation of the path tracing algorithm. The basic implementation already contains some optimised sampling strategies such as multi-dimensional N-rooks sampling and importance sampling with Russian roulette.

The technique was tested on a simple scene of a room with coloured walls and a waxed floor. The room contains a white cube, a slightly specular green cylinder and a glass sphere (Fig. 2). Images were computed at a resolution of 100×100 pixels with 10 samples per pixel and compared against a reference image which was computed at 500 samples per pixel. The RMS error metric was used to measure the variance of the images:

$$RMS = \sqrt{\frac{\sum_p (L_p - L_{p,ref})^2}{N}}$$

Figure 3 shows how the ambient term affects the variance of the resulting images. Several images were computed using the same number of samples per pixel but with increasing estimates for the ambient term. For simplicity the same estimate was used for all objects in the scene.

An ambient term of 0 corresponds to the original path tracing algorithm. As expected from the theory the variance decreases with the introduction of a larger ambient term. It reaches a minimum at the optimal estimate and then increases again. For this example the RMS error is reduced with a maximum of almost 10% as compared to simple path tracing.

The variance can be further reduced by a few percent by estimating the ambient term more accurately for each of the individual objects or regions in the scene, either manually or in a preprocessing step. If the scene is illuminated indirectly by means of some spots pointing to the ceiling the reduction increases to 14%. This result may be expected since the ambient term specifically improves the accuracy for indirect lighting effects.

Another test with an outdoor scene under an overcast sky shows a more spectacular reduction of the RMS error by 87%. Note that the hemisphere is usually not sampled separately as a light source because of its size. Instead it is treated as a source of indirect lighting. The ambient term then proves to be an effective control variate for the skylight.

6 Conclusions

We have presented a variance reducing technique for Monte Carlo ray tracing which is based on an estimated ambient lighting term. In the recursive ray tracing process indirectly reflected radiance values are computed as a sum of two terms: reflected radiance resulting from this ambient term and a correction to this term which is computed in the remainder of the recursive process. In a theoretical discussion we have proven the mathematical correctness of the technique and looked at its potential for various stochastic ray tracing approaches.

Fig. 2. Test scene used for measuring the reduction of the variance.

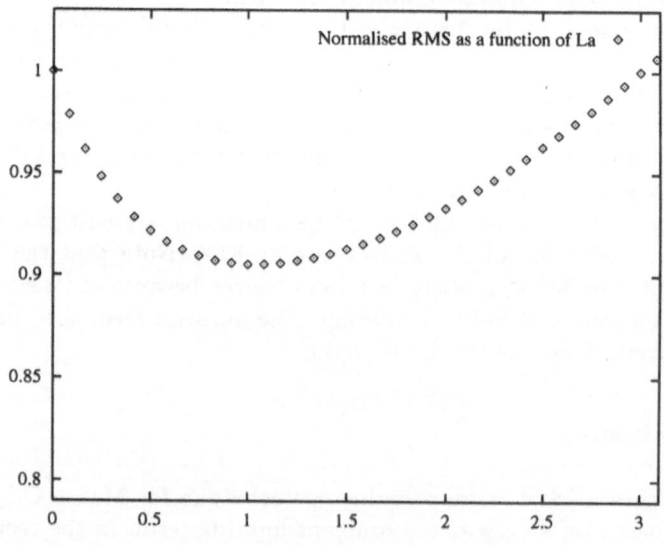

Fig. 3. The introduction of an ambient term reduces the variance for a fixed number of samples per pixel. The variance reaches a minimum at the optimal estimate.

Practical tests have shown that there really is a reduction of the variance. The improvement depends on the quality of the estimate of the ambient lighting and may be modest. Still, the technique has some distinct advantages:

- It mainly improves the rendering of diffuse interreflection, which has always been one of the weak points of Monte Carlo ray tracing. Because the convergence rate of Monte Carlo methods is generally limited to a slow $\sqrt{N}$ any reduction of the variance is more than welcome.
- The extra computational work involved is negligible since no extra rays have to be cast.
- Although an optimal ambient lighting term may be hard to find even a conservative estimate will improve the convergence. A simple preprocessing step may suffice for this purpose.
- Integration with other variance reducing techniques such as stratified sampling is straightforward. If importance sampling cannot be applied because of the complexity of the *brdf*s the technique may offer an even larger improvement. The only requirement is that the *brdf* can be integrated over the hemisphere.

The technique should also prove useful in related Monte Carlo algorithms. More in specific we are currently investigating its application in bi-directional path tracing [13, 14].

7 Acknowledgements

The first author would like to acknowledge the financial support by a grant from the Belgian "Instituut tot Aanmoediging van Wetenschappelijk Onderzoek in Nijverheid en Landbouw" (I.W.O.N.L. #910184). Implementation was done on equipment kindly made available by Hewlett Packard Belgium.

References

1. T. Whitted, "An improved illumination model for shaded display," *Communications of the ACM*, vol. 23, no. 6, 1980.
2. R. Cook, T. Porter, and L. Carpenter, "Distributed ray tracing," *Computer Graphics*, vol. 18, no. 3, pp. 137–145, 1984.
3. J. Kajiya, "The rendering equation," *Computer Graphics*, vol. 20, no. 4, pp. 143–150, 1986.
4. G. Ward, F. Rubinstein, and R. Clear, "A ray tracing solution for diffuse interreflection," *Computer Graphics*, vol. 22, no. 4, pp. 85–92, 1988.
5. P. Shirley and C. Wang, "Distribution ray tracing: Theory and practice," in *Proceedings of the Third Eurographics Workshop on Rendering*, (Bristol, UK), pp. 33–43, May 1992.
6. M. Lee, R. Redner, and S. Uselton, "Statistically optimized sampling for distributed ray tracing," *Computer Graphics*, vol. 19, no. 3, pp. 61–67, 1985.
7. P. Shirley, *Physically Based Lighting Calculations for Computer Graphics*. PhD thesis, University of Illinois, Nov. 1990.

8. P. Shirley and C. Wang, "Direct lighting by monte carlo integration," in *Proceedings of the Second Eurographics Workshop on Rendering*, (Barcelona, Spain), May 1991.

9. B. Lange, "The simulation of radiant light transfer with stochastic ray-tracing," in *Proceedings of the Second Eurographics Workshop on Rendering*, (Barcelona, Spain), May 1991.

10. M. Kalos and P. Whitlock, *Monte Carlo Methods*. Wiley & Sons, 1986.

11. J. Hammersly and D. Handscomb, *Monte Carlo Methods*. Chapman and Hall, 1964.

12. Y. Shreider, ed., *The Monte Carlo Method*. Pergamon Press, 1966.

13. E. Lafortune and Y. Willems, "Bi-directional path tracing," in *Proceedings of CompuGraphics*, (Alvor, Portugal), pp. 145–153, Dec. 1993.

14. E. Lafortune and Y. Willems, "A theoretical framework for physically based rendering," *Computer Graphics Forum*, vol. 13, pp. 97–107, June 1994.

An Importance Driven Monte-Carlo Solution to the Global Illumination Problem

Philippe Blasi, Bertrand Le Saëc, Christophe Schlick

Laboratoire Bordelais de Recherche en Informatique, 351 cours de la libération, 33405 Talence, France

Abstract

We propose a method for solving the global illumination problem with no restrictive assumptions concerning the behaviour of light either on surface or volume objects in the scene. Surface objects are defined either by facets or parametric patches and volume objets are defined by voxel grids which define arbitrary density distributions in a discrete tridimensional space. The rendering technique is a Monte-Carlo ray-tracing based radiosity which unifies the processing of objects in a scene, whether they are surfacic or volumic. The main characteristics of our technique are the use of separated Markov chains to prevent the explosion of the number of rays and an optimal importance sampling to speed-up the convergence.

1 Introduction

Solving the global illumination problem is necessary to achieve photorealism in image synthesis [7, 16, 14]. To account for all complex reflection/transmission phenomena on surface objects, recent models proposed in computer graphics include more and more physics, using theoretical light distribution functions to go beyond the ideal specular and/or ideal diffuse case [5, 19, 20, 15]. Another step toward photorealism has been the inclusion of absorption/scattering phenomena created by volume objects such as clouds, haze, fog [8, 12, 13, 3]. In this paper, we propose a progressive Monte-Carlo ray-tracing based radiosity that enable rendering of surface and volume objects with general light distribution functions and multiple reflection/transmission/absorption/scattering phenomena. This method can be viewed as a merging of a stochastic interpretation of [9] and an improved version of [1]. The first one is a progressive radiosity technique for surface objects with general reflectance functions. The second one is a ray-tracing algorithm for volume objects with arbitrary density distributions and multiple scattering. The method described in this paper is a two pass method (one view independent and one view dependent) that unifies the processing of surface and volume objects.

2 Rendering Equations

The generation of realistic pictures involves two equations : the *image rendering equation* (Equation 1) and the *scene rendering equation* (Equation 2). The first one defines the illumination of a given pixel in the image. It is essentially a mean over several integration dimensions (pixel width, pixel height, lens radius, lens angle, shutter time). The second defines the radiance of each couple (P, V) where P is a point and V a direction of the scene. It is a Fredholm equation that expresses the light transport in the environment. See [1] for a more complete explanation of these equations.

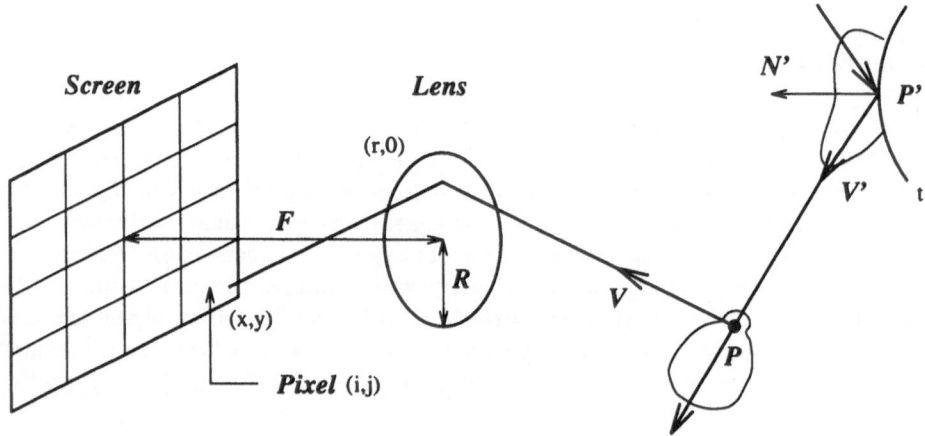

Fig. 1. Image rendering and scene rendering equations.

$$I(i,j) = \frac{1}{T\pi R^2} \int_x \int_y \int_r \int_\theta \int_t K_V(M, P) \, L(P, V) \, dx \, dy \, r \, dr \, d\theta \, dt \quad (1)$$

$$L(P, V) = L_E(P, V) + \int_{V' \in \mathcal{V}} K_S(P, V, V') \, K_V(P, P') \, L(P', V') \, dV' \quad (2)$$

- $I(i, j)$: Illumination of pixel (i, j)
- $L(P, V)$: Radiance leaving point P in direction V
- $L_E(P, V)$: Self radiance leaving point P in direction V
- $K_S(P, V, V')$: Surface scattering factor at P between directions V and V'
- $K_V(P, P')$: Volume attenuation factor between points P and P'
- $\mathcal{V}$: Set of directions for incident light (solid angle 4π)
- $T\pi R^2$: Normalization factor (T is the shutter time and R is the lens radius)
- dV' : Differential solid angle element surrounding direction V'

We consider these two equations on a somewhat particular point of view (see [1] for a more detailed version of the following discussion). A point P where light interacts with matter can be either on a surface object or inside a volume object. The $K_S(P, V, V')$ — surface scattering factor — coefficient expresses the distribution of energy in space at a scattering point P. It is the ratio of radiances between two directions V and V' at P. This coefficient enables to unify the behavior of light on objects whether they are surfacic or volumic by considering that transmission and reflection at a point P are only particular cases of scattering. The $K_V(P, P')$ coefficient — volume attenuation factor — expresses the attenuation of light traveling through a participating medium. It is the ratio of radiances between two scattering points P and P' (in the vaccum, K_V yields 1). P and P' are supposed to be two successive scattering points, therefore the only physical phenomenum that can occur between these points is absorption. Thus K_V is given by Bouguer's law restricted to absorption :

$$K_V(P, P') = e^{-\int_P^{P'} \alpha\, \rho(P'')\, dP''} \tag{3}$$

where α is the absorption coefficient and $\rho(P)$ is the density at the point P. At a scattering point P, the expression of K_S depends whether P belongs to a surface or a volume object :

— on a surface object,

$$K_S(P, V, V') = (N.V)\, R(P, V, V') \tag{4}$$

where N is the normal vector to the surface at point P and $R(P, V, V')$ the bidirectional reflectance transmittance distribution function (BRTDF) of the surface.

— inside a volume object,

$$K_S(P, V, V') = \frac{1}{4\pi}\, \gamma\, \varphi(V, V') \qquad \text{and} \qquad \gamma = \frac{\sigma}{\alpha + \sigma} \tag{5}$$

where $\varphi(V, V')$ is the phase function of the object, γ the albedo, σ is the scattering coefficient and α the absorption coefficient.

For a surface object, the location of scattering points can be explicitly computed using the intersection of the ray and the surface. For a volume object, this calculation cannot be done because only the density of matter is known. More precisely, volume objects are defined as a set of particles whose position in space is random, but whose distribution is known. Thus locations of scattering points are computed in a probabilistic way, using a *probability of interception* of a ray by a particle. The probability of interception increases as a function of the density, the scattering coefficient and the distance covered by the ray in the object since the last scattering point. In Bouguer's law, the scattering coefficient expresses the fraction of incoming energy which is lost by scattering. Therefore it is natural to define the probability of interception $\omega(P, P')$ as :

$$\omega(P, P') = 1 - e^{-\int_P^{P'} \sigma\, \rho(P'')\, dP''} \tag{6}$$

In Equation 6, $\omega(P, P')$ is function of the wavelength, due to the spectral dependence of σ. For algorithmic reasons (a ray carries several spectral samples), it is more convenient to have a wavelength independent probability of interception. Therefore, we rather use either an average or a weighted average scattering coefficient $\bar{\sigma}$ for the definition of $\omega(P, P')$:

$$\bar{\sigma} = \frac{1}{n} \sum_{i=1}^{n} \sigma_{f_i}, \quad \text{or} \quad \bar{\sigma} = \frac{1}{m} \sum_{i=1}^{n} r_{f_i} \sigma_{f_i}, \quad \text{with} \quad m = \sum_{i=1}^{n} r_{f_i} \quad (7)$$

where $\{f_1, \ldots, f_n\}$ is the set of the sample frequencies and r_f the energy value at frequency f carried by the ray. Finally, in the particular case where density between P and P' is constant, Equation 6 becomes :

$$\omega(\delta) = 1 - e^{-\bar{\sigma} \rho \delta} \quad (8)$$

where ρ is the density and δ the distance between P and P'. Notice that when $\rho = 0$ (outside the volume object, for instance) the probability of interception is null, as expected.

3 Resolution of the Rendering Equations

In the computer graphics literature, many techniques can be found to solve a more or less simplified form of the rendering equations. Among them, several methods based on a Monte-Carlo evaluation of these equations, combined with a ray-tracing scheme, have been presented [2, 7, 16, 10]. These techniques have shown to be, not only easy to implement, but also well-adapted to a large class of situations. The main advantage of Monte-Carlo techniques is that they enable to solve multidimensional integral equations (like rendering equations are) as if they were monodimensional, by using separated Markov chains [4, 7]. On the other hand, the main drawback of these techniques is the convergence speed which may be, for the general case, as low as $O(n^{1/d})$ where n is the number of samples and d is the number of dimensions of the equation.

Several techniques have been developped for Monte-Carlo methods to speed-up the convergence [4]. One classical technique is *importance sampling* (sometimes called weighted sampling). The idea behind importance sampling is to use more samples in the parts of the domain where the signal is high, and less samples where the signal is low. More precisely, for a given distribution function f, an *optimal importance sampling* can be obtained from a uniform sampling by using the inverse function F^{-1} of the repartition function F associated with f. So, any valuation of $t = F^{-1}(u)$, where u is a uniform random variable, provides a stochastic weighted value of t (see [16, 17] for some applications of this result in computer graphics).

In our context, the role of the distribution function is played by the surface scattering factor. Several expressions for this factor can be found (given by different theories in physics) but, unfortunately, none of them is integrable and inversible, and thus cannot provide optimal sampling.

The solution that we propose to circumvent this limitation is to approximate theoretical expressions by more simpler functions which are integrable and inversible. We have developped an approximation technique [14] which enables such simplifications while staying in good accuracy with the original functions. This scheme has been applied both for light scattering on surface objects [15] and on volume objects [1]. These results are shortly recalled hereafter (for more complete explanations, the reader is invited to refer [15] and [1]).

3.1 Scattering Factor on Surface Objects

In our model, light reflection/transmission on a surface object is totally defined by two parameters. The first one, $\gamma \in [0, 1]$, is the albedo of the material (ratio of reflected energy relative to incident energy). In fact, to account for spectral variations, we actually define several γ, one for each sample wavelength (e.g. three with the RGB model). The second one, $r \in [0, 1]$, is the roughness of the surface which defines the relative amount of diffuse and specular behaviours (the surface is perfectly specular when $r = 0$, and perfectly diffuse when $r = 1$). It should be noted that these two parameters are sufficient only when the material has homogeneous optical properties (such as metal). For material with heterogeneous properties (such as plastic), several couple of (γ, r) may be defined, one for each homogeneous surface that composes the material). The formulation of the scattering factor is :

$$K_S(P, V, V') = \frac{1}{4\pi} \gamma \frac{r}{(1 + rt^2 - t^2)^2} \qquad \text{with} \qquad t = (N \cdot H) \qquad (9)$$

where N is the normal vector of the surface at point P and H is the classical half-vector between V and V' (used for instance, in the Cook-Torrance model).

As said, this formulation provides an optimal importance stochastic sampling for t starting from a uniform random variable $u \in [0, 1]$ (once t is computed, the random direction of the scattered ray is quite easy to derive [15]) :

$$t = \sqrt{\frac{u}{r - ru + u}} \qquad (10)$$

3.2 Scattering Factor on Volume Objects

In our model, light reflection/transmission on particles of a volume objects has quite a similar expression. It is also defined by two parameters : $\gamma \in [0, 1]$ which is the albedo of the material, and $k \in [-1, 1]$ which enables to vary continuously between perfect forward scattering ($k > 0$), isotropic scattering ($k = 0$) and backward scattering ($k < 0$). The formulation of the scattering factor is :

$$K_S(P, V, V') = \frac{1}{4\pi} \gamma \frac{1 - k^2}{(1 - ks)^2} \qquad \text{with} \qquad s = (V \cdot V') \qquad (11)$$

Here again, an optimal importance stochastic sampling for s (and thus a random direction for the scattered ray, see [1]) can be obtained from a uniform random variable $u \in [0, 1]$:

$$s = \frac{2u + k - 1}{2ku - k + 1} \tag{12}$$

The continuum between isotropic (or perfectly diffuse) and Dirac (or perfectly specular) scattering provided by the two previous formulations is the main characteristic of our models. Indeed, having such a continuum will enable us to put a threshold for r or k. Objects for which this coefficient is above (resp. below) the threshold will be called *specular* (resp. *diffuse*). These two families of objects will be treated differently by the algorithm.

4 Description of the Method

4.1 Overview

We propose a progressive ray-tracing based Monte-Carlo radiosity with distribution functions generalized to participating media. This method accounts for surface/surface, volume/surface and volume/volume interactions. As usual for radiosity algorithms, surface objects are divided into patches for which constant optical properties are assumed. Volume objects are modelled as tridimensional grids with constant density for a voxel. Such grids may be generated by fractal algorithms similar to those described in [11] or by physically based algorithms.

During the first pass, the most energetic object is chosen and rays are cast according to its distribution function. When a ray hits a *specular* object, its energy is immediatly reflected back to the scene. When it hits a *diffuse* object, the incident energy is stored into a storage structure. When a ray travels through a volume object, the algorithmic process described in [1] is used. The ray progresses incrementaly with uniform steps. At each step, its energy is attenuated by $K_V(P, P')$ using the distance covered since the last step and using the local density of the object. Moreover, scattering may occur according to a probability of interception associated with the media. In order to cast a new ray carrying the scattered energy, the phase function is used as a weighting function for a Monte-Carlo sampling process.

During the second pass which is view-dependent, visualization rays starting from the view point are sent towards each pixel of the screen and travel straight through the scene. If the hit object is diffuse, we get the radiance of the object. If it is specular, we cast into the scene a reflected visualization ray. Here again, when a ray travels through a volume object, the algorithm process described in [1] is used. The ray progresses incrementaly voxel by voxel. At each step, the attenuation of the ray due to the current voxel is computed.

4.2 Storage Consideration

The storage of radiances with their directions is an expensive memory consuming problem. Several solutions have been proposed in the past for environments composed of surface objects (sampled spheres [9, 16] or spherical harmonics [18, 20]). The memory cost is already high for environments containing only surface objects and becomes prohibitive for environments with volume objects. Consequently, we have decided to store radiances not inside the volume itself, but on its surface (we define the surface of a volume object as the boundary between null density voxels and the others voxels of the volume object). Thus, the storage is no more expensive than for surfaces and reduces the number of accesses to volume data. As a counter part, we cannot place anymore the observer inside the volume object. Moreover, we have to increase the number of rays traveling through the volume object to get an accurate sampling of the energy leaving it. Note that this storage is particularly interesting for almost opaque volume objects, such as dense clouds. Indeed, in that case, most of rays are "reflected" by the cloud as if it was surfacic.

In our implementation, we store incident energies on a sphere sampled into meridians and parallels (an hemisphere is sufficient for opaque surface objects). The resolution of the sampling depends on the specularity of the material. The number of samples must increase with the specularity. For perfect diffuse surfaces, we do not need the direction of incident energies, so we can only use one sample for the sphere. For specular or nearly specular objects, this storage becomes too much expensive. Fortunately, it corresponds to the case where the distribution function is very narrow (Dirac-like) and for which the Markov chain process without storage is very efficient.

Usually, a ray intersects a closed object twice : one when it enters the object and one when it leaves it. As far as the storage is concerned, we consider that a ray hits the surface of a volume object only when it is already inside of the object. In the same way, a visualization ray hits the surface of a volume object only when it comes from the outside of the object.

4.3 Illumination Pass

During the illumination pass of the algorithm, the most energetic storage unit (either a surface patch or a volume boundary voxel) is chosen. Then, for each sample of the storage sphere with an energy greater than a given threshold, rays are sent according to the scattering distribution of the object (or to its goniometrical distribution for the self-emitted radiance). The number of rays is simply the ratio of the energy of the sample divided by the ε value (eventually, one can put an upper bound on the number of rays sent for a given sample). Then, whether the ray hits :

- a specular or nearly specular object, we cast into the scene one reflected ray according to the distibution function of the object.
- a diffuse or nearly diffuse object, we store the incident energy with its direction using the sampled sphere associated to the object.

When a ray travels through a volume object, it progresses incrementaly in steps of uniform length. At each step, the energy carried by the ray is scaled by the attenuation factor. Then we compute the probability of interception of the ray using the length of the step and the average density of the object along that step. If there is no interception, the ray is simply propagated a step further in the same direction. If there is an interception, we perform an importance sampling of the phase function to cast a new ray propagating the scattered energy from the scattering point (see Section 3).

At the end of the illumination pass, the incident energies stored on the sampled spheres are converted into emitted energies using the distribution function of the object. These new samples will be used during the visualization pass.

Algorithm of the Illumination Pass

For each patch P of a surface object
    Initialize the energy : $E_P = 0$
For each voxel V of the surface of a volume object
    Initialize the energy : $E_V = 0$
Choose the most energetic patch P
While $E_P >$ THRESHOLD
    Compute the number N of rays to cast
    For each ray R
        Initialize the energy of R : $E_R = E_P/N$
        Cast stochastically the ray R according to
        the distribution function : CastRay (R)
    End-For
    Choose the most energetic patch P
End-While

function CastRay(Ray R)
    Switch R hits :
        - a *specular* surface object O :
            Propagate stochastically the ray R' according to
            the distribution function : CastRay (R')
        - a *diffuse* surface object O :
            Store the incident energy E_R with its direction
        - a *volume* object O :
            While $E_R >$ THRESHOLD and R is still in O
                Attenuate the energy $E_R = e^{-\alpha\rho\delta} E_R$ where
                $\delta =$ distance in V and $\rho =$ density of V
                Use the probability of interception $\omega(\delta)$ to decide
                if scattering occurs at the current point
                If there is not scattering then
                    Propagate the ray R in the same direction
                else
                    Propagate stochastically a new ray R'
            End-While
            If $E_R >$ THRESHOLD

Store the energy in the last encountered voxel $V : E_V = E_V + E_R$
Propagate the ray in the scene : CastRay(R)
End-Switch
End-Function

4.4 Visualization Pass

During the visualization pass of the algorithm, rays are sent from the viewer toward each pixel of the screen. Their attenuation factor is initialised to 1. Then, whether the visualization ray hits :

- a specular or nearly specular object, we cast into the scene one reflected/ transmitted ray according to the distribution function of the patch. The radiance get by this ray will be scaled by the albedo of the surface.
- a diffuse or nearly diffuse object, the directional radiance is computed using the sampled sphere associated to the patch.

When a ray travels through a volume object, the visualization ray progresses incrementaly, voxel by voxel, until it hits a surface or goes out the volume object. At each step, we scale the attenuation factor of the visualization ray by the volume attenuation of the current step. This attenuation is calculated using the complete Bouguer law :

$$e^{-\int_P^{P'} (\alpha + \sigma)\, \rho(P'')\, dP''} \tag{13}$$

Indeed, during the illumination pass, we only store the energies of rays scattered by the volume object. Now, we have to get the energies that have travelled through the volume object without being scattered. The radiance of objects located inside or behind the volume object will be scaled by the attenuation factor of the ray.

Algorithm of the Visualization Pass

For each pixel P
Initialize the radiance of $R : L_R = 0$
Initialize the attenuation of $R : A = 1$
Send a visualization ray R from the eye : CastVisuRay (R)
End-For

function CastVisuRay (Ray R)
Switch R hits :
- a *specular* surface object O :
Propagate stochastically the ray R' according to
the distribution function : CastVisuRay (R')
- a *diffuse* surface object O :

      Add the directional radiance of the patch : $L_R = L_R + A\ L_P$
- a *volume* object O :
      Add the directional radiance of the voxel : $L_R = L_R + A\ L_V$
      While $A >$ THRESHOLD and R is still in O
          Scale the attenuation $A = Ae^{-\alpha\rho\delta}$
            where $\delta =$ distance covered in V and $\rho =$ density of V
      End-While
      If $A >$ THRESHOLD CastVisuRay(R)
End-Function

5 Conclusion

We have presented a progressive ray-tracing based radiosity algorithm for environments including surface or volume objects with general reflectance functions and arbitrary density distributions. It accounts for surface/surface, surface/volume and volume/volume energy exchanges. A simple (but unfortunately expensive) data structure is used to store directional energy exchanges in order to circumvent the limitation to isotropic exchanges. The algorithm also simulates in the general case (*ie* multiple scattering) of the behavior of light traveling through participating media. The last characteristic of the method is that it provides optimal importance sampling for the Monte-Carlo evaluation by using specific approximated functions to describe the behaviour of light on surface or volume objects. For any additional information (e.g. complete experimentation results), please contact the first author.

Aknowledgments

The present work is supported by the *Université Bordeaux I*, the *Centre National de la Recherche Scientifique* and the *Conseil Régional d'Aquitaine*.

References

1. P. Blasi, B. Le Saëc, C. Schlick, *A Rendering Algorithm for Discrete Volume Density Objects*, Proc. EUROGRAPHICS'93, p103-116, 1993.
2. R.L. Cook, *Stochastic Sampling in Computer Graphics*, ACM Transactions on Graphics, v5, n1, p51-72, 1986.
3. D.S. Ebert, R.E.Parent, *Rendering and Animation of Gaseous Phenomena*, Proc. SIGGRAPH 90, Computer Graphics, v24, n4, p357-366, 1990.
4. J.M. Hammerley, D.C. Handscomb, *Monte-Carlo methods*, Wiley, 1964.
5. X.He, K.Torrance, F.Sillion, D.Greenberg, *A Comprehensive Physical Model for Light Reflection*, Proc. SIGGRAPH 91, Computer Graphics, v25, n4, p187-196, 1991.
6. M. Inakage, *Volume Tracing of Atmospheric Environments*, Visual Computer, p104-113, 1991.

7. J.T. Kajiya, *The Rendering Equation*, Proc. SIGGRAPH 86, Computer Graphics, v20, n3, p143-145, 1986.
8. J.T. Kajiya, B. Von Hertzen, *Ray Tracing Volume Densities*, Proc. SIGGRAPH 84, Computer Graphics, v18, n3, p165-174, 1984.
9. B. Le Saëc, C. Schlick, *A Progressive Ray Tracing based Radiosity with General Reflectance Functions*, Proc. First Eurographics Workshop on Rendering, p103-116, 1990.
10. Thomas J. V. Malley, *A Shading Method for Computer Generated Images*, MS Thesis, Univ. of Utah, June 1988.
11. H.O. Peitgen, D. Saupe, *The Science of Fractal Images*, Springer Verlag, 1988.
12. H.E. Rushmeier, K.E. Torrance, *The Zonal Method for calculating Light Intensities in Presence of Participating Medium*, Proc. SIGGRAPH 87, Computer Graphics, v21, n4, p293-302, 1987.
13. G. Sakas, *Fast Rendering of Arbitrary Distributed Volume Densities*, Proc. EUROGRAPHICS'90, p519-530, 1990.
14. C. Schlick, *Divers éléments pour une synthèse d'images réalistes*, PhD Thesis, Université Bordeaux 1, 1992.
15. C. Schlick, *An Inexpensive BDRF Model for Physically Based Rendering*, to be presented at EUROGRAPHICS'94.
16. P.S. Shirley, *Physically Based Lighting Calculations for Computer Graphics*, PhD Thesis, University of Illinois, 1990.
17. P.S. Shirley, C Wang, *Distribution RayTracing : Theory and Practice*, Proc. Third Eurographics Workshop on Rendering, 1992.
18. F.Sillion, J.Arvo, S.Westin, D.Greenberg, *A Global Illumination Solution for General Reflectance Distribution*, Proc. SIGGRAPH 91, Computer Graphics, v25, n4, p187-196, 1991.
19. G.J.Ward, *Measuring and Modeling Anisotropic Reflection*, Proc. SIGGRAPH 92, Computer Graphics, v26, n2, p265-272, 1992.
20. S.Westin, J.Arvo, K.Torrance, *Predicting Light Reflection from Complex Surfaces*, Proc. SIGGRAPH 92, Computer Graphics, v26, n2, p255-264, 1992.

Importance-driven Monte Carlo Light Tracing

Philip Dutré, Yves D. Willems

Department of Computer Science, Katholieke Universiteit Leuven
Celestijnenlaan 200A, B-3001 Heverlee, Belgium

1 Abstract

One possible method for solving the global illumination problem is to use a particle model, where particles perform a random walk through the scene to be rendered. The proposed algorithm uses this particle model, but computes the illumination of the pixels in a direct manner. In order to optimise the sampling process, adaptive probability density functions are used. The result is that particles are shot to those regions with a high potential capability. This algorithm has some advantages, such as the absence of a mesh and the possibility to handle all types of light-surface interactions with the same method.

2 Introduction

The global illumination problem is formulated by the well-known rendering equation (Kajiya 1986). Different methods have been proposed to solve this equation: Monte Carlo Path Tracing, which is in fact an application of distributed ray tracing (Cook et al. 1984, Shirley and Wang 1991, 1992); various two-pass methods which combine a radiosity and a ray tracing pass (Chen et al. 1991, Sillion and Puech 1989, Wallace et al. 1987); methods based on particle tracing (Pattanaik and Mudur 1992), which are related to solutions presented in recent heat transfer literature (Brewster 1992).

Our method is based on the simulation of the particle model of light, and propagates particles that are generated at the light sources. During the computation of the path followed by the particle, illumination contributions are directly gathered at relevant pixels. Our algorithm is a probabilistic "shooting" algorithm. The sampling is based on the bidirectional reflection distribution functions (BRDF) at the reflecting surfaces, and on an adaptive probability density function (PDF) at the light sources. The latter is initialised as a uniform sampling function, but is refined during the execution of the algorithm.

3 Mathematical Description

3.1 The Potential Equation

The flux of light leaving a given set S, consisting of points and associated directions around those points, can be written as:

$$\Phi(S) = \int_A \int_{\Omega_x} L(x \to \Theta) W_e(x \leftarrow \Theta) \cos(\Theta, n_x) d\omega_\Theta d\mu_x \quad (1)$$

The function $W_e(x \leftarrow \Theta)$ equals 1 if (x, Θ) belongs to the set, 0 otherwise. In order to solve the global illumination problem, we have to compute the fluxes corresponding to each set we are interested in. In a classic radiosity algorithm, each patch with the entire hemisphere forms a separate set. In a ray tracing algorithm, those points and directions which are visible to a pixel form a separate set. We will refer to these sets as pixel sets. A pixel set is a set of pairs (x, Θ), for which $L(x \to \Theta)$ directly contributes to the flux through the pixel.

As pointed out by Pattanaik (1993a, 1993b), the adjoint of the rendering equation (the adjoint is referred to as the potential equation), can be used to express the illumination of a specific surface in an environment. The potential equation is very well suited to describe shooting algorithms. The flux of a set is then written as:

$$\Phi(S) = \int_A \int_{\Omega_x} L_e(x \to \Theta) W(x \leftarrow \Theta) \cos(\Theta, n_x) d\omega_\Theta d\mu_x \quad (2)$$

The potential $W(x \leftarrow \Theta)$ (sometimes also referred to as importance) expresses what fraction of the total energy emitted at (x, Θ) contributes to the flux of the set S. The potential $W(x \leftarrow \Theta)$ satisfies the following transport equation:

$$W(x \leftarrow \Theta) = W_e(x \leftarrow \Theta) + \int_{\Omega_{p(x,\Theta)}} W(p(x, \Theta) \leftarrow \Psi) f_r(\Theta, x, \Psi) \cos(\Psi, n_{p(x,\Theta)}) d\omega_\Psi \quad (3)$$

By computing the potential W for each elementary light source, we can derive the flux for a certain set S (be it a patch or pixel set), and thus obtain a value for its perceived radiance. Determining the value of W for each differential light source is a shooting process, since this computation starts at the light sources and simulates the propagation of light in a scene. If we want to apply a Monte Carlo technique to solve (2), we have to generate samples at the light sources (we will refer to these samples as particles). For each particle, W needs to be evaluated, using (3). This latter is a Fredholm equation of the second kind, which can be evaluated by a random walk over the entire domain. The random walk consists of pairs $(x_0, \Theta_0), (x_1, \Theta_1), ..., (x_l, \Theta_l)$ where $x_{i+1} = p(x_i, \Theta_i)$ and Θ_{i+1} is sampled using $f_r(\Theta_i, x_{i+1}, \Psi) \cos(\Psi, n_{x_{i+1}})$ as a subcritical PDF for Ψ. This procedure leads to the following estimator for $W(x_0 \leftarrow \Theta_0)$:

$$\langle W(x_0 \leftarrow \Theta_0) \rangle = \sum_{i=0}^{l} W_e(x_i \leftarrow \Theta_i) \quad (4)$$

However, very few of the generated particles will eventually end up as belonging to the set we are interested in $(W_e \neq 0)$, unless the set in question is very large.

3.2 The Next Event Estimator

The technique known as next event estimator (Coveyou 1967, Pattanaik 1993a) tries to solve the problem that very few random walks will eventually contribute to the overall result. We define a modified potential $V(x \leftarrow \Theta)$:

$$W(x \leftarrow \Theta) = W_e(x \leftarrow \Theta) + V(x \leftarrow \Theta) \tag{5}$$

where

$$
\begin{aligned}
V(x \leftarrow \Theta) &= \int_{\Omega_{p(x,\Theta)}} W(p(x,\Theta) \leftarrow \Psi) f_r(\Theta, x, \Psi) \cos(\Psi, n_{p(x,\Theta)}) d\omega_{\Psi} \\
&= \int_{\Omega_{p(x,\Theta)}} W_e(p(x,\Theta) \leftarrow \Psi) f_r(\Theta, x, \Psi) \cos(\Psi, n_{p(x,\Theta)}) d\omega_{\Psi} \\
&\quad + \int_{\Omega_{p(x,\Theta)}} V(p(x,\Theta) \leftarrow \Psi) f_r(\Theta, x, \Psi) \cos(\Psi, n_{p(x,\Theta)}) d\omega_{\Psi} \\
&= V_e(x \leftarrow \Theta) + \int_{\Omega_{p(x,\Theta)}} V(p(x,\Theta) \leftarrow \Psi) f_r(\Theta, x, \Psi) \cos(\Psi, n_{p(x,\Theta)}) d\omega_{\Psi} \tag{6}
\end{aligned}
$$

$V(x \leftarrow \Theta)$ can be considered as the contribution of the radiance $L(x \rightarrow \Theta)$ to the flux of the set, taking into account at least one reflection on a secondary surface.

The next event estimator technique is especially useful when $W_e \neq 0$ for very few points $(p(x, \Theta), \Psi)$. If these points are known, $V_e(x \leftarrow \Theta)$ can become a very simple expression that can be evaluated analytically.

By substituting (5) in (2) the flux can now be written as:

$$
\begin{aligned}
\Phi(S) &= \int_A \int_{\Omega_x} L_e(x \rightarrow \Theta) W(x \leftarrow \Theta) \cos(\Theta, n_x) d\omega_\Theta d\mu_x \\
&= \int_A \int_{\Omega_x} L_e(x \rightarrow \Theta) W_e(x \leftarrow \Theta) \cos(\Theta, n_x) d\omega_\Theta d\mu_x \\
&\quad + \int_A \int_{\Omega_x} L_e(x \rightarrow \Theta) V(x \leftarrow \Theta) \cos(\Theta, n_x) d\omega_\Theta d\mu_x \\
&= \Phi_d(S) + \Phi_i(S) \tag{7}
\end{aligned}
$$

$\Phi(S)$ is expressed as the sum of two terms. The first term Φ_d describes the direct illumination of the light sources. A point belonging to a light source contributes directly to the flux of the set only if $W_e \neq 0$. The second term Φ_i describes the indirect illumination, through one or more reflections.

4 Algorithm

The proposed light tracing algorithm will compute estimates for all fluxes associated with each pixel set. Our algorithm will use a Monte Carlo evaluation for the integral equations (7) and (6). Some integrals require the evaluation of $W_e(x \leftarrow \Theta)$. If the eye consists of a single point, there is only one value of Θ

for each x for which $W_e(x \leftarrow \Theta)$ is possibly equal to 1. In order to evaluate $W_e(x \leftarrow \Theta)$, we just have to trace a ray from x towards the eyepoint, and check for intersecting objects and pixel containment (Fig. 1). Therefore, some integrals degenerate to a single discrete value. The evaluation of $V_e(x \leftarrow \Theta)$ (6) becomes very straightforward, as well as the evaluation of the inner integral of $\Phi_d(S)$ (7).

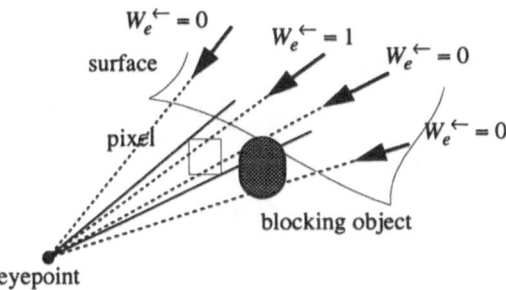

Fig. 1. Evaluation of $W_e(x \leftarrow \Theta)$: trace a ray towards the eye, and check for intersecting objects and pixel containment.

4.1 Evaluation of $\Phi(S)$

In order to evaluate $\Phi_d(S)$ using a Monte Carlo technique, we have to generate different samples $x_j (j = 1..N)$. However, $\Phi_i(S)$ also requires a direction Θ_j to be sampled. Therefore, we will generate pairs (x_j, Θ_j) to evaluate Φ_i, and use the same x_j to evaluate Φ_d. To generate x_j, we will use a PDF proportional to the emitted power of the light sources. This implies that a bright light source will be sampled more often than a weak one. Initially, Θ_j is sampled uniformly over the entire hemisphere around x_j. At regular steps during the algorithm, this PDF will be changed in order to reduce the variance (more on this in section 4.3). Once we have (x_j, Θ_j), we need to evaluate $W_e(x_j \leftarrow \Theta_j)$ and $V(x_j \leftarrow \Theta_j)$.

4.2 Evaluation of $V(x_j \leftarrow \Theta_j)$

$V(x_j \leftarrow \Theta_j)$ is given by (9), which is a Fredholm equation of the second kind. Such an equation can be stochastically evaluated by using a random walk. We consider $f_r(\Theta, x, \Psi)cos(\Theta, n_x)$ as a subcritical PDF for Θ_{i+1}. Due to the physical properties of the BRDF f_r, this is a valid assumption. We are therefore certain that the random walk will stop. By using the BRDF as the basis for the PDF, directions important to the reflection of incoming power are sampled more often.

The procedures above provide us with an algorithm to estimate the flux and the radiance associated with a given pixel set (Fig. 2). However, we are not interested in the flux of only one pixel set, but we want to compute fluxes of all pixel sets associated with all pixels of the screen. We can define a separate $W_e(S_{pixel})$ for each individual pixel set. If we evaluate each random walk taking all possible $W_e(S_{pixel})$ into account, then each random walk actually contributes to all different pixel sets. In practice this implies tracing rays towards the eye, checking for any intervening objects, and determining the correct pixel for which the contribution takes any effect.

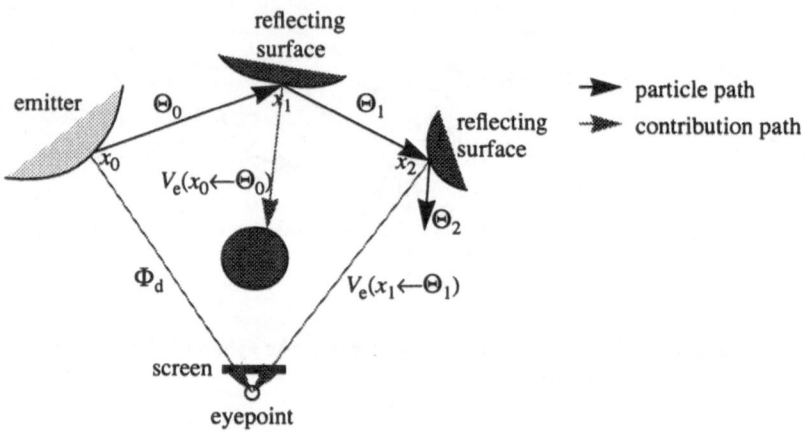

Fig. 2. Particles make a random walk through the environment. At each intersection point, a contribution for the relevant pixel is computed.

4.3 Adaptive Probability Density Functions

As a general principle for reducing the variance in Monte Carlo evaluations, the general shape of the PDF should resemble the shape of the function to be integrated. In our algorithm, the function V is part of the integrand of both Φ_d and V. It would be very interesting if we could give our PDF a similar shape to V when generating particles at the light sources. Unfortunately, the only way to gain information about the shape of V is by actually evaluating it, which we wanted to do more efficiently in the first place. Lepage (1978, Press et al. 1992) proposes an adaptive MC algorithm that adapts the PDF so that it resembles the function to be integrated. The PDF is constructed using the following principles:

- The PDF is a stepwise function. Initially, the PDF is uniform over the entire domain to be integrated.
- Each interval of the PDF has an equal chance of being selected. The size of an interval determines the actual probability of a single point belonging to that interval being selected.
- After each iteration (an iteration steps evaluates the integral using the current PDF), the PDF is updated by adjusting the size of the intervals (Fig. 3).

This is done in such a way that the estimated value of the integral in each interval is equal. If the size of the intervals doesn't change within certain limits, the "optimal" PDF is reached.

- The results of the different iterations can be combined into a single estimated value of the integral.

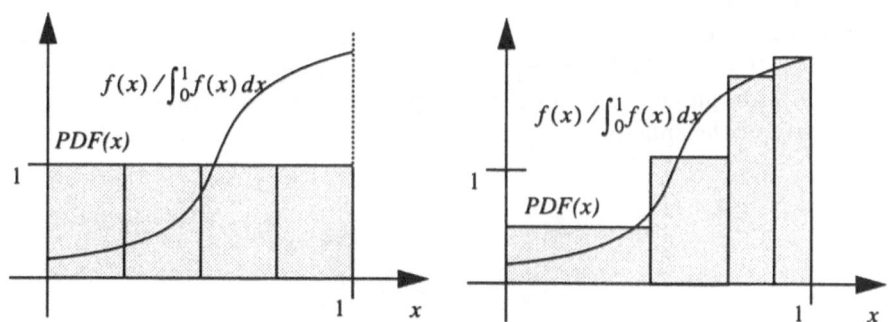

Fig. 3. Initial uniform PDF (left) and PDF after one or more iterations (right). The size of the intervals determines the probability function.

We have extended this algorithm to two dimensions (to be able to sample a direction on a hemisphere), by using a k-d tree. Whenever the dividing line between interval "leaves" is stabilised, this dividing line is frozen and the two intervals are recursively subdivided. This subdivision scheme allows for a flexible stepwise PDF.

We have applied this adaptive PDF algorithm to the sampling of the light sources. The function to be integrated is $L_e(x \rightarrow \Theta)W(x \leftarrow \Theta)\cos(\Theta, n_x)$, using random walks. After each iteration, each consisting of an appropriate number of particles, the PDF for each light source is refined using the principles outlined above. The net result is that more particles are shot in directions that contribute more to the overall flux of the screen. The stochastic sampling is therefore driven by the importance function W.

5 Results

We have implemented this algorithm using the following restrictions:

- Light sources are point light sources with a uniform radiance distribution.
- BRDFs are modelled using a Phong-like reflection model.
- Adaptive PDFs are used at the light sources.

A testscene is shown in Fig. 4. Two lightsources, on the left and right walls, are partially obscured by lamp shades. A third lightsource is positioned behind the viewer. Initially, all particles are shot uniformly in all directions around the lightsources, but after several refinements of the PDFs, particles have a higher probability of being shot in those directions that contribute to the illumination of the screen. For the light sources covered by the spheres, this implies that less particles are shot "into" the sphere, and more are shot "into" the scene. Fig. 5 shows the distribution of particles for the light source on the left wall, plotted in (u_1, u_2) space (a direction on the hemisphere is generated as $(2\pi u_1, arccos(1 - 2u_2))$, with u_1 and u_2 being uniform random numbers over $[0..1]$). The directions going "into" the scene are marked. The lower left corner represents the samples directed to the back wall, the lower right corner represents the samples directed to the front. The middle lower region marks the samples which are shot to the left wall. All samples located in the upper part correspond to directions pointing to the inside of the sphere.

Fig. 4. The testscene has two partially obscured lightsources on both walls. After several iterations, more particles should be directed upwards than can be expected from a uniform sampling of the directions around a lightsource.

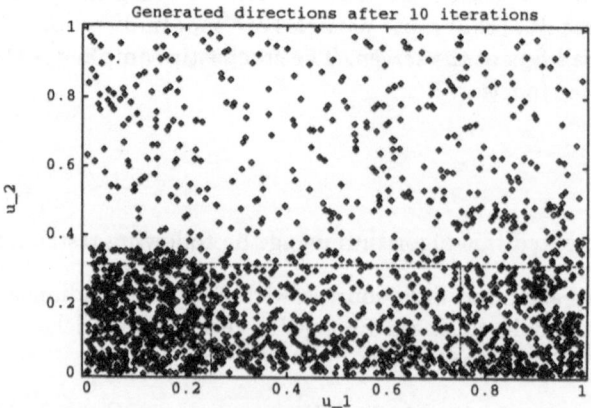

Fig. 5. Samples generated for the light source on left wall.

Figure 6 plots the average number of contributions to the screen per intersection point. Each iteration step is computed with an additional 50,000 samples generated at the light sources. The plot shows the result of only the last iteration, and also the overall result, taking all samples into account. It is clear that the hits which contribute to the screen increase with increasing number of iteration steps, and thus lower the variance of the estimate of the flux through each pixel. Other testscenes give similar results.

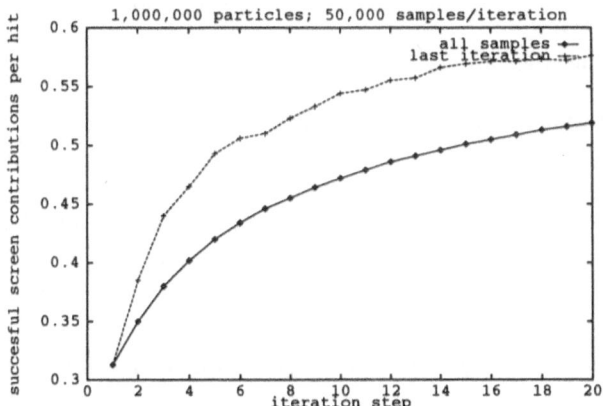

Fig. 6. Screen contributions per path vs number of iterations.

6 Discussion

The presented algorithm computes the global illumination by shooting particles from the light sources. Both the integrals expressing the fluxes and transport quantities are evaluated using Monte Carlo sampling. This means that all light transport (diffuse, specular) is carried out in a uniform way. All light paths are generated correctly, and the algorithm is therefore able to compute effects such as glossy and diffuse reflections, soft shadows and colour bleeding.

The algorithm is also the dual of the classic path tracing algorithm. Path tracing uses the next event estimator in order to solve the rendering equation. Light tracing uses the same approach, but solves the potential equation.

The algorithm tries to optimise the sampling process at the light sources by using adaptive PDFs. The PDF is represented by a two-dimensional step function, and is hierarchically built up using a k-d structure. The advantage of using this approach is clear: the new generated particles are shot in those directions that contribute the most to the screen. Thus, the potential function is actually used to guide the sampling process. Currently, the PDFs are only adapted at the light sources, but this technique can be extended to surface patches as well. The net result is that more particles are shot towards regions with high potential, and at the same time the PDF is a rough estimate of the actual potential function. This optimised sampling process can also be applied to path tracing. The approach used by Shirley (1991), where light sources are selected when shooting shadow rays, is related to this principle.

7 Conclusion

We have presented a stochastic rendering algorithm based on particle tracing, using adaptive PDFs.
Advantages of the method are:

- All kinds of light transport are handled in a uniform way.
- No mesh is required.
- All light paths are generated correctly.
- Particles are shot in directions with a high potential capability

Disadvantages are:

- The algorithm is view dependent.
- The quality of the images strongly depends on the number of particles being shot.
- High frequency details such as reflections, refractions or caustics are difficult to render accurately.

Future work includes extending the adaptive PDFs to all surfaces, and introducing the same principles to path tracing and bidirectional path tracing (Lafortune 1994). The algorithm can also be adapted to account for other sets, e.g. radiosity patches.

8 Acknowledgements

This text presents research results of the Belgian incentive program "Information Technology" - computer science of the future, initiated by the Belgian State, Prime Minister's Service, Science Policy Office. The scientific responsibility is assumed by its authors.

References

Brewster, Q.: Thermal Radiative Transfer & Properties. J.Wiley and Sons (1992).
Chen, S., Rushmeier, H., Miller, G., Turner D.: A Progressive Multi-Pass Method for Global Illumination. Computer Graphics (SIGGRAPH '91 Proceedings), 25(4) (1991) 164-174
Cook, R., Porter, T., Carpenter, L.: Distributed Ray Tracing. Computer Graphics (SIGGRAPH '84 Proceedings), 18(3) (1984) 137-145

Coveyou R., Cain V., Yost K.: Adjoint and importance in monte carlo applications. Nuclear Science and Engineering, 27 (1967) 219-234

Kajiya, J.: The Rendering Equation. Computer Graphics (SIGGRAPH '86 Proccee-dings), 20(4) (1986) 143-150

Lafortune, E., Willems, Y.: A Theoretical Framework for Physically Based Rendering, Computer Graphics Forum, Special Issue on Rendering, 13(2) (1994) 97-107

Lepage, G.: A New Algorithm for Adaptive Multidimensional Integration. Journal of Computational Physics, 27 (1978) 192-203

Pattanaik, S., Mudur, S.: Computation of Global Illumination by Monte Carlo Simula-tion of the Particle Model of Light. Proceedings of the 3rd Eurographics Workshop on Rendering, (1992) 71-83

Pattanaik, S., Mudur, S.: The Potential Equation and Importance in Illumination Com-putations, Computer Graphics Forum, 12(2) (1993a)

Pattanaik, S.: Computational Methods for Global Illumination and Visualisation of Complex 3D Environments, PhD Thesis, Birla Institute of Technology and Science, Pilani, India (1993b)

Press, W., Teukolsky, S., Vetterling, W., Flannery, B.: Numerical Recipes in Fortran, 2nd Edition, (1992) Cambridge University Press, 309-314

Shirley, P., Wang, C.: Direct Lighting by Monte Carlo Integration. Proceedings of the 2nd Eurographics Workshop on Rendering (1991)

Shirley, P., Wang, C.: Distribution Ray tracing: Theory and Practice, Proceedings of the 3rd Eurographics Workshop on Rendering (1992)

Sillion, F., Puech, C.: A General Two-Pass Method Integrating Specular and Diffuse Reflection. Computer Graphics (SIGGRAPH '89 Proceedings), 23(3) (1989) 335-344

Wallace, J., Cohen, M., Greenberg, D.: A Two-Pass Solution to the Rendering Equa-tion: A Synthesis of Ray tracing and Radiosity Methods. Computer Graphics (SIG-GRAPH '87 Proceedings), 21(4) (1987) 311-320

Appendix: Symbols & Units

Φ	flux [Watt]
$L(x \rightarrow \Theta)$	outgoing radiance at point x in direction Θ [Watt m^{-2} sr^{-1}].
$L_e(x \rightarrow \Theta)$	self-emitted outgoing radiance at point x in direction Θ [Watt m^{-2} sr^{-1}].
$W(x \leftarrow \Theta)$	incident potential at point x in direction Θ.
$W_e(x \leftarrow \Theta)$	initial incident potential at point x in direction Θ.
$d\mu_x$	differential surface area around x.
$d\omega_\Theta$	differential solid angle around Θ.
A	total area of all surface points in the environment.
Ω_x	hemisphere around point x.
$p(x, \Theta)$	the closest point "seen" by x in direction Θ.
n_x	normal at point x
$f_r(\Theta, x, \Phi)$	the Bidirectional Reflection Distribution Function (BRDF) at x, with incoming direction Θ and outgoing direction Φ [sr^{-1}].

Part IV

Radiosity

A New Stochastic Radiosity Method for Highly Complex Scenes

László Neumann[1], *Martin Feda*[2], *Manfred Kopp*[2], *Werner Purgathofer*[2]

[1] Integra Kft., Budapest, Hungary
[2] Technical University of Vienna, Vienna, Austria

Abstract

This paper presents a linear-time radiosity algorithm for very complex environments. The new algorithm is based on a progressive refinement iteration process with stochastic instead of deterministic convergence. Each iteration step simulates one interreflection step for all patches similar to Jacobi iteration, but with an approximate interreflection matrix rather than with the exact one. The stochastic shooting method is described, which computes such approximate interreflection matrices at very low computational cost. The efficiency of the algorithm can be further increased by several variance reduction methods.

1 Introduction

The radiosity algorithm is a powerful method for photorealistic rendering. It is based on solving a linear system of radiosity equations, where the radiosity values of the patches are the unknowns [5].

Unfortunately, the computation time of the radiosity algorithm for complex scenes is very high. Several modifications of the original algorithm have been described to reduce the computational complexity, e.g. [2, 3, 10, 7, 4]. However, these methods are still unsuitable for very complex scenes containing millions of patches.

The first radiosity implementations used Gauss-Seidel or Jacobi-iteration to solve the set of radiosity equations. Both iteration methods require the entire form factor matrix. Therefore they can be used only for simple scenes. Most of the state-of-the-art methods are based on the progressive refinement algorithm [3]. This algorithm is equivalent to Southwell iteration [6], a method known in numerical mathematics for solving linear systems of equations. The advantage of Southwell iteration for radiosity is that it is not necessary to store the entire matrix of form factors, only one column of the matrix associated with one shooting patch is computed on-the-fly at each iteration. Nevertheless, Southwell iteration is very slow in general numerical applications compared to other iterative methods such as Gauss-Seidel iteration or Jacobi iteration for solving systems of equations. This is why it is not used in numerical mathematics. Progressive refinement radiosity is theoretically an $O(N^2)$ algorithm, where N denotes the number of patches. It approaches $O(N)$ only for scenes with dominating direct illumination by a few light sources.

This paper describes a stochastic iteration method for radiosity evaluation designed for highly complex scenes, where the number of patches is on the order of hundreds of thousands or millions. After the definition of stochastic convergence we will show that our new algorithm converges stochastically to the correct radiosity solution. The algorithm combines the advantages of Southwell and Jacobi iteration: only a fixed number of columns of the form factor matrix have to be computed on-the-fly at each iteration similar to Southwell iteration, while the required number of iterations is comparable to Jacobi iteration. Experiments have shown that the computation time for comparable results is significantly reduced compared to conventional progressive refinement radiosity. In fact, solutions with sufficient accuracy can be obtained in linear time. The fundamentals of the new algorithm were presented in [8, 9].

2 Mathematical Background of the New Stochastic Method

Radiosity simulates the diffuse interreflections in an environment by solving the system of radiosity equations:

$$B_i = E_i + \rho_i \cdot \sum_{j=1}^{N} F_{ij} \cdot B_j \tag{1}$$

Several iterative methods can be used to obtain the solution: Gauss-Seidel iteration [5], Jacobi iteration, and Southwell iteration which is identical to the progressive refinement approach [3, 6]. The convergence requirements of these methods are always met in radiosity problems, because the system of radiosity equations is diagonally dominant: the form factors F_{ij} for each patch i sum up to at most one, and surface reflectance is always less than one.

The system of equations (1) can be written in a general form as follows:

$$x = A \cdot x + b \tag{2}$$

Under requirements invariably met in radiosity problems, the solution of this system of equations (2) can be written as a Neumann series:

$$x = b + A \cdot b + A^2 \cdot b + \ldots \tag{3}$$

In the radiosity context, the term b of the Neumann series corresponds to the self-emission, the term $A \cdot b$ to the direct illumination, the term $A^2 \cdot b$ to indirect illumination via one intermediate reflector, and so on.

Jacobi iteration is the simplest solution method. At each iteration step, the approximation of the solution is improved by the following iteration formula:

$$x^{(k)} = A \cdot x^{(k-1)} + b \tag{4}$$

With an initial vector $x^{(0)} = b$ this iterative formula leads exactly to the partial sums of the Neumann series. Unfortunately, the computation of the full matrix A is too time consuming for very complex scenes, as it contains all form factors. Furthermore, it cannot be handled because of its high memory requirements.

The idea presented here is to use stochastic convergence instead of deterministic convergence. Stochastic convergence is defined as follows: the intermediate solution vectors $x^{(k)}$ of a stochastic method converge stochastically to vector x, if for arbitrary positive ε:

$$\lim_{k \to \infty} P\left(\|x^{(k)} - x\| \geq \varepsilon\right) = 0 \tag{5}$$

where P denotes probability.

Stochastic convergence can be used to reduce the computational costs drastically. The full interreflection matrix A is replaced by different approximate interreflection matrices A_k at each iteration step k, where the expected value E of each approximate interreflection step $A_k \cdot x$ is identical to the exact interreflection step $A \cdot x$, i.e. A_k is chosen so that:

$$E\left[A_k \cdot x\right] = A \cdot x \tag{6}$$

Note that $E\left[A_k\right] = A$ is not required to meet criterion (6). Useful approximate matrices A_k can be generated much faster than the full matrix A. Details on generating $A_k \cdot x$ are described in the next section. However, if A_k is used instead of A for Jacobi iteration in formula (4), $x^{(k)}$ does not converge stochastically, because different approximate matrices A_k are used at each iteration step k. This becomes clear by expanding the first iterations of iteration formula (4) with A_k instead of A:

$$\begin{aligned}
x^{(1)} &= b + A_1 \cdot b \\
x^{(2)} &= b + A_2 \cdot b + A_2 \cdot A_1 \cdot b \\
x^{(3)} &= b + A_3 \cdot b + A_3 \cdot A_2 \cdot b + A_3 \cdot A_2 \cdot A_1 \cdot b
\end{aligned} \tag{7}$$

The first solution $x^{(1)}$ contains the first-order term $A_1 \cdot b$, while $x^{(2)}$ and $x^{(3)}$ contain first-order terms $A_2 \cdot b$ and $A_3 \cdot b$, respectively. In the same way, $x^{(2)}$ and $x^{(3)}$ contain different second-order terms, and so on. Therefore the iteration results $x^{(k)}$ are not convergent.

Stochastic convergence can be achieved only if all terms of the partial sum $x^{(k-1)}$ are contained in the new partial sum $x^{(k)}$. This means that new terms of any order n must not replace the nth order terms of the previous partial sums, but they have to be combined, e.g. by averaging:

$$x^{(1)} = b + A_1 \cdot b$$

$$x^{(2)} = b + \frac{1}{2} \cdot (A_1 + A_2) \cdot b + A_2 \cdot A_1 \cdot b \tag{8}$$

$$x^{(3)} = b + \frac{1}{3} \cdot (A_1 + A_2 + A_3) \cdot b +$$

$$\frac{1}{3} \cdot (A_2 \cdot A_1 + A_3 \cdot A_1 + A_3 \cdot A_2) \cdot b + A_3 \cdot A_2 \cdot A_1 \cdot b$$

Since all $A_k \cdot x$ have the same expected value $A \cdot x$, the iteration is guaranteed to converge stochastically to the correct solution. It is important to note that each iteration k improves the accuracy of the solution in two ways: the variance of terms already contained in $x^{(k-1)}$ is improved in $x^{(k)}$, and a new term of order k is added.

Reducing the variance of a nth order term means in the radiosity context, that the nth order interreflection corresponding to this term is more accurately simulated than in the previous intermediate solution $x^{(k-1)}$. The reduction of the variance by averaging approximate matrices A_k of identical expected value $E[A_k \cdot x] = A \cdot x$ becomes clear by the following fact:

$$\lim_{n \to \infty} \frac{1}{n} \cdot \sum_{k=1}^{n} A_k \cdot x = A \cdot x \tag{9}$$

Equation (9) can be generalized for n^{th} order terms. By that it can be shown that the iteration converges stochastically to the correct solution.

In addition to the variance reduction, each iteration k adds a new term of order k, which represents one additional step of diffuse interreflection in the radiosity context: while $x^{(1)}$ accounts for self-emission and direct illumination only, the approximation of indirect illumination via one intermediate reflector is contained in $x^{(2)}$, the approximation of indirect illumination via two intermediate reflectors is contained in $x^{(3)}$, etc.

Unfortunately, it is impossible to compute the average terms for any order n with the correct weighting factors as in (8). The numerical result $x^{(1)}$ cannot be split up into separated terms, and therefore the different terms of order n generated in subsequent iterations cannot be averaged with correct weighting factors. So other averaging methods have to be found which do not require to manipulate the single terms of the partial sums.

We propose the following iteration formula, which is simple to handle and memory efficient, because it does not require any additional storage for averaging:

$$x^{(k)} = (1 - \tau_k) \cdot x^{(k-1)} + \tau_k \cdot \left[A_k \cdot x^{(k-1)} + b \right] \tag{10}$$

where $\{\tau_k\}$ is an appropriate series which converges to 0. For example, the harmonic series can be used for $\{\tau_k\}$:

$$\tau_k = \frac{1}{k} \tag{11}$$

Using equations (10) and (11), the partial sums of the first three iterations are:

$$x^{(1)} = b + A_1 \cdot b$$
$$x^{(2)} = b + \frac{1}{2} \cdot (A_1 + A_2) \cdot b + \frac{1}{2} \cdot A_2 \cdot A_1 \cdot b \tag{12}$$
$$x^{(3)} = b + \frac{1}{3} \cdot (A_1 + A_2 + A_3) \cdot b +$$
$$\left(\frac{1}{3} \cdot A_2 \cdot A_1 + \frac{1}{6} \cdot A_3 \cdot A_1 + \frac{1}{6} \cdot A_3 \cdot A_2 \right) \cdot b + \frac{1}{6} \cdot A_3 \cdot A_2 \cdot A_1 \cdot b$$

The low-order terms in (12) contain the average of matrices, just as in (8). However, higher order terms are not correctly averaged, because the weighting factors of matrices or of products of matrices do not sum up to one. However, the sum of weighting factors for each term converges to one, as the iteration progresses. Therefore the iteration process based on formulas (10) and (11) is guaranteed to converge stochastically to the correct solution. More details of the theoretical background of our method are given in [9].

3 The Stochastic Shooting Method

This section describes a method to compute $A_k \cdot x^{(k-1)} + b$ with approximate interreflection matrices A_k that meet criterion (6). We call this method "stochastic shooting method". It is designed for highly complex scenes and very efficient: its computational complexity for evaluating $A_k \cdot x$ is only $O(N)$ instead of $O(N^2)$ for the exact evaluation of $A \cdot x$ (N is the number of patches in the scene). The new method works with radiant power values $P_i = B_i \cdot Area_i$ (in Watt) rather than with radiosity values B_i, as is implicitly done by conventional progressive refinement radiosity as well. Therefore it is convenient to reformulate the radiosity equation (1) by using the reciprocity principle (13) in terms of power (14):

$$Area_i \cdot F_{ij} = Area_j \cdot F_{ji} \tag{13}$$

$$P_i = W_i + \rho_i \cdot \sum_{j=1}^{N} F_{ji} \cdot P_j \tag{14}$$

$W_i = E_i \cdot Area_i$ is the self-emitted power of patch i.

The idea of stochastic shooting is to select a fixed number M of shooting patches for each iteration step. The selection is made stochastically by importance sampling, where the probability of a patch to be selected is proportional to its radiant power. These M shooting operations form one stochastic shooting step. A useful number of shooting patches at each step is e.g. $M = 500$, that means that $M \ll N$. The M shooting patches act as representatives of all other patches. Therefore they do not simply shoot their own power as in progressive refinement radiosity - this would violate criterion (6) - but they shoot equal portions of the total radiant power of all patches in the scene. The expected value of such a shooting step is equal to the exact result of one interreflection step, where all patches are distributing their own power. Therefore the stochastic shooting method meets criterion (6).

It is important to note that no "unshot" power values are involved in the stochastic shooting method, because it is similar to Jacobi iteration, but not to Southwell iteration as conventional progressive refinement radiosity. Therefore the M shooting patches are selected according to the current power values P_i. Bright patches with high power P_i are selected with higher probability than patches with low power. Since the power P_i is already represented by this selection probability, all shooting patches have to shoot the same amount of power. Since the M shooting patches are representatives of the entire scene, the total power P_{total} of all N patches in the scene has to be shot from the M shooting patches in M equal portions to meet criterion (5). The power shot from each one of the M shooting patches is given by:

$$X = \frac{1}{M} \cdot \sum_{i=1}^{N} P_i = \frac{1}{M} \cdot P_{total} \tag{15}$$

It is possible that importance sampling selects one patch several times for one iteration step, especially if it is very bright. In any case, M different shooting patches have to be selected, but patches which are selected several times shoot multiple portions of power. Generalizing formula (15), the power shot from a patch j which is selected M_j times is given by:

$$X_j = M_j \cdot \frac{\sum_{i=1}^{N} P_i}{\sum_{i=1}^{N} M_i} = M_j \cdot \frac{P_{total}}{\sum_{i=1}^{N} M_i} \tag{16}$$

Note that $M_j = 0$ for most of the N patches. $\sum_{i=1}^{N} M_i = M$ if each one of the M shooting patches is selected only once by importance sampling, otherwise $\sum_{i=1}^{N} M_i > M$.

In the first iteration it might be impossible to find M different shooting patches, if there are less than M light sources, while all the other patches are dark. In this case, or if there are some dominating light sources emitting most of the self-emitted power, the light sources should shoot their power to the environment in a preprocessing step by conventional deterministic shooting, as discussed in section 5.

In analogy to Jacobi iteration (4), $A_k \cdot x^{k-1} + b$ is evaluated for each patch by summing up the self-emitted power and the incoming power at iteration k, weighted by the form factors. Note that the incoming power is not added to the previous values as in progressive refinement radiosity (Southwell iteration). Therefore no unshot power values are required.

4 Implementation

The new stochastic algorithm using averaging formula (10) and without the preprocessing step is illustrated in the following pseudo-code description:

for all patches i:
$P_i := W_i$
while not converged:
{
select M shooting patches by importance sampling proportional P_i
compute total power P_{total} in the environment
determine τ_k
for all patches i:
{
$P_i := (1 - \tau_k) \cdot P_i + \tau_k \cdot W_i$ */* first part of*
formula (10) */
}
for all shooting patches j:
{
compute all form factors F_{ji} for shooting patch j
compute portion X_j of total power P_{total} shot from j by eq. (16)
for all receiving patches i:
$P_i := P_i + \tau_k \cdot \rho_i \cdot F_{ji} \cdot X_j$ */* second part of formula (10) */*
}
display Gouraud interpolated image
}

The form factors are computed by hemi-cubes in our implementation [1], but other methods are possible, e.g. ray traced form factors [12].

The iteration formula (10) is split up into two parts here. The reason is that in this way no additional storage is required, while a direct implementation of formula (10) requires separated storage for the old and the new solutions ($x^{(k-1)}$ and $x^{(k)}$, respectively). In this implementation, the first part scales the old solution and the self-emitted part according to (10), while the second part scales and adds the power received at this iteration.

Importance sampling is implemented in linear time as follows: a cumulative distribution function F is defined by

$$F(j) = \frac{\sum_{i=1}^{j} P_i}{\sum_{i=1}^{N} P_i} \tag{17}$$

Obviously, $F(0) = 0$ and $F(N) = 1$. We now define regular steps $\Delta = \frac{1}{M}$ and a random starting value $y_1 = r \cdot \Delta$, where r is a random value of uniform distribution in the interval $(0, 1)$. Given $y_i = y_1 + (i - 1) \cdot \Delta$. Patch j is selected as shooting patch if

$$F(j-1) \leq y_i < F(j) \tag{18}$$

Importance sampling is illustrated in fig.1.

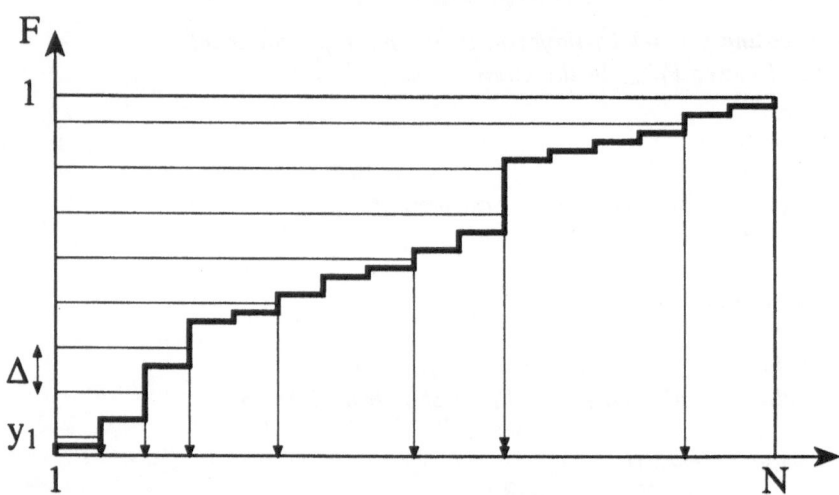

Fig. 1. Importance sampling.

The advantage of this stratified technique to perform importance sampling is that it scatters the M shooting patches throughout the environment, if the numbering of patches corresponds to the objects in the scene. Therefore, the M shooting patches are good representatives of the environment. The selection of M representative illuminators among N patches can be interpreted as some kind of grouping.

Fig.1 also shows that very bright patches can be selected several times in one iteration step. In this case, this method does not select M different patches, as it is shown in fig.1: M is 8 in this example, but only 7 different patches are selected, because one patch is selected twice. If the number of different shooting patches is significantly less than M, the missing number of patches should be selected in a second pass with new Δ and y_1 to improve the accuracy, provided that there are sufficient other candidates that were not selected.

For generating color images, the color band of the rgb triple with highest power is determined for each patch and used for the computation of P_{total} and for importance sampling. The shooting patches shoot the full power X_j only in this color band, while in the other color bands X_j is attenuated according to the ratio of actual power values.

5 Enhancements

The basic idea of the new method can be varied and enhanced in many details. Some of these extensions are described in this section.

Instead of the harmonic set used in formula (11), other series of τ_k values can be used. The disadvantage of the harmonic set is that only the coefficients of the first order elements $A_i \cdot b$ sum up to one, as it can be seen in (12). That means that indirect illumination effects are underestimated. This problem can be solved by preceding the harmonic set by an arbitrary number of "1"s, e.g. one to three of them. For example, the series $\tau_k = \{1, 1, \frac{1}{2}, \frac{1}{3}, \ldots\}$ contains one preceding "1" and leads to the following partial sums in the first three iterations:

$$
\begin{aligned}
x^{(1)} &= b + A_1 \cdot b \\
x^{(2)} &= b + A_2 \cdot b + A_2 \cdot A_1 \cdot b \\
x^{(3)} &= b + \frac{1}{2} \cdot (A_2 + A_3) \cdot b + \frac{1}{2} \cdot (A_2 \cdot A_1 + A_3 \cdot A_2) \cdot b + \frac{1}{2} \cdot A_3 \cdot A_2 \cdot A_1 \cdot b
\end{aligned}
\tag{19}
$$

It can be seen that the coefficients of second order terms sum up to one here, and that the coefficient of the third order term is significantly increased. In general, each "1" preceding the harmonic set increases the maximum order of terms by one, for which the coefficients sum up to one. On the other hand, this method reduces the number of considered terms, thus increasing the variance. For example, the first order term of $x^{(3)}$ in (19) contains only two approximate matrices, while in (12) three matrices are considered.

If the scene contains a relatively small number of light sources or some dominating light sources with high self-emittance, importance sampling will probably select the light sources as shooting patches at each iteration, thus increasing the variance of the solution. This problem can be solved by deterministic shooting in a preprocessing step. Each of the brightest light sources shoots its self-emitted power in this preprocessing step as in conventional progressive refinement radiosity. This self-emitted power must not be considered in the subsequent stochastic iteration, because it is already distributed. This is the only case where unshot power values appear in our algorithm: the unshot powers of light source patches, which were received from other shooting patches in the preprocessing step, act as new self-emittance values for the stochastic shooting method. For image rendering purposes, the self-emitted power distributed in the preprocessing step has to be added to the power values computed by stochastic iteration to get the total power of the patches, because the power already distributed in the preprocessing step is not considered by stochastic iteration. For patches not processed by deterministic shooting, the power received in the preprocessing step (unshot power) acts as self-emittance.

Instead of starting the iteration with $x^{(0)} = b$, a better estimate for $x^{(0)}$ can be obtained by the ambient light described in [3]. The new starting vector is given by $x^{(0)} = b + x_{amb}$. The ambient light can furthermore be used for overshooting in the preprocessing step. Each patch selected in the preprocessing step shoots not only its self-emitted power, but also some estimated power representing power received from other patches. The ambient light can be used to estimate this additional power [4]. Shooting more than the actual power results in negative unshot power. Since the unshot power after the preprocessing step acts as self-emittance for the stochastic shooting algorithm, it must be adapted to handle negative power in the following manner: absolute values of power are used both for computing P_{total} and for importance sampling. If a patch j with negative power is selected for shooting, it shoots the same amount of power as all of the M patches, but negative power $-X_j$ instead of positive power X_j.

With the algorithm outlined in section 4, the images are updated after each iteration, each iteration consisting of M shooting operations. Therefore, the image update rate is relatively low. To increase the image update rate, intermediate images can be generated. The power values corresponding to the radiosities displayed in these images can be obtained by:

$$j_{x}{}^{(k)} = \left(1 - \tau_k \cdot \frac{j}{M}\right) \cdot x^{(k-1)} + \tau_k \cdot \left[{}^{j}A_k \cdot x^{(k-1)} + \frac{j}{M} \cdot b\right] \qquad (20)$$

$j_{x}{}^{(k)}$ denotes the intermediate result after j shooting operations of the iteration k, ${}^{j}A_k$ is an approximate matrix containing j columns corresponding to the j processed shooting patches (${}^{M}x^{(k)} = x^{(k)}$ and ${}^{M}A_k = A_k$).

6 Results

Figures 3-6 (see color plate 7) show a test scene consisting of 338,000 triangles, rendered with different methods. Figures 3 and 4 demonstrate the inefficiency of conventional progressive refinement: figure 3 shows direct illumination only, shooting the 3,144 light sources. For figure 4 15,000 shooting steps were performed, but the solution is nearly identical to direct illumination only, because conventional progressive refinement radiosity converges very slowly. Figure 5 shows the same solution with 15,000 shooting steps, but with adding ambient light for display [3]. Figure 6 shows the stochastic solution, spending the same computational expense as for figure 4 and 5. The computation time was 35 hours on an Iris Indigo with MIPS R4000 processor for each one of figures 4-6.

Receiving patches very close to one of the shooting patches tend to be too bright in the stochastic solution, possibly leading to irritating artifacts, which disappear very slowly as the iteration progresses. Such artifacts can be seen for example in the corners of rooms, as in figure 6. This problem is inherent to the stochastic shooting method. One rather expensive method to attack this problem is to repeat the complete solution process with different random numbers for importance sampling, resulting in several radiosity solutions, which are almost equal, but where artifacts appear at different places. The minimal radiosity value of patches from these solutions is used for rendering. Other methods are still under development.

Three different solutions were computed to generate figure 6, each one using 10 stochastic iteration steps with $M = 500$, so that the total number of hemicubes is 15,000, as for figures 4 and 5. For each patch, the minimum radiosity value from these three solutions was used for display to eliminate the artifacts described above.

Figures 7 and 8 (see color plate 7) show a test scene consisting of 294,000 patches. Figure 7 shows the deterministic solution using 10,000 conventional iterations without ambient light, while figure 8 shows the stochastic solution with 1000 shooting patches in the preprocessing step and 9 stochastic iterations with $M = 1000$. Thus, the number of hemi-cubes is 10,000 for both methods, the computation time was 25 hours.

Interreflections are represented much stronger in the solution computed by stochastic shooting. Therefore the images displaying the stochastic solution are much brighter than the corresponding images displaying the deterministic solution without ambient light, where most interreflections are still missing. Color bleeding effects are also more visible in images displaying the stochastic solution. This can be seen best in figures 7-8 on the ceiling from the bluish floor.

We cannot give an exact error evaluation for complex test scenes, because it would require the exact radiosity solution. However, for some scenes it is easy to determine the exact solution analytically: we use the interior of a cube consisting of 480,000 triangles of equal size, where the emission of each triangle is 1, and the reflectance is 50%. The exact radiosity solution for each triangle is 2. The stochastic shooting algorithm was performed with 500 shooting patches in the preprocessing step, and 9 stochastic iterations with M=500. Fig.2 shows the average error of stochastic shooting and conventional progressive refinement radiosity with corresponding numbers of shooting patches. Conventional progressive refinement radiosity converges very slowly. After 5000 shooting patches, approximately 1% of the total power is shot. Stochastic shooting converges much faster. The preprocessing step leads to a reduction of efficiency for this scene, because there are no dominating light sources, but all patches have equal self-emissions.

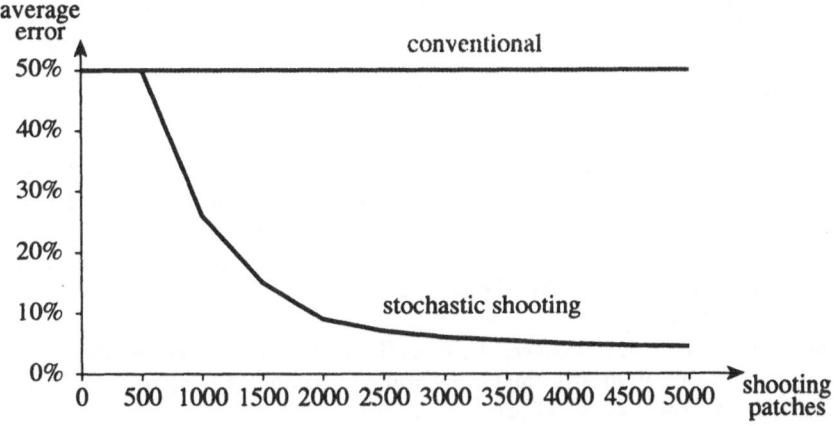

Fig. 2. Average errors of stochastic shooting and conventional progressive radiosity.

7 Conclusion and Future Trends

This paper describes a novel stochastic approach for linear-time solution of diffuse radiosity problems for very complex environments. It converges stochastically to the correct solution.

Of course, this method has its limits. For example, let a city be illuminated by one hundred thousand lamps. At each iteration at most some thousand of these lamps can be considered. Light deficiency will appear in the neighborhood of a lamp not picked out, while light excess will appear close to selected lamps. Both cases are especially troublesome for a lamp near the point of view. View-independent radiosity solutions for such scenes seem to be too time consuming on current hardware. Therefore importance driven methods should be considered [11].

Other variance reduction methods may be based on the information accumulated at previous iterations. Optimal determination of τ_k exploiting this information seems promising, but also other averaging methods should be considered. Alternatives to the stochastic shooting method for approximating $A \cdot x$ should also be investigated. An other interesting field of future research is to enhance the algorithm to non-diffuse environments.

Variance reduction by hierarchical patch subdivision is also considered to be an essential field of future research.

Receiving patches very close to one of the shooting patches tend to be too bright, thus possibly leading to irritating artifacts. Current research is devoted to this problem, and will be continued in the future.

Acknowledgments

Thanks to A. Neumann for his help for this work by mathematical discussions, to C. Kelemen for his suggestions for the development of the stochastic shooting method, and to P. Shirley, J. Kalinowski, J. Sas, and G. Bajda for test scenes.

References

1. Cohen, M., Greenberg, D.: The Hemi-Cube - A Radiosity Solution for Complex Environments. Computer Graphics (ACM SIGGRAPH '85 Proceedings) 19(3), (1985).
2. Cohen, M., Greenberg, D., Immel, D., Brock, P.: An Efficient Radiosity Approach for Realistic Image Synthesis. IEEE Computer Graphics and Applications 6(2),   (1986).
3. Cohen, M., Chen, E., Wallace, J., Greenberg, D.: A Progressive Refinement Approach to Fast Radiosity Image Generation. Computer Graphics (ACM SIGGRAPH '88 Proceedings) 22(4),   (1988).
4. Feda, M., Purgathofer, W.: Accelerating Radiosity by Overshooting. Proceedings of 3rd Eurographics Workshop on Rendering, Bristol, UK (1992).

 5. Goral, C., Torrance, K., Greenberg, D.,Battaile, B.: Modeling the Interaction
    of Light between Diffuse Surfaces. Computer Graphics (ACM SIGGRAPH '84
    Proceedings) 18(3),   (1984).
 6. Gortler, S., Cohen, M.: Solving the Radiosity Linear System. Communicating
    with Virtual Worlds, Proceedings of Computer Graphics International 93, N.
    and D. Thalmann (editors), Springer (1993).
 7. Hanrahan, P., Saltzmann, D., Aupperle, L.: A Rapid Hierarchical Radiosity
    Algorithm. Computer Graphics (ACM SIGGRAPH '91 Proceedings) 25(4),
    (1991).
 8. Neumann, L.: Monte Carlo Radiosity. Lecture at the 4th Eurographics Work-
    shop on Rendering as part of the special session *Computer Graphics Research
    in Eastern Europe*, Paris, France (1993).
 9. Neumann, L.: Monte Carlo Radiosity. Paper submitted to *Computing* (1994).
10. Recker, R., George, D., Greenberg, D.: Acceleration Techniques for Progressive
    Refinement Radiosity. Computer Graphics 24(2),   (1990).
11. Smits, B., Arvo, J., Salesin, D.: An Importance-Driven Radiosity Algorithm.
    Computer Graphics (ACM SIGGRAPH '92 Proceedings) 26(4),   (1992).
12. Wallace, J., Elmquist, K., Haines, E.: A Ray Tracing Algorithm for Progres-
    sive Radiosity. Computer Graphics (ACM SIGGRAPH '89 Proceedings) 23(3),
    (1989).

Constructing Solvers for Radiosity Equation Systems

Wei Xu[1], Donald S. Fussell[2]

[1] Department of Mathematics, University of Texas at Austin, TX 78712, USA
[2] Department of Computer Sciences, University of Texas at Austin, TX 78712, USA

1 Introduction

In computer graphics, many approaches to determining the illumination in an environment of light emitters and Lambertian reflectors employ a piecewise constant approximation to the radiosity function, leading to a linear system with n^2 coefficients (the form factors) given n surface elements over which the function is assumed constant. Approaches of this type have collectively been called *classical radiosity* [Go1]. In the past ten years, several iterative techniques for solving such systems have been developed. While initially, Gauss-Seidel iteration was used to solve such systems [Go1], more recent work employs relaxation techniques which can improve the efficiency of each step in the iteration, so that only $O(n)$ computations are needed per iteration rather than the $O(n^2)$ required by Gauss-Seidel and similar techniques [Co1, Fe1, Go2, Sh1, Xu1]. This efficiency has made classical radiosity practical for moderately complex environments. In this paper, we provide a common mathematical treatment of these more efficient iterative solvers, which we henceforth call *linear iteration* (LI) solvers. Note that linear in this context refers to the complexity of a single iteration in the solution of a classical radiosity system with $O(n^2)$ coefficients and not to any reduction in the overall number of interactions required to achieve a given error bound as is done in hierarchical [Ha1] and wavelet [Go1] methods.

The progressive radiosity(PR) algorithm, presented by Cohen et al. in 1988[Co1], is the first LI method specifically designed to solve radiosity systems, although it was later shown to be equivalent to Southwell's relaxation method [Go2]. Subsequently, Feda presented an overshooting algorithm which converges much faster than the PR method in some cases. However, Feda provided no mathematical analysis of his algorithm, and since the algorithm involves "negative radiance shooting" in almost all circumstances, it is not obvious that it converges in general. To solve the convergence problem, Shao et al. [Sh1] and Gortler et al. [Go2] developed their own new overshooting algorithms independently. Their methods are similar in that both of them are based on a combination of radiance gathering and shooting among parts of the environment at each iteration. Moreover, they are both *positive* overshooting methods, which means no negative radiance interchanges are needed.

Although the positive overshooting methods have been proven to be convergent, they do not converge as fast as Feda's method in some cases [Go2]. Recently, the authors gave a new overshooting algorithm (called Xu's method in this paper), which is based on a general mathematical analysis of radiosity equation systems [Xu1]. Experimental results indicate that the new method converges faster than existing methods in all cases tested. In [Xu1], we also gave a modified version of Feda's method which outperforms Feda's original method experimentally, and we have shown that both Xu's method and the modification of Feda's method are convergent under certain conditions. Our modification to Feda's method removes an unreasonable restriction on the magnitude of radiance increments allowed, which hinders the convergence of the algorithm. Since the main ideas of Feda's original algorithm and our modification are the same, unless otherwise specified, "Feda's method" henceforth will refer to both versions of Feda's method.

In the remaining sections of this paper, we describe the radiosity problem in a way that allows a uniform mathematical treatment of all these methods. We discuss misconceptions that have hindered the development of more effective overshooting techniques. We show how existing LI solvers can be understood as variants of a general iterative solution algorithm. We then show that many of these systems are related to each other in that they are essentially the same techniques applied to different transformed linear systems using various preconditioners. We then describe experimental results on a benchmark scene which confirm the results in [Xu1] indicating that our method converges faster than previous methods on a variety of scenes. These results also demonstrate that the original algorithm of Feda fails to converge on the test scene, while our modification of this algorithm converges very rapidly.

2 Background

2.1 Problem Definition

The classical radiosity equation system used in computer graphics is

$$\mathbf{M}\mathbf{x} = \mathbf{b} \tag{1}$$

or, equivalently,

$$\mathbf{D}\mathbf{M}\mathbf{D}^{-1}(\mathbf{D}\mathbf{x}) = \mathbf{D}\mathbf{b} \tag{2}$$

based on the reciprocity relation $A_i F_{i,j} = A_j F_{j,i}$,
   where
   $\mathbf{M} = \mathbf{I} - \mathbf{F} \in \mathbf{R}^{n \times n}$, $\mathbf{I}$ is the nth order identity matrix,
   $\mathbf{F} = (f_{i,j})_{n \times n} \in \mathbf{R}^{n \times n}$, $f_{i,j} = \rho_i F_{i,j}$,
   $\mathbf{b} = (b_1, \cdots, b_n)^T \in \mathbf{R}^n$,
   $\mathbf{D}$ is the diagonal matrix with $A_1, \ldots, A_n$ as its diagonal elements,
   and
   ρ_i: the reflectivity of the ith patch, $0 < \rho_i < 1$,

$F_{i,j}$:the form-factor from the ith patch to the jth patch satisfying $F_{i,i} = 0$ and $\sum_{j=1}^{n} F_{i,j} \equiv 1$,

b_i : the emission of the ith patch, $b_i \neq 0$ means the ith patch is a light source,

A_i: the area of the ith patch in the system,

$\mathbf{x} = (x_1, \cdots, x_n)^T \in \mathbf{R}^n$ is the vector of radiosities of all patches.

We use A to denote the total area of all n patches: $A = \sum_i A_i$. In the following sections, we assume $\mathbf{x}$ to be an approximation of the true solution $\mathbf{x}^*$ of e.q. (1) and define the corresponding *residual* $\mathbf{r} = (r_1, \ldots, r_n)^T$ by $\mathbf{r} = \mathbf{b} - \mathbf{Mx}$, which is equivalent to $\mathbf{M}(\mathbf{x}^* - \mathbf{x}) = \mathbf{r}$.

By convention, unless specified, matrices are represented by bold capital letters, vectors by bold small letters and scalars by plain letters.

2.2 Negative Shooting and Unshot Energy

In computer graphics, the radiosity equation system (1) can be regarded as the equilibrium power balance of all patches in the environment emitting and receiving radiances among themselves. When we get an approximate solution $\mathbf{x}$, it means that $\mathbf{x}$ is an intermediate stage in the process of reaching equilibrium. In previous methods [Co1, Fe1, Go2, Sh1, Xu1], r_i is called the "unshot energy" of the ith patch after x_i has been shot from the patch. In overshooting methods, r_i could be negative. Since radiant energy is always positive, the negativity of r_i can easily lead the the conclusion that negative shooting is bad for the convergence of solvers. This seems to be a primary reason for the development of positive overshooting methods [Go2, Sh1].

To understand negative shooting, we must first distinguish between *incorrect shooting* and *negative shooting*. Radiance shot from a patch, say the ith patch, at iteration p, is said to be incorrect if it makes $|x_i^{(p)} - x_i^*| > |x_i^{(p-1)} - x_i^*|$. On the other hand, radiance shot from patch i at iteration p is negative if $x_i^{(p-1)} > x_i^{(p)}$, that is, if the increment to x_i is negative. We emphasize here that negative shooting is NOT necessarily incorrect. In fact, in our numerical experiments, we have found that very few (less than 1% of) negative increments are incorrect in either Feda's or Xu's methods. Another factor leading to a misunderstanding of negative shooting is the term "unshot energy." In numerical analysis, the vector $\mathbf{r}$ is called the "residual." In computer graphics, $\mathbf{r}$ is called "unshot energy" because $\mathbf{r}$ appears to account for all the nonequilibrium radiosity of all patches in the environment. Actually, however, the ideal shooting radiance for a shooting patch i is $x_i^* - x_i$, which is in general not the same as $\mathbf{r}_i$. Therefore, we should call $x_i^* - x_i$ the unshot energy, which means shooting this quantity will obtain the true solution x_i^* on the ith patch. Since $\mathbf{r} = (\mathbf{I} - \mathbf{F})(\mathbf{x}^* - \mathbf{x})$, we see that the relationship between signs of elements in $\mathbf{r}$ and signs of elements in $\mathbf{x}^* - \mathbf{x}$ is quite complicated[Xu1]. For these reasons, in this paper, we call $\mathbf{r}$ the residual and $x_i^* - x_i$ the unshot energy.

3 General LI Solvers

Notice that the coefficient matrix in e.q. (1) is row diagonally dominant while the coefficient matrix in e.q. (2) is column diagonally dominant. The diagonal dominance of radiosity equation systems guarantees that $\mathbf{M}$ is invertible, and $\mathbf{M}^{-1}$ can be represented as the Neumann series [Ki1]

$$\mathbf{M}^{-1} = \sum_{k=0}^{\infty} \mathbf{F}^k. \tag{3}$$

Therefore,

$$\mathbf{x}^* = \sum_{k=0}^{\infty} \mathbf{F}^k \mathbf{b}. \tag{4}$$

The term $\mathbf{F}^k \mathbf{b}$ in the equation above represents the illumination of $\mathbf{b}$ passed through k reflections in all possible ways among all patches in the environment.

3.1 Some Important Matrices

As a foundation for further discussion of LI solvers for radiosity equation systems, we now present some matrices which are necessary for our formulation of existing techniques. Although some of the algorithms covered were not expressed in matrix form originally, this formulation will allow us to see the relationship among them more clearly.

Let

$$\mathbf{M}_i = \mathbf{I} - \mathbf{F}_i \tag{5}$$

where

$$\mathbf{F}_i = \begin{pmatrix} 0 & \cdots & \rho_1 F_{1,i} & \cdots & 0 \\ 0 & \cdots & \rho_2 F_{2,i} & \cdots & 0 \\ \vdots & \cdots & \vdots & \cdots & \vdots \\ \rho_i F_{i,1} & \cdots & 0 & \cdots & \rho_i F_{i,n} \\ \vdots & \cdots & \vdots & \cdots & \vdots \\ 0 & \cdots & \rho_{n-1} F_{n-1,i} & \cdots & 0 \\ 0 & \cdots & \rho_n F_{n,i} & \cdots & 0 \end{pmatrix} \tag{6}$$

for some fixed i and

$$\tilde{\mathbf{M}} = \mathbf{I} - \tilde{\mathbf{F}} \tag{7}$$

where

$$\tilde{\mathbf{F}} = \begin{pmatrix} \rho_1 \frac{A_1}{A} & \cdots & \rho_1 \frac{A_n}{A} \\ \vdots & \cdots & \vdots \\ \rho_n \frac{A_1}{A} & \cdots & \rho_n \frac{A_n}{A} \end{pmatrix} = \begin{pmatrix} \rho_1 \\ \vdots \\ \rho_n \end{pmatrix} \left(\frac{A_1}{A}, \ldots, \frac{A_n}{A} \right). \tag{8}$$

$$\tag{9}$$

It is easy to verify that

$$\tilde{\mathbf{M}}^{-1} = \mathbf{I} + \frac{1}{1 - \rho_{ave}} \tilde{\mathbf{F}} \tag{10}$$

and

$$\tilde{\mathbf{F}}^2 = \rho_{ave} \tilde{\mathbf{F}}, \tag{11}$$

where

$$\rho_{ave} = \frac{1}{A} \sum_{j=1}^{n} \rho_j A_j \leq \max_i \rho_i \tag{12}$$

is the area-weighted reflectivity of the environment. We also define

$$\mathbf{W} = \mathbf{I} + \mathbf{F} + (\tilde{\mathbf{F}}^2 + \tilde{\mathbf{F}}^3 + \tilde{\mathbf{F}}^4 + \cdots) = \mathbf{I} + \mathbf{F} + \tilde{\mathbf{F}}(\tilde{\mathbf{M}}^{-1} - \mathbf{I}) = \mathbf{I} + \mathbf{F} + \frac{\rho_{ave}}{1 - \rho_{ave}} \tilde{\mathbf{F}}. \tag{13}$$

We can now express the Ambient term defined in [Co1] as follows

$$Ambient = \frac{\sum_j A_j r_j}{A - \sum_j A_j \rho_j}$$

$$= \frac{1}{\rho_i(1 - \rho_{ave})} \mathbf{e}_i^T \tilde{\mathbf{F}} \mathbf{r} \quad for \ all \ i.$$

where $\mathbf{e}_i = (0, \ldots, 1, \ldots, 0)^T$. Thus matrix $\tilde{\mathbf{F}}$ is closly related to the Ambient. We will see later that $\tilde{\mathbf{F}}$ is central to the matrix representation of Feda's method, although Feda did not give this matrix in his original paper. Notice that $\tilde{\mathbf{F}}$ is a reasonable approximation of $\mathbf{F}$ based on the knowledge of form-factors; how good an approximation depends, of course, on the configuration of the environment. Matrix $\mathbf{M}_i$ was first used by Gortler el al. in [Go2]. Matrix $\mathbf{W}$ approximates $\mathbf{M}^{-1}$ by substituting $\tilde{\mathbf{F}}$ for $\mathbf{F}$ in all high order terms in the Neumann series expansion of $\mathbf{F}^{-1}$.

3.2 A General LI Solver

Iterative solvers for a linear system $\mathbf{Ax} = \mathbf{b}$, are generally of the following form [Ba1, Ki1]

> Initialize $\mathbf{x} = \mathbf{0}$ and $\mathbf{r} = \mathbf{b}$
> *while* not convergent *do*
>   Choose $\Delta\mathbf{x}$
>   Update $\mathbf{x} \leftarrow \mathbf{x} + \Delta\mathbf{x}$
>   Update $\mathbf{r} \leftarrow \mathbf{r} - \mathbf{A}\Delta\mathbf{x}$

If both $\mathbf{A}$ and $\Delta\mathbf{x}$ are dense, then calculating residuals costs $O(n^2)$. Our goal is to use only $O(n)$ computation per iteration. Thus, we must choose the vector $\Delta\mathbf{x}$ such that it has only $O(1)$ nonzero elements. Typically, we choose $\Delta\mathbf{x}$ to be a vector with only one nonzero element. The magnitude of $\Delta\mathbf{x}$ of course depends on the residuals at each iteration. If we choose $\Delta\mathbf{x}$ to be a vector with only its ith element nonzero, then the best choice of $\Delta\mathbf{x}$ is the unshot energy

$[\mathbf{e}_i^T(\mathbf{x}^* - \mathbf{x})]\mathbf{e}_i = (\mathbf{e}_i^T \mathbf{A}^{-1}\mathbf{r})\mathbf{e}_i$. Since $\mathbf{A}^{-1}$ is not easy to calculate, we substitute another matrix, say $\mathbf{G}$, which can be calculated quickly, as an approximation to $\mathbf{A}^{-1}$ to obtain the increment $\Delta\mathbf{x}$. We need to find $\mathbf{G}$ as close to $\mathbf{A}^{-1}$ as possible, while using no more than $O(n)$ time in the computation of $\mathbf{G}$. The following is a outline of our General LI Solver for the system $\mathbf{Ax} = \mathbf{b}$.

General LI Solver

Step 1: initialization: $\mathbf{x}^{(0)} = \mathbf{0}$ and $\mathbf{r}^{(0)} = \mathbf{b}$

Step 2: *while* not convergent *do*

        Step 2.1:choose i and an increment $\Delta x^{(p)} = \mathbf{e}_i^T \mathbf{Gr}^{(p)}$

        Step 2.2:update $\mathbf{x}^{(p+1)} = \mathbf{x}^{(p)} + \Delta x^{(p)}\mathbf{e}_i$

        Step 2.3:update $\mathbf{r}^{(p+1)} = \mathbf{r}^{(p)} - \Delta x^{(p)}\mathbf{Ae}_i$

Step 3: output $\mathbf{x}^{(p)} + \mathbf{r}^{(p)}$ as the final solution

Note that our discussion of LI solvers is in terms of a general system of equations $\mathbf{Ax} = \mathbf{b}$ instead of specifically e.q. (1). We will see in the next section that the use of this general method on transformed systems, which are different systems than that of e.q. (1), leads to interesting methods for solving the radiosity problem.

How well this algorithm performs depends primarily on two things, selecting the shooting patch i and finding a matrix $\mathbf{G}$ close to $\mathbf{A}^{-1}$. Based on this algorithm and the matrices defined above, we can clearly see the relationships among the existing iterative radiosity methods. All five previous methods can be regarded as the general solver applied to e.q. (1), with different choices of $\mathbf{G}$ to approach $\mathbf{A}^{-1}$ and methods for selecting i as described in the following table [Xu1]. [3]

method	How to choose i	G
PR:	$r_i^{(p)} = \|\|\mathbf{Dr}^{(p)}\|\|_\infty$	$\mathbf{I}$
Shao:	$r_i^{(p)} = \|\|\mathbf{Dr}^{(p)}\|\|_\infty$	$\mathbf{I} + \mathbf{F}$
Gortler:	$r_i^{(p)} = \|\|\mathbf{Dr}^{(p)}\|\|_\infty$	$\mathbf{M}_i^{-1}$ (depending on index i)
Feda:	$r_i^{(p)} = \|\|\tilde{\mathbf{M}}^{-1}\mathbf{Dr}^{(p)}\|\|_\infty$	$\tilde{\mathbf{M}}^{-1}$
Xu:	$r_i^{(p)} = \|\|\tilde{\mathbf{M}}^{-1}\mathbf{Dr}^{(p)}\|\|_\infty$	$\mathbf{W}$

Table 1. Choosing $\mathbf{G}$ and i in the five methods.

In order to achieve fast convergence, the matrix $\mathbf{G}$ must be as close to $\mathbf{M}^{-1}$ as possible. From the Neumann series, we know that $\mathbf{I}$ and $\mathbf{I} + \mathbf{F}$ are two simple

---

[3] There are slight differences between the algorithms listed here and the original ones for the sake of implementation, but the main ideas and rates of convergence are the same. Note that $\|\|\mathbf{x}\|\|_\infty = \max_{1 \le i \le n} |x_i|$ where $\mathbf{x} \in \mathbf{R}^n$.

approximations to $\mathbf{M}^{-1}$, while the higher order terms in the series are too costly to calculate. The matrices $\tilde{\mathbf{M}}^{-1}$ and $\mathbf{W}$ are also approximations of $\mathbf{M}^{-1}$ if $\tilde{\mathbf{F}}$ is close to $\mathbf{F}$:

$$\tilde{\mathbf{M}}^{-1}\,\mathbf{M} = (\sum_{k=0}^{\infty} \tilde{\mathbf{F}}^k)(\mathbf{I} - \mathbf{F}) = \mathbf{I} + (\sum_{k=0}^{\infty} \tilde{\mathbf{F}}^k)(\tilde{\mathbf{F}} - \mathbf{F}) \tag{14}$$

$$\mathbf{W}\,\mathbf{M} = (\mathbf{I} + \mathbf{F} + \sum_{k=2}^{\infty} \tilde{\mathbf{F}}^k)(\mathbf{I} - \mathbf{F}) = \mathbf{I} + \tilde{\mathbf{F}}^2 - \mathbf{F}^2 + (\sum_{k=2}^{\infty} \tilde{\mathbf{F}}^k)(\tilde{\mathbf{F}} - \mathbf{F}) \tag{15}$$

The matrix $\mathbf{M}_i^{-1}$, which acts as an approximation of $\mathbf{M}^{-1}$ in Gortler's method [Go2], is very close to the matrix $\mathbf{I} + \mathbf{F}$:

$$\mathbf{e}_i^T \mathbf{M}_i^{-1} \mathbf{r} = \frac{r_i + \rho_i \sum_j F_{i,j} r_j}{1 - \sum_j \rho_i \rho_j F_{i,j} F_{j,i}}$$
$$\approx r_i + \rho_i \sum_j F_{i,j} r_j + o(n^{-1})$$
$$\approx \mathbf{e}_i^T (\mathbf{I} + \mathbf{F})\mathbf{r}$$

It is therefore not surprising that experiments indicate that Gortler's and Shao's methods show similar performance.

As we know, at a certain stage, a shooting patch i has a residual radiosity r_i. If we shoot r_i to the environment, then two kinds of radiance will return to patch i, the radiance reflected by patch j ($j \neq i$) directly and the radiance reflected among several patches before returning to the shooting patch i. Therefore, rather than just shooting the residual radiosity as the increment at a particular iteration step, if we can estimate these two kinds of returned radiance and add them to the residual as the increment for the step, we can reduce the overall number of iterations required. That is the main idea of overshooting. All four overshooting methods (Feda's, Gortler's, Shao's and Xu's) differ mainly in how these two kinds of returned radiance are estimated. According to the equations above, all five solvers listed in the table fall into three categories based on their estimation of the returning radiance.

1. No returned radiance is predicted, this give the PR method, which does not overshoot.
2. Only directly returned radiance is predicted, this gives Shao's and Gortler's methods.
3. Both kinds of returned radiance are predicted, this gives Feda's and Xu's methods.

The main difference between Feda's and Xu's method is that Xu's method estimates the first kind of returned radiance more precisely than Feda's does. As we predicted, the experiments showed that the third category generally converges faster than the second does, while the second converges faster than the first does.

3.3 Transformed Systems

When we apply our general LI solver to e.q. (1), we usually get the matrix $\mathbf{G}$ from the Neumann series of $\mathbf{M}^{-1}$. Obviously, the smaller $||\mathbf{F}||_\infty$ is[4], the faster the series (4) converges. One way to make $||\mathbf{F}||_\infty$ smaller is to use a *transformed system* [Ba1] of the form

$$\mathbf{CM}\,\mathbf{x} = \mathbf{Cb}. \tag{16}$$

The matrix $\mathbf{C}$ in e.q. (16) is called the preconditioner matrix. Ideally $\mathbf{C}$ should be $\mathbf{M}^{-1}$, but if $\mathbf{M}^{-1}$ is difficult to calculate, we wish to choose the best approximation that we can afford to calculate. Generally speaking, it is not easy to get a good preconditioner $\mathbf{C}$ without a great deal of computation. Even if we get a good $\mathbf{C}$, calculating the new coefficient matrix $\mathbf{CM}$ is still expensive. Our goal is to use only linear time per iteration, so we cannot afford to do a general matrix multiplication, taking at least $O(n^2)$ time, at each iteration. However, for radiosity systems, we do have a nice preconditioner, matrix $\tilde{\mathbf{M}}$. According to e.q. (10) and the simple structure of $\tilde{\mathbf{F}}$, the computation of the matrix product $\tilde{\mathbf{F}}\mathbf{y}$ requires only $O(n)$ operations for any vector $\mathbf{y}$. Moreover, $\tilde{\mathbf{M}}^{-1}$ is a good approximation to $\mathbf{M}^{-1}$ because of e.q. (14).

Using transformed systems gives us a better understanding of the relationships among the solution algorithms. Simple solvers applied on a transformed system can generate sophisticated solvers for the original equations. Using these ideas, we can show the following relationships.

- If all patches are the same size, then PR applied to a transformed system produces Feda's method (with our modification).
- Shao's method applied to a transformed system produces the matrix $\mathbf{G}$ of Xu's method.

To show the first result, we look at the transformed equation

$$\tilde{\mathbf{M}}^{-1}\mathbf{DMD}^{-1}(\mathbf{Dx}) = \tilde{\mathbf{M}}^{-1}\mathbf{Db}. \tag{17}$$

We denote e.q. (17) by $\mathbf{Sy} = \mathbf{u}$ where $\mathbf{S} = \tilde{\mathbf{M}}^{-1}\mathbf{DMD}^{-1}$, $\mathbf{y} = \mathbf{Dx}$, $\mathbf{u} = \tilde{\mathbf{M}}^{-1}\mathbf{Db}$ and we let $\mathbf{q} = \tilde{\mathbf{M}}^{-1}\mathbf{Dr}$.

Applying the PR method to this equation yields

$$\mathbf{y}^{(p+1)} = \mathbf{y}^{(p)} + (\mathbf{e}_i^T \mathbf{q}^{(p)})\mathbf{e}_i \tag{18}$$

and

$$\mathbf{q}^{(p+1)} = \mathbf{q}^{(p)} - (\mathbf{e}_i^T \mathbf{q}^{(p)})\mathbf{Se}_i. \tag{19}$$

If we multiply $\mathbf{D}^{-1}$ and $\mathbf{D}^{-1}\tilde{\mathbf{M}}$ on the left sides of the two equations respectively, we immediate obtain

$$\mathbf{x}^{(p+1)} = \mathbf{x}^{(p)} + (\mathbf{e}_i^T \tilde{\mathbf{M}}^{-1}\mathbf{Dr}^{(p)})\mathbf{D}^{-1}\mathbf{e}_i$$
$$= \mathbf{x}^{(p)} + (\mathbf{e}_i^T \tilde{\mathbf{M}}^{-1}\mathbf{r}^{(p)})\mathbf{e}_i$$

---

[4] Note that $||\mathbf{A}||_\infty = \max_{1 \le i \le m} \sum_{j=1}^n |a_{i,j}|$, where $\mathbf{A} \in \mathbf{R}^{m \times n}$.

and

$$r^{(p+1)} = r^{(p)} - (e_i^T \tilde{M}^{-1} D r^{(p)}) D^{-1} \tilde{M} S e_i$$
$$= r^{(p)} - (e_i^T \tilde{M}^{-1} r^{(p)}) e_i.$$

The new equations are exactly the formulae of Feda's method applied to e.q. (1). The equations above are true because D is a constant number times the identity matrix under the assumption that all patches are of equal size.

To show the second result, let us examine matrix G in our general linear solver when we apply Shao's method to the transformed system

$$(I + \frac{1}{1 - \rho_{ave}} \tilde{F}) M x = (I + \frac{1}{1 - \rho_{ave}} \tilde{F}) b \tag{20}$$

i.e.

$$[I - (F - \frac{1}{1 - \rho_{ave}} \tilde{F} + \tilde{F} F)] x = (I + \frac{1}{1 - \rho_{ave}} \tilde{F}) b. \tag{21}$$

Recall that in Shao's method matrix $G = I + F$ for the system $(I - F)x = b$. If we apply Shao's method on the system (20), the residuals of the two equation systems satisfy $q = (I + \frac{1}{1 - \rho_{ave}} \tilde{F}) r$, where q and r are the residuals of e.q. (20) and e.q. (1) respectively. Then the new matrix G is

$$G = (I + F - \frac{1}{1 - \rho_{ave}} \tilde{F} + \tilde{F} F)(I + \frac{1}{1 - \rho_{ave}} \tilde{F})$$

$$\approx (I + F - \frac{1}{1 - \rho_{ave}} \tilde{F} + \tilde{F}^2)(I + \frac{1}{1 - \rho_{ave}} \tilde{F})$$

$$= (I + F - \tilde{F})(I + \frac{1}{1 - \rho_{ave}} \tilde{F})$$

$$\approx I + F - \tilde{F} + \frac{1}{1 - \rho_{ave}} \tilde{F} + \frac{1}{1 - \rho_{ave}} \tilde{F}^2 - \frac{1}{1 - \rho_{ave}} \tilde{F}^2$$

$$= I + F + \frac{\rho_{ave}}{1 - \rho_{ave}} \tilde{F}$$

$$= W.$$

Note that in the equations above, we use $\tilde{F} F \approx \tilde{F}^2$.

While Xu's method is similar to Shao's method in the choice of G, but applied to the system of e.q. (20) rather than e.q. (1), it does not use Shao's method of choosing the shooting patch. This is done in a manner similar to that of Feda.

It is important to notice that the transformed system of e.q. (17) has a different meaning from the original system of e.q. (1). Feda's method is an overshooting method for the system of e.q. (1), and it may generate negative residuals of e.q. (1). However, our modification of Feda's method is the PR method (positive increments, no overshooting) with respect to the system of e.q. (17). Thus, its residuals with respect to e.q. (17) are all positive. We can therefore show that it converges under reasonable conditions [Xu1], just as we can for Xu's method. This demonstrates that under proper conditions, negative increments are not necessarily incorrect, as we have discussed above. The two versions of Feda's method differ in that Feda's original method used an ambient term related to the residuals of e.q. (17) to bound the magnitude of the increments. That was an error caused by confusing the two formulations. We cannot use a term from e.q. (17) to bound a similar term in e.q. (1). They mean different things. In fact, when overshooting with respect to e.q. (1) is done, there can be negative residuals of e.q. (1) for many patches, and this can cause Feda's ambient term to be zero when there is still much energy remaining to be distributed. This can prevent Feda's original method from converging, as the experimental results in the next section demonstrate.

4 Experimental Results

We have implemented all of these algorithms in C by modifying the global illumination package of Sumant Pattanaik of the Indian National Centre for Software Technology. Figures 2 through 9 contain images produced using these implementations on a test scene provided by Peter Shirley of Indiana University. The figures show a simple interior scene with a light source on the ceiling and a table with four chairs on the floor. The original environment is composed of 402 patches. They are subdivided into 1384 patches in our tests. In order to make the comparisons visually clearer, no ambient light terms are used in displaying any of the figures. In order to save space, we do not provide separate images when they are visually indistinguishable (even though they are not identical numerically). The convergence criterion for all methods is that the RMS error across all patches be less than 10^{-6}, where the RMS error is given by

$$RMS = \sqrt{\frac{\sum A_i (x_i^* - x_i)^2}{A}}.$$

The total number of iteration steps to convergence was, for Xu's method: 2104, for Feda's method (modified): 2853, for Gortler's method: 3584, for Shao's method: 3607, for progressive radiosity: 6392, and for Feda's method (original): >20,000.

To get a more detailed idea of the performance of the algorithms, their rates of convergence are shown in Figure 1. In the figure, the horizontal axis represents the number of iterations performed for each algorithm, and the vertical axes represents the RMS error of the current approximate solution. The experiment shows that Feda's original method does not converge in this case. The reason is that the control term in the method is very small after about 2000 iterations. It also shows the performance differences among the three classes of methods that use different estimates of returned radiance, as discussed above. PR converges significantly more slowly than the other methods since it does not use overshooting at all. Gortler's and Shao's methods, whose performance is indistinguishable on the graph, both estimate directly returned radiance. Feda's and Xu's methods, which converge fastest, use a more global estimate of returned radiance.

RMS

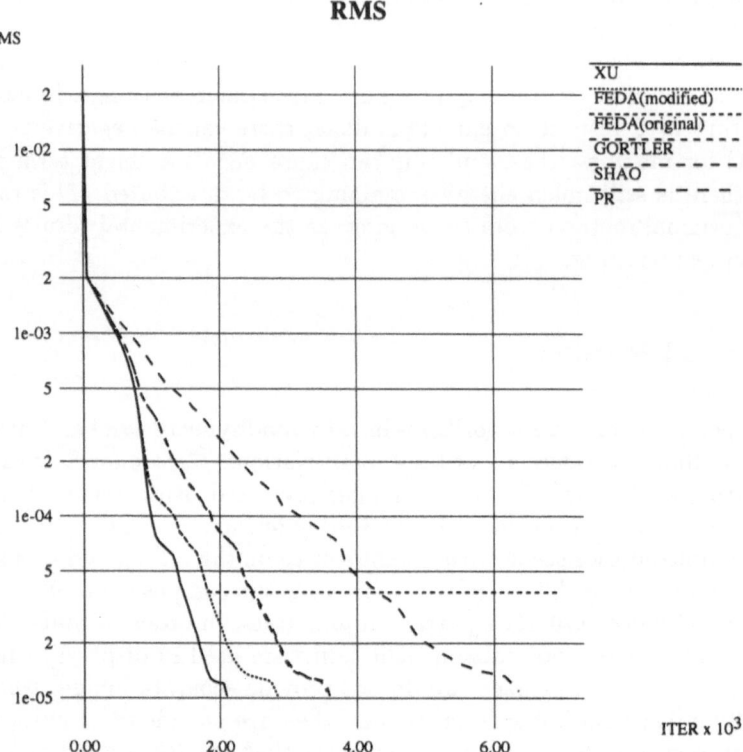

Fig. 1. Convergence Comparison.

Figures 2–4 show the results after 100 iterations. Figures 5–7 show the results after 300 iterations. Figures 2–4 indicate that the five methods are using two very different criteria for choosing shooting patches.

4.1 Computational Requirements

For each iteration, the amount of work done by PR, Shao's, Gortler's, Feda's and Xu's methods are proportional to $2n$, $3n(average)$, $4n(average)$, $5n$ and $7n$ respectively [Xu1]. Since calculating form factors is the greatest expense in each iteration for these methods if they are recalculated on the fly, the time required to obtain the solution strongly depends on the number of iterations needed. In this case, Xu's method is expected to be the fastest one in the cases we have tested[Xu1]. If all form-factors are pre-calculated, then the differences between the methods are smaller, and the fastest time may not coincide with the fewest iterations.

Fig. 2. Left: PR - 100 Iterations. Right: Shao's and Gortler's Methods, 100 Iterations.

Fig. 3. Left:Feda's and Xu's methods, 100 Iterations Right: PR - 300 Iterations.

Fig. 4. Left: Shao's and Gortler's Methods, 300 Iterations. Right: Feda's and Xu's Methods, 300 Iterations.

5 Conclusions

We have analyzed transformed radiosity systems and presented a general LI solver, which gives us a new way to systematically understand fast iterative solvers, and, hopefully, to search for new ones. We have also proved that Feda's method is equivalent to the PR method on a transformed system, and that our previously developed method is similar to Shao's method on a transformed system in that it uses the same matrix G for computing increments, while it shares with Feda's method the choice of i, the shooting patch for each iteration. We believe that this treatment provides a clearer understanding of the relationships among solvers for classical radiosity equation systems than has been available thus far.

References

[Ba1] Barrett, R., Berry, M., Chan, T., Demmel, J., Donato, J., Dongarra, J., Eijkhout, V., Pozo, R., Romine, C. and van der Vorst, H., *Templates for the Solution of Linear Systems: Building Blocks for Iterative Methods*,SIAM, 1994

[Co1] Cohen, M., Chen, S., Wallace, J. and Greenberg, D., A Progressive Refinement Approach to Fast Radiosity Image Generation, *ACM Computer Graphics* **22**(1988), 75–84.

[Fe1] Feda, M., Purgathofer, W., Accelerating Radiosity By Overshooting, in 1992 Eurographics Rendering Workshop (June 1992), Consolidation Express, Bristol England, 21–32.

[Go1] Goral, C.M., Torrance, K.E., Greenberg, D.P., and Battaile, B. Modelling the Interction of Light between Diffuse Surfaces, , *Computer Graphics* **18**(1984), 212–222.

[Go1] Gortler, S., Schröder, P., Cohen, M. and Hanrahan, P., Wavelet Radiosity, *Computer Graphics* **27**(1993), 221–230.

[Go2] Gortler, S., Cohen, M. and Slusallek, P., Radiosity and Relaxation Methods, Technical Report, Computer Science Department, Princeton University, 1993 (to appear in *IEEE CG & A*).

[Ha1] Hanrahan, P., Salzman, D. and Aupperle, L., A Rapid Hierarchical Radiosity Algorithm, *Computer Graphics* **25** (1991), 197–206.

[Ki1] Kincaid, D. and Cheney, W., *Numerical Analysis*, Brooks/Cole Publishing Company, 1990.

[Sh1] Shao, M.Z., and Badler, N.I., Analysis and Acceleration of the Progressive Refinement Radiosity Method, Proceedings of the 1993 Eurographics Rendering Workshop.

[Xu1] Xu, W. and Fussell, D., A Fast Solver of Radiosity Equation Systems, To be appeared in the Proceedings of Pacific Graphics'94/CADDM'94, August. 1994, Bei-Jing, China.

New Efficient Algorithms with Positive Definite Radiosity Matrix

László Neumann[1], *Robert F. Tobler*[2]

Budapest H-1122, Maros u. 36, Hungary
Technische Universität Wien, Vienna, Austria

Abstract

New efficient algorithms will be presented for solving diffuse radiosity problems, involving advantages of progressive radiosity. Demonstration of the algorithms and of their convergence relies on the new form of the radiosity equations, with a positive definite matrix. The methods have been tested with a new error formula, the (area-weighted) average relative error. The form with a symmetric, positive definite matrix penetrates into the gist of the radiosity problem deeper than the former radiosity or power variable equations. At the same time this makes it possible to apply several algorithms well-known from numerical analysis. In general, the positive definite form leads to algorithms, which are mathematically handleable, and of proven convergence and effectiveness.

1 Introduction

Solution of the diffuse radiosity problem will be considered, actually looking back to a decade. In the first four years, exclusively "full matrix" methods have been applied (Gauss-Seidel, Jacobi), e.g. [1]. Thereafter the progressive radiosity was introduced [2], then the overshooting method [4], beyond of being methods offering faster convergence, also permitted to solve relatively more extensive problems using "on-the-fly" form factor computation. At last, recent trends comprise the methods of hierarchical radiosity [7] and Monte Carlo radiosity [10] suiting also larger systems.

All the earlier methods applied the known, classic, *radiosity* variable equations, with other than symmetrical, positive definite matrices, where it can be proven that the matrix row norm is less than 1.

The Southwell algorithm – although mostly it is applied with the radiosity variable form – is the simplest to write in terms of *power* variable equations. Also this is neither symmetric, nor positive definite, but its matrix column norm is less than 1.

In this paper, a form of *positive definite* matrix will be introduced, by simply transforming the known radiosity equation system. A minimum-maximum estimation will be given for its *eigenvalues*. Thereafter two algorithms unknown in numerical analysis, developed in 1981 [9], will be applied for solving the radiosity problem.

These methods rely on the possibility to define a *scalar product* and so-called C-orthogonality by means of an arbitrary positive definite matrix C. Actually, the *directions C-orthogonal to hyperplanes representing rows of the equation system exactly coincide with the coordinate directions*. That is, similarly to relaxation-type shooting and overshooting methods, a single coordinate is altered in an elementary step, in course of a C-orthogonal projection.

In case of closed environments, there is the possibility for a special C-orthogonal step *requiring no form factor computation*. Here all the radiosities are altered at once, by the same value (*constant radiosity step*).

The scalar product also defines a norm, the so-called *energetic norm*. This paper will consider algorithms converging in this norm. This norm – somewhat simplified – penalizes the error of the given patch partly in proportion to its area, and partly in inverse proportion to its radiosity. That is, it approximates the *relative error* weighted by the surface, the error formula to be introduced in this paper, corresponding to the *logarithmic nature of human visual perception*. Thereby it is much better suited to describe the error of an approximate radiosity solution or of an approximate image than the previously applied error formulae.

2 Positive Definite Radiosity Matrix

The diffuse radiosity equation system, in classic form, with the usual notation:

$$B_i = E_i + \rho_i \cdot \sum_{j=1}^{n} F_{ij} B_j \tag{1}$$

The system of equation (1) can be written in a general form as follows: $\mathbf{Ax} = \mathbf{e}$, where $x_i = B_i$, $e_i = E_i$ furthermore $a_{ii} = 1$ and if $i \neq j$, then $a_{ij} = -\rho_i F_{ij}$.

In the following it is assumed that there is no perfectly black or white patch. That is, there are numbers $\epsilon_1 > 0$ and $\epsilon_2 > 0$ for which it is true for any subscript i $(i = 1, \ldots, n)$, that $\epsilon_1 \leq \rho_i \leq 1 - \epsilon_2$.

Starting from equation (1) , let us multiply row i by $\frac{A_i}{\rho_i}$:

$$\frac{A_i}{\rho_i} \cdot B_i = \frac{A_i}{\rho_i} \cdot E_i + A_i \cdot \sum_{j=1}^{n} F_{ij} B_j \tag{2}$$

Theorem 1

The matrix of equation (2) is *symmetric and positive definite*.

Proof

Let us write the system of equation (2) in a more concise form $\mathbf{C}\mathbf{x} = \mathbf{b}$. Now $\mathbf{x}$ is a vector of radiosity values: $x_i = B_i$, and the constant vector of the right-hand side is $b_i = \frac{A_i}{\rho_i} \cdot E_i$. The diagonal elements of matrix $\mathbf{C}$ are: $c_{ii} = \frac{A_i}{\rho_i}$, and for $i \neq j$: $c_{ij} = c_{ji} = -A_i F_{ij} = -A_j F_{ji}$.

This means that matrix $\mathbf{C}$ is symmetric, derived from the known reciprocity of form factors:

$$A_i F_{ij} = A_j F_{ji} \tag{3}$$

Sine $\mathbf{C}$ is symmetric, it has real eigenvalues. The Gerschgorin theorem permits to estimate minimum and maximum eigenvalues. Eigenvalues being real, instead of circles in the plane of complex numbers, we only have to deal with intervals. The i-th interval is contained in I below:

$$I_i = \left[A_i \cdot \left(\frac{1}{\rho_i} - 1 \right), A_i \cdot \left(\frac{1}{\rho_i} + 1 \right) \right] \tag{4}$$

In determining I, an essential characteristic of form factors has been made use of:

$$\sum_{j=1}^{n} F_{ij} \leq 1 \tag{5}$$

Every eigenvalue is contained in the union of these intervals, so it is simple to make a (rough) estimation for the lowest and the highest eigenvalue:

$$\lambda_{min} \geq \min_i A_i \cdot \left(\frac{1}{\rho_i} - 1 \right)$$

$$\lambda_{max} \leq \max_i A_i \cdot \left(\frac{1}{\rho_i} + 1 \right) \tag{6}$$

$\lambda_{min} > 0$, since $\rho_i \leq 1 - \epsilon_2 < 1$. Thereby it has been proven that $\mathbf{C}$ is positive definite.

3 Orthogonal Projection Method

3.1 Fundamentals of the Method

Let us start from an arbitrary linear equation system, with a non-singular matrix $\mathbf{A}$. Rows of the equation system of form $\mathbf{A}\mathbf{x} = \mathbf{e}$ define hyperplanes of n-dimensional space. The common point of these hyperplanes is the solution $\mathbf{x}$ of the equation system. Hyperplanes may be written in the form $\langle \mathbf{a}_i, \mathbf{x} \rangle = e_i$, $(i = 1, \ldots, n)$, where vector $\mathbf{a}$ is row i of matrix $\mathbf{A}$, and notation "$\langle , \rangle$" denotes the scalar product. Gist of the orthogononal projection method consists in starting from an arbitrary vector $\mathbf{x}^{(0)}$, then selecting the hyperlane the farthest from $\mathbf{x}^{(0)}$, or later, from the actual iteration point $\mathbf{x}^{(k)}$. Let $\mathbf{a}_i$ be the normal to hyperplane i. Let point $\mathbf{x}^{(k+1)}$ be the *orthogonal projection* of vector $\mathbf{x}^{(k+1)}$ on hyperplane i. That is, one proceeds from $\mathbf{x}^{(k)}$ in direction $\mathbf{a}_i$ until reaching hyperplane i. The bidimensional case is illustrated in figure 1. Let D_k be the distance of point $\mathbf{x}^{(k)}$ from the solution $\mathbf{x}$. Hence:

$$D_k = \|\mathbf{x} - \mathbf{x}^{(k)}\| \tag{7}$$

and d_k the distance of $\mathbf{x}^{(k)}$ from the selected hyperplane. Now, according to the Pythagorean theorem:

$$D_{k+1}^2 = D_k^2 - d_k^2 \tag{8}$$

Obviously, inasmuch as the farthest plane is selected, the algorithm converges to the solution at a geometrical rate. The convergence rate depends on the norm of matrix $\mathbf{A}^{-1}$, omitting details. Slower convergence may also be guaranteed if not the farthest plane is selected but all the planes are affected cyclically, or maybe for other rules of selection. Geometric rate of convergence may be guaranteed for an *overprojection* as seen in figure 2 if there is a $|p_k| < 1 - \epsilon$. In this case a simple step will be worse but the complete iteration may be accelerated. An acceleration may also result from omitting the resriction for p_k in certain projections [9]. Its details will not be considered here. In case of overprojection, equation (8) becomes:

$$D_{k+1}^2 = D_k^2 - (1 - p_k^2) \cdot d_k^2 \tag{9}$$

Let i be the subscript of the selected hyperplane:

$$d_k = \frac{e_i - \langle \mathbf{a}_i, \mathbf{x}^{(k)} \rangle}{\|\mathbf{a}_i\|} = \frac{r_i^{(k)}}{\|\mathbf{a}_i\|} \tag{10}$$

Beyond of yielding the distance d affected by a sign, equation (10) also contains the definition of the row-wise error $r_i^{(k)}$ affected by a sign. According to figure 1:

$$\mathbf{x}^{(k+1)} = \mathbf{x}^{(k)} + d_k \cdot \mathbf{a}_i^0 \tag{11}$$

Making use of equation (10) this can be written as:

$$\mathbf{x}^{(k+1)} = \mathbf{x}^{(k)} + \frac{r_i^{(k)}}{\|\mathbf{a}_i\|^2} \cdot \mathbf{a}_i \tag{12}$$

Obviously, equation (12) is simplified by norming normal vectors of the hyperplanes, so as to become unit vectors.

Let us consider, how error vector components change after projection. By definition:

$$r_j^{(k+1)} = b_j - \langle \mathbf{a}_j, \mathbf{x}^{(k+1)} \rangle \tag{13}$$

Making use of equation (12):

$$r_j^{(k+1)} = r_j^{(k)} - \frac{r_i^{(k)}}{\|\mathbf{a}_i\|^2} \cdot \langle \mathbf{a}_j, \mathbf{a}_i \rangle \tag{14}$$

$$D_{k+1}^2 = D_k^2 - d_k^2$$

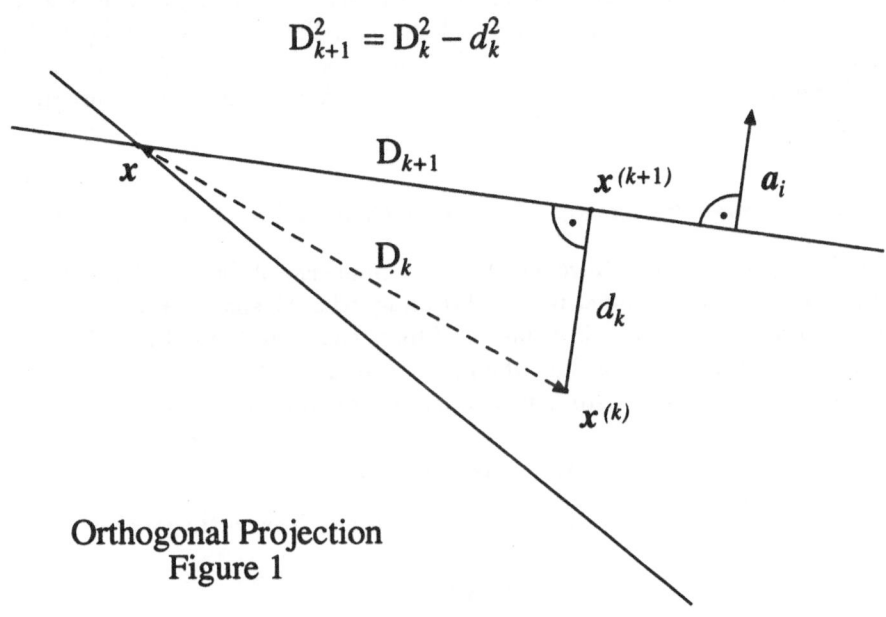

Orthogonal Projection
Figure 1

$$D_{k+1}^2 = D_k^2 - (1 - p_k^2)d_k^2$$

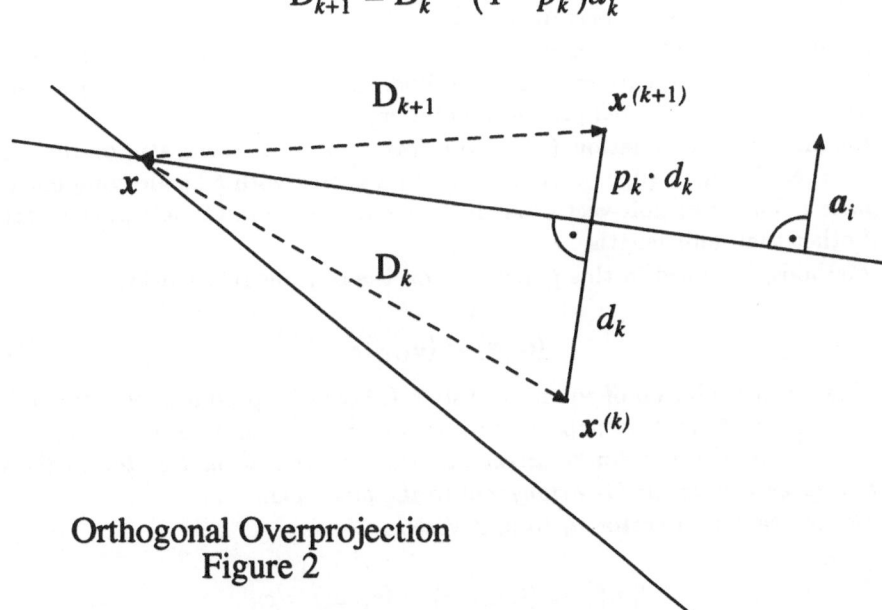

Orthogonal Overprojection
Figure 2

Applying these results above to equations (1) or (2) would require the computation of the entire matrix for renewing the error vector. Since this is a "full-matrix" method, it cannot be considered efficient. The solution lending efficiency to the algorithm above, where it is sufficient to calculate a single column of the matrix per iteration step for computing the new error vector (like in progressive radiosity) will be presented in the following section.

3.2 Orthogonal Projection Method with Positive Definite Matrix

Note that in the method above, nowhere was made use of the fact that the metric defined by the scalar product is a Euclidean metric, the space a Euclidean space. All the formulae keep remain valid for Hilbert spaces of finite dimensions [9].

In particular, let us consider the scalar product below, that can be defined in terms of an arbitrary, symmetrical, positive definite matrix $\mathbf{C}$:

$$\langle \mathbf{a}, \mathbf{b} \rangle_C = \langle \mathbf{Ca}, \mathbf{b} \rangle = \langle \mathbf{a}, \mathbf{Cb} \rangle \tag{15}$$

According to this scalar product, vectors a and b are orthogonal if:

$$\langle \mathbf{a}, \mathbf{b} \rangle_C = 0 \tag{16}$$

For a C-orthogonality as defined by equation (16), C-metrics may be introduced:

$$\|a\|_C^2 = \langle \mathbf{a}, \mathbf{a} \rangle_C = \langle \mathbf{Ca}, \mathbf{a} \rangle \tag{17}$$

called also *energetic norm* in the special literature. The metric space defined by it will be called C- *metric space* in the following text. This metric is applied in proving the convergence of several methods known in numerical analysis (such as gradient and conjugated gradient methods).

Let us consider equation (2) of the form $\mathbf{Cx} = \mathbf{b}$. Row i is of the form $\langle \mathbf{c}_i, \mathbf{x} \rangle = b_i$. Let $\mathbf{u}_i = (0, 0, \ldots, 0, 1, 0, \ldots, 0)$ a vector with a single component 1 at place i. The term unit vector has been avoided since in C-metrics this vector is of other than unit length.

Methods discussed in this paper rely on the obvious relationship:

$$\langle \mathbf{c}_i, \mathbf{x} \rangle = \langle \mathbf{u}_i, \mathbf{x} \rangle_C \tag{18}$$

That is, the solution of equation system (2) may be produced as intersection of planes in the C-metric space with normal vectors – vectors $\mathbf{u}_i, (i = 1, 2, \ldots, n)$ – that are just the *coordinate directions*. Namely, the *normal vector in the C-metric space is a vector C- orthogonal to the given plane*.

Let us transform vector $\mathbf{u}_i$ to unit vector:

$$\|\mathbf{u}_i\|_C^2 = \langle \mathbf{Cu}_i, \mathbf{u}_i \rangle = \langle \mathbf{c}_i, \mathbf{u}_i \rangle = c_{ii} \tag{19}$$

$\mathbf{u}_i^0$ is a unit vector in C-metrics:

$$\mathbf{u}_i^0 = \frac{1}{\|\mathbf{u}_i\|_C} \cdot \mathbf{u}_i \tag{20}$$

For vector $\mathbf{x}^{(k)}$ of an arbitrary iteration procedure, the error of row i is:

$$r_j^{(k)} = b_j - \langle \mathbf{u}_j, \mathbf{x}^{(k)} \rangle_C \tag{21}$$

The distance of $\mathbf{x}^{(k)}$ from hyperplane j in C-metrics, according to equations (10) and (19) is:

$$d_k = \frac{r_j^{(k)}}{\|\mathbf{u}_j\|_C} = r_j^{(k)} \cdot \left(\frac{A_j}{\rho_j}\right)^{-\frac{1}{2}} \tag{22}$$

In equation (22) a value corresponding to matrix $\mathbf{C}$ in equation (2) has been established. For orthogonal projection, the hyperplane with the *highest* $|d_k|$ *value is selected*. In this case the distance from the solution is shortest after the projection in C-metrics (according to equation (8)).

Let i be the subscript of the selected hyperplane. After orthogonal projection, the value of the approximate solution vector is obtained from equaiton (11). Projection being of direction $\mathbf{u}_i$, a single coordinate i of the approximate solution is changed:

$$\mathbf{x}^{(k+1)} = \mathbf{x}^{(k)} + d_k \cdot \mathbf{u}_i^0 \tag{23}$$

That is, for equation (2), according to equation (22):

$$x_i^{(k+1)} = x_i^{(k)} + r_i^{(k)} \cdot \left(\frac{A_i}{\rho_i}\right)^{-1} \tag{24}$$

According to equation (14) the components of the error vector after projection $(j = 1, 2, \ldots, n)$ are:

$$r_j^{(k+1)} = r_j^{(k)} - \frac{r_i^{(k)}}{\|\mathbf{u}_i\|_C^2} \cdot \langle \mathbf{u}_j, \mathbf{u}_i \rangle_C = r_j^{(k)} - \frac{r_i^{(k)}}{\|\mathbf{u}_i\|_C^2} \cdot c_{ij} \tag{25}$$

For matrix $\mathbf{C}$ in equation (2) and for the selected i: $r_i^{(k+1)} = 0$ and if $j \neq i$:

$$r_j^{(k+1)} = r_j^{(k)} + r_i^{(k)} \cdot \rho_i \cdot F_{ij} \tag{26}$$

3.3 A Special Hyperplane for Closed Environments

Let us introduce vector 1:

$$\mathbf{1} = (1, 1, \ldots, 1) \tag{27}$$

Summing up rows of the equation system with a positive definite matrix $\mathbf{C}$, making use of equation(18):

$$\sum_{j=1}^{n} \langle \mathbf{u}_j, \mathbf{x} \rangle_C = \langle \mathbf{1}, \mathbf{x} \rangle_C \tag{28}$$

The sum of components of constant vector $\mathbf{b}$ in equation (2) is:

$$\sum_{j=1}^{n} \frac{A_j}{\rho_j} \cdot E_j = \sum_{j=1}^{n} r_j^{(0)} = R^{(0)} \tag{29}$$

The equation of the new hyperplane is:

$$\langle \mathbf{1}, \mathbf{x} \rangle_C = R^{(0)} \tag{30}$$

Of course, rows of the equation system may be formed into an arbitrary linear combination, to be joined to the set of original hyperplanes. But the sum above is the only one *not to require form factor computation* in orthogonal projection on it, then in renewing the error vector!

Transforming equation (30):

$$\langle \mathbf{1}, \mathbf{x} \rangle_C = \langle \mathbf{C1}, x \rangle = \langle \mathbf{h}, \mathbf{x} \rangle \tag{31}$$

where components of $\mathbf{h}$:

$$h_i = \sum_{j=1}^{n} c_{ij} = \frac{A_i}{\rho_i} - A_i \cdot \sum_{j=1}^{n} F_{ij} = A_i \cdot \frac{1 - \rho_i}{\rho_i} \tag{32}$$

i.e. the hyperplane equation is:

$$\sum_{i=1}^{n} A_i \cdot \frac{1 - \rho_i}{\rho_i} \cdot B_i = \sum_{i=1}^{n} \frac{A_i}{\rho_i} \cdot E_i \tag{33}$$

where $B_i = x_i$.

In deducing equation (32) a closed environment has been assumed, that is, $\sum F_{ij} = 1$. Let us introduce notation $H = \sum h_j$. Be $\mathbf{x}^{(k)}$ C-orthogonally projected on hyperlane (30):

$$\mathbf{x}^{(k+1)} = \mathbf{x}^{(k)} + D \cdot \mathbf{1}^0 \tag{34}$$

According to equation (10) the sign affected distance from this hyperplane is:

$$D = \frac{R^{(k)}}{\|\mathbf{1}\|_C} = \frac{R^{(k)}}{H^{\frac{1}{2}}} \tag{35}$$

By admitting hyperplane (30) among original hyperplanes, the rule of selection is modified so as to require cyclic testing of distance $d_j(j = 1, 2, \ldots, n)$ and D, and to select the maximum absolute value, then projecting on the plane belonging to it. Making use of equation (35), equation (34) may be written as:

$$\mathbf{x}^{(k+1)} = \mathbf{x}^{(k)} + \frac{R^{(k)}}{H} \cdot \mathbf{1} \tag{36}$$

Thereby a new-type iteration step has been found that, in contrast to the step of relaxation, *simultaneously alters all coordinates* of $\mathbf{x}^{(k)}$. Namely, every coordinate varies by the same value $\frac{R^{(k)}}{H}$. This kind of step is named *constant radiosity step*.

Using equation (14), alteration of errors of the original planes following this step may be computed:

$$r_j^{(k+1)} = r_j^{(k)} - \frac{R^{(k)}}{H} \cdot h_j \tag{37}$$

The other error-refreshing formula expresses the modification of the hyper-plane error after projection on a conventional plane i:

$$R^{(k+1)} = R^{(k)} - r_i^{(k)} \cdot (1 - \rho_i) \tag{38}$$

The following will be a recapitulation in two algorithms of the methods in chapter 3. The first one (Algorithm- I) is the version without a special hyper-plane, the second one suits only closed environments (Algorithm-II), since it uses the new hyperplane. In course of the tests, this latter proved to be much more efficient that the first one (tested in two rules of selection).

Both algorithms also make use of parameter p_k of overprojection, discussed in equation (9).

There is another feature in this algorithm deserving attention. Fundamental interpretation of free parameter $p_k = 0$. But also in case $|p_k| < 1 - \epsilon$, geometrical rate of convergence may be safeguarded. According to tests, the algorithm is fastest for low positive values, that is, for a *slight overrelaxation*. In case of $p = -1$ there is a standstill, while for $p = 1$, there is C-orthogonal mirroring to the selected plane. For $|p| = 1$, the distance from the solution in C-metrics is invariant.

4 Algorithms

4.1 Relaxation-type Algorithm (Algorithm-I)

According to statements in chapter 3.2:

Start:

$$B_i^{(0)} = 0 \quad \text{radiosity} \quad [Wm^{-2}] \quad (i = 1, 2, \ldots, n)$$
$$r_i^{(0)} = \frac{A_i}{\rho_i} \cdot E_i \quad \text{error vector} \quad [W] \quad (i = 1, 2, \ldots, n)$$
$$k = 0$$

Step 1: Selection of patch [1]:

$$d_i^{(k)} = r_i^{(k)} \cdot \left(\frac{A_i}{\rho_i}\right)^{-\frac{1}{2}} \qquad (i = 1, 2, \ldots, n)$$

Selection of patch-subscript i:

$$d = \max|d_i^{(k)}| \to i,$$

if $d \leq$ given $eps \to$ END.

Step 2: *only for the selected subscript i:*

$$B_i^{(k+1)} = B_i^{(k)} + (1 + p_k) \cdot r_i^{(k)} \cdot \left(\frac{A_i}{\rho_i}\right)^{-1}$$

p_k is an arbitrary constant: $|p_k| \leq 1 - \epsilon, 0 < \epsilon \leq 1$

Step 3: *new values of error vector components*

$$r_j^{(k+1)} = r_j^{(k)} + (1 + p_k) \cdot r_i^{(k)} \cdot \rho_i F_{ij} \qquad (j = 1, 2, \ldots, n; j \neq i)$$
$$r_i^{(k+1)} = -p_k \cdot r_i^{(k)}$$
$$k := k + 1$$

GOTO Step 1

Let us consider the illustrative content of the algorithm above. At first glance, it seems to be very similar to other overshooting algorithms. Evidently it is a *relaxation method*. But there are a few essential differences to the previously known methods. The error vector is already at the start *not the unshot power* due to self-illumination, but its ρ_i-th part. That is, the importance of darker patches increases. The factor $\left(\frac{A_i}{\rho_i}\right)^{-\frac{1}{2}}$ which is used in the rule of selection, seems to be rather courious without knowledge of the theoretical background (see equation (22)). Note also that updating the error vector uses *the same ρ_i for all j*. The error vector looses its simple physical interpretation during the iteration steps and can only be understood in the context of the given mathematical background.

In the concept of distance of the C-metric space, and in all steps of the algorithm above, inverse proportionality to ρ_i is of importance. It is close to the approach to relative error, to be introduced below as alternative to the known error *RMS*.

---

[1] Modifying the rule of selection according to the one below leads to a Southwell algorithm proven to converge to the positive definite form, *differing in purport from the Southwell (shooting) method in its usual form*. Furthermore, it converges for an arbitrary p_k for $|p_k| \leq 1 - \epsilon$.

The modified rule of selection: $\max|r_i^{(k)}| \to i$, if max value $\leq$ given $eps \to$ END.

4.2 Average Relative Error (ARE)

In looking at an image, because of the *logarithmicity of perception*, the same perception difference is due to a radiosity difference of 5 Wm^{-2} on a surface of 50 Wm^{-2} radiosity, as a difference of 1 Wm^{-2} on a surface of 10 Wm^{-2} radiosity. The error formula introduced in this paper is the "Average Relative Error" (ARE) [2] where B_j is the exact solution:

$$ARE = \sum_{j=1}^{n} a_j \cdot \frac{|B_j^{(k)} - B_j|}{B_j} \quad where \quad a_j = \frac{A_j}{\sum_{k=1}^{n} A_k} \quad (39)$$

It is assumed that for every j, $B_j \geq \epsilon > 0$, that is, there is no optically independent, unilluminated part system or absolutely black patch. To support advantages of this error formula, let us consider a set of patches forming perceptually even gray steps (uniform scale) in a wall surface of homogeneous illumination. Now – at a fair approximation – the series of reflectivities is an exponential series, with logarithms forming an arithmetic series. Obviously, *relative errors* have to be limited for the sake of perceiving the uniform scale. The relative error formula is also better suited for managing colour deviations.

4.3 Relaxation-type Algorithm (Algorithm-I)

According to the equations in chapter 3.2 and 3.3:

Notations:

$$h_j = \frac{A_j}{\rho_j} \cdot (1 - \rho_j) \quad (i = 1, 2, \ldots, n)$$

$$H = \sum_{j=1}^{n} h_j$$

Start:

$$B_i^{(0)} = 0 \quad radiosity \quad [Wm^{-2}] \quad (i = 1, 2, \ldots, n)$$
$$r_i^{(0)} = \frac{A_i}{\rho_i} \cdot E_i \quad error\ vector \quad [W] \quad (i = 1, 2, \ldots, n)$$
$$R^{(0)} = \sum_{j=1}^{n} r_j^{(0)}$$
$$k = 0$$

---

[2] For a scene not divided into patches relative errors have to be sampled at a uniform distribution on the surface to form their arithmetical mean. In case of subdivision into patches, sampling limit exactly corresponds to weighting by surface, provided the radiosity within a patch is constant (conforming to finite approximation).

Step 1: Selection rule:

$$d_i^{(k)} = r_i^{(k)} \cdot \left(\frac{A_i}{\rho_i}\right)^{-\frac{1}{2}} \qquad (i = 1, 2, \ldots, n)$$

Selection of patch-subscript i:

$$d = \max |d_i^{(k)}| \to i,$$

if $d \le$ given $eps \to$ END.

$$D = R^{(k)} \cdot H^{-\frac{1}{2}}$$

if $|D| < d$ then Step 2A else Step 2B

Step 2A: *only for the selected subscript i:*

$$B_i^{(k+1)} = B_i^{(k)} + (1 + p_k) \cdot r_i^{(k)} \cdot \left(\frac{A_i}{\rho_i}\right)^{-1}$$

p_k is an arbitrary constant: $|p_k| \le 1 - \epsilon,\ 0 < \epsilon \le 1$

new values of error vector components

$$r_j^{(k+1)} = r_j^{(k)} + (1 + p_k) \cdot r_i^{(k)} \cdot \rho_i F_{ij} \qquad (j = 1, 2, \ldots, n; j \ne i)$$
$$r_i^{(k+1)} = -p_k \cdot r_i^{(k)}$$
$$R^{(k+1)} = R^{(k)} - (1 + p_k) \cdot r_i^{(k)} \cdot (1 - \rho_i)$$
$$k := k + 1$$

GOTO Step 1

Step 2B: *constant radiosity step*

$$B_j^{(k+1)} = B_j^{(k)} + (1 + p_k) \cdot R^{(k)} \cdot H^{-1} \qquad (j = 1, 2, \ldots, n)$$

p_k is an arbitrary constant: $|p_k| \le 1 - \epsilon,\ 0 < \epsilon \le 1$

new values of error vector components

$$r_j^{(k+1)} = r_j^{(k)} - (1 + p_k) \cdot h_j \cdot R^{(k)} \cdot H^{-1} \qquad (j = 1, 2, \ldots, n; j \ne i)$$
$$R^{(k+1)} = -p_k \cdot R^{(k)}$$
$$k := k + 1$$

GOTO Step 1

The algorithm above makes use of the closed environment. In such cases the solution lies always in a special hyperplane (see equation (33)):

$$\sum_{j=1}^{n} h_j \cdot B_j = R^{(0)} \tag{40}$$

C-orthogonal projection to this plane is the constant radiosity step in Step 2B. This recent-type step alters every radiosity value by the *same constant* , and permits to update the error vector *without form factor computation*. In the algorithm above, here and there a constant radiosity step is interlaced between steps in Algorithm-I.

5 Ambient Term

By analogy to the ambient term introduced in progressive radiosity [2], an approximate solution is wanted for display, that can be computed in knowledge of the approximate solution vector $\mathbf{x}^{(k)}$ and error vector $\mathbf{r}^{(k)}$. There is: $\mathbf{C}\mathbf{x}^{(k)} = \mathbf{b} - \mathbf{r}^{(k)}$ and $\mathbf{C}\mathbf{x}_{res}^{(k)} = \mathbf{r}^{(k)}$, where $\mathbf{x}_{res}^{(k)}$ is the solution of the "residuum" problem. The exact solution is: $\mathbf{x} = \mathbf{x}^{(k)} + \mathbf{x}_{res}^{(k)}$. Ambient term formulae are various assessments for vector $\mathbf{x}_{res}^{(k)}$. To compute the ambient term, the equation of form (2) will be abandoned for the classic form (1). In equations of the form $\mathbf{A}\mathbf{x} = \mathbf{e}$, $x_i = B_i$ and $e_i^{(k)} = r_i^{(k)} \cdot \frac{\rho_i}{A_i} = \rho_i \cdot r_i^{(k)} \cdot A_i^{-1}$.

The roughest assessment is a single Jacobi iteration step made for the residuum problem. Now, $x_{res,i}^{(k)} \approx e_i^{(k)} = \rho_i \cdot r_i^{(k)} \cdot A_i^{-1}$.

A much better approximation is obtained in the form:

$$x_{res,i}^{(k)} \approx e_i^{(k)} + \rho_i \cdot \gamma^{(k)} = \rho_i \cdot (r_i^{(k)} \cdot A_i^{-1} + \gamma^{(k)}) \tag{41}$$

That is – in lack of other *a priori* information – the part other than e has to be *proportional to the reflectivity* of each patch. For the residuum problem the hyperplane equation may be written according to equations (29) through (32):

$$\langle 1, \mathbf{x}_{res} \rangle_C = \langle \mathbf{h}, \mathbf{x}_{res} \rangle = R^{(k)} \tag{42}$$

Hence:

$$\sum_{j=1}^{n} h_j \cdot x_{res,j}^{(k)} = \sum_{j=1}^{n} r_j^{(k)} \tag{43}$$

Just as the solution of the original equations lies on hyperplanes (30) and (40), the solution of the residuum problem lies on hyperplane (43). Thereby parameter $\gamma^{(k)}$ can be determined, making use of equation (41):

$$\gamma^{(k)} = \frac{\sum_{j=1}^{n} r_j^{(k)} \cdot \rho_j}{\sum_{j=1}^{n} A_j \cdot (1 - \rho_j)} \tag{44}$$

In the algorithms above, after step k, the following radiosity value may be applied for display (considering $B_{res,i}^{(k)} = x_{res,i}^{(k)}$):

$$^dB_i^{(k)} = B_i^{(k)} = \rho_i \cdot (r_i^{(k)} \cdot A_i^{-1} + \gamma^{(k)}) \tag{45}$$

Remember that the ambient term formula of the classic shooting (Southwell) method applied as reference problem of the tests had to be somehow "approximated" by the formula above, for the sake of comparability. Obviously, not the first ambient term formula in [2] has been applied, since it is a rough approximation. The formula has been applied, stripped of the unshot term, similarly to equation (41), and only resultants of higher-order reflections have been computed, making use of ρ_{avg}. This form of the classic ambient term yielded – to our surprise – after mathematical deduction a result perfectly identical to equation (45)! Also this deeper relationship points to the importance of the hyperplane equation valid to closed environments.

It has been investigated how much the ambient term image according to equation (45) improves if preceded by a constant radiosity step of arbitrary size (a hyperplane step). It was rather curious to find that the sum of constant radiosity step and of the ambient term is *independent* of the size of constant radiosity step. So it seems quite useless to intercalate such a step. It appears in figure 3 that after the hyperplane step, the curve of error of the ambient term image starts horizontally, since after the constant radiosity step the ambient term image according to equation (45) does not change. On the other hand, error vector **r** is completely restructured, and later, the favourable effect of the hyperplane step becomes gradually manifest.

6 Results and Future Trends

The methods have been tested in a simple, closed environment. The scene was a cube in a parallelepipedic room, the patches numbered $n = 988$. The number of patches with self-emission was 25, $\rho_{avg} = 0.659$, and $0.0445 \le \rho_i \le 0.887$. A method has been applied to correct symmetricity errors arising in hemi-cube computations so that row sums of form factors remain 1. Perspectively, the effect of symmetricity error has to be examined, and/or analytic form factor computation is suggested.

Four algorithms have been tested, applying the classic shooting method as reference. Thereafter followed the Southwell algorithm with the positive definite matrix, as well as Algorithm I and Algorithm II above.

All of the methods with positive definite matrix offered *maximum efficiency for some overrelaxation* . Further research is required to determine efficient p_k series coping with the given problem.

Relative errors of the four methods above with and without ambient term can be seen in figure 3. *Algorithm-II appears to be much more efficient than the* other methods. It was astonishing to see how the reference method, the positive definite version of Southwell algorithm, and Algorithm-I yielded similar results either with or without ambient term, although the *selected patch series were*

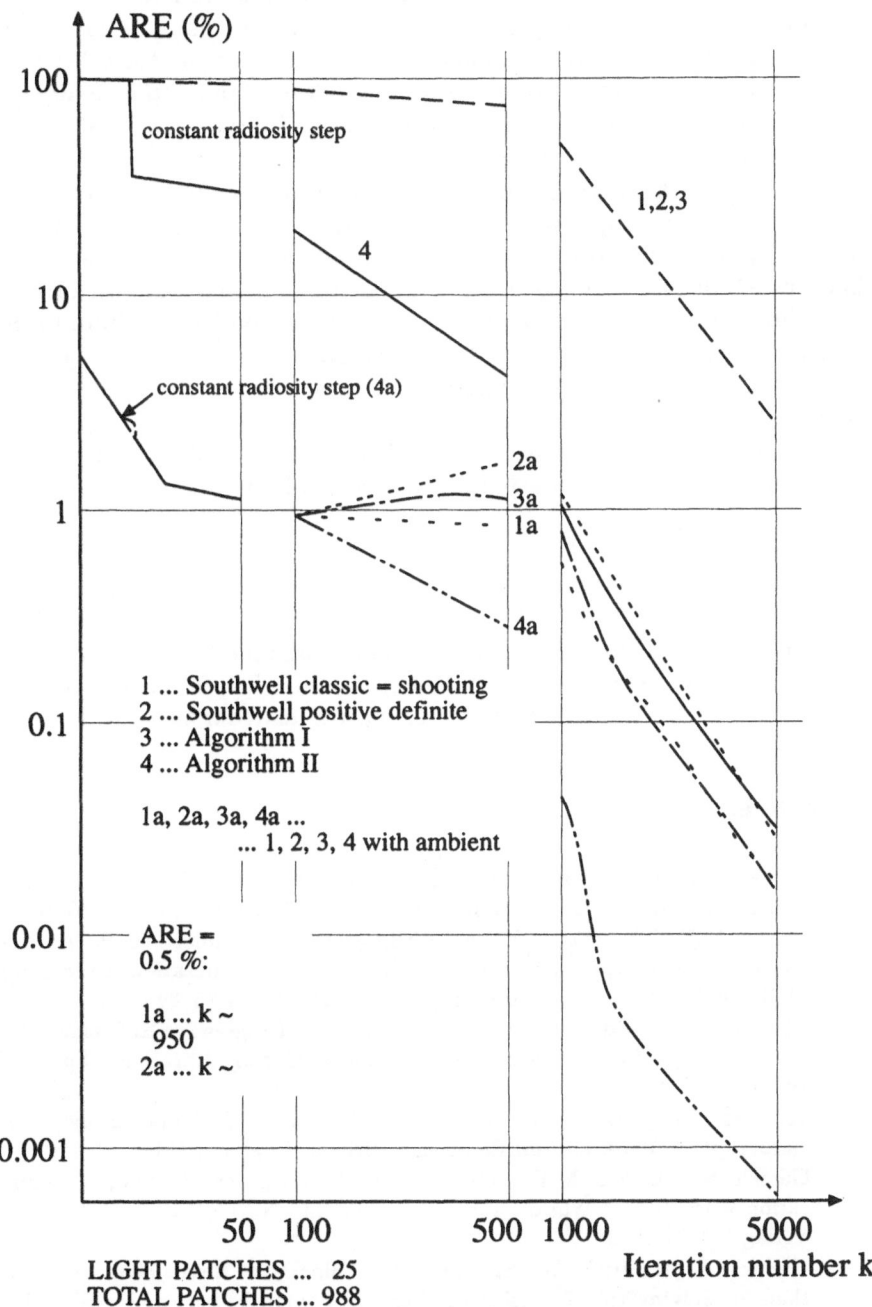

Figure 3

different in the three cases. In future, further tests have to be made, to compare the introduced algorithms with the known overshooting methods.

As matter of fact, this paper has a double result as gist. On one hand, *an efficient algorithm for closed environments* has been found, on the other hand, a *deepgoing mathematical procedure and background to examine this family of methods*. Since these were missing from earlier special literature, several algorithm arose intuitively, without convergence proofs.

In addition to the methods considered, the positive definite form is likely to offer several efficient applications in the future. So may be, on the one hand, orthogonal projection procedures in subspaces of $m \ll n$ dimensions of a space defined by C-metrics. On the other hand, several methods known in the numerical literature, with the stipulation of symmetric positive definite form, for instance, the gradient and the conjugated gradient method. Investigations in this scope are pursued in cooperation with Prof. Werner Purgathofer and his co-workers.

A further possibility of generalization is offered by investigation of positive definite forms of radiosity for separable and general non-diffuse reflectance.

Acknowledgements

The authors are indebted to *Attila Neumann* (Budapest), and *Prof. Werner Purgathofer* (Technische Universitat Wien) for their helpful comments, and to *Manfred Kopp* (Wien) for the form factor matrix made for the test.

References

[1]   Cohen, M.F., Greenberg, D.P.: The Hemi-cube: A Radiosity Solution for Complex Environments, ACM Computer Graphics, 19(3), (August 1985) 26–35

[2]   Cohen, M.F., Shenchang, E.Ch., Wallace, J.R., Greenberg, D.P.: A Progressive Refinement Approach to Fast Radiosity Image Generation, Proceedings of SIGGRAPH'88, In Computer Graphics, 22(4), (1988) 75–84

[3]   Chalmers, A., Paddon, D.: Parallel Processing of Progressive Refinement Radiosity, In Second Eurographics Workshop on Rendering, Barcelona, Spain, (May 1991)

[4]   Feda, M., Purgathofer, W.: Accelerating Radiosity by Overshooting, In Third Eurographics Workshop on Rendering, Bristol, England, (May 1992)

[5]   Gortler, S.J., Cohen, M.F.: Solving the Radiosity Linear System, In Communication with Virtual Worlds, Editors: Thalmann, N.M, Thalmann, D., Springer Verlag (1993) 78–88

[6]   Greiner, G., Heidrich, W., Slussalek, Ph.: Blockwise Refinement - A New Method for Solving the Radiosity Problem, In Fourth Eurographics Workshop on Rendering, Paris, (June 1993) 233–245

[7]   Hanrahan, P., Salzman, D., Aupperle, L.: A Rapid Hierarchical Radiosity Algorithm, Proceedings of SIGGRAPH'91, In Computer Graphics, 25(4), (1991) 197–206

[8]   Min-Zhi Shao, Badler, N.I.: Analysis and Acceleration of Progressive Refine-
       ment Radiosity Mehtod, In Fourth Eurographics Workshop on Rendering, Paris,
       (June 1993) 247–258
[9]   Neumann, L.: Orthogonal Projection Algorithms in Hilbert Spaces, Techni-
       cal Report (in Hungarian). Computer and Automation Institute, Hungarian
       Academy of Sciences, Budapest, (1981)
[10]   Neumann, L.: Monte Carlo Radiosity, Lecture delivered at the Fourth Euro-
       graphics Workshop on Rendering, Paris, (June 1993), submitted to Computing
       (Springer Verlag)

Adaptive Mesh Refinement with Discontinuities for the Radiosity Method

W. Stürzlinger

Johannes Kepler University, A-4040 Linz, Austria

Abstract

The radiosity method simulates the interaction of light between diffuse reflecting surfaces, thereby accurately predicting global illumination effects. One of the main problems of the original algorithm is the inability to represent correctly the shadows cast onto surfaces. Adaptive subdivision techniques were tried but the results are not good enough for general purposes. The conceptually different discontinuity meshing algorithm produces exact pictures of shadow boundaries but is computationally expensive. The newly presented adaptive discontinuity meshing method combines the speed of adaptive subdivision with the quality of the discontinuity meshing method.

1 Introduction

Radiosity has become a popular method for image synthesis due to its ability to generate images of high realism. It was first introduced to computer graphics by Goral [GTGB84]. The radiosity method models the interaction of light between diffuse surfaces ("patches"). These patches are used to store the radiosity on the respective part of the surface. The global illumination is then approximated by formulating a linear equation system for the interaction of radiosity between the patches. The progressive refinement method [CCWG88] uses a reordering of the solution process to speed up the calculation. This method works as follows: An iteration step distributes ("shoots") the radiosity of the patch with the maximum unshot radiosity to all other patches in the environment. Displaying the results after each iteration step provides the user with progressively refined approximations to the resulting picture.

To describe the influence the illumination of one patch onto another, a value - called formfactor - must be computed. These formfactors were first computed using the relatively inexact hemicube method. Wallace [WEH89] improved the accuracy by using analytic approximations for small parts of the shooting patch and ray tracing for the visibility calculations.

Another noteworthy property of the radiosity method is that it computes the illumination globally, i.e. independent of the camera position. After the radiosity algorithm has finished the scene can be viewed on a graphic workstation from arbitrary viewpoints.

2 Previous Research on Adaptive Subdivision

2.1 Patches and Elements

A drawback of the original radiosity method is the large number of patches needed to capture important detail such as shadow boundaries accurately as more patches increase the computational needs significantly.

Cohen [CGIB86] proposed a two-level hierarchy to partially overcome this problem. The patches are further subdivided into elements. The illumination is computed for the elements and are also used to display the final image. The average of the element radiosities gives a good approximation to the radiosity of the respective patch. The errors caused by shooting the radiosity from patches are sufficiently small.

Hanrahan [HSA91] generalized the subdivision hierarchy to multiple level and used an adaption of n-body problem algorithms to speed up the calculations.

2.2 Adaptive Subdivision

The radiosity algorithm with patches and elements yields unsatisfactory results when applied to general scenes as one cannot determine in advance which level of subdivision will be needed to store the illumination across a surface correctly for every possible viewpoint.

Adaptive subdivision is used to overcome this problem (see e.g. [VP91, LBT92, PWWP93]). The mesh is refined locally if the radiosity values at the element vertices vary to much or in regions with a high radiosity gradient across elements [VP91]. Such elements are considered unevenly lit, the mesh is subdivided and new radiosity values are computed for the added elements. Afterwards the algorithm is recursively applied to the new mesh elements.

This improved technique may still yield visually annoying artefacts because the resulting mesh density varies (too) quickly near shadow boundaries causing interpolation errors in the final image. A restricted quadtree scheme (see e.g. [CW93]) can be used to ensure a gradually varying mesh density.

Fortunately it is not necessary to compute the illumination for all sampling points in every iteration. In surface regions evenly lit by the current shooter only the radiosity of the original elements and associated sampling needs to be calculated. The radiosity of samples created earlier because of uneven illumination by the shooting patch of a previous iteration can be interpolated from the vertices of the original element, if the current shooter lights it evenly. This method avoids a steady increase of sample contributions to be calculated, which would cause a slowdown of subsequent iterations.

2.3 Discontinuity Meshing

A better approach would use the exact shadow boundaries for the mesh subdivision [PWWP93]. The umbra and penumbra regions can be computed exactly for a patch casting a shadow onto a plane when lit by a polgonal lightsource. The penumbra region is separated from the umbra region and the fully lit part by line segments (see Figure 1). The illumination function has discontinuities of first or second order across these line segments (see e.g. [He92, LTG92]).

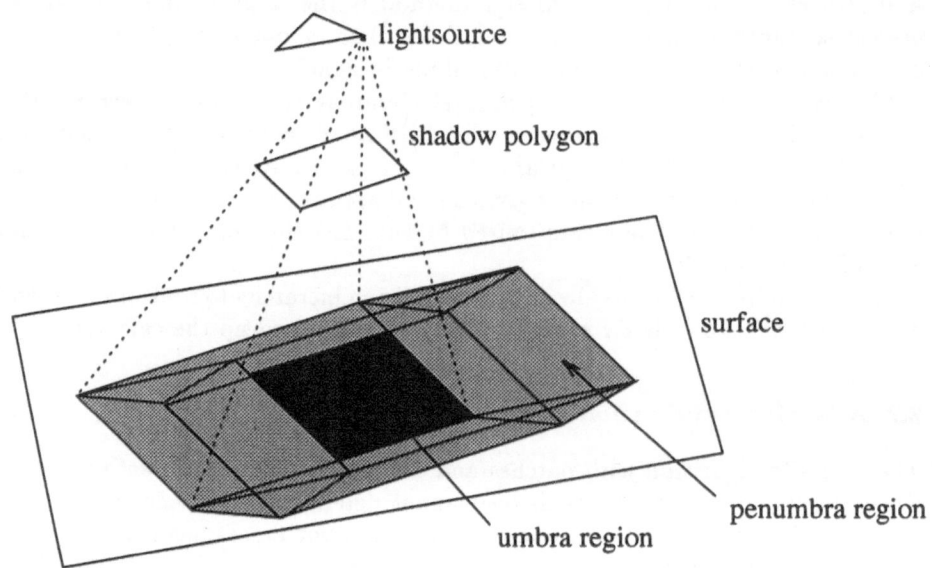

Fig. 1. Penumbra and umbra regions.

Lischinski [LTG92] presented an algorithm which calculates all shadow boundaries. Shadows cast by the current shooter onto all other surfaces are constructed exactly. The use of a BSP-tree (Binary Space Partition tree, see [FKN80]) optimizes this costly operation. The contribution of the current shooter is stored in a separate mesh. This mesh is "added" to the overall mesh after each iteration.

Heckbert [He92] calculated the shadow boundaries using a different approach based on wedges and a sweep line algorithm.

3 Adaptive Discontinuity Meshing

3.1 Motivation

The major drawback of adaptive subdivision is the fact that the required subdivision level depends on the viewing perspective of the final image. Therefore, this method is not well suited for high quality interactive viewing environments. On the one hand artifacts become noticeable at shadow boundaries near the camera (due to insufficient subdivision). On the other hand surfaces far away from the camera can do with much coarser subdivision. Therefore, the distance of a surface to the camera could be used to compute a maxmimum subdivision level. However, this method only applies to static images.

Philips [PWWP93] remarked that adaptive subdivision produces good results if exact shadow boundaries are used to subdivide the mesh but reasoned that they are too expensive to calculate.

The runtimes reported by Lischinski [LTG92] for discontinuity meshing are not far from dominating the whole illumination computation time even though a BSP-tree is used to speed up the calculation. One reason is that all discontinuity segments are calculated, regardless if noticeable or not. Shadow boundaries such as those caused by small objects close to lightsources will be practically invisible in the final images and there is no real need to compute and store them.

3.2 Adaptive Discontinuity Meshing

Adaptive discontinuity meshing is a combination of an adaptive subdivision algorithm and the discontinuity meshing method. Formfactors are calculated by raytracing [WEH89]. The subdivision algorithm is modified to use a different test and subdivision strategy. If a shadow boundary crossing an element is detected the exact shadow boundary is computed and used for mesh subdivision. As an example the shaded surface elements in figure 2 have been subdivided by the shadow boundaries which cross them.

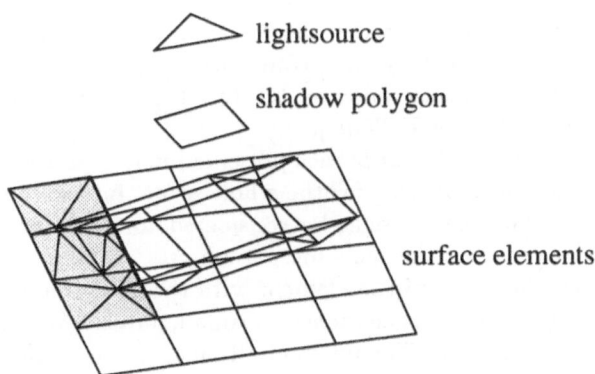

Fig. 2. Adaptive discontinuity meshing in progress.

The adaptive discontinuity meshing algorithm proceeds as follows:

First the illumination for a regular grid of sampling points is computed. The visibility of the shooting patch is determined by raycasting and those patches which obstruct the shooting patch are remembered ("light blockers"). In addition a flag stores if the shooter is fully invisible from the sample. Knowing the blocking patches for all vertices of an element it can be determined if it is potentially crossed by a shadow boundary.

Adaptive discontinuity meshing uses the following test and subdivision procedure for each element:

1. If the shooting patch is invisible from all vertices of the element then it is assumed shadowed as a whole and no further action is taken.
2. If the shooter is fully visible from all vertices and the radiosities at the vertices differ significantly the element is subdivided regularily. Then the test is applied to each of the generated (sub-)elements.
3. If the shooting patch is fully visible and the element is uniformly lit no further action is taken.
4. If the maximum difference of the vertex-radiosities is small the element is assumed to be lit uniformly and the algorithm takes no further action.
5. The number of blocking patches for the element is computed.
   (a) If too many patches (e.g. more than 4) cause shadow boundaries on the element it is subdivided regularily. Then the test is reapplied to each of the generated (sub-)elements.
   (b) Otherwise the respective shadow boundary segments for each of the blockers are constructed and the element is subdivided accordingly. This alternative is also chosen if the subdivision level reaches a user-supplied maximum.

The calculation of the shadow boundaries requires a representation of the locations where the visibility of the shooting patch changes. These locations correspond to wedges defined by the geometries of the shooting patch and the patch which causes the shadow and can be stored in a shadow BSP-tree. For a more thorough discussion see [LTG92].

In contrast to Lischinski the approach presented in this paper does not require to construct the shadow BSP-tree for the whole scene. Instead only two patches (the shooter and a "blocker") must be considered for the construction of the shadow BSP-tree caused by the blocking patch.

By intersecting the plane of the element with the BSP-tree a set of discontinuity segments is generated. As elements are small, only a few of these segments will cross the current element. The union of all shadow boundaries of all blocking patches is then used to partition the element into triangles.

The BSP-trees which were used to compute shadow boundaries are stored for the duration of the current iteration, as they might be needed for neighbouring elements. 2d- and 3d-bounding volumina for elements are used to accelerate the detection of potential shadow boundary segments.

The principal advantage of this new algorithm is that it creates considerably less elements than the original adaptive subdivision algorithm. Most shadow boundaries are represented exactly after the first subdivision step thereby avoiding the need for further subdivision in many cases. Only in complicated cases (e.g. multiple intersecting shadow boundaries) the algorithm subdivides deeper.

Instead of relying on heuristics only the algorithm classifies most cases unambiguously by using information already gathered by the visibility test. Therefore, this adaptive subdivision algorithm detects shadow boundaries crossing elements more reliably than the previously published methods.

Due to better shadow boundary detection, the threshold for unevenly lit elements can be set higher than in the original adaptive subdivision algorithm as shadow boundaries are already explicitly accounted for.

Primary lightsources and strong secondary lightsources cause the most prominent discontinuities. These will be detected reliably by the algorithm. Unnoticeable i.e. weak shadow boundaries are ignored and cause no discontinuity segments to be generated. In contrast to Lischinski [LTG92] who used the heuristic of computing the discontinuities only for the primary lightsources, this algorithm computes shadow boundaries only where neccessary, i.e. where they are visible in the final images or walk through environment.

3.3 Improved Adaptive Discontinuity Meshing

Due to the regular grid of the original elements aliasing effects can occur (e.g. small sharp shadow details might be missing).

In a surface region with changing lightning conditions the mesh density will vary abruptly causing interpolation artifacts. Such artifacts can be avoided by using a scheme analogous to the restricted quadtree. If the subdivision levels of neighbouring elements differ by more than one the respective element is subdivided and the algorithm is applied recursively.

Many artifacts appear also at the boundary of a region where elements were split by discontinuity segments and others were not (e.g. figure 3), The artifacts are caused by t-vertices and can be avoided by the anchoring scheme described by Baum [BRW89].

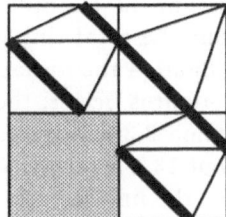 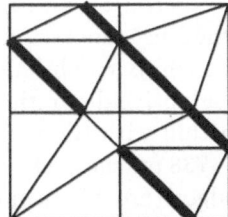

Fig. 3. T-vertices (left) and anchoring (right). Discontinuity segments are drawn in bold.

The techniques presented in section 2.2 are used to avoid a steady increase of sample contributions to be computed.

3.4 Reconstruction of the Illumination Function

One method for reconstructing the illumination function from the radiosity values is by linear interpolation across elements known as Gouraud shading – a polygon display method often implemented in hardware on graphic workstations. The resulting illumination function is continuous in value (C^0). This technique allows an interactive walkthrough of the environment.

As illumination varies smoothly across surfaces (except at shadow boundaries) higher order reconstruction methods can be used, as an alternative. Lischinski [LTG92] used quadratic and Salesin [SLR92] cubic Bezier-triangles. Both approaches exploit the precalculated discontinuities to correctly approximate the illumination function. The reconstruction algorithm of Salesin [SLR92] provides a C^1-smooth interpolation of the surface illumination.

4 Implementation and Results

Our simple test scene consisted of a cube floating above a plane lighted by two lightsources was modeled (analguous to [LTG92]).

Figure 4 shows the mesh in the upper part and a Gouraud shaded version in the lower part of the picture. The pictures were generated without the modifications discussed in section 3.3. The statistics for the two versions are given in the following table, where AS stands for the original adaptive subdivision method and ADM stands for the new adaptive discontinuity meshing method. Times are given in seconds for a SGI Indigo R3000 for the first two interations (corresponding to the two lightsources).

	AS 1. iter	AS 2. iter	ADM 1. iter	ADM 2. iter
Total number of elements	1361	2057	326	828
Iteration time (sec)	4	3	4	5

The mesh created by the adaptive discontinuity meshing algorithm consist of considerably less elements compared to the original adaptive subdivision algorithm, resulting also in less memory usage. Due to the more complex shadow boundary detection and subdivision algorithm the adaptive discontinuity meshing method uses more time per element but the total times used by both algorithms are compareable. As can be seen in figure 4 the visual quality of the result of the adaptive discontinuity meshing method is better, though.

The algorithm with the modifications of section 3.3 was tested with a scene consisting of 4738 patches. The method took about 13 % longer than the adaptive subdivision algorithm. The timings are given for the first iteration.

	AS	ADM
Total number of elements	104689	35897
Iteration time (sec)	559	630

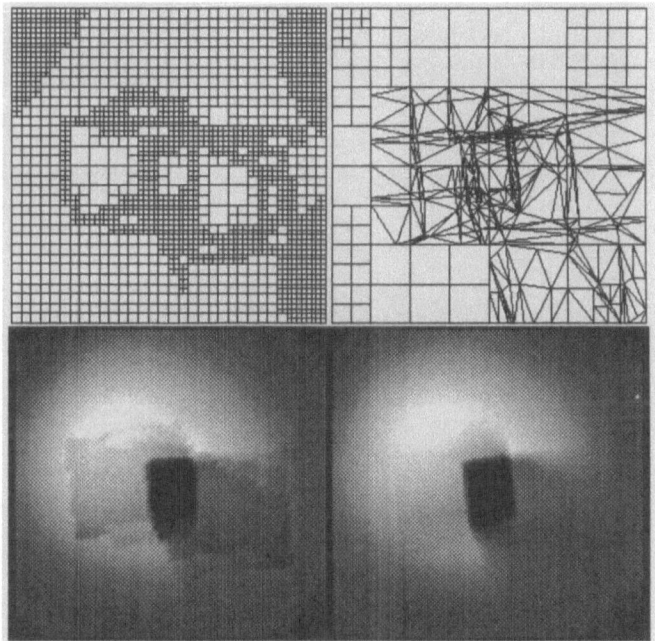

Fig. 4. Adaptive subdivision (left) and adaptive discontinuity meshing (right).

However the visual quality of the resulting image (see figure 5) is superior to the image computed by ordinary adaptive subdivision.

5 Conclusion and Further Extensions

The adaptive discontinuity meshing method presented in this paper combines the speed of adaptive subdivision with the image quality of the discontinuity meshing method.

- Compared to the adaptive subdivision method the adaptive discontinuity meshing algorithm delivers a result in compareable time.
- Significantly fewer elements are generated which reduces memory requirements.
- Due to the improved shadow boundary representation the resulting images are visually more accurate.
- This method introduces an new approach for reliable adaptive subdivision criteria.
- Adaptive discontinuity meshing can be used as an extension to existing radiosty systems and/or parallel implementations of the radiosity algorithm (e.g. [St94]).

Fig. 5. Complex scene with adaptive discontinuity meshing.

In this paper only Gouraud shading was used for the resulting images. The potential effect of higher order interpolation methods remains to be investigated.

Hierarchical discontinuity meshing [LTG93] is another practicable way to improve image quality and to obtain the image quickly as well. A noteable disadvantage of all hierarchical methods reported by [Ca94, To94] are significant problems in parallelizing them for distributed memory machines.

5.1 Acknowledgements

The author thanks G. Schaufler for reading an early version.

References

[BRW89]   Baum, D. R., Rushmeier, H. E., Winget, J. M.: Improving Radiosity Solutions through the Use of Analytically Determined Form-Factors. Computer Graphics (SIGGRAPH '89) **23**:3 (1989) 51-60

[Ca94]   Carter, M.: Private communications.

[CGIB86]   Cohen, M., Greenberg, D. P., Immel, D. S., Brock, P. J.: An Efficient Radiosity Approach for Realistic Image Synthesis. IEEE Computer Graphics and Applications **6**:3 (March 1986) 26-35

[CCWG88]   Cohen, M., Chen, S. E., Wallace, J. R., Greenberg, D. P.: A Progressive Refinement Approach to Fast Radiosity Image Generation. Computer Graphics (SIGGRAPH '88) 22:4 (1988) 75–84

[CW93]   Cohen, M. F., Wallace, J. R.: Radiosity and Realistic Image Synthesis. Academic Press (1993)

[FKN80]   Fuchs, H., Kedem, Z. M., Naylor, B.: On Visibile Surface Generation by a Priori Tree Structures. Computer Graphics (SIGGRAPH '80) 14:3 (July 1980) 124–133

[GTGB84]   Goral, C. M., Torrance, K. E., Greenberg, D. P., Battaile, B.: Modelling the Interaction of Light Between Diffuse Surfaces. Computer Graphics (SIGGRAPH '84) 18:3 (1984) 212–222

[He92]   Heckbert, P.: Discontinuity Meshing for Radiosity. Third Eurographics Workshop on Rendering (May 1992) 203–226

[HSA91]   Hanrahan, P., Salzman, D., Aupperle, L.: A Rapid Hierarchical Radiosity Algorithm. Computer Graphics (SIGGRAPH '91) 25:4 (July 1991) 197–206

[LBT92]   Languenou, E., Bouatouch, K., Tellier, P.: An adaptive Discretization Method for Radiosity. Proceedings of Eurographics 1992 11:3 (1992) 205–216

[LTG92]   Lischinski, D., Tampieri, F., Greenberg, D. P.: A Discontinuity Meshing Algorithm for Accurate Radiosity. IEEE Computer Graphics and Applications 12:6 (Nov 1992) 25–39

[LTG93]   Lischinski, D., Tampieri, F., Greenberg, D. P.: Combining Hierarchical Radiosity and Discontinuity Meshing Computer Graphics (SIGGRAPH '93) 27:4 (August 1993) 199–208

[PWWP93]   Philips, S., Worrall, A., Willis, C., Paddon, D.: Adaptive Mesh Refinement for the Radiosity Method. Proceedings of Compugraphics (1993) 178–186

[SLR92]   Salesin, D., Lischinski, D., DeRose, T.: Reconstructing Illumination Functions with Selected Discontinuities. Third Eurographics Workshop on Rendering (May 1992) 99–112

[St94]   Stürzlinger, W., Wild, C.: Parallel Progressive Radiosity with Parallel Visibility Computations, Winter School of Computer Graphics 94 (Plzen, CZ) (Feb. 1994) 66–74

[To94]   Tobler, R. F.: Private communications.

[VP91]   Vedel, C., Puech, C.: A testbed for adaptive subdivision in progressive radiosity, Second Eurographics Workshop on Rendering (May 1991)

[WEH89]   Wallace, J. R., Elmquist, K. A., Haines, E. A.: A Ray Tracing Algorithm for Progressive Radiosity. Computer Graphics (SIGGRAPH '89) 23:3 (July 1989) 315–324

Optimizing Discontinuity Meshing Radiosity

Neil Gatenby, W. T. Hewitt

Computer Graphics Unit, MCC, University of Manchester, Oxford Road, Manchester M13 9PL, UK

1 Introduction

Discontinuity meshing radiosity is no longer new to the Computer Graphics community. When trying to closely model, with patches, the *true* radiance function over some surface, it is now well established that errors are inevitable if patch boundaries take no account of discontinuities in the true radiance function [16, 13, 5].

Lischinski et al. [14], following on from Heckbert's earlier work [16], presented a Discontinuity Meshing Radiosity (DMR) system which stored a polygonal scene in a Binary Space Partitioning (BSP) tree [7, 6]. The presence of the BSP tree allowed efficient evaluation of discontinuity edges by utilizing routines which visit polygons in front-to-back order.

Since then, DMR has been incorporated into Hierarchical Radiosity (HR) [11, 12] by first obtaining a coarse global solution, using elements whose boundaries lie along known discontinuity edges, then refining this solution locally (for display) by extracting some information from the coarse solution, and re-calculating various other quantities [15].

This paper presents an incorporation of HR into DMR[1]. When modelling the radiance function across a surface, all discontinuity edges are included in the mesh. When evaluating the contribution from a surface whose radiance is represented by such a mesh, a piecewise constant hierarchical representation of the radiance is used, keeping accuracy high, complexity linear, and computational costs low.

The approach is a Progressive Refinement Radiosity (PRR) algorithm [4], which evaluates the radiance across the whole scene due to the unshot energy from one surface only, and keeps moving onto another bright surface and repeating this evaluation, until convergence.

Three optimizations of the DMR algorithm are presented in this paper:

Shadow Classification A careful track is kept of which regions in a discontinuity mesh can actually *see* all of the current source, which can only see

---

[1] Note: 'HR into DMR', not 'DMR into HR' as per [15]

part of it, and which have their view of the source completely blocked. This information (which can be deleted when finished with) allows efficient computation of radiance values, as occlusion testing is only necessary for points which are known to lie in penumbra regions.

An Efficient Sampling Strategy When shooting from a surface which is not a primary light source, the radiance across the shooter may well be varying rapidly over its surface, making it expensive to sample. A piecewise constant hierarchical representation of the shooter radiance is introduced, to improve the efficiency of the sampling process.

Layering When two different sources produce two different meshes on the surface of some receiver, previous algorithms have *merged* the two meshes into one. In the approach outlined here, meshes are *layered* in an effort to avoid the computational costs of merging, and to allow the disposal of less important layers as the solution progresses.

2 Discontinuity Meshing

The actual *meshing* of the polygons in the scene, which ensures that element boundaries coincide with various discontinuities the radiance function may exhibit, proceeds almost exactly as described in [14].

The algorithm begins by building a BSP tree from the parallelograms that make up the scene. Next, a powerful emitter is chosen, as per conventional PRR. This source polygon is used to generate a number of VE (vertex-edge) and EV (edge-vertex) shadow wedges[2], each of which represents a region across which it is expected that the radiance function due to the chosen emitter will exhibit a discontinuity of some sort. A more detailed description of shadow wedges can be found in [14]. Before describing any more specifics here, a description of the data structure used to store the discontinuity edges is presented:

2.1 Data Structure

Evaluating discontinuity edges is all very well, but not very useful unless they can be stored in a data structure which allows one to efficiently recover previously hard-earned information. Like Lischinski et al. [14], the structure used is a combination of a 2D-BSP tree[3], and a Winged Edge Data Structure (WEDS [1]). Each internal node of the uvBSP tree contains the (u,v) line equation of an edge in the WEDS, each leaf node of the tree points to a WEDS face. This structure is referred to as a *DM texture*, and is used to represent the radiance across the `receiver` polygon due to the current `source`, figure 1.

3 Shadow Classification

What has been described so far differs hardly at all from what is described in [14]: The scene is stored in a BSP tree, allowing efficient shadow wedge and

---

[2] EEE events are ignored in this implementation

[3] Hereinafter referred to as a 'uvBSP tree'.

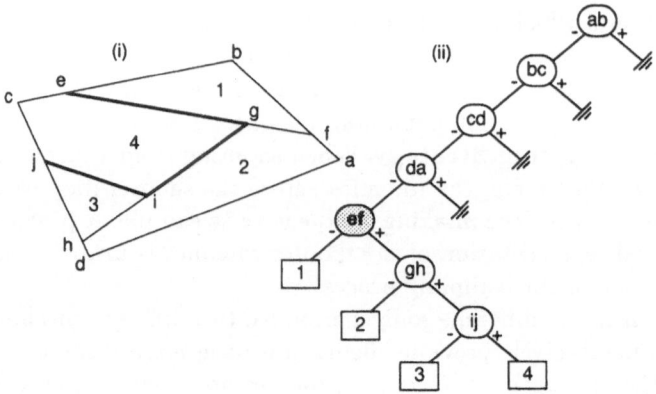

Fig. 1. (i) A polygon, showing discontinuity and construction edges. (ii) The uvBSP tree representing the polygon, with the polygon's 'root' node shown shaded.

discontinuity edge computation, and a data structure is in place to efficiently store the edges, and the regions which the edges delineate. What *is* apparent, though, is that after having gone to a lot of trouble to locate and store these edges, which are the crucial lines in any shadow region, *no* information about what actually *caused* the shadow has been stored.

In the algorithm described here, as well as storing a degree of discontinuity, each shadow wedge carries information about which occluder caused it, and whether the wedge bounds the occluder's umbra volume, penumbra volume, or not. Originally, it was believed that by tagging each discontinuity edge[4] with the shadow classification of its causal wedge (**umb**, **pen**, or neither), together with the relevant occluder, it would be possible to tour the boundaries of the WEDS faces formed by these discontinuity edges and determine whether the face was lit, in penumbra or in umbra with respect to the current source. Whilst this initial algorithm worked well for simple scenes, it tends to *under*classify shadow regions in more complex scenes [8].

3.1 Minimal Candidate Lists

Having built the topological half of a DM texture, it is necessary to evaluate the contribution of the source at various points in the texture. In an effort to establish which polygons, if any, lie between a sample point and the source, previous DMR algorithms [14, 15] have culled the entire scene by the source plane, the receiver plane, and then further culled those polygons that remained. However, it should be noted that a minimal occluder candidate list can be found by examining the order in which the scene BSP nodes were visited when generating the VE discontinuity wedges, figure 2.

A bitmask stored with each node can be used to keep track of whether the node was found to be front-facing or back-facing with respect to each source

---

[4] Found by intersecting a shadow wedge with the polygons in the scene

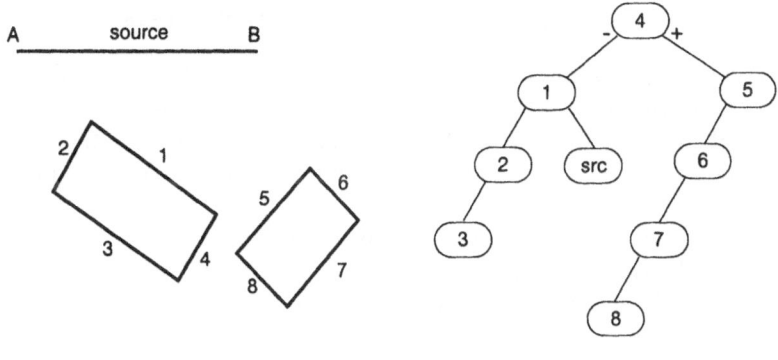

front-to-back(A) = 1, 2, 3_{BF}, 4_{BF}, 5, 8, 7_{BF}, 6_{BF}

front-to-back(B) = 1, 3_{BF}, 2_{BF}, 4_{BF}, 5, 6, 8_{BF}, 7_{BF}

Fig. 2. A simple scene, its BSP tree, and two front-to-back orderings taken at the source vertices.

vertex. Nodes which face zero source vertices receive no contribution whatsoever from the source (polygons 3,4 & 7 in figure 2). Nodes which face all source vertices can see all of the source (occlusion by other polygons aside - polygons 1 & 5, figure 2). Nodes which face some, but not all, source vertices lie in a plane which splits the source polygon (polygons 2, 6 & 8, figure 2). To establish an occluder candidate list for all the polygons at a BSP node n, simply find the union of all the nodes that come before n in any of the orderings containing it[5]. A proof is provided in the appendix. This (relatively short) candidate list can be now be culled by the source and receiver planes and further culled using either shaft-culling [10, 15], frustum-culling [14], or (as we have done) using shadow visibility BSP trees [2, 3].

It is interesting to note that these front-to-back orderings can also be used when generating EV wedges to give an efficient method of finding which polygons can clip the wedge between the source's E and the polygon's V.

3.2 Shadow Visibility BSP trees

Shadow visibility BSP (SVBSP) trees are used to store the umbra and penumbra volumes of each original scene polygon. Readers unfamiliar with SVBSP trees should consult [2, 3]. SVBSP trees, rather than shaft culling [10], are used because:

1. The planes needed to build the trees are found when discontinuity meshing; no extra work is needed.
2. The amount of culling work done is the same as shaft culling.

---

[5] A node will not appear in an ordering if the src vertex in question lies in the plane of the node.

3. The trees can be further used to shadow classify WEDS faces.

The second point is interesting: Given a receiver, and a candidate list of m occluders, shaft culling involves comparing each of these polygons with between four and eight planes. Comparing the receiver to the penumbra SVBSP tree of each candidate also involves between $4m$ and $8m$ polygon/plane comparisons, hence the same amount of work.

Those polygons whose penumbra volumes miss the receiver are taken off the candidate list. Those that remain are compared to the uvBSP tree of the receiver, in order to classify each WEDS face as being either lit, or in penumbra. Those found to be in penumbra are compared with the occluder's umbra volume (if it casts an umbra on the receiver at all).

The result of this classification is that every WEDS face is tagged as being either lit, in penumbra, or in umbra[6], and has a list of the polygons that are causing that shadow state.

Now, for each WEDS vertex, one can establish whether it lies in a lit region, a penumbra region, or an umbra region, by examining the shadow classification of the faces that surround it. If the point lies in penumbra, one can establish a target list of occluders from the surrounding faces, making the radiance evaluation at the vertex very efficient. No evaluation is needed for umbra sample points, and no occluder list is needed for lit sample points.

4 DM textures

Having built the uvBSP tree and WEDS for a DM texture, all the WEDS faces are classified as being either lit, in penumbra, or in umbra, and the penumbra/lit faces are triangulated so that bivariate quadratic elements can be used to model the radiance across each one. In order to fit such an element, a radiance value has to be found for each face vertex and for the mid-point of each face edge (see section 4.1). Once this has been done, the mesh is refined where necessary (see section 4.2), and any new faces that are generated get their six boundary radiance values evaluated. It is now possible to delete all the shadow information stored at the WEDS faces & vertices, to save space. Indeed, the whole WEDS structure can be replaced by a much simpler, and smaller, structure, whose sole purpose is to store quadratic elements.

Next, for each face of the refined mesh, a radiance-weighted average of the face's six boundary points (3 vertices, 3 edge mid-points) is found, and stored with the face. Also stored with the face is the average of the six boundary radiance values, and the face's (u, v)-area. These three values (position, radiance, (u, v)-area) are filtered up the uvBSP tree, the values at a node n being:

$$A_n = A_{n_-} + A_{n_+};$$
$$L_n = \frac{A_{n_-} L_{n_-} + A_{n_+} L_{n_+}}{A_n};$$

---

[6] Faces bounded by D^0 edges need not undergo this classification.

$$x_n = \frac{A_{n_-} L_{n_-} x_{n_-} + A_{n_+} L_{n_+} x_{n_+}}{A_{n_-} L_{n_-} + A_{n_+} L_{n_+}}$$

Note that the (u, v)-area of the root node will always be 1. Each node represents a region of the polygon, the (u, v)-area gives the fraction of the total polygon area that this regions takes up. The radiance (L_n) and position (x_n) have been chosen so that they can combine to give the *best possible* primary estimate when integrating over the region represented by the node.

4.1 Sampling a DM texture

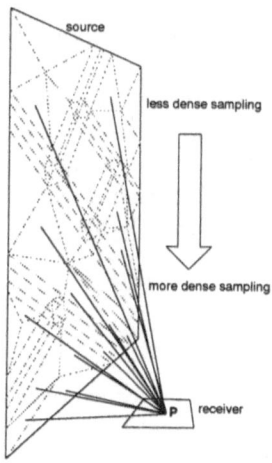

Fig. 3. Sampling a DM texture. The more important the contribution, the more work.

Assume that the current shooting polygon, src, has its unshot radiance represented by a DM texture. In order to evaluate the radiance at a point **P** due to this texture, first evaluate the solid angle Ω_{src} subtended at **P** by src, using the algorithm described in [9]. Now, if x_{src} is the position stored at the root of src's uvBSP tree (the shaded node in figure 1(ii)), L_{src} the radiance value stored there, and θ_{rcv} the angle between the surface normal at **P** and $(x_{src} - P)$, then $L_{src}. \cos\theta_{rcv}.\Omega_{src}$ is an estimate for the unoccluded contribution of the texture, at **P**. If this value is greater than some small user-defined ε, then recurse down the tree, until the estimated contribution at each node is small enough (see figure 3). Psuedo-code for a routine sample, which does exactly this, is:

```
float sample ( DMtexture *tree, Pt3 *P, Pt3 *norm, float omega, float eps
{
  float tmp;

  tmp = tree->rad * tree->uvArea * omega * eval_cos(tree->x, P, norm);
```

```
    if ( tmp > eps )
      return ( sample ( tree->neg, P, norm, omega, eps )
             + sample ( tree->pos, P, norm, omega, eps ) );
    else
      return ( tmp * vis(P, tree->x) );
}
```

Note that the estimate for the solid angle subtended by a region of the tree, at $\mathbf{P}$, is the product of the region's (u, v)-area with $\Omega_{\mathbf{src}}$. This is not exact, but certainly seems as valid as the circular disc and bounding sphere approximations which abound [17, 12, 15].

Note that the sample position $\mathbf{x_n}$, stored at each node of the uvBSP tree has been carefully chosen so that it is close to highly radiant parts of the surface, and far from less radiant parts. This means that the error when using this point for a primary estimate is minimal – the point is close to ($\sim$ accurate) the regions which might produce large errors, and far from ($\sim$ inaccurate) those which can't.

If a leaf node is reached before the estimated contribution is small enough (say the estimate is k times bigger then ε), then k samples can be taken within the triangular leaf, as per conventional direct lighting algorithms [18]. This approach is still being researched.

4.2 Refining a DM texture

Having evaluated all six radiance values for every leaf in the DM texture of rcv, does the mesh need refining at all? Should the leaf be split into smaller regions? Consider the three vertices $\mathbf{P_0}$, $\mathbf{P_1}$ and $\mathbf{P_2}$ of the leaf. It is easy to evaluate the three direction vectors $(\mathbf{x_{src}} - \mathbf{P_0})$, $(\mathbf{x_{src}} - \mathbf{P_1})$, and $(\mathbf{x_{src}} - \mathbf{P_2})$. These can be passed to the solid angle evaluation routine [9] to find $\Omega_{\mathbf{leaf}}$; the solid angle subtended by the leaf at $\mathbf{x_{src}}$. Furthermore, if $\mathbf{x_{rcv}}$ is the radiance-weighted average of the leaf's six boundary points, and $\theta_{\mathbf{src}}$ is the angle subtended at $\mathbf{x_{src}}$ between $(\mathbf{x_{rcv}} - \mathbf{x_{src}})$ and the src surface normal, then ...

$$L_{\mathbf{leaf}} \cdot \cos \theta_{\mathbf{src}} \cdot \Omega_{\mathbf{leaf}}$$

... can be compared with ε. If it is small enough, no subdivision takes place, otherwise the leaf node is split into smaller regions. This criterion is still the subject of work in progress, and may change.

5 Complexity

5.1 Layering DM textures

Combining DM textures is costly. If L sources each cast $O(n)$ discontinuity edges onto a surface, the cost of meshing the surface and including these edges is $O((Ln)^2) = O(L^2 n^2)$. The cost of storing the L textures separately is $O(Ln^2)$.

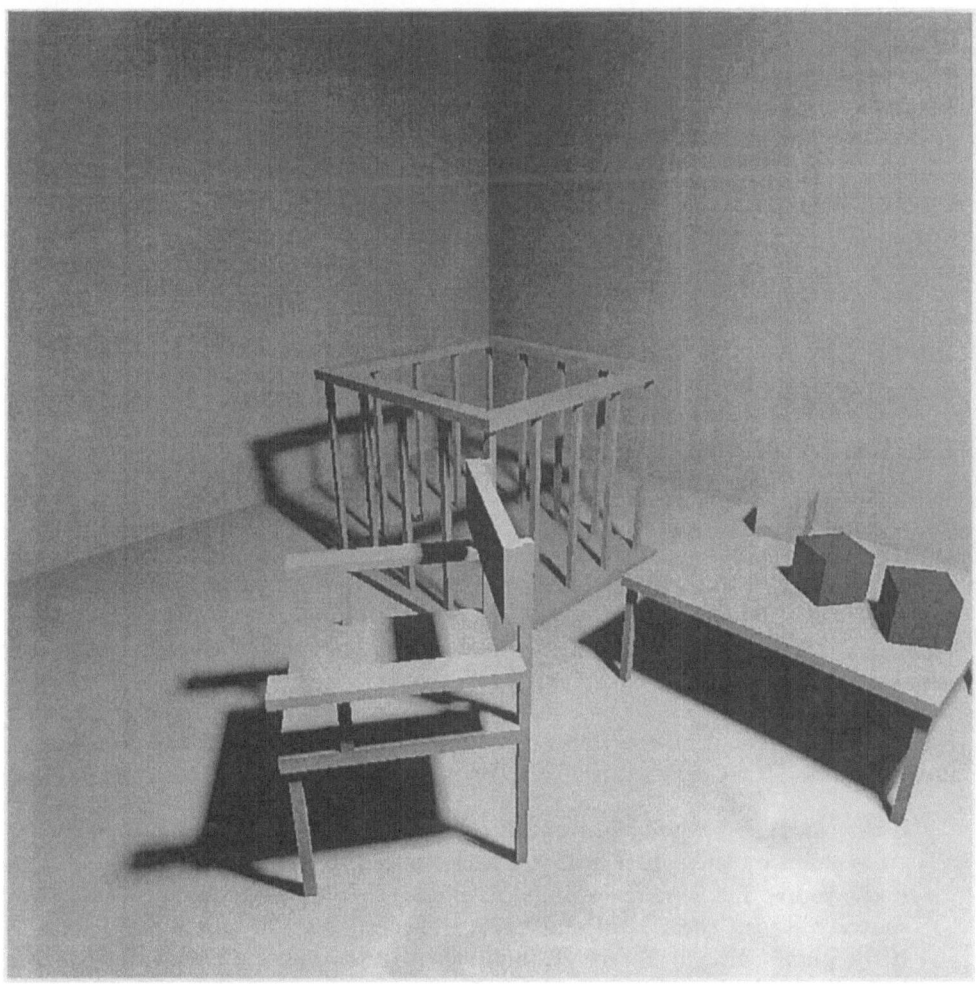

Fig. 4. An example scene: A single area light source illuminating a child's playroom. This took 173.5 seconds to render (800x800 pixels), most of which (132.5 secs) was ray tracing.

DM textures are stored separately, and those which become insignificant compared to the others being stored get merged into a single quadtree *base texture*. This means that early iterations, which later get swamped by others, will be stored for as long as they are significant, and then stored at a much reduced cost. Sampling m DM textures simply involves sampling each one, and returning the sum. Current research is examining the storage and access overheads of this approach, as opposed to combining the textures.

5.2 Algorithm Complexity

Suppose the `sample` routine terminates at p points in a tree. If each leaf node is now split into a 1000 tiny leaves, the sampling will still stop at the same p nodes in the tree. The authors feel the complexity of the algorithm is linear.

Closing Remarks: The authors would like to thank the staff in the Computer Graphics Unit for their help in producing this paper: In particular, Mr Fenqiang Lin. Neil Gatenby acknowledges the financial assistance of the Science and Engineering Research Council.

6 Appendix: Minimal Candidate Lists

Definition 1. An ordered list of BSP tree nodes, found by touring the scene BSP tree in front-to-back order, with respect to some point **P**, is referred to as the *tree ordering of* **P**.

Proposition 1 *If the point* **P** *lies somewhere on a source polygon, then given a tree ordering of* **P** *which list two nodes n_i and n_j in the order "... n_i ... n_j ...", there is at least one tree ordering, evaluated at a vertex of the source polygon, which lists these nodes in the same order.*

Proof. Let the node n be the youngest common ancestor of the two nodes n_i, n_j in the scene BSP tree. Possibly $n = n_i$ or $n = n_j$.

- If the source lies wholly in front of the partitioning plane stored at n, then every point on the source will visit these nodes in the same order.
- If the source lies wholly behind this plane, then again, every point on the source will visit these nodes in the same order.
- If the plane cuts the source polygon, then those points on the source lying in front of the plane will visit the nodes in one order, and those lying behind the plane will visit the nodes in the opposite order. Either way, the relevant order will have been captured by the tree ordering taken at one of the source vertices.

This concludes the proof.

References

1. Bruce G. Baumgart. A Polyhedron Representation for Computer Vision. *AFIPS Proceedings*, 44:589–596, May 1975.
2. Norman Chin and Steven Feiner. Near Real-Time Shadow Generation Using BSP Trees. *ACM Computer Graphics*, 23(3):99–106, July 1989.
3. Norman Chin and Steven Feiner. Fast Object-Precision Shadow Generation for Area Light Sources Using BSP Trees. *ACM Computer Graphics*, 26:21–30, May 1992. Special Issue on *1992 Symposium on Interactive 3D Graphics*.

 4. Michael F. Cohen, Shenchang Eric Chen, John R. Wallace, and Donald P. Green-
    berg. A Progressive Refinement Approach to Fast Radiosity Image Generation.
    ACM Computer Graphics, 22(4):75–84, August 1988.
 5. Michael F. Cohen and John R. Wallace. *Radiosity and Realistic Image Synthesis*.
    Academic Press Professional, 1993.
 6. Henry Fuchs, Gregory D. Abram, and Eric D. Grant. Near Real-Time Shaded
    Display of Rigid Objects. *ACM Computer Graphics*, 17(3):65–72, 1983.
 7. Henry Fuchs, Zvi M. Kedem, and Bruce F. Naylor. On Visible Surface Generation
    by *a priori* Tree Structures. *ACM Computer Graphics*, 14(3):124–133, 1980.
 8. Neil Gatenby. *Incorporating Hierarchical Radiosity into Discontinuity Meshing
    Radiosity*. PhD thesis, University of Manchester, 1994. To appear.
 9. Neil Gatenby and W. T. Hewitt. Concerning the Solid Angle Subtended by a
    Convex Polygon at a Point. 1994. Internal Paper, Computer Graphics Unit,
    University of Manchester.
10. Eric A. Haines and John R. Wallace. Shaft Culling for Efficient Ray-Traced Ra-
    diosity. In *Proceedings of the Second Eurographics Workshop on Rendering*. EU-
    ROGRAPHICS, May 1991.
11. Pat Hanrahan and David Salzman. A Rapid Hierarchical Radiosity Algorithm for
    Unoccluded Environments. In *Proceedings of the First Eurographics Workshop on
    Photosimulation, Realism and Physics in Computer Graphics*. EUROGRAPHICS,
    May 1990.
12. Pat Hanrahan, David Salzman, and Larry Aupperle. A Rapid Hierarchical Ra-
    diosity Algorithm. *ACM Computer Graphics*, 25(4):197–206, August 1991.
13. Paul Heckbert. Discontinuity Meshing for Radiosity. In *Proceedings of the 3rd
    Eurographics Workshop on Rendering*. EUROGRAPHICS, May 1992.
14. Dani Lischinski, Filipo Tampieri, and Donald P. Greenberg. Discontinuity Mes-
    hing for Accurate Radiosity. *IEEE Computer Graphics & Applications*, 12(6):25–
    39, November 1992.
15. Dani Lischinski, Filipo Tampieri, and Donald P. Greenberg. Combining Hierarchi-
    cal Radiosity and Discontinuity Meshing. In *COMPUTER GRAPHICS Procee-
    dings, Annual Conference Series*, pages 199–208. ACM SIGGRAPH, New York,
    August 1993.
16. Paul S. Heckbert. *Simulating Global Illumination Using Adaptive Meshing*. PhD
    thesis, University of California, Berkeley, June 1991. Dept. of Electrical Enginee-
    ring and Computer Sciences.
17. John R. Wallace, Kells A. Elmquist, and Eric A. Haines. A Ray Tracing Algo-
    rithm for Progressive Refinement Radiosity. *ACM Computer Graphics*, 23(3):315–
    324, July 1989.
18. Changyaw Wang. Physically Correct Direct Lighting for Distribution Ray Tracing.
    In *Graphics Gems III*, pages 307–313. Academic Press, 1992.

Simplifying the Representation of Radiance from Multiple Emitters

George Drettakis

iMAGIS / IMAG, B.P. 53, F-38041 Grenoble Cedex 9, France

Abstract

In recent work radiance function properties and discontinuity meshing have been used to construct high quality interpolants representing radiance. Such approaches do not consider the combined effect of multiple sources and thus perform unnecessary discontinuity meshing calculations and often construct interpolants with too fine subdivision. In this research we present an extended structured sampling algorithm that treats scenes with shadows and multiple sources. We then introduce an algorithm which simplifies the mesh based on the interaction of multiple sources. For unoccluded regions an a posteriori simplification technique is used. For regions in shadow, we first compute the maximal umbral/penumbral and penumbral/light boundaries. This construction facilitates the determination of whether full discontinuity meshing is required or whether it can be avoided due to the illumination from another source. An estimate of the error caused by potential simplification is used for this decision. Thus full discontinuity mesh calculation is only incurred in regions where it is necessary resulting in a more compact representation of radiance.

1 Sampling Illumination from Multiple Sources

To accurately render scenes illuminated by area light sources, it is necessary to represent the illumination on surfaces by a simpler, approximating function, even when considering only direct illumination. Piecewise polynomial interpolants are often chosen for this purpose. Such representations are an essential requirement for global illumination computation, in particular for the finite-element style approaches (e.g. [Zatz93, GSCH93]), which extend the radiosity-based method [CoGr85].

In the interpolant construction algorithms presented to date, much effort has been devoted to correctly treating shadow boundaries and identifying the behaviour of radiance. These methods have thus achieved high quality representation of illumination using simple functions. However, despite the significant advances in the field, little has been done to actually compensate for the cumulative effects of illumination from multiple emitters, be they light sources or secondary reflectors.

The importance of identifying these interactions is easy to see: when a single source is present, it may cast a detailed shadow which may require significant computation to represent correctly. However, if a second source illuminates the same region in an unobstructed fashion, the shadow will be "washed out" leaving little need for the detailed representation. This phenomenon is illustrated in Fig. 1(a) and (b) (see colour section), in which one and two sources illuminate the environment respectively.

Fig. 1. (a) One Source and (b) Two Source Images.

In this paper we propose a solution to this problem, by extending the techniques developed for discontinuity meshing and structured sampling [DrFi93, DrFi94, Dret94]. Throughout we consider only environments of diffusely reflecting surfaces lit by diffusely emitting sources. In the following section we present relevant previous work; we then present the extended structured sampling approach. We then briefly describe the two-pass discontinuity meshing algorithm which incurs the cost of full discontinuity meshing only in the regions required. In the sections that follow, we describe the simplification criteria for two sources, first for the intersection of unoccluded regions and then for the intersection of penumbral/unoccluded regions. For both cases we present first results of a prototype implementation. We then present the extension to multiple sources and summarise the results of the paper.

2 Previous Work

In previous work, the approximations used to represent radiance or radiosity have generally been guided by the requirements of the global illumination calculations. A simpler approach to constructing radiance representations is to examine illumination from a single emitter. The first such approach, in which the nature or structure of radiance for unoccluded regions is examined, was presented by Campbell and Fussell [Camp91]. They observed that radiance for these environments displays a single maximum. This idea was extended by Drettakis and Fiume [DrFi93], who constructed quadratic or linear interpolants tensor-product interpolants which can be shown to satisfy tight error bounds.

It has recently been shown that the computation of shadow boundaries, which are subsequently used to guide interpolant construction, is fundamental for high quality approximation of illumination. The first such work was performed in [Camp91] in which the boundary between penumbral and unoccluded regions was computed. The resulting mesh was then used to build an approximation of radiance of constant-radiance triangular elements. Similar work was performed by Chin and Feiner [ChFe92]. Lischinski et al. [LiTG92] were the first to consider discontinuity surfaces interior to the penumbra, that signify a change in the topological view of the light source (e.g. the appearance or disappearance of a vertex or an edge in the visible portion of the source). They subsequently built a triangulation of the receiver surfaces based on the subdivision of this mesh, and constructed quadratic interpolants over these triangles. A different algorithm was presented by Heckbert [Heck92], in which a similar mesh is computed. Lischinski et al. [LiTG92] also merged the meshes from multiple sources, but no simplification was attempted. In this paper we extend the approach de-

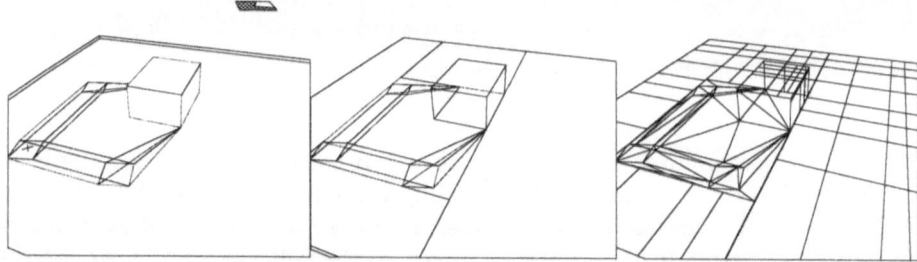

Fig. 2. (a) Mesh and Backprojection (b) Segmentation into Light and Penumbra and (c)Triangular/Tensor Product Interpolants.

veloped in [DrFi94, Dret94]. In this approach the *complete discontinuity mesh* is calculated: the environment is segmented into regions (mesh *faces*), in which the topological structure of the visible region of the source does not change. An abstract representation of the visible part of source, called a *backprojection*, is stored with each face. An example of such a mesh is shown in Fig. 2(a), where the backprojection of the point marked with a cross is shaded on the source. In [Dret94], the complete mesh is used to construct linear and quadratic interpolants representing radiance in the penumbra. In addition, the structured sampling approach of [DrFi93] was extended ([Dret94]) to handle environments with shadows in the following way. First all regions of shadow are identified and enclosed in a bounding box. Such a regular region enclosing a region of penumbral and umbral faces is called a *penumbral group*. The remaining parts of the receivers (which are unoccluded) are segmented into parallelograms (Fig. 2(b)) on which the structured sampling algorithm is used to create tensor-product interpolants as in [DrFi93] (Fig. 2(c)). Notice in Fig. 2(c) how in the regions of penumbra triangular interpolants are used, while in the unoccluded regions sparse tensor product representations suffice.

3 Extending Structured Sampling for Multiple Emitters

For the purpose of computing reference images in scenes with multiple sources, the discontinuity mesh from each source can be computed independently, and stored with the surface. When rendering using ray-casting, each mesh is queried, the backprojection retrieved for each mesh corresponding to each source and the exact radiance value computed.

To obtain the merged mesh due to several sources, the meshes corresponding to each source are combined. This is performed simply by adding the faces of one mesh into the other. If two light regions with tensor-products are combined, the merged region will contain tensor-product interpolants, while in ever other case (penumbra or umbra combined with penumbra, penumbra or umbra combined with unoccluded) the resulting mesh faces will be triangulated and a combined interpolant built.

By using the structured algorithm in [DrFi93] the radiance function in unoccluded regions for each source is split into regions in which the radiance is well behaved. The algorithm then creates quadratic interpolants and guarantees that the interpolants satisfies tight error bounds. Thus, the combined illumination function over the intersection of two light regions will continue to satisfy these error bounds. Similarly, for the other regions the combination of triangular or tensor-product interpolants is also guaranteed to give high quality results, since the regions have been segmented based on the complete discontinuity mesh.

Because of the guaranteed error bounds for the interpolants representing unoccluded illumination, we can safely use these approximations in our calculations for simplification (see below), instead of the more expensive direct illumination calculation.

4 Two-Pass "On Demand" Discontinuity Meshing

The main cost of the complete discontinuity meshing algorithm is due to the relatively large number of discontinuity surfaces that must be traced in the environment. In addition, it is necessary to search for the existence of discontinuity surfaces (either edge-vertex wedges (EV) or triple-edge quadric surfaces (EEE)), formed by edges and vertices not on the source. To reduce the cost of this computation, we must reduce the number of surfaces traced into the environment.

To do this we separate the mesh computation into two phases: first, the computation of the boundary between light and penumbra, and an estimate of the region between umbra and penumbra, and second the full computation of all discontinuity surfaces interior to the penumbra *only* when required. We call the boundary between penumbra and light the maximal boundary, and the boundary between umbra and penumbra the minimal boundary. The combined maximal and minimal boundary is called the *extremal* boundary.

4.1 Extremal Boundary Approximation

The computation of the maximal boundary can be performed exactly, since it is formed exclusively by EV surfaces [Camp91]. Thus these events can be identified in constant time for each object, and subsequently propagated into the environment. The minimal boundary can include EEE events [Tell92], which can be treated by the method described in [DrFi94].

As an example consider the scene shown in Fig. 3. On the left we see the full discontinuity mesh, and on the right the extremal boundary.

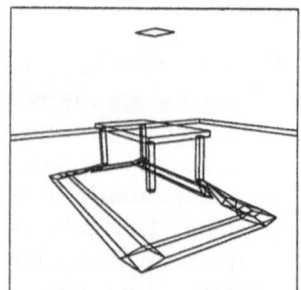 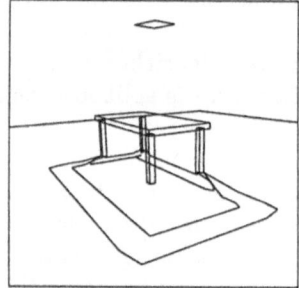

Fig. 3. Complete Mesh vs. Extremal Boundary.

The number of discontinuity surfaces traced through the environment is thus reduced significantly. In addition, since no internal detail of the mesh is computed, all non-emitter events are ignored, and the search time for such events is eliminated.

The computation time for the extremal boundary is significantly reduced compared to the computation of the full mesh. In Table 1 we compare the cost of complete discontinuity meshing to the cost of the extremal boundary for the scenes shown in Fig. 2 and Fig. 3, as well as two other more complex scenes. As we can see, the cost of the complete mesh computation is three to four times higher than the just the extremal boundary. It is thus evident that large gains can be achieved if the complete mesh need be computed only when required.

Table 1. Computation time for Complete Mesh and Extremal Boundary

Scene	Polygons	Complete Mesh	Extremal Boundary	Ratio Complete/ Boundary
Box Scene	14	0.74 sec	0.16 sec	4.6
Table Scene	36	1.01 sec	0.31 sec	3.2
Desk Scene	182	17.20 sec	4.42 sec	3.8
Desk & Chair Scene	288	35.20 sec	9.20 sec	3.8

4.2 Local Complete Mesh Construction

As discussed earlier, one of the goals of the approach presented here is to compute portions of the discontinuity mesh only when necessary. The discontinuity meshing algorithm presented in ([Dret94, DrFi94]) is particularly well suited to such an extension.

Given a convex region defined on a receiver for which the complete mesh is desired, a convex volume defined by the source and that region is defined. Using the same spatial subdivision structure as in [DrFi94], the objects contained in this volume can be found efficiently.

To create the full mesh *locally* in the desired region of the receiver, the discontinuity meshing algorithm of [DrFi94] is applied using only the objects within the volume. In this manner, a much smaller number of discontinuity surfaces are traced (only those corresponding to edges and vertices of the selected objects), and the number and expense of searches for non-emitter events is also limited.

5 Simplification Criteria

In this section we discuss the simplification criteria used when two meshes are combined. In Section 6 we show how this applies to an arbitrary number of sources.

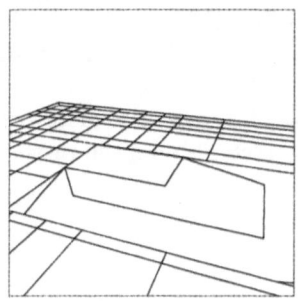 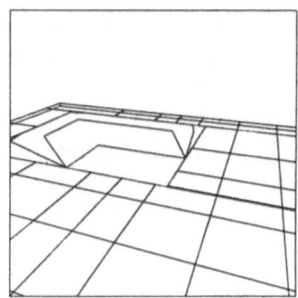

Fig. 4. Simplified Meshes for Box Scene.

Consider a source S_1 and a source S_2. We assume that we have computed the extremal boundaries for the discontinuity mesh for each source, that the environment has been segmented into parallelogram regions of light and penumbra/umbra. We also assume that the structured sampling algorithm has been applied, subdividing the regions of light. In each such unoccluded region a biquadratic tensor product interpolant has been built, which represents the radiance function accurately within strict error bounds. We call each such mesh the simplified mesh for source S. In Fig. 4 we show the simplified mesh for each source for the scene of Fig. 1 (see colour section).

Given the two meshes, M_1 and M_2 respectively, we proceed to "add" M_2 into M_1. Merging is performed this way purely for reasons of algorithmic simplicity. There are three cases that must be treated:

1. Merging light faces of M_1 with light faces of M_2.
2. Merging light faces of one mesh with penumbral faces of the other.
3. Merging penumbral faces of one mesh with penumbral faces of the other.

For the first case, since we have the structured representation in the form of tensor product interpolants for both meshes, we use an a posteriori error estimation to determine whether simplification can be performed. For the second case, we determine the regions of the penumbral group for which complete meshing is necessary. For the third case we currently perform no simplification.

5.1 Light-Light Simplification

The simplest case is the insertion of an unoccluded (light) face F_2 of M_2, into the mesh M_1. The mesh M_1 is searched to find all faces contained inside the boundary of the face F_2 being added. Call these faces $\{f_1, f_2, ..., f_n\}$. Within each such light face f_i of mesh M_1, a (structured) biquadratic interpolant $s_i^1(x, y)$ has been defined. Correspondingly, the structured interpolant in F_2 is $s_2^2(x, y)$.

To determine whether simplification is possible, we proceed to construct two biquadratic interpolants: first a high quality representation of the combined radiance with the region of F_2, denoted $s_\cap(x, y)$ and second a simplified representation, $\tilde{s}(x, y)$. The error incurred by the simpler interpolant (compared to the high-quality interpolant) is used to determine whether simplification can be achieved.

The high-quality interpolant $s_\cap(x, y)$ is defined as follows, in a piecewise fashion over each f_i (this is the interpolant created when combining the meshes as in Section 3):

$$s_\cap = s_2^2(x, y) + s_i^1(x, y), (x, y) \in f_i \tag{1}$$

Since the interpolants $s_i^j(x, y), j = 1, 2$ already constructed are good approximations of the actual radiance function, $s_\cap(x, y)$ is considered to be an accurate approximation of the combined function over the entire domain $F_2 = \cup f_i$.

The second interpolant $\tilde{s}(x, y)$ is defined over F_2 as a simple 9-point biquadratic tensor product, for which the midpoints are used as internal defining nodes. The nodal values are found by querying $s_\cap(x, y)$.

To determine whether the combined illumination from two sources can be represented accurately by the simplified interpolant $\tilde{s}(x, y)$, we use standard approximation theoretic error estimate [Pren89]. As a first approach we compute the L_2-norm of the difference of the simplified and the accurate interpolants.

For the L_2-norm the following quantity is computed:

$$L_2 = \sqrt{\int\int_{F_2} (\tilde{s}(x, y) - s_\cap(x, y))^2 dxdy} \tag{2}$$

This integral is computed in a piecewise fashion over each tensor product domain f_i. Since both $\tilde{s}(x, y)$ and $s_\cap(x, y)$ are quadratic functions, the integral of Eq.(2) can be computed analytically. In practice, the analytic expression is large and numerically unstable, so a two-dimensional Gauss-Legendre quadrature rule is used. In many cases, the quadrature can give exact results.

If the L_2-norm is less than a user-specified tolerance, the edges of the faces f_i are removed, and radiance in the domain of F_2 is represented by the simplified interpolant $\tilde{s}(x, y)$.

In Fig. 5, we show the result of the simplification criteria applied to a scene of two sources with no shadows. In Fig. 5(a) the original mesh is shown. From Fig. 5(b) it can be seen that T-vertices have been introduced into the mesh. To ensure C^0 continuity, T-vertices are treated as "slave-nodes". First all interpolants of simplified faces are constructed. For each T-vertex, the corresponding value of the neighbouring simplified interpolant replaces the previously assigned nodal value. In Fig. 6(a) (in the colour section) we show the image rendered using

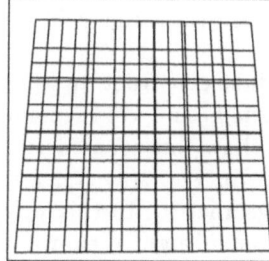 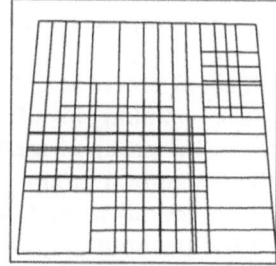

Fig. 5. (a) Original Unoccluded Mesh, and (b) Simplified Mesh.

the original full mesh interpolant. In Fig. 6(b) the result of the construction of the continuous interpolants for the simplified mesh is shown. As can be seen, the resulting images show little difference. However, a more graded variation between simplified and unsimplified regions would be beneficial, using a form of restricted meshing.

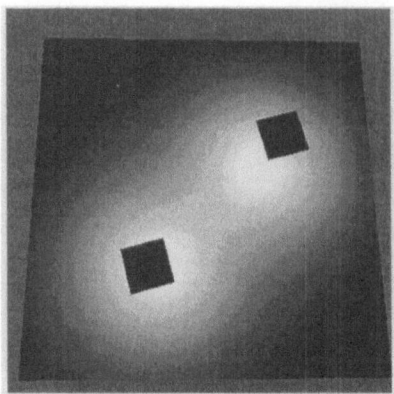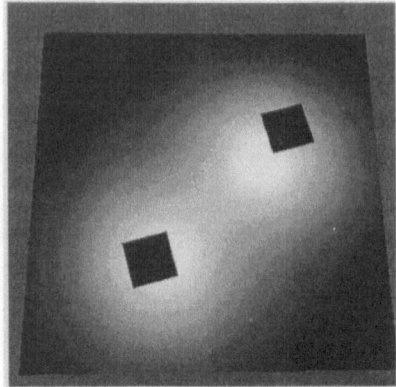

Fig. 6. Images for (a) Original and (b) Simplified Unoccluded Meshes.

5.2 Light-Penumbra Simplification

Consider a penumbral group of a mesh M_P caused by source S_P and a set of light faces of the mesh M_L caused by source S_L, which are contained or cut the penumbral group. We wish to add the light faces into the mesh M_P, and to determine the regions of the penumbral group for which the complete discontinuity mesh must be computed. In contrast to the light-light case, we do not have an accurate representation of the radiance in the penumbra.

To determine whether detailed mesh computation is required, we first construct a medium quality approximation $\hat{s}_{\cap}(x, y)$ to the radiance in the penumbra, using the extremal boundary, within each light face of M_L. This piecewise approximation takes into account the extremal boundaries of the various sources, and its use is equivalent to the accurate interpolant $s_{\cap}(x, y)$ for the light-light case. We then construct the simplified interpolant by defining a single biquadratic tensor product $\tilde{s}(x, y)$. The simplification criteria used are the same as in the light-light case.

The construction of $\hat{s}_{\cap}(x, y)$ proceeds as follows. We first construct an independent mesh defined by the bounding box of the penumbral group. We then add in the extremal boundary of the group of mesh M_P. We show this construction for the box scene and the penumbral group of one source in Fig. 7(a) (refer to Fig. 4(a) and Fig. 1 (colour section) to understand the geometry). In this way, a coarse segmentation of the penumbral group into regions of light, penumbra and umbra has been achieved.

For each vertex inserted into the independent mesh the appropriate illumination value due to source S_P is assigned. For the vertices on the maximal boundary or in the unoccluded regions this is the direct unoccluded illumination from S_P and for the points on the minimal boundary the value is 0. We then insert all the light faces of M_L that intersect or are contained in the penumbral group boundary (Fig. 7(b)). For the resulting vertices the value of unoccluded illumination is retrieved from the appropriate interpolants of M_L, but it is then necessary to add the appropriate (penumbral) value due to the source S_P. For regions of

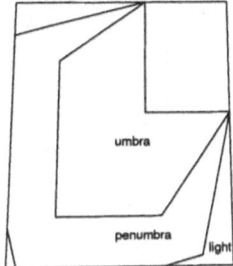 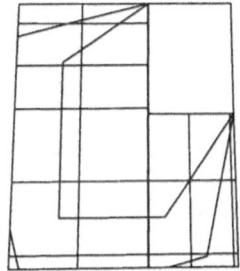 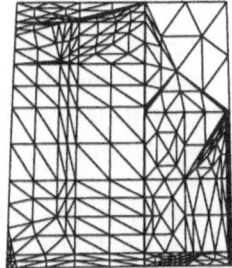

Fig. 7. Mesh for Error Testing: (a) Maximal/Minimal Boundary of penumbral group of M_P, (b) Light faces of M_L added, (c) Triangulation (domain of $\hat{s}_\cap(x,y)$).

umbra and light (due to source S_P) this can be found simply. For vertices in regions within the penumbra however it is necessary to retrieve an estimate of the radiance value. This can be achieved by estimating the derivative value of radiance (see below).

The resulting combined mesh is then triangulated (Fig. 7(c)), and the piecewise elements of the interpolant $\hat{s}_\cap(x,y)$ are built. Interior nodal values are computed either directly (if in a region of light or umbra) from the appropriate interpolants in M_L and M_P, or are averages of the neighbouring nodes if the node is within the penumbra.

For each region corresponding to a light face F_L, the interpolant $\tilde{s}(x,y)$ is constructed. This interpolant is a simple 9-point bi-quadratic Lagrange interpolant. The values for nodes corresponding to vertices in the combined mesh have already been assigned and those that remain are found by querying the interpolant $\hat{s}_\cap(x,y)$. We then compute the L_2-norm error in the same manner as for the unoccluded case for the triangles of $\tilde{s}(x,y)$ which lie in umbra or penumbra. The integral is computed over each triangle included in the domain of the light face F_L. If the L_2 error is less than the predefined tolerance, the edges of F_L are inserted into M_P, the extremal boundary edges contained in F_L are removed from the mesh M_P and radiance within this region is represented by the simplified interpolant.

If the error is greater than the user specified tolerance, the region of the original light face is marked as requiring further meshing. After processing all light faces, the complete mesh is locally computed only for the regions required.

5.3 First Implementation and Discussion

To verify the algorithm, we have implemented the light-penumbra simplification by first computing the complete mesh, and then simplifying the mesh where appropriate. The full construction of the extremal boundary and the simplification algorithm have been implemented as described above, with the exception of the local backprojection estimate. Instead, for the light-face vertices within penumbra, the exact penumbral radiance is retrieved from the (complete) mesh of source S_P.

As mentioned above, for the penumbral regions only the portions of the simplified mesh in penumbra or umbra are taken into consideration for the L_2-norm computation. As noted in [Dret94], edges leading to a singular vertex display a particularly rapid variation. To correctly account for this, in faces for which singular edges exist the light faces are also considered in the L_2-norm calculation.

The results of the implementation are shown in Fig. 8. We first show the unsimplified combined mesh (a), and then the simplified mesh for tolerance values 0.005 and 0.001 respectively (b) and (c). The corresponding shaded images

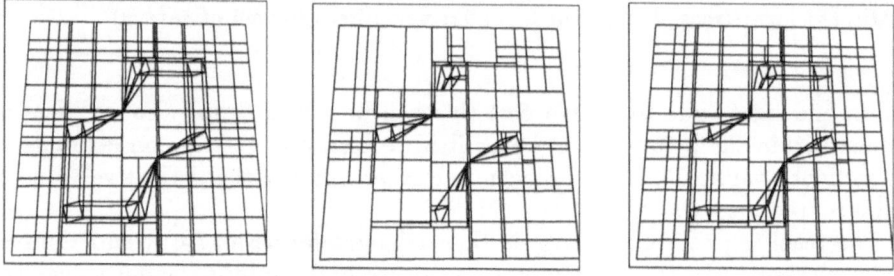

Fig. 8. (a) Unsimplified Combined Mesh and Simplified Mesh for (b) Tolerance 0.005 and (c) 0.001.

are shown in Fig. 9(a),(b) in the colour section. The results of a more complicated test are shown in Fig. 10 to 12. The complete mesh and resulting image are shown in Fig. 10, and the reduced meshes and images in Fig. 11 and 12 for tolerances equal to 0.1 and 0.005 respectively.

Fig. 9. Images of Simplified Meshes (a) Tolerance = 0.005, (b) Tolerance = 0.001.

Overall the method shows promising first results. Little difference can be seen in the simplified images compared to complete mesh image for the simple scene (Fig. 1 (b)), and the simplification appears to occur in desirable regions

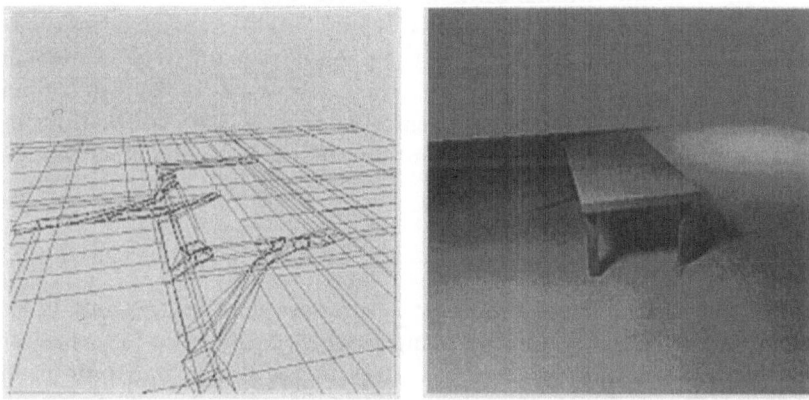

Fig. 10. (a) Complete Table Mesh and (b) Complete Table Image.

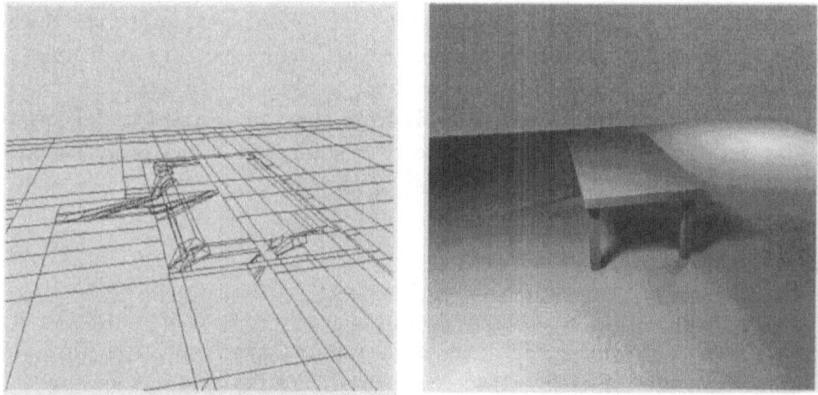

Fig. 11. (a) Table Scene Mesh with Tol = 0.1 (b) Resulting Image.

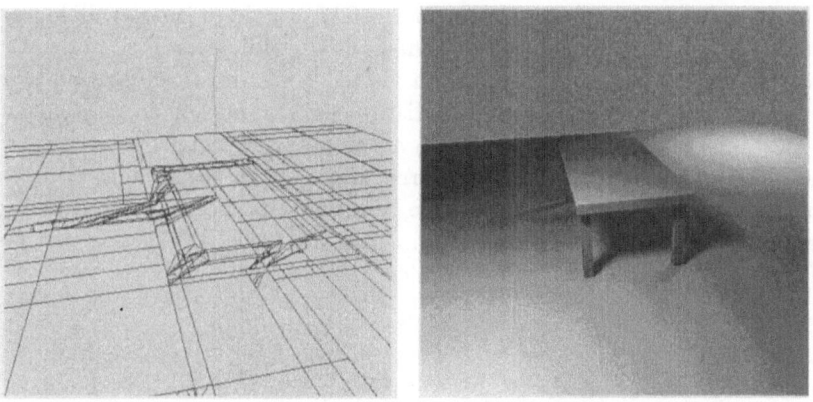

Fig. 12. (a) Table Scene Mesh with Tol = 0.005 (b) Resulting Image.

of the mesh as the tolerance grows. Similarly the simplified images for the table scene (Fig. 11, 12) appear to maintain relatively high quality, since simplification occurs in the regions in which the detail of the penumbra is not very important.

In the tests performed it can be seen that the use of the L_2-norm can sometimes cause undesirable simplification (e.g., the shadow boundary of the front leg in Fig. 11(a)). A possible solution is to maintain the extremal boundary instead of substituting with a tensor product.

5.4 Penumbral Radiance Estimates

Given the maximal and minimal boundary we propose here an estimate of the radiance at any point in the penumbra using local backprojection information. By construction, the minimal or maximal edges of the discontinuity mesh include information about the local change of the backprojection. Thus a good estimate of the radiance at a point P, known to be in penumbra, can be found by approximation.

To perform this approximation we first find the edge on the minimal boundary for which the two endpoints are closest to P. We then calculate the backprojection into the penumbra locally in a direction defined by the midpoint of the minimal edge and the point P. Given the backprojection, we estimate the radiance derivative, then build a Hermite cubic from the values and the derivative estimates, and determine the radiance value at P using the cubic. Experimental verification will determine the quality of this approach.

6 Treating Multiple Sources

The simplification algorithm begins by computing the extremal boundary for each of the n sources in the scene. The light regions are computed, and the structured algorithm run for each surface. The result is a list of simplified meshes for each surface: $\{M_1, ..M_n\}$. The algorithm proceeds by merging the first two meshes. The combined mesh M_c is then merged with mesh M_3 etc.

For a pair $\{M_c, M_j\}$ we first insert the light faces of M_j into the mesh . If a light face of M_j contains exclusively light faces of M_c, or there is a parallelogram subregion of M_j with this property, the light-light simplification is applied. The penumbral regions of both meshes are then visited, and the simplification algorithm is run for each penumbral group. A list of regions marked as "potentially requiring meshing" is stored, together with a pointer to the appropriate source. In addition, the interpolant $\hat{s}_\cap(x, y)$ is stored and used in subsequent tests for error bound checking. If a subsequent source eliminates the need for the meshing, the corresponding regions are deleted from the list. At the end of this process, there will be a list of regions for which the complete mesh is applied.

7 Conclusions

In this paper we have presented an algorithm which allows more compact representation of radiance due to multiple emitters based on careful error analysis, and allows the cost of discontinuity meshing to be deferred until it is required.

To achieve this goal, the L_2-norm is used to compare an accurate representation of radiance over a domain with a simpler one. When the simpler interpolant satisfies a given error tolerance, it is used. For regions with unobstructed views of all sources, this is performed as an a posteriori step. For regions in penumbra for one source and light for another, a low-quality discontinuity mesh is first computed, and an approximation to radiance built, which is then compared to a simpler interpolant. Results of a first implementation show promising reduction of the mesh, and good quality images when using the simplified interpolant.

For the future, it is extremely interesting to apply these ideas to complex environments with many sources, to determine the savings, both in the representation of unoccluded regions, but more importantly in the computation time for discontinuity meshing. The subsequent step is the usage of these algorithms in a global illumination context, since for secondary reflection the need for complete meshing is highly unlikely.

8 Acknowledgments

The author is a post-doctoral fellow hosted by INRIA, under an ERCIM fellowship. Many of the ideas presented originate in the authors' Ph.D. thesis [Dret94] at the University of Toronto, under the supervision of Prof. Eugene Fiume. The software system used for the implementation includes many software components written by researchers at the Dynamic Graphics Project at Toronto.

References

[Camp91] Campbell, A. T. III, Fussell, D. S.: An Analytic Approach to Illumination with Area Light Sources, Technical Report TR-91-25, Computer Science Dept., University of Texas at Austin, August 1991.

[ChFe92] Chin N., Feiner S.: Fact Object Precision Shadow Generation for Area Light Source using BSP Trees, ACM Computer Graphics (SIGGRAPH Symp. on Interactive 3D Graphics), March 1992.

[CoGr85] Michael F., Greenberg D. P. : The Hemi-cube, A Radiosity Solution For Complex Environments, ACM Computer Graphics (SIGGRAPH '85 Proceedings), Vol. 19, No. 3, July 1985.

[DrFi93] Drettakis G., Fiume E. L. : Accurate and Consistent Reconstruction of Illumination Functions Using Structured Sampling, Proceedings of the Eurographics Conference, Barcelona, Spain, September 1993.

[DrFi94] Drettakis, G., Fiume E. L. : A Fast and Accurate Shadow Algorithm for Area Light Sources Using Backprojection ACM SIGGRAPH Computer Graphics, Annual Conference Series, July 1994.

[Dret94] Drettakis G.: Structured Sampling and Reconstruction of Illumination for Image Synthesis Ph.D. Thesis, Dept. of Computer Science, University of Toronto, also available as CSRI Tech. Report-293 (ftp site ftp.csri.toronto.edu:csri-technical-reports/293), January 1994.

[GSCH93] Gortler S. J., Schroeder P., Cohen M. F., Hanrahan P.: Wavelet Radiosity, ACM SIGGRAPH Computer Graphics, Annual Conference Series, August 1993.

[HaSA91] Hanarahan P., Salzman D., Aupperle L.: A Rapid Hierarchical Radiosity Algorithm, ACM Computer Graphics (SIGGRAPH '91 Proceedings).

[Heck92] Heckbert P.: Discontinuity Meshing for Radiosity, 3rd Eurographics Workshop on Rendering, Bristol, UK May 1992.

[HeWi91] Heckbert P., Winget, J. M.: Finite Element Methods for Global Illumination, EECS/University of California Berkeley, Report No. UCB/CSD 91/643, July 1991.

[LiTG92] Lischinski D., Tampieri F., Greenberg D. P.: Discontinuity Meshing for Accurate Radiosity, IEEE Computer Graphics and Applications, November 1992.

[NiNa83] Nishita, T., Nakamae, E. : Half-tone Representation of 3-D Objects Illuminated by Area Sources or Polyhedron Sources, Compsac, Proc. IEEE 7th Intl. Comp. Soft and Applications Conference, 237–242, November 1983.

[Pren89] Prenter, P.M.: Splines and Variational Methods, John Wiley and Sons, New York, 1989.

[SaLD92] Salesin D., Lischinski D., DeRose T. : Reconstructing Illumination Functions with Selected Discontinuities, 3rd Eurographics Workshop on Rendering, Bristol, UK May 1992.

[Tell92] Teller S.: Computing the Antipenumbra of an Area Light Source ACM Computer Graphics (SIGGRAPH 92 Proceedings), July 1992.

[Zatz93] Zatz H. R.: Galerkin Radiosity: A Higher Order Solution Method for Global Illumination, ACM Computer Graphics (SIGGRAPH '93 Proceedings), August 1993.

Part V

Wavelets

Haar Wavelet: A Solution to Global Illumination With General Surface Properties

Sumanta N. Pattanaik, Kadi Bouatouch

IRISA, Campus de Beaulieu, 35042 Rennes Cedex, France

Abstract

This paper presents a method for solving the problem of global illumination for general environments, using projection of the radiance function on a set of orthonormal basis functions. Wavelet scaling functions form this basis set. The highlights of the paper are : it (i) points out the difficulty associated with the straightforward projection of the integral operator associated with the radiance equation and proposes a method for overcoming this difficulty, (ii) gives the data structure and algorithm for illumination solution in environments containing diffuse and non-diffuse reflecting surfaces, and (iii) proposes the use of bi-orthogonal wavelet for the radiance function reconstruction at the time of rendering. Actual implementation has been carried out using the Haar wavelet basis. The main reason for using Haar basis is that it makes the projection of the integral operator, as well as the computation of the inner product of the integral kernel with its basis functions much simpler. However, the algorithm and data structures presented are not restricted to the Haar basis alone.

1 Introduction

Computation of global illumination in an environment requires the solution of linear integral equations. In general, closed form solution does not exist for such equations. So, one resorts to numerical solution methods. Projection method [1] is one such numerical solution method. One comes across the very first explicit use of this method for the global illumination solution in [2]. Much recently [3, 4, 5] there has been a greater surge of interest in application of this method to the illumination problem. These methods defer in their choice and the number of basis functions for carrying out the projection. Of the various choices of basis functions the wavelets seem to have the edge over others [3, 6] because (i) the hierarchical decomposition and reconstruction characteristics [7] of wavelets allows the use of variable number of basis functions in the projection of functions involved in the same integral equation, (ii) they provide a handle [8] for adaptively deciding on the number of basis functions. So far, the application of

wavelets (or for that matter of projection methods) to the illumination problem
has been limited to the solution of radiosity equation.

In this paper we have attempted to use wavelet projection method for solution of the general radiance equations. The work presented here may be seen as
bringing the brute-force discretisation method of [9] and hierarchical discretisation method of [10] into the framework of functional projection technique. It thus
opens up scopes of using higher order basis functions for use in projection-based
illumination computation methods.

The organisation of the paper is as follows. We first describe the general
radiance equation. Then discuss the functional projection and pose the difficulty
involved in projecting the integral operator involved in the equation. We then
propose a solution using wavelet basis function, in particular using Haar wavelet
basis function. We then provide the data structure and algorithm for the solution
of radiance equation using this projection.

2 Three Point Radiance Equation

Radiance from a point $\bar{x}'$ of a surface p towards the point $\bar{x}''$ of surface q,
$L_{pq}(\bar{x}', \bar{x}'')$, can be written as [11] :

$$L_{pq}(\bar{x}', \bar{x}'') = \epsilon_{pq}(\bar{x}', \bar{x}'') + \sum_r \int_{A_r} \kappa_{rpq}(\bar{x}, \bar{x}', \bar{x}'')L_{rp}(\bar{x}, \bar{x}')d\bar{x} \qquad (1)$$

where $\epsilon_{pq}(\bar{x}', \bar{x}'')$ is the radiance due to emission from $\bar{x}'$ along $\bar{x}''$, $\bar{x}$ is a point
on the surface r $i.e$ $\bar{x} \in A_r$,

$$\kappa_{rpq}(\bar{x}, \bar{x}', \bar{x}'') = \frac{f_p(\bar{x}', \Theta_{\bar{x}\bar{x}'}, \Theta_{\bar{x}'\bar{x}''})\cos\theta_{\bar{x}\bar{x}'}\cos\theta_{\bar{x}'\bar{x}}}{|\bar{x}\bar{x}'|^2}v(\bar{x}, \bar{x}')$$

f is the surface $brdf$, $v(\bar{x}, \bar{x}')$ is the visibility between $\bar{x}$ and $\bar{x}'$.
Solution of equation (1) using projection method will require the expansion of
the functions and the integral operator involved in the equation in some basis.
Orthonormal wavelet scaling functions $\phi_{J,k}$ with compact support [12] at some
appropriate resolution J can form such basis. For the convenience of explanation,
in the following discussions of this section, we shall assume the environment to
be 2D (flatland). Also for the uniformity in the variable space, we shall change
the radiance equation to a parametric form as follows:

$$L_{pq}(u', u'') = \epsilon_{pq}(u', u'') + \sum_r \int_{u=0}^1 K_{rpq}(u, u', u'')L_{rp}(u, u')du \qquad (2)$$

where $K_{rpq}(u, u', u'') = \kappa_{rpq}(x, x', x'')\frac{dx}{du}$ and the parameters u, u', u'' ranging
between 0 and 1 span the flatland surfaces r, p and q respectively. By simi-
lar reasoning, in 3D space $K_{rpq}()$ will be a 6 variate function with parameters
u, v, u', v', u'', v'' and each u, v pair taking the value in a unit square will span
the full area of the surface.

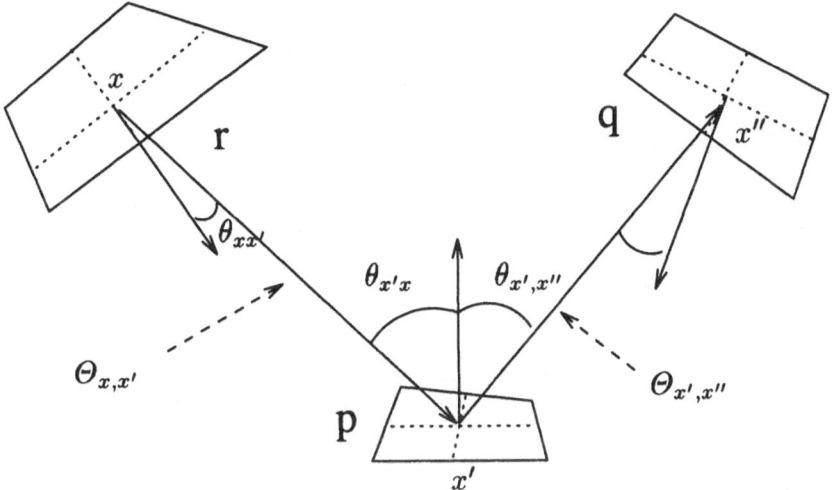

Fig. 1. Three point geometry.

Now the expansion of the radiance and the kernel functions can simply be written as:

$$L(u', u'') = \sum_{k,l} L_{k,l}^J \phi_{J,k}(u')\phi_{J,l}(u'') \tag{3}$$

$$K(u, u', u'') = \sum_{k,l,m} K_{k,l,m}^J \phi_{J,k}(u')\phi_{J,l}(u'')\phi_{J,m}(u) \tag{4}$$

where coefficients of expansion $L_{k,l}^J$ and $K_{k,l,m}^J$ are inner product of the functions $L()$ and $K()$ respectively with their corresponding basis functions. *i.e.*

$$L_{k,l}^J = \langle L(u', u''), \phi_{J,k}(u')\phi_{J,l}(u'')\rangle$$

$$K_{k,l,m}^J = \langle K(u, u', u''), \phi_{J,k}(u')\phi_{J,l}(u'')\phi_{J,m}(u)\rangle$$

However, unlike in the case of diffuse radiance equation [3, 6], such straightforward expansion of the integral operator in equation (2) is difficult. This difficulty arises because the integration is over one variable where as the radiance function inside is a function of two variables. Thus the expansion leads to:

$$\int_u K(u, u', u'')L(u, u')du$$

$$= \int_u \left[\sum_{k,l,m} K_{k,l,m}^J \phi_{J,k}(u')\phi_{J,l}(u'')\phi_{J,m}(u) \sum_{m',k'} L_{m',k'}^J \phi_{J,k'}(u')\phi_{J,m'}(u) \right] du$$

$$= \sum_{k,l,m} K_{k,l,m}^J \phi_{J,k}(u')\phi_{J,l}(u'') \sum_{m',k'} \phi_{J,k'}(u')L_{m',k'}^J \int_u \phi_{J,m}(u)\phi_{J,m'}(u)du$$

$$= \sum_{k,l,m} K^J_{k,l,m} \phi_{J,k}(u')\phi_{J,l}(u'') \sum_{k'} \phi_{J,k'}(u')L^J_{m,k'}$$

The derivation of the last step is due to the orthonormality of the function ϕ, which implies that $\int_u \phi_{J,m}(u)\phi_{J,m'}(u)du = \delta_{m,m'}$. So the summation term over m' disappears. However, unlike the expansion of other functions in the equation (2), the right hand side of the above equation is not a linear combination of only $\phi_{J,k}(u')\phi_{J,l}(u'')$'s.

The compact support of the function ϕ simplifies the above equation a bit further to give:

$$\int_u K(u,u',u'')L(u,u')du = \sum_{k,l,m} K^J_{k,l,m}\phi_{J,l}(u'') \sum_{k'=k-M+1}^{k+M-1} \phi_{J,k}(u')\phi_{J,k'}(u')L^J_{m,k'}$$

where M is the number of vanishing moments of the wavelet function.
Luckily, it is possible to express each of the $\phi_{J,k}(u')\phi_{J,k'}(u')$ terms in the above equation as a linear combination of $\phi_{J,n}(u')$'s [13]. Particularly, with scaling function in the Haar basis, such expansion is simply the following.

$$\sum_{k'=k-M+1}^{k+M-1} \phi_{J,k}(u')\phi_{J,k'}(u') = \phi_{J,k}(u')\phi_{J,k}(u') = 2^{J/2}\phi_{J,k}(u')$$

Here k' takes only one value which is k. This is because in the Haar basis $M = 1$ and $\phi_{J,k}(u')$ has a constant value of $2^{J/2}$ within its support.
Thus, now we can write the expansion of the integral operator as:

$$\int_u K(u,u',u'')L_{rp}(u,u')du = 2^{J/2} \sum_{k,l} \phi_{J,k}(u')\phi_{J,l}(u'') \sum_m K^J_{k,l,m}L^J_{m,k} \quad (5)$$

As the integral term in equation (2) actually represents the reflected radiance, we shall refer to it as $\hat{L}_{rpq}(u',u'')$ and will thus have the following expression.

$$\hat{L}_{rpq}(u',u'') = 2^{J_{rpq}/2} \sum_{k,l} \phi_{J_{rpq},k}(u')\phi_{J_{rpq},l}(u'') \sum_m K^{J_{rpq}}_{k,l,m} L^{J_{rpq}}_{m,k} \quad (6)$$

$\hat{L}_{rpq}()$ carries subscript rpq because it represents reflected radiance from a point u' on surface p towards the point u'' on surface q, due to the incoming radiance from all the points u of surface r. Similarly, J_{rpq} is the appropriate resolution for the expansion of the kernel K_{rpq} using the wavelet scaling function. The method of finding appropriate J_{rpq} will be given in the subsequent section.

Now we can rewrite equation (2) for the geometry in figure 1 as:

$$L_{pq}(u',u'') = \epsilon_{pq}(u',u'') + \hat{L}_{rpq}(u',u'') \quad (7)$$

Using the expansions given in equations (3) and (6) we arrive at the following set of linear equations.

$$L^{J_{rpq}}_{k,l} = \epsilon^{J_{rpq}}_{k,l} + 2^{J_{rpq}/2} \sum_m K^{J_{rpq}}_{k,l,m} L^{J_{rpq}}_{m,k} \quad (8)$$

Allowing for the contribution from more than one surface r, *i.e.*,

$$L_{pq}(u', u'') = \epsilon_{pq}(u', u'') + \sum_r \hat{L}_{rpq}(u', u'') \tag{9}$$

we will have the linear equation set :

$$L_{k,l}^{J_{rpq}} = \epsilon_{k,l}^{J_{rpq}} + \sum_r 2^{J_{rpq}/2} \sum_m K_{k,l,m}^{J_{rpq}} L_{m,k}^{J_{rpq}} \tag{10}$$

Similarly for every pair of surfaces p, q in the environment we will have its corresponding linear set. All these linear equations can be solved together by using an iterative method discussed in the following section.

We have come across similar linear equation formulations for the global illumination involving glossy surfaces in [10]. However, there is a significant difference between the formulations. The linear expression of [10] has been derived by multiplying both sides of equation (2) by a term $G(\bar{x}', \bar{x}'')dx''dx'$ and integrating the resulting equation over the surface p and surface q. *i.e.*:

$$\int_{A_p} \int_{A_q} L_{pq}(\bar{x}', \bar{x}'')G(\bar{x}', \bar{x}'')d\bar{x}''d\bar{x}' = \int_{A_p} \int_{A_q} \epsilon_{pq}(\bar{x}', \bar{x}'')G(\bar{x}', \bar{x}'')d\bar{x}''d\bar{x}'$$

$$+ \sum_r \int_{A_p} \int_{A_q} \int_{A_r} \kappa_{rpq}(\bar{x}, \bar{x}', \bar{x}'')\, L_{rp}\, (\bar{x}, \bar{x}')d\bar{x}G(\bar{x}', \bar{x}'')d\bar{x}''d\bar{x}' \tag{11}$$

where $G(\bar{x}', \bar{x}'') = \frac{\cos \theta_{x'x} \cos \theta_{x'x''}}{|\overline{x'x''}|^2} v(\bar{x}', \bar{x}'')$.

This integration actually leads to an expression of the total flux reaching surface q due to the surface p. If the surfaces p, q and r are very small (*i.e.* the environment has been prediscretised to small patches) and the radiance function over patch p towards the patch q is constant and that over patch r towards the patch p is constant then the both side of the equation (11) can be divided by $\int_{A_p} \int_{A_q} G(\bar{x}', \bar{x}'')d\bar{x}''d\bar{x}'$ to give a simple linear radiance equation. Thus, in [10] the linear equations represent the expressions for the *pre-assumed constant* radiance over a *small patch* towards another *small patch* in an prediscretised environment; whereas in our derivation the linear equations represent the expression for the coefficients of expansion of the radiance function projected over the wavelet basis functions.

3 Environment with Diffuse and Non-diffuse Surfaces

The formulations derived in the previous section assumes general reflection properties for all the surfaces in the environment. As far as the computational complexity is concerned, it may be beneficial to assume that the environment also contains surfaces with diffuse reflection/emission properties. The benefit arises from the directional independence of the radiance from the diffuse surfaces. So for diffuse surfaces the general radiance expression (2) simplifies to:

$$L_p(u') = \epsilon_p(u') + \sum^{nd} \int_{u=0}^1 K_{rp}(u, u')L_{rp}(u, u')du + \sum^d \int_{u=0}^1 K_{rp}(u, u')L_r(u)du$$

where nd and d are respectively the number of non-diffuse and diffuse surfaces in the environment and p is the diffuse surface,

$$K_{rp}(u, u') = \rho_p(x')\frac{\cos\theta_{x'x}\cos\theta_{xx'}}{\pi\left|\bar{xx'}\right|^2}\frac{dx}{du}$$

and $\rho_p(x')$ is the diffuse reflectivity.

Similar equation can be written for the non-diffuse surface. Projecting such equations on the wavelet basis, we will arrive at the following linear set of equations

$$L_k^{J_{rp}} = \epsilon_k^{J_{rp}} + \sum_r^{nd} 2^{J_{rp}/2}\sum_m K_{k,m}^{J_{rp}}L_{m,k}^{J_{rp}} + \sum_r^d\sum_m K_{k,m}^{J_{rp}}L_m^{J_{rp}} \quad \text{for } p \text{ diffuse} \quad (12)$$

and

$$L_{k,l}^{J_{rpq}} = \epsilon_{k,l}^{J_{rpq}} + \sum_r^{nd} 2^{J_{rpq}/2}\sum_m K_{k,l,m}^{J_{rpq}}L_{m,k}^{J_{rpq}} + \sum_r^d\sum_m K_{k,l,m}^{J_{rpq}}L_m^{J_{rpq}} \quad \text{for } p \text{ nondiffuse.}$$
$$(13)$$

We now proceed to give a solution method for the global illumination in an environment, using equations (12) and (13).

4 Solution

The data structure and algorithm given in this section are the extensions to our earlier work for diffuse environment [6].

4.1 Data Structure

We start with the data structure for the surface.

```
typedef struct {
    Geom geometric_information;
    Opt optical_information;
    typedef struct INTERACTION{
        void *kernel;                    /* Pointer to 2Point/3Point struct.*/
        struct INTERACTION *next;
    }Interaction *interaction;
    struct{
        int J_pq;                        /* Max interaction resolution.*/
        float *[L_{k,l}^{J_pq}], *[\epsilon_{k,l}^{J_pq}];    /* Projection Coeffs.*/
    }*radiance;
}Surface;
```

$[L_{k,l}^{J_{pq}}]$ and $[\epsilon_{k,l}^{J_{pq}}]$ in the data type $Surface$ are the coefficients of projection of radiance and emittance function respectively and have an hierarchical structure. There are $(J_{pq}+1)$ levels in the hierarchy. Each level $J \in [0, J_{pq}]$ has $up\ to$[1]

---

[1] As we shall see later, though in principle there can be so many coefficients the actual number will depend on the interaction of the 2Point or 3Point kernel.

2^{4J} coefficients. The values of $[L^{J_{pq}}_{k,l}]$ are set after each gathering by the surface. For diffuse surfaces only a single structure of *radiance* is necessary. Whereas for each specular surface there will be n such structures where n is the number of surfaces visible to the specular surface.

```
/*  Structure to hold relevant 2 point interaction informations.*/
typedef struct {
    int J_pr;          /* Resolution of interaction.*/
    int p, k,l;        /* p : surface-id, k,l ∈ [1,2^J_pr] its indices.*/
    int r, i,j;        /* r : surface-id, i,j ∈ [1,2^J_pr] its indices.*/
    float K^J_pr_i,j,k,l;  /* Coeff of 2 point interaction p ↔ r */
}2Point;               /*  = ⟨K(),φ_J,i()φ_J,j()φ_J,k()φ_J,l()⟩.*/
/*  Structure to hold relevant 3 point interaction informations.*/
typedef struct {
    int J_rpq;         /* Resolution of interaction.*/
    int k, l;          /* k,l ∈ [1,2^J_rpq] indices of p.*/
    int q, m,n;        /* q : receiver, m,n ∈ [1,2^J_rpq] its indices.*/
    int r, i,j;        /* r : emitter, i,j ∈ [1,2^J_rpq] its indices.*/
    float K^J_rpq_i,j,k,l,m,n; /* Coeff of 3 point interaction r → p → q */
}3Point;               /*  =⟨K(),φ_J,i()φ_J,j()φ_J,k()φ_J,l()φ_J,m()φ_J,n()⟩.*/
```

4.2 Algorithm

```
wavelet_radiance()
begin
  compute_kernel();
  Initialise_radiance_coefficients();
  Compute_radiance_solution();
end.
compute_kernel()
begin
  for each mutually visible surface pair (p,r) do
    if diffuse(p) or diffuse(r) then
      Compute_2point_Kernel(0,r,1,1,p,1,1);
    if non_diffuse(p)
      Compute_3point_Kernel(0,r,1,1,p,1,1,q,1,1) ∀ q visible to p;
    if non_diffuse(r)
      Compute_3point_Kernel(0,p,1,1,r,1,1,q,1,1) ∀ q visible to r;
    endif;
  endfor; /* for each surface pair */
end;
```

The procedures `Compute_2point_Kernel` and `Compute_3point_Kernel` compute the resolution for projection and compute the projection coefficients of the kernel.

The resolution computation is carried out adaptively starting with $J = 0$ and progressively incrementing the J till the kernel smoothness condition is satisfied [6]. The outline of these two algorithms are as follows:

Compute_2point_Kernel$(J, \mathbf{p}, k, l, \mathbf{r}, i, j)$
begin

  Compute $K^{J+1}_{i',j',k',l'}$ /* *by Numerical quadrature.* */

  $\forall\ i' \in [2i-1, 2i],\ j' \in [2j-1, 2j],\ k' \in [2k-1, 2k]$ and $l' \in [2l-1, 2l]$;

  Compute $\left[{}^{\xi}D^{J}_{i,j,k,l}\right]^{\xi=I,II,...,XV}$ from $K^{J+1}_{i',j',k',l'}$'s [2] ;

               /* *Hierarchical Decomposition* */

  if $\left({}^{\xi}D^{J}_{i,j,k,l} \leq Threshold\right) \forall \xi$ **then**

    Compute $K^{J}_{i,j,k,l}$ from $K^{J+1}_{i',j',k',l'}$;/* *Hierarchical Decomposition* */
    set $J_{pr} = J$;

    $2point$ = **new**(**2Point**); *$2point$ = $\left\{ J_{pr}, \mathbf{p}, (k, l), \mathbf{r}, (i, j), K^{J_{pr}}_{i,j,k,l}\right\}$;

    $(\mathbf{p}).interaction$ = **new**(**struct Interaction**);
    $(\mathbf{r}).interaction$ = **new**(**struct Interaction**);
    $(\mathbf{p}).interaction.kernel$ = $(\mathbf{r}).interaction.kernel$ = $2point$;

  else *Compute_2point_Kernel*$(J+1, \mathbf{p}, k', l', \mathbf{r}, i', j')$
      $\forall\ i' \in [2i-1, 2i],\ j' \in [2j-1, 2j],\ k' \in [2k-1, 2k],\ l' \in [2l-1, 2l]$;

  endif;

end;

Compute_3point_Kernel$(J, \mathbf{r}, i, j, \mathbf{p}, k, l, \mathbf{q}, m, n)$
begin

  Compute $K^{J+1}_{i',j',k',l',m',n'}$ /* *By numberical quadrature technique.* */

  $\forall\ i' \in [2i-1, 2i],\ j' \in [2j-1, 2j],\ k' \in [2k-1, 2k],\ l' \in [2l-1, 2l],$
      $m' \in [2m-1, 2m],\ n' \in [2n-1, 2n]$;

  Compute $\left[{}^{\xi}D^{J}_{i,j,k,l,m,n}\right]^{\xi=I,II,...,CXIII}$ from $K^{J+1}_{i',j',k',l',m',n'}$'s [3] ;

      /* *Hierarchical Decomposition* */

  if $\left({}^{\xi}D^{J}_{i,j,k,l,m,n} \leq Threshold\right) \forall \xi$ **then**

    Compute $K^{J}_{k,l,m,n}$ from $K^{J+1}_{i',j',k',l',m',n'}$'s;/* *Hierarchical Decomposition* */
    set $J_{rpq} = J$;

    $3point$ = **new**(**3Point**);

    *$3point$ = $\left\{ J_{rpq}, (k, l), \mathbf{q}, (m, n), \mathbf{r}, (i, j), K^{J_{rpq}}_{i,j,k,l,m,n}\right\}$;

    $(\mathbf{p}).interaction$ = **new**(**struct Interaction**);
    $(\mathbf{p}).interaction.kernel$ = $3point$;

  else *Compute_3point_Kernel*$(J+1, \mathbf{p}, k', l', \mathbf{r}, i', j', \mathbf{q}, m', n')$
        $\forall\ i' \in [2i-1, 2i],\ j' \in [2j-1, 2j], k' \in [2k-1, 2k],$
        $l' \in [2l-1, 2l],\ m' \in [2m-1, 2m],\ n' \in [2n-1, 2n]$;

  endif;

end;

---

[2] ${}^{\xi}D^{J}_{i,j,l}$ is the inner product of $K()$ with the wavelet function ${}^{\xi}\Psi$. In wavelet basis for each multi-variate scaling function there are $2^m - 1$ number of wavelet basis functions where m is the number of variates.

[3] As discussed earlier, for a function with 6 variables there are $2^6 - 1 = 63$ wavelet basis functions.

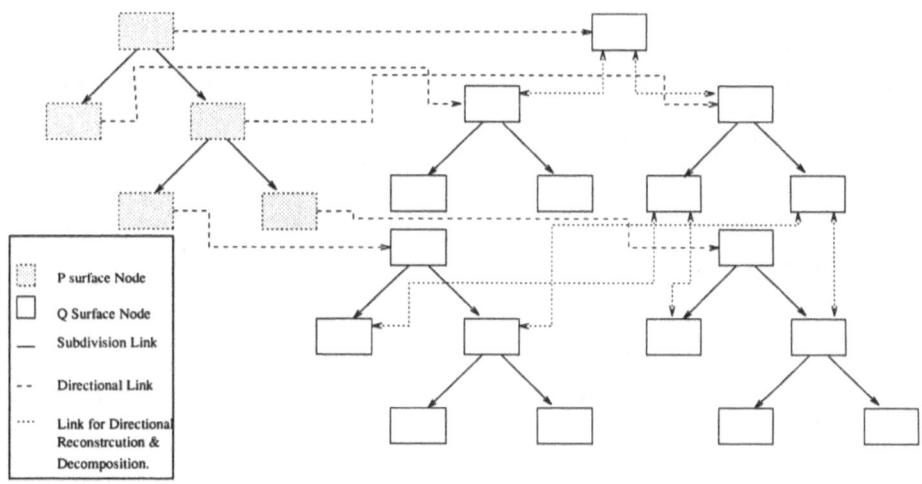

Fig. 2. The data-structure to handle Directional Radiance.

In the procedure given above the increment in the resolution of the wavelet basis means the regular subdivision of the surface in the parametric domain. Depending on whether a two-point or a three-point kernel is being handled, 2 or 3 surfaces will be subdivided simultaneously. This seems to be inappropriate when some of the surfaces involved in the interaction are disproportionately small. This problem arises because of the uniform parameterisation of the surfaces. Each of the interacting surfaces is a unit square in the parameter space. However, the actual area may be significantly different from each other. To minimise the problem we use a concept of *virtual resolution*. When refinement is necessary, the resolution of the largest of the interacting surfaces is actually incremented, (*i.e.* it is subdivided) whereas for the other two only the virtual resolution is incremented (*i.e.* they are not subdivided. If originally a surface is assumed to span a unit area in the parametric domain, after the increment of the virtual resolution the same surface is assumed to span one a quarter area in the same parametric domain). As the resolution of only one of the surfaces is actually incremented, the computational complexity of the adaptive kernel projection is substantially reduced, but care must be taken while computing the projection. To be precise, both for specular and diffuse interaction kernel only 2^2 operations are carried out at each iteration step instead of the 2^6 in the case of specular and 2^4 in the case of diffuse kernel. The consequence of this change is that the data-structure for handling the directional radiance in *surface* becomes a bit more complicated. Figure 2 gives the pictorial representation of this modified data structure.

```
   compute_radiance_solution()
begin
 repeat
   done = true;
   for each surface p do/*Gather radiance through all interaction links.*/
     if diffuse(p) then
```

$[T_{k,l}^J] = [(\mathbf{p}).\epsilon_{k,l}^J];$ /* T : temp struct to gather.*/

```
     for each interaction of p do
```

from $(\mathbf{p}).interaction$ get $\left\{ J_{pr}, (k,l), \mathbf{r}, (i,j), K_{i,j,k,l}^{J_{pr}} \right\};$

$K = K_{i,j,k,l}^{J_{pr}};$

if diffuse($\mathbf{r}$) then $L\_from\_r = (\mathbf{r}).L_{i,j}^{J_{pr}}$

$\qquad\qquad\qquad$ else $L\_from\_r = 2^{J_p} \times (\mathbf{r}).L_{i,j,k,l}^{J_{rp}}[\mathbf{p}];$

$T_{k,l}^{J_{pr}}$ += $K \times L\_from\_r;$

```
     endfor; /* for each interaction of p */
```

2d_resonstruct_decompose(J_p, T);

if $ABS(T_{1,1}^0 - (\mathbf{p}).L_{1,1}^0) > Threshold$ then

```
       done = false;
```

$\left[(\mathbf{p}).L_{k,l}^J \right] = \left[T_{k,l}^J \right];$

```
     endif;
     else /* non-diffuse surface */
```

$\left[T_{k,l,m,n}^J[\mathbf{q}] \right] = \left[(\mathbf{p}).\epsilon_{k,l,m,n}^J[\mathbf{q}] \right] \; \forall \; \mathbf{q} \; ;$ /* T : temp struct to gather.*/

```
     for each interaction of p do
```

from $(\mathbf{p}).interaction$ get $\left\{ J_{rpq}, (k,l), \mathbf{q}, (m,n), \mathbf{r}, (i,j), K_{i,j,k,l,m,n}^{J_{rpq}} \right\};$

$K = K_{i,j,k,l,m,n}^{J_{rpq}};$

if diffuse($\mathbf{r}$) then $L\_from\_r = (\mathbf{r}).L_{m,n}^{J_{rp}}$

$\qquad\qquad\qquad$ else $L\_from\_r = 2^{J_p} \times (\mathbf{r}).L_{i,j,k,l}^{J_{rpq}}[\mathbf{p}];$

$T_{k,l,m,n}^{J_{rpq}}[\mathbf{q}]$ += $K \times L\_from\_r;$

```
     endfor; /* for each interaction of p */
```

3d_reconstruct_decompose($J_{pq}, T[\mathbf{q}]$) $\forall$ $\mathbf{q}$;

```
     for each q do
```

if $ABS(T_{1,1,1}^0[\mathbf{q}] - (\mathbf{p}).L_{1,1,1,1}^0)[\mathbf{q}] > Threshold$ then

```
         done = false;
```

$\left[(\mathbf{p}).L_{k,l,m,n}^J[\mathbf{q}] \right] = \left[T_{k,l,m,n}^J[\mathbf{q}] \right] \; ;$

```
       endif;
     endfor; /* for each q */
   endif;
   endfor; /* for each p */
 until (done);
end;
```

5 Results

We have applied the method discussed to simple environments. For the environment shown in figure 3 with an emitter, a reflector and a receiver we have given here two images. Images have been created to show the direction independent radiance distribution over the receiving surface due to the changing reflecting property of the reflector. The specular surface has been modeled as rolled aluminum using Ward's reflection model [14]. Figure 4 is created by associating diffuse reflection property with the reflector. For this the algorithm generated 4616 two point nodes and 205346 two point interactions. Figure 5 is created by associating specular reflection property to the reflector. It required 986 two point nodes, 16301 two point interactions, 420625 three point directional nodes and 335811 three point interactions.

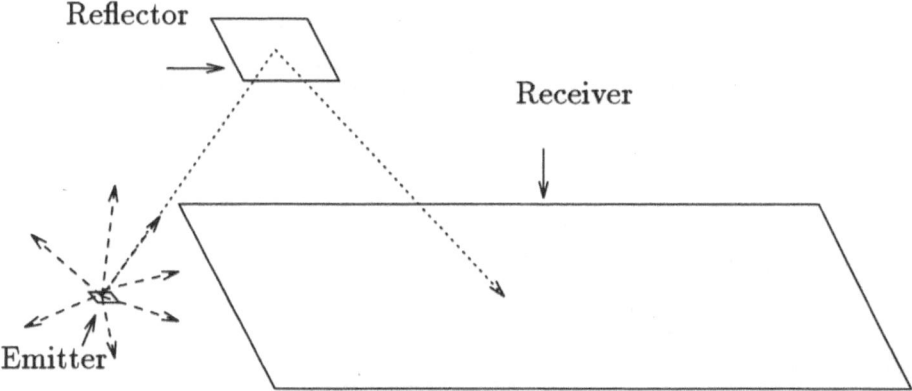

Fig. 3. Simple scene for demonstration.

6 Discussions

In spite of the effort of making the projection as accurate as possible, one makes the approximation by choosing a non-zero threshold and by choosing a limit on the maximum resolution J. In our case we had chosen the threshold as 0.0001 and the maximum resolution as 8. In the process, we have been able to capture the diffuse radiance distribution almost accurately when the reflector is diffuse (Figure 4). However, the same is not true when the reflector is specular (Figure 5). So for a better rendering of the computed image, smoothing in some form or other is necessary. Instead of choosing some extraneous smoothing procedure, we propose to carry out the function reconstruction using bi-orthogonal wavelets[15], with

Fig. 4. Diffuse Reflector.

Fig. 5. Specular Reflector.

which smoothing comes naturally. Using bi-orthogonal wavelets the expansion of a function is as follows:

$$f = \sum < f, \phi_{J,k} > \phi'_{J,k}$$

where each of the basis sets $\{\phi_{J,k}\}$ and $\{\phi'_{J,k}\}$ is not necessarily orthogonal in itself but they are orthogonal to each other. *i.e.*

$$< \phi_{J,k}, \phi'_{J,k'} >= \delta_{kk'}$$

In our application, as one of the basis set is already Haar basis ($\{\phi_{J,k}\}$), all we need is another wavelet basis set which is orthogonal to Haar. At present we are experimenting with spline wavelet basis, which is orthogonal to Haar [16], as the $\{\phi'_{J,k}\}$ for the radiance reconstruction during rendering.

The radiance function computed by the method discussed in this paper is defined from a point on a surface to a point on another surface. So if the final purpose of the computation is rendering, which is most often the case, then it is necessary that the computation be carried out in an enclosure. However, if one is interested in rendering only one or a few number of particular view(s), then the enclosure requirement can be avoided by introducing the eye piece as a hypothetical surface into the environment [11, 10]. This hypothetical surface is capable of receiving illumination, so takes part in the 3 point interactions, but does not obstruct or reflect the illumination.

The algorithm discussed above is still not fast enough for a general environment. We attribute is to the fact that the surface subdivision is entirely dependent on the kernel. Though theoretically it seems to be correct, it may be an overkill in the cases where the real contribution of the interacting surfaces to each other is not very significant. The knowledge of this information may help us in deciding on a coarser subdivision (*i.e.* lower resolution) by appropriate choice of the threshold in the kernel computation. As we do not have the exact information, one better way will be to carry out the kernel determination interactively along with the process. That is, we follow an illumination shooting step instead of a gathering step. As in the usual shooting operation we start with the emitting surface(s) and then proceed to the bright-most surface till the unshot energy is minimum. The kernel computation also precedes in the same fashion, starting along with the emitter and then with the brightmost surface and so on. Adapting the algorithm given above to shooting requires minimal change.

References

1. L. M. Delves and J. L. Mohamed. *Computational Methods for Integral Equations.* Cambridge University Press, 1985.
2. Paul Heckbert. *Simulating Global Illumination Using Adaptive Meshing.* PhD thesis, June 1991.
3. Steven Gortler, Peter Schroder, Michel F. Cohen, and Pat Hanrahan. Wavelet radiosity. *Computer Graphics (SIGGRAPH '93 Proceedings),* 27(4):221–230, 1993.

4. Harold R. Zatz. Galerkin radiosity. *Computer Graphics (SIGGRAPH '93 Procee- dings)*, 27(4):213–220, 1993.

5. Roy Troutman and Nelson L. Max. Radiosity algorithms using higher order finite element methods. *Computer Graphics (SIGGRAPH '93 Proceedings)*, 27(4):209– 212, 1993.

6. Sumanta N. Pattanaik and Kadi Bouatouch. Fast wavelet radiosity method. *Computer Graphics Forum, Special Eurographics '94 Conference Proceedings Issue*, Sept. 1994.

7. Stephane G. Mallat. A theory for multiresolution signal decomposition: the wa- velet representation. *IEEE Transactions on PAMI*, 11(7):674–693, 1989.

8. G. Beylkin, R. Coifman, and V. Rokhlin. Fast wavelet transforms and numerical algorithms i. *Communications on Pure and Applied Mathematics*, XLIV:141–183, 1991.

9. Dave S. Immel, Michael Cohen, and Donald P. Greenberg. A radiosity method for non-diffuse environments. *Computer Graphics (SIGGRAPH '86 Proceedings)*, 20(4):133–142, Aug. 1986.

10. Larry Aupperle and Pat Hanrahan. A hierarchical illumination algorithm for sur- faces with glossy reflections. *Computer Graphics (SIGGRAPH '93 Proceedings)*, 24(4):155–162, August 1993.

11. Christian Bouville, Kadi Bouatouch, Pierre Tellier, and Xavier Pueyo. A theoreti- cal analysis of global illumination models. *Proceedings Eurographics Workshop on Photosimulation, Realism and Physics in Computer Graphics*, 53–66, June 1990.

12. Ingrid Daubechies. Orthonormal bases of compactly supported wavelets. *Com- munications on Pure and Applied Mathematics*, XLI:909–996, 1988.

13. Bernard Delyon and Anatoli Juditsy. *personal communication*, IRISA, 1994.

14. Gregory J. Ward. Measuring and modeling anisotropic reflection. *Computer Gra- phics (SIGGRAPH '92 Proceedings)*, 26(4):265–272, 1992.

15. Albert Cohen, Ingrid Daubechies, and J.-C. Feauveau. Biorthogonal bases of compactly supported wavlets. *Communications on Pure and Applied Mathema- tics*, XLV:485–560, 1992.

16. Bernard Delyon. *Ondelettes Orthogonales et Biorthogonales*. Technical Report, IRISA, Rennes, No. 732, November 1993.

Wavelet Radiance

Per Christensen, Eric Stollnitz, David Salesin, Tony DeRose

University of Washington, Seattle WA 98195, USA

Abstract

In this paper, we show how wavelet analysis can be used to provide an efficient solution method for global illumination with glossy and diffuse reflections. Wavelets are used to sparsely represent radiance distribution functions and the transport operator. In contrast to previous wavelet methods (for radiosity), our algorithm transports light directly among wavelets, and eliminates the pushing and pulling procedures.

The framework we describe supports curved surfaces and spatially-varying anisotropic BRDFs. We use importance to make the global illumination problem tractable for complex scenes, and a final gathering step to improve the visual quality of the solution.

1 Introduction

Radiosity algorithms assume that all reflection is ideally diffuse. This assumption, while making the computation of global illumination more tractable, ignores many important effects, such as glossy highlights and mirror reflections. Though more expensive, the simulation of directional reflection is essential for realistic image synthesis.

One promising approach to solving directional light transport is the finite element method, as pioneered by Immel *et al.* [16] and Shao *et al.* [21], and later refined by Sillion *et al.* [22]. Recently, Gortler *et al.* [14] and Schröder *et al.* [20] proposed an algorithm based on wavelets that focuses effort on the significant energy transfers, for the simpler case of radiosity. These works use the "non-standard" decomposition of the transport operator, and represent radiosity as a weighted sum of scaling functions. The non-standard decomposition forces light interactions to be between basis functions at the same level of detail. In addition, it requires the use of "*Push*" and "*Pull*" procedures to distribute radiosity among levels of a hierarchy in each iteration.

Building on this work, we have developed a four-dimensional wavelet representation for spatially- and angularly-varying radiance distributions. However, in contrast to the approach taken by Gortler *et al.*, our algorithm uses the "standard" decomposition of the transport operator, and represents radiance in terms of wavelets rather than scaling functions. Our method allows light interactions between different levels of detail, and does not require pushing and pulling procedures.

We also incorporate importance-driven refinement, as described by Smits *et al.* [23] for radiosity, to avoid unnecessary work in computing viewpoint-dependent solutions of complex scenes. In addition, our implementation supports curved surfaces and anisotropic bidirectional reflectance distribution functions. The framework we describe naturally accommodates spatial variations, described by texture maps, in both emission and reflectance. Finally, to improve the visual quality of the image, a final gathering step is used [19].

2 Finite Elements for Radiance

In this section, we briefly review the equation that governs light transport, and describe how the finite element method can be used to compute approximate solutions.

2.1 Radiance

Let x, y, and z be points in space. *Radiance* $L(y \rightarrow z)$ is defined as the power emanating from y, per unit solid angle in the direction towards z, per unit projected area perpendicular to that direction.

At equilibrium, radiance satisfies the following transport equation [10]:

$$L(y \rightarrow z) = L^e(y \rightarrow z) + \int_x f_r(x, y, z) \, G(x, y) \, L(x \rightarrow y) \, dx. \tag{1}$$

In this equation, $L^e(y \rightarrow z)$ is the *emitted radiance* from y in the direction towards z, and dx is an infinitesimal area around point x. The term $f_r(x, y, z)$ is the *bidirectional reflectance distribution function*, or BRDF, describing the ratio of reflected radiance (in the direction towards z) to the differential irradiance (from the direction of x) that produces it. Finally, the *geometric term* $G(x, y)$ is given by

$$G(x, y) \equiv V(x, y) \cdot \frac{\cos\theta_x \cos\theta_y}{||x - y||^2},$$

where $V(x, y)$ is a *visibility term* that is 1 or 0, depending on whether or not x and y are visible to one another, and θ_x and θ_y are the angles between the line segment xy and the respective normals of differential areas at x and y. The geometric term describes how radiance leaving a differential area at x in the direction towards y arrives as differential irradiance at y.

The transport equation (1) can be rewritten in operator form as

$$L = L^e + \mathcal{T}L. \tag{2}$$

Here, the *transport operator* T is defined by

$$(TL)(y \to z) \equiv \int_x f_r(x, y, z) G(x, y) L(x \to y) dx,$$

where $(TL)(y \to z)$ denotes the result of T operating on $L(x \to y)$ to produce a function whose argument is $(y \to z)$.

2.2 Discretization

Let $\mathbf{B}(x \to y) = (b_1(x \to y), b_2(x \to y), ...)$ be a basis for the space of radiance distributions. The unknown radiance distribution can be projected onto the basis $\mathbf{B}$ by writing L as a series expansion,

$$L(x \to y) = \sum_{i=1}^{\infty} \ell_i \, b_i(x \to y).$$

This equation can be written in matrix form as $L(x \to y) = \mathbf{B}(x \to y)\mathbf{L}$, where $\mathbf{L}$ is an infinite column matrix whose i-th entry is ℓ_i. When no confusion can arise, we suppress the arguments and simply write $L = \mathbf{BL}$.

In the original formulation of radiosity, piecewise-constant functions were used as a basis [13]. In subsequent work on radiosity, Zatz [26] and Troutman and Max [24] used orthogonal polynomials, and Gortler *et al.* [14] used wavelets. In the more general context of radiance, the distribution of light leaving a patch has both spatial and angular variation. Immel *et al.* [16] used piecewise-constant basis functions for both spatial and angular variation. Later, Sillion *et al.* [22] used spherical harmonics for the angular variation and piecewise-constant basis functions for the spatial variation. In Sect. 3 we motivate and introduce our choice of basis, a wavelet basis for both spatial and angular variation.

Regardless of the choice of basis functions, we can obtain a system of equations for the unknown entries of $\mathbf{L}$ by substituting $L = \mathbf{BL}$ and $L^e = \mathbf{BL}^e$ into the transport equation (2), and using linearity of the operator T to yield

$$\mathbf{BL} = \mathbf{BL}^e + T(\mathbf{BL}) = \mathbf{BL}^e + (T\mathbf{B})\mathbf{L}.$$

Let $\langle f \,|\, g \rangle$ denote the standard inner product, $\int_{yx} f(x \to y) g(x \to y) dx \, dy$. If $\mathbf{F} = (f_1, f_2, ...)$ and $\mathbf{G} = (g_1, g_2, ...)$ are two row matrices of functions, let $[\langle \mathbf{F} \,|\, \mathbf{G} \rangle]$ be the matrix whose ij-th entry is $\langle f_i \,|\, g_j \rangle$. For clarity, we assume an orthonormal basis throughout this paper (the introduction of dual basis functions is necessary for non-orthonormal bases [7, 20]). By applying the linear operator $[\langle \mathbf{B} \,|\, \cdot \rangle]$ to both sides of the equation above and using orthonormality of the basis functions, we arrive at the infinite system of linear equations

$$\mathbf{L} = \mathbf{L}^e + \mathbf{TL}, \tag{3}$$

where $\mathbf{T} = [\langle \mathbf{B} \,|\, T\mathbf{B} \rangle]$ is an infinite matrix representing the transport operator T. The rs-th entry of $\mathbf{T}$ is a *transport coefficient*, representing the influence of the coefficient of b_s on the coefficient of b_r. It can be written explicitly as

$$T_{r \leftarrow s} = \langle b_r \,|\, T b_s \rangle = \int_{xyz} b_r(y \to z) f_r(x, y, z) G(x, y) b_s(x \to y) dz \, dy \, dx, \tag{4}$$

where the notation $r \leftarrow s$ is to emphasize that $T_{r \leftarrow s}$ represents the influence of the *sender* s on the *receiver* r.

3 A Wavelet Basis for Radiance

In this section we construct a basis for efficiently representing radiance distributions. Recent results by Beylkin *et al.* [4, 5], Alpert [1], Gortler *et al.* [14], Hanrahan *et al.* [15] and others indicate that significant performance gains can be achieved using a multiresolution basis. We first present some background on multiresolution analysis, and then describe one-dimensional wavelet bases and how they can be extended to four-dimensional bases for radiance distributions.

3.1 Multiresolution Analysis

Multiresolution analysis as formulated by Mallat [17] provides a framework for studying multiresolution bases. There are two basic ingredients for a multiresolution analysis: an infinite chain of nested linear function spaces $V^0 \subset V^1 \subset V^2 \subset \cdots$ and an inner product $\langle f \mid g \rangle$ defined on any pair of functions $f, g \in V^j$. The space V^j contains functions of resolution j, with resolution increasing as j increases. *Scaling functions* refer to bases for the spaces V^j. A function can be approximated by a sum of scaling functions.

Alternatively, we can represent the same approximation as coarse scaling functions in V^0 along with detail at finer and finer resolutions. Detail is represented by functions in the *orthogonal complement spaces* W^j defined by

$$W^j \equiv \{ f \in V^{j+1} \mid \langle f \mid g \rangle = 0 \ \ \forall g \in V^j \}.$$

Wavelets refer to bases for the orthogonal complement spaces W^j; the spaces W^j are therefore called *wavelet spaces*.

Orthogonal complements are often written as $V^{j+1} = V^j \oplus W^j$ since, intuitively, wavelet space W^j includes the functions that are in V^{j+1} but "missing" from V^j. More formally, any function $f^{j+1} \in V^{j+1}$ can be written uniquely as an orthogonal decomposition $f^{j+1} = f^j + f_\perp^j$, where $f^j \in V^j$ and $f_\perp^j \in W^j$. The space V^j can be fully decomposed as

$$V^j = V^0 \oplus W^0 \oplus \cdots \oplus W^{j-1}.$$

A *multiresolution basis* for V^j can be formed by selecting a scaling function basis for V^0 and wavelet bases for the spaces $W^0, ..., W^{j-1}$. The scaling functions spanning V^0 represent coarse variation, while the wavelets provide detail at increasing resolutions.

For a more complete introduction to wavelets and their applications in computer graphics, see DeRose *et al.* [11].

3.2 Choice of Wavelet Basis

The simplest multiresolution basis in one dimension is the Haar basis [14]. The space V^j consists of piecewise-constant functions on $[0,1]$ with discontinuities at $\{0, 1/2^j, 2/2^j, ..., 1\}$. The space V^j is spanned by the Haar scaling functions $\phi_i^j(u)$ while the wavelet space W^j is spanned by piecewise-constant wavelets $\psi_i^j(u)$. A few Haar scaling functions and wavelets are shown in Fig. 1.

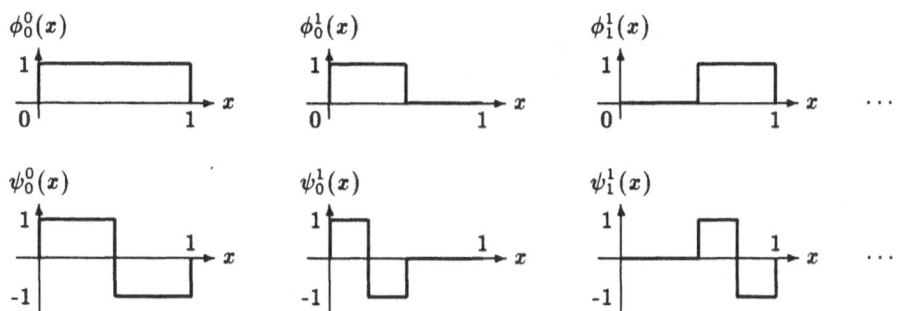

Fig. 1. Haar scaling functions ϕ_i^j and wavelets ψ_i^j.

There are many alternatives to the Haar basis, each with advantages and disadvantages. One requirement for an efficient adaptive algorithm is the availability of fast quadrature formulas for the scaling functions and wavelets (and their duals, if non-orthonormal bases are used). In addition, due to the high dimensionality of the radiance transport problem, it is advantageous to have only one scaling function in space V^0: a single scaling function leads to a single interaction between two patches at the coarsest level, while (as shown in Sect. 3.3) having two one-dimensional scaling functions leads to 16 four-dimensional scaling functions, requiring 256 interactions between two patches at the coarsest level. Finally, bounded-interval wavelets are preferable to wavelets with unbounded support, since it is unclear how radiance distributions would be artificially extended beyond the geometric extent of surface patches.

Among the wavelet bases that have the advantages outlined above, there are both continuous and discontinuous choices. There are currently two families of bounded-interval continuous wavelets available in the literature: Daubechies wavelets adapted to the bounded interval [9], and bounded-interval B-spline wavelets [8]. Note that having continuous basis functions on each patch is not sufficient to ensure a continuous solution: continuity must also be enforced across boundaries of adjacent patches, or else the basis functions must be defined over complex shapes with arbitrary topology (for example, the complex floor shape in Fig. 4, see color plate 8).

We have experimented with bounded-interval B-spline wavelets [7], Daubechies wavelets, and the Haar basis. Of these, the Haar basis has many advantages, including orthogonality, compact support, and simple quadrature formulas. Alt-

hough "flatlets" [14] have more vanishing moments[1] than the Haar basis, flatlets
have wider support, requiring costly quadrature formulas. "Multiwavelets" [14]
are constructed from higher-order polynomials, which also require costly quadrature formulas. The main disadvantage of the Haar basis, its discontinuities,
can be ameliorated by performing a final gathering step during rendering [19].

3.3 A Four-dimensional Wavelet Basis

Four-dimensional basis functions are required for representing radiance distributions: two variables describe spatial variation across a surface, and two variables
describe angular variation. As is common, we split the surfaces into patches
such that the spatial variables on each patch can be parameterized on the unit
square $[0,1]^2$. The domain of the radiance distributions is then $[0,1]^2 \times H^2$,
where H^2 is the unit hemisphere. By mapping H^2 onto $[0,1]^2$, we can use tensor
products of one-dimensional basis functions for angular variations, just as we do
for spatial variations.

We use *gnomonic projection* to map between points in H^2 and points on
a disc with radius $\pi/2$. As shown in Fig. 2(a), gnomonic projection maps great
circles through the pole of H^2 to radial lines, and preserves arc length along these
curves. We use this map because it is easily computed and introduces only mild
distortion. This projection is followed by a radial "stretch" of the disc to exactly
cover the unit square, as shown in Fig. 2(b). The composition of these mappings
is a continuous and invertible mapping between H^2 and the unit square.

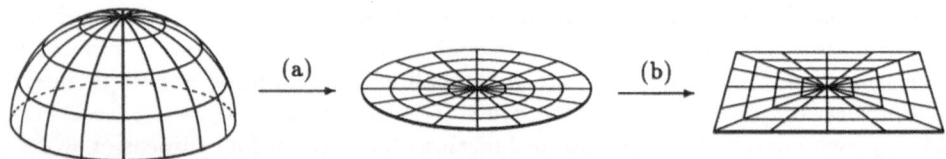

Fig. 2. Mapping the hemisphere to the unit square: we use gnomonic projection (a),
followed by a radial "stretch" (b).

Sillion *et al.* [22] use spherical harmonics as basis functions for angular variations in radiance. These functions have the advantage of being naturally defined
on the sphere, thereby eliminating the need for projection to the plane. The
number of basis functions to represent a directional radiance distribution with
spherical harmonics is comparable to the number needed in the Haar wavelet
basis, so there is no immediate advantage of using the Haar wavelet basis. However, the Haar wavelets have local support while spherical harmonics have global

---

[1] As discussed in Alpert [1] and Gortler *et al.* [14], an increased number of vanishing moments will increase the sparsity of the discrete approximation of a smooth
operator.

support. Therefore, the transport matrix is dense for a spherical harmonics basis but sparse for a Haar wavelet basis.

We use the "non-standard" wavelet basis [4], constructed from tensor products of univariate basis functions as follows. Let $\mathbf{u} = (u_1, u_2, u_3, u_4)$ denote a point in $[0, 1]^4$, and let $\mathbf{i} = (i_1, i_2, i_3, i_4)$ denote a 4-component multi-index of integers. The four-dimensional scaling functions for V^j take the form

$$\phi\phi\phi\phi_{\mathbf{i}}^{j}(\mathbf{u}) \equiv \phi_{i_1}^{j}(u_1)\, \phi_{i_2}^{j}(u_2)\, \phi_{i_3}^{j}(u_3)\, \phi_{i_4}^{j}(u_4).$$

That is, the scaling functions for resolution j consist of all possible products of the one-dimensional scaling functions for resolution j. The four-dimensional wavelets spanning the orthogonal complement W^j are formed by taking all other products of scaling functions and wavelets for resolution j. These wavelets consist of 15 types:

$$\phi\phi\phi\psi_{\mathbf{i}}^{j}(\mathbf{u}),\quad \phi\phi\psi\phi_{\mathbf{i}}^{j}(\mathbf{u}),\quad \phi\phi\psi\psi_{\mathbf{i}}^{j}(\mathbf{u}),\quad \ldots ,\quad \psi\psi\psi\psi_{\mathbf{i}}^{j}(\mathbf{u}).$$

We take as our basis $\mathbf{B}$ the set of basis functions spanning $V^0, W^0, W^1, \ldots$ for each patch in the scene.

4 A Wavelet Radiance Algorithm

We now turn to our wavelet-based radiance solution method. In some respects, our algorithm is similar to the approach described by Gortler $et\ al.$ [14] for wavelet radiosity. However, there are a number of ways — in addition to the higher dimensionality — in which our algorithm differs significantly from previous radiosity work. Most significantly, our use of the standard operator decomposition permits refinement of links at either end. We also describe how our refinement oracle serves to drive an adaptive quadrature scheme.

4.1 Main Algorithm

Initially, we project L^e into space V^0, the space spanned by the scaling functions, to give $\tilde{L}^e$. We also compute (as described in Sect. 4.2) the entries of $\mathbf{T}$ corresponding to interactions of scaling functions in V^0 with one another, giving $\tilde{\mathbf{T}}$. Quantities with a tilde are approximate, both because they represent truncated versions of infinite matrices and because they are computed numerically.

The main part of the algorithm alternates between computing an approximate radiance solution $\tilde{L}$ and improving the finite representation of the transport operator $\tilde{\mathbf{T}}$:

> **procedure** $WaveletRadiance(\tilde{\mathbf{T}}, \tilde{\mathbf{L}}^e)$:
> $\tilde{\mathbf{L}} \leftarrow \tilde{\mathbf{L}}^e$
>   **repeat**
> $\tilde{\mathbf{L}} \leftarrow GaussSeidel(\tilde{\mathbf{T}}, \tilde{\mathbf{L}}, \tilde{\mathbf{L}}^e)$
> $\tilde{\mathbf{T}} \leftarrow Refine(\tilde{\mathbf{T}}, \tilde{\mathbf{L}})$
>   **until** visual convergence of $\tilde{\mathbf{L}}$
> **end procedure**

The main loop iterates until *visual convergence* is achieved, that is, until further refinement does not change the computed image significantly. We use Gauss-Seidel iteration to solve an approximate version of the discrete transport equation (3) given by

$$\tilde{L} = \tilde{L}^e + \tilde{T}\tilde{L}.$$

The main algorithm calls on a *refinement oracle*, described in Sect. 4.3, to refine the radiance transport matrix.

Just as in previous hierarchical radiosity algorithms [10], the matrices $\tilde{T}$, $\tilde{L}$, and $\tilde{L}^e$ are never formed explicitly. Entries of $\tilde{L}$ and $\tilde{L}^e$ are associated with the surface patches, while entries of $\tilde{T}$ are stored as "links" between radiance coefficients.

Note that the algorithm presented by Gortler *et al.* [14] requires "*Push*" and "*Pull*" procedures to distribute transported radiosity among the levels of a hierarchy between Gauss-Seidel iterations. By using the standard operator decomposition and representing radiance in terms of wavelets rather than scaling functions, our algorithm eliminates the pushing and pulling procedures. On the other hand, the non-standard operator decomposition is in theory more sparse than the standard decomposition for an operator that is smooth. It is not clear whether or not this theoretical advantage of the non-standard decomposition has a practical implication for an operator like the light transport operator, which is only piecewise-smooth.

4.2 Computing Transport Coefficients

Each transport coefficient $T_{r \leftarrow s}$ is defined in Equation (4) as an inner product that results in a six-dimensional integral. For example, the influence of wavelet $\psi\phi\psi\phi^j_{i,s}(\mathbf{u}_s)$ on wavelet $\psi\phi\phi\phi^j_{i,r}(\mathbf{u}_r)$ is $T_{r \leftarrow s} = \langle \psi\phi\phi\phi^j_{i,r} \mid T\psi\phi\psi\phi^j_{i,s} \rangle$. If we write $\mathbf{u} = (x, \omega)$, where $x = (u_1, u_2)$ denotes spatial components and $\omega = (u_3, u_4)$ denotes angular components, then the inner product takes the form

$$T_{r \leftarrow s} = \langle \psi\phi\phi\phi^j_{i,r} \mid T\psi\phi\psi\phi^j_{i,s} \rangle \tag{5}$$

$$= \int \psi\phi\phi\phi^j_{i,r}(x_r, \omega_r)\, f_r(x_s, x_r, \omega_r)\, G(x_s, x_r)\, \psi\phi\psi\phi^j_{i,s}(x_s, \omega_s)\, d\omega_r\, dx_r\, dx_s$$

$$= \int \left[\int \psi\phi\phi\phi^j_{i,r}(x_r, \omega_r)\, f_r(x_s, x_r, \omega_r)\, d\omega_r \right] G(x_s, x_r)\, \psi\phi\psi\phi^j_{i,s}(x_s, \omega_s)\, dx_r\, dx_s.$$

Here ω_s is considered to be a function of x_s and x_r, since the direction at the sender must lie along the line between sending and receiving positions. Note that only the BRDF and the receiving basis function depend on ω_r. Our numerical integration routine samples these two functions in its innermost loop, while the remaining functions are evaluated only as the positional variables change.

We approximate integrals such as the one above using (slightly jittered) uniform sampling of the integrand. More accurate rules such as Gauss-Legendre or Gauss-Kronrod quadrature could also be used [7, 14, 26].

4.3 Refinement

In many applications of wavelets in numerical analysis, the goal is to obtain a sparse representation of a given matrix, thereby making repeated matrix–vector multiplications much faster [4]. In wavelet-based approaches to global illumination, the cost of explicitly constructing an entire transport matrix far outweighs the expense of any matrix–vector multiplications that follow. Therefore, it is essential to restrict the number of computed transport coefficients.

The goal of the refinement oracle is to determine where to refine $\tilde{T}$ to better approximate T. The two most important sources of error are:

- *truncation error* due to significant entries missing from $\tilde{T}$, and
- *quadrature error* in computing the entries of $\tilde{T}$.

In this section we describe how our oracle reduces truncation error. Section 4.4 outlines a method for simultaneously reducing quadrature errors.

Our refinement oracle uses concepts from the brightness refinement criterion for hierarchical radiosity [15] and the oracle used by Gortler *et al.* for wavelet radiosity [14]. The idea is to estimate the amount of light that would be transported if a new transport coefficient were to be added to $\tilde{T}$. If this quantity falls below some threshold, then it is likely that the expensive computation of the transport coefficient can be avoided without resulting in significant error in the solution.

For a given link λ between a pair of basis functions, we separately consider refining at the sending end and at the receiving end of λ. In either case, we multiply a sending basis function coefficient by an estimate of the transport coefficient for the link λ_{new} under consideration. In our implementation, the transport coefficient for λ_{new} is estimated by the variation in the kernel evaluations for λ. (This variation is stored along with the transport coefficient on link λ.) By contrast, Gortler *et al.* use a polynomial interpolant rather than sample variation to estimate kernel smoothness.

Suppose the oracle decides to refine the receiving end of a link. Then new links are created as follows: When refining a link to a scaling function in space V^0, links to all 15 wavelets in space W^0 are created. When refining a link to a wavelet in space W^j, links to the overlapping wavelets of the same type in W^{j+1} are created. (In the case of the Haar basis, $2^4 = 16$ new links are created.) A similar process occurs when the oracle decides refinement is needed at the sending end of a link.

Note that our refinement procedure can refine each end of a link independently, and in our algorithm links are never destroyed. The approach described by Gortler *et al.* removes a link at one level of the hierarchy and replaces it with multiple links at a finer level of detail, thereby refining both ends simultaneously.

4.4 Adaptive Quadratures

If we always use a numerical integration rule of high accuracy to compute transport coefficients, effort may be wasted evaluating the kernel for many interactions that have little effect on the final image. On the other hand, the significant coefficients have to be computed accurately; otherwise, the solution will not converge to the correct value. It is therefore advantageous to use an adaptive integration technique that reduces error only for significant transport coefficients.

For time efficiency, we would like to store the values of all kernel evaluations that have already been computed in order to reuse them for improved quadratures. Unfortunately, space limitations prohibit this approach. Instead, we store only the evaluations from the most recently computed transport coefficient. These new kernel evaluations can be used to update any transport coefficient whose sending and receiving basis functions overlap with those of the new transport coefficient.

When a transport coefficient $T_{r \leftarrow s}$ is refined and a new entry $T_{r' \leftarrow s'}$ is computed, we check whether or not a transport coefficient between basis functions with the same supports as r' and s' has already been computed. If so, we need do no more; if not, the samples used to compute $T_{r' \leftarrow s'}$ are used to update $T_{r \leftarrow s}$. Updating a transport coefficient is done in two steps. First, the original samples of the integrand within the supports of r' and s' are recomputed and subtracted from $T_{r \leftarrow s}$. Next, the new kernel evaluations are multiplied by the appropriate basis functions, weighted by area, and added to $T_{r \leftarrow s}$. This approach to adaptive quadrature is less expensive than simply recomputing $T_{r \leftarrow s}$ more accurately upon refinement, since we reuse the costly kernel samples whenever possible.

Although we have only implemented this adaptive integration technique for the Haar basis, it could be extended to other wavelet bases. However, it is not immediately apparent how this approach would generalize to integration rules using non-uniform sampling.

5 Implementation Features

In this section, we describe features of our implementation. Objects in the scene can consist of flat quadrilaterals and tensor-product Bézier patches, and can have isotropic or anisotropic reflection. The light sources can have spatial and angular variation. We use importance to restrict refinement to the light transports that influence the final image the most, and employ a final gathering step to improve the visual quality of the solution.

5.1 Surface Geometry

Any parametric surface representation can be used by our algorithm, so long as we are able to compute a position, surface normal, and differential area associated with a given parametric point (u_1, u_2), and determine the intersection of a ray with the surface. Our implementation currently handles tensor-product Bézier patches and quadrilaterals. It would also be straightforward to add non-uniform rational B-spline surfaces. The images in Fig. 3 (see color plate 8) show a teapot consisting of 28 Bézier patches.

5.2 Reflection Models and Texture Maps

We use the Ward isotropic and anisotropic reflection models [25] since they are physically valid and fast to evaluate. Examples of this reflection model can be seen in Fig. 3 (see color plate 8). In addition, we use spatially varying reflectances to simulate details of the materials in the scene. We take the BRDF to be the product of a spatially-varying texture and the angular variation of the Ward model. Figure 4 (see color plate 8) demonstrates both texture-mapped and anisotropic reflectance functions.

In the course of numerically approximating a transport coefficient, the geometric term and the BRDF are sampled at a number of points. The reflectance for each point is determined by a look-up in a texture map, multiplied by the angular variation given by Ward's model. Gershbein *et al.* [12] present an alternative approach, using wavelet decompositions of textures for radiosity.

5.3 Light Sources

By storing the wavelet decomposition of an image as the initial coefficients on a patch, we can model a light source that emits a spatially-varying radiance (like a television screen). In general, not all coefficients of the emitting image will have links from them, but the coefficients are ready to be transported into the scene if the refinement procedure so decides. This technique allows a complex environment to be displayed using simple geometry.

A simple approach to angular variation is to let the emission depend upon direction. For example, we model "spotlights" using a Phong-like function, in which emission is proportional to some power of the cosine of the angle between the emission direction and the surface normal of the patch. The spotlights appear dark from most directions because of the very narrow distribution of light they emit.

We demonstrate the use of spotlights and a spatially-varying emitter (the outdoor environment seen through the window) in Fig. 4(see color plate 8). More complex effects such as a slide projector or sunlight through a stained-glass window could be modeled by combining spatial and angular variations in an emitter.

5.4 Importance

In order to maintain a tractably small problem for complex scenes, we use importance-driven refinement for a view-dependent solution. Importance was described in Smits *et al.* [23] for radiosity and in Christensen *et al.* [6], Aupperle and Hanrahan [3], and Pattanaik [18] for radiance. Briefly, importance measures the fraction of light leaving a point that will reach the eye.

The algorithm combines estimates of importance and radiance to drive the global solution, allowing it to exploit view-dependent information as part of an adaptive refinement scheme. We use exitant directional importance [6], since it satisfies the same transport equation as radiance. Importance can therefore be discretized in the same manner as radiance and transported by the same links. The only difference between importance and radiance is that radiance is emitted by light sources, while exitant directional importance is emitted by the eye.

Smits *et al.* [23] showed that importance gives a substantial speed-up for a complex diffuse scene. For glossy reflections, the gain in speed is even greater, due to the directionality of radiance and importance: a directional interaction is refined only if the amount of transported radiance *in that direction* is both large and important. Note that we can get arbitrarily large speed-ups, compared to a solution obtained without using importance, by choosing a sufficiently complex scene where many parts do not contribute significantly to the final image.

The first three images of Fig. 4 (see color plate 8) show a complex scene viewed from above. The radiance emitted by the spotlights and reflected in the scene is shown in Fig. 4(a). Importance is emitted from the eye and reflected to the important parts of the scene, as shown in Fig. 4(b). This picture demonstrates how small a fraction of the model significantly influences the solution visible from the eye. Figure 4(c) is a gray-scale encoding of the number of links between the basis functions on each surface patch. This "refinement image" verifies that most work is performed in areas that are both bright and important.

5.5 Final Gather

Following the ideas that Reichert [19] used for radiosity, we have implemented a final radiance gathering step. For each pixel in the image, we perform a final gathering of light to the surface point that corresponds to the midpoint of the pixel. For each sending basis function, we evaluate a simplified version of the integral in Equation (5). Since the receiving position is fixed and the radiance is reflected towards the eye, the integration is over only sending positions.

Formally, this final gather corresponds to changing to a piecewise-constant basis, where the support of each basis function is the projection of a pixel onto a surface in the scene. This basis is tailored to be visually pleasing. The final gather smooths the discontinuities in the wavelet representation and makes highlights, textures, and shadows crisper. The improvement brought about by the final gather can be seen by comparing Figs. 4(d) and 4(e) (see color plate 8).

Another way of thinking about the final gathering step is in the context of distribution ray tracing. When a ray emanating from the eye intersects a surface in the scene, a group of reflected rays are traced from the intersection point to points on other surfaces in the scene. A constant number of rays are cast to the support of each basis function in the radiance solution, so the directions of the rays are guided by the radiance solution,. Thus, the most refined areas of the radiance solution are sampled the most by the distribution of reflected rays. Note that the costly "explosion" of the number of recursive bounces used in distribution ray tracing is avoided, and that the final gather requires no additional memory.

6 Results

As a test scene, we used a maze of hallways with a glossy Bézier-patch teapot in the center (see Fig. 4, color plate 8). The scene consists of 152 patches, including 28 Bézier patches, and has 8,802 mutually visible pairs of patches. The teapot's reflectance function is anisotropic with specularities $\alpha_u = 0.2$ and $\alpha_v = 0.5$, specular reflectivity $\rho_s = (0.1, 0.1, 0.1)$, and diffuse reflectivity $\rho_d = (0.2, 0.15, 0)$. The illumination consists of 24 "spotlights," patches that emit directional radiance. There is a patch outside the window that emits light according to a scanned image of an outdoor scene, giving the appearance of a full environment beyond the window. There is also a small patch representing the eye in the hallway in front of the teapot. The eye patch emits importance in the direction of the teapot, just like a spotlight emits light.

Running times on a DEC Alpha machine were approximately five minutes to compute the initial transport coefficients between scaling functions in V^0, then 110 minutes to iterate the main algorithm and refine as far as V^4 in important parts of the scene, and 15 minutes to render a 600×600 image using ray casting and evaluation of the solution. The final gather takes another two hours, so the time for the final gather is comparable to the computation time for the solution.

Note the interreflections: there is significant color bleeding from the brick walls to the dim ceiling, and the white squares on the pedestal are reflected in the bottom of the teapot. Also note the glossy highlights on the teapot.

7 Conclusion

We have presented an efficient method for simulating light transport in an environment with diffuse and glossy reflections. We use wavelet basis functions to represent the four-dimensional radiance distribution associated with surfaces in a scene. Wavelets adapt to the solution, so in areas with little spatial or angular variation a coarse solution is computed, and in areas with greater detail a more refined solution is found.

In contrast to previous algorithms for wavelet radiosity, we use a standard decomposition of the transport operator, and we represent radiance as a weighted sum of wavelets rather than scaling functions. We do not use pushing and pulling procedures, and we are able to refine just that end of a link for which the estimated improvement is greatest. In order to obtain accurate numerical integration without the expense of extraneous samples, we have also developed adaptive integration rules for the transport coefficients.

Radiance transport is formulated as a multidimensional Fredholm integral equation of the second kind. Thus, our approach may benefit other fields in which such equations arise — numerical analysis, finite element analysis, and particle transport simulation, for example.

There are a number of areas in which we foresee future work. A comparison of wavelet bases for radiance should examine rates of convergence, quadrature expense and accuracy, continuity properties, and the amount of work required to obtain a solution of a given accuracy. Standard and non-standard operator decomposition should be compared for a piecewise-smooth kernel typical of global illumination with partial occlusion. It would also be interesting to compare wavelets for two-point transport with a three-point transport algorithm, as described by Aupperle and Hanrahan [2, 3] for piecewise-constant basis functions. Finally, an investigation of the final gathering step should determine whether or not it improves the numerical accuracy of the solution in addition to improving its visual appearance.

There are many possible extensions to the present algorithm. Wavelet bases are not suited to the representation of ideal specular reflections. Instead, a ray tracing step for ideal specular reflection could be incorporated in the same fashion as in Sillion *et al.* [22]. Furthermore, surfaces that transmit light in addition to reflecting it could be incorporated into our algorithm by using a wavelet basis defined for the entire sphere of directions.

Acknowledgements

This work was supported by NSF Presidential and National Young Investigator awards (CCR-8957323 and CCR-9357790), an NSF Graduate Research Fellowship, the University of Washington Graduate Research Fund (award 75-1721), the Technical University of Denmark, and the Danish Research Council.

References

1. Bradley K. Alpert. *Sparse Representations of Smooth Linear Operators.* PhD thesis, Yale University, 1990.
2. Larry Aupperle and Pat Hanrahan. A hierarchical illumination algorithm for surfaces with glossy reflection. In *Proceedings of SIGGRAPH'93*, pages 155–162, August 1993.
3. Larry Aupperle and Pat Hanrahan. Importance and discrete three point transport. In *Proceedings of the Fourth Eurographics Workshop on Rendering*, pages 85–94, June 1993.
4. G. Beylkin, R. Coifman, and V. Rokhlin. Fast wavelet transforms and numerical algorithms I. *Communications on Pure and Applied Mathematics*, 44:141–183, 1991.
5. G. Beylkin, R. R. Coifman, and V. Rokhlin. Wavelets in numerical analysis. In Mary Beth Rushkai et al., editors, *Wavelets and Their Applications*, pages 181–210. Jones and Bartlett, 1992.
6. Per H. Christensen, David H. Salesin, and Tony D. DeRose. A continuous adjoint formulation for radiance transport. In *Proceedings of the Fourth Eurographics Workshop on Rendering*, pages 95–104, June 1993.
7. Per H. Christensen, Eric J. Stollnitz, David H. Salesin, and Tony D. DeRose. Importance-driven wavelet radiance. Technical Report 94-01-05, Department of Computer Science and Engineering, University of Washington, January 1994.
8. Charles K. Chui and Ewald Quak. Wavelets on a bounded interval. *Numerical Methods of Approximation Theory*, 9:53–75, 1992.

9. A. Cohen, I. Daubechies, and J. C. Feauveau. Biorthogonal bases of compactly supported wavelets. *Communications on Pure and Applied Mathematics*, 45:485–500, 1992.

10. Michael F. Cohen and John R. Wallace. *Radiosity and Realistic Image Synthesis*. Academic Press Professional, Cambridge, Massachusets, 1993.

11. Tony D. DeRose, David H. Salesin, and Eric J. Stollnitz. Wavelets for computer graphics: A primer. In *SIGGRAPH'94 Computational Representations of Geometry Course Notes*, July 1994.

12. Reid Gershbein, Peter Schröder, and Pat Hanrahan. Textures and radiosity: Controlling emission and reflection with texture maps. In *Proceedings of SIGGRAPH'94*, pages 51–58, July 1994.

13. Cindy M. Goral, Kenneth E. Torrance, Donald P. Greenberg, and Bennett Battaile. Modeling the interaction of light between diffuse surfaces. In *Proceedings of SIGGRAPH'84*, pages 213–222, July 1984.

14. Steven J. Gortler, Peter Schröder, Micheal F. Cohen, and Pat Hanrahan. Wavelet radiosity. In *Proceedings of SIGGRAPH'93*, pages 221–230, August 1993.

15. Pat Hanrahan, David Salzman, and Larry Aupperle. A rapid hierarchical radiosity algorithm. In *Proceedings of SIGGRAPH'91*, pages 197–206, July 1991.

16. David S. Immel, Michael F. Cohen, and Donald P. Greenberg. A radiosity method for non-diffuse environments. In *Proceedings of SIGGRAPH'86*, pages 133–142, August 1986.

17. Stephane Mallat. A theory for multiresolution signal decomposition: The wavelet representation. *IEEE Transactions on Pattern Analysis and Machine Intelligence*, 11(7):674–693, July 1989.

18. Sumanta N. Pattanaik. *Computational Methods for Global Illumination and Visualisation of Complex 3D Environments*. PhD thesis, Birla Institute of Technology and Science, 1993.

19. Mark C. Reichert. A two-pass radiosity method driven by lights and viewer position. Master's thesis, Program of Computer Graphics, Cornell University, Ithaca, New York, January 1992.

20. Peter Schröder, Steven J. Gortler, Micheal F. Cohen, and Pat Hanrahan. Wavelet projections for radiosity. In *Proceedings of the Fourth Eurographics Workshop on Rendering*, pages 95–104, June 1993.

21. Min-Zhi Shao, Qun-Sheng Peng, and You-Dong Liang. A new radiosity approach by procedural refinements for realistic image synthesis. In *Proceedings of SIGGRAPH'88*, pages 93–102, August 1988.

22. François X. Sillion, James R. Arvo, Stephen H. Westin, and Donald P. Greenberg. A global illumination solution for general reflectance distributions. In *Proceedings of SIGGRAPH'91*, pages 187–196, July 1991.

23. Brian E. Smits, James R. Arvo, and David H. Salesin. An importance-driven radiosity algorithm. In *Proceedings of SIGGRAPH'92*, pages 273–282, July 1992.

24. Roy Troutman and Nelson L. Max. Radiosity algorithms using higher order finite elements. In *Proceedings of SIGGRAPH'93*, pages 209–212, August 1993.

25. Gregory J. Ward. Measuring and modeling anisotropic reflection. In *Proceedings of SIGGRAPH'92*, pages 265–273, July 1992.

26. Harold R. Zatz. Galerkin radiosity. In *Proceedings of SIGGRAPH'93*, pages 213–220, August 1993.

Wavelet Methods for Radiance Computations

Peter Schröder, Pat Hanrahan

Department of Computer Science, Princeton University

Abstract

This paper describes a new algorithm to compute radiance in a synthetic environment. Motivated by the success of wavelet methods for radiosity computations we have applied multi wavelet bases to the computation of radiance in the presence of glossy reflectors. We have implemented this algorithm and report on some experiments performed with it. In particular we show that the convergence properties of basis functions with 1–4 vanishing moments are in accordance with theoretical predictions. As in the case of wavelet radiosity we find higher order bases to have advantages. However, the cost scaling due to the higher dimensionality of the problem is such that the higher order bases only become competitive for very high precision requirements. In practice we rarely go beyond piecewise linear functions.

1 Introduction

One of the main areas of computer graphics research concerns the analysis and synthesis of the propagation of light in a given scene. The goal of this research is the development of efficient algorithms to compute "photo-realistic" images of non-existent scenes. Much attention has been devoted to the diffuse case and a number of radiosity algorithms have been proposed. Two developments in that area, higher order Galerkin schemes [10, 11, 26, 25], and hierarchical approaches [9] have recently been unified using wavelets [8, 19].

Only few results have been reported on attempts to solve the more general rendering equation [13]. There have been some attempts at extending radiosity to handle specular or glossy reflections [12, 20, 21, 14] or to use finite element methods directly to solve the rendering equation [22]. All of these have suffered from high computational complexity and consequently extremely long simulation times.

Significant progress in the reduction of the overall computational order of the radiance problem occurred recently when Aupperle and Hanrahan [2] extended their earlier hierarchical radiosity work to radiance. The success of this approach and the success of the earlier extension of hierarchical radiosity to wavelet radiosity suggests that the tools of wavelet analysis and the sparse realization of operators in wavelet bases should allow for similar improvements when brought to bear on the radiance equation.

In this paper we describe our implementation of a higher order hierarchical Galerkin algorithm using multi wavelet bases [1] to solve for radiance in the presence of glossy reflectors. We examine a number of test configurations for which we have independent means of computing a correct answer (since they are single bounce configurations) and quantify the convergence behavior of piecewise constant, linear, quadratic, and cubic bases.

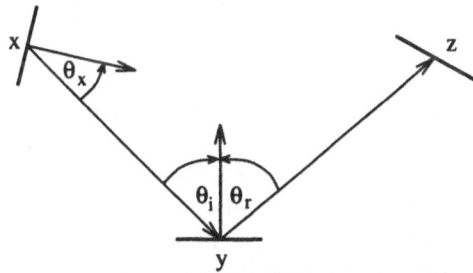

Fig. 1. Geometry of the canonical three point transport with radiance originating at some surface X and being reflected at Y in the direction of Z.

2 The radiance equation

In this section we describe the particular parameterization of the radiance equation that we are using and the linear system which results from applying a Galerkin method to it. Throughout $\mathbf{x}$, $\mathbf{y}$, and $\mathbf{z}$ will describe points on surfaces, where radiance originates at $\mathbf{x}$ and is reflected at $\mathbf{y}$ in the direction of $\mathbf{z}$ (see Figure 1). Typically there are parameters intrinsic to a surface which parameterize these quantities, but we will abstract from that fact in the following discussion to simplify the notation.

There are two common ways of parameterizing the radiance equation. One, which we will call the *directional* parameterization makes (outgoing) radiance a function of a point on a given surface and a direction attached at this point

$$L_o(\mathbf{y}, \omega) = L_o^e(\mathbf{y}, \omega) + \int_{H^2} f_r(\omega', \mathbf{y}, \omega) L_o(\mathbf{x}(\mathbf{y}, \omega'), -\omega') \, \mathbf{n}_y \cdot d\omega'$$

where we have made the dependence of $\mathbf{x}$, the point visible from $\mathbf{y}$ in the direction ω', explicit. $\mathbf{n}_y$ gives the normal of the surface at $\mathbf{y}$.

The *spatial* parameterization describes L_o as a function of two points on a given pair of surfaces

$$L_o(\mathbf{y}, \mathbf{z}) = L_o^e(\mathbf{y}, \mathbf{z}) + \int_{M^2} f_r(\mathbf{x}, \mathbf{y}, \mathbf{z}) L_o(\mathbf{x}, \mathbf{y}) G(\mathbf{x}, \mathbf{y}) \, dA_x$$

In both cases the symbol L_o^e describes emitted radiance and f_r denotes the BRDF. G is the geometry factor accounting for visibility and the differential element to differential element form factor. We use the symbol H^2 as shorthand for the hemisphere above a surface point and M^2 as the symbol for the union of all surfaces in the scene.

Independent of the parameterization used we can write the radiance transport operator as

$$(1 - \mathcal{T})L_o = (1 - \mathcal{S} \circ \mathcal{G})L_o = L_o^e$$

The operator symbol $\mathcal{G}$ describes the transformation of outgoing radiance L_o at $\mathbf{x}$ into incoming radiance L_i at $\mathbf{y}$, $\mathcal{G}L_o = L_i$. The scattering of incident radiance is denoted with the symbol $\mathcal{S}$ and corresponds to the surface local multiplication of incoming radiance L_i with the BRDF f_r followed by integration over the hemisphere. Consequently we have $\mathcal{S}L_i = L_o$. Note that both $\mathcal{G} = \mathcal{G}^+$ and $\mathcal{S} = \mathcal{S}^+$ are self adjoint with respect to the canonical inner product measure on line space ($d\mu = d\omega \cdot d\mathbf{A}$). For the former this follows from symmetry while for the latter it is a consequence of Helmholtz reciprocity. It follows that $\mathcal{T}^+ = \mathcal{G} \circ \mathcal{S}$.

From now on we will use the symbol L to stand for outgoing radiance since our algorithm will compute outgoing radiances.

A Galerkin approach to the inversion of $1 - \mathcal{T}$ projects the operator into a subspace spanned by some finite basis [6]. Assuming an orthonormal (w.r.t. the *parameter domain*) basis a linear system of the following form results

$$\forall i, j : \quad l_{ij} = l_{ij}^e + \sum_{mn} T_{ijmn} l_{mn}$$

for some unknown expansion coefficients l_{ij} of L.

Choosing a spatial parameterization, and hence a basis, of the form $\{N_i(\mathbf{x})\} \times \{N_j(\mathbf{y})\}$ we have $L(\mathbf{x}, \mathbf{y}) = \sum_{mn} l_{mn} N_m(\mathbf{x}) N_n(\mathbf{y})$. The transport coefficients T_{ijmn} are then defined as

$$T_{ijmn} = \langle \mathcal{T}(N_i N_j), N_m N_n \rangle$$
$$= \int_{\mathbf{z}} \int_{\mathbf{y}} \int_{\mathrm{M}^2} k^s(\mathbf{x}, \mathbf{y}, \mathbf{z}) N_m(\mathbf{x}) N_n(\mathbf{y}) N_i(\mathbf{y}) N_j(\mathbf{z}) \, d\mathbf{x} \, d\mathbf{y} \, d\mathbf{z}$$

where $k^s(\mathbf{x}, \mathbf{y}, \mathbf{z}) = f_r(\mathbf{x}, \mathbf{y}, \mathbf{z}) G(\mathbf{x}, \mathbf{y}) \frac{dA_x}{dx}$ is the *spatial kernel*. Note that the coefficients T_{ijmn} appear to be eight dimensional since $\mathbf{y}$ occurs twice. However, the integral is still only over six dimensions as one would expect. Using this observation we may split off one of the basis functions in $\mathbf{y}$, say N_n and interpret the T_{ijmn} as expansion coefficients of a modified spatial kernel function k_n^s

$$k_n^s(\mathbf{x}, \mathbf{y}, \mathbf{z}) = k^s(\mathbf{x}, \mathbf{y}, \mathbf{z}) N_n(\mathbf{y}) \approx \sum_{ijm} T_{ijmn} N_m(\mathbf{x}) N_i(\mathbf{y}) N_j(\mathbf{z}) \qquad (1)$$

In the case of a directional parameterization the basis set would typically be of the form $\{N_i(\mathbf{x})\} \times \{N_j(\omega)\}$ with $L(\mathbf{x}, \omega) = \sum_{mn} l_{mn} N_m(\mathbf{x}) N_n(\omega)$. The spatial parameterization only had three free parameters $(\mathbf{x}, \mathbf{y}, \mathbf{z})$ in a natural way. The directional parameterization starts out with four parameters $(\mathbf{x}, \omega', \mathbf{y}, \omega)$.

Since only points $\mathbf{x}$ and $\mathbf{y}$ which "look at each other" will couple across the integral however this parameterization too has only three free parameters as expected. For example, one can chose to express $\mathbf{x}$ as a function of $(\mathbf{y}, \omega')$ or ω' as a function of $(\mathbf{x}, \mathbf{y})$, resulting in two different expressions for T_{ijmn}

$$
\begin{aligned}
T_{ijmn} \\
&= \langle T(N_i N_j), N_m N_n \rangle \\
&= \int_\omega \int_\mathbf{y} \int_{\mathrm{M}^2} k^d(\omega', \mathbf{y}, \omega) N_m(\mathbf{x}) N_n(\omega') N_i(\mathbf{y}) N_j(\omega)\, dx\, dy\, d\omega \\
&= \int_\omega \int_\mathbf{y} \int_{\mathrm{H}^2} k^d(\omega', \mathbf{y}, \omega) N_m(\mathbf{x}) N_n(\omega') N_i(\mathbf{y}) N_j(\omega)\, d\omega'dy\, d\omega
\end{aligned}
$$

with the *directional kernel* $k^d(\omega', \mathbf{y}, \omega) = f_r(\omega', \mathbf{y}, \omega) \mathbf{n}_y \cdot \omega'$.

Once again the T_{ijmn} admit to an interpretation as coefficients in the expansion of a modified kernel function k_n^d

$$
k_n^d(\mathbf{x}, \mathbf{y}, \omega) = k^d(\omega'(\mathbf{x}, \mathbf{y}), \mathbf{y}, \omega) N_n(\omega'(\mathbf{x}, \mathbf{y})) \approx \sum_{ijm} T_{ijmn} N_m(\mathbf{x}) N_i(\mathbf{y}) N_j(\omega) \quad (2)
$$

and k_m^d

$$
k_m^d(\omega', \mathbf{y}, \omega) = k^d(\omega', \mathbf{y}, \omega) N_m(\mathbf{x}(\mathbf{y}, \omega')) \approx \sum_{ijn} T_{ijmn} N_n(\omega') N_i(\mathbf{y}) N_j(\omega) \quad (3)
$$

2.1 Discussion of parameterizations

When trying to decide which parameterization of radiance to use a number of issues arise which we will turn to now. Both spatial and directional parameterizations share the feature that the Galerkin method effectively expands kernel functions which are *modified*. In the case of the spatial parameterization we saw above (Equation 1) that instead of expanding k^s we end up expanding k_n^s. In the directional case we gave two choices (Equations 2, 3) k_n^d and k_m^d. In any case the original kernel is multiplied with one of the basis functions. As a consequence the properties of the *modified* kernel function determine the behavior of the algorithm. For example, suppose we use piecewise polynomial functions as bases. In that case the modified kernel will be of higher polynomial order.

A major practical difference between the two parameterizations arises immediately when computing the quadratures inherent in the definition of T_{ijmn}. Suppose our bases have finite support, as is most often the case. The 6D integral of the spatial parameterization can be evaluated in a straightforward way with a product quadrature rule since the domain of the integrand is a 6D hypercube. We say that the supports of the basis functions *match* by definition (see the 2D illustration on the left in Figure 2). This is not the case for the directional parameterization.

Suppose we consider some basis function on surface X with support $(\mathbf{x}, \omega')$ (see the 2D illustration on the right in Figure 2). This rectangle of support in

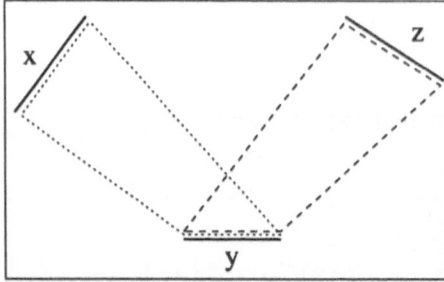 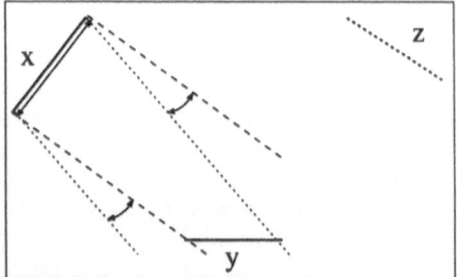

Fig. 2. Illustration of the matchup of support between basis functions. On the left basis functions with spatial parameterization. Their supports (dotted respectively dashed outlines) match at Y. On the right basis functions with directional parameterizations. A basis function with spatial support on X and some directional support (spread of angles) does not match up cleanly with the spatial support of Y.

parameter space corresponds to a (convolution) cone of directions in world space. The only time there is any exchange between X and a basis function on Y is when the spatial support of Y intersects this cone. This intersection will in general be awkwardly shaped with respect to the spatial support y of a chosen basis function on Y. Similarly, if we choose to fix x and y to correspond to the spatial support of some basis functions we will only have exchange for that portion of directions $\omega'(\mathbf{x}, \mathbf{y})$ which overlap the directional support ω' of the basis function on X. Again a region which is generally awkwardly shaped. Consequently product rules are hard to apply and suffer from precision problems [16].

On the other hand in the absence of real clustering algorithms using a spatial parameterization makes the number of basis functions for a given patches' outgoing radiance an a priori function of the input complexity. However, it is not clear how much this difference bears out in practice since the directional approaches still need to identify and process all primitives inside the directional support of a given patches' basis function. Further research and comparison of methods is needed to fully assess the impact of this difference.

2.2 Non-standard realization of the operator

When using wavelets to realize integral operators we need to distinguish between the types of bases used as well as the type of realization of the integral operator itself. These are separate issues and either one admits to so called *standard* and *non-standard* treatments. In particular we are using a non-standard realization of the operator as was done in the original wavelet radiosity work [19, 8].

Using a non-standard realization of the operator has a number of consequences

- transport due to different sources needs to be consolidated with a push/pull operation
- refinement proceeds by replacing earlier (coarser) couplings

- a simple recursive procedure provably accounts for all important transports (for tree wavelets)
- the number of necessary coefficients is $O(n)$ versus $O(n \log n)$, where n is the number of elements [4].

These issues are further compounded by the independent issues associated with primal and dual bases. For example, if the dual hierarchy does not have vanishing moments then this by itself causes the need for a wavelet up/down transformation independent of the standard or non-standard realization of the operator itself. Since we are using orthonormal bases we will not discuss primal versus dual bases here (for a discussion of these issues in the context of radiosity see [19]).

One of the major issues in any wavelet based algorithm is the enumeration of all important couplings. For tree wavelets (neighboring wavelets have no overlapping support) this is straightforward as wavelets and their supports are uniquely identified with sections of geometry (elements). A simple recursive procedure [9, 8] considers the coupling between surfaces and naturally accounts for all energy transfers while maintaining some error threshold

```
ProjectKernel( Basis ij, Basis mn )
  error = Oracle( ij, mn );
  if( Accept( error ) || RecurLimit( ij, mn ) )
    Tijmn = Quadrature( ij, mn );
  else
    if( PreferredSubdivision( ij, mn ) == ij )
      ForAllChildren( c, ij )
        ProjectKernel( c, mn );
    else
      ForAllChildren( c, mn )
        ProjectKernel( ij, c );
```

Tree wavelets also make it possible to work with the smooth functions exclusively instead of having to use various combinations of smooth and detail functions, simplifying the implementation.

It is not immediately clear how to use wavelets with overlapping support in this recursive enumeration scheme. The basic difficulty arises from the need to insure that all power is accounted for once and only once. For overlapping wavelets the standard realization of the operator is simpler. In the standard realization there is no overrepresentation of bases at the different levels of resolution. Consequently refinement proceeds by adding a detail function wherever the error criterion is not met. The standard realization does require couplings between all levels of the hierarchy however [4], resulting in the $O(n \log n)$ complexity. Whether the extra factor of $\log n$ is very noticeable for the regimes in which radiosity or radiance computations are performed is an open question of research.

After the initial setup of transport links there is typically refinement in successive iterations of the solver. In a tree wavelet scheme, such as the one we use, links are *replaced* upon refinement by child (finer) links. Using a standard realization of the operator, refinement would proceed by *adding* child links. Replacing coarser links with finer links has clear implications for the error analysis. The earlier links were found to contain too much error and replaced by links with lesser error. In the standard realization finer links are added to decrease the representation error. The difficulty arises from the fact that there is numerical error in the quadrature proportional to some power of the subdivision level. This error remains in the earlier link but is reduced for the newly added, finer links. Further research is needed to understand how these differences in error behavior express themselves in the fidelity of the final solution.

3 Implementation

In this section we discuss some of the implementation details which arose in our approach and how we addressed them.

As mentioned above we use a spatial parameterization with multi wavelet (piecewise polynomial) bases. This approach is a direct extension of the earlier wavelet radiosity work reported in [8, 19]. The main difference is the added number of dimensions. Coefficients of basis functions are not tied to individual surfaces anymore but rather to pairs of surfaces. There are still links which govern the exchange of power. Instead of links only between surface elements there are now also links between pairs of surface elements (with the middle surface matching up). The resulting data structures follow closely the ideas presented by Aupperle and Hanrahan in [2]. A refinement procedure refines links as before based on an oracle while gathering occurs across links (both inter surface and inter surface-pairs). Visibility is determined as described by Teller and Hanrahan [24]. The actual code is a strict superset of our earlier wavelet radiosity code. The quadrature used is straightforward Gaussian quadrature [18]. Since we use a spatial parameterization simple product rules suffice. The Push and Pull code is identical save for the fact that it extends over more dimensions.

In the following sections we address some individual details associated with our particular implementation of the radiance solver.

3.1 Shading model

As a BRDF we use a sum of a pure diffuse component and a microfacet model. We use the approximation to the Beckmann distribution together with an approximation of the Smith shadowing factor and an anisotropy control term all proposed by Schlick [17]

$$f_r(t, v, v', w) = \frac{g(v)g(v')}{4\pi v v'} z(t) a(w)$$

$$g(v) = \frac{v}{r + v(1 - r)}$$

$$z(t) = \frac{r}{(1 - t^2(1 - r))^2}$$

$$a(w) = \sqrt{\frac{p}{p^2 + w^2(1 - p^2)}}$$

where $t = H \cdot N$ is the cosine of the angle between the local surface normal and the half angle vector between incoming and outgoing directions; v and v' are the cosines of the incoming and outgoing directions respectively with the normal; w gives the cosine of the half angle vector with the preferred direction of the anisotropy model. The parameters $r, p \in [0, 1]$ control roughness and anisotropy respectively. The Fresnel factor was set to one. The images in Figure 8 (see color plate 9) show the use of the anisotropy factor. The approximation as given is not normalized and its hemispherical reflectance is not independent of incoming angle. However, its hemispherical reflectance is bounded and a simple normalization, which is a function of the roughness parameter, suffices to avoid energy gain.

3.2 Importance

Recently a number of papers in the graphics community [23, 3, 5, 15] have shown that the computation of illumination for a given scene can be greatly accelerated if we give up our goal of producing a view independent solution and instead compute a view dependent solution. Because of the great demand placed on computational resources by radiance computations we included this acceleration technique in our algorithm.

Since importance is a quantity which is propagated under the same operator as radiance it is an easy matter to include importance as a fourth "color" channel in the simulation. This follows directly from the fact that both $\mathcal{G}$ and $\mathcal{S}$ are self adjoint.

Let R describe the response of our sensor (e.g. eye, CCD) to *incoming* radiance at some point $\mathbf{x}$ from a direction $\boldsymbol{\omega}$. Define $\tilde{L}_o$ to be the solution to the formal operator equation $(1 - T)\tilde{L}_o = R$. The response of our sensor to the incoming radiance L_i is described as

$$
\begin{aligned}
\langle R, L_i \rangle &= \langle (1 - T)\tilde{L}_o, L_i \rangle \\
&= \langle \tilde{L}_o, (1 - T^+)L_i \rangle \\
&= \langle \tilde{L}_o, (1 - \mathcal{G} \circ \mathcal{S})\mathcal{G}L_o \rangle \\
&= \langle \tilde{L}_o, \mathcal{G}(1 - \mathcal{S} \circ \mathcal{G})L_o \rangle \\
&= \langle \mathcal{G}\tilde{L}_o, (1 - T)L_o \rangle \\
&= \langle \tilde{L}_i, L_o^e \rangle
\end{aligned}
$$

The last equation shows the well known fact that the response of our sensor to incoming radiance can be computed from the incoming radiance at the light sources due to the formal transport problem which arises when treating the sensor as a radiance source with "emittance" profile R. This also explains why we can use the same algorithm to solve both for importance and radiance: importance is *defined* as the solution to the same operator equation as radiance, only the boundary condition is different.

Since we are using importance refinement each scene consists of a sequence of geometric primitives (quadrilaterals in our current implementation) one of which is our "CCD" camera and the only source of R emittance. The final image results by evaluating the basis functions anchored at the CCD camera.

3.3 Oracle and refinement

Our recursive refinement procedure is driven by an error estimate for a given transport as well as the magnitude of radiance at the source end of a transport coupling and the importance at the receiver end of the transport. The error estimate for the coupling is determined by a a polynomial oracle similar to the one described in [8]. In the case of radiance the polynomial estimator extends over 6 dimensions rather than 4, but the basic logic remains the same. The samples of the kernel function generated as part of the quadrature routine are used to construct an interpolating polynomial. This polynomial is measured against the actual kernel function using a number of new sample points. The resulting error estimate is augmented by a geometric analysis. The geometric analysis was inspired by the observations that Aupperle and Hanrahan [2] made. Very peaked BRDF functions are easily missed if only a small number of samples of the integrand are taken. To decrease the chance of aliasing problems due to missing this peak we have augmented the oracle with a geometric analysis.

For a given triplet of surfaces exchanging power we consider the range of outgoing angles on X, incoming angles on Y, and outgoing angles on Y using straightforward geometric analysis (see [2]). The resulting ranges of angles are used in an interval evaluation of the shading model itself giving max and min values of f_r over the surfaces in question. This spread in the value of f_r is used as a weight of the error estimate derived by the polynomial oracle. Let ϵ be this estimate. We scale it by

$$1 + r(1 - r)(f_{r_{\max}} - f_{r_{\min}})$$

The factor or r normalizes the BRDF since its peak value is proportional to r^{-1}. The factor $(1 - r)$ insures that the penalty scaling increases for more peaked BRDF functions where the danger of aliasing is much larger.

This augmented oracle has been very successful in finding the peak of a BRDF and insuring the sufficient subdivision occurs around the peak. Figure 3 shows the oracle in progress. Notice the detail in the meshing as the error threshold is lowered. In particular for very peaked reflectances ($r = 0.001$) we can see in the images "islands" of fine meshing in the region of the reflection peak. Another example for anisotropic reflectors is shown in the images at the top of Figure 8 (see color plate 9). Notice in particular how the mesh follows the high anisotropy gradients of the reflection (most noticeable in the green part).

3.4 Separation of directional and isotropic radiance

In environments which contain both purely diffuse and glossy reflectors it is desirable to distinguish between diffuse and glossy transport. This approach avoids

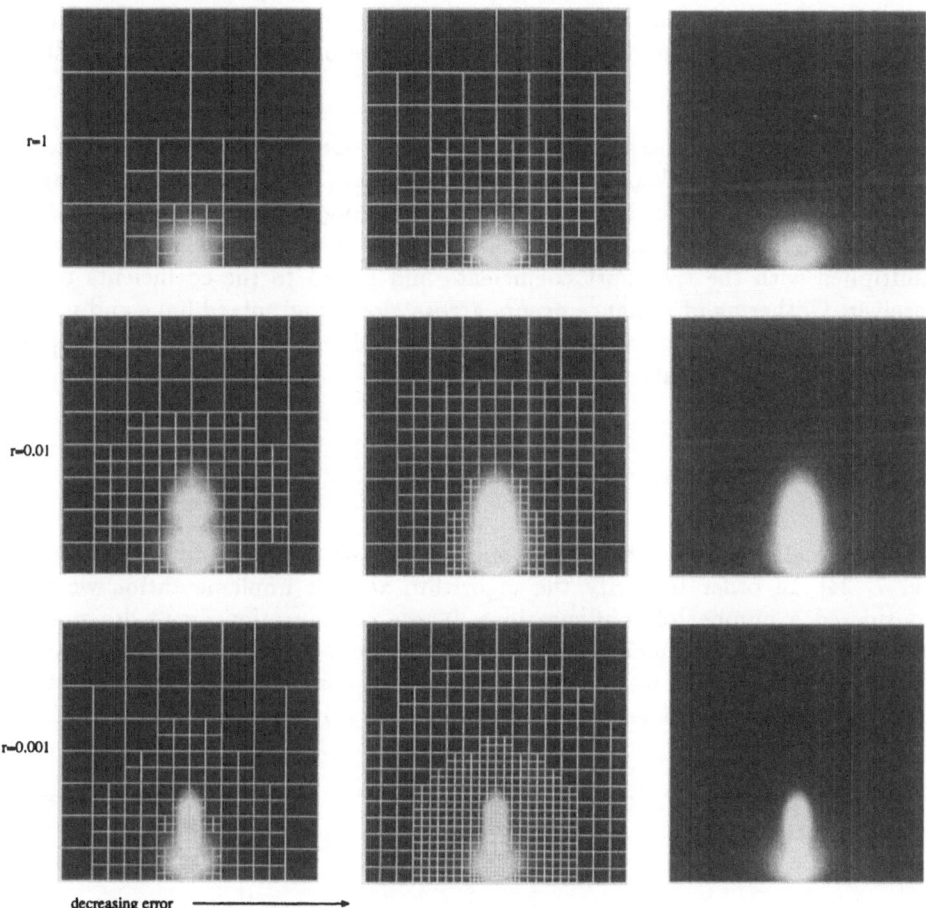

Fig. 3. Images of small source/reflector test configuration for different roughness values ($r = 1, 0.01, 0.001$) and different error criteria (10%, 1%, final accuracy).

the cost of the extra directional dimensions in transports which are independent of direction, for example reflection off a diffuse surface.

We take advantage of this by classifying a given link into one of the following categories. A link is called

- *diffuse* if both source and destination are diffuse. In this case only the usual radiosity couplings T_{ijmn}, $j = 0$ and $n = 0$, need to be computed and associated with the given link
- *glossy* if the receiver element exhibits glossy reflection. In this case the source may itself be diffuse or glossy. The diffuse case is simply characterized by coupling coefficients T_{ijmn} for which $n = 0$. This corresponds to writing $L(\mathbf{x}, \mathbf{y}) = \frac{B(\mathbf{x})}{\pi}$ and only using the constant basis function in $\mathbf{y}$. Otherwise these transports are characterized by the full range of subindices on T_{ijmn} and represent the canonical case with all coefficients computed

– *mixed* if a glossy source interacts with a diffuse reflector. In this case the set T_{ijmn} reduces to one for which $j = 0$ and we only compute the remaining T_{ijmn}.

During the solution process radiosity coefficients are kept at elements while radiance coefficients are kept in a separate tree data structure corresponding to the hierarchy of radiance basis functions. Gathering is performed across diffuse links just as in radiosity, i.e. the radiosity of the source is moved across the link, multiplied with the transport coefficients and added to the coefficients of the receiver. Gathering of radiance occurs across glossy and mixed links and is only distinguished by the dimensionality of the quantities being moved and multiplied with coupling coefficients.

4 Results

The above algorithm has been implemented as part of our rendering testbed [8, 19, 7, 24]. In order to verify the algorithm and its implementation we have considered a number of configurations. These configurations were designed to both stress the numerical algorithms and to be verifiable in an independent manner. In this section we describe three of these configurations and give results from simulations which show behavior consistent with a theoretical analysis.

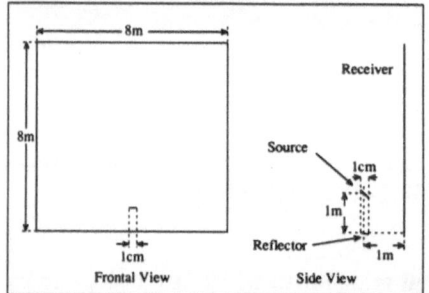 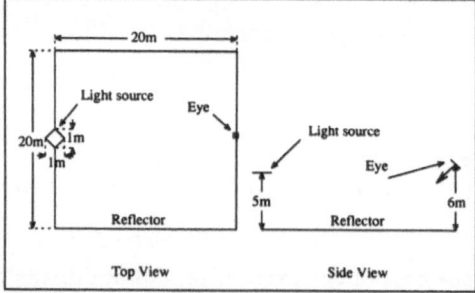

Fig. 4. Left: Geometry of small source/reflector test configuration. The source is inclined 45° to avoid any direct illumination of the receiver wall. The reflector is inclined 15° to cause a significant intersection between the directional lobe of the BRDF and the receiver wall. Right: Geometry of large area source/reflector configuration. The source is parallel to the reflector at the far end, while the eye is inclined by 45° towards the reflector.

The first test configuration is shown on the left in Figure 4. A diffuse emitter is placed above a glossy reflector. We examine the irradiance on a diffuse receiver wall. Due to the relative orientations any transport to the wall has to occur across a single bounce off the reflector, creating an intersection of the directional lobe of the BRDF with the wall. The irradiance on the wall is equal to

$$E(\mathbf{z}) = \int_{A_r} \int_{A_s} f_r(\mathbf{x}, \mathbf{y}, \mathbf{z}) G(\mathbf{x}, \mathbf{y}) \frac{B(\mathbf{x})}{\pi} G(\mathbf{y}, \mathbf{z}) \, dA_x \, dA_y$$

where $\mathbf{x}$ is located on the source A_s, $\mathbf{y}$ on the reflector A_r, and $\mathbf{z}$ on the receiver wall. Because of the relative ratio of size of source/reflector and the distance to the receiver wall a one point quadrature rule will incur an error on the order of 10^{-4}. In other words, the irradiance on the receiver follows the pointwise evaluation of f_r itself to within 10^{-4}. This is used as the reference solution to which to compare our computed solution. Note further that $f_r(\mathbf{x}, \mathbf{y}, \mathbf{z}) G(\mathbf{y}, \mathbf{z})$ has a very high dynamic range. f_r itself ranges from unity (directions which have only a diffuse contribution) to $\frac{1}{r}$. G ranges over 2 orders of magnitude due to the denominator ranging from $(1m)^2$ to $(9m)^2$. The particular value of r used for the graphs in Figure 5 was 0.01.

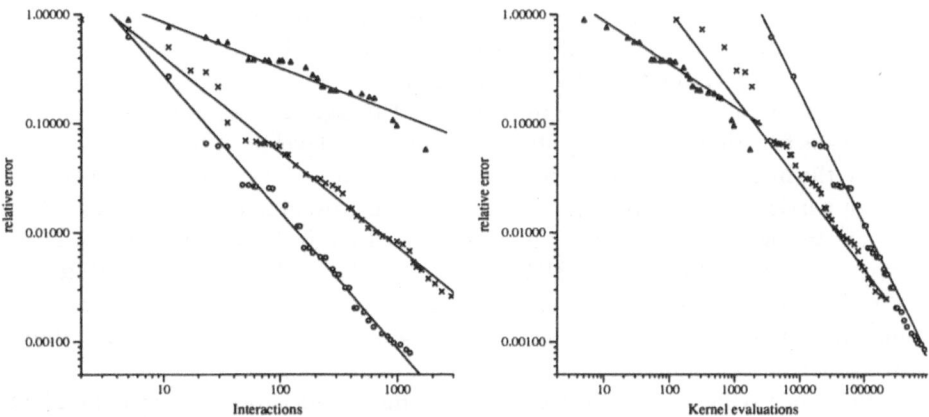

Fig. 5. Relative L^1 error for the small source/reflector configuration (on the left of Figure4) as a function of number of interactions allocated by the oracle and used for transport. From top to bottom we plotted multi wavelets of 1, 2, and 3 vanishing moments. On the left as a function of coefficients and on the right normalized to kernel evalutations.

Figure 5 shows the convergence behavior of multi wavelet bases with $M = 1, 2, 3$ vanishing moments. The error is relative L^1 error defined as

$$\frac{\int_{A_w} \|E(z) - \hat{E}(z)\| \, dA_z}{\int_{A_w} \|E(z)\| \, dA_z}$$

where $\hat{E}(z)$ denotes the computed solution. This integral itself is evaluated with a repeated trapezoid rule 3 subdivision levels finer than the irradiance computation. In this way any error incurred in computing the error integral itself is prevented from contaminating our convergence measurements. The independent variable in the resulting graph (left side) gives the number of couplings allocated by our oracle and the associated radiance/importance refinement procedure and consequently used during the computation of transport.

The plot shows clearly the convergence behavior of the three different types of bases. The data points have been fitted with lines. The resulting slopes have ratios very close (within 3%) to 1 : 2 : 3 which are the theoretically predicted ratios for the given order of basis functions. However, when plotting the data in this way we are ignoring the increasing work necessary for higher order quadratures which are required by higher order basis functions. Figure 5 on the right shows the same data, but this time plotted as a function of the number of kernel evaluations which more closely measures the actual work performed by the algorithm. Due to the sixth order scaling of the samples for a 6 dimensional quadrature rule the higher order basis function data points are moved over to the right. In fact the quadratic basis function data points move over so far that quadratic bases only become competitive at very high accuracy requirements.

The images in Figure 3 show the oracle in progress. The top row shows the perfectly diffuse case ($r = 1$), the middle row a more directional case of $r = 0.01$ and the bottom row a very peaked BRDF for $r = 0.001$. In each row the first image has an error on the order of 10%, the second on the order of 1% and both show the associated meshing. The final image shows final accuracy with linear basis functions at a finest allowed subdivision level of $25cm$. We can clearly observe the increased meshing where the kernel function has the highest variance. Note in particular the separating "islands" of fine meshing as r is decreased. One is in an area where the variance is dominated by diffuse reflection the other in the area where the lobe of the BRDF intersects the wall. The pattern of light on the wall shows clearly the pinching off of the peak in the directional lobe of the reflectance function as r is decreased and demonstrates the action of non-diffuse transport.

One aspect which is not stressed by the above configuration is any significant area integration over the light source or the reflector surface. The difficulty with such a configuration is the need to find an independent means of verifying the computed answer. We now turn to such a configuration.

Figure 4 shows a diagram of a diamond shaped light source over a base polygon on the right. The light source is located at the far end, while the eye is at the near end looking down at an angle of 45°. A picture of this configuration can be seen in Figure 7. The roughness parameter was set to $r = 0.01$ for a fairly peaked response. There is also a diffuse component of $d = 0.1$ which can be seen at the far end right below the light source. The error in the computed solution was estimated by an independent integration module which evaluated the radiance at a given point on the reflector with respect to the eye by using a 7th order Gauss quadrature over the light source. Evaluating this function pointwise at a grid 3 levels below the subdivision grid on the reflector produced a numerical answer with significantly higher precision than our computed solution. The convergence results are plotted in Figure 6 for multi wavelets of $m = 1, 2, 3, 4$ vanishing moments respectively. Once again we can see the characteristic convergence rates (fitted lines).

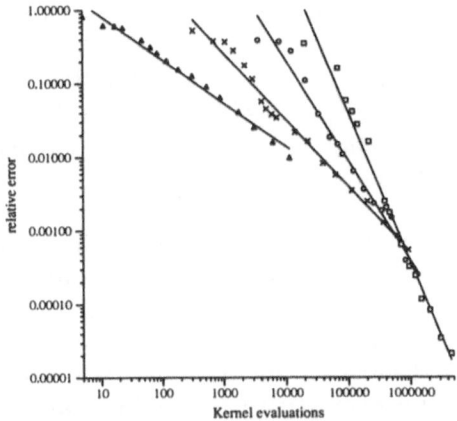

Fig. 6. Relative L^1 error for the configuration on the right of Figure 4 as a function of kernel evaluations. From left to right we plotted multi wavelets of $m = 1, 2, 3, 4$ vanishing moments.

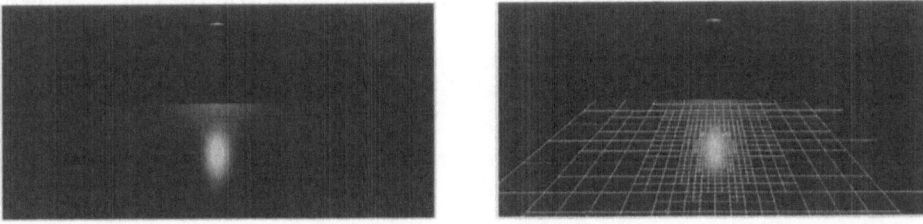

Fig. 7. Images of large area source/reflector test configuration. On the left the radiance as seen from the eye; on the right the induced meshing ($r = 0.01$; linear basis functions).

Finally we added an anisotropy factor to the shading model [17] and used 3 colored light sources to show the resulting reflections. Figure 8 (see color plate 9) shows a rendered image of this configuration on the top left and with the corresponding meshing on the reflector on the top right. Note the fine level of subdivision in the areas where the radiance changes most rapidly. This simulation used linear basis functions, a roughness parameter of $r = 0.1$, and an anisotropy factor of $p = 0.1$. The preferred direction of the anisotropy model ("scratches") was given by the family of hyperbolas $x * y = \pm c$ (note the singularity in the middle). The sequence of images in Figure 8 (see color plate 9) shows a spatial plot of the resulting radiance field by rotating the eye $90°$ around the model.

5 Conclusion

In this paper we have described a new algorithm for the computation of radiance in the presence of glossy reflectors using multi wavelet bases. The resulting algorithm has been shown to converge to the correct results in a number of test

configurations. The rate of convergence is consistent with the theoretically predicted rate.

As was done in the earlier work concerning wavelet radiosity [8, 19] we have
in effect extended an earlier hierarchical technique to higher orders: in the case of
radiosity the work reported in [9] and in the case of radiance the work reported
in [2] . The benefits are similar. The quality of the computed images increases
markedly when going from piecewise constant bases to piecewise linear (or higher). In the case of radiosity the work per entry in the matrix system scales as a
fourth power of the number of kernel evaluations, while in the case of radiance
it scales as a sixth power. In the case of radiosity this led to a relationship between user experienced work and error which clearly favored higher order basis
functions. In the case of radiance this tradeoff is not so clear. Higher order basis functions only become competitive at very high precision requirements (see
Figures 5, 6). In practice we have found that the cost increase for linear basis
functions is not too high while yielding much better looking pictures. So far we
have employed quadratic bases only for the plotting of the graphs. Cubic bases
are prohibitively expensive. Unless some major optimizations in the code can be
found we do not expect cubic bases to find much application because of their
high cost.

The radiance problem remains hard and costly to compute. Considerable
research remains to be done to accelerate algorithms which compute the light
transport in the presence of glossy reflectors. We do believe that hierarchical
techniques will have a place in the repertoire of such algorithms. Interesting
areas for further investigations include

- comparisons between the directional and spatial parameterizations
- comparisons between standard and non-standard realizations
- overlapping wavelets

Acknowledgments

We would like to thank Seth Teller for major code contributions to the GUR
testbed; Larry Aupperle, Wim Sweldens, Steven Gortler, and Michael Cohen for
many fruitful discussions regarding implementation ideas, wavelets, and earlier
radiance algorithms; David Laur for production help. Support was provided by
Apple, Silicon Graphics, the Scientific Visualization Department at GMD, and
the NSF (contract no. CCR 9207966).

References

1. ALPERT, B., BEYLKIN, G., COIFMAN, R., AND ROKHLIN, V. Wavelet-like Bases for the Fast Solution of Second-kind Integral Equations. *SIAM Journal on
   Scientific Computing 14*, 1 (January 1993).
2. AUPPERLE, L., AND HANRAHAN, P. A Hierarchical Illumination Algorithm for
   Surfaces with Glossy Reflection. In *Computer Graphics Annual Conference Series
   1993* (August 1993), Siggraph, pp. 155–162.

3. AUPPERLE, L., AND HANRAHAN, P. Importance and Discrete Three Point Transport. In *Fourth Eurographics Workshop on Rendering* (June 1993), Eurographics, pp. 85–94.

4. BEYLKIN, G., COIFMAN, R., AND ROKHLIN, V. Fast Wavelet Transforms and Numerical Algorithms I. *Communications on Pure and Applied Mathematics 44* (1991), 141–183.

5. CHRISTENSEN, P. H., SALESIN, D. H., AND DEROSE, T. A Continuous Adjoint Formulation for Radiance Transport. In *Fourth Eurographics Workshop on Rendering* (June 1993), Eurographics, pp. 95–104.

6. DELVES, L. M., AND MOHAMED, J. L. *Computational Methods for Integral Equations.* Cambridge University Press, 1985.

7. GERSHBEIN, R. S., SCHRÖDER, P., AND HANRAHAN, P. Textures and Radiosity: Controlling Emission and Reflection with Texture Maps. In *Computer Graphics Annual Conference Series, 1994* (1994).

8. GORTLER, S., SCHRÖDER, P., COHEN, M., AND HANRAHAN, P. Wavelet Radiosity. In *Computer Graphics Annual Conference Series 1993* (August 1993), Siggraph, pp. 221–230.

9. HANRAHAN, P., SALZMAN, D., AND AUPPERLE, L. A Rapid Hierarchical Radiosity Algorithm. *Computer Graphics 25*, 4 (July 1991), 197–206.

10. HECKBERT, P. S. *Simulating Global Illumination Using Adaptive Meshing.* PhD thesis, University of California at Berkeley, January 1991.

11. HECKBERT, P. S. Radiosity in Flatland. *Computer Graphics Forum 2*, 3 (1992), 181–192.

12. IMMEL, D. S., COHEN, M. F., AND GREENBERG, D. P. A Radiosity Method for Non-Diffuse Environments. *Compuber Graphics 20*, 4 (August 1986), 133–142.

13. KAJIYA, J. T. The Rendering Equation. *Computer Graphics 20*, 4 (1986), 143–150.

14. LESAEC, B., AND SCHLICK, C. A Progressive Ray-tracing-based Radiosity with General Reflectance Functions. In *Photorealism in Computer Graphics (Proceedings Eurographics Workshop on Photosimulation, Realism and Physics in Computer Graphics)* (June 1990), K. Bouatouch and C. Bouville, Eds., Springer Verlag, pp. 101–114.

15. PATTANAIK, S. *Computational Methods for Global Illumination and Visualization of Complex 3D Environments.* PhD thesis, Birla Institute of Technology and Science, Pilani, India, February 1993.

16. PER H. CHRISTENSEN, ERIC J. STOLLNITZ, D. H. S., AND DEROSE, T. D. Importance-Driven Wavelet Radiance. Tech. Rep. 94-01-05, University of Washington, Seattle, January 1994.

17. SCHLICK, C. A customizable reflectance model for everyday rendering. In *Fourth Eurographics Workshop on Rendering* (June 1993), Eurographics, pp. 73–83.

18. SCHRÖDER, P. Numerical Integration for Radiosity in the Presence of Singularities. In *Fourth Eurographics Workshop on Rendering* (1993).

19. SCHRÖDER, P., GORTLER, S. J., COHEN, M. F., AND HANRAHAN, P. Wavelet Projections For Radiosity. In *Fourth Eurographics Workshop on Rendering* (June 1993), Eurographics, pp. 105–114.

20. SHAO, M.-Z., PENG, Q.-S., AND LIANG, Y.-D. A New Radiosity Approach by Procedural Refinements for Ralistic Image Synthesis. *Computer Graphics 22*, 4 (August 1988), 93–101.

21. SHIRLEY, P. A Ray Tracing Method for Illumination Calculations in Diffuse Specular Scenes. In *Proceedings of Graphics Interface 90* (May 1990), Canadian

Information Processing Society, pp. 205–212.

22. SILLION, F. X., ARVO, J. R., WESTIN, S. H., AND GREENBERG, D. P. A Global Illumination Solution for General Reflectance Distributions. *Computer Graphics 25*, 4 (July 1991), 187–196.

23. SMITS, B. E., ARVO, J. R., AND SALESIN, D. H. An Importance Driven Radiosity Algorithm. *Computer Graphics 26*, 2 (August 1992), 273–282.

24. TELLER, S., AND HANRAHAN, P. Global Visibility Algorithms for Illumination Computations. In *Computer Graphics Annual Conference Series 1993* (August 1993), Siggraph, pp. 239–246.

25. TROUTMAN, R., AND MAX, N. Radiosity Algorithms Using Higher-order Finite Elements. In *Computer Graphics Annual Conference Series 1993* (August 1993), Siggraph, pp. 209–212.

26. ZATZ, H. R. Galerkin Radiosity: A Higher Order Solution Method for Global Illumination. Master's thesis, Cornell University, August 1992.

Part VI

Dynamic Solutions
and Walkthroughs

Efficient Radiosity in Dynamic Environments

David Forsyth, Chien Yang, Kim Teo

University of Iowa, Iowa City, IA 52242, USA

Abstract

A method of determining radiosity in an environment containing moving objects, is described. This method uses the hierarchical techniques of Hanrahan *et al.* to obtain a static solution. Hanrahan's techniques efficiently create a hierarchical meshing of the environments geometry, and create links from element to element based on the magnitude of the form-factor between the elements. These ideas extend naturally to a dynamic environment, as only three atomic editing operations are required to update a hierarchy when an object moves: a link can be moved up or down the hierarchy, or a link can be occluded. Our algorithm exploits these simple editing processes to maintain the hierarchy, and then uses an iterative technique to solve the resulting linear system. The approach is extremely efficient, requiring little work between frames. **Keywords:** Radiosity, Computer Graphics.

1 Introduction

Diffuse interreflections are a source of various substantial effects in the radiance of scenes. Reproducing these effects appears to be essential to creating realistic renderings of scenes [14]. Diffuse interreflections are accurately modelled by a Fredholm equation of the second kind, which gives the radiance of a patch as that on the patch due to the source alone plus that on the patch arising from coupling to other patches.

Consider a set of surfaces in space, parametrised as $\mathbf{x}(\mathbf{u})$, where u is a two-dimensional vector of parameters. Every surface reflects light onto every other surface within a line of sight; the resulting radiance of the collection is:

$$N(\mathbf{u}) = N_0(\mathbf{u}) + \rho(\mathbf{u}) \int_S K(\mathbf{u}, \mathbf{v}) N(\mathbf{v}) dA$$

where $N(\mathbf{u})$ is the radiance at $\mathbf{u}$, $N_0(\mathbf{u})$ is the "initial radiance" at $\mathbf{u}$ (that is, the radiance at $\mathbf{u}$ if all other surface patches are absent), $\rho(\mathbf{u})$ is the reflectance at $\mathbf{u}$ and $K(\mathbf{u}, \mathbf{v})$ is the *form factor* from patch $\mathbf{v}$ to patch $\mathbf{u}$. K expresses the gain in transferring radiance from patch $\mathbf{v}$ to patch $\mathbf{u}$, and has the form:

$$K(\mathbf{u}, \mathbf{v}) = \frac{1}{\pi} \frac{(\mathbf{n}(\mathbf{u}).d_{uv})(\mathbf{n}(\mathbf{v}).d_{vu}) View(\mathbf{u}, \mathbf{v})}{(d_{uv}.d_{uv})^2}$$

where $d_{uv} = \mathbf{x}(\mathbf{v}) - \mathbf{x}(\mathbf{u})$ and $View(\mathbf{u}, \mathbf{v})$ is one if there is a line of sight from $\mathbf{u}$ to $\mathbf{v}$, and zero if there is not. Analytical results are hard to establish, though some exist [5]. The $View$ term is discontinuous and bears a complicated relationship to shape, and the relationship between an object's shape and its radiance - the main matter to study - is exceptionally complex due to the form of the kernel.

1.1 Numerical Solutions

Usually, finite elements are used in constructing radiosity solutions, and the main thrust of work has been on point collocation methods using constant elements. The result is an $O(n^2)$ algorithm, where the dominant problem is computing the approximation to the kernel. Galerkin methods, though analytically elegant, tend to be inappropriate as a result of the extra integrations required, but have recently become more popular (e.g. [18]). Typical recent approaches to obtaining efficient numerical solutions include: **progressive radiosity**, where an incremental approximate solution follows from allowing elements to "shoot" light onto every other patch [3, 13]; and **importance-driven radiosity** where for a particular view of a radiosity solution, an adjoint equation is used to determine the patches that make the most crucial contribution to that view [17]. When constant elements are used, the solution is smoothed using an interpolatory scheme to avoid a harlequin appearance. Achieving aesthetically pleasing solutions this way is often rather difficult, as human observers tend to be insensitive to the accuracy (in, say, an L^2 norm) of a solution, but highly sensitive to certain kinds of error, typical of this form of method. These effects are well illustrated in a recent text-book on the subject, which also develops the theory in reasonable detail [4].

Hierarchical Radiosity Using an analogy with the recent fast numerical techniques for the n-body problem (e.g. [6], and in a different form, [8]). Hanrahan *et al.* [10] recently constructed a *hierarchical radiosity algorithm* which is extremely efficient. Hanrahan's approach takes a system of polygons, and constructs a hierarchy of elements using a quadtree, with a polygon at the root of each tree. Links are constructed between elements of the hierarchy which have a different root by testing the form-factor between the elements (which also falls off as the reciprocal square of distance); if it is smaller than some threshold, a link is established (figure 1). Elements are then given an initial radiance, and radiosity is propagated along these links using a simple "up-and-down" algorithm. This approach is efficient, because it allows multiple representations of the same radiator, and because it constructs links which have the same radiometric significance (rather than having elements at either end be the same size).

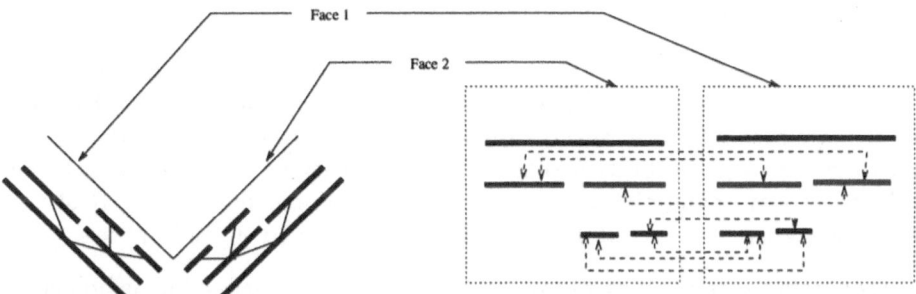

Fig. 1. The left half of the figure shows an element hierarchy superimposed on a simple translationally symmetric geometry - a gutter formed by two plane walls at 45°. The symmetry has been integrated out. Elements are given as thick lines, and the geometry is drawn using thin lines; the relationship in the hierarchy is given by the position of the elements. The right half shows the element-element links for a particular threshold in this geometry.

2 Radiosity in Dynamic Environments

The obvious approach to obtain a radiosity solution for a sequence of pictures of an environment containing moving objects is computing a new radiosity solution for each frame is recognised to be hopelessly inefficient, because it does not use the information contained in the previous solution. Baum *et al.* attributed the temporal coherence of the kernel and of solutions to object coherence, and exploited it to obtain a factor of 25 speedup for image sequences where all moving objects and their paths were known in advance, by computing static relationships in a preprocessing pass [1]. George *et al.* use the concept of *negative energy*; when an object moves, some patches distribute negative energy to account for the new shadows now cast by the patch [7]. Incremental information about form-factors and solutions is not accumulated; however, Müller and Schöffel gained efficiency by using sophisticated data structures to keep track of occlusion and repropagation information [15]. Chen [2] reformulated progressive radiosity to address dynamic environments; in his approach, when an object moves, affected patches compute incremental form-factor terms, and propagate incremental radiosity. Each patch that has contributed to the existing solution must then re-shoot its incremental radiosity. The approach is particularly appropriate for interactive modelling systems, as it is not necessary to wait for the algorithm to converge before an object is moved again.

Hanrahan's method does not address a dynamic environment, but its efficiency is extremely attractive. There is a natural way to extend the method to a dynamic environment, which appears to be quite efficient. This approach assumes that objects are neither created nor destroyed, but is otherwise quite general. The key to the approach is a study of the behaviour of links as objects move.

2.1 Link Activities

An element hierarchy can be updated to reflect a movement by relatively simple editing. At any timestep, the hierarchy of elements for polygons that have not moved since the last frame, and the links between those elements, do not change over time; the only possibility is that elements can become temporarily occluded. Links to or from dynamic objects are more interesting, but display relatively simple behaviour. The possibilities for both dynamic and static links are:

- **Occlusion initiated or terminated:** in this case, where a link is broken by occlusion, the form-factor across the link may be modified or zeroed (if the link is completely occluded), but the link is retained as the occlusion may disappear later; if the occlusion disappears, the form-factor can be restored. These events can occur for either static or dynamic links (figure 2).
- **Promoting a link:** as polygons move away from one another, the form factor between elements falls off; for sufficiently distant polygons, the form factor may become so low that a link can move up the hierarchy to larger elements. If a link moves up the hierarchy, then it may be possible to reap some elements from the base of the hierarchy (for example, figure 3). This is easily accomplished, as the condition can be detected when the link is moved. This event can occur only for a dynamic link (figure 3).
- **Demoting a link:** as polygons move closer, the form-factor increases, and elements may need to be split and their children linked to maintain numerical accuracy. If a link moves down the hierarchy, elements may need to be created; again, this is easily accomplished, as the condition can be detected when the link is moved. This event can occur only for a dynamic link (figure 3).

Once it is known that only a limited range of events can occur at a link, it is important to be able to predict which links are affected in the next frame; with an effective prediction component, the algorithm takes the following form:

- Establish a hierarchy of elements and links for the geometry in the first frame. For each time-step:
  1. Predict which links will be promoted, which will be demoted, and which experience an occlusion event.
  2. Update only those links, and edit the hierarchy to reflect promotions and demotions.
  3. Use a prediction of the solution (usually an extrapolate based on previous solutions) to start an iterative solver.

Note that the solution process and the process of editing the hierarchy do not depend on the classification of links as static or as dynamic. The classification is extremely important for predicting link events, which can have a significant effect on efficiency. In our experience with implementation, the dominant cost is in occlusion testing, and it is important to be able to predict effectively which links will have their form-factors changed by occlusions, to avoid examining each link at each step.

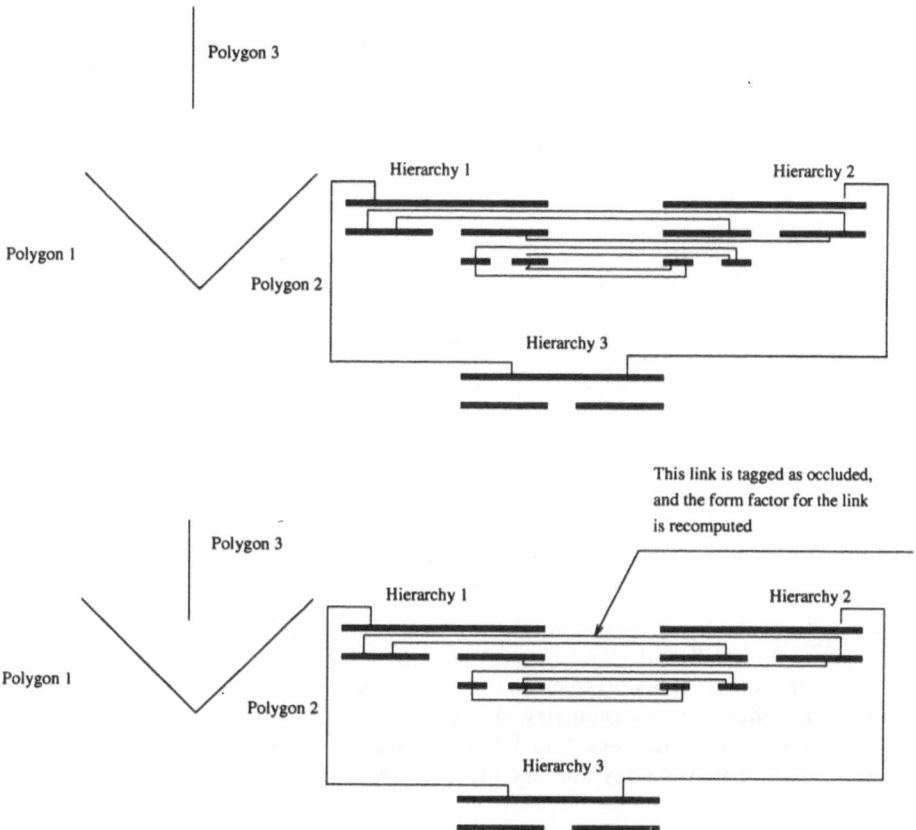

Fig. 2. As polygon 3 approaches 1 and 2, it occludes links across the hierarchies of elements; these links are marked as being occluded, and the form factor is recomputed. Even if the link has form-factor zero, it is retained for future reference as polygon 3 might move away.

Figure 4 (see color plate 10) shows dynamic link events for an orthogonal gutter being approached by a patch (the translational symmetry has been integrated out). Figures are read top to bottom, left to right. The links, shown in pink, are to the centre of the relevant element in the hierarchy, and are drawn as lines joining element centres. Links to the patch are dynamic, others are static. In the first frame, many links go the centre of the patch (hence, to the top element in the hierarchy); by the second frame, these links have been demoted, and so are represented as going to the centre of each half of the patch. As the patch gets closer to the gutter, more links are demoted, and links move to lower levels of the hierarchy, and so move to points given by finer subdivisions of the patch.

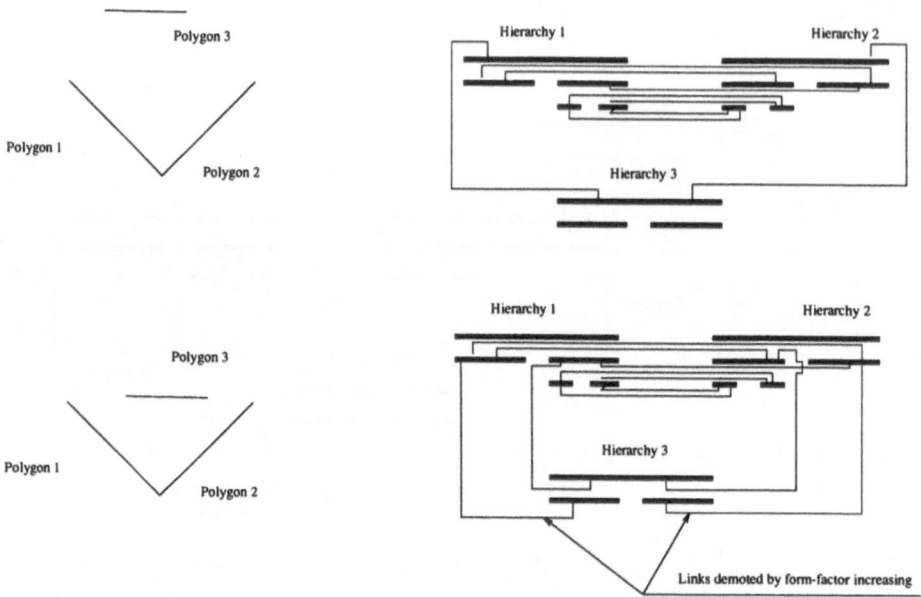

Fig. 3. As the geometry changes from the top to the bottom, the links between elements of hierarchies 1 and 2 and elements of hierarchy 3 are demoted because polygon 3 approaches the other two polygons and the form-factors increase. Promotion is the reverse of this effect; as the geometry changes from the bottom to the top, the links between elements of hierarchies 1 and 2 and elements of hierarchy 3 are promoted, because polygon 3 moves away and the form-factors decrease.

2.2 Predicting Link Events

Our present implementation predicts link events using an inefficient but conservative strategy. It is known in advance which objects are dynamic, and dynamic and static links are treated differently. To date, we have worked only with geometrical layouts that guarantee that static links are not occluded (for example, a static room with a moving light in the ceiling), thereby bypassing the problem of predicting occlusion events with static links.

The two columns on the left in figure 5 (see color plate 11) show a motion sequence, with the light moving around the ceiling. The mesh elements with links to the light source are shown to the right of the relevant frame; these are the only dynamic links. The figures should be read from top to bottom. Note how dynamic links are demoted as the light approaches a wall, and promoted as it leaves. In the present, early, implementation, all dynamic links have their form-factors recomputed; more sophisticated prediction algorithms will reduce this extra work. The figures were rendered using a Gouraud shading of a Delaunay triangulation of the sample points. Timing information appears in table 1. The two right hand columns show a motion sequence, with the light moving around the ceiling. In the central column, the dynamic links are reinspected at each step; in far right-hand column, links are extrapolated up to seven frames ahead, to predict events. Form-factor values are also extrapolated. This leads to a deterioration in rendering quality for some speed-up.

The results in the left-hand columns of figure 5 (see color plate 11) are derived from an implementation where each dynamic link is tested at each step; clearly, this is an inefficient approach. Results in the right-hand column of figure 5 are obtained from an implementation where dynamic link events are predicted by linear extrapolation. For each dynamic link, a linear extrapolate predicts the frame at which the next link event will occur. This frame is recorded in the link; until that frame is reached, the form-factor and occlusion terms are obtained by a linear extrapolate. When the frame at which an event is predicted, is reached, the form-factor is re-evaluated. The oldest form-factor value involved in the extrapolation is discarded, and the new value is incorporated. The results compare reasonably well in quality, for some speed-up (table 1).

3 Results

Our present implementation works for an environment where static links will not be occluded, so that predicting static occlusion events is unnecessary. Link promotion and demotion are dealt with by re-examining all dynamic links at each time-step. The geometry used consists of a three-walled room, with a floor, no ceiling, and a box lying on the floor, with a light source moving around in the plane of the ceiling. In the lefthand columns of figure 5 (see color plate 11), the sample points of the radiosity solution are Delaunay triangulated and these triangles are Gouraud shaded. This approximation technique causes some annoying perceptual effects, particularly Mach bands and occasional disruptions in the geometry of the isophotes due to a non-unique triangulation, but has the merit of being fast and efficient; furthermore, if the triangulation is done in the frame of the faces, it is affine covariant, meaning that it supports reasonable changes in viewpoint without the radiance appearing to slip across surfaces. As the timings in table 1 show, the per-frame timing is extremely fast, with a relatively low initial cost. We are presently exploring the prospects for better approximation techniques that run as fast or faster.

Figure 5 and table 1 also show results for a slightly different geometry, where polygons are flat-shaded; in the central column of figure 5, each dynamic link is re-inspected at every step, whereas in the right-hand column, the link formfactors are extrapolated for up to seven frames in advance. The deterioration in image quality is accompanied by a slight improvement in speed.

4 Future Work

Predicting link events is a significant outstanding problem. Visualizing link events as a process where objects enter or leave shafts that run between two elements, or where the shaft geometry changes, appears to be productive. This view can be generalised to a more sophisticated approach to the problem of predicting link events by constructing and maintaining a database, which can

Sequence	Number of frames	Average time per frame	Standard deviation	Time to set up and solve frame 1
Gouraud shaded corridoor	109	3.81 s	0.760 s	30.95 s
Cubical room	20	4.21 s	1.36 s	22.24 s
Cubical room with extrapolation	20	3.92 s	0.845 s	19.74 s

Table 1. Timing information for the three sequences rendered. The time to set up and solve frame 1 is representative of the time required to solve a given frame from scratch; this is substantially larger than the average time taken to solve for radiosity and render a frame, indicating that there are substantial savings to be had in reusing radiosity information. Note that extrapolating form-factors gives about a 7 % saving in the average time taken to render a frame, and substantially reduces the standard deviation; this is probably because extrapolation is poor at predicting events when many elements appear or disappear from view. There are typically 5000-6000 polygons in each frame.

answer the query "Which shafts pass through this region of space?". The database is constructed by decomposing free space surrounding objects into cells of various sizes; each cell records the shafts passing through the cells, and hence the links that might be occluded if an object passes through the cell. This means that, by tracking the path of a moving object, the links between static objects that will be occluded by the object can be quickly and efficiently identified and recomputed.

This approach does not address the problem of objects occluding dynamic links, as it appears to be difficult to update the shaft database quickly when the ends of the shafts move. We are at present experimenting with an approach where dynamic link occlusions are managed by extrapolation, and static link events by a spatial database. In particular, this system will not require dynamic and static objects to be separated in advance. When an object moves, it will be erased from the static database and treated as a dynamic object; if it remains stationary for a sufficient number of frames, it will be reinserted into the static database.

As the results show, hierarchical techniques are not effective in preserving the discontinuities in a radiosity solution. The dynamics of these discontinuities are complicated, and maintaining a discontinuity based mesh in a dynamic environment appears to be extremely difficult; it may be simpler and more effective to predict the discontinuities at each frame, and then impose them on the solution in a "cleaning-up" pass after the solution for a frame has been determined. It appears unlikely that any coherence in the discontinuities can be effectively exploited. Post-processing solution meshes to demote links that transfer too much energy would also improve the solutions. The adaptations made to the mesh in this way could be maintained in the same way that dynamic links are maintained. We expect them to show substantial frame-to-frame coherence. Clustering groups of polygons that interact, as in the work of Sillion [16], and lazy evaluation of links between hierarchy elements, as in the work of Holzschuch *et al.*, both appear to offer substantive savings. A substantial source of these savings appears to be *domain decomposition*, where the geometry is segmented into sets whose radiometric interactions can be approximated easily; we intend to investigate principled techniques for domain decomposition.

Acknowledgements

We are grateful for instructive and helpful comments, including further references, from anonymous referees, and from Andrew Zisserman. This research was carried out at the University of Iowa Department of Computer Science, supported in part by a National Science Foundation Young Investigator Award with matching funds from GE, Eugene Rikel, Rockwell International and Tektronix.

References

1. Baum, D.R., Wallace R.W., Cohen M.F., Greenberg D.P. "The Back-Buffer: An Extension of the Radiosity-Method to Dynamic Environments," *The Visual Computer*, **2**,5, 1986, pp. 298-306.
2. Chen, S.E. "Incremental Radiosity: An Extension of Progressive Radiosity to an Interactive Image Synthesis System," *Computer Graphics (SIGGRPAH '90 proceedings)*, **24**, 4, 1990, pp. 135-144.
3. Cohen, M., Chen, S.E., Wallace, J.R., and Greenberg, D.P. A progressive refinement approach to fast radiosity image generation. Computer Graphics (SIGGRAPH '88 Proceedings) 22:4 (Aug 1988), pp. 75-84.
4. Cohen, M.F. and Wallace, J.R., *Radiosity and realistic image synthesis*,Academic, 1993.
5. Forsyth, D.A. and Zisserman, A.P. "Shape from shading in the light of mutual illumination,", *Image and Vision Computing*, AVC special issue, 42-49,1990.
6. Greengard, L. (1988) The rapid evaluation of potential fields in particle systems. MIT Press, Cambridget, MA.
7. George, D.W., Sillion, F.X., and Greenberg, D.P. "Radiosity redistribution for dynamic environments." IEEE Computer Graphics and Applications 10:4 (July 1990), pp. 26-34.
8. Hackbusch, W. and Nowak, Z.P., "On the fast matrix multiplication in the boundary element method by panel clustering," *Numer. Math.*, **54**, 463-491, 1989
9. Haines, E. A., and Wallce, J.R. Shaft Culling for efficient ray-traced radiosity. In Second Eurographics Workshop on Rendering (Barcelona, Spain, May 1991).
10. Hanrahan, P., Salzman, D. and Aupperle, L., "A rapid hierarchical radiosity algorithm," SIGGRAPH-91, 197-206, 1991.
11. Holzschuch, N., Sillion, F.X. and Drettakis, G., "An efficient progressive refinement strategy for hierarchical radiosity," this volume.
12. Koenderink, J.J. and Van Doorn, A.J., "Geometrical modes as a general method to treat diffuse interreflections in radiometry," *J. Opt. Soc. Am.*, **6**, 1, 1987, pp15-31.

13. Lischinski, D., Tampieri, F., and Donald, D.P., "Discontinuity meshing for accurate radiosity". *IEEE Computer Graphics and applications* (November 1992) pp. 25-39.

14. Meyer, G.W. "Color calculations for and perceptual assessment of computer graphic images," PhD thesis, Program of Computer Graphics, Cornell University, 1986.

15. Müller, S. and Schöffel, F., "Fast radiosity propagation for interactive virtual environments using a shadow-form-factor-list," this volume.

16. Sillion, F.X. "Clustering and volume scattering for hierarchical radiosity calculations," this volume.

17. Smits, B. E., Arvo, J. R., and Salesin, D. H. An importance-driven radiosity algorithm. Computer Graphics (SIGGRAPH '92 Proceedings) 26:4 (July 1992), pp. 273-282.

18. Zatz, H.R. "Galerkin radiosity: A higher order solution method for global illumination." Master's Thesis, Program of Computer Graphics, Cornell University, Aug. 1992.

Fast Radiosity Repropagation For Interactive Virtual Environments Using A Shadow-Form-Factor-List

Stefan Müller, Frank Schöffel

Fraunhofer Institute for Computer Graphics, Wilhelminenstr. 7, 64283 Darmstadt, Germany

Abstract

The radiosity method became a very important tool in order to enable photorealistic rendering in virtual reality systems. Based on the geometric description of a scene, the view-independent illumination is computed in a preprocess and colors are assigned to each patch vertex. These virtual environments look very impressive, but any interaction with the scene geometry or its materials results in a time expensive recalculation of the radiosity simulation. This leads to the common phrase:

Radiosity scenes are like museums,
you may look around, but do not touch anything!

In this paper, a new algorithm is presented to overcome this problem. The algorithm is based on the fact that most of the information needed for the radiosity repropagation after any scene modification was already computed during the radiosity preprocess. Therefore, the radiosity method is extended by storing shadow- and form-factor-information in an efficient data structure, the so-called shadow-form-factor-list (SFFL). We describe how the SFFL can be used to minimize the recomputation time after any scene modification. Moreover, very important information about scene coherence is included within the SFFL. Thus, an efficient traversal of the SFFL helps to repropagate radiosity only in those parts of the scene, that are affected by the model change.

1 Introduction

Virtual reality (VR) characterizes a fascinating technology, which enables the user to experience computer simulated data immersively. Using modern graphics hardware, we are able to render even complex scenes with several frames per second, taking textures and direct illumination of "hardware light sources" into account. However, the quality of these images does not satisfy user requirements in many cases. Because of missing shadows and the simple illumination simulation, it is often very difficult to orientate oneself and to understand the contents of the virtual environments. The radiosity method [13], [10], [11] can be used to overcome this problem. After subdividing the surfaces of the scene geometry in a set of patches, the global illumination can be simulated in a preprocess. The resulting vertex colors of the patches can then be mapped as textures onto the surrounding surface without losing any rendering performance. Some VR-systems are using this technology [2], especially for virtual presentations of architecture and interior design. One problem still remains: whenever there is a change in position, shape or attributes of any object in the scene, the entire illumination process has to be repeated. But even modern workstation processors are not fast enough to compute a radiosity solution within an acceptable response time. Thus, the fascinating image quality provided by a radiosity preprocess can only be supported for static virtual environments.

Interacting with any object of the scene tends to be local and affects only small parts of the illumination process. The challenge therefore is to reuse information which is already provided by the radiosity preprocess and exploiting coherences of the scene, in order to identify small parts affected by the change. Buckalew & Fussell [7] suggested such an idea for ray-tracing purposes. Illumination links are determined by connecting visible surfaces in a preprocess and are used to update scene modifications progressively. Baum et al. [3] presented a radiosity based algorithm for dynamic environments where the paths of moving objects have been predefined. This approach is restricted to the usage of the hemi-cube algorithm [9] and is unfortunately limited to animation sequences.

Another method was presented by Chen [8] and George et al. [12]. Starting from an existing radiosity solution computed using the progressive refinement radiosity algorithm [10], any change in the scene results in the computation of an *incremental radiosity* (the difference of the existing radiosity and the new radiosity corresponding to the change). The incremental radiosity is then *redistributed* (following the nomenclature of George et al.) in the same manner as distributing the unshot radiosity in the progressive refinement process. For example, turning off a light source will result in shooting *negative light* from the light source. Both algorithms proved to be faster than repeating the radiosity process from scratch. However, the obtained results are still too slow for virtual environments, because valuable CPU-time is wasted for recalculating information already computed during the progressive refinement step.

Our new algorithm combines the advantages of both ideas by recording information computed during the illumination preprocess in a shadow-form-factor-list. Starting from an existing radiosity solution only iterations affected by any change in the environment are repeated (*repropagated*), adopting the concept of incremental radiosities. Thus, radiosity changes can be identified easily and updated very fast. This process is also in the spirit of progressive refinement and runs independently of the rendering loop.

2 The Extended Progressive Refinement Method

The progressive refinement method [10] solves the diffuse global-illumination problem iteratively for environments made up of polygonal patches. At each iteration t, the patch with the most unshot radiosity is chosen as the *shooting patch* (marked with the index s_t). Form-factors from the shooting patch to all patches of the environment have to be computed next. The unshot and absolute radiosities of each patch i at iteration t (with $t \geq 1$) are given by the following iterative equations:

Absolute radiosity: $\qquad\qquad B_i^t = B_i^{t-1} + \rho_i \cdot \Delta B_{s_t}^{t-1} \cdot F_{i,s_t}$ $\qquad\qquad$ (1)

Unshot radiosity: $\qquad\qquad \Delta B_i^t = \Delta B_i^{t-1} + \rho_i \cdot \Delta B_{s_t}^{t-1} \cdot F_{i,s_t}$ $\qquad\qquad$ (2)

where:

$B_i^0 = \Delta B_i^0 = E_i$: $\qquad\qquad$ the starting values for the absolute and the unshot radiosities are set to the patch emission.

$\Delta B_{s_t}^{t-1} = \max\{\Delta B_i^{t-1}\}$: the patch with the maximum unshot radiosity after iteration t-1 is selected as the shooting patch (s_t) for iteration t.

$\Delta B_{s_t}^t = 0$: $\qquad\qquad$ after shooting at iteration t, the unshot radiosity of patch s_t is set to zero.

The unshot radiosity that was distributed to the environment at iteration t is also denoted as ΔB^t, whereby $\Delta B^t = \Delta B_{s_t}^{t-1}$.

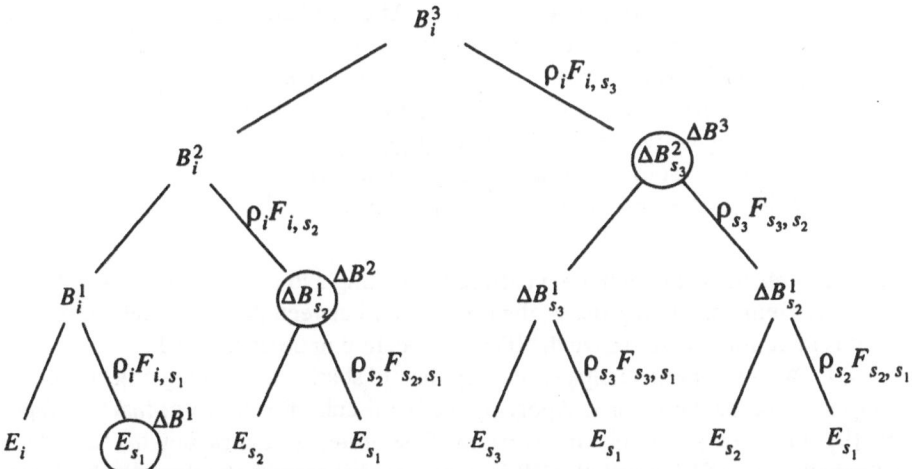

Fig. 1. The absolute radiosity of patch i after 3 iterations. Patch-IDs are represented by subscripts, iteration numbers by superscripts. IDs of shooting patches are marked with an index s_t, where t is the iteration number. The unshot radiosities distributed to patch i at each iteration are circled.

An example of the first three iterations of the absolute radiosity of any patch i is given in Fig. 1. Regarding the lower left subtree, the absolute radiosity of patch i at the first iteration is obtained from its emission plus the unshot radiosity of the shooting patch (s_1) at iteration 1 (weighted by the factor connected to the right branch). At iteration 2, the absolute radiosity B_i^2 depends on the unshot radiosity of sending patch s_2, which depends on the unshot radiosity of patch s_1 etc. The tree for the unshot radiosity values can be determined analogously.

For a presentation of a scene in VR we compute n progressive refinement iterations in a preprocess (n might be user defined or automatically decided by defining a threshold of the maximum unshot radiosity that has to be distributed to the scene). As we can see in Fig. 1, the precomputed radiosities have to be updated, if the user changes reflectivities, emissions or form-factors within the *iteration-trees* of all patches. Usually, such a change will not affect all precomputed information, like unshot radiosities or form-factors. Therefore, a first approach would be to extend the progressive refinement preprocess by storing unshot radiosities and form-factors in an efficient data structure. After any scene modification, the same iterations are repeated again by updating only the data affected by the change.

Although this method seems to be faster than starting the entire radiosity simulation from scratch, there remain two problems: first, the repropagation would start with a non-illuminated scene, ignoring the existing radiosity distribution. Secondly, this approach is still too slow, because all iterations are repeated, which is not necessary in most cases. For example, if the reflectivity of patches is changed, which did not shoot during the progressive refinement process, it would be sufficient to update their radiosities and no iteration has to be repeated.

Therefore, we adopt the concept of incremental radiosities of George et al. [12] and Chen [8]. Starting from the existing radiosity solution, any scene modification results in the computation of incremental radiosities. After updating the *primary* effects, the same iterations as in the preprocess are repeated by adding incremental radiosities to the existing radiosity values, but only if the iteration is affected by the change. This process is called *repropagation* (in contrast to the *redistribution* method of George et al., where the progressive refinement is continued from the existing solution). This method is also in the spirit of progressive refinement (e.g., if an object is moved, the old shadow disappears and the new shadow is added independently of the rendering loop).

If an object obstructs the light path between a sending and a receiving patch during the progressive refinement preprocess, the form-factor between them becomes zero. In this case it is more important to save the ID of the occluding object instead of the form-factor itself. This information helps to identify the old shadow of moving objects very fast during the repropagation pass. Applying the hemi-cube for the form-factor computation [9] does not yield this information. Therefore, a ray-tracing based radiosity method similar to Wallace et al. [17] is used. Starting from a shooting patch, shadow-feelers are sent towards all patch midpoints of the environment. If a receiving patch is visible from the shooting patch, the form-factor is computed by the prism method [4]. Otherwise the ID of the occluding object is returned. To speed up the intersection calculation, the bounding volume hierarchy suggested by Kay & Kajiya [16] is used in combination with a priority-queue for an efficient traversal.

We now describe how the progressive refinement method is extended in order to keep information needed for the repropagation pass. All iterations are recorded in a shooting list, while the shadow- and form-factor-information is saved in a shadow-form-factor-list. The radiosity update and the repropagation pass are described in section 3.

Shooting List and Shadow-Form-Factor-List

The shooting list (SL) is a dynamic array containing the data displayed in Fig. 2. For each iteration t during the radiosity preprocess (with $1 \leq t \leq n$, where n is the total number of iterations) a shooting patch is selected and its ID and its unshot radiosity are recorded in the SL. For each shooting patch the index of its first SL-entry (*SL-index*) is assigned to the patch data structure. If a patch is selected as a shooter again, the next-pointer of its last SL-entry is set to the next SL-entry (e.g., in Fig. 2 the shooting patches of iteration 1 and 3 are identical. The SL-index of this patch points to the SL-entry 1, while the next-pointer of SL-entry 1 points to SL-entry 3).

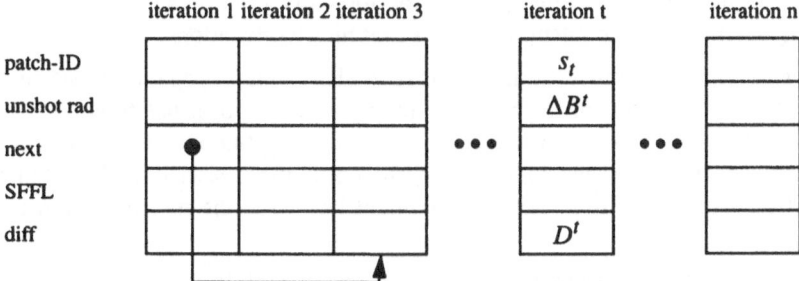

Fig. 2. The shooting list. For each iteration, the ID and the unshot radiosity of the shooting patch is recorded. The next-entry points to the next SL-entry of this patch within the shooting list. SFFL contains a pointer to the shadow-form-factor-list. The incremental radiosity (*diff*) is explained in the repropagation section.

At each iteration, shadow-feelers are shot from the midpoint of the selected shooting patch towards each patch midpoint of the environment. For all receiving patches, the form-factor between the shooting and the receiving patch is stored in a shadow-form-factor-list (SFFL), if there is no obstacle between them. Otherwise, the ID of the occluding object is stored (see Fig. 3).

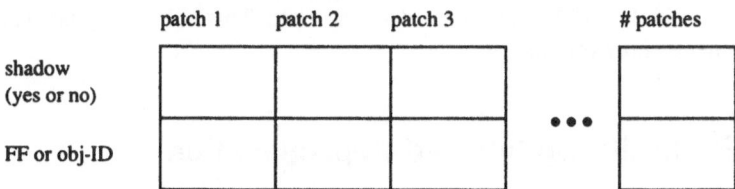

Fig. 3. The shadow-form-factor-list. For each patch the first boolean entry describes, whether the second entry contains a form-factor between this patch and the shooting patch (of the related iteration), or the ID of an occluding object.

Note, that the SFFL can be used to speed up the progressive refinement step. If a patch is selected as a shooting patch again, the existing form-factors can be reused following the SL-index of this patch. However, we need to copy the SFFL for any further SL-entry of this patch instead of pointing to the first instance in order to guarantee a consistent repropagation pass (see section 4 for further details).

Memory Requirements and Efficiency

The amount of additional memory required by this approach is:

- All allocated SFFLs: #iterations • #patches • 8 byte
- SL: #iterations • 20 byte
- Additional SL-index at each patch: #patches • 4 byte

In our current VR-system, the upper limit for the number of patches is around 20 000, in order to enable a real-time walk-through with an acceptable frame-rate on an SGI Reality Engine. Using 100 iterations in the radiosity preprocess, around 16 MB are needed, which is not a problem on today's graphics workstations.

As we can see, the memory requirements (and also the repropagation time) depend on the number of iterations of the radiosity preprocess. The user has to choose between image quality and system response time by controlling this number. However, this is not really a problem because in VR it is sufficient in most cases to use only a few iterations by adjusting an user controlled ambient term (see the results section for more details).

In order to identify the shadow of a moving object rapidly during the repropagation pass, only one shadow-feeler is sent from each receiving patch to the current sending patch. Therefore, no partial occlusion is taken into account. However, these shadow-feelers lead to correct values, if an intelligent patch subdivision algorithm is used, which guarantees small patches at high radiosity gradients [1], [11].

Some VR-systems distinguish between *static* and *dynamic* objects in order to speed up the collision detection. The user can only interact with *dynamic* objects, which are especially marked in an input file by defining their physical behavior or their degrees of freedom for user interaction. For these systems it is useful to extend the shadow-feeler concept. If a *dynamic* object is detected as an obstacle between a shooting and a receiving patch, the shadow test is continued by preferring the storage of *static* occluding objects within the SFFL rather than *dynamic* ones. This helps to update shadows of modified objects more efficiently.

3 Fast Radiosity Update and Repropagation

Any scene modification results in the computation of incremental radiosities which are applied for updating two kinds of effects. The *primary* effects are directly related to the existing absolute radiosities B_i^n and eventually to the existing unshot radiosities ΔB_i^n of the modified patches, if they have not been selected as shooting patches during the radiosity preprocess. Otherwise, we have to assign the incremental radiosities to the related SL-entries and to update all *secondary* effects by a repropagation pass. It is important to emphasize that all existing absolute and unshot radiosities as well as all SL- and SFFL-entries have to be restored in a consistent manner to be able to continue the progressive refinement process if necessary.

In this section, the evaluation of incremental radiosities caused by a material change and the update of the primary effects are described. It is followed by the explanation of the repropagation pass. This pass is also used for handling geometry changes, which will be described in the next section.

Changing Patch Emission E

After changing a radiosity emission, the incremental radiosity D is computed by subtracting the old emission value from the new one:

$$D = E^{\text{new}} - E^{\text{old}} \tag{3}$$

Usually, patch emissions belong to surface materials. If we change a material emission, we have to identify all patches i referencing this material. For each patch i the existing radiosity is updated by:

$$B_i^{n, \text{new}} = B_i^n + D \tag{4}$$

The unshot radiosities of these patches are also obtained by adding D to the existing unshot radiosities ΔB_i^n, but only if these patches did not shoot any radiosity during the preprocess (i.e., if their SL-index is undefined). Otherwise, D is added to the *diff*-entry of the first SL-item of each patch i (see Fig. 2) by dereferencing its SL-index. In this case, the incremental radiosities need to be repropagated after updating all primary effects.

Changing Patch Reflectivity ρ

If we change the reflectivity of a material, we also have to identify all patches i referencing this material. If the value of the old reflectivity was not equal zero, the incremental radiosity D_i is given by:

$$D_i = (\rho^{\text{new}} - \rho^{\text{old}}) \cdot \frac{B_i^n - E_i}{\rho^{\text{old}}} \qquad \text{if } \rho^{\text{old}} \neq 0 \tag{5}$$

Otherwise, the incremental radiosity D_i is evaluated by repeating the n iterations for all patches i and exploiting the form-factors stored within the SFFLs:

$$D_i = \rho^{\text{new}} \sum_{t=1}^{n} \Delta B^t F_{i, s_t} \qquad \text{if } \rho^{\text{old}} = 0 \tag{6}$$

For each patch i, the existing radiosities are again updated by:

$$B_i^{n,\,new} = B_i^n + D_i \tag{7}$$

If the SL-index of i is not defined (the patch did not shoot any radiosity during the pre-process), D_i is also added to the existing unshot radiosities ΔB_i^n. Otherwise, the update process is more complex as in the previous paragraph, because now we have to restore the existing unshot radiosities and the *diff*-entries of <u>all</u> SL-entries of this patch.

The new unshot radiosity is given by[1]:

$$\Delta B_i^{n,\,new} = \frac{\rho^{new}}{\rho^{old}} \Delta B_i^n \tag{8}$$

Then, the first iteration t_1, where patch i was selected as a shooting patch, is obtained by dereferencing its SL-index. The incremental radiosity D^{t_1} added to the *diff*-item of SL-entry t_1 is given by[2]:

$$D^{t_1} = (\rho^{new} - \rho^{old}) \cdot \frac{\Delta B^{t_1} - E_i}{\rho^{old}} \tag{9}$$

For all other SL-entries t' of patch i, $D^{t'}$ is added to the related *diff*-entries[3]:

$$D^{t'} = (\rho^{new} - \rho^{old}) \cdot \frac{\Delta B^{t'}}{\rho^{old}} \tag{10}$$

After updating all primary effects, the incremental radiosities need to be repropagated.

Repropagation

As described in the previous paragraphs, the update of primary effects might result in *diff*-entries within the SL, which means those incremental radiosities have to be repropagated.

Therefore, we start at the first entry of the SL with an incremental radiosity (*diff*) not equal zero. For each patch of the environment, the incremental radiosity for this iteration has to be added to its existing radiosity by reusing the form-factors stored in the

---

[1] If ρ^{old} is zero, the unshot radiosity of i has to be recomputed by an equation similar to Eq. 6 adding over all entries from its last SL-entry plus 1 until n.

[2] If ρ^{old} is zero, Eq. 6 is applied by adding over all entries from 1 until t_1-1.

[3] If ρ^{old} is zero, Eq. 6 is applied by adding over all entries from the index of its previous shot plus 1 until t'-1.

related SFFL. The radiosity change of any receiving patch i at iteration t is given by the following equation (note that the new reflectivity value has to be used).

$$B_i^{n, \text{new}} = B_i^n + \rho_i \cdot D^t \cdot F_{i, s_t} \tag{11}$$

If patch i does not appear as a shooter in the SL at an iteration greater than t, the unshot radiosity of this patch can be updated in the same way. Otherwise, we have to find this iteration t' (starting with the SL-index of patch i and following the *next*-pointers within the SL until we find an iteration $t' > t$) and the incremental radiosity $D^{t'}$ is updated by:

$$D^{t', \text{new}} = D^{t'} + \rho_i \cdot D^t \cdot F_{i, s_t} \tag{12}$$

Finally, the unshot radiosity stored in the SL at iteration t is updated by

$$\Delta B^{t, \text{new}} = \Delta B^t + D^t \tag{13}$$

and the incremental radiosity is deleted:

$$D^t = 0 \tag{14}$$

The entire process is repeated with the next SL-entry with an incremental radiosity unequal zero, until the end of the SL is reached.

Example

The update- and repropagation-algorithm can be illustrated by a simple example as shown in Fig. 4. Three iterations are preprocessed; the order of the shooting patches is 1, 2 and 3. The radiosity of patch 4 is examined; its iteration-tree is similar to the one displayed in Fig. 1. We describe the repropagation after changing the emission of patch 1.

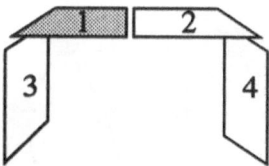

Fig. 4. A simple environment consisting of four patches. Patches 1 and 2 are light sources with an emission greater than zero. Three iterations are recorded in the SL; the order of the shooting patches is 1, 2, 3. Note, that the form-factor between 1 and 2 is zero.

First, the primary effect of patch 1 after modifying E_1 is taken into account by adding the incremental radiosity to its existing value (see Eq. 3 and Eq. 4). The SL-index of patch 1 points to the first SL-entry. Therefore, the incremental radiosity is also added to the *diff*-entry of the first SL-item. The actual situation of patch 4 is shown in Fig. 4.a (see Fig. 1 for more details about the iteration-tree). The black color indicates the validity of the already computed radiosity values at each node, that can be guaranteed at this repropagation step.

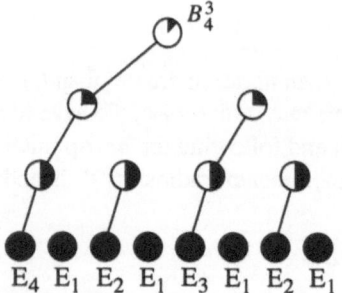

E_4 E_1 E_2 E_1 E_3 E_1 E_2 E_1

Fig. 4.a. After processing the primary effect, all emission values become valid. The *diff*-entry at iteration 1 corrects the already propagated unshot radiosity, but is not yet "linked" (repropagated) to the existing results.

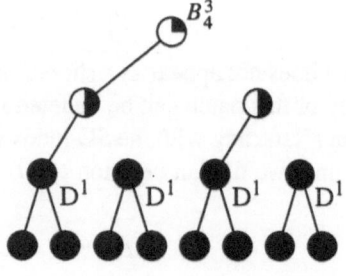

Fig. 4.b. The incremental radiosity D^1 is added to the existing radiosity of patch 4 and to the following SL-*diff*-entries (displayed as a link).

In Fig. 4.b the first repropagation step is displayed. D^1 is added to the existing radiosity of patch 4 (using Eq. 11) and D^2 and D^3 at the second and third SL-entry are increased (using Eq. 12). Note, that D^2 remains zero, since no radiosity was propagated from patch 1 towards patch 2.

The second step normally updates the values shown in Fig. 4.c. In our example, the value of D^2 is zero. Therefore, we continue with the last step by adding D^3 to the existing radiosity of patch 4.

All other patches are processed in the same manner. As we can see, the repropagation pass needs only two steps and no form-factor has to be recalculated.

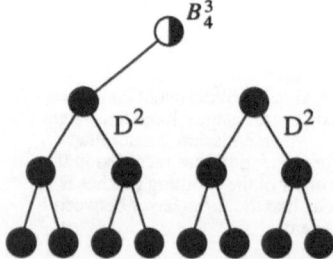

Fig. 4.c. D^2 is zero, therefore no propagation is executed.

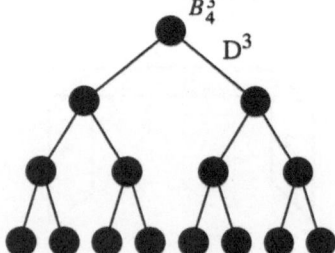

Fig. 4.d. During the last step the incremental radiosity D^3 is added to the existing radiosity of patch 4.

Pseudo-Code

The repropagation algorithm is described in the following pseudo-code:

*function **repropagate***
{

    for each entry t *of the shooting list with* $D^t \neq 0$:
    {

        for each patch i:
        {

$$F_{i, s_t} = SFFL_t(i)$$

$$B_i^{n, new} = B_i^n + \rho_i \cdot D^t \cdot F_{i, s_t}$$

            if i *shot radiosity at iteration* t' *with* t' > t:

$$D^{t', new} = D^{t'} + \rho_i \cdot D^t \cdot F_{i, s_t}$$

            else

$$\Delta B_i^{n, new} = \Delta B_i^n + \rho_i \cdot D^t \cdot F_{i, s_t}$$

        }

        $\Delta B^{t, new} = \Delta B^t + D^t$

        $D^t = 0$

    }
}

4 Changing Scene Geometry

Geometry changes are more time consuming tasks than attribute changes, since form-factors have to be recomputed. Any geometry change can be reduced to a *delete-object* and an *add-object* problem, whereby an object consists of a list of patches. If the user activates an object (e.g., by grabbing it with the data-glove) in order to move it or to change its shape, the object is deleted from the illumination simulation. If the user deactivates the object after finishing his interaction, it is added to the illumination process again. We have to solve four kinds of problems:

delete-object

- the patch radiosities of the deleted object have to be removed (this task can be neglected, since these patch radiosities will be recomputed after adding the object to the scene again).

- the old shadow of the deleted object has to be removed by shooting additional light into its old shadow area.

add-object

- The patch radiosities of the added object have to be updated.

- The new shadow has to be added to the scene by shooting negative light into the new shadow area.

The challenge is to identify radiosity changes caused by the mentioned tasks very fast and to exploit as many existing form-factors within the SFFL as possible. A shadow might appear according to each shooting patch. Therefore, we have to consider all entries t of the SL.

The radiosity update process is very similar to the one described in the previous section. Any geometry change results in the computation of incremental radiosities, which are directly applied to the existing radiosities of the affected patches and their SL-entries, if these patches have been selected as shooting patches during the radiosity preprocess.

If shooting patches are changed, all SFFL-entries related to these patches become invalid. In this case there is no other way than recomputing their SFFLs.

We only describe the evaluation of the incremental radiosity D caused by the modeling change. After each step, the existing radiosities have to be updated by applying Eq. 4. The unshot radiosity of each modified patch i is obtained by adding D to the existing unshot radiosities ΔB_i^n, but only if this patch did not shoot any radiosity at an iteration t' with $t' > t$. Otherwise, D is added to the *diff*-entry of iteration t'. Finally, the incremental radiosities need to be repropagated in a repropagation pass, as described in the previous section. The repropagation pass only needs to be processed once after accumulating all incremental radiosities caused by a *delete-object-* and an *add-object*-operation.

Delete Shadow

For each iteration the IDs of objects, which obstructed the light path from a shooting patch to any receiving patch, are recorded within the SFFL. Therefore, removing the shadow of the selected object (O_{select}) from the environment becomes an easy task. For each entry t of the SL, we have to check all SFFL-entries. If O_{select} is found as an occluding object at SFFL-index i, we have to send a new shadow-feeler from the sending patch s_t towards patch i. If another obstacle is detected, the SFFL-entry is replaced by the new object-ID. Otherwise the new form-factor F_{i, s_t} is computed and stored in the SFFL. The incremental radiosity is then determined by:

$$D_i = \rho_i \cdot \Delta B^t \cdot F_{i, s_t} \tag{15}$$

Note, if a patch appears multiple times within the SL (it was selected as a shooting patch more than once), there is a copy of the SFFL at each SL-entry. Otherwise the information about the occluding objects would become inconsistent after the first SFFL update. However, the new form-factors only need to be computed for the first SFFL-copy and can be reused for all other SL-entries of this patch.

Add Shadow

For each entry t of the SL, we have to rapidly identify all patches which are occluded by the new object (O_{select}) according to the shooting patch s_t. Therefore, a shadow-volume [14] is constructed from each shooting patch s_t to determine a list of candidate objects. For each patch i of a candidate object we check the SFFL, whether i is already occluded by another object. If not, a shadow-feeler is sent towards s_t, which only needs to be tested against the new object. If O_{select} is hit by this ray, Eq. 15 is again applied to determine the incremental radiosity by reusing the old form-factor of the SFFL-entry. Finally, the SFFL- entry is replaced by O_{select}.

If an object is deleted and added again to the environment, it only appears as an occluding object within the SFFLs, if no other object obstructs the light path between the related sending and receiving patch. Thus, moving this object again might be updated faster, because shadow-feelers are only tested, if they are really necessary. If the VR-system distinguishes between static and dynamic objects, this effect helps to minimize the recomputation time by preferring the storage of static objects as occluding objects within the SFFL rather than dynamic ones (as mentioned in the section "Memory Requirements and Efficiency").

Update Patch Radiosities of Moving Objects

After adding an object to the scene, we have to remove the old illumination from its surface patches by exploiting the old SFFLs. Then, the new radiosities are computed and the SFFL-entries are restored. For each shooting patch s_t of the SL, all patches i of the selected object are considered.

For the evaluation of the incremental radiosities, we have to distinguish four cases:

1. Patch i was occluded before the change, but is visible from s_t now: we have to compute the new form-factor and store it in the SFFL.

$$D_i = \rho_i \cdot \Delta B^t \cdot F_{i,s_t}^{new} \qquad (16)$$

2. Patch i was visible before the change, but is occluded now by an object O_{hit}: we have to replace the old form-factor of the SFFL-entry by O_{hit}.

$$D_i = -\rho_i \cdot \Delta B^t \cdot F_{i,s_t}^{old} \qquad (17)$$

3. Patch i was visible before and remains visible: the new form-factor has to be computed and the SFFL-entry is replaced.

$$D_i = \rho_i \cdot \Delta B^t \cdot \left(F_{i,s_t}^{new} - F_{i,s_t}^{old} \right) \qquad (18)$$

4. Patch i was occluded before and is now occluded by another object: the SFFL-entry is replaced by the new object-ID and no radiosity is modified.

$$D_i = 0 \tag{19}$$

As discussed in the previous paragraph, a shadow volume is constructed from a shooting patch over the added object, in order to find the new shadow more efficiently. This volume can also be exploited to speed up the shadow-tests for the patches of the moved objects.

Moving a Shooting Patch

If patches are moved, which appear as shooting patches within the SL, the related SFFLs have to be recomputed. For each receiving patch i the same four cases as discussed in the previous paragraph are distinguished. But now, all entries of the SFFL are updated in contrast to the previous case, where only the SFFL-entries of the moved patches have been recalculated.

5 Repropagation vs. Redistribution

Our proposed repropagation algorithm repeats the same iterations as in the radiosity preprocess after any scene modification. The advantage of this method is, that most of the already precomputed data can be reused for a fast radiosity update and the recomputation effort is obviously minimized. But for the effectiveness of this approach it is very important to obtain as much information in the preprocess as possible. If the user switches on a light source which had been turned off during the radiosity preprocess, more progressive refinement iterations would be necessary after the repropagation pass. In this case, the system is able to suggest further iterations, because all absolute and unshot radiosities as well as all SL- and SFFL-entries are updated in a consistent manner during the repropagation pass. Thus, the user could still control image quality during the VR-presentation. On the other hand, the system could suggest a "garbage collection" of the SL, if shooting patches become unimportant after a scene modification (e.g., when a shooting patch is shadowed by a moved object).

Most of the described problems can be avoided if the user already takes care at the radiosity preprocess that all important patches appear within the SL (by switching on all light sources, adding all objects to the scene, setting all reflectivities unequal zero and selecting the iteration number accordingly). Another possibility would be to extend the SL by interactively selecting patches which have to be processed during the radiosity preprocess in order to obtain the important data needed for the interactive VR-session.

The redistribution approach of George et al. [12] and Chen [8] overcomes this problem by continuing the progressive refinement anyway after each scene modification. Sophisticated algorithms are presented to identify the shooting patches, which might contribute negative radiosity to the scene. The concept of our proposed SFFL can easily be adopted to speed up the redistribution algorithm as well (i.e., identifying patches occluded by moving objects and reusing already computed form-factors). But since an arbitrary patch might be selected as a shooting patch in the redistribution pass, the SFFL will fail frequently and new form-factors from the new shooting patch to all receiving patches have to be computed. By yielding always correct results, this algorithm will usually need more computing time.

It seems that our repropagation algorithm is better suited for the requirements of VR, while the redistribution method is more important for lighting simulation programs. In the field of VR, the system response time is more important than image quality. Using the repropagation method, the user can avoid time demanding form-factor calculations by controlling the described parameters of the radiosity preprocess. He is able to decide between fast interaction feed-back or high image quality during the VR-presentation.

6 Results

The algorithm we have presented is integrated into our interactive lighting simulation program GENESIS, which combines radiosity-, ray-tracing- and fast rendering-facilities. The system allows interactive walk-through and any kind of scene modification, like changing surface attributes (colors, radiosity-emissions, textures, etc.), improving scene topology (e.g., defining object hierarchies) or moving objects (translating, rotating, scaling). GENESIS is mainly used as a preprocessor for preparing CAD-data for a photorealistic presentation in our VR-system [2]. It is also used as a research testbed for the development of new algorithms in order to improve rendering-speed and -quality for virtual environments.

The user is able to specify the number of radiosity iterations or a convergence threshold for the maximum unshot radiosity that has to be distributed. During the radiosity process, the described SL- and SFFL-entries are obtained automatically. Any radiosity recalculation is executed concurrently to the rendering loop. After changing surface attributes or activating respectively deactivating objects, a recalculation process is started, while the user is able to continue navigating through the virtual environment. In our current implementation, the interaction is restricted to one modification at a time, i.e. the user can only modify the scene, if the last repropagation process is finished.

An approach, which proved to be very useful for VR, is the usage of virtual point light sources as fake radiosity emitters. These are defined as normal point light sources and treated first during the radiosity preprocess. From each point light source, shadow-feelers are sent towards all patch midpoints, similar to a progressive refinement step. The form-factor calculation is reduced to a cosine term, as in the traditional Phong-illumination-model, and a user-defined ambient term is adjusted to the scene. Thus, the illumination results are similar to those using hardware shading facilities. But shadows of objects appear and rendering becomes faster, because no more shading has to be processed. For the scenes of Fig. 7 - Fig. 10 (see color plate 12) only the direct illumination of virtual point light sources has been used. Thus, the number of iterations and the repropagation time have been reduced drastically while getting a very good image quality. After processing all virtual light sources, the normal radiosity process can be continued in order to take interreflection into account.

Several tests were conducted to determine the effectiveness of the proposed algorithm. All of the timing data were obtained from performing the computation on a Silicon Graphics 310 Reality Engine. The displayed scenes are typical VR-environments rendered with more than 10 frames/sec. For all presented images, only the direct illumination of emitting patches (Fig. 5 and Fig. 6, see color plate 12) or virtual point light sources (Fig. 7 - Fig. 10, see color plate 12) have been used, in order to demonstrate the image quality already achieved after a small number of iterations. For better comparison, the time values after 100 iterations are displayed, too.

Model	#patches	rend. time frames / sec	additional memory		radiosity preprocess	
			dir. ill.	100 iter.	dir. ill.	100 iter.
VR lab (fig. 5)	14 675	12	0.6 MB (4 iter.)	12 MB	42 sec (4 iter.)	434 sec
airport (fig. 7)	15 734	11	0.7 MB (5 iter.)	13 MB	136 sec (5 iter.)	785 sec
office (fig. 9)	11 296	13	0.5 MB (5 iter.)	10 MB	63 sec (5 iter.)	347 sec

Table 1. Information about the test scenes; the additional memory requirements needed for the SFFLs are also shown.

In Table 1 detailed information about the models is displayed, which had been used for the tests. The time needed to update the radiosity distribution after several scene modifications is shown in Table 2.

Model	model change	dir. ill.	100 iter.
VR lab (fig. 6)	moving chair	1.5 sec	20 sec
	moving terminal	0.7 sec	12 sec
	dimming 2 light sources	0.3 sec	5 sec
airport (fig. 8)	changing reflectivity	0.2 sec	0.2 sec
office (fig. 10)	deleting table and chairs	0.6 sec	6 sec

Table 2. Radiosity update times.

As we can see, the update of attribute changes can be performed nearly in real-time, while the repropagation time after moving, adding or deleting objects depends drastically on the amount of scene patches and the number of precomputed iterations: the more patches already shot during the preprocess, the more shadows have to be updated. Thus, the user can decide between high image quality or short interaction response time by controlling radiosity preprocess parameters.

7 Conclusions and Further Work

We have extended the progressive refinement radiosity method by saving information computed during the radiosity preprocess in an efficient data structure. The new repropagation algorithm exploits this data and scene coherences to update the existing radiosity solution when a change in the environment takes place. The algorithm is well suited for the requirements of VR and enables the usage of radiosity methods also in dynamic virtual environments. The user is able to decide between very high image quality or very fast system response after any scene modification within the VR-presentation by controlling preprocess parameters.

If the user changes surface attributes, the radiosity values can be updated nearly in real-time. The shadow of a moving object is updated concurrently to the rendering loop after the object is activated or deactivated. To support better user interaction, a fast feed-back should be provided, like a fake shadow [6] which can be created in real-time during the object movement.

Our current implementation is restricted to one modification at a time. Before modifying the scene, the user has to wait until the previous repropagation is finished. Future research should include a sophisticated log-mechanism suggested by George et al. [12] or a geometry-queue technique described by Chen [8] by accumulating all changes and updating them in an efficient manner.

Typically, the patch subdivision is well suited for a static virtual environment. Moving an object into areas of low patch resolutions might result in disagreeable scene artifacts. Therefore, the combination of our repropagation algorithm with mesh redistribution [1], adaptive meshing techniques [5] or hierarchical radiosity [15] is an important point for future research.

8 Acknowledgements

Many thanks to Dirk Reiners and Matthias Unbescheiden for their constant support and implementation of important tools of Genesis. Thanks to Alex Prilop, Hans Joseph and Peter Fritzen for careful proofreading of the first version of this paper.

The VR lab was modelled by Rolf Kruse assisted by Eva Irrek. Thanks to Wilkhahn and Markus Huth from Cad&Art for supporting us with the office- and the airport scene.

References

1. Águas, Miguel P.N., Stefan Müller, "Mesh Redistribution in Radiosity," 4th Eurographics Workshop on Rendering, Paris, France, June 1993, pp. 327 - 335.
2. Astheimer, Peter, Wolfgang Felger, Stefan Müller, "Virtual Design: A Generic VR System For Industrial Applications," *Computers & Graphics*, Vol. 17, No. 6, December 1993, pp. 671 - 678.
3. Baum, Daniel R., John R. Wallace, Michael F. Cohen, Donald P. Greenberg, "The Back-Buffer: An Extension of the Radiosity-Method to Dynamic Environments," *The Visual Computer*, Vol. 2, No. 5, 1986, pp. 298-306.
4. Baum, Daniel R., Holly E. Rushmeier, J. M. Winget. "Improving Radiosity Solutions Through the Use of Analytically Determined Form-Factors," *ACM Computer Graphics (SIGGRAPH '89 Proceedings)*, Vol. 23, No. 3, July 1989, pp. 325-334.
5. Baum, Daniel R., S. Mann, K. P. Smith, J. M. Winget, "Making Radiosity Usable: Automatic Preprocessing and Meshing Techniques for the Generation of Accurate Radiosity Solutions", *ACM Computer Graphics (SIGGRAPH '91 Proceedings)*, Vol. 25, No. 4, July 1991, pp. 51-60.
6. Blinn, James F., "Jim Blinn´s Corner: Me and My (Fake) Shadow," *IEEE Computer Graphics & Applications*, Vol. 8, No. 1, July 1988, pp. 82 - 86.
7. Buckalew, Chris, Donald Fussell, "Illumination Networks: Fast Realistic Rendering with General Reflectance Functions," *ACM Computer Graphics (SIGGRAPH '89 Proceedings)*, Vol. 23, No. 3, July 1989, pp. 89-98.
8. Chen, Shenchang E., "Incremental Radiosity: An Extension of Progressive Radiosity to an Interactive Image Synthesis System," *ACM Computer Graphics (SIGGRAPH '90 Proceedings)*, Vol. 24, No. 4, August 1990, pp. 135-144.
9. Cohen, Michael F., Donald P. Greenberg, "The Hemi-Cube: A Radiosity Solution for Complex Environments," *ACM Computer Graphics (SIGGRAPH '85 Proceedings)*, Vol. 19, No. 3, July 1985, pp. 31-40.
10. Cohen, Michael F., Shenchang Eric Chen, John R.Wallace, Donald P. Greenberg, "A Progressive Refinement Approach to Fast Radiosity Image Generation," *ACM Computer Graphics (SIGGRAPH '88 Proceedings)*, Vol. 22, No. 4, August 1988, pp. 75-84.
11. Cohen, Michael F., John R.Wallace, *Radiosity and Realistic Image Synthesis*, Academic Press Professional, New York, 1993.
12. George, David W., François X. Sillion, Donald P. Greenberg, "Radiosity Redistribution for Dynamic Environments," *IEEE Computer Graphics & Applications*, Vol. 10, No. 4, July 1990, pp. 26 - 34.
13. Goral, Cindy M., Kenneth E. Torrance, Donald P. Greenberg, Bennet Battaile, "Modeling the Interaction of Light Between Diffuse Surfaces," *ACM Computer Graphics (SIGGRAPH '84 Proceedings)*, Vol. 18, No. 3, July 1984, pp. 213-222.
14. Haines, Eric A., John R.Wallace, "Shaft Culling for Efficient Ray-Traced Radiosity," 2nd Eurographics Workshop on Rendering, Barcelona, Spain, May 1991.
15. Hanrahan P., D. Salzman, L. Aupperle, "A Rapid Hierarchical Radiosity Algorithm", *ACM Computer Graphics (SIGGRAPH '91 Proceedings)*, Vol. 25, No. 4, July 1991, pp. 197 - 206.
16. Kay, T. L., James T. Kajiya, "Ray Tracing Complex Scenes," *ACM Computer Graphics (SIGGRAPH '86 Proceedings)*, Vol. 20, No. 4, August 1986, pp. 269-278.
17. Wallace, John R., Kells A. Elmquist, Eric A. Haines, "A Ray Tracing Algorithm For Progressive Radiosity," *ACM Computer Graphics (SIGGRAPH '89 Proceedings)*, Vol. 23, No. 3, July 1989, pp. 315-324.

An Efficient Progressive Refinement Strategy for Hierarchical Radiosity

Nicolas Holzschuch, François Sillion, George Drettakis

iMAGIS / IMAG, B.P. 53, F-38041 Grenoble Cedex 9, France

Abstract

A detailed study of the performance of hierarchical radiosity is presented, which confirms that visibility computation is the most expensive operation. Based on the analysis of the algorithm's behavior, two improvements are suggested. Lazy evaluation of the top-level links suppresses most of the initial linking cost, and is consistent with a progressive refinement strategy. In addition, the reduction of the number of links for mutually visible areas is made possible by the use of an improved subdivision criterion. Results show that initial linking can be avoided and the number of links significantly reduced without noticeable image degradation, making useful images available more quickly.

1 Introduction

The radiosity method for the simulation of energy exchanges has been used to produce some of the most realistic synthetic images to date. In particular, its ability to render global illumination effects makes it the technique of choice for simulating the illumination of indoor spaces. Since it is based on the subdivision of surfaces using a mesh and on the calculation of the energy transfers between mesh elements pairs, the basic radiosity method is inherently a costly algorithm, requiring a quadratic number of form factors to be computed.

Recent research has focused on reducing the complexity of the radiosity simulation process. Progressive refinement has been proposed as a possible avenue [1], whereby form factors are only computed when needed to evaluate the energy transfers from a given surface, and surfaces are processed in order of importance with respect to the overall balance of energy. The most significant advance in recent years was probably the introduction of hierarchical algorithms, which attempt to establish energy transfers between mesh elements of varying size, thus reducing the subdivision of surfaces and the total number of form factors computed [4, 5].

Since hierarchical algorithms proceed in a top-down manner, by limiting the subdivision of input surfaces to what is necessary, they first have to establish a number of top-level links between input surfaces in an "initial linking" stage. This results in a quadratic cost with respect to the number of input surfaces, which seriously impairs the ability of hierarchical radiosity systems to deal with environments of even moderate complexity. Thus a reformulation of the algorithm is necessary in order to be able to simulate meaningful architectural spaces of medium complexity (several thousands of input surfaces). To this end the questions that must be addressed are: What energy transfers are significant? When must they be computed? How can their accuracy be controlled?

The goal of the research presented here is to extend the hierarchical algorithm into a more progressive algorithm, by identifying the calculation components that can be delayed or removed altogether, and establishing improved refinement criteria to avoid unnecessary subdivision. Careful analysis of the performance of the hierarchical algorithm on a variety of scenes shows that the visibility calculations dominate the overall compute time.

Two main avenues are explored to reduce the cost of visibility calculations: First, the cost of initial linking is reduced by delaying the creation of the links between top-level surfaces until they are potentially significant. In a BF refinement scheme this means for instance that no link is established between dark surfaces. In addition, a form factor between surfaces can be so small that it is not worth performing the visibility calculation.

Second, experimental studies show that subdivision is often too high. This is a consequence of the assumption that the error on the form factor is of magnitude comparable to the form factor itself. In situations of full visibility between surfaces, relatively large form factors can be computed with good accuracy.

2 Motivation

To study the behaviour of the hierarchical algorithm, we ran the original hierarchical program [5] on a set of five different interior environments, varying from scenes with simple to moderate complexity (from 140 to 2355 input polygons). The scenes we used were built in different research efforts and have markedly different overall geometric properties. By using these different scenes, we hope to identify general properties of interior environments. We thus hope to avoid, or at least moderate, the pitfall of unjustified generalisation that oftens results from the use of a single scene or a class of scenes with similar properties to characterise algorithm behaviour. The scenes are: *"Full office"*, which is the original scene used in [5], *"Dining room"*, which is "Scene 7" of the standard set of scenes distributed for this workshop, *"East room"* and *"West room"*, which are scenes containing moderately complex desk and chair models, and finally *"Hevea"*, a model of a hevea tree in a room. Table 2 gives a short description and the number of polygons n for each scene. Please refer to Figs. 1, 3, 5 and 9-12 for a computed view of the test scenes.

Name	n	Description
Full Office	170	The original office scene
Dining room	402	A table and four chairs
East room	1006	Two desks, six chairs
West room	1647	Four desks, ten chairs
Hevea	2355	An hevea tree with three light sources

Table 1. Description of the five test scenes.

2.1 Visibility

The first important observation we make from running the algorithm on these test scenes is the quantification of the cost of visibility calculations in the hierarchical algorithm. As postulated in previous work [9, 6], visibility computation represents a significant proportion of the overall computation time. In the graph shown in Fig. 1, the percentages of the computation time spent in each of the five main components of the hierarchical algorithm are presented. "Push-pull" signifies the time spent traversing the quadtree structure associated with each polygon, "Visibility" is the time spent performing visibility calculations, both for the initial linking step and subsequent refinement, "Form Factors" is the time spent performing the actual unoccluded form factor approximation calculation, "Refine" is the time spent updating the quadtree for refinement, and finally "Gather" shows the cost of transferring energy across the links created between quadtree nodes (interior or leaves) [5]. The graph in Fig. 1 shows that

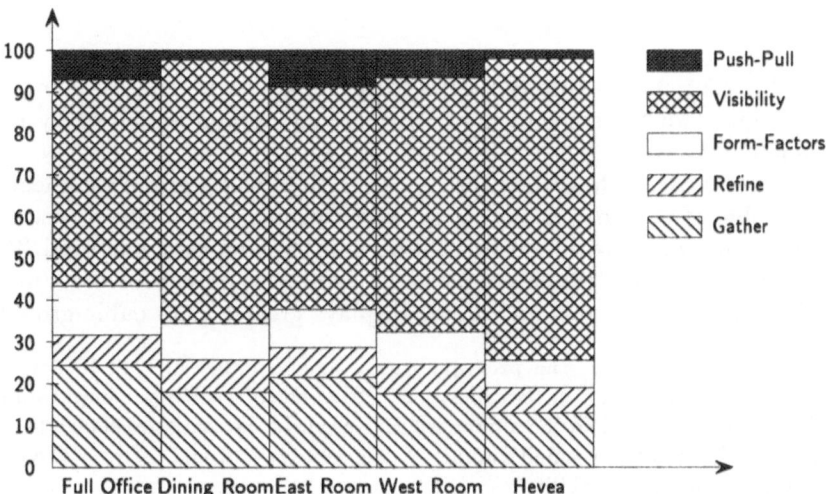

Fig. 1. Relative time spent in each procedure.

visibility calculations dominate the computation in the hierarchical algorithm[1]. Of course this is relative to the algorithm used. A better approach, e.g. with a pre-processing step, as in Teller et al. [9] could probably reduce the relative importance of visibility.

2.2 Initial Linking

The second important observation concerns the actual cost of the initial linking step. As mentioned in the introduction, this cost is at least quadratic in the number of polygons, since each pair of input polygons has to be tested to determine if a link should be established. Since this step is performed before any transfer has commenced, it is a purely geometric visibility test, in this instance implemented by ray-casting. The cost of this test for each polygon pair can vary significantly, depending on the nature of the scene and the type of ray-casting acceleration structure used. In all the examples described below, a BSP tree is used to accelerate the ray-casting process.

Name	n	Total Time	Initial Linking
Full office	170	301	5.13
Dining room	402	4824	436
East room	1006	587	194
West room	1647	1017	476
Hevea	2355	4253	1597

Table 2. Total computation time and cost of initial linking (in seconds).

Table 2.2 presents timing results for all test scenes. The total computation time is given for ten steps of the multigridding method described by Hanrahan et al [5].[2].

These statistics show that the cost of initial linking grows significantly with the number of polygons in the scene. The dependence on scene structure is also evident, since the growth in computation time between *East room* and *West room* is actually sublinear, while on the other hand the growth of the computation time between *West room* and *Hevea* displays greater than cubic growth in the

---

[1] In its current version, the program uses a fixed number of rays to determine the mutual visibility between two polygons. The cost of visibility computation is thus roughly proportional to the number of rays used. In the statistics shown here, 16 rays were used, a relatively small number. Using more rays would increase the percentage of time devoted to visibility tests.

[2] The k'th step of the multigridding method is typically implemented as the k'th "bounce" of light: the first step performs all direct illumination, the second step all secondary illumination, the third all tertiary illumination etc.

number of input polygons. For all tests of more than a thousand polygons, it is clear that the cost of initial linking becomes overwhelming. Invoking this cost at the beginning of the illumination computation is particularly undesirable, since a useful image cannot be displayed before its completion. Finally, we note that recent improvements of the hierarchical radiosity method by Smits et al. [8] and Lischinski et al. [6] have allowed significant savings in refinement time, but still rely on the original initial linking stage. Thus initial linking tends to become the most expensive step of the algorithm[3].

Another interesting observation can be made concerning the number of top-level links (links between input polygons) for which the product BF never becomes greater than the refinement threshold $\varepsilon_{\text{refine}}$ over the course of the ten refinement steps[4]. Figure 2 shows the percentage of such links during the first ten iterations. A remarkably high percentage of these links never becomes a candidate for refinement: after 10 steps, between 65% and 95% of the links have not been refined. A significant number of those links probably have very little impact on the radiosity solution.

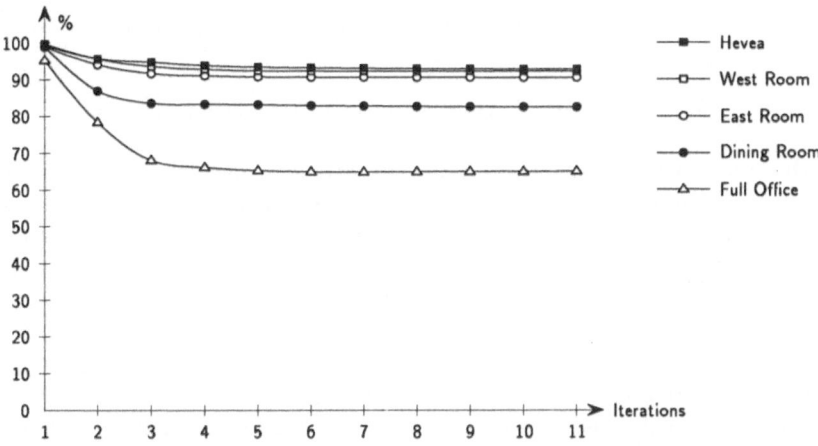

Fig. 2. Percentage of links for which BF does not exceed $\varepsilon_{\text{refine}}$.

What can be concluded from the above discussion? First, if the initial linking step can be eliminated at the beginning of the computation, a useful solution becomes available much more quickly, enhancing the utility of the the hierarchical method. Second, if the top-level links are only computed when they contribute significantly to the solution, there is the potential for large computational savings from eliminating a large number of visibility tests.

---

[3] For example Lischinski et al. report a refinement time of 16 minutes for an initial linking time of 2 hours and 16 minutes.

[4] This is the ε used in the original formulation.

2.3 Unnecessary Refinement

The third important observation made when using the hierarchical algorithm is that unnecessary subdivision is incurred, especially for areas which do not include shadow boundaries. This observation is more difficult to quantify than the previous two. To demonstrate the problem we present an image of the *Dining room* scene, and the corresponding mesh (see Fig. 1 and 2). The simulation parameters were $\varepsilon_{\text{refine}} = 0.5$ and $MinArea = 0.001$.

As can be seen in Fig. 2, the subdivision obtained with these parameters is such that acceptable representation of the shadows is achieved in the penumbral areas caused by the table and chairs. However, the subdivision on the walls is far higher than necessary: the illumination over the wall varies very smoothly and could thus be represented with a much coarser mesh. In previous work it was already noted that radiance functions in regions of full illumination can be accurately represented using a simple mesh based on the structure of illumination [2].

If this unnecessary subdivision is avoided, significant gains can be achieved since the total number of links will be reduced, saving memory, and since an attendant reduction of visibility tests will result, saving computation time.

3 Lazy Evaluation of the Top-level Interactions

In this section a modification of the hierarchical algorithm is proposed, which defers the creation of links between top-level surfaces until such a link is deemed necessary. The basic idea is to avoid performing any computation that does not have a sizable impact on the final solution, in order to concentrate on the most important energy transfers. Thus it is similar to the rationale behind progressive refinement algorithms. At the same time it remains consistent with the hierarchical refinement paradigm, whereby computation is only performed to the extent required by the desired accuracy.

To accomplish this, a criterion must be defined to decide whether a pair of surfaces should be linked. In our implementation we use a specific threshold $\varepsilon_{\text{link}}$ on the product BF. Top-level links are then created *lazily*, only once the linking criterion is met during the course of the simulation.

3.1 Description of the Algorithm

In the original hierarchical radiosity algorithm, two polygons are either mutually invisible, and thus do not interact, or at least partially visible from each other and thus exchange energy. We introduce a second qualification, whereby a pair of polygons is either *classified* or *unclassified*. A pair will be marked *classified* when some information is available regarding its interaction. Initially, all pairs of polygons are marked as unclassified.

At each iteration, all unclassified pairs of polygon are considered: First their radiosity is compared to $\varepsilon_{\text{link}}$. If they are bright enough, we check (in constant time) if they are at least partially facing each other. If not, the pair is marked as classified and no link is created. If they are facing, we compute an approximation of their form factor, without a visibility test. If the product of the form factors and the radiosity is still larger than $\varepsilon_{\text{link}}$, we mark the pair of polygons as classified, and compute the visibility of the polygons. If they are visible, a link is created using the form factors and visibility already computed. Thus a pair of polygons can become classified either when a link is created, or when the two polygons are determined to be invisible. Figure 3 shows a pseudo-code listing of both the Initial Linking phase and the Main Loop in the original algorithm [5] and Fig. 4 gives the equivalent listing in our algorithm.

```
Initial Linking
for each pair of polygons (p, q)
    if p and q are facing each other
        if p and q are at least partially visible from each other
            link p and q
Main Loop
for each polygon p
    foreach link l leaving p
        if B × F > εrefine
            refine l
    foreach link l leaving p
        gather l
```

Fig. 3. The Original Algorithm.

The threshold $\varepsilon_{\text{link}}$ used to establish top-levels interactions is not the same as the threshold used for BF refinement, $\varepsilon_{\text{refine}}$. The main potential source of error in our algorithm is an incomplete balance of energy. Since energy is transfered across links, any polygon for which some top-level links have not been created is retaining some energy, which is not propagated to the environment.

When recursive refinement is terminated because the product BF becomes smaller than $\varepsilon_{\text{refine}}$, a link is always established, which carries some fraction of this energy (the form factor estimate used in the comparison against $\varepsilon_{\text{refine}}$ is an upper bound of the form factor). On the other hand, when two top-level surfaces are not linked because the product BF is smaller than $\varepsilon_{\text{link}}$, all the corresponding energy is "lost". It is thus desirable to select a threshold such that $\varepsilon_{\text{link}} < \varepsilon_{\text{refine}}$. In the examples shown below we used $\varepsilon_{\text{link}} = \varepsilon_{\text{refine}}/5$.

The classified/unclassified status of all pairs of input surfaces requires the storage of $\frac{n(n-1)}{2}$ bits of information. We are currently working on compression techniques to further reduce this cost[5].

---

[5] The storage cost for the classified bit represents 62 kb for a thousand surfaces, 25 Mb for twenty thousand surfaces.

```
Initial Linking
for each pair of polygons (p, q)
    record it as unclassified
Main Loop
    for each unclassified pair of polygons (p, q)
        if p and q are facing each other
            if B_p > ε_link or B_q > ε_link
                compute the unoccluded FF
                if B × F > ε_link
                    link p and q
                    record (p, q) as classified
            else record (p, q) as classified
    for each polygon p
        for each link l leaving p
            if B × F > ε_refine
                refine l
        for each link l leaving p
            gather l
```

Fig. 4. Pseudo-code listing for our algorithm.

3.2 Energy Balance

Since radiosity is mainly used for its ability to model light interreflection, it is important to maintain energy consistency when modifying the algorithm. An issue raised by the lazy linking strategy is that "missing" links, those that have not been created because they were deemed insignificant, do not participate in energy transfers. Thus each gather step only propagates some of the energy radiated by surfaces.

If the corresponding energy is simply ignored, the main result is that the overall level of illumination is reduced. However a more disturbing effect can result for surfaces that have very few (or none) of their links actually established: these surfaces will appear very dark because they will receive energy only from the few surfaces that are linked with them.

The solution we advocate in closed scenes is the use of an *ambient term* similar to the one proposed for progressive refinement radiosity [1]. However the distribution of this ambient term to surfaces must be based on the estimated fraction of their interaction with the world that is missing from the current set of links. The sum of the form factors associated with all links leaving a surface gives an estimate of the fraction of this surface's interactions that is actually represented. Thus, in a closed scene, its complement to one represents the missing link. Using this estimate to weight the distribution of the ambient energy, the underestimation of radiosities can be partially corrected: surfaces that have no links will use the entire ambient term, whereas surfaces with many links will be only marginally affected.

However, since form factors are based on approximate formulas, the sum of all form-factors can differ from one, even for a normally linked surface. This comes from our *BF* refinement strategy: we accept that the form-factor on a link between two dark surfaces be over-estimated, or under-estimated. This may results in energy loss, or creation. If the error we introduced by not linking some surfaces is of the same order – or smaller – than the one due to our lack of precision on the form-factor estimation, using the ambient term will not suffice to correct the energy inbalance.

To quantify the influence of those errors on the overall balance of energy, we compute the following estimate of the incorrect energy:

$$\mathcal{E}_{E_T} = \sum_p |1 - F_p| B_p A_p \tag{1}$$

where A_p is the area of polygon p, B_p its radiosity and F_p the sum of the form factors on all links leaving p. This can be compared to the total energy present in the scene:

$$E_T = \sum_p B_p A_p \tag{2}$$

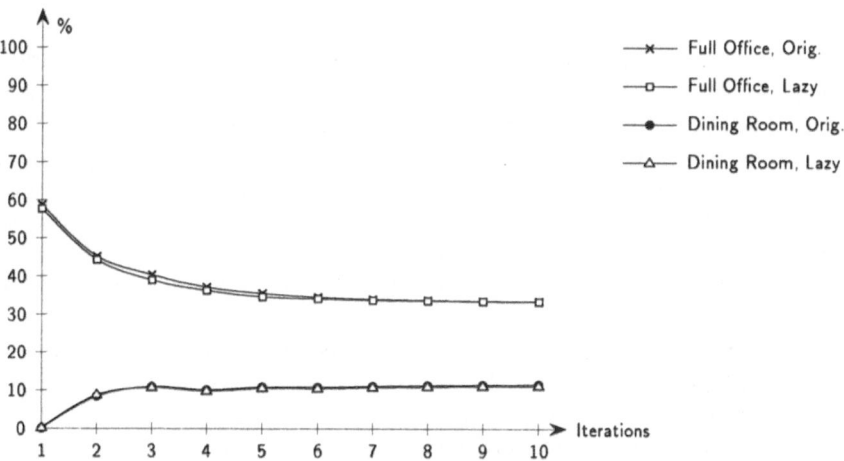

Fig. 5. Incorrect Energy $\mathcal{E}_{E_T}/E_T$.

Figure 5 shows a plot of the ratio $\mathcal{E}_{E_T}/E_T$ for the *Dining Room* scene and the *Full Office*, for both the original algorithm and our algorithm. Note that the error can be significant, but is mainly due to the original algorithm.

4 Reducing the Number of Links

The refinement of a link is based on the estimation of an associated error bound. Various criteria have been used that correspond to different error metrics, including the error in the form factor [4], the error in the radiosity transfer [5], and the impact of the error in the radiosity transfer on the final image [8].

All these criteria implicitly assume that the error in the form factor estimate is equivalent to the magnitude of the form factor itself. While this is true for infinitesimal quantities, in many instances it is possible to compute a reasonable estimate of a relatively large form factor. In particular this is true in situations of full visibility between a pair of surfaces.

Consider two patches p and q. A bi-directionnal link between them carries two form factor estimates $F_{p,q}$ and $F_{q,p}$. If we refine the link by dividing p in smaller patches p_i of area A_i (e.g. in a quadtree), the definition of the form factor

$$F_{u,v} = \frac{1}{A_u} \int_{A_u} \int_{A_v} G(dA_u, dA_v) dA_u dA_v \tag{3}$$

where G is a geometric function, implies that the new form factors verify:

$$F_{p,q} = \frac{1}{A_p} \left(\sum_i A_i F_{p_i,q} \right) \tag{4}$$

$$F_{q,p} = \sum_i F_{q,p_i} \tag{5}$$

These relations only concern the exact values of the form factors. However they can be used to compare the new form factor estimates with the old ones, and determine *a posteriori* wether refinement was actually required. If the sum of the F_{q,p_i} is close to the old $F_{q,p}$, and they are not very different from one another, little precision was gained by refining p. Moreover, if $F_{p,q}$ is close to the average of the $F_{p_i,q}$, and the $F_{p_i,q}$ are not too different from one another, then the refinement process did not introduce any additional information. In this case we force p and q to interact at the current level, since the current estimates of form factors are accurate enough.

In our implementation we only allow reduction of links in situations of full visibility between surfaces. We compute the relative variation of the children form factors, which we test against a new threshold $\varepsilon_{\text{reduce}}$. We also check that the difference between the old form factor $F_{p,q}$ and the sum of the $F_{p_i,q}$, and the difference between $F_{q,p}$ and the average of the F_{q,p_i} are both smaller than $\varepsilon_{\text{reduce}}$.

If we note $F_{u,v}$ our current estimation of the form-factor between two patches u and v, and assuming we want to refine a patch p in p_i, we note:

$$F_{p,q}^{\min} = \min_i(F_{p_i,q}) \qquad F_{q,p}^{\min} = \min_i(F_{q,p_i})$$

$$F_{p,q}^{\max} = \max_i(F_{p_i,q}) \qquad F_{q,p}^{\max} = \max_i(F_{q,p_i})$$

$$F_{p,q}' = \frac{1}{A_p} \left(\sum_i A_i F_{p_i,q} \right) \qquad F_{q,p}' = \sum_i F_{q,p_i}$$

and we refine p if any of the following is true:

$$\frac{F_{p,q}^{\max} - F_{p,q}^{\min}}{F_{p,q}^{\max}} > \varepsilon_{\text{reduce}} \qquad \frac{F_{q,p}^{\max} - F_{q,p}^{\min}}{F_{q,p}^{\max}} > \varepsilon_{\text{reduce}}$$

$$\frac{|F_{p,q}' - F_{p,q}|}{F_{p,q}'} > \varepsilon_{\text{reduce}} \qquad \frac{|F_{q,p}' - F_{q,p}|}{F_{q,p}'} > \varepsilon_{\text{reduce}}$$

The decision to cancel the subdivision of a link is based purely on geometrical properties, therefore it is permanent. The link is marked as "un-refinable" for the entire simulation.

The check whether a link is worth refining involves the computation of form factor estimates to and from all children of patch p. Thus the associated cost in time is similar to that of actually performing the subdivision. If a single level of refinement is avoided by this procedure, there will be little gain in computation time, but the reduction in the number of links will yield memory savings. But if link reduction happens "early enough", several levels of refinement can be avoided. In our test scenes, an implementation of this algorithm reduced significantly the number of quadtree nodes and links (see Fig. 6), with a slightly smaller reduction in computation time because of the cost of the extra form factor estimates (see Fig. 7).

5 Results

5.1 Lazy Linking

Figures 3 in coulour section shows the same scene as in Fig. 1, computed using the lazy linking strategy of Sect. 3. Note that it is visually indistinguishable from its original counterpart. Figure 4 plots the absolute value of the difference between these two images.

5.2 Reduction of the Number of Links

To measure the performance of the reduction criterion, we computed the ratio of the number of quadtree nodes (surface elements) obtained with this criterion, to the number of nodes obtained with the original algorithm. The graph in Fig. 6a plots this ratio against the number of iterations. Note that an overall reduction by nearly a factor of two is achieved for all scenes. Figure 6b shows a similar ratio for the number of links. This global reduction of the number of objects involved leads to a similar reduction of the memory needed by the algorithm, thus making it more practical for scenes with more polygons.

Figure 7 shows the ratio of the computation times using the improved criterion and the original algorithm. The reduction of the number of links has a dramatic impact on running times, with speedups of more than 50%.

Figures 5 and 6 show the image obtained after link reduction. Note the variation in the mesh on the walls, and the similarity of the shaded image with the ones in Figs. 1 and 3. Figure 7 plots the absolute value of the difference between the image produced by the original algorithm and the image obtained after link reduction. Note that part of the differences are due to the lazy linking strategy of Sect. 3. So Figure 8 shows the difference between lazy linking and reduction of the number of links.

1. The Original Algorithm.

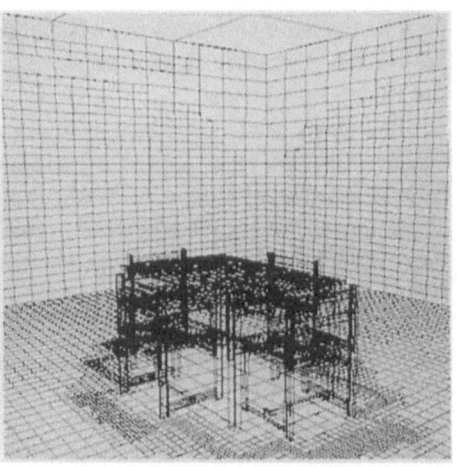

2. The Grid Produced.

3. With Lazy Linking.

4. Diff. Between 1. and 3. (×8).

5. With Link Reduction.

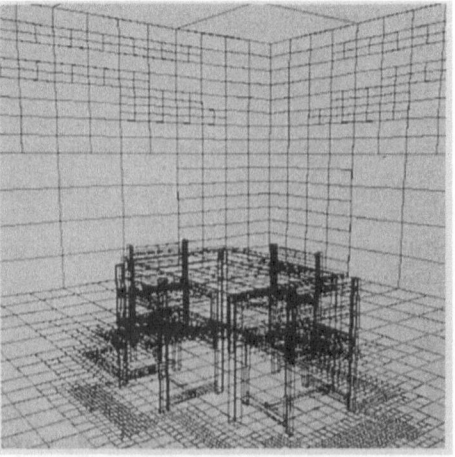

6. The Grid Produced.

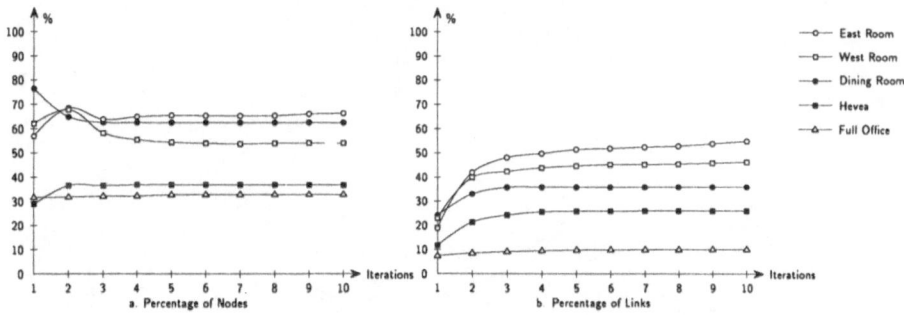

Fig. 6. Percentage of nodes and links left after reduction.

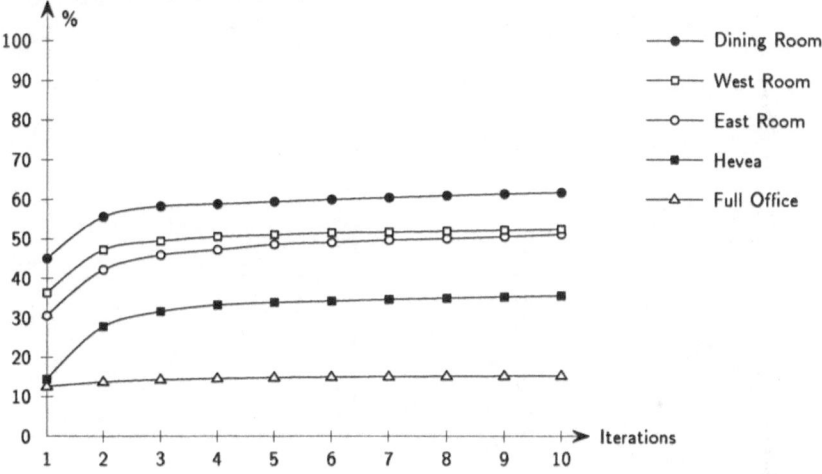

Fig. 7. Percentage of computation time using link reduction.

5.3 Overall Performance Gains

Timing results are presented in Table 5.3. As expected, a significant speedup is achieved, particularly for complex scenes. For all scenes, ten iterations with lazy linking took less time to compute than the first iteration alone with the original algorithm. Finally, using lazy linking and reduction produces a useful image in a matter of minutes even for the most complex scenes in our set.

6 Conclusions and Discussion

We have presented the results of an experimental study conducted on a variety of scenes, showing that visibility calculations represent the most expensive portion of the computation. Two improvements of the hierarchical algorithm were proposed. The first modification creates top-level links *lazily*, only when it is

7. Diff. Between 1. and 5. (×8).

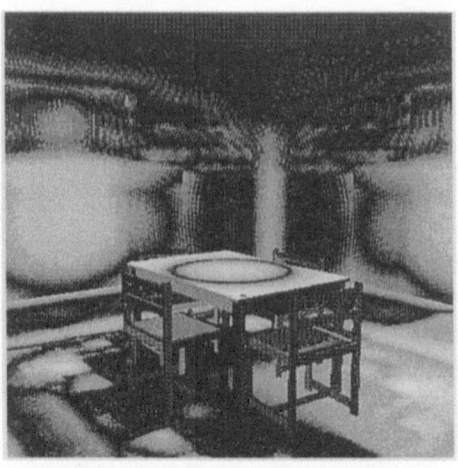

8. Diff. Between 3. and 5. (×8).

9. Full Office.

10. East Room.

11. West Room.

12. Hevea.

Name	n	Original Algorithm		with Lazy Linking...		and Reduction	
Full office	170	301 s	(242 s)	287 s	(234 s)	43 s	(30 s)
Dining room	402	4824 s	(4191 s)	4051 s	(3911 s)	657 s	(552 s)
East room	1006	587 s	(378 s)	377 s	(191 s)	193 s	(59 s)
West room	1647	1017 s	(752 s)	514 s	(277 s)	270 s	(101 s)
Hevea	2355	4253 s	(2331 s)	1526 s	(847 s)	543 s	(122 s)

Table 3. Time needed for ten iterations (and time for producing the first image).

established that the proposed link will have a definite impact on the simulation. With this approach the hierarchical algorithm still remains quadratic in the number of input surfaces, but no work and very little storage is devoted to the initial linking phase. The resulting algorithm is more progressive in that it produces useful images very quickly. Note that the quadratic cost in the number of input surfaces can only be removed by clustering methods [7].

An improved subdivision criterion was introduced for situations of full visibility between surfaces, which allows a significant reduction of the number of links.

Future work will include the simplification of the hierarchical structure due to multiple sources and subsequent iterations. A surface that has been greatly refined because it receives a shadow from a given light source can be fully illuminated by a second source, and the shadow become washed in light.

Better error bounds, both on form factor magnitude and global energy transfers, should allow even greater reduction of the number of links. Accurate visibility algorithms can be used to this end, by providing exact visibility information between pairs of surfaces.

7 Acknowledgments

George Drettakis is a post-doc hosted by INRIA and supported by an ERCIM fellowship. The hierarchical radiosity software was built on top of the original program kindly provided by Pat Hanrahan.

References

1. Cohen, M. F., Chen, S. E., Wallace, J. R., Greenberg, D. P.: A Progressive Refinement Approach to Fast Radiosity Image Generation. SIGGRAPH (1988) 75–84
2. Drettakis, G., Fiume, E.: Accurate and Consistent Reconstruction of Illumination Functions Using Structured Sampling. Computer Graphics Forum (Eurographics 1993 Conf. Issue) 273–284
3. Goral, C. M., Torrance, K. E., Greenberg, D. P., Bataille, B.: Modeling the Interaction of Light Between Diffuse Surfaces. SIGGRAPH (1984) 213–222

4. Hanrahan, P. M., Salzman, D.: A Rapid Hierarchical Radiosity Algorithm for Un-occluded Environments. *Eurographics Workshop on Photosimulation, Realism and Physics in Computer Graphics*, June 1990.
5. Hanrahan, P. M., Salzman, D., Auperle, L.: A Rapid Hierarchical Radiosity Algorithm. SIGGRAPH (1991) 197–206
6. Lischinski, D., Tampieri, F., Greenberg, D. P.: Combining Hierarchical Radiosity and Discontinuity Meshing. SIGGRAPH (1993)
7. Sillion, F.: Clustering and Volume Scattering for Hierarchical Radiosity calculations. *Fifth Eurographics Workshop on Rendering*, Darmstadt, June 1994 (in these proceedings).
8. Smits, B. E., Arvo, J. R., Salesin, D. H.: An Importance-Driven Radiosity Algorithm. SIGGRAPH (1992) 273–282
9. Teller, S. J., Hanrahan, P. M.: Global Visibility Algorithm for Illumination Computations. SIGGRAPH (1993) 239–246

Efficient Re-rendering of Naturally Illuminated Environments

Jeffry S. Nimeroff[1], *Eero Simoncelli*[1], *Julie Dorsey*[1,2]

[1] Department of Computer and Information Science
[2] Department of Architecture
University of Pennsylvania, Philadelphia PA 19104, USA

Abstract

We present a method for the efficient re-rendering of a scene under a directional illuminant at an arbitrary orientation. We take advantage of the linearity of the rendering operator with respect to illumination for a fixed scene and camera geometry. Re-rendering is accomplished via linear combination of a set of pre-rendered "basis" images. The theory of steerable functions provides the machinery to derive an appropriate set of basis images. We demonstrate the technique on both simple and complex scenes illuminated by an approximation to natural skylight. We show re-rendering simulations under conditions of varying sun position and cloudiness.

1 Introduction

In recent years, researchers have begun to treat the simulation of natural illumination (overcast or clear skylight [15]) with global illumination algorithms [15, 22]. A major difficulty with modeling daylight is that the direction of the sun varies continuously throughout the day. In addition, cloud conditions may also change (e.g., from clear to overcast). This paper addresses the problem of efficient dynamic re-rendering of a scene under such changes.

An example application of the technique is in the rendering of naturally illuminated architectural environments. In order to qualitatively assess a daylit interior, designers need to see subtle lighting effects such as soft shadowing, indirect illumination, and color bleeding. These effects are generally only available through costly global illumination algorithms. For instance, in order to compute an animation of the appearance of an interior space during the course of a typical day, one would need to compute a global solution at each of a large number of time steps corresponding to a sequence of sun directions. Furthermore, varying the sky conditions (e.g. cloudiness) would require an entirely new animation with new global solutions.

Rather than computing a global solution for each time step, we describe a technique for computing a time-independent basis—a small number of global solutions—that suffice to simulate the entire animation. The theory of steerable functions provides the means to construct the basis images (one per solution) needed for rendering via linear combination.

2 Linearity of Rendering

For our formulation, the rendering operator R takes an illumination description $L(\hat{u})$ (the illuminant intensity as a function of illumination direction $\hat{u}$), a scene and camera geometry G, and yields an image I:

$$R(L(\hat{u}), G) \rightarrow I \ . \tag{1}$$

Since the geometry G is fixed, an individual rendering operator can be thought of as existing for each chosen geometry. We denote this operator as:

$$R_G(L(\hat{u})) \rightarrow I \ . \tag{2}$$

If one is willing to discount physical and quantum optics and work with static scene geometries, the rendering operation is linear with respect to the illumination [11, 8, 4] operator. More specifically, rendering obeys the rules of *superposition*:

- the image resulting from an additive combination of two illuminants is just the *sum* of the images resulting from each of the illuminants independently,
- multiplying the intensity of the illumination sources by a factor α results in a rendered image that is multiplied by the same factor.

What is the advantage of this linearity? Consider an illuminant constructed as the combination of simpler "basis" illumination functions $L_i(\hat{u})$,

$$L(\hat{u}) = \sum_{i=1}^{N} \alpha_i L_i(\hat{u}) \ . \tag{3}$$

Linearity allows us to write the desired rendered image as a linear combination of images rendered under each of the basis functions:

$$R_G(L(\hat{u})) = R_G \left(\sum_{i=1}^{N} \alpha_i L_i(\hat{u}) \right) = \sum_{i=1}^{N} \alpha_i R_G(L_i(\hat{u})) \ . \tag{4}$$

The $R_G(L_i(\hat{u}))$ constitute a set of images rendered under each of the basis illuminants $L_i(\hat{u})$. The equation states that we may compute an image for any linear combination of the basis illuminants via a linear combination of these pre-rendered images.

3 Choosing the Illuminant Basis

In order to make use of this property, we must select an appropriate *basis set* of illumination functions $L_i(\hat{\mathbf{u}})$. Some desirable properties for this set of functions are as follows:

1. The basis functions should be general enough to form any light source we desire (via linear combination).
2. The number of basis functions, N, should be small, since this corresponds to the number of basis images we must actually render.
3. For each illumination function that can be represented, we should also be able to compute (via linear combination) the same function rotated by any three-dimensional rotation. In other words, the (linear) space of illumination functions that we represent should be *rotation-invariant*.

The first two of these properties have conflicting requirements: the smaller the number of basis functions, the less flexibility we have in the variety of representable illuminants. This is true of any sort of function expansion, such as Taylor or Fourier series approximations.

The last property is a more explicit and restricted version of the first property and is not necessary for linear combinations. Nevertheless, it is extremely useful in the case of sunlight illuminants, since the direction of the sun varies along a path on a sphere. This property places a strong constraint on the functions known as "steerability" [9]. A steerable function is one that can be written as a linear combination of rotated versions of itself. Freeman and Adelson [9] have developed a theory of such functions and demonstrated their use in two-dimensional image processing problems. For the purposes of the present paper, we will develop a set of steerable functions in three dimensions and demonstrate their use as illumination basis functions for the linear re-rendering problem.

3.1 Steerable Functions: Directional Cosine Example

We begin by illustrating the idea of steerability using the simplest form of steerable function. Let $c(\hat{\mathbf{u}}; \hat{\mathbf{s}})$ be defined as:

$$c(\hat{\mathbf{u}}; \hat{\mathbf{s}}) = \hat{\mathbf{u}} \cdot \hat{\mathbf{s}} \ ,$$

where $\hat{\mathbf{s}}$ and $\hat{\mathbf{u}}$ are unit vectors in $\mathbb{R}^3$ and $(\cdot)$ indicates an inner product. We consider $c()$ as a function on the sphere parameterized by the unit vector $\hat{\mathbf{u}}$, with $\hat{\mathbf{s}}$ a fixed direction vector. Clearly, the function computes the cosine of the angle between a point on the sphere and the fixed direction $\hat{\mathbf{s}}$. We therefore refer to this as a *directional cosine* function.

We can expand the equation as:

$$\begin{aligned} c(\hat{\mathbf{u}}; \hat{\mathbf{s}}) &= s_x(\hat{\mathbf{u}} \cdot \hat{\mathbf{e}}_x) + s_y(\hat{\mathbf{u}} \cdot \hat{\mathbf{e}}_y) + s_z(\hat{\mathbf{u}} \cdot \hat{\mathbf{e}}_z) \\ &= s_x c(\hat{\mathbf{u}}; \hat{\mathbf{e}}_x) + s_y c(\hat{\mathbf{u}}; \hat{\mathbf{e}}_y) + s_z c(\hat{\mathbf{u}}; \hat{\mathbf{e}}_z) \ , \end{aligned} \qquad (5)$$

where the $\hat{\mathbf{e}}_*$ are the unit vectors corresponding to the three Euclidean coordinate axes, and s_* are the components of $\hat{\mathbf{s}}$. We have written the directional cosine function in direction $\hat{\mathbf{s}}$ as *a linear combination of directional cosines* along the three coordinate axes. That is, we can compute *any* rotated version of this function via linear combinations of a *fixed set* of rotated copies. We say that the set of three functions, $c(\hat{\mathbf{u}}; \hat{\mathbf{e}}.)$, constitute a *steerable basis set*.

Of course, there is nothing particularly special about the coordinate axis directions $\{\hat{\mathbf{e}}_x, \hat{\mathbf{e}}_y, \hat{\mathbf{e}}_z\}$. We could choose *any* three non-coplanar directions, $\{\hat{\mathbf{s}}_1, \hat{\mathbf{s}}_2, \hat{\mathbf{s}}_3\}$, and still perform this computation. The easiest way to see this is by working from (5). We can write $c(\hat{\mathbf{u}}; \hat{\mathbf{s}}_i)$ for each i in terms of the axis cosine functions:

$$c(\hat{\mathbf{u}}; \hat{\mathbf{s}}_i) = s_{i,x} c(\hat{\mathbf{u}}; \hat{\mathbf{e}}_x) + s_{i,y} c(\hat{\mathbf{u}}; \hat{\mathbf{e}}_y) + s_{i,z} c(\hat{\mathbf{u}}; \hat{\mathbf{e}}_z) \ .$$

This is a set of three linear equations, which we can write in matrix form as:

$$\begin{pmatrix} c(\hat{\mathbf{u}}; \hat{\mathbf{s}}_1) \\ c(\hat{\mathbf{u}}; \hat{\mathbf{s}}_2) \\ c(\hat{\mathbf{u}}; \hat{\mathbf{s}}_3) \end{pmatrix} = \mathbf{M}_3 \begin{pmatrix} c(\hat{\mathbf{u}}; \hat{\mathbf{e}}_x) \\ c(\hat{\mathbf{u}}; \hat{\mathbf{e}}_y) \\ c(\hat{\mathbf{u}}; \hat{\mathbf{e}}_z) \end{pmatrix} \ ,$$

where $\mathbf{M}_3$ is a 3×3 matrix containing the vectors $\hat{\mathbf{s}}_i$ as its rows.

If the three vectors $\hat{\mathbf{s}}_i$ are non-coplanar, they span $\mathbb{R}^3$, and we can invert the matrix $\mathbf{M}_3$ to solve for the axis cosines:

$$\begin{pmatrix} c(\hat{\mathbf{u}}; \hat{\mathbf{e}}_x) \\ c(\hat{\mathbf{u}}; \hat{\mathbf{e}}_y) \\ c(\hat{\mathbf{u}}; \hat{\mathbf{e}}_z) \end{pmatrix} = \mathbf{M}_3^{-1} \begin{pmatrix} c(\hat{\mathbf{u}}; \hat{\mathbf{s}}_1) \\ c(\hat{\mathbf{u}}; \hat{\mathbf{s}}_2) \\ c(\hat{\mathbf{u}}; \hat{\mathbf{s}}_3) \end{pmatrix} \ .$$

Given the axis cosines, we can compute *any* directional cosine function via (5):

$$c(\hat{\mathbf{u}}; \hat{\mathbf{s}}) = \hat{\mathbf{s}}^T \mathbf{M}_3^{-1} \begin{pmatrix} c(\hat{\mathbf{u}}; \hat{\mathbf{s}}_1) \\ c(\hat{\mathbf{u}}; \hat{\mathbf{s}}_2) \\ c(\hat{\mathbf{u}}; \hat{\mathbf{s}}_3) \end{pmatrix} \ .$$

Thus, we have an expression for computing the directional cosine in any direction $\hat{\mathbf{s}}$ from the cosines in three fixed but arbitrary non-coplanar directions, $\hat{\mathbf{s}}_i$.

3.2 Directional Cosine Polynomials

The steerable basis we have derived is not yet suitable as an illuminant basis, since the functions take on both positive and negative values. We can form a simple steerable illuminant basis by simply adding unity to these:

$$\begin{aligned} L(\hat{\mathbf{u}}; \hat{\mathbf{s}}) &= 1 + c(\hat{\mathbf{u}}; \hat{\mathbf{s}}) \\ &= 1 + s_x c(\hat{\mathbf{u}}; \hat{\mathbf{e}}_x) + s_y c(\hat{\mathbf{u}}; \hat{\mathbf{e}}_y) + s_z c(\hat{\mathbf{u}}; \hat{\mathbf{e}}_z) \ . \end{aligned}$$

The function L is written as a sum of *four* terms. This equation is still not in a steerable form, but we can write it steerably using the same trick as before. We choose four arbitrary non-coplanar unit vectors $\{\hat{s}_1, \hat{s}_2, \hat{s}_3, \hat{s}_4\}$, write four linear equations for L in each of these directions, and invert this to get:

$$L(\hat{u}; \hat{s}) = \begin{pmatrix} 1 \\ s_x \\ s_y \\ s_z \end{pmatrix}^T \mathbf{M}_4^{-1} \begin{pmatrix} L(\hat{u}; \hat{s}_1) \\ L(\hat{u}; \hat{s}_2) \\ L(\hat{u}; \hat{s}_3) \\ L(\hat{u}; \hat{s}_4) \end{pmatrix} , \tag{6}$$

where $\mathbf{M}_4$ is now the matrix:

$$\mathbf{M}_4 = \begin{pmatrix} 1 & s_{1,x} & s_{1,y} & s_{1,z} \\ 1 & s_{2,x} & s_{2,y} & s_{2,z} \\ 1 & s_{3,x} & s_{3,y} & s_{3,z} \\ 1 & s_{4,x} & s_{4,y} & s_{4,z} \end{pmatrix} .$$

The directional cosine functions described thus far are quite broad in their extent: the magnitude of each function is significant over a large fraction of the sphere. When used for purposes of scene illumination, these functions may be too diffuse. How can we build narrower illuminants? One simple generalization can be achieved by considering polynomials of directional cosine functions.

Consider a general second order polynomial of the directional cosine function defined in (5):

$$\begin{aligned} f(\hat{u}; \hat{s}) &= a_0 + a_1(\hat{u} \cdot \hat{s}) + a_2(\hat{u} \cdot \hat{s})^2 \\ &= a_0 \\ &\quad + a_1[s_x u_x + s_y u_y + s_z u_z] \\ &\quad + a_2\,[s_x^2(u_x^2) + 2s_x s_y(u_x u_y) + 2s_x s_z(u_x u_z) \\ &\quad\quad + s_y^2(u_y^2) + 2s_y s_z(u_y u_z) + s_z^2(u_z^2)] \ . \end{aligned} \tag{7}$$

As in the previous section, this equation may be placed in steerable form by considering a set of 9 direction vectors $\{\hat{s}_i | i \in [1,9]\}$:

$$f(\hat{u}; \hat{s}) = \begin{pmatrix} 1 \\ s_x \\ s_y \\ s_z \\ s_x^2 \\ s_x s_y \\ s_x s_z \\ s_y^2 \\ s_y s_z \\ s_z^2 \end{pmatrix}^T \mathbf{M}_9^{\#} \begin{pmatrix} f(\hat{u}; \hat{s}_1) \\ f(\hat{u}; \hat{s}_2) \\ f(\hat{u}; \hat{s}_3) \\ f(\hat{u}; \hat{s}_4) \\ f(\hat{u}; \hat{s}_5) \\ f(\hat{u}; \hat{s}_6) \\ f(\hat{u}; \hat{s}_7) \\ f(\hat{u}; \hat{s}_8) \\ f(\hat{u}; \hat{s}_9) \end{pmatrix} ,$$

where the rows of the matrix M_9 contain the combinations of the $\hat{s}_i$ found in each of the terms of (7). The symbol # indicates a least-squares pseudo-inverse operation. This is used in place of a standard matrix inverse: the matrix M_9 is not of full rank because the functions $f(\hat{u}; \hat{s}_i)$ do not span the full space of second order polynomials. Nevertheless, the interpolation of (7) is exact.

The function $f(\hat{u}; \hat{s})$ may be made narrower (through proper choice of the a_k) than the first order polynomial of the previous section. But note that we have paid a price for this: we now require nine basis functions for steerability as opposed to four. This is a fundamental tradeoff in steerable basis sets: *a narrower steerable function requires a larger number of basis functions.* [3]

4 Bases for Natural Illumination

In this section, we discuss the design of illuminant basis sets for approximating sunlight. We consider overcast skylight and clear skylight separately and then discuss general skylight.

4.1 Overcast Skylight

Overcast skylight [6, 15] is the illumination that emanates from the sun but is completely absorbed and re-radiated by the atmosphere (clouds) before illuminating the scene. It is a function that describes an overcast/cloudy day. The function has a cosine falloff relative to a fixed point (zenith) but does not depend on the sun's position in the sky:

$$L(\hat{u}) = L_z(1 + 2(u_z))/3 \ , \tag{8}$$

where u_z is the z-component of $\hat{u}$, and L_z is an overall illumination constant. Since the orientation of this function never changes, there is no need to construct a steerable basis for it.[4]

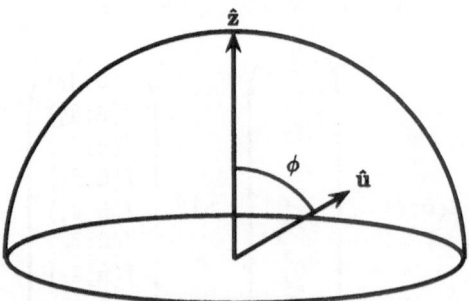

Fig. 1. Overcast skylight geometry.

---

[3] In two dimensions, this is simply a restatement of the Nyquist criterion for sampling of bandlimited signals [20].

[4] We could construct a basis of size 4 using (6).

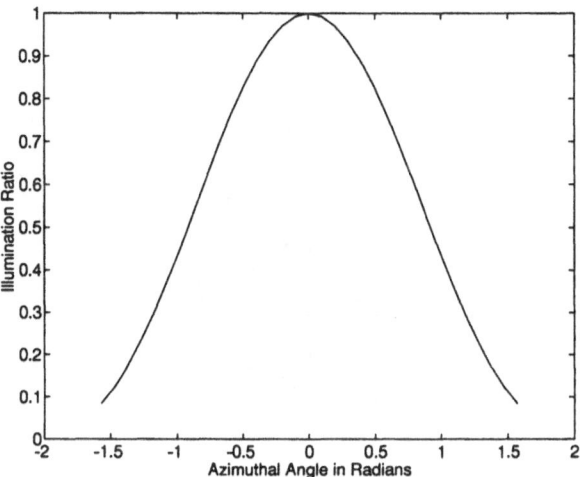

Fig. 2. Overcast skylight distribution.

4.2 Clear Skylight

Clear skylight [1, 15] describes the distribution of the sun's energy on a clear day. It is very complex and is dependent on the sun's position in the sky and on the direction relative to a fixed point (zenith):

$$L(\hat{\mathbf{u}}; \hat{\mathbf{s}}) = L_z \frac{(0.91 + 10 \exp(-3 \arccos(\hat{\mathbf{u}} \cdot \hat{\mathbf{s}})) + 0.45(\hat{\mathbf{u}} \cdot \hat{\mathbf{s}})^2)(1 - \exp(-0.32/u_z))}{0.274(0.91 + 10 \exp(-3 \arccos(s_z)) + 0.45(s_z^2))} ,$$

$$(9)$$

where $\hat{\mathbf{s}}$ is the unit vector pointing to the sun.

4.3 Steerable Sunlight Approximation

In order to re-render naturally illuminated scenes via linear combinations of rendered images, a steerable approximation to the clear skylight function in (9) must be constructed. We rewrite the equation as:

$$
\begin{aligned}
L(\hat{\mathbf{u}}; \hat{\mathbf{s}}) &= \left[\frac{L_z}{0.274(0.91 + 10 \exp(-3 \arccos(s_z)) + 0.45(s_z^2))} \right] \\
&\quad \cdot [1 - \exp(-0.32/u_z)] \\
&\quad \cdot \left[0.91 + 10 \exp(-3 \arccos(\hat{\mathbf{u}} \cdot \hat{\mathbf{s}})) + 0.45(\hat{\mathbf{u}} \cdot \hat{\mathbf{s}})^2 \right] \\
&= L_1(\hat{\mathbf{s}}) \cdot L_2(\hat{\mathbf{u}}) \cdot L_3(\hat{\mathbf{u}} \cdot \hat{\mathbf{s}}) \ .
\end{aligned}
$$

In order to compute $L(\hat{\mathbf{u}}; \hat{\mathbf{s}})$ from a set of illuminants $L(\hat{\mathbf{u}}; \hat{\mathbf{s}}_i)$, note that only L_3 must be steerable. L_2 is a function of $\hat{\mathbf{u}}$ only and does not affect the steerability.

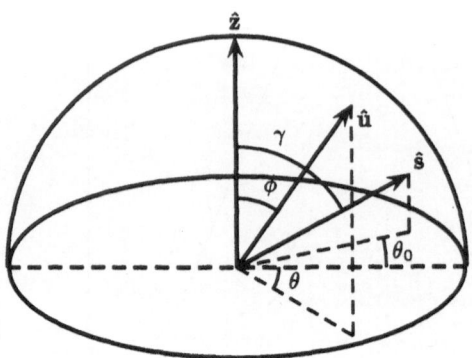

Fig. 3. Clear skylight geometry.

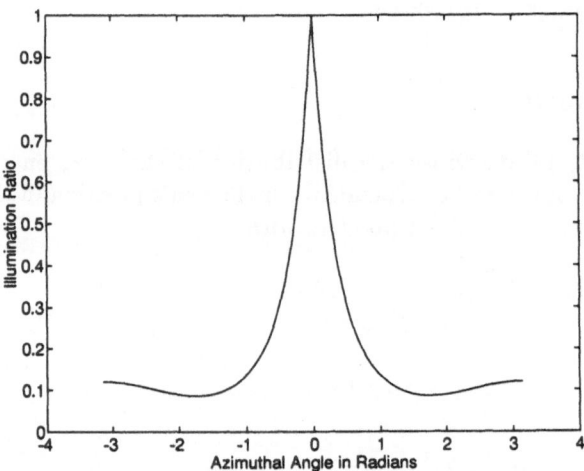

Fig. 4. Clear skylight distribution for sun at zenith.

L_1 is a function of $\hat{s}$ only and acts as an illumination scaling constant. Therefore the steerable form of $L(\hat{u}; \hat{s})$ may be written as:

$$L(\hat{u}; \hat{s}) = L_1(\hat{s}) \cdot \sum_i \left(\alpha_i(\hat{s}) \cdot \overbrace{L_2(\hat{u}) \cdot \underbrace{L_3(\hat{s}_i \cdot \hat{u})}_{\text{Steerable}}}^{\text{Basis lights}} \right) . \tag{10}$$

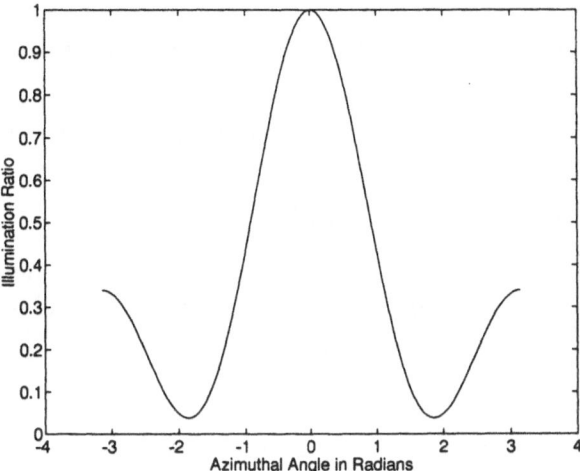

Fig. 5. Approximated clear skylight distribution at zenith.

We must construct a steerable approximation to the function L_3. For purposes of this paper, we use a second order approximation:

$$L_3(\hat{\mathbf{u}} \cdot \hat{\mathbf{s}}) = 0.91 + 10 \exp(-3 \arccos(\hat{\mathbf{u}} \cdot \hat{\mathbf{s}})) + 0.45(\hat{\mathbf{u}} \cdot \hat{\mathbf{s}})^2$$
$$\approx 0.5012 + 1.9116(\hat{\mathbf{u}} \cdot \hat{\mathbf{s}}) + 3.3911(\hat{\mathbf{u}} \cdot \hat{\mathbf{s}})^2 \ . \tag{11}$$

This steerable function requires a basis set of size ten. We note again that higher order polynomials would provide better approximations at the expense of a larger basis set requiring additional executions of the costly global illumination algorithm.

Using the linearity of the rendering operator and (10) we can write an expression for re-rendering an image for any sun direction $\hat{\mathbf{s}}$ from the images rendered under 9 different sun directions s_i:

$$R_G(L(\hat{\mathbf{u}}; \hat{\mathbf{s}})) = L_1(\hat{\mathbf{s}}) \cdot \sum_i \alpha_i(\hat{\mathbf{s}}) \frac{R_G(L_2(\hat{\mathbf{u}}) \cdot L_3(\hat{\mathbf{s}}_i \cdot \hat{\mathbf{u}}))}{L_1(\hat{\mathbf{s}}_i)} \ , \tag{12}$$

where the α_i are the components of:

$$\begin{pmatrix} 1 & s_x & s_y & s_z & s_x^2 & s_x s_y & s_x s_z & s_y^2 & s_y s_z & s_z^2 \end{pmatrix} \mathbf{M}_9^\# \ . \tag{13}$$

4.4 General Skylight

As demonstrated above, a steerable approximation for an overcast day requires a first-order expansion, while the clear day requires a second-order expansion. To generate an image for a partially overcast day, we have to gradually phase in the second order terms. This can be done by linearly interpolating between the two sets of coefficients.

Let b be a number in $[0, 1]$ indicating the brightness of the day (1=sunny, 0=cloudy). Let

$$v_0 = (\begin{matrix} \beta_0 & 0 & 0 & \beta_1 & 0 & 0 & 0 & 0 & \beta_2 \end{matrix}) \ ,$$

and

$$v_1(\hat{s}) = (\begin{matrix} 1 & s_x & s_y & s_z & s_x^2 & s_x s_y & s_x s_z & s_y^2 & s_y s_z & s_z^2 \end{matrix}) \ ,$$

where $v_1(\hat{s})$ is the interpolation vector for the clear skylight function with sun in direction $\hat{s}$, and v_0 is the interpolation vector that gives a least-squares best fit to the overcast skylight function (8). Then let

$$v(\hat{s}, b) = (1 - b)v_0 + bv_1(\hat{s}).$$

The interpolation functions α_i in (12) are the components of:

$$v(\hat{s}, b)\mathbf{M}^{\#}.$$

5 Implementation and Results

Figure 6 provides an overview of our approach. There are two main components to the system: the pre-processing stage, which entails computing the basis images using a renderer, and the post-processing phase, which involves re-rendering the scene at a specific time of day under desired sky conditions (e.g. overcast or clear).

Once the basis images have been computed, the scene can be quickly re-rendered based on a new sun position and desired sky conditions. This is accomplished by performing a linear combination of the basis images, given the coefficients for the sun direction and sky definition. Thus, a designer can see a variety of lighting configurations throughout a typical day or observe an animation of these effects in the time required to combine the basis images together. That is, no calls to the costly global illumination operator are required for this interaction.

We used the illuminant approximation of (11) to generate our set of nine basis images for a sample architectural scene.

The set of $\hat{s}_i$ used were

$$
\begin{pmatrix} \hat{s}_1 \\ \hat{s}_2 \\ \hat{s}_3 \\ \hat{s}_4 \\ \hat{s}_5 \\ \hat{s}_6 \\ \hat{s}_7 \\ \hat{s}_8 \\ \hat{s}_9 \end{pmatrix}
=
\begin{pmatrix}
(\ \ 0.0000, & 0.0000, & 1.0000\ ) \\
(\ \ 0.9102, & 0.0000, & 0.4142\ ) \\
(\ \ 0.0000, & 0.9102, & 0.4142\ ) \\
(-0.9102, & 0.0000, & 0.4142\ ) \\
(\ \ 0.0000, & -0.9102, & 0.4142\ ) \\
(\ \ 0.6436, & 0.6436, & -0.4142\ ) \\
(-0.6436, & 0.6436, & -0.4142\ ) \\
(-0.6436, & -0.6436, & -0.4142\ ) \\
(\ \ 0.6436, & -0.6436, & -0.4142\ )
\end{pmatrix}
.
$$

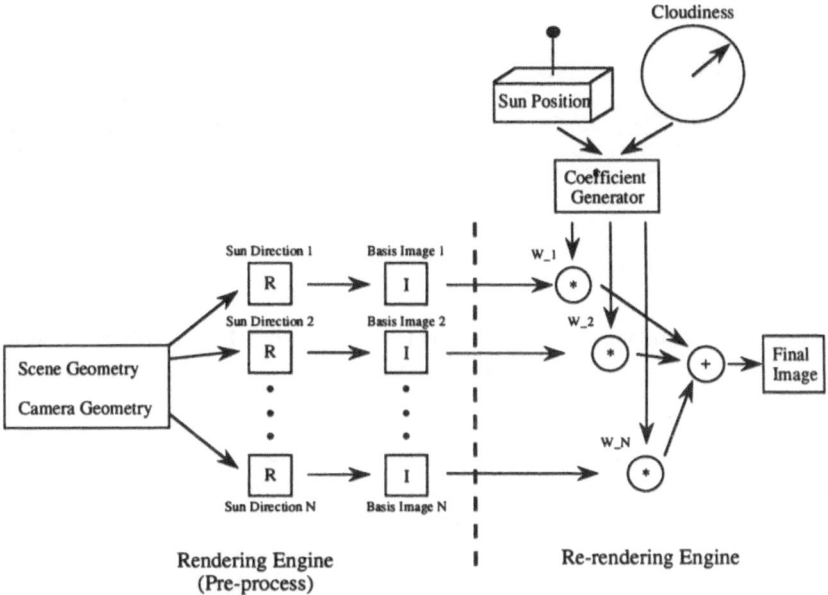

Fig. 6. Implementation architecture.

For each sun position $\hat{s}_i$, an image was rendered using a multi-pass global illumination algorithm. The renderer combines a progressive radiosity pass to simulate diffuse lighting effects and a stochastic ray-tracing pass to simulate specular effects. The rendering was performed on a 50 MHz SGI Crimson VGXT with 64 megabytes of RAM. Each 640 by 486 image took approximately one hour to complete with a nine hour total rendering/setup time. Once the initial nine hour rendering phase is performed, re-rendering time becomes negligible (approximately one second per image, not including I/O).

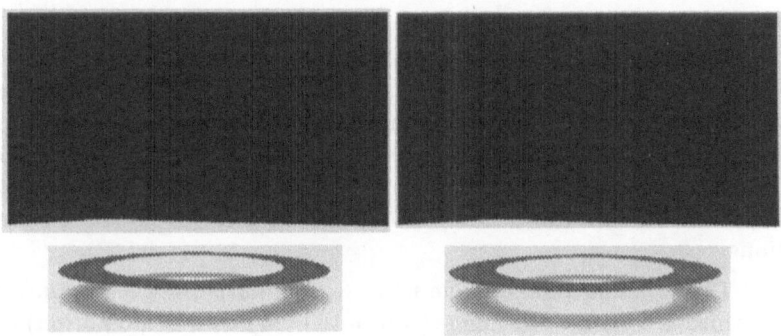

Fig. 7. a) Rendered image; b) re-rendered image (linear combination of nine basis images).

Fig. 8. CIE standard.   **Fig.9.** Steerable second   **Fig.10.** Steerable fourth
                              order approximation.   order approximation.

It is important to note that our rendering times are representative of a global illumination (progressive radiosity) simulation running to convergence. However, our re-rendering implementation does not require this. The basis images can be computed with virtually any rendering algorithm—affording the possibility to trade quality for time. For example, during the early design stages of a building design, one could use a local illumination model or a very coarse global illumination solution to minimize the time required to compute the basis images. Later, when greater precision is necessary, more accurate images could be used. Also, we could use a larger number of basis images to get a more exact description of the daylight distribution function.

Figure 7 shows two images. The first is an image of a simple scene rendered with our sunlight model. The second has the sun at the same location as the first, but is a linear combination of the basis images for the scene. The RMS error calculated on these two images is negligable ($>$ 0.008).

Figures 8 - 10 shows three images. The first is an image of a simple scene rendered with the CIE standard clear day function. The second image uses our second order approximation to the CIE standard and the third uses a fourth order approximation. As we increase the order of our approximation we can more closely match the CIE standard function. In the limit, our approximation is exact.

Figure 11 shows a sequence of eighteen images corresponding to a sequence of sun positions during the course of a day. This is the prototypical example for showing the benefit of our approach. Once the small number of basis images are computed, obtaining a rendering of the environment with a new sun position and sky description is reduced to a fast image combination step. Thus, the process is very interactive and alleviates many of the problems involved with constructing animations.

Figure 12 show four images. The first two are basis images (actually rendered). The third is a sunny-day image (computed via linear combination) with the sun position between that of the two basis images. The fourth is a cloudy-day image also computed via linear combination.

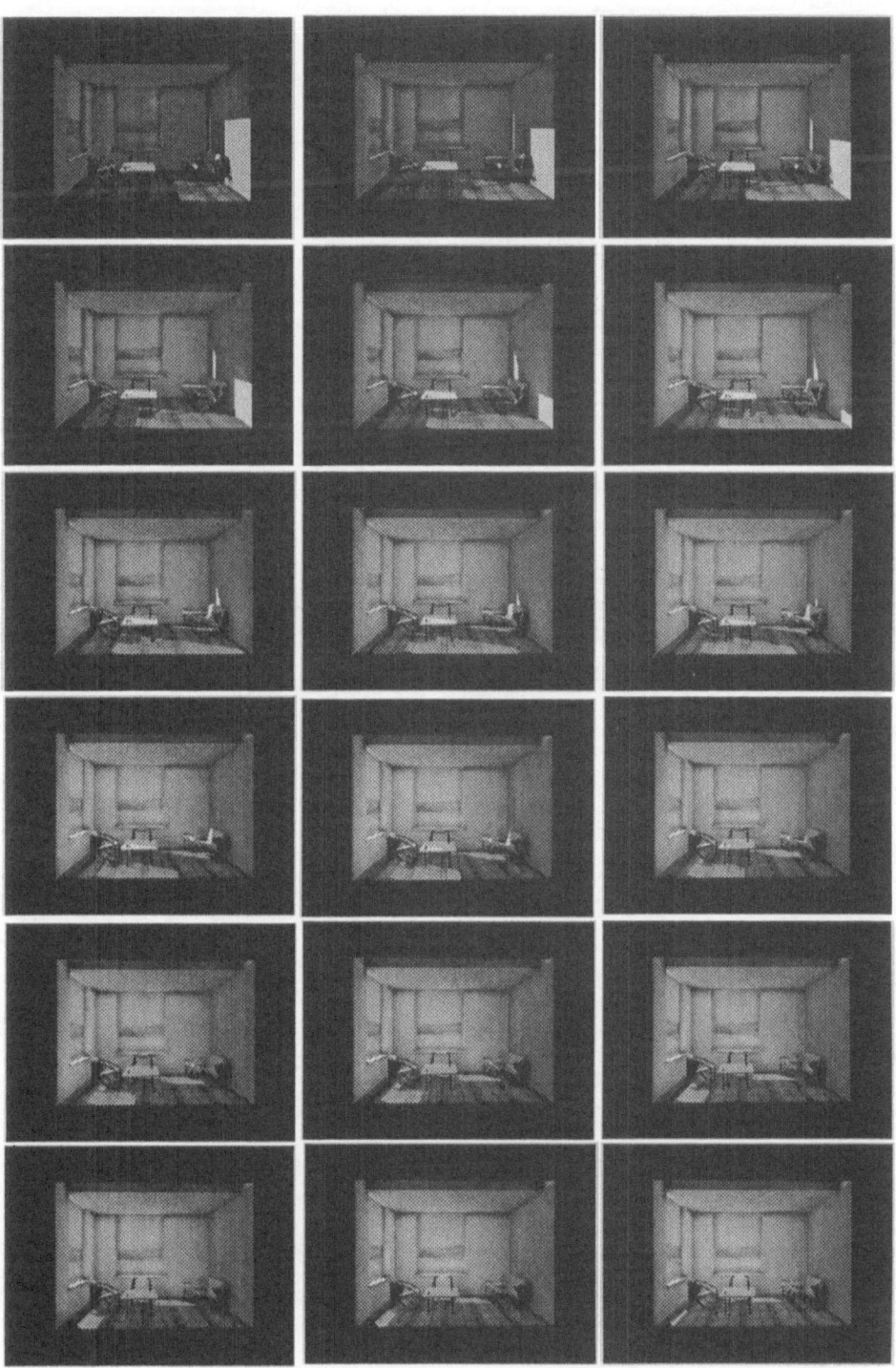

Fig. 11. Sun from 7:00am through 11:15am in 15 minute increments. Each of these 18 images is computed via linear combination of the 9 basis images.

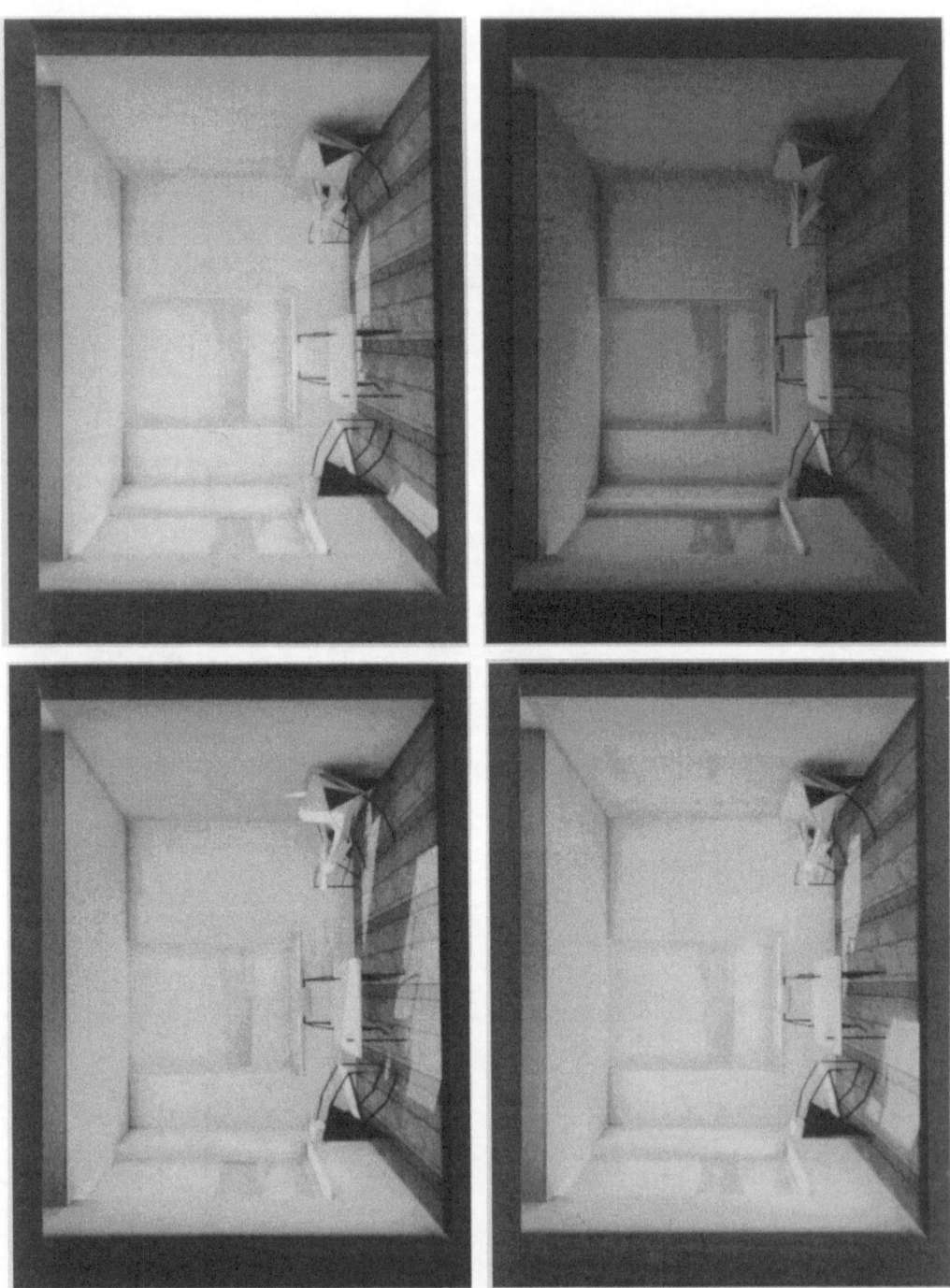

6 Discussion

We have presented a method for the fast re-rendering of naturally illuminated scenes using linear combinations of pre-rendered images. The method requires a set of "basis" illumination functions. In general, this set is unconstrained, but we have imposed a constraint of steerability in order to guarantee that the set of representable illuminants is rotationally invariant. This constraint is particularly useful when modeling natural illumination functions.

Our method allows for an interactive edit-render cycle by eliminating calls to the renderer once the basis images have been computed. This provides the user with the ability to animate naturally illuminated scenes in a fraction of the time that it would require with conventional methods. The limitation of the method is that efficiency requires broad extended illuminants. Narrower illuminants require a larger basis set and consequently more pre-rendering computation.

Several interesting research directions remain. First, for most environments, constructing the approximation of sunlight over the entire sphere is not necessary. Interiors are rarely exposed to sunlight from all directions as they often contain a limited number of openings. Additional work is necessary to quantify the relationship between basis size, basis quality, and spatial coverage. Second, we would like to take advantage of common computation between the different renderings. Recomputing the geometric relationships between objects is unnecessary in a static environment. Third, the approach can extended to use the vertex radiosities as a basis set. This would allow images to be created on the fly for any camera position. Although certain aspects of our approach require further investigation, our preliminary results indicate that this method offers a promising solution to daylight simulation.

References

1. CIE Techinical Committee 4.2. Standardization of luminance distribution on clear skies. CIE Publication No. 22, Commission International de L'Eclairaze, Paris, 1973.
2. John M. Airey, John H. Rohlf, and Frederick P. Brooks, Jr. Towards image realism with interactive update rates in complex virtual building environments. In *Computer Graphics (1990 Symposium on Interactive 3D Graphics)*, volume 24, pages 41–50, March 1990.
3. Chris Buckalew and Donald Fussell. Illumination networks: Fast realistic rendering with general reflectance functions. In *Computer Graphics (SIGGRAPH '89 Proceedings)*, volume 23, pages 89–98, July 1989.
4. I. W. Busbridge. *The Mathematics of Radiative Transfer*. Cambridge University Press, Bristol, 1960.
5. Shenchang Eric Chen. Incremental radiosity: An extension of progressive radiosity to an interactive image synthesis system. In *Computer Graphics (SIGGRAPH '90 Proceedings)*, volume 24, pages 135–144, August 1990.
6. IES Daylighting Committee. Recommended practice of daylighting. *Lighting Design and Application*, 9(2):45–58, 1979.

7. Julie Dorsey. *Computer Graphics Techniques for Opera Lighting Design and Simulation.* PhD thesis, Cornell University, Program of Computer Graphics, Ithaca, NY, January 1993.

8. Julie Dorsey, James Arvo, and Donald Greenberg. Interactive design of complex time-dependent lighting. Submitted for publication, 1994.

9. William T. Freeman and Edward H. Adelson. The design and use of steerable filters. *IEEE Transactions on Pattern Analysis and Machine Intelligence,* 13(9):891–906, September 1991.

10. Gene H. Golub and Charles F. Van Loan. *Matrix Computations.* Johns Hopkins University Press, Baltimore, MD, 1989.

11. James T. Kajiya. The rendering equation. In *Computer Graphics (SIGGRAPH '86 Proceedings),* volume 20, pages 143–150, August 1986.

12. James T. Kajiya. Radiometry and photometry for computer graphics. In *SIGGRAPH '90 Advanced Topics in Ray Tracing Course Notes.* ACM Press, August 1990.

13. Claus Muller. *Spherical Harmonics.* Springer-Verlag, New York, NY, 1966.

14. Jeffry S. Nimeroff, Eero Simoncelli, Julie Dorsey, and Norman I. Badler. Rendering spaces for architectural environments. Submitted to Presence, the Journal of Virtual Reality and Teleoperators, April 1994.

15. Tomoyuki Nishita and Eihachiro Nakamae. Continuous tone representation of three-dimensional objects illuminated by sky light. In *Computer Graphics (SIGGRAPH '86 Proceedings),* volume 20, pages 125–132, August 1986.

16. P Perona. Deformable kernels for early vision. In *IEEE Comp. Soc. Conf. Computer Vision and Pattern Recognition,* pages 222–227, Maui, 1991.

17. Chris Schoeneman, Julie Dorsey, Brian Smits, James Arvo, and Donald Greenberg. Painting with light. In *Computer Graphics (SIGGRAPH '93 Proceedings),* volume 27, pages 143–146, August 1993.

18. Carlo H. Séquin and Eliot K. Smyrl. Parameterized ray tracing. In *Computer Graphics (SIGGRAPH '89 Proceedings),* volume 23, pages 307–314, July 1989.

19. Eero P. Simoncelli. *Distributed Analysis and Representation of Visual Motion.* PhD thesis, Massachusetts Institute of Technology, Department of Electrical Engineering and Computer Science, Cambridge, MA, January 1993. Also available as MIT Media Laboratory Vision and Modeling Technical Report #209.

20. Eero P. Simoncelli, William T. Freeman, Edward H. Adelson, and David J. Heeger. Shiftable multi-scale transforms. *IEEE Trans. Information Theory,* 38(2):587–607, March 1992. Special Issue on Wavelets.

21. Gilbert Strang. *Introduction to Applied Mathematics.* Wellesley-Cambridge Press, Wellesley, MA, 1986.

22. Gregory J. Ward. The radiance lighting simulation system. In *Computer Graphics (SIGGRAPH '94 Proceedings),* volume 28, July 1994.

Texture Mapping as an Alternative for Meshing During Walkthrough Animation

Karol Myszkowski, Tosiyasu L. Kunii

The University of Aizu, Aizu-Wakamatsu, 965-80 Japan

Abstract

Mesh-based radiosity calculation requires many mesh elements to reconstruct subtle details of shading. On the other hand, the excessive number of polygons slows down rendering, impairing the sensation of interactivity when a user-navigated walkthrough in complex environment is performed. When distribution of illumination over a scene is to be quickly rendered, then the Gouraud shaded polygon becomes an inefficient drawing primitive, which can be successfully replaced by texture mapping.

This paper proposes an application of texture mapping to reconstruct the shading of surfaces in the scene regions where distribution of illumination is extremely complex. Mesh-based Gouraud shading is used to visualize the remaining surfaces, exhibiting simple illumination, usually constituting the majority of the scene. As a result, many mesh elements can be eliminated, compared to traditional approaches, and image display can be done significantly faster. Also, the improvement of shading quality is possible by recalculating illumination and storing the results as textures in scene regions where a mesh-based approach produces shading artifacts. Experiments performed have shown that application of this idea pays off on high-end workstations, when hardware supported texture mapping is available.

1 Introduction

Walkthrough animation is a very effective tool for analysis and presentation of design, which is extensively used in architecture, interior, and lighting applications. Images generated during walkthrough should not only be nice looking, but also true. This means that the appearance of an object constructed in reality on the basis of the design should be similar to its virtual analog on the computer display. The important aspect of image reliability is physically-based lighting simulation performed for a modeled scene. To this end the radiosity method is often applied which produces maps of illumination for the whole scene as a result of view-independent calculations. Usually radiosity data are stored at the vertices of a polygonal mesh which becomes quite complex when fine shading details are reconstructed. On the other hand, the complexity of the mesh impairs the speed of image display, which affects the impression of smooth motion during walkthrough animation.

Visibility computations performed by scan conversion hardware on the level of polygons seems to be the most critical bottleneck in walkthrough animation. Many algorithms suitable to architectural applications have been developed to reduce the number of polygons fed to the geometry engine, e.g., visibility culling [8], and level-of-details control [6, 13]. Texture mapping is also used to simplify geometry of the model and enhance realism of visualized surfaces by application of scanned photos of actual construction materials.

The new generation of graphics accelerators is designed as texture mapping machines, significantly reducing performance penalties for texturing. The quality of texturing is very high due to application of minification and magnification filters, which are provided with no penalty at all (e.g., SGI's *RealityEngine²*). In view of these trends of graphic hardware development, various applications of texture mapping have become more and more attractive [9].

In this paper, we discuss an application of textures to reconstruct the shading of surfaces as a solution alternative to traditional mesh-based storage and Gouraud shading performed during an interactive walkthrough. Textures cover surfaces exhibiting the most complex illumination, and eliminate many mesh elements used in traditional approach. As a result the image display can be performed faster. Also, improvement in shading quality is possible by recalculating illumination for textures where mesh-based approach produces shading artifacts.

The following section presents the previous works. Then texture generation as well as rendering issues are discussed. Also, some techniques for improving the quality of texture-based shading are proposed. Finally, experimental results are shown.

2 Previous Research

The idea of using textures to store illumination data is not new. Arvo [2] proposed *illumination maps* to store radiosity for diffuse surfaces encountered by rays traced from light sources toward the scene. Heckbert [10] introduced *radiosity textures (rexes)*, which adaptively adjust the density of sample points to match the complexity of radiosity distribution. During rendering Heckbert performed bilinear interpolation to fill image pixels covered by texels, or averaging when projection of texels on the image plane is smaller than the size of pixel. Vedel [15] also used sampling-based data structure and reconstructed radiosity by an elliptical filter which was oriented perpendicularly to the radiosity gradient.

The common denominator of all these approaches is the elimination of mesh by separating geometrical and radiosity data. These techniques are suitable for generation of still images where resolution of textures can be precisely estimated (Heckbert proposed a *size pass* to record screen size information in each rex).

In walkthrough animation this assumption does not hold, and extremely high texture magnifications for close-up views can be expected. Another problem is texture storage required by the discussed algorithms for complex scenes. Usually, the distribution of radiosity over the scene is non-uniform, and in many regions can be easily reconstructed by a small number of mesh elements. In these regions, the application of textures is not efficient. Heckbert proposes quadtree structure of his rexes to control locally the number of radiosity samples, which solves the problem of texels density adaptation. However, this structure is not supported by standard capabilities of graphical hardware, and hence cannot be efficiently used during image display. The algorithm proposed in this paper overcomes the above problems, and performs well in applications where different views of the scene are needed.

3 Textures vs. Meshing

Most existing radiosity algorithms rely on geometrical models built of a polygonal mesh. The initial mesh is further subdivided in the course of lighting simulation to reconstruct shadow borders, regions of penumbra, and other regions exhibiting high radiosity gradients. Two basic approaches of mesh subdivision are used by radiosity algorithms: *a priori* and *a posteriori* methods [5]. *A priori* methods reconstruct explicitly umbra and penumbra borders on the basis of purely geometrical considerations, resulting in moderate numbers of mesh elements [3, 11, 12]. However, adaptive meshing is still needed when radiosity gradients have no connections with scene geometry, e.g., for gradients produced by light sources described by complex goniometrical diagrams (see a spot of light on the floor in Fig. 1a, color plate 13). *A posteriori* algorithms exploit progressively updated knowledge of scene illumination to make decisions concerning mesh subdivision, and usually tend to oversubdivide regions in proximity of abrupt changes of radiosity distribution [4, 16].

A priori and a posteriori meshing methods are usually applied to traditional shading; however, in lighting design applications the color fringe convention of image display is very common (Fig. 2a, color plate 13). Interactive walkthrough is a very effective tool for inspection of distribution of illumination in all interesting regions of the scene. In order to secure appropriate quality of images, the initial mesh should be adaptively subdivided on the basis of pseudo-colors assigned to the vertices (Fig. 2b, color plate 13). Depending on the particular color settings, which correspond to illumination thresholds, the number of mesh elements in some scene regions can be quite big.

All of the discussed methods generate a large number of mesh elements in scene regions where distribution of illumination is complex. Elimination of some of these elements without impairing the shading quality is crucial to speed up image display. To this end, regions exhibiting complex mesh are detected, and replaced by corresponding textures imitating mesh-based shading. We call these textures *shading textures* to stress the fact that we store in textures, ready to display RGB values instead of radiosity.

3.1 Mesh Postprocessing

Fast texture mapping performed by specialized hardware is currently available exclusively on high-end graphical workstations. Application of shading textures for speeding up walkthrough animation makes sense when such hardware can be utilized. In the solution proposed by this paper, textures are generated optionally by a separate module, which processes the mesh produced during lighting simulation. The resulting shading textures and simplified mesh are used during an interactive walkthrough.

The mesh postprocessing approach makes the creation of textures totally independent on the adaptive mesh subdivision. Also, as the mesh is already known, the scene regions to be replaced by textures can be optimally chosen taking into account the number of eliminated mesh elements, required texture resolution, and the size of texture buffer (i.e., memory specially dedicated to store textures). It should be noted that if the size of all textures exceeds the size of buffer, then swapping between the main memory and the texture memory seriously degrades the performance of the image display.

At the first step of the mesh postprocessing the whole scene is scanned and regions exhibiting high concentrations of elements are identified. The basis for this scanning is an initial, coarse mesh, built in our implementation exclusively of triangles (this restriction does not limit the applicability of the technique when other mesh elements besides triangles are used). Coplanar triangles are grouped into pairs which form quadrilaterals, preferable rectangles. The latter case occurs frequently in architectural applications, allowing efficient use of the whole texture, since most of texels fall inside the scene region to be replaced by this texture. For every quadrilateral the number of children (split triangles) per unit surface area ($E_{density}$) is calculated.

Two main parameters should be decided: (1) the resolution of texture (T_{res}), and (2) the threshold number of mesh elements to be eliminated (E_{thr}); both parameters are related to unit surface area. In the simplest case the user specifies both parameters, but then no control of overflow of the texture memory is provided. When T_{res} is fixed, then quadrilaterals with highest $E_{density}$ are subsequently replaced by textures as long as the texture buffer is not overflown. When E_{thr} is given, then all quadrilaterals which satisfy the condition $E_{density} \geq E_{thr}$ are covered by textures. In such a case, T_{res} is adjusted taking into account the total surface area covered by textures and the texture buffer size.

The next stage of postprocessing is texture generation. Graphical hardware is used to speed up this task, and to prevent some numerical problems which may arise when different approaches are utilized to display images acquired as textures, and a final image based on these textures. Gouraud shaded image of the quadrilateral to be replaced by texture as well as its coplanar neighborhood is displayed and then grabbed from the frame buffer memory. The longest edge of the quadrilateral is aligned with the texture border to minimize the number of texels falling outside this polygon. At the same time mapping parameters are calculated, which assign coordinates in texture space to corresponding vertices of the quadrilateral. Optionally, neighboring quadrilaterals can be merged into

stripes, which are covered by single texture. In such a case the number of textures
is reduced, as well as the number of borders between textured regions.

Prior to walkthrough animation, shading textures are loaded into the texture
memory. In order to get the best performance, all textures used to display a single
frame should be stored in the texture buffer. When textures overflow the buffer,
then management of the texture memory should be done by the application
software; otherwise a random memory swap is done at the operating system
level. The topic of the texture buffer management is beyond the scope of this
paper, and the rest of this discussion assumes that all textures fit in texture
memory.

3.2 Image Display

Two techniques are selectively used during image display: Gouraud shading for
the original mesh, and texture mapping for regions covered by shading texture.
The following problems can be expected during image generation:

- lack of shading continuity on the border:
  - between Gouraud shaded and textured regions,
  - between independent, neighboring textures;
- blurring of fine shading details like sharp shadow borders.

These deficiencies become very annoying when textures are magnified for
close-up views; the magnification is higher, the the degradation of the image
quality is stronger. On the other hand, restricted size of texture memory makes the storage of high resolution textures impossible. Therefore some measures
become important for improving the quality of magnified textures.

Shading Continuity Problems with shading continuity usually arise in regions
of high radiosity gradients and non-linear radiosity distribution. Our experiments
have shown that discontinuity can be significantly reduced when vertices of quadrilateral correspond exactly to the centers of texels (this condition can be met
at all vertices only for rectangles). Of course, the color of such texels should be
the same as the color assigned to the vertices. In a practical implementation,
pixel/texel matching between the two different algorithms should be achieved:
(1) Gouraud shading which produces texture, (2) texture mapping itself, which
assigns this texture back to the same location. On some hardware platforms it
may happen that interpolation of color during Gouraud shading is not performed
for sample points exactly corresponding to the centers of pixels. The hard-wired
algorithms of Gouraud shading and texture mapping cannot be modified, so the
only choice is manipulation of the viewport position during texture acquisition,
and adjustment of the texture coordinates assigned to vertices.

Merging of neighboring quadrilaterals into a stripe covered by a single texture
eliminates many potential borders between textures. When creation of such a
stripe is not justified, because a high percentage of texels fall outside the region
to be covered by the texture, then the best shading match is achieved when

the resolution of neighboring textures is the same. This assumption holds in our current implementation, where texture resolution is a function of the covered surface area.

Texture Magnification An inherent feature of texture magnification is blurring of fine shading details. When such texture is visible in the foreground of the image, then degradation of image quality becomes intolerable, even for fast changing views in an animated sequence. On the other hand, blurred details in the background are less objectionable. Moreover, when the meshing algorithm is not perfect, and some subtle shading details are incomplete, e.g., missing segments of sliver-like shadows, then delicate blurring can even improve (in subjective terms) the overall image appearance.

The blurring effect can be significantly improved when some non-standard features of texture mapping are available, like "texture sharpen" and "detail texture" features [7]. In the texture sharpen case, no additional storage is needed, and the user can model the shape of extrapolation curve, which usually should be clamped to a magnification order 3–5 for best visual results. Figure 3 (color plate 14) presents mesh-based shading, ordinary and sharpened textures for magnification ratio 3967 (refer to formula (1)).

However, even these advanced texture mapping features, currently offered exclusively by high-end workstations, cannot solve the blurring problem. In these circumstances, the simplest solution is to control the magnification factor, and use ordinary mesh when magnification exceeds a threshold specified by the user. Such a threshold can be specified globally for the whole scene, or adaptively on the basis of texture complexity, via the size of the smallest mesh element replaced by the texture. In addition, shadow information can be used, which is stored as a binary value (shadow on/off) for each vertex and for all light sources. When shadow status corresponding to the same light source is different for neighboring vertices, then a high frequency texture pattern can be expected, and a more strict threshold of magnification should be used. (Some analogies to Sillion's mesh subdivision criterion can be found [14].)

The texture magnification can be evaluated when distance from the eye point to the textured object is known. As the magnification inspection should be done for all textures, the simplification of calculations becomes crucial. The definition of texture magnification M can be expressed by the following formula:

$$M = \frac{t_{area}}{p_{area}} \tag{1}$$

where t_{area} and p_{area} are the size of the area of textured surface covered by a single texel and pixel, respectively. The value of t_{area} does not depend on the observer's position, and is stored for every shading texture. The value of p_{area} should be recalculated for all textures and for every frame of the animated sequence:

$$p_{area} = p_{aspect\_ratio} \left(\frac{d \tan(\alpha/2)}{v_{res}/2} \right)^2 = C d^2 \tag{2}$$

where p_{aspect_ratio} is the pixel aspect ratio, d is the distance between the eye position and the center of region covered by texture (coordinates of such points are stored for every texture), α is the vertical viewing angle, and v_{res} is the vertical resolution of image. The term C is constant for given camera position, and can be pre-calculated once per frame.

The proposed magnification check does not take into account visibility frustum. It is assumed, however, that visibility culling is performed, and most of the polygons outside the pyramid of vision have already been eliminated by an algorithm using object-space coherence [8]. The resolution of textures should be as high as possible in order to minimize the probability of excessive magnification. The algorithm for automatic adjustment of T_{res} for fixed E_{thr} proposed in §3.1 maximizes the resolution of textures for a given size of the texture buffer.

Duality of shading performed alternately by original mesh or shading texture can be used as a form of level-of-detail (LOD) control performed during walkthrough animation. Both texture magnification factor and load of display pipeline can decide when the faster texture mapping should replace the mesh, even at expense of a lower image quality.

3.3 Refinement of Texture Quality

As already mentioned, most meshing algorithms used in practical applications miss some fine shading details or reconstruct them inaccurately, e.g., shadows thrown by leaves of a plant. In these affected areas, distribution of radiosity can be recalculated from scratch, transformed to RGB values, and stored in the shading texture, replacing poor quality mesh-based images as proposed in previous sections. Radiosity sampling is performed at locations corresponding to texels rather than vertices of mesh. Some similarities to image generation by ray tracing may be found. All advantages related with sampling-based approach are available, e.g., jittering, adaptive supersampling, Pixel Selected Ray Tracing [1] etc. Moreover, it is possible to draw upon knowledge about scene illumination acquired during the adaptive mesh splitting.

The basic problem is how to get continuity on the border between the sampling-based texture and its Gouraud shaded neighborhood. The problem of continuity can be partially eliminated when the texture acquired from mesh-based image and the sampling-based texture are blended. The blending function (2-D matrix of values in the range [0,1], which correspond to each texel) suppresses the influence of the sampling-based texture in the proximity of its border with coplanar Gouraud shaded mesh element. The closer to the texture border, the higher is the weight of the mesh-based texture; away from the border the mesh-based texture is totally ignored. This technique produces reasonable results when the quality of mesh-based shading is good, and requires only local corrections. Otherwise, all coplanar elements should be replaced by a single sampling-based texture.

4 Results

Experimental analysis has been performed on the $ONYX$ workstation (Silicon Graphics, Inc.) equipped with $RealityEngine^2$ graphics accelerator. The main goal of the experiment was the evaluation of the image display speed traded-off by the quality of resulting images.

Image display speed as a function of E_{thr} control parameter was considered. A practical penalty introduced by texture mapping was also measured in our application. Figure 1a (color plate 13) presents the scene used in our experiments. The scene was originally built from 8646 triangles, and then adaptively subdivided into 81285 mesh elements (Fig. 1b, color plate 13). The scene regions covered by 350 shading textures are visualized in green in Fig. 1c, color plate 13 ($E_{thr} = 20$). Control parameter T_{res} was fixed to 32 by 32 texels. It is the maximal texture's resolution because the biggest quadrilateral in the scene is taken as the surface unit area. Resolution of other textures is scaled proportionally to the surface area, preserving number of texels per square meter of the scene. $RealityEngine^2$ internally scales textures to a resolution which is a power of 2 (4, 8, 16, etc.). This rule is also followed during texture generation in order to have more reliable control over memory used by shading textures. All statistics of texture memory presented below take into account memory extension by the factor 1/3, which is related to the texture filtration technique called MipMap [7], which is performed by default on $RealityEngine^2$. Three components textures (8-bits per component) have been used.

E_{thr}	$Time$ [sec.]	T_{ratio} [%]	$Penalty$ [%]	$E_{eliminated}$	E_{ratio} [%]	$Textures$ $Number$	$Memory$ $Size$ [kB]
100	0.293	157.0	1.3	30584	160.3	125	384.4
50	0.219	210.0	2.7	43530	215.3	265	530.5
20	0.199	231.1	4.0	47040	237.4	350	696.7
10	0.194	237.0	5.1	47814	242.8	406	810.1
4	0.193	238.7	6.2	48124	245.1	471	942.4

Table 1. Statistics of texture-based image display

Table 1 presents the timings of image display (refer to column $Time$) with various values of E_{thr}, while the timing of Gouraud shading for this scene was 0.460 seconds; T_{ratio} is the ratio of timings for Gouraud shading and textures. The penalty for texturing ($Penalty$) is measured as the relative difference of image generation times for the same mesh with and without textures. The speedup of image display is proportional to the number of eliminated mesh elements ($E_{eliminated}$); E_{ratio} is the ratio of the number of triangles to be displayed for Gouraud shading and textures. A comparison of T_{ratio} and E_{ratio} reveals that the penalty for texturing slightly affects the overall algorithm performance, especially for small E_{thr}. The last two columns present the number of textures and the memory used as a function of E_{thr}. Taking into account that up to 4 MB of texture memory is available on the *RealityEngine*[2] graphics accelerator, there is still room to create many additional textures, and to apply the presented technique to more complex scenes. Texture generation is relatively fast, e.g., postprocessing of 350 textures took 46.5 seconds ($E_{thr} = 20$).

The experimental results presented so far have shown that application of shading textures significantly reduces time of image display. The question arises: *What price, in terms of image quality, should be paid for smoother walkthrough animation?* A quantitative comparison of images generated using shading textures to traditional approach based on Gouraud shading is presented in Table 2. A histogram of textured pixels exhibiting the same differences of RGB δ between textured and Gouraud shaded images is calculated as:

$$\delta = abs(P_i^{texture} - P_i^{gouraud}) \tag{3}$$

where $P_i^{texture}$, $P_i^{gouraud}$ are averages of pixel's RGB for textured and Gouraud shaded images. It is assumed that the range of possible values of δ is [0,255]. Table 2 presents percentages of pixels for $\delta = 0, 1, 2$ and $\delta > 2$. δ_{max} describes the maximum difference of RGB between textured and Gouraud shaded pixels. Also, *RMS Error* (4) is introduced as the global measure of texturing quality

$$RMS\ Error = \sqrt{\frac{\sum_{i=1}^{n} \delta_i^2}{n}} \tag{4}$$

where n is the number of pixels covered by textures.

Error measures were calculated for various values of T_{res}. Formula (1) is used to calculate the maximum and the average magnification ratios (M_{max} and M_{avr}). The same scene is used (Fig. 1a, color plate 13); 42.1% of the whole image is covered by 350 textures (Fig. 1c, color plate 13). Figure 1d shows the error introduced by textures comparing to mesh-based approach for $T_{res} = 32$ by 32 texels. The intensity of pixels is magnified for better visibility preserving proportions to the error values.

T_{res}	M_{max}	M_{avr}	RMS	$\delta = 0$ [%]	$\delta = 1$ [%]	$\delta = 2$ [%]	$\delta > 2$ [%]	δ_{max}
256 x 256	1.14	0.05	2.228	36.1	57.2	3.1	3.2	39
128 x 128	4.58	0.18	2.059	36.3	57.3	3.2	3.2	41
64 x 64	15.52	0.77	2.027	43.0	51.8	2.4	2.8	52
32 x 32	73.96	3.03	2.382	48.0	45.8	2.6	3.6	54
16 x 16	295.84	12.04	3.632	43.0	47.3	4.3	5.4	64
8 x 8	1182.67	48.16	4.140	24.9	47.5	13.5	14.1	82

Table 2. Statistics of the texture-based image quality

The best image matching has been obtained for $T_{res} = 64$ by 64 texels, i.e., when average magnification of texture is close to 1. This means that filtration performed on strongly minified textures is a source of some minor discrepancies. The big values of δ_{max} are produced near sharp shadow borders, as a result of texture blurring.

In terms of subjective comparison of images by people, an evident degradation of image quality has been observed for textures 8 by 8 texels, mainly because of discontinuities of shading on the texture borders. For higher resolution textures, differences near the shadow regions have been noticed, but in general the image quality has been acceptable.

Also, a generation of sampling-based shading textures has been investigated. The results for two scenes are presented: a Room and a Cafeteria. Figures 4a (color plate 14) and 5a (color plate 15) present Gouraud shading based images of scene regions exhibiting many subtle shadows, which in some cases are poorly reconstructed by mesh. Figures 4b (color plate 14) and 5b (color plate 15) show the corresponding images where sampling-based textures had been used. Significant quality improvement can be observed in the latter case. No problems with continuity on the borders of sampling-based textures are visible when moderate magnification of textures is performed (for the scene Room: $M_{max} = 16.9$ and $M_{avr} = 4.5$). In Figs. 4c and 5c, blue regions are covered by the sampling-based textures, while green regions mark textures using Gouraud shading. Ray-traced images with accurate shadows are given for reference (Figs. 4d and 5d). The scene Cafeteria was built from 1338324 triangles. 459656 triangles were replaced by 2782 shading textures. 188 textures were recalculated on the sampling basis. Texture preprocessing took 5692 seconds.

5 Conclusions

We have presented an application of texture mapping as a drawing primitive complementary to Gouraud shaded polygons traditionally used for fast rendering of radiosity images. The basic premise of the proposed method is the elimination of many mesh elements, which can be replaced by a single texture covering a scene region exhibiting complex illumination. Since the penalty for texture mapping on high-end workstations is relatively small, the speed up of image display is nearly proportional to the number of polygons replaced by textures.

The main drawback of the proposed solution is degradation of image quality when a texture is excessively magnified. However, these situations can be easily detected, and traditional mesh techniques can be applied. Notwithstanding, the accuracy of the image can be significantly improved when texture is created on the basis of illumination sampling instead of a mesh-based image exhibiting shading artifacts.

The experiments have shown that the technique proposed can be efficiently applied to an interactive walkthrough in moderately complex environments. When the problem of texture buffer management is efficiently solved, then this algorithm is suitable for huge scenes too.

One may expect that when texturing limitations (especially the size of the texture memory and texture sharpening algorithms) are overcome by future generations of graphical hardware, then radiosity data can be stored directly in textures [10], eliminating mesh storage completely. However, taking into account current possibilities of graphical equipment, the approach proposed in this paper seems to be a reasonable trade-off for practical applications.

6 Acknowledgements

The models of room and cafeteria were provided by Sigma Design, Inc., and Nikken, Inc., respectively, and then rendered by Koji Tsuchiya. Turbo Beam Tracing software developed by INTEGRA, Inc., was used by the authors as a testbed for shading textures implementation.

The authors would like to thank colleagues from The University of Aizu, Oleg Okunev and Michael Cohen, for reviewing the manuscript. Special thanks for helpful discussions go to Akira Fujimoto.

References

1. T. Akimoto, K. Mase, A. Hashimoto, and Y Suenage. Pixel selected ray tracing. *Eurographics'89 Proceedings (Hamburg, Germany)*, pages 39–50, September 1989.
2. J. R. Arvo. Backward ray tracing. *SIGGRAPH'86 Course Notes: Developments in Ray Tracing*, 12, August 1986.
3. A. Campbell and D. Fussell. Adaptive mesh generation. *Computer Graphics (SIGGRAPH'90 Proceedings)*, 24(4):155–164, August 1990.
4. M. F. Cohen, D. P. Greenberg, D. S. Immel, and P. J. Brock. An efficient radiosity approach for realistic image synthesis. *IEEE CG&A*, 6(3):26–35, March 1986.
5. M. F. Cohen and J. R. Wallace. *Radiosity and Realistic Image Synthesis*. Academic Press Professional, London, 1993.
6. T. A. Funkhouser and C. H. Sequin. Adaptive display algorithm for interactive frame rates during visualization of complex virtual environments. *Computer Graphics (SIGGRAPH'93 Proceedings)*, 27:247–254, August 1993.
7. Silicon Graphics, editor. *Graphical Library Programming Guide*. Document Number 007-1680-010. Silicon Graphics, Inc., 1992.
8. N. Greene, M. Kass, and G. Miller. Hierarchical z-buffer visibility. *Computer Graphics (SIGGRAPH'93 Proceedings)*, 27:231–238, August 1993.
9. P. Haeberli and M. Segal. Texture mapping as a fundamental drawing primitive. *Fourth Eurographics Workshop on Rendering (Paris, France)*, pages 259–266, June 1993.
10. P. Heckbert. Adaptive radiosity textures for bidirectional ray tracing. *Computer Graphics (SIGGRAPH'90 Proceedings)*, 24(4):145–154, August 1990.
11. P. Heckbert. Discontinuity meshing for radiosity. *Third Eurographics Workshop on Rendering (Bristol, UK)*, pages 203–226, May 1992.
12. D. Lischinski, F. Tampieri, and D. P. Greenberg. Discontinuity meshing for accurate radiosity. *IEEE CG&A*, 12(6):25–39, November 1992.
13. J. Rossignac and P. Borrel. Multi-resolution 3d approximations for rendering complex scenes. *Second Conference on Geometric Modeling in Computer Graphics (Genova, Italy)*, pages 453–465, June 1993.

14. F. Sillion. Detection of shadow boundaries for adaptive meshing in radiosity. *Graphics Gems II, J. Arvo, Ed., Academic Press, San Diego*, pages 311–315, 1991.
15. C. Vedel. Improved storage and reconstruction of light intensities on surfaces. *Third Eurographics Workshop on Rendering (Bristol, UK)*, pages 113–121, May 1992.
16. C. Vedel and C. Puech. A testbed for adaptive subdivision in progressive radiosity. *Second Eurographics Workshop on Rendering (Barcelona, Spain)*, May 1991.

BRUSH as a Walkthrough System for Architectural Models

Bengt-Olaf Schneider, Paul Borrel, Jai Menon, Josh Mittleman, Jarek Rossignac

IBM T.J. Watson Research Center, P.O. Box 704, Yorktown Heights, NY 10598

Abstract

Brush provides an interactive environment for the real-time visualization and inspection of very large mechanical and architectural CAD databases. It supports immersive and non-immersive virtual reality walkthrough applications (for example, when validating or demonstrating to a customer an architectural concept) and detailed design reviews of complex mechanical assemblies such as engines, plants, airplanes, or ships.

Brush achieves interactive response times by selecting from multiple-resolution representations for each object, computed automatically by simplifying the original data. Simplified models reduce the cost of displaying small details that do not significantly affect the image, allowing navigation through models comprising hundreds of thousands of triangles.

A natural gesture-driven interface allows mouse or space-ball control of the camera for intuitive walkthrough in architectural scenes. Simple facilities for editing and sequencing camera positions along with automatic animation of camera trajectories between key-frames enable the construction, demonstration, and archive of pre-programmed walkthrough sequences.

1 Introduction

Today, architects face a wide range of constraints and requirements when designing new buildings or remodeling and renovating existing structures. Such requirements are imposed on the architect by the existing building codes and the customers. Some examples follow:

- *Environmental Impact Studies* often demand that the architect convincingly demonstrate the effect of his design. For example, constructing a new office building might obstruct the view from existing buildings.
- *Shadows* cast by buildings on the ground and on other buildings must be considered when predicting the impact a new building will have on neighboring structures. Shadow analysis must be done for different times of the day and the year.

- *Customers* will often understand the character and proportions of a building more easily if they are able to take a virtual stroll through the new building. Today, many design firms attempt to satisfy these requests with canned video presentations.
- *Visibility and Accessibility* are important properties of architectural spaces. For instance, in lecture halls and theaters it is important that the stage area be clearly visible from all seats.

Such requirements, in addition to traditional demands like structural and thermal analysis, put a heavy load on today's architects and civil engineers. Meeting these requirements will permit architects to bid more competitively for contracts and to provide better and more timely service to customers. By providing interactive manipulation and simulation, computer graphics uniquely assists designers in addressing these concerns.

Brush is an interactive environment for real-time visualization and inspection of very large architectural and mechanical CAD models. **Brush** was designed specifically to provide designers with a quick path to shaded, three-dimensional, interactive rendering of their models. It therefore presents the user with a set of interaction paradigms that are intuitive and natural for a given task. **Brush** automates many of the cumbersome details of managing large geometric data sets and chosing optimized rendering modes to achieve interactive response time, and thus hides their complexity from the user.

In this paper we will describe some of the underlying algorithms of **Brush** and how they are used in architectural applications. The remainder of this paper will introduce **Brush** and explain how it addresses some of these problems. First we summarize alternative approaches to the problem. Then, we give a brief overview of the architecture of **Brush**. The follwing sections provide a more detailed description of the interaction and animation capabilities offered by **Brush**. We then report briefly the performance achieved with **Brush** and its current status. The last section describes how **Brush** addresses some real-world architectural problems.

2 Prior Work

The fundamental computational problem for interactive visualization of large models is to reduce the amount of geometry to be processed by the renderer enough to allow interactive update rates of the display. Two principal techniques are available to accomplish these goals: level of detail management and efficient determination of visibility.

Various systems have been proposed recently to address these problems. In [2] a system is described for interactive walkthroughs of models which lend themselves to be partitioned into cells, e. g. rooms, connected by portals, e. g. doors. The method consumes extensive resources during preprocessing of the scene. Reportedly [3], preprocessing of a scene with 250,000 polygons took about 6 hours and generated 58 MB of visibility data. This system was combined with a level-of-detail management system [1] that employs a cost-benefit heuristic to minimize frame-rate variations.

An improved visibility algorithm based on a hierarchical z-buffer was described in [3]. The algorithm combines partitioning object-space using an octree to cull invisible portions of the model with a pyramidal z-buffer. The pyramidal z-buffer provides a z profile at different resolutions to quickly reject polygons that are know to be hidden by already rendered polygons. The method incurs extra cost for constructing the octree and for maintaining the pyramidal z-buffer. For complex scenes this cost is recovered by more efficient rejection of hidden polygons. To make best use of this method, it requires features in the graphics hardware that are not commonly available today.

Iris Performer™[4] is a programming library that uses a hierarchical data structure to organize the model into smaller parts each of which has an associated bounding volume. This data structure is used to optimize culling and rendering of the model. It is the responsibility of the programmer to organize the data structure such that Performer can make good use of it. To improve run-time performance, the designer can provide several representations of an object with varying amount of detail. Performer selects the appropriate level of detail automatically.

3 System Overview

Figure 1 shows a simplified block diagram of the system architecture of **Brush**. Models are imported through import bridges that interface **Brush** to different CAD systems and interchange formats. A preprocessor analyzes the model geometry and automatically constructs bounds and simplified representations of the objects in the scene, and converts the data into a format optimized for fast rendering. The **Brush** display engine manages the dynamic selection of objects to be displayed and controls the rendering process. The user can interact and control the display process at any time through different user-interface channels.

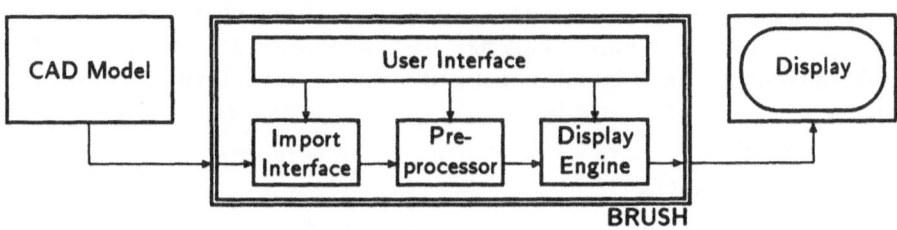

Fig. 1. System architecture of Brush.

3.1 Import interfaces.

CAD models of architectural or engineering designs can be imported from various commercial design systems or through different file formats, e. g. Catia^{TM}, AES^{TM}, Pro/ENGINEER^{TM}, DXF^{TM}, STL^{TM}. The Brush native import format is based on the concept of instantiation of solids described as polyhedra, thus providing a simple though versatile interface to import from different design systems and/or to convert data represented in different formats.

The import facilities in Brush allow the user to select one or several models from the CAD database. The ability to load and display different models at the same time enables the visualization of interactions among those models. Each import bridge preserves source information about the model such as colors, tags, or hierarchy by automatically constructing meaningful names and (optionally) collecting objects into groups.

3.2 Simplification.

The objective of Brush is to provide readily-available high-performance visualization of CAD data. To this end, Brush uses different levels of detail for each part of the model when rendering the image. In contrast to many other rendering systems, Brush assumes the burden of constructing the various levels of detail and computes them *automatically* when it reads the model for the first time.

The simplification technique works directly from the polyhedral boundary models. It is not limited to smooth surfaces and does not rely on the capability of a CAD system to produce tesselations that approximate curved surfaces to different accuracies. It is therefore capable of eliminating or simplifying details involving many surfaces and can simplify objects directly designed as polyhedral models. Visually accurate simplified models of mechanical parts can typically be rendered in only 5% of the time necessary to render the originals.

The simplification algorithm employs a 3D grid to cluster vertices in the original model that can be collapsed in order to derive a simplified version of that model with fewer vertices. A more detailed description of the algorithm can be found in [5]. This technique is especially effective because it directly addresses one of the main performance bottlenecks in today's graphics systems: vertex processing. This applies particularly to complex scenes where the average polygon is very small. Then the rasterization cost is low and the cost for vertex processing dominates. Figure 5 and figure 6 (color plate 16, courtesy of IBM Germany) compare the original model and the same model with 10 times less triangles.

3.3 Display Engine

Brush achieves high rendering performance by reducing unnecessary processing of the model. For instance, Brush maintains a tight bound for every instance of an object which is used to cull objects the clipping volume. This procedure avoids loading the graphics hardware with geometry data for objects ultimately not visible on the screen.

Brush provides an automatic constant-frame-rate display mode, which selects the simplification level to use for each instance depending on its visual importance in the current frame. The user may adjust the overall quality, trading off performance and visual accuracy. Less accurate models may be used for quickly finding a good viewpoint or for previewing a walkthrough animation. The accurate models are used for inspection of details or for recording images or animations. The user may also override the automatic mode and select particular solids or groups of solids to be displayed with full detail, while others (considered background information) are displayed with less detail or are hidden altogether.

Brush provides two automatic modes for selecting the levels of detail. In *Constant Quality Mode*, Brush strives to maintain a constant subjective image quality by selecting levels of detail based on the size of the objects as they appear on the screen. In *Constant Update Mode*, the levels of detail for the objects are chosen so that Brush best meets a user-specified target number of triangles to be displayed; this algorithm gives preference to objects that appear large on the screen and less weight to objects that cover only a small fraction of the screen.

To sustain interactive response time, Brush automatically switches to simplified representations whenever the user requests changes in the image, e. g. view point changes. During pauses in the user's interaction, Brush uses the idle time to prepare a full-quality image in the backbuffer, thus always trying to give the highest quality images within the time constraints specified by the user's interaction pattern.

4 User Interaction

Brush provides the user with a simple yet powerful set of tools to navigate and manipulate the model. These tools are available through different user-interfaces: dialog boxes with icons symbolizing the actions or direct-manipulation using one of the many supported input devices (see below).

The following paragraphs will outline those user interaction paradigms and concepts that apply to the architectural domain.

Navigation Paradigms. Brush provides several modes for moving the camera (view point) to accommodate various preferences or circumstances. For example, a user perceives motion differently when looking at a mechanical part or when touring an architectural scene.

The preferred mode for inspecting (small) mechanical parts is the *Inspect Mode* where all motions occur relative to the part; the user interacts with the model as if he were holding it in his hand at arm's length.

The preferred mode for touring architectural scenes is the *Walkthrough Mode*. In this mode, user input, e. g. mouse motions, are mapped in a very intuitive manner to simple camera movements (go forward or backward, turn left or right, look up or down...) to provide users with the virtual reality effect of walking through a scene (such as a room, store, building, plant, plane, or ship) while keeping their feet solidly on the ground. For instance, the user can adjust his viewing direction to look upwards but will still move parallel to the ground instead of leaving the ground to follow his line of sight. Real-time realistic motion provides vital cues for understanding and evaluating the aesthetics or the validity of complex structures.

Direct Manipulation. Besides standard graphical user-interface elements like sliders and push buttons, **Brush** offers the user the option of having his gestures translated directly into manipulations of the objects or the viewpoint. These gestures vary for different input devices. For mouse input, for example, diffe-rent button combinations are mapped to actions like **translate viewpoint** or **rotate object**. Devices with six degrees of freedom, like the Spaceball^{TM}or the Polhemus^{TM}tracker, support these actions even more intuitively.

Brush can support several such input devices simultaneously. The user can chose the optimal direct-manipulation method for a given action. For example: rotations of the object could be performed using the Spaceball, object translati-ons with the mouse, while the user position and viewing direction are captured with a head tracker.

Depending on the input device and the task at hand, users prefer different interpretation of their input. In *Position Mode* the input is proportional to the change of position or orientation; for example the object will follow the cursor. In *Velocity Mode* the input is interpreted as a rate of change: the larger the user input, e. g. mouse displacement, the faster the position and/or orientation change. **Brush** also offers the combination of both methods. Small input is in-terpreted in Position Mode and large inputs in Velocity Mode. This *Combined Mode* is useful, for instance, for positioning an object first roughly (in Velocity Mode) and then accurately (in Position Mode).

Selection and Grouping. Solids may be selected through simple graphical interaction (e. g. picking with the mouse) or by entering the solid name. Select-by-name allows the user to choose a solid or a set of related solids by entering an exact solid name or by entering a filter that matches one or more solid names. The names of selected solids allow the user to identify the original part in the database. Because most models of architectural scenes or mechanical assemblies are constructed from thousands of solids, **Brush** offers efficient grouping mecha-nisms. The display characteristics of an entire group may be changed in one step. For example, the group may be temporarily made invisible, or may be replaced by a simple approximating shape. Groups are constructed by collecting selected solids. This selection may be performed through mouse picking, through filters on solid names, or by editing a 3D box in the model. The user can place this selection box in the scene, adjust its position and dimensions, and then select all solids which intersect the box. This feature is particular useful for interference and assembly inspection and analysis. Groups may also be combined with other groups.

The user will frequently want to examine only part of model and hide the remaining solids, either to achieve greater graphics performance or to unclutter the image. He may wish to highlight some parts of the model by setting their colors or to force some parts to be displayed in their original geometry while allowing the rest to vary according to their importance in the scene. **Brush** provides a simple, hierarchical scheme which allows the user to set display characteristics for single solids, groups of solids, or the entire scene. Display characteristics include level of detail, color, and visibility.

Realism. Architectural details are more easily appreciated if additional visual clues are given to the viewer. Stereoscopic display greatly helps in achieving realism and in developing an intuitive understanding of a scene. **Brush** supports stereoscopic display in several forms: Immersive display using head-mounted displays and non-immersive display using either a projection screen together with polarized glasses or stereo directly off the monitor together with LCD shutter glasses.

As explained earlier, shadows provide important information on how buildings and structural features impact the surrounding buildings. **Brush** provides interactive rendering of floor shadows. The sun's position can either be specified explicitly or animated. These two options allow analysis of particular lighting conditions as well as an efficient means to inspect the shadow coverage over the course of a full day. Figure 3 (color plate 16, courtesy of IBM France) shows a model of the Abbey of Cluny rendered with floor shadows.

Both, geometry and materials are equally important to appreciate an architectural design. **Brush** can apply textures to different parts of the model to satisfy the need for realistically looking images of the design. **Brush** enables the architect to explore various design alternatives for the choice of materials by simply selecting different material textures from a wide selection of textures. Figure 7 (color plate 16, courtesy of IBM Germany) shows how wood and marble textures have been applied to a model.

5 Animation

Simple key-presses or mouse clicks allow the user to store up to 100 camera set-ups in numbered camera registers for later use. Cameras can be stored and recalled easily. Because an abrupt change of the view to a previously stored camera could leave the viewer disoriented, **Brush** moves smoothly between views by interpolating in a natural manner so that the user can keep track of the change. The interpolation scheme and the number of interpolation steps can be controlled by the user.

A walkthrough or animation sequence can be prepared for demonstration to customers or for design review by storing a sequence of camera setups along the desired camera trajectory. The walkthrough may be played back at various speeds and with controlled accuracy.

To define an animation, the user enters a sequence of cameras using the camera register numbers. A simple animation control grammar allows the user to repeat subsequences, to change the number of steps between key frames (i. e. speed), and to modify the animation in a variety of other ways. For example, one could easily specify that the camera should approach a scene, turn three times around it, then zoom in on some detail. Animation control resembles that of a VCR, allowing the user to start and stop at any time and to single-step through the animation. The user can globally control the speed of the animation and the method of interpolation in between stored views.

6 Implementation

Brush is currently available to selected customers in a beta test version for IBM and Silicon Graphics platforms. With its unique simplification technology and adaptive level of detail selection algorithm, Brush regularly improves the perceived rendering performance of the underlying hardware by about an order of magnitude. The following table illustrates this ability and summarizes performance data for some example models (see figures 2, 3, 4 on color plate 16, courtesy of the Olympic Winter Games):

Model	Triangle count	Platform	Rendering time	
			Original	Const. Update
Frauenkirche	229,687	1	267 sec	14 sec
		2	64 sec	5 sec
		3	31 sec	5 sec
Cluny	685,724	1	711 sec	69 sec
		2	181 sec	17 sec
		3	81 sec	21 sec
Ice rink	201,296	1	196 sec	8 sec
		2	60 sec	4 sec
		3	23 sec	2 sec

Platform 1   IBM RS/6000 Mod. 530, High-Perf. 3D Adapter
Limit set to 5,000 triangles
Platform 2   IBM RS/6000 Mod. 560 with a GTO Adapter
Limit set to 8,000 triangles
Platform 3   SGI 4D with VGX graphics options
Limit set to 12,000 triangles

All times are for animations containing 10 consecutive frames.

7 Applications

Brush has been used successfully in a number of applications:

The Frauenkirche in Dresden is currently being reconstructed from old plans and drawings. The initial capture of the model was done using Catia. Brush has directly imported the **Catia** data and has provided interactive renderings of the church early in the project. Architects and project managers can already provide guided tours through the virtual Frauenkirche, giving visitors today an impression of what the reconstructed church will look like several years from now.

The interactive and intuitive navigation facilities of **Brush** were used to select viewpoints of the Olympic sites in Lillehammer/Norway. These views were later used in the production of an IBM TV commercial for the 1994 Olympic Winter Games. The original CAD models were constructed in **AES** from where they were directly imported into **Brush**.

8 Conclusion

We have described **Brush**, a walkthrough system for large mechanical and architectural CAD models. **Brush** employs automatic object simplification and adaptive level of detail selection to achieve interactive frame rates for models that cannot be rendered interactively with today's graphics hardware.

Brush is seamlessly integrated with popular CAD systems and provides designers with a quick path from their CAD system to a shaded three-dimensional view of their design.

Brush provides important functions and features that help architects and interior designers to quickly visualize and demonstrate their designs. This allows to evaluate and verify designs in early design stages. Powerful navigation and rendering facilities let the user interactively inspect their designs in 3D.

References

1. Thomas A. Funkhouser, Carlo H. Séquin, *Adaptive Display Algorithm for Interactive Frame Rates During Visualization of Complex Virtual Environments*, Proc. Siggraph 1993, Computer Graphics 26, pp. 247-254
2. Seth J. Teller, Carlo H. Séquin, *Visibility Preprocessing for Interactive Walkthroughs*, Proc. Siggraph 1991, Computer Graphics 25, 4, (August 1991), pp. 61-69
3. Ned Greene, Michael Kass, Gavin Miller, *Hierarchical Z-Buffer Visibility*, Proc. Siggraph 1993, Computer Graphics 26, pp. 231-238
4. Patricia McLendon, *IRIS Performer Programming Guide*, Silicon Graphics, Document Number 0070-1680-010, 1992
5. Jarek Rossignac, Paul Borrel, *Multi-resolution 3D Approximations for Rendering Complex Scenes*, in B. Falcidieno and T.L. Kunii (Eds.), *Modeling in Computer Graphics*, Springer-Verlag, 1993.

Environment Mapping for Efficient Sampling of the Diffuse Interreflection

Erik Reinhard, Lucas U. Tijssen, Frederik W. Jansen

Faculty of Technical Mathematics and Informatics, Delft University of Technology, Julianalaan 132, 2628BL Delft, The Netherlands

Abstract

Environment mapping is a technique to compute specular reflections for a glossy object. Originally proposed as a cheap alternative for ray tracing, the method is well suited to be incorporated in a hybrid rendering algorithm. In this paper environment mapping is introduced to reduce the amount of computations involved in tracing secondary rays. During rendering, instead of tracing the secondary rays all through the scene, values are taken from the maps for the rays that would otherwise hit distant objects. This way the quality of the image is retained while providing a cheap alternative to stochastic brute force sampling methods. An additional advantage is that due to the local representation of the entire 3D scene in a map, parallelising this algorithm should result in a good speed-up and high efficiency.

1 Introduction

In the past, a number of approaches to rendering have been proposed. Image quality and speed are the two main goals set in the computer graphics community. If speed is the dominant factor, e.g. in flight simulators and architectural walk-throughs where images must be produced in real-time, z-buffer-based algorithms and hardware can be used. By using a radiosity pre-processing, a more realistic shading can be obtained. Disadvantages are that specular reflection can not be modelled and that the quality of the solution strongly depends upon the resolution of the radiosity mesh.

The other approach to rendering is the use of sampling algorithms, such as ray tracing or ray tracing based radiosity. There are several versions of two-pass algorithms which consist of a radiosity and a ray tracing pass. These hybrid algorithms differ in the amount of sampling done during the rendering pass. The standard two-pass algorithm only samples specular reflection during rendering, while the radiosity values are used for diffuse reflection and direct lighting (Sillion and Puech 1989; Wallace et al. 1987). An extended version also samples direct light during rendering (Shirley 1990, 1991; Chen et al. 1991; Kok and Jansen

1991) and finally, diffuse light may be sampled in the rendering stage in addition to specular reflection and direct light (Rushmeier 1988; Chen et al. 1991).

Sampling of indirect light allows the simulation of intricate reflection details. However, in complex environments this method will be very expensive and moreover it may bring about aliasing problems. To make aliasing less visible and to obtain a reasonable estimate of the indirect diffuse reflection, either a huge number of samples has to be taken, or stochastic techniques may be applied. Stochastic sampling effectively turns aliasing into noise, which is less perceptible to the human eye.

However, a large number of samples is still needed. Therefore, using today's hardware, it is not possible to compute an image interactively with these methods. There are two approaches to reduce computation times of high quality rendering algorithms. First the algorithm can be optimised by reducing the number of redundant computations. Examples of such improvements are spatial subdivision techniques (Glassner 1989) and grouping (Rushmeier 1993; Kok 1993). Second, rendering algorithms may provide good opportunities to be efficiently implemented on multicomputers.

An implementation of a hybrid algorithm on a distributed memory MIMD computer will likely present problems when the scenes to be rendered are large. Then the scene database can not be replicated with every processor due to memory restrictions. Some distribution scheme will have to be applied instead. Objects can be assigned to the processors randomly, completely ignoring scene coherence. A better idea is to base the object distribution upon a spatial subdivision structure. Then the objects that are contained within a region of the environment, are assigned to the same processor. A task is executed by the processor that holds the relevant data in its local memory. This data parallel solution may, however, give rise to excessive load imbalances. Another approach is to schedule the computation tasks in a demand driven way, but then processors may need to request data from other processors, resulting in large communication overheads. This is in particular the case for secondary rays where data coherence is low.

In order to solve both sampling and parallelisation problems, we propose to use environment mapping in an adapted form. Where in Blinn and Newell (1976) environment mapping is presented as a cheap alternative for ray tracing, in our approach, which is similar to (Greene 1986), environment mapping is part of a hybrid rendering algorithm to handle secondary rays efficiently. The sampling related problems are solved by pre-filtering the maps. The communication problem is releaved by providing a means to efficiently store information of remote objects in a local environment map. Thus data retrieval becomes a local process, which removes the need to link data management and task scheduling. Therefore, a more flexible parallel implementation may be achieved.

The complete rendering algorithm consists of three separate stages. First, a standard radiosity preprocessing is performed. A coarse mesh is used in this stage, as in subsequent stages only a rough estimate of patch radiances is needed. In the second stage, objects are grouped and for each group an environment map is generated. This is a view independent operation. The map generation may be viewed as a pre-processing of secondary rays. Normally, the origin of secondary rays is determined by the intersection point of a primary ray and a surface. During map building, all rays are traced from the centre point. However, as in the rendering stage secondary rays are generally not traced from the centre point, an error will occur. How to keep this error small is discussed in the following section. In the last stage the scene is rendered using environment maps and radiances.

The map generation and rendering stages are presented in greater detail in the next section. Experiments with an implementation of the environment mapping algorithm are discussed subsequently, while in the last section conclusions are drawn.

2 Method

The environment mapping technique was first introduced to computer graphics by Blinn and Newell (1976). It is a method to enhance an object with reflections without explicitly tracing secondary rays. This is accomplished by projecting the 3D environment onto a 2D environment map that surrounds the glossy object. Instead of intersecting secondary rays with objects, an index in the environment map is computed from the surface normal of the object and the angle of the incoming ray (see Figure 1). Environment mapping can also be used to reflect digitised photographs in objects.

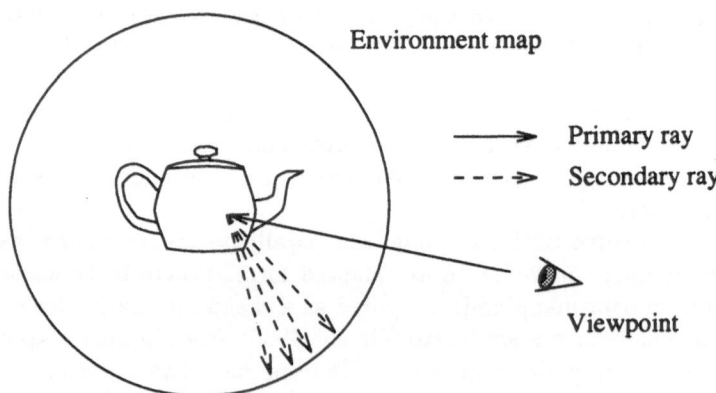

Fig. 1. For every secondary ray, a look-up in the environment map is done, instead of casting secondary rays.

Following (Miller and Hoffman 1984), in (Greene 1986) environment mapping was augmented with filtering capabilities to support a more general reflection model with both diffuse and specular reflection. The single environment map was replaced by a cube with six maps that were placed around the object. For each of the six maps, a mip-map was generated. They are indexed according to the specularity of the object that the maps surround. Mip-mapping is a pre-filtering method (Williams 1983) that filters colour arrays, such as texture maps or environment maps.

In the environment mapping algorithm as proposed in this paper, the emphasis is on cost reduction of tracing secondary rays, as suggested in (Hall 1986). To achieve this, the scope of these rays is limited to the boundaries of the cube on which the maps are projected. Within these limits, rays are actually traced, as other objects within the cube may be hit first. Because most of the scene is outside the cube, many intersection computations do not have to be performed. This suggests that the smaller the cube is, the greater the savings, as more objects will be on the outside.

However, this also increases the error that environment mapping introduces, because the maps are generated with respect to the centre of the cube, but due to the size of the object(s) within the cube, secondary rays generally do not originate from the centre of the cube. Therefore, the size of the cube is preferably large with respect to the objects within. Also, the objects for which environment mapping is a suitable technique, are relatively small and cubicly shaped. Another error source is the distance of outside objects to the environment map. The closer these objects are to the environment map, the smaller the error.

As long as the condition of small and cubic objects is satisfied, there is no objection to clustering multiple objects together and to assigning them a single environment map. Good candidates for clustering are for example plants, keyboards and generally small objects with much detail. Not very suitable are long stretched objects such as floors and walls etc.

Environment mapping consists of two distinct stages. First the maps must be generated and then the maps can be used in the rendering phase. During the generation of the environment maps, first the centre of the clustered object is determined. Then around this centre point a large cube is placed on which six environment maps will be projected, one for each side. The resolution of the maps should be high enough to capture sufficient detail for the subsequent rendering stage. Especially specular surfaces need detailed environment maps. From the centre point a number of rays are shot through each map element. Only objects outside the maps are intersected with these rays. A map entry is generated by performing standard ray tracing. After the map entries have been computed, the mip-maps are built by recursively down-filtering the environment maps. This completes the view-independent map generation.

In the rendering stage, for each pixel primary rays are shot, which gives rise to a large number of secondary rays. In our algorithm, with the exception of shadow testing point light sources and selected area light sources, these functions are largely performed by sampling the environment maps. According to the angle of incidence of the primary ray and the bi-directional reflection distribution function (brdf) of a surface, a number of secondary rays are spawned and traced within the scope of the surrounding cube.

An example of possible trace paths is given in Figure 2. Both teapot and table possess an environment map. A primary ray hits the teapot and spawns secondary rays. Some of these rays will hit the table. For these rays according to the brdf of the table, new rays are spawned which are bounded by the environment map belonging to the table.

The distribution of secondary rays is determined by the brdf of the surface, i.e. more rays are sent in the reflected direction than in other directions. Therefore, the angle between neighbouring rays is smaller in the reflected area. Figure 3 shows two brdf's, where the one on the left belongs to a surface that is partly diffuse and partly specular. The brdf on the right belongs to a completely diffuse surface. Because the environment maps are mip-mapped, the filter level must be computed before an entry can be calculated. The brdf determines the angle between successive rays (Figure 3) and this angle provides a means to determine the mip-map level. The closer the rays are together, the less filtering is needed. For more diffuse areas, stronger filtered versions of the environment map should be used. The link between brdf and index level is depicted in Figure 4.

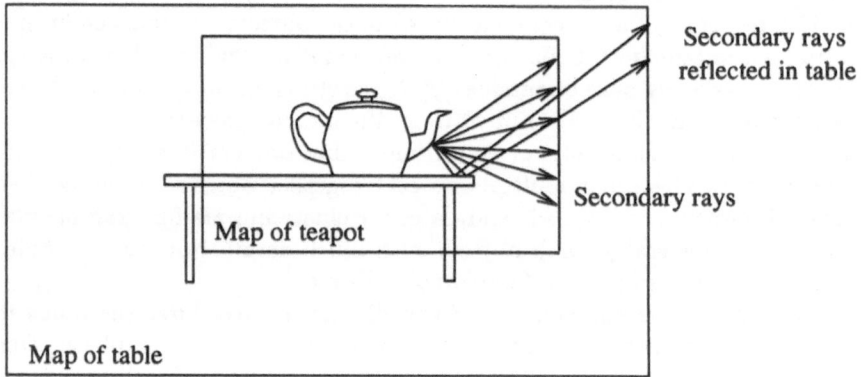

Fig. 2. Example of possible paths of secondary rays.

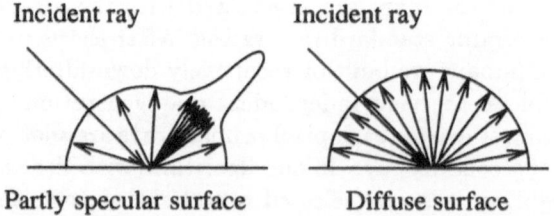

Fig. 3. Secondary rays spawned according to angle of incidence and brdf.

Because no directed shooting is used for both building the environment maps and sampling the maps, there is no guarantee that point light sources are sampled accurately. Even if they are traced separately during the generation of the maps,

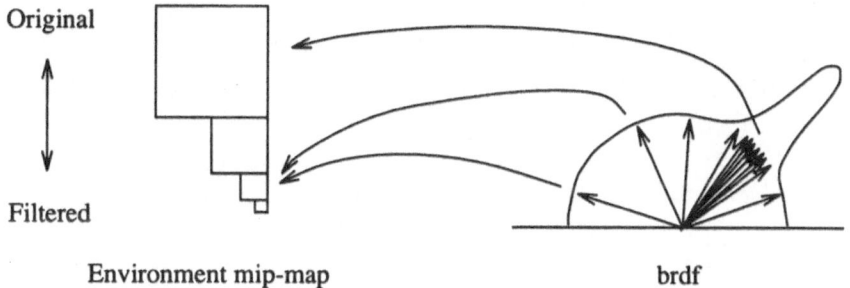

Fig. 4. Brdf determines mip-map index level.

point light sources are not well represented in the map. Therefore, these light sources are traced in the rendering stage, partly bypassing the environment maps. Also, sources that are selected for source sampling are kept outside the map in order to keep the amount of noise low.

Pure specular surfaces may be handled separately as well, given the fact that the error introduced by using environment maps is largest for perfect mirrors. Finally, the advantage of having a limited scope for secondary rays becomes less when the objects outside the environment map are located close to the environment map. These examples show that environment mapping is most suitable in those cases where sampling does not significantly influence the quality of the image.

3 Experiments

Tests have been performed to establish the image quality that can be achieved using environment mapping. Also, the method is compared with respect to quality and rendering times with two two-pass radiosity algorithms. The first shoots primary rays and uses the pre-computed radiosity values to avoid any diffuse secondary rays. Also source selection is performed to limit the number of secondary shadow rays. In the remainder, this algorithm will be called 'source selection' (Kok and Jansen 1991). The second algorithm taking part in the comparison, shoots primary rays and for each object/primary ray intersection, both diffuse and specular secondary rays are shot. However, instead of shooting tertiary diffuse rays, the pre-computed radiosity values are used. The number of shadow rays is limited by using source selection. This algorithm is also known as 'one-level path tracing' (Rushmeier 1988); in this paper to be abbreviated as 'path tracing'.

All tests have been performed on a test scene consisting of a table on which a ball is placed. The table is in a room with a textured ceiling and four area light sources. The table has an environment map, so that the walls and the ceiling are outside the map and the table and the ball are inside the map. The objects outside are projected onto the map, which is shown in Figure 5.

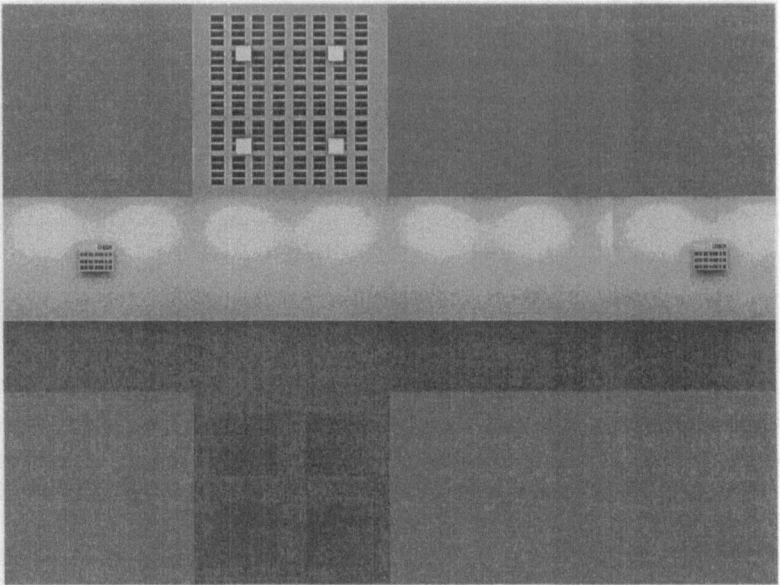

Fig. 5. Environment map generated for table in test environment.

Two potential sources for errors have been defined in the preceding paragraph. These are the finite resolution of the maps and the discrepancy between the origin of secondary rays during map generation and rendering. The test scene (with a specular reflecting table top) has been rendered using different map resolutions, results of which are shown in Figure 6. The rendering times for these pictures are given in Table 1[1]. The effect of differences between the origin of rays during map generation and rendering can be varied by enlarging the environment map with respect to the table. In Figure 7, the size of the environment map is increased from left to right. Corresponding rendering times are shown in Table 1.

These images show that when the resolution is chosen too low, aliasing occurs. For this test environment, which is a worst case in the sense that the camera-point is zoomed in on a specular reflecting table, a resolution of at least 512 x 512 is needed to generate acceptable images. For more distant view points a lower resolution can be used. The same holds for more diffuse objects.

The amount of time needed to generate the environment maps quadruples when doubling the resolution in both u and v directions. This is in accordance with expectations, as four times as many rays are cast. Actual rendering times do not vary as a function of the map resolution, because the number of secondary

---

[1] All rendering has been performed on a Silicon Graphics Indigo.

[2] The resolution is the number of map entries in both u and v directions. The distance ratio is 1 : 12.5.

[3] The ratios given in these columns are the size of the table divided by the distance of the centre point of the environment map. The resolution of the map is 512 x 512.

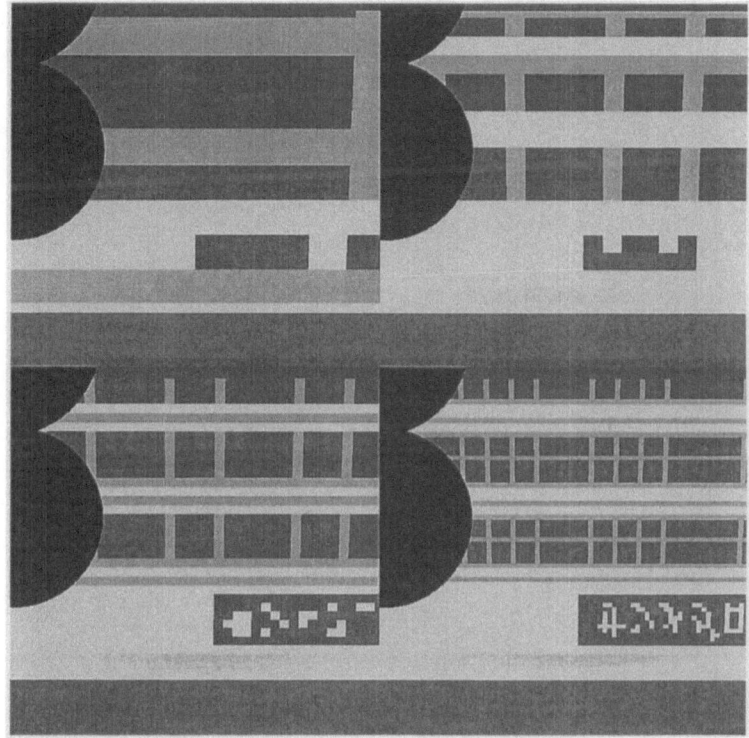

Fig. 6. Test scene rendered with increasing environment map resolution. The table top is a purely specular reflector.

rays that are traced remains constant.

Varying the distance between table and environment map, it turns out that the dislocation of objects outside the environment map becomes within bounds when the distance ratio is around 1 : 10. If the map is placed more closely to the table, the dislocation of the reflection increases.

During rendering the effect of the size of the maps on the rendering times is less significant. Here, smaller environment maps mean slightly shorter rendering times. This result is opposite to the relation between size and map generation time, because now a smaller map allows secondary rays to be traced along a shorter distance.

The test scene as used in the preceding test has been used for the comparison with the afore mentioned algorithms as well. The table top, however, is now 20% specular reflecting and 80% diffuse. In Figure 8, the results of the algorithms are shown. Both the environment mapping and the path tracing picture exhibit colour bleeding between the ball and the table and the ball casts a more accurate and darker shadow upon the table than is the case with the source selection algorithm. The ball also receives more reflected light from the table. These effects can be attributed to the diffuse sampling performed by the environment mapping

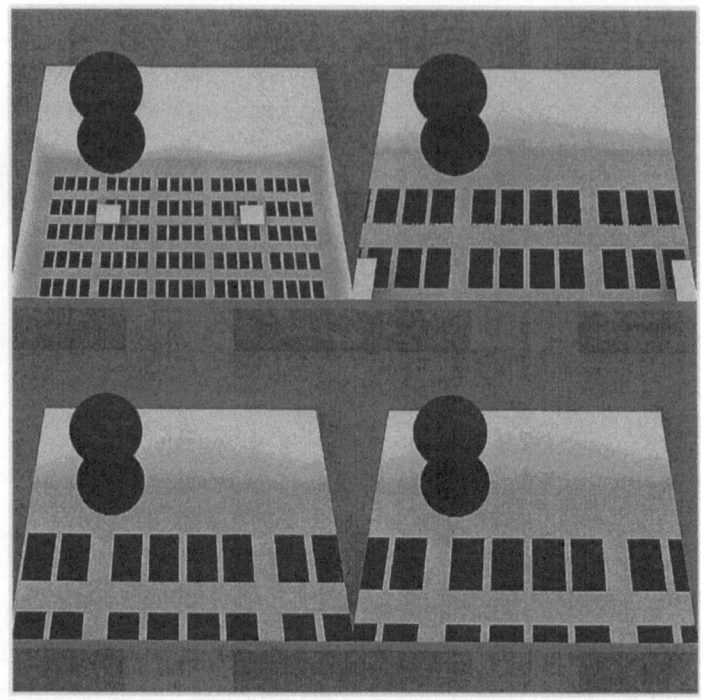

Fig. 7. Test scene rendered with increasing map size. The table top is a purely specular reflecting surface.

and path tracing algorithms. As the shading is completely independent of the local radiosity mesh, artifacts due to insufficient meshing are thus avoided with this algorithms.

The number of rays for each algorithm are given in Table 3 and the rendering times are given in Table 3. For this simple test scene, the differences are not very prominent. For more complex environments the rendering times for the environment mapping algorithm will not increase much, while the rendering times for path tracing will grow significantly. The environment map generation times are expected to grow slowly with increasing scene complexity, while the source selection algorithm's time complexity is relatively independent of the scene to be rendered.

4 Discussion

Environment mapping is a technique which can be incorporated in a ray tracing based radiosity algorithm. With the exception of elongated objects, environment

---

[4] Number of rays per pixel or per map element.
[5] Number of rays generated per intersection.

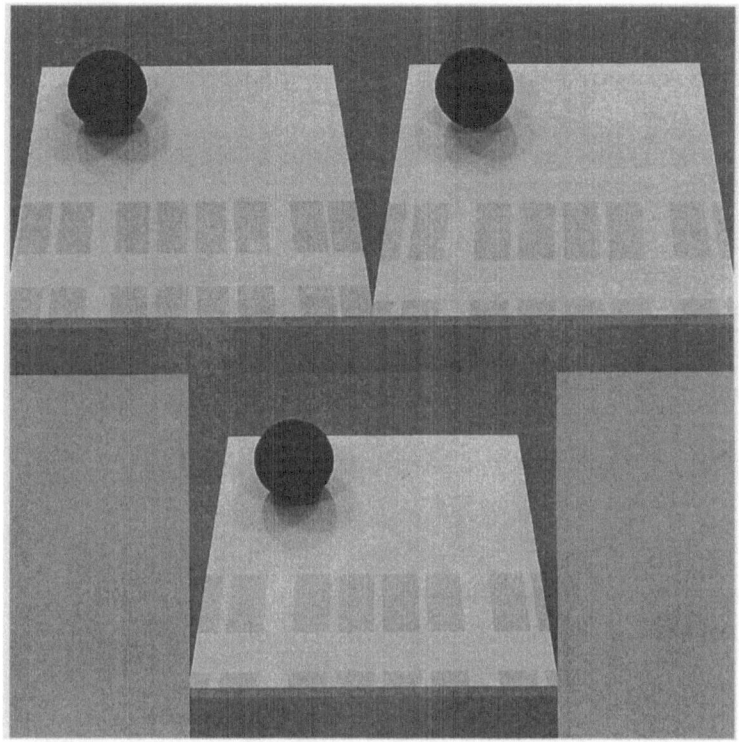

Fig. 8. Qualitative comparison of hybrid rendering algorithms. In the upper left the three stage environment mapping algorithm, the result of the source selection algorithm is to the right and the path tracing picture is below.

Fig. 9. Qualitative comparison of hybrid rendering algorithms. The three stage environment mapping algorithm (left), the result of the source selection algorithm (middle) and the one-level path tracing algorithm (right).

	Resolution[2]				Distance ratio[3]			
	64	128	256	512	1 : 1.25	1 : 5	1 : 10	1 : 14
Radiosity	9 : 45	9 : 45	9 : 45	9 : 45	9 : 45	9 : 45	9 : 45	9 : 45
Env. gen.	0 : 16	1 : 05	4 : 22	17 : 23	31 : 28	23 : 00	17 : 59	16 : 42
Rendering	6 : 51	6 : 54	6 : 53	6 : 55	9 : 35	9 : 33	9 : 44	9 : 49
Total	16 : 52	16 : 44	21 : 00	33 : 53	50 : 38	42 : 12	37 : 28	36 : 16

Table 1. Rendering times in min:sec for test scene using different environment map resolutions and different distances between centre point and map

Type of ray	Env. mapping		Source sel.	Path Tr.
	Map gen.	Rend.		
Primary[4]	1	1	1	1
Shadow[5]	16	16	16	16
Diffuse[5]	0	100	0	100
Specular[5]	1	1	1	1

Table 2. Number of rays shot

mapping can be used for single objects or groups of objects. Three important parameters that influence the accuracy of the images are the resolution of the maps, the distance between the centre point and the environment maps and the location of objects outside the environment maps. The resolution needs to be highest for perfect mirrors, while a lower resolution is sufficient for glossy and diffuse surfaces.

The distance between maps and the centre point depends on the size of the objects for which the maps are generated. If the ratio between these two is chosen too small, then the reflected surroundings appear dislocated. With respect to the quality of the images, both environment mapping and path tracing allow more accurate shadows due to the diffuse sampling that is performed during rendering. In addition, these methods are capable of handling more complicated brdf's than source selection, which splits a surface's reflection properties into a specular and

Pass	Env. mapping	Source sel.	Path Tr.
Radiosity	9 : 45	9 : 45	9 : 45
Env. map generation	1 : 50 : 52	n.a.	n.a.
Rendering	7 : 17 : 43	5 : 39 : 08	11 : 17 : 36
Total	9 : 08 : 20	5 : 48 : 53	11 : 27 : 21

Table 3. Timings of the the rendering algorithms in hour:min:sec

a diffuse component of which the latter is taken from the radiosity mesh.

A disadvantage may be that this rendering technique requires more memory, as in addition to the scene description, a number of possibly large environment maps need to be stored. However, if a similar qualitative result were to be obtained without environment mapping, a much finer radiosity mesh would be needed, which largely cancels out the memory disadvantage of environment mapping.

Due to the more local data references made during rendering, environment mapping is better suited for parallel implementation than the source selection and path tracing algorithms. Each processor in a MIMD computer could be assigned a number of objects with their associated environment maps. This results in an object space subdivision where all objects within an environment cube, are physically stored with the same processor. Rendering can then be accomplished with minimal communication requirements, as only primary rays need to be distributed and results must be transferred to the frame buffer. Secondary rays may also induce communication, but all diffuse and specular secondary rays are handled locally. For the generation of the environment maps, communication between processors will still be required. However, the number of rays needed in this stage is relatively small compared with the amount of sampling which would otherwise be needed during rendering.

As only a sequential implementation of the environment mapping algorithm exists, our future plans include implementing this algorithm on a transputer system. Performance and scalability issues will then be examined. The ability to use more accurate brdf's has not been fully exploited yet in the implementation discussed in the preceding paragraph. Therefore, inclusion of more realistic brdf's remains work to be done. Finally, we would like to extend this algorithm so that large flat objects can be handled correctly as well.

References

Blinn, J. F., Newell, M. E.: Texture and reflection in computer generated images, Communications of the ACM 19(10), 542–547, (1976).

Chen, S. E., Rushmeier, H. E., Miller, G., Turner, D.: A progressive multi-pass method for global illumination, Computer Graphics 25(4), 165–174, (1991).

Glassner, A. S.: An Introduction to Ray Tracing, Academic Press, San Diego (1989).

Greene, N.: Environment mapping and other applications of world projections, IEEE Computer Graphics and Applications (1986) 21–29.

Hall, H.: Hybrid Techniques for Rapid Image Synthesis, course notes, SIGGRAPH '86: Image Rendering Tricks, (1986).

Kok, A. J. F., Jansen, F. W.: Source selection for the direct lighting computation in global illumination, in Proceedings Eurographics Workshop on Rendering, Barcelona, Spain (1991).

Kok, A. J. F.: Grouping of patches in progressive radiosity, in M. Cohen, C. Puech , F. Sillion, eds, Fourth Eurographics Workshop on Rendering, Paris, France, 221–231 (1993).

Kok, A. J. F., Jansen, F. W., Woodward, C.: Efficient, Complete Radiosity Ray Tracing Using a Shadow-coherence Method, The Visual Computer, 10(1993) 19–33.

Miller, G. S., Hoffman, C. R.: Illumination and Reflection Maps: Simulated Objects in Simulated and Real Environments, SIGGRAPH '84: Advanced Computer Graphics Animation Seminar Notes, (1984)

Rushmeier, H. E.: Realistic Image Synthesis for Scenes with Radiatively Participating Media, PhD thesis (1988).

Rushmeier, H. E., Patterson, C., Veerasamy, A.: Geometric Simplification for Indirect Illumination Calculations, Graphics Interface '93, 227–236 (1993).

Shirley, P.: A Ray Tracing Method for Illumination Calculation in Diffuse Specular Scenes, Graphics Interface '90, 205–212 (1990).

Shirley, P.: Physically Based Lighting Calculations for Computer Graphics, PhD thesis, Urbana-Champaign (1991).

Sillion, F., Puech, C.: A general two-pass method integrating specular and diffuse reflection, ACM Computer graphics (1989), SIGGRAPH '89.

Wallace, J. R., Cohen, M. F., Greenberg, D. P.: A two-pass solution to the rendering equation: A synthesis of ray tracing and radiosity methods, ACM Computer Graphics 21(4), 311–320, (1987), SIGGRAPH '87.

Williams, L.: Pyramidal parametrics, ACM Computer Graphics 17(3), 1–11, (1983).

Colour Plates

Colour Plate 2

**A Model for Fluorescence
and Phosphorescence**
Page 60–70

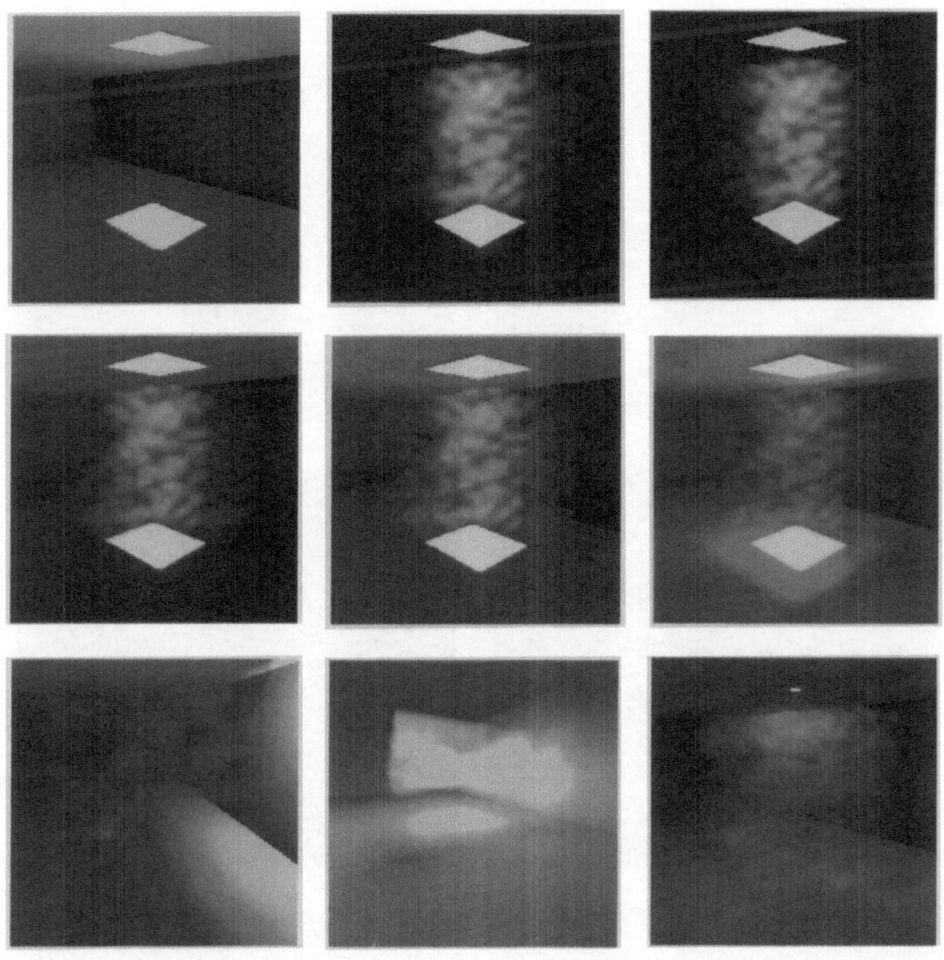

Colour Plate 4

**Efficient Light Propagation
for Multiple Anisotropic Volume Scattering**
Page 87–104

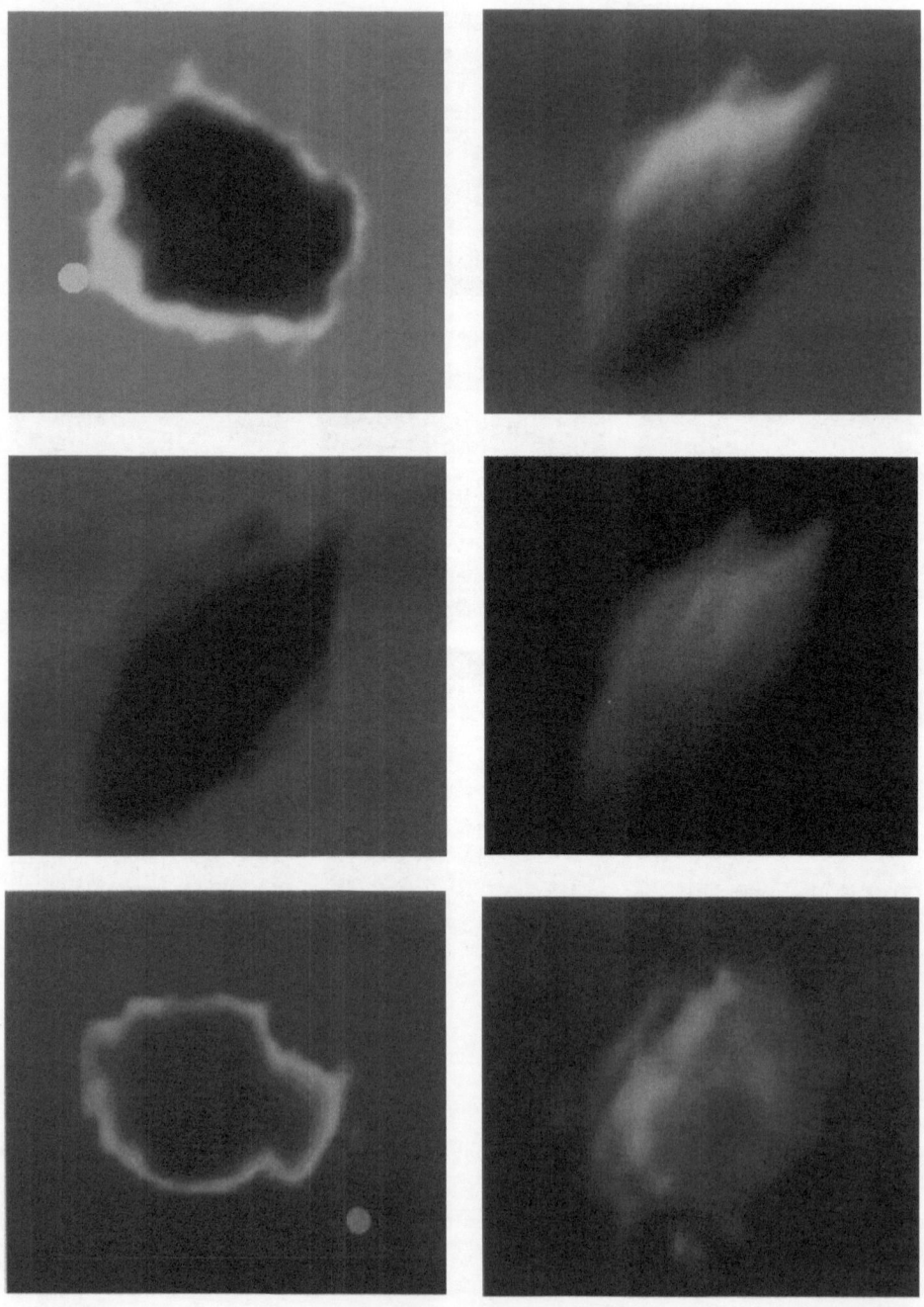

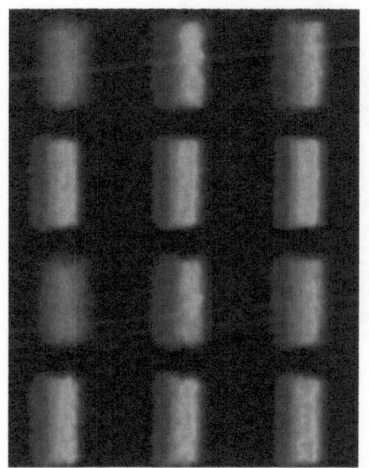

a   b

(a) Example spectra resulting from different spectral sampling schemes. Top 6: each initial ray spawns 2, 3, 4, 6, 8 and 16 refracted rays with wavelength randomly distributed in the 380–780 nm range. Bottom 6: single refracted ray with 2, 3, 4, 6, 8, 16 spectral samples and (b) the test scene with 2 light sources, one colimated behind the viewer and one directly above.

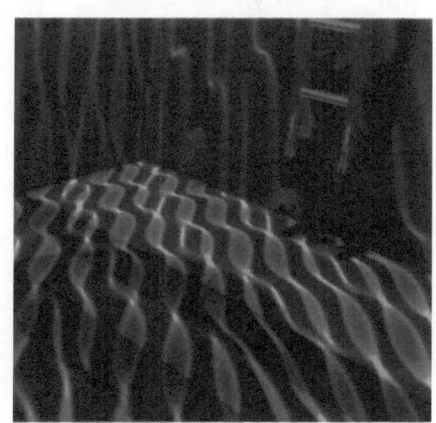

a   b

View of swimming pool from (a) above and (b) below.

Colour Plate 6

Rayvolution: An Evolutionary
Ray Tracing Algorithm
Page 136–144

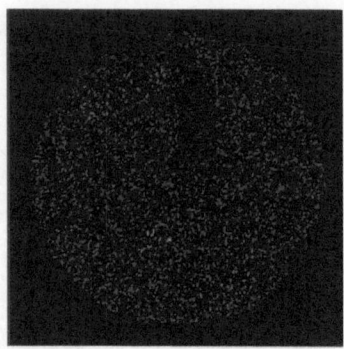 

Left: Monte-Carlo ray distribution. Right: Corresponding evolved ray distribution.

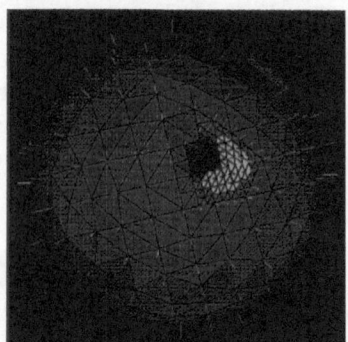 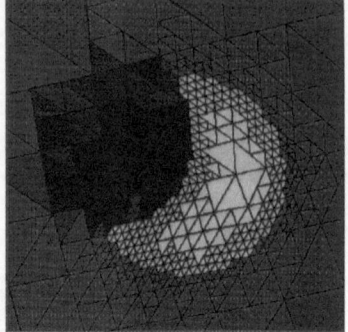

Left: Hemisphere represented as a population of triangles. Right: Evolved hemisphere stratification in detail.

Left: Image generated by Monte-Carlo integration. Right: Corresponding image generated by evolutionary stratification.

Colour Plate 8

Wavelet Radiance

Page 293–307

a b c

Ward's reflection model: (**a**) anisotropic reflection, $\alpha_u = 0.1$, $\alpha_v = 0.5$; (**b**) isotropic reflection, $\alpha_u = \alpha_v = 0.2$; (**c**) anisotropic reflection, $\alpha_u = 0.5$, $\alpha_v = 0.1$.

 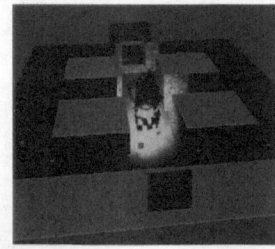 

a b c

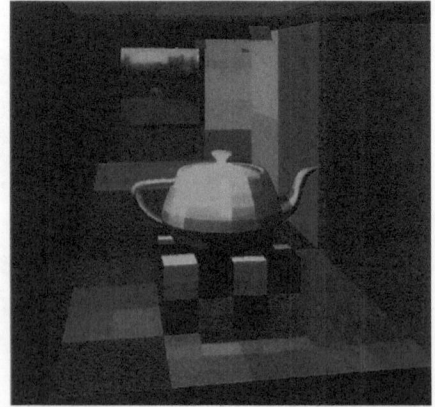 

d e

Solutions for a complex scene: (**a**) radiance seen from above; (**b**) importance seen from above; (**c**) gray-scale representation of refinement; (**d**) radiance solution without final gather; (**e**) radiance solution with final gather.

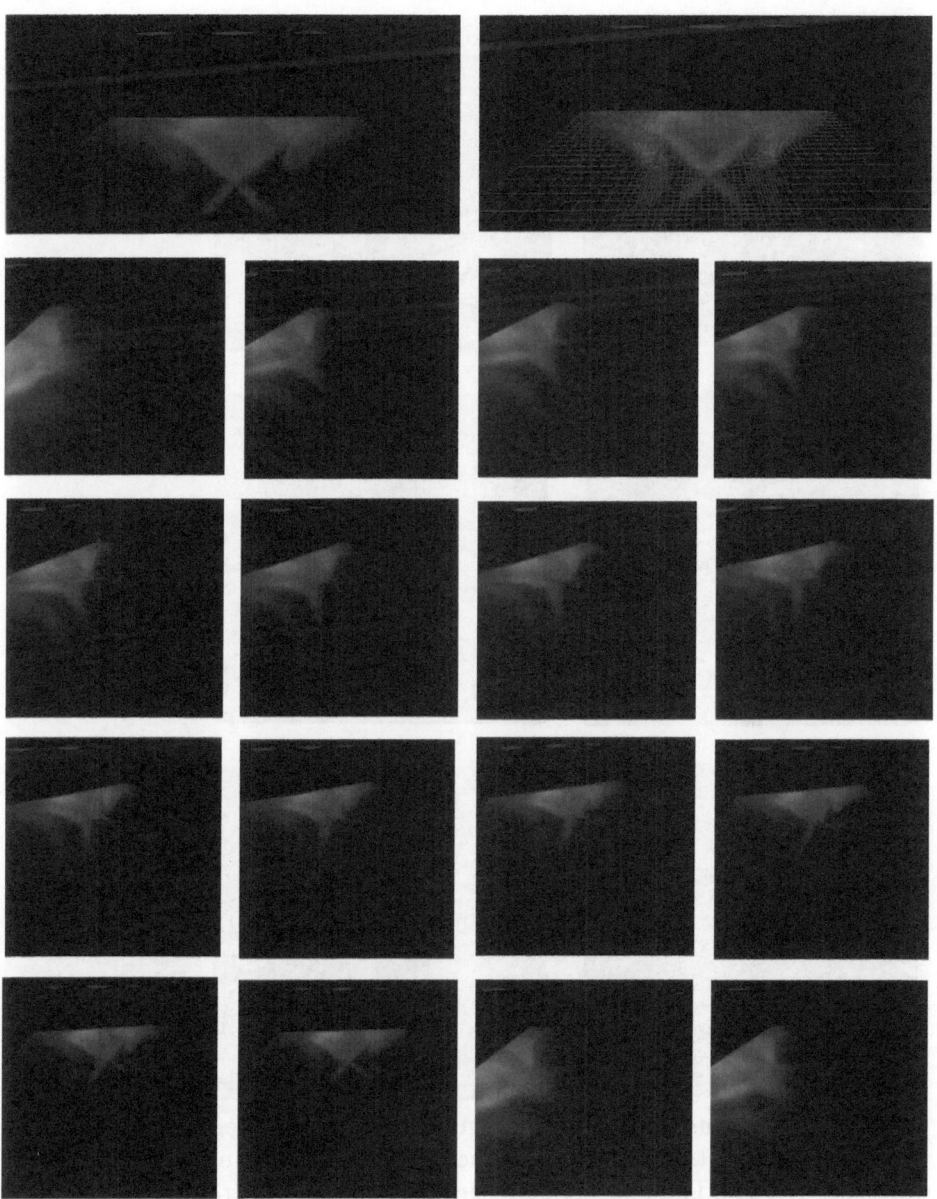

The top left shows a configuration with three light sources and an anisotropic reflector; the top right the included meshing. Below a sequence illustrating a spatial plot of the radiance field induced by the three coloured light sources as the view point changes ($r = 0.1$, $p = 0.1$; linear basis functions).

Colour Plate 10

Efficient Radiosity
in Dynamic Environments
Page 327–336

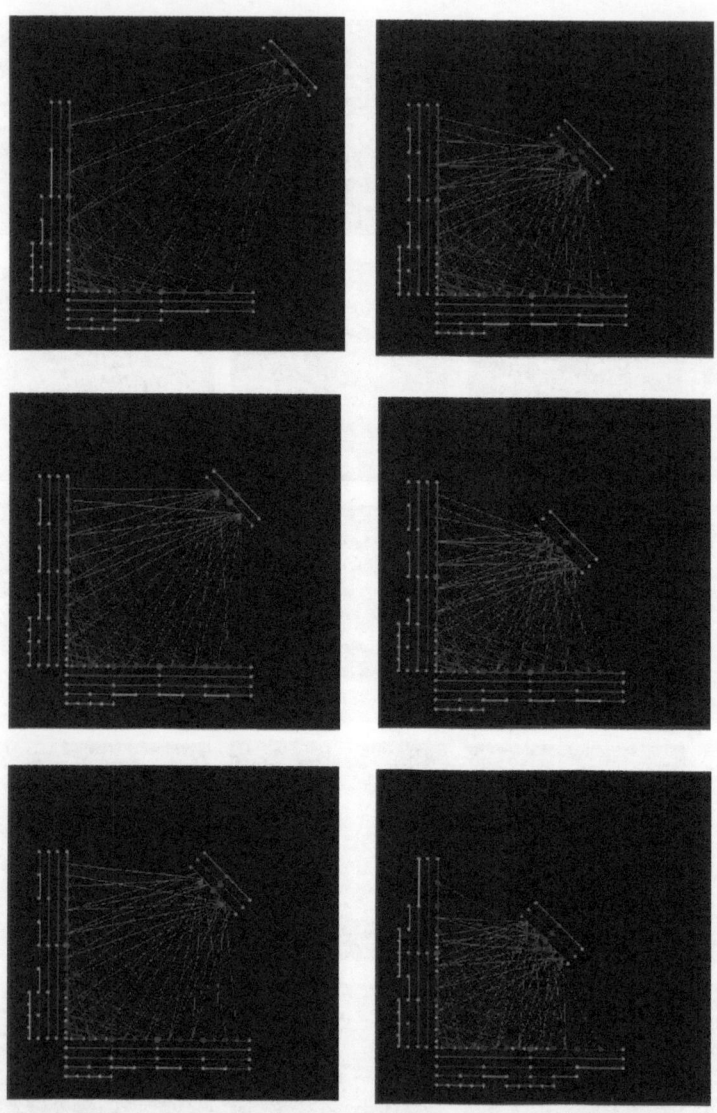

Dynamic links events for an orthogonal gutter being approached by a patch . The links (in pink) are to the centre of the relevant hierarchy element. Links to the patch are dynamic, others are static. In the first frame many links go to the centre of the patch (to hierarchy element). As the patch gets closer to the gutter, links are demoted and move to the lower hierarchy levels.

Left: Motion sequence with the light moving around the ceiling. Mesh elements with light-source links are shown to the right of each image. Note the changes in the dynamic links.

Right: Dynamic links reinspected at each step. In far right column links and form factors are extrapolated up to seven frames ahead to predict events.

Colour Plate 12

Fast Radiosity Repropagation
For Interactive Virtual Environments Using A Shadow-Form-Factor-List
Page 337–354

The model of the VR lab of Fraunhofer IGD.

The same scene after moving the terminal and a chair.

The model of the airport waiting area of Abu Dhabi. In this scene, five virtual point light sources have been used.

The same scene after changing the reflectivity of the seats.

The model of the cabinet of the president of the European Parliament. In this scene five virtual point light sources have been used.

The same room after deleting the conference table and the chairs.

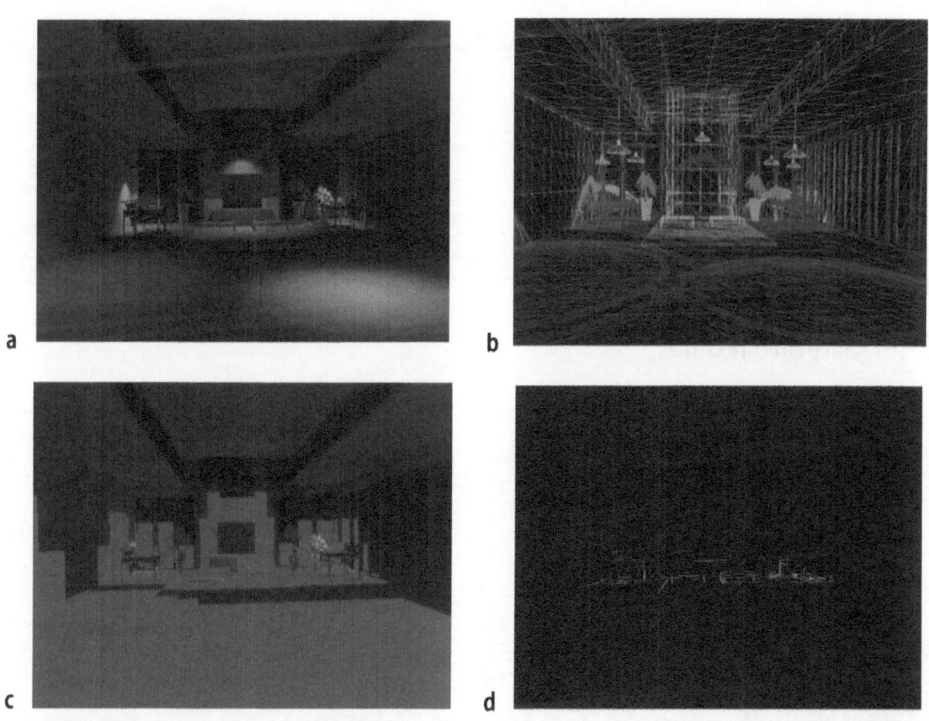

Room. A comparison of mesh-based vs. texture-based shading: (**a**) mesh-based Gouraud shading, (**b**) the corresponding mesh, (**c**) the scene regions replaced by textures (green), (**d**) differences between mesh-based and texture-based images.

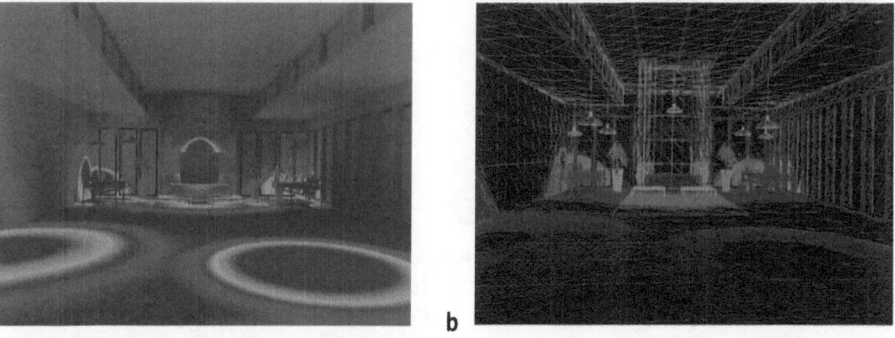

Room. The scene luminance distribution in the colour fringe convention: (**a**) colour-fringe image, (**b**) corresponding mesh.

Colour Plate 14

Texture Mapping as an Alternative for Meshing During Walkthrough Animation
Page 387–398

Texture magnification: (**a**) mesh-based Gouraud shading, (**b**) ordinary texture, (**c**) sharpened texture.

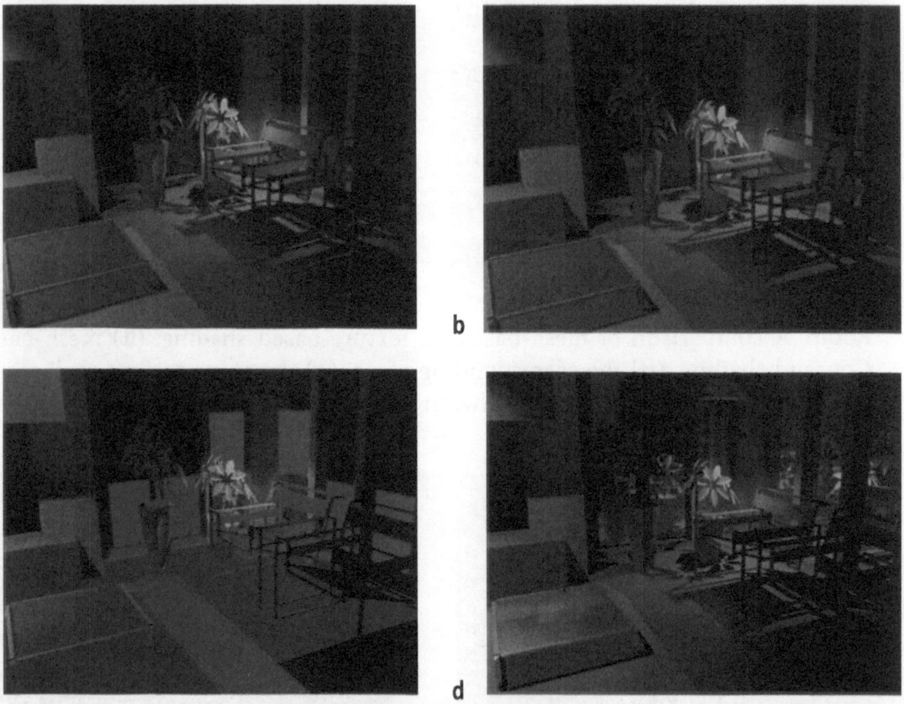

Room. Close-up view for shadows: (**a**) mesh-based Gouraud shading, (**b**) texture-based shading, (**c**) the scene regions replaced by texture (green – mesh-based texture, blue – sampling-based texture), (**d**) reference ray tracing image.

**Texture Mapping as an Alternative
for Meshing During Walkthrough Animation**
Page 387–398

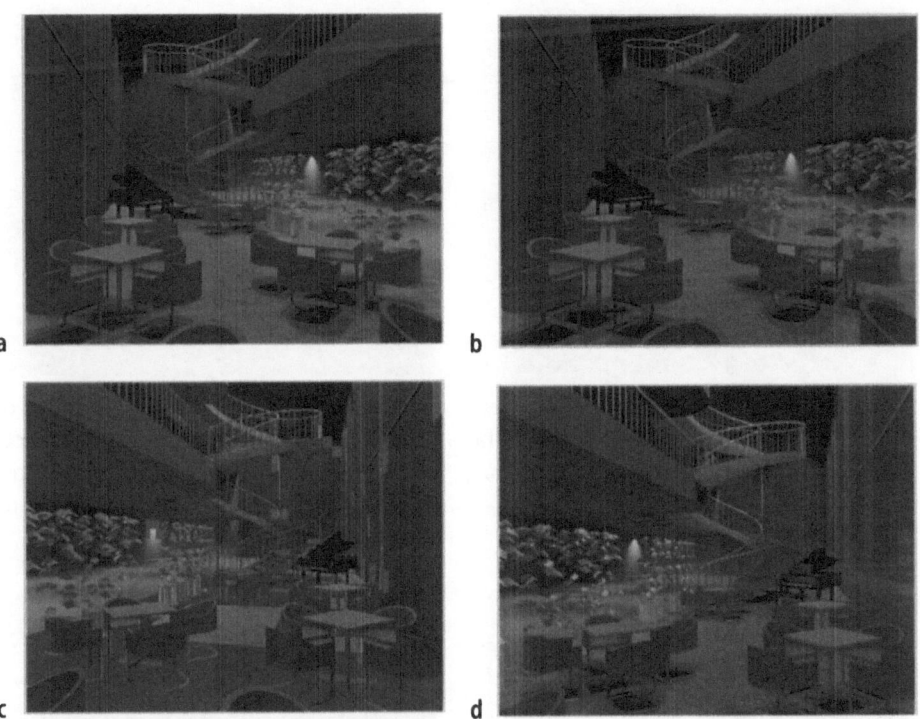

Cafeteria. Close-up view for shadows: (**a**) mesh-based Gouraud shading, (**b**) texture-based shading, (**c**) the scene regions replaced by texture (green – mesh-based
texture, blue – sampling-based texture), (**d**) reference ray tracing image.

Colour Plate 16

Model of the Frauenkirche in Dresden, Germany. Courtesy of IBM Germany. The model contains about 230 000 triangles.

Computer reconstruction of the abbey of Cluny, France. Courtesy of IBM France. The model contains about 680 000 triangles, and has been rendered with floor shadows.

Icerink at the Olympic site in Lillehammer, Norway. Courtesy of the Olympic Winter Games. The model contains about 200 000 triangles.

Interior of the Frauenkirche in Dresden, Germany. Courtesy of IBM Germany. Full detail, about 125 000 triangles.

Interior of the Frauenkirche in Dresden, Germany. Courtesy of IBM Germany. Simplification, about 10 000 triangles.

Interior of the Frauenkirche in Dresden, Germany. Courtesy of IBM Germany. Full detail with textures.

List of Authors

Markus Beyer
Fraunhofer Institute for
Computer Graphics,
Wilhelminenstraße 7,
64283 Darmstadt, Germany

Philippe Blasi
Laboratoire Bordelais de Recherche
en Informatique, Univerist Bordeaux I,
351, Cours de la Lebration 33405
TALENCE Cedex, France

Paul Borrel
IBM T. J. Watson Res. Ctr.,
P.O. Box 704, Yorktown Heights,
NY 10598, USA

Kadi Bouatouch
Institut de Recherche en
Informatique et Systmes Alatoires,
Campus Universitaire de Beaulieu,
35042 Rennes Cedex, France

Michael Chelle
Institut de Recherche en
Informatique et Systmes Alatoires,
Campus Universitaire de Beaulieu,
35042 Rennes Cedex, France

Kenneth Chiu
Indiana University,
Dept. of Computer Science,
Lindley Hall, Bloomington,
IN 47405, USA

Per Christensen
University of Washington,
Apartment 408, 4225 11th Ave. NE,
Seattle, WA 98105, USA

Steven Collins
Reilly Institute,
Trinity College,
Dept. of Computer Science,
Dublin 2 Ireland

Tony DeRose
University of Washington,
3940 Wallingford Ave. N,
Seattle, WA 98103, USA

Julie Dorsey
University of Pennsylvania,
Dept. of Computer and
Information Science,
200 South 33rd St., Philadelphia,
PA 19104-6389, USA

George Drettakis
iMAGIS / IMAG, B. P. 53,
38041 Grenoble Cedex 09, France

Philip Dutré
Katholieke Universiteit Leuven,
Dept. Computerwetenschappen,
Celestijnenlaan 200 A,
3001 Heverlee, Belgium

Martin Feda
Institute of Computer Graphics,
TU Vienna, Wiedner Hauptstr. 7/186/2,
1040 Vienna, Austria

David Forsyth
The University of Iowa,
Dept. of Computer Sciences,
14 MacLean Hall, Iowa City,
IA 52242-1419, USA

Donald Fussell
University of Texas at Austin,
Dept. of Mathematics,
Austin, Texas 78712, USA

Neil Gatenby
Computer Graphics Unit,
Manchester Computing Centre,
The University of Manchester,
Oxford Road, Manchester M13 9PL,
United Kingdom

Andrew Glassner
Xerox PARC,
3333 Coyote Hill Road,
Palo Alto, CA 94304, USA

Leonidas Guibas
Stanford University,
Dept. of Computer Science,
Robotics Laboratory,
Stanford, CA 94305-2140 USA

Pat Hanrahan
Princeton University,
Dept. of Computer Science,
35 OldenSt.. Princeton,
NJ 08544-2087, USA

W. Hewitt
Computer Graphics Unit,
Manchester Computing Centre,
The University of Manchester,
Oxford Road, Manchester M13 9PL,
United Kingdom

Nicolas Holzschuch
iMAGIS / IMAG, B. P. 53,
38041 Grenoble Cedex 09, France

Frederik Jansen
Delft University of Technology,
Faculty of Technical Mathematics
and Informatics, Julianalaan 132,
2628 BL Delft, The Netherlands

Manfred Kopp
Institute of Computer Graphics,
TU Vienna, Wiedner Hauptstr. 7/186/2,
1040 Vienna, Austria

Tosiyasu Kunii
The. University of Aizu,
Tsuruga, Ikki-machi,
Aizu-Wakumatsu City,
Fukushima, 965-80, Japan

Brigitta Lange
Fraunhofer Institute for
Computer Graphics,
Wilhelminenstraße 7,
64283 Darmstadt, Germany

Eric Lafortune
Katholieke Universiteit Leuven,
Dept. Computerwetenschappen,
Celestijnenlaan 200 A,
3001 Heverlee, Belgium

Eric Languenou
Institut de Recherche en
Informatique et Systmes Alatoires,
Campus Universitaire de Beaulieu,
35042 Rennes Cedex, France

Nelson Max
L-301, Lawrence Livermore National
Lab., P.O. Box 808,
Livermore, CA 94550, USA

Jai Menon
IBM T. J. Watson Res. Ctr.,
P.O. Box 704, Yorktown Heights,
NY 10598, USA

Josh Mittleman
IBM T. J. Watson Res. Ctr.,
P.O. Box 704, Yorktown Heights,
NY 10598, USA

Stefan Müller
Fraunhofer Institute for
Computer Graphics,
Wilhelminenstraße 7,
64283 Darmstadt, Germany

Karol Myszkowski
The University of Aizu,
Tsuruga, Ikki-machi,
Aizu-Wakumatsu City,
Fukushima, 965-80, Japan

Jeffry S. Nimeroff
University of Pennsylvania,
Dept. of Computer and Information
Science, 200 South 33rd St.,
Philadelphia, PA 19104-6389, USA

Laszlo Neumann
Maros u. 36,
H-1122 Budapest, Hungary

Sumanta N. Pattanaik
Institut de Recherche en
Informatique et Systmes Alatoires,
Project SIAMES,
Campus Universitaire de Beaulieu,
35042 Rennes Cedex, France

Werner Purgathofer
Institute of Computer Graphics,
TU Vienna, Karlsplatz 13/186,
1040 Vienna, Austria

Erik Reinhard
Delft University of Technology,
Faculty of Technical Mathematics
and Informatics, Julianalaan 132,
2628 BL Delft, The Netherlands

Jarek Rossignac
IBM T. J. Watson Res. Ctr.,
P.O. Box 704, Yorktown Heights,
NY 10598, USA

Holly Rushmeier
National Institute of Science
and Technology, Rm. B-146, Bldg. 225
Gaithersburg, MD 20899 USA

Bertrand Le Saëc
Laboratoire Bordelais de
Recherche en Informatique,
Univerist Bordeaux I, 351,
Cours de la Lebration,
33405 TALENCE Cedex, France

Georgios Sakas
Fraunhofer Institute for
Computer Graphics,
Wilhelminenstraße 7,
64283 Darmstadt, Germany

David Salesin
University of Washington,
3940 Wallingford Ave. N,
Seattle, WA 98103, USA

Christophe Schlick
Laboratoire Bordelais de
Recherche en Informatique,
Univerist Bordeaux I, 351,
Cours de la Lebration,
33405 TALENCE Cedex France

Peter Schröder
Princeton University,
Dept. of Computer Science,
35 OldenSt.. Princeton,
NJ 08544-2087, USA

Frank Schöffel
Fraunhofer Institute for
Computer Graphics,
Wilhelminenstraße 7,
64283 Darmstadt, Germany

Francois Sillion
iMAGIS / IMAG, B. P. 53,
38041 Grenoble Cedex 09,
France

Eero Simoncelli
University of Pennsylvania,
Dept. of Computer and
Information Science,
200 South 33rd St., Philadelphia,
PA 19104-6389, USA

Peter Shirley
Indiana University,
Dept. of Computer Science,
Lindley Hall, Bloomington,
IN 47405, USA

Bengt-Olaf Schneider
IBM T. J. Watson Res. Ctr.,
P.O. Box 704, Yorktown Heights,
NY 10598, USA

Eric Stollnitz
University of Washington,
Apartment 301,
3940 Wallingford Ave. N,
Seattle, WA 98103, USA

Wolfgang Stürzlinger
Johannes Kepler Universität Linz,
Inst. für Informatik,
Abt. f. graph. und parallele DV,
Altenbergerstr. 69,
4040 Linz, Austria

Kim Teo
The University of Iowa,
Dept. of Computer Sciences,
14 MacLean Hall, Iowa City,
IA 52242-1419, USA

Lucas U. Tijssen
Delft University of Technology,
Faculty of Technical Mathematics
and Informatics, Julianalaan 132,
2628 BL Delft, The Netherlands

Robert F. Tobler
Institute of Computer Graphics,
TU Vienna, Wiedner Hauptstr. 7/186/2,
1040 Vienna, Austria

Eric Veach
Stanford University,
Dept. of Computer Science,
Robotics Laboratory,
Stanford, CA 94305-2140 USA

Yves Willems
Katholieke Universiteit Leuven,
Dept. Computerwetenschappen,
Celestijnenlaan 200 A,
3001 Heverlee, Belgium

Wei Xu
University of Texas at Austin,
Dept. of Mathematics,
Austin, Texas 78712, USA

Chien Yang
The University of Iowa,
Dept. of Computer Sciences,
14 MacLean Hall, Iowa City,
IA 52242-1419, USA

Focus on Computer Graphics

(Formerly EurographicSeminars)

User Interface Management and Design. Edited by D. A. Duce, M. R. Gomes, F. R. A. Hopgood, J. R. Lee. VIII, 324 pages, 117 figs., 1991

Advances in Computer Graphics Hardware III. Edited by A. A. M. Kuijk. VIII, 214 pages, 88 figs., 1991

Advances in Object-Oriented Graphics I. Edited by E. H. Blake, P. Wisskirchen. X, 218 pages, 74 figs., 1991

Advances in Computer Graphics Hardware IV. Edited by R. L. Grimsdale, W. Straßer. VIII, 276 pages, 124 figs., 1991

Advances in Computer Graphics VI. Images: Synthesis, Analysis, and Interaction. Edited by G. Garcia, I. Herman. IX, 449 pages, 186 figs., 1991

Intelligent CAD Systems III. Practical Experience and Evaluation. Edited by P. J. W. ten Hagen, P. J. Veerkamp. X, 270 pages, 116 figs., 1991

Graphics and Communications. Edited by D. B. Arnold, R. A. Day, D. A. Duce, C. Fuhrhop, J. R. Gallop, R. Maybury, D. C. Sutcliffe. VIII, 274 pages, 84 figs., 1991

Photorealism in Computer Graphics. Edited by K. Bouatouch, C. Bouville. XVI, 230 pages, 118 figs., 1992

Advances in Computer Graphics Hardware V. Rendering, Ray Tracing and Visualization Systems. Edited by R. L. Grimsdale, A. Kaufman. VIII, 174 pages, 97 figs., 1992

Multimedia. Systems, Interaction and Applications. Edited by L. Kjelldahl. VIII, 355 pages, 129 figs., 1992. Out of print

Advances in Scientific Visualization. Edited by F. H. Post, A. J. S. Hin. X, 212 pages, 141 figs., 47 in color, 1992

Computer Graphics and Mathematics. Edited by B. Falcidieno, I. Herman, C. Pienovi. VII, 318 pages, 159 figs., 8 in color, 1992

Rendering, Visualization and Rasterization Hardware. Edited by A. Kaufman. VIII, 196 pages, 100 figs., 1993

Visualization in Scientific Computing. Edited by M. Grave, Y. Le Lous, W. T. Hewitt. XI, 218 pages, 120 figs., 1994

Photorealistic Rendering in Computer Graphics. Edited by P. Brunet, F. W. Jansen. X, 286 pages, 175 figs., 1994

From Object Modelling to Advanced Visual Communication. Edited by S. Coquillart, W. Straßer, P. Stucki. VII, 305 pages, 128 figs., 38 in color, 1994

Photorealistic Rendering Techniques. Edited by G. Sakas, P. Shirley, S. Müller. X, 448 pages, 155 figs., 16 color plates, 1995